A Concise

Windows 8

Guide for Homes and Corporates

Vivek Nayyar

A Concise Windows 8 Guide for Homes and Corporates by Vivek Nayyar

Published by **Vivek Nayyar (Senior Windows Administrator and Chief Editor, Elerion LLC** and **Technical Head, Siskin Technologies, India**).

This book is dedicated to my loving dad ***Mr. V. K. Nayyar*** *whose abilities have always inspired me to do something different, and in the loving memory of my mom* ***Late Mrs. Indu Nayyar*** *who always wanted me to rise and shine.*

- Vivek Nayyar

Acknowledgements

I am thankful to all those who devoted their time and shared their experiences during the creation of this book. Entire credit for the success of this book goes to them only.

The three closest people who always supported me are:

Mr. Tarun Kandpal
Systems Administrator
India

Ms. Swagata Bharali
Branch Manager
India

Mr. Navneet Mehta
State Head
India

About the Author

Vivek Nayyar

Vivek Nayyar has 8+ years' experience in academic and corporate IT training and systems administration on Microsoft and Virtualization platforms.Today he works as Senior Windows Administrator and Chief Editor at Elerion LLC., Slovakia and Technical Head at Siskin Technologies, India. He also works as LAN Consultant and provides remote support to various IT oriented organizations around the globe. He has written several IT related blogs and articles on Microsoft Windows (Client Operating Systems and Network Operating Systems) and VMware. He has been working on Windows platform since 2001. He has authored a few other books on Windows 7, Windows 8 and Windows Group Policies.

Contents at a Glance

Table of Contents

Introduction

'A Concise Windows 8 Guide for Homes and Corporates' is a screenshots enriched 'Must-Have' guide book written to serve as one-stop-shop for home users, desktop engineers, systems administrators, IT scholars, and all others who currently use or are planning to use Windows 8.

Apart from guiding Windows 8 users, administrators, engineers and scholars, this guide book also covers the concepts of every given option in detail. This gives them a fair idea of how Windows operating systems work, which further helps them in understanding and working with almost all versions of Windows.

This guide book is in very simple and easy-to-understand language, and is deliberately written in this way to let the readers get the most out of it.

Readers can send their suggestions and/or feedbacks to: **vivek.nayyar1107@gmail.com**

CHAPTER 1:

INSTALLATION & PREPARATION

Install Microsoft Windows 8

Introduction to Microsoft Windows 8

Microsoft Windows 8 is the latest operating system released by Microsoft. This operating system is a successor of Microsoft Windows 7. Microsoft Windows 8 is a client operating system and can become member of the domains once it is connected to the network and configured appropriately.

Microsoft has modified the interface of the operating system. For example, Start menu is replaced with the Metro UI Start screen. Apart from the modifications in the interface, locations of some options are also changed. Modifications that can be seen in Microsoft Windows 8's interface can help users and administrators work on the operating system more easily and comfortably while using touchscreen devices such as Tablet PCs, Windows mobile phones, etc.

To know more about Microsoft Windows 8's modified interface, refer to the lesson 'The New Interface' later in this chapter.

Microsoft Windows 8 Installation

Just like any other software application, Microsoft Windows 8 must also be installed on the computer system before it can be used. The process of installing any operating system, including Microsoft Windows 8, is slightly different as compared to the process involved to install any other software application that runs on the operating system. The installation process of Microsoft Windows 8 involves several steps that help administrators customize the operating system to best fit their requirements once it is installed.

In order to install Microsoft Windows 8, administrators must verify the minimum system requirements of the computer on which they plan to install the operating system, and they must also check the compatibility of the attached hardware devices with the operating system. The best way to check the compatibility of the hardware with the operating system is to check the Hardware Compatibility List or HCL that can be found online.

Minimum System Requirements to Install Microsoft Windows 8

In order to install Microsoft Windows 8 on a computer, the computer must meet the following hardware requirements:

- Processor - 1 GHz or above
- Physical Memory (RAM) - 2 GB (Recommended), 1 GB (Minimum)
- Hard Disk Space - 20 GB (Recommended), 15 GB (Minimum)
- Screen Resolution - 1366 x 768
- Graphics Support - DirectX 9
- Optical Media Drive - DVD Drive

How to Install Microsoft Windows 8

Once the minimum system requirements are met, steps given below must be followed to install Microsoft Windows 8 on the computer:

1. Start the computer and enter into the BIOS setup.

2. Configure the computer to boot from DVD.
3. Insert Microsoft Windows 8 bootable installation media.
4. Reboot the computer with DVD support.
5. On the displayed screen, click **Next**.

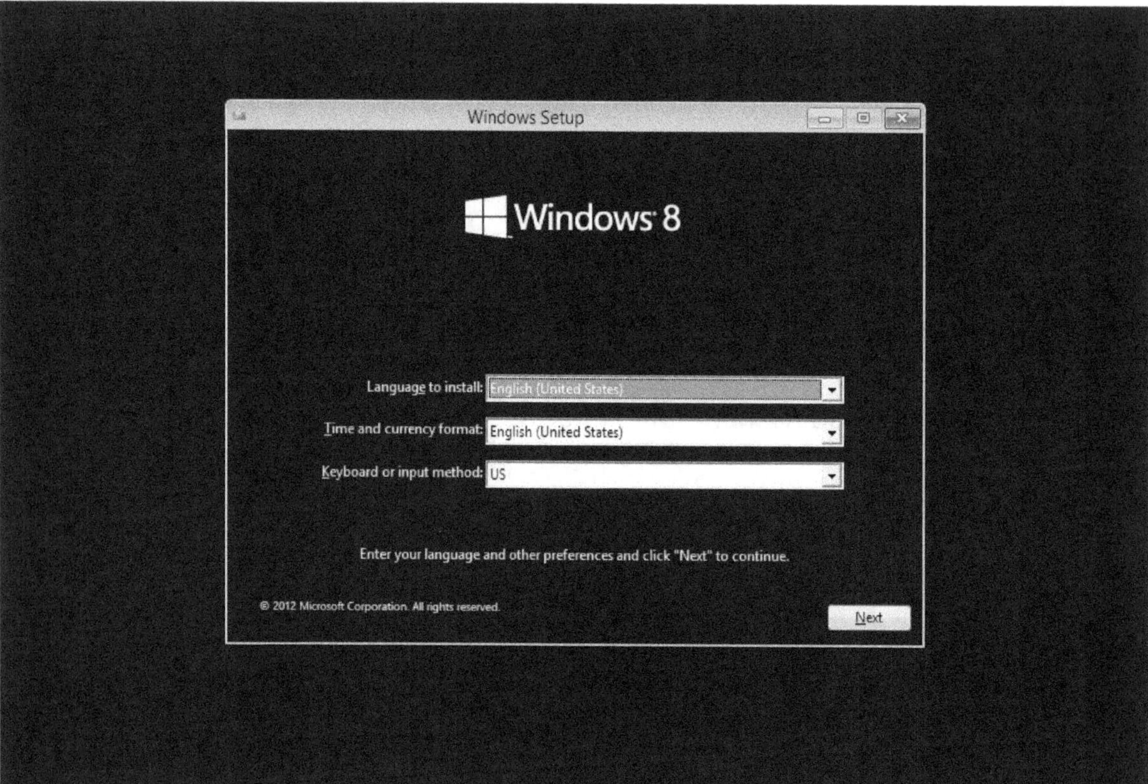

6. On the next window, click **Install now**.

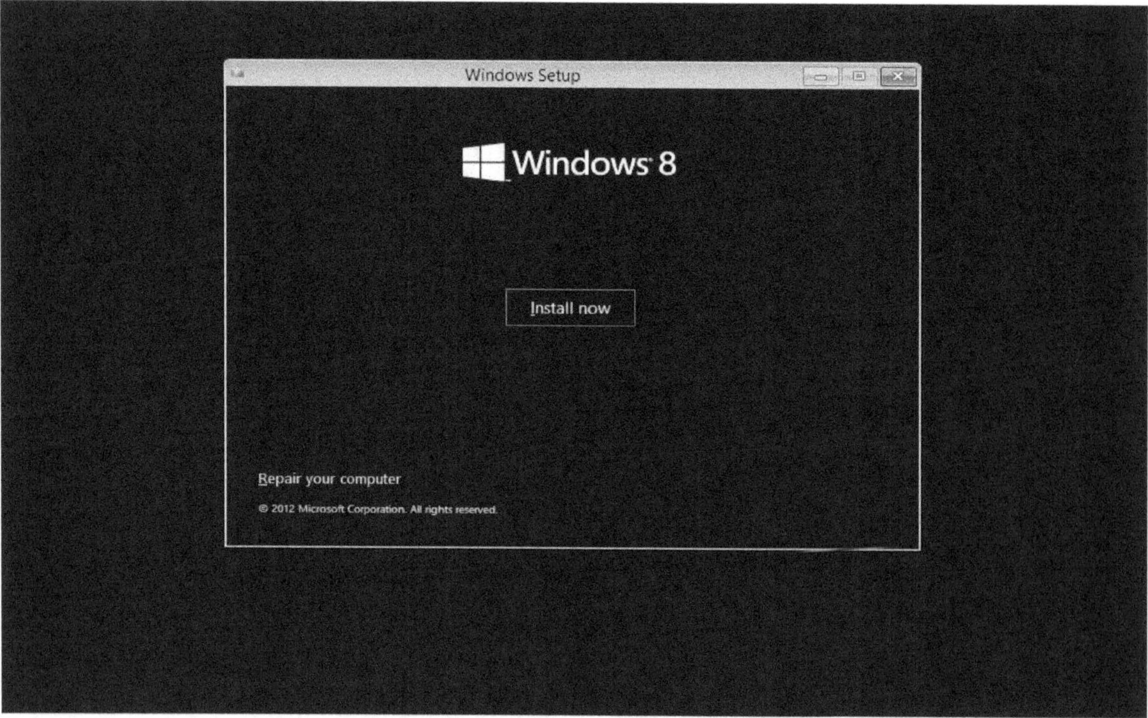

7. On next page, type the 25-character product key and click **Next**.

8. On the **License terms** page, check **I accept the license terms** checkbox and click **Next**.

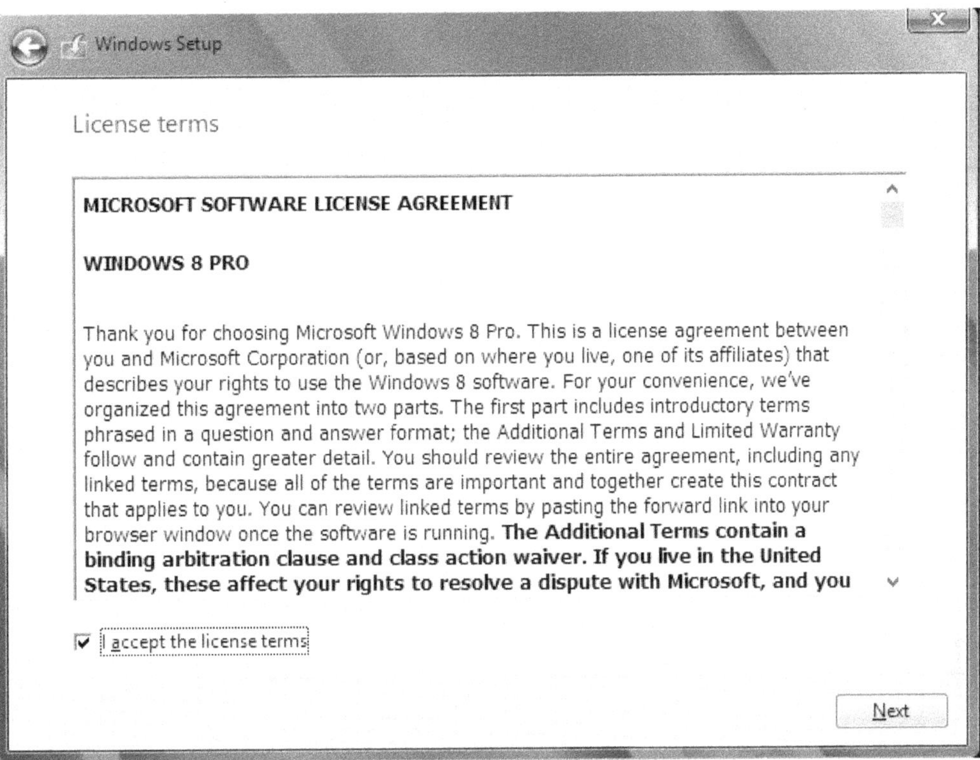

9. On **Which type of installation do you want** page, click **Custom: Install Windows only (advanced)** option.

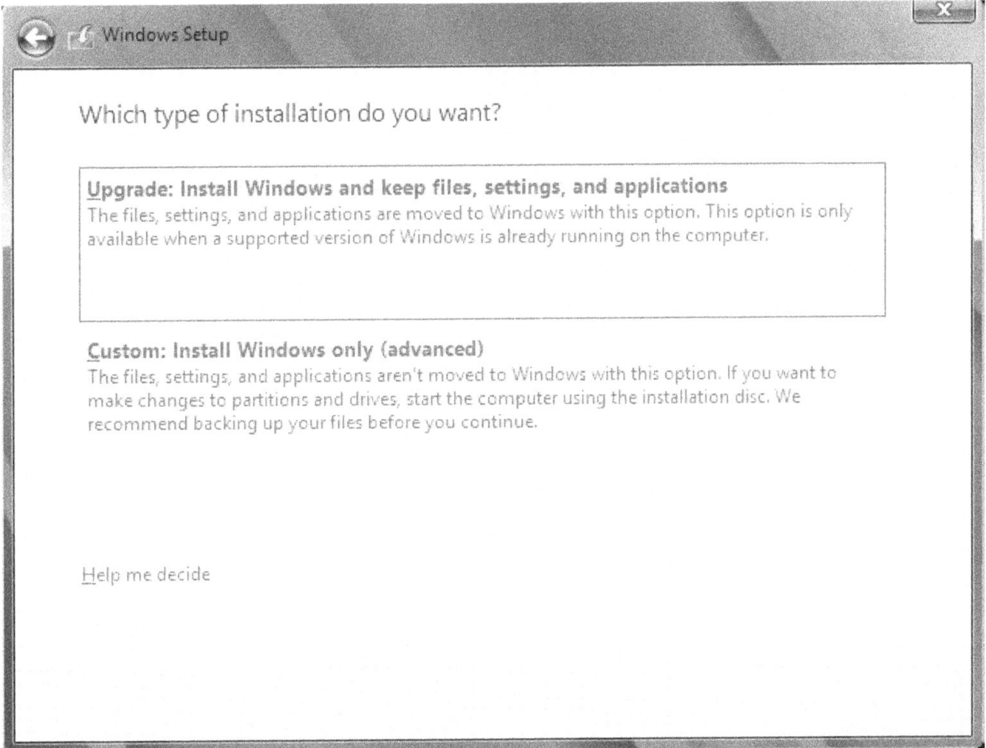

10. On **Where do you want to install Windows** page, click to select the hard disk drive where Windows 8 is to be installed and click **Next** to assign full disk space

to the system drive (C:). Alternatively, **Drive options (advanced)** option can also be clicked to create partitions in the hard disk drive before clicking **Next** button.

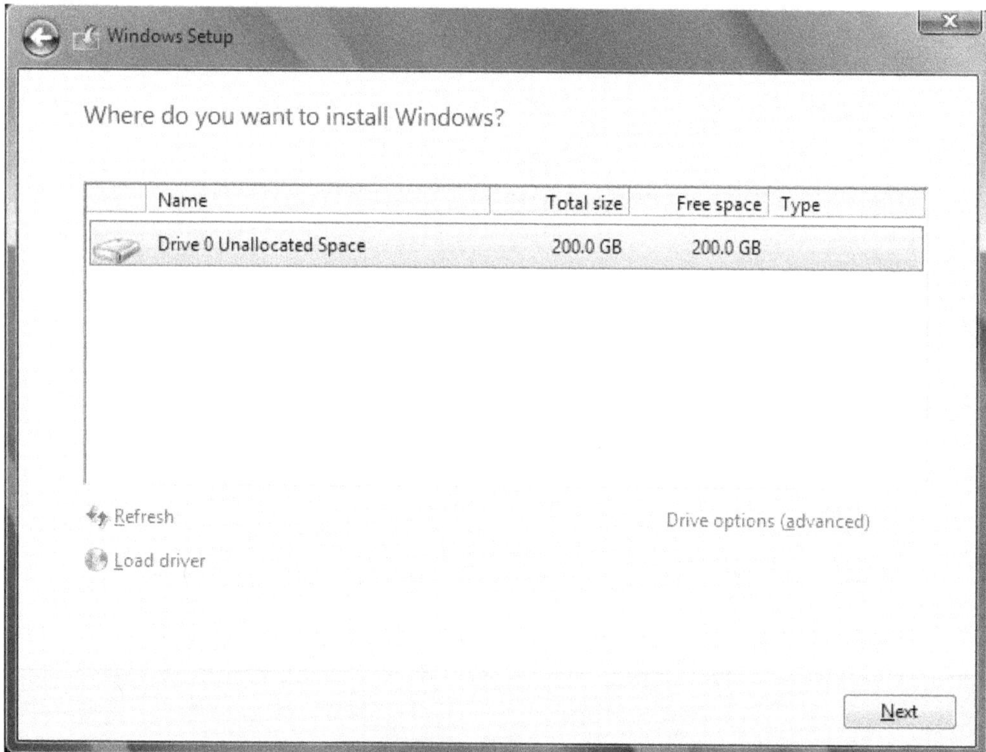

11. On the **Installing Windows** page, wait till Windows gets installed and the computer restarts.

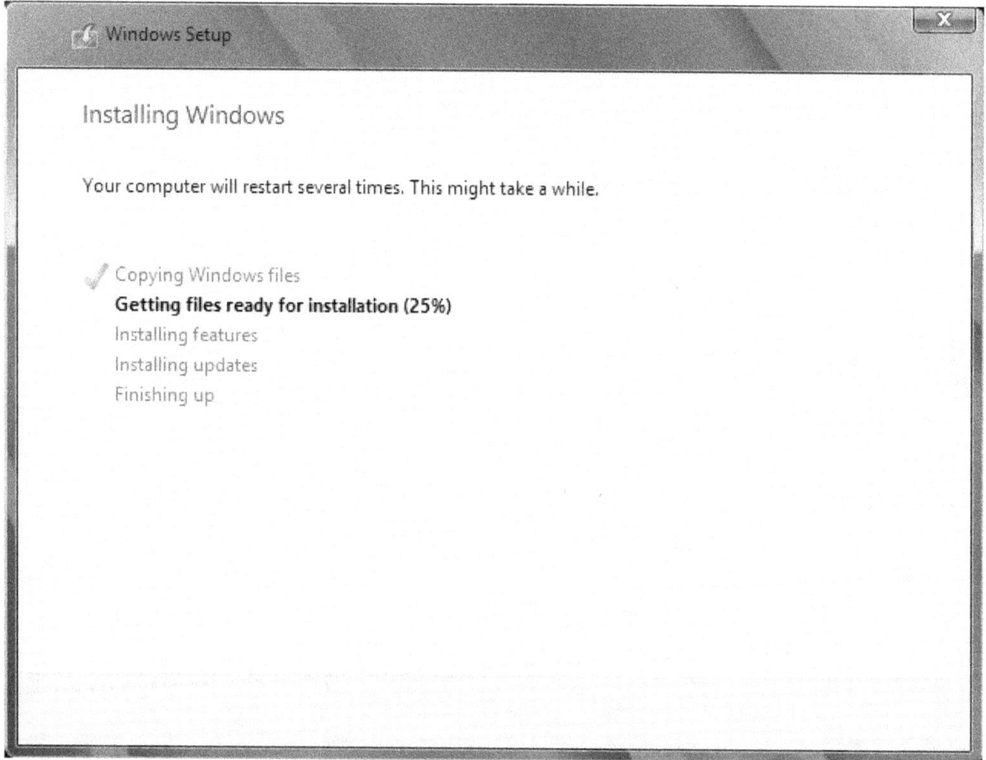

Note: *While restarting, if the screen displays the message, '**Press any key to boot from CD or DVD**', do **NOT** press any key. Let the system restart on its own or the system will start the installation process right from the beginning.*

12. On **Personalize** window, choose the color scheme from the available colors.
13. In the **PC name** field, specify a unique name for the Windows 8 computer.

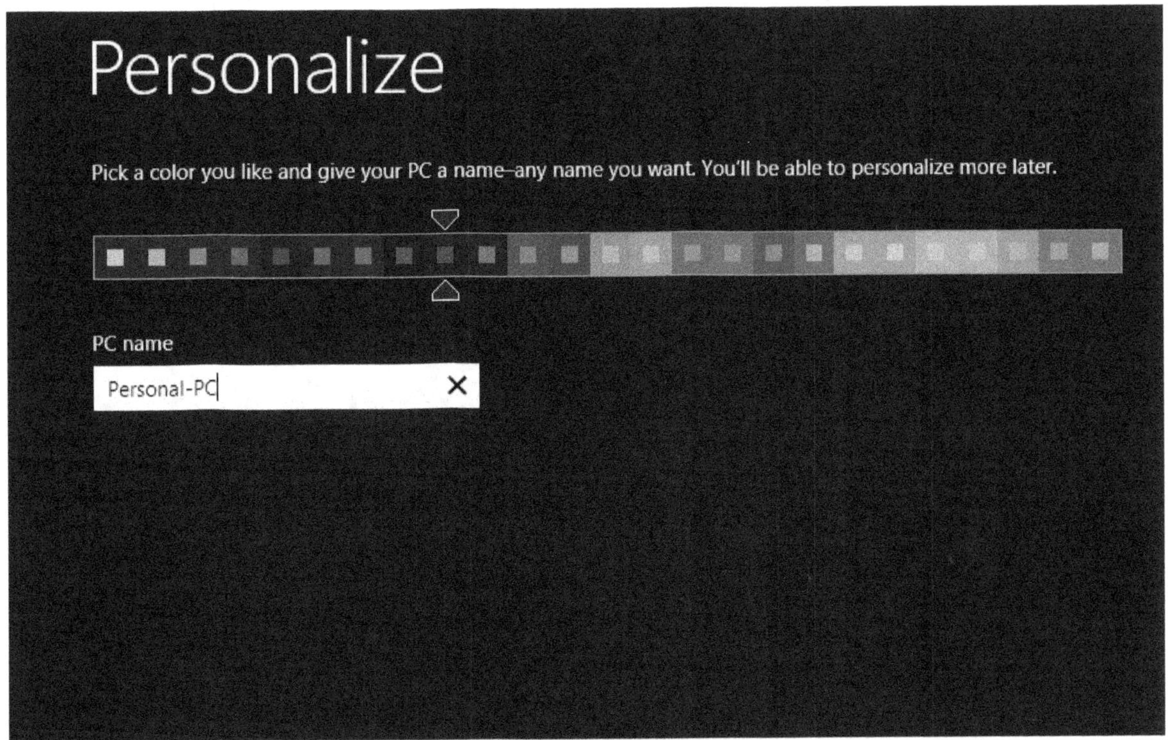

Note: *Users and administrators can give any name to the computer as long as the same name is not given to any other computer in the common network. Unique name is required to establish network connectivity between the computers.*

14. Click **Next** when done.
15. On the **Settings** window, click **Customize** button to configure Windows 8 granularly before start using it. Alternatively, **Use express settings** button can also be clicked to use the default settings and continue with the finalizing process.

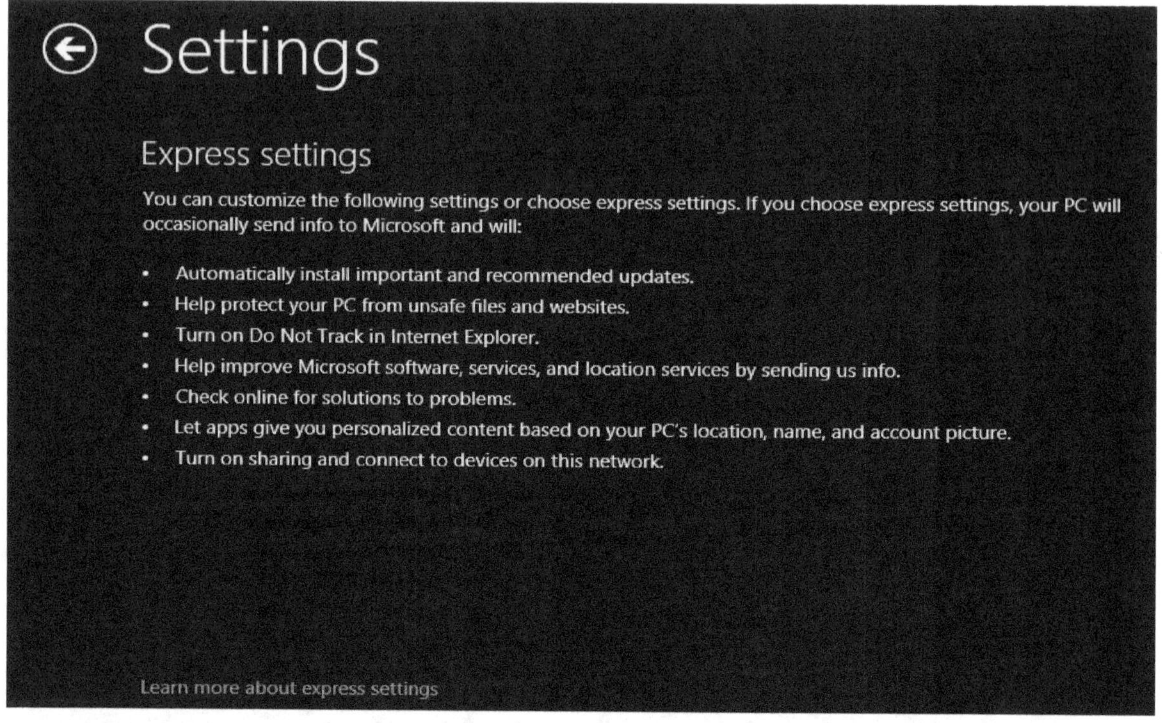

Note: *Settings can be configured after Windows is successfully installed on the computer. Administrative credentials are required to do so.*

16. On **Help protect and update your PC** window, make appropriate adjustments to the settings and click **Next**.

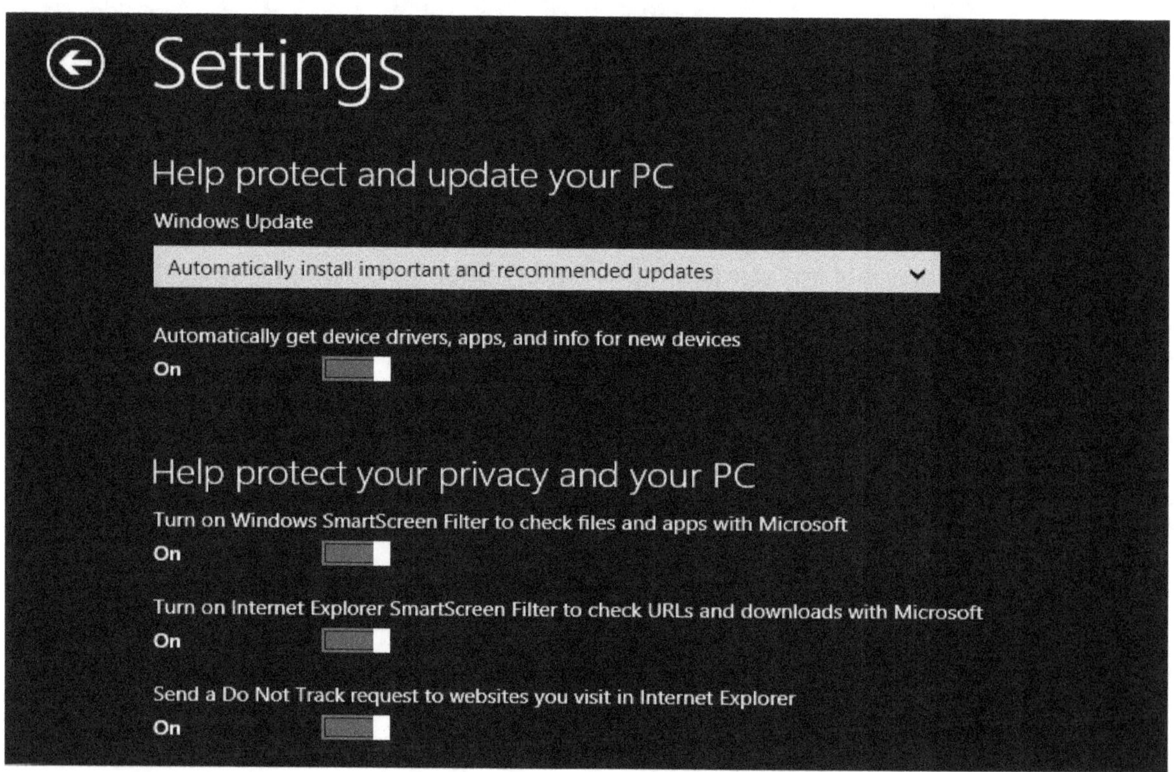

17. On **Send Microsoft info to help make Windows and apps better** window, make appropriate changes as desired and click **Next**. Alternatively, default settings

can also be left intact and **Next** button can be clicked without making any changes to the settings.

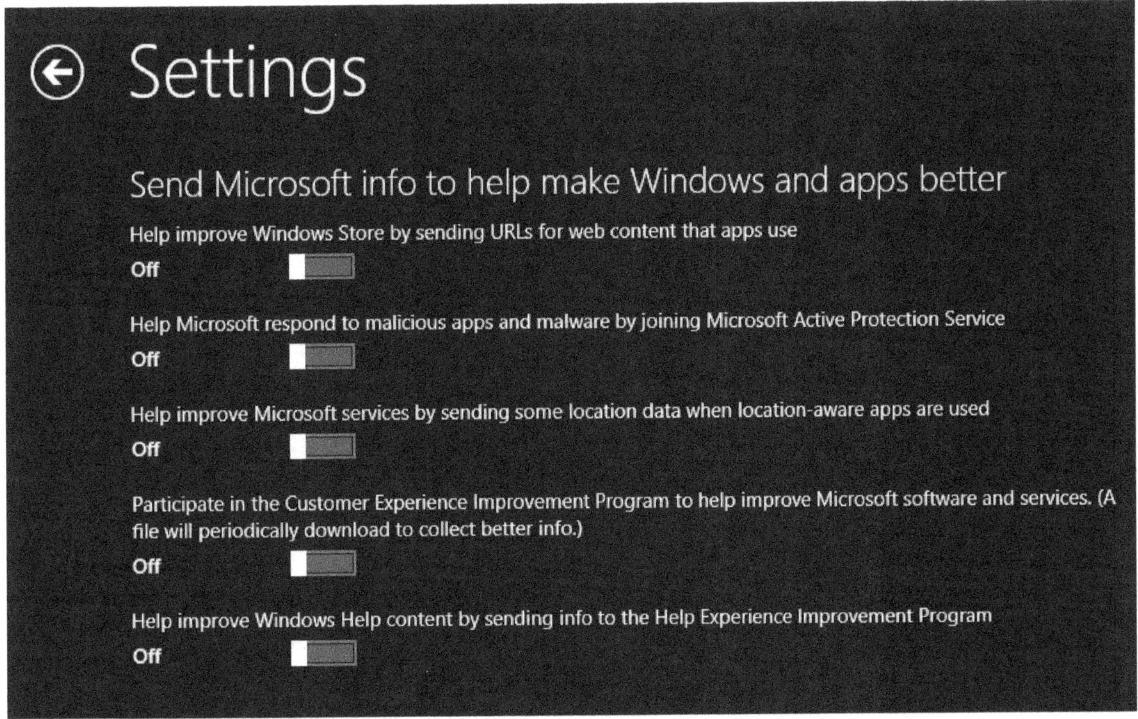

18. On **Check online for solutions to problems** window, make appropriate changes to the settings as desired and click **Next**. Alternatively, default settings can also be left intact and **Next** button can be clicked without making any changes to the settings.

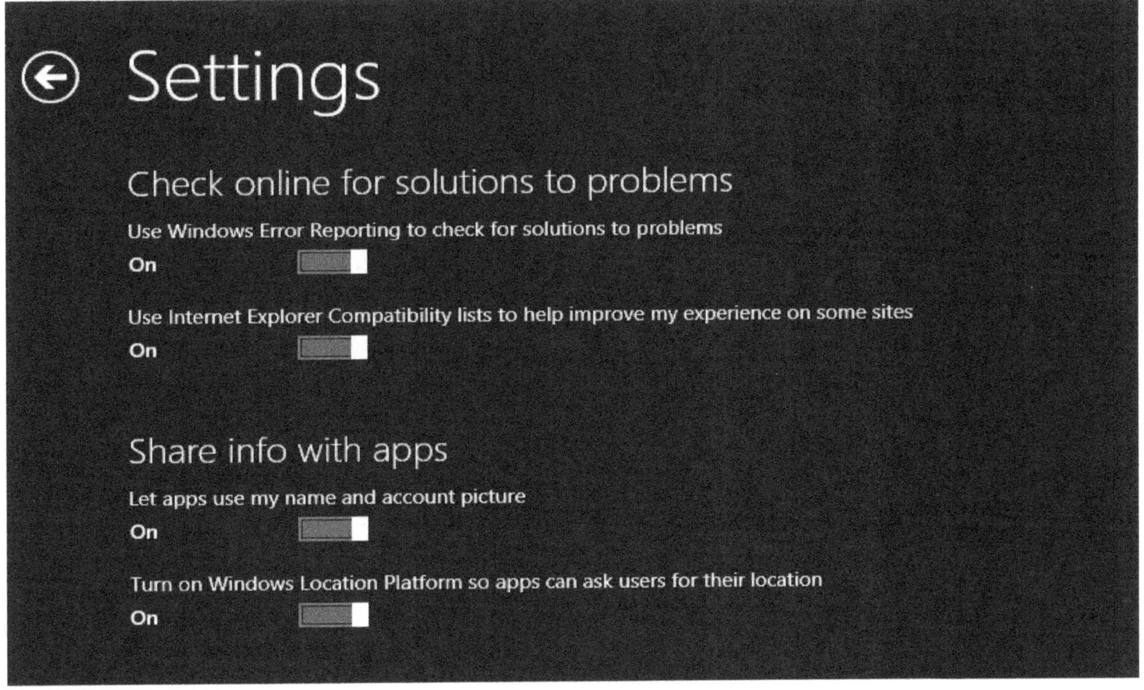

19. On **Sign in to your PC** window, populate the **User name**, **Password**, **Reenter password** and **Password hint** fields with appropriate values as desired.

Sign in to your PC

If you want a password, choose something that will be easy for you to remember but hard for others to guess.

User name Michael

Password ••••••

Reenter password ••••••

Password hint a

Note: *User name specified here will automatically become member of 'Administrators' group and will get unrestricted privileges on the computer.*

20. Click **Finish** when done to finalize Windows 8 settings and configurations.

21. Once things have been finalized, the user account that was created in step 19 will be logged on automatically and will be displayed with the **Start** screen.

The New Interface

Microsoft Windows 8 has entirely a new look and a different interface. The new interface has several modifications and provides users a different way to interact with the operating system.

Some of the newly added elements in Microsoft Windows 8, that are expected to be used by majority of people worldwide are discussed below:

- **Lock Screen** - Lock Screen is the very first window that is displayed on the monitor screen after the computer is successfully booted. Because of Calendar app, Lock Screen displays time, day of the week, date and current month. Lock Screen also displays Internet connection status. Calendar app can be removed from the lock screen by going to 'PC settings' > 'Personalize'. Other apps can be added and/or Lock Screen's background image can be changed from this window as well. Desktop or laptop users can use their mouse or touch pads to drag the Lock Screen up. People who use touchscreen computers, Tablet PCs or Windows phones can swap their fingers up to hide the Lock Screen. Once the Lock Screen is hidden, users can then provide the passwords for their accounts on the displayed logon screen.
- **Password Reveal** - This new feature in Microsoft Windows 8 allows users to view the typed password by clicking the Password Reveal option. Password Reveal option is represented by an eye icon that is available at the right end of the password field and only appears when users start typing their passwords. In order to view the typed password, users must click and hold the mouse button on the eye icon. The password remains revealed as long as the eye icon is clicked. As soon as users release the mouse button, the password gets hidden (masked) again.
- **Start Screen** - One of the major modifications in Microsoft Windows 8 is the Metro UI Start screen. Start screen has replaced the Start button that was available in pre-Windows 8 operating systems. Start screen contains several tiles which, when clicked, initiate their corresponding apps. Start screen also consists of the shortcut icons to the applications that administrators install on a Windows 8 computer. In case the shortcut icon of any installed application is not visible in the Start screen, users can manually pin the icon in order to make it accessible with ease.
- **The Four Corners** - The new interface that Microsoft Windows 8 has is specially designed for Tablet PCs and touchscreen monitors. Considering this, the interface of the operating system is designed in a way that users can swap their fingers or move the mouse to any of the four corners of the screen to get different options. Every corner of the monitor screen displays a separate window/pane when a mouse is hovered to it. Mouse can be hovered to any of the four corners of the window while being on any window. However, different options, thumbnails, or other window specific features related to the same options can be seen while being on different windows. Windows/panes that each corner of the Start and desktop screen displays is:

> **When on Start Screen:**

>> **Top Left Corner** - When mouse is hovered to the top left corner of the Start screen, a thumbnail of the previous window is displayed. If the mouse pointer is hovered to top left corner and then moved down a bit, a thumbnail view (small icons) of all the opened windows can be seen. Users can click (left-click) any one of them to go to that particular window. Optionally, users can right-click any of the icons and from the context menu, they can click 'Close' to close the window.

***Note:** If no window (including the desktop screen) has been opened after the system boot, nothing is displayed when the mouse is hovered to the top left corner while being on Start screen.*

>> **Bottom Left Corner** - When mouse is hovered to the bottom left corner while being on the Start screen, a thumbnail of the desktop screen is displayed. When the mouse is hovered to the bottom left corner and is moved up a bit, a thumbnail view (small icons) of all the opened windows can be seen. Users can click (left-click) any one of them to go to that particular window. Optionally, they can right-click any of the icons and from the context menu they can click 'Close' to close the window. If users right-click at the bottom left corner of the Start screen, various options are displayed in the context menu. The options that the context menu contains are Run, Computer Management, Command Prompt, Command Prompt (Admin), etc.

Note: *Thumbnail of the desktop screen is displayed on the bottom left corner of the Start screen only when the desktop has been opened previously. If the computer has recently booted, and users hover mouse to the bottom left corner, since no window has been opened, nothing is displayed at all.*

>> **Top/Bottom Right Corner** - While being on the Start screen, when the mouse is hovered to the top or bottom right corner of the window, the options pane is displayed. The pane contains five icons which, when clicked, open different panes or screens that allow users to perform different tasks on the computer. The options that appear, and their brief description are as below:

- **Search** - When this option is clicked, Apps screen appears and users can click on the desired app to initiate it. Users can also type the name of the desired feature, a file or an app in the Search pane that appears in the left and has Apps field to type the desired entity's name.
- **Share** - While being on Start screen, if Share option is clicked, Windows 8 allows users to share any selected app or tile with other people by linking it to the Microsoft Store. Users must right-click the app or tile in order to select it before clicking 'Share' option from the options pane.

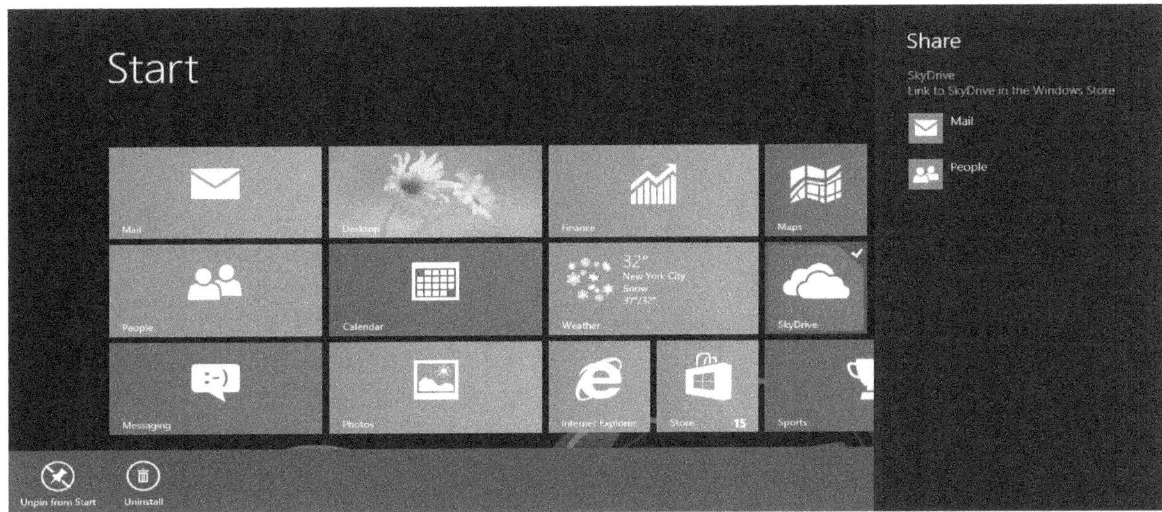

- **Start** - While being on Start screen, clicking this option does nothing at all. However if users have previously opened the desktop window, clicking this option while being on Start screen opens the desktop screen. On the desktop window, when Start option is clicked, it opens the Start screen. In other words if the desktop screen has been opened previously, this option works as a toggle switch between the Start screen and the desktop window.
- **Devices** - While be on Start screen, when this option is clicked, a pane in the left is opened and users can select the secondary monitor with which the current monitor screen can be shared.
- **Settings** - When Settings option is clicked while being on the Start screen, Start screen specific options are displayed in the left pane. By default Tiles and Help options are displayed in the upper section of the pane. The lower section of the pane remains the same even when the Settings option is clicked while being on the Start screen or Desktop window. Options that the lower section of the Settings pane contains include Network icon, Volume icon, Brightness (to adjust the brightness of the display, but is only available Windows 8 is installed on the devices that support the feature), Notifications, Power button (computer can be restarted, shut down, hibernated or put to sleep mode using this option), Change PC settings and Keyboard icon (to display the keyboard layout - US English is selected by default).

> **When on Desktop Window:**

>> **Top Left Corner** - When mouse is hovered to the top left corner of the screen, a thumbnail of the previous window is displayed. If the mouse pointer is hovered to top left corner and then moved down a bit, a thumbnail view (small icons) of all the opened windows can be seen. Users can click (left-click) any one of them to go to that particular window. Optionally, they can right-click any of the icons and from the context menu, they can click 'Close' to close the window.

Note: *If no window (except the desktop screen) has been opened, nothing is displayed when the mouse is hovered to the top left corner.*

>> **Bottom Left Corner** - When mouse is hovered to the bottom left corner while being on the desktop screen, a thumbnail of the Start screen is displayed. When the mouse is hovered to the bottom left corner and is moved up a bit, a thumbnail view (small icons) of all the opened windows can be seen. Users can click (left-click) any one of them to go to that particular window. Optionally, they can right-click any of the icons and from the context menu they can click 'Close' to close the window. If users right-click anywhere at the bottom left corner of the desktop screen, various options are displayed in the context menu. The options that the context menu contains are Run, Computer Management, Command Prompt, Command Prompt (Admin), etc.

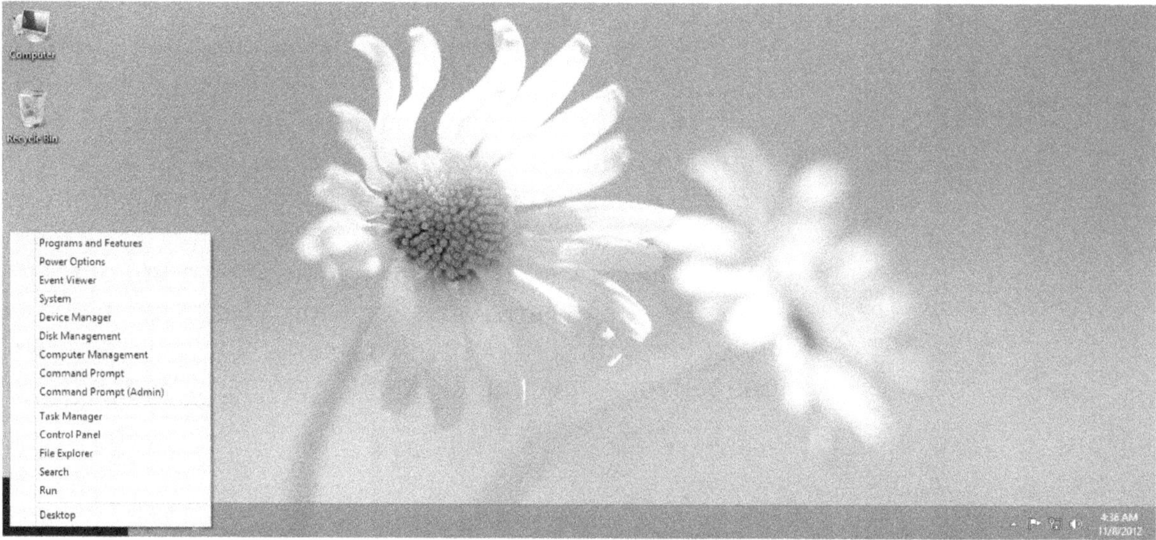

>> **Top/Bottom Right Corner** - While being on the desktop screen, when the mouse is hovered to the top or bottom right corner of the window, the options pane is displayed. The pane contains five icons which, when clicked, open different panes or screens that allow users to perform different tasks on the computer. The options that appear, and their brief description are as below:

- **Search** - When this option is clicked, Apps screen appears and users can click on the desired app to initiate it. Users can also type the name of the desired feature, a file or an app in the Search pane that appears in the left and has Apps field to type the desired entity's name.
- **Share** - While being on the desktop screen, if Share option is clicked, a Share pane appears in the left displaying that users can't share anything from the desktop screen.
- **Start** - While being on desktop screen, clicking on this option opens the Start screen. On the Start screen, when Start option is clicked, it opens the desktop window. In other words, this option

works as a toggle switch between the Start screen and the desktop window.

- **Devices** - While being on desktop screen, when this option is clicked, a pane in the left is opened and users can select the secondary monitor with which the display of current monitor can be shared.
- **Settings** - When Settings option is clicked while being desktop window, computer specific and most commonly used configuration options are displayed in the Settings pane in the left. Options that are displayed in the upper section of the pane are Control Panel, Personalization, PC info and Help. The lower section of the pane remains the same even when the Settings option is clicked while being on Start screen or Desktop window. Options that the lower section of the Settings pane contains include Network icon, Volume icon, Brightness (to adjust the brightness of the display, but is only available when Windows 8 is installed on the devices that support the feature), Notifications, Power button (computer can be restarted, shut down, hibernated or put to sleep mode using this option), Change PC settings and Keyboard icon (to display the keyboard layout - US English is selected by default).

- **File Explorer** - File Explorer is the icon that is available in the taskbar which, when clicked, opens Libraries window. In pre-Windows 8 operating systems, this icon was called Windows Explorer.
- **Modified Window** - Any window that users open in windows explorer has modified interface. Every time an object that resides in the window is clicked, its corresponding commands can be viewed in the Manage menu that appears in the menu bar at the top of the window. Manage menu is displayed next to other menus. When Manage menu is clicked, the available options can be seen and accessed from the displayed ribbon.
- **Modified Copying and Moving Options** - When an object is copied or moved to a different location, apart from displaying close button abort the process, the copy or move box also displays pause button. Pause button can be used to

temporarily halt the copying or moving process. After pausing copying or moving process, it can be resumed by clicking resume button.

- **Network Locations** - Unlike Windows 7, Windows 8 does not allow administrators to change network locations (at least not that easily). When a Windows 8 computer is connected to the Internet, its network location is automatically set to Private. On the other hand, when the computer is not connected to the Internet, the network location automatically changes to Public. In order to change the network location manually, administrators must modify the group policies settings of Windows 8 computer.
- **Windows Store** - Windows Store is an online marketplace from where Windows 8 users can download and install free and paid apps. In order to install apps from Windows Store, users must provide Microsoft account's credentials. Windows Store can be accessed by clicking the Store tile that is available in the Start screen.
- **Microsoft Account** - Windows 8 allows users to log on to the computer using a globally accepted Microsoft account. Microsoft account is an e-mail address registered with Microsoft. Users can use any e-mail address to register it with Microsoft. As soon as an e-mail address is registered, it becomes Microsoft account and can be used to log on to Windows 8 or to access Windows Store and apps. Users can also create a new e-mail address with Hotmail.com or Live.com which automatically becomes Microsoft account as soon as it is created.

Add or Remove Desktop Icons

Introduction to the Desktop Icons

When Microsoft Windows 8 is installed, it is only the Recycle Bin that is available on the desktop screen. Microsoft designed Windows 8's default user profile this way to keep the desktop neat and tidy, which makes it easier for the users to work on Windows. If users are experienced and are old users of Microsoft Windows, using the OS without commonly used icons on the desktop would not be a problem for them. On the other hand, users who are new to computer field and/or are new to the Microsoft platform, it might be challenging for them to operate Windows without the icons.

To make things easier, it is recommended that users should that the most frequently used icons on their desktop screens. Some of the commonly used icons are, Computer, Control Panel, etc.

How to Add or Remove Desktop Icons?

In order to add or remove commonly used icons from the desktop screen in Microsoft Windows 8, steps given below must be followed:

1. Log on to Microsoft Windows 8 computer with any account.
2. From the **Start** screen, click **Desktop** tile.
3. On the desktop screen, right-click anywhere.
4. From the context menu, click **Personalize**.
5. From the **Personalization** window, click **Change desktop icons** from the left pane.
6. On the **Desktop Icon Settings** box, check or uncheck the checkboxes representing the icons that are to be placed or removed from the desktop respectively.

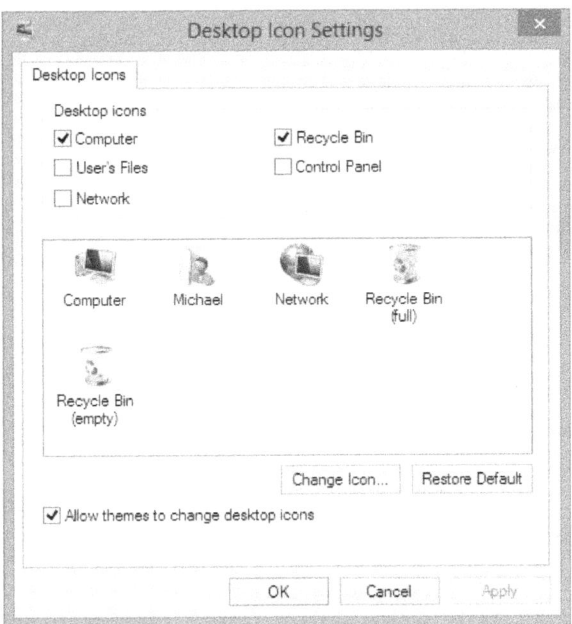

7. Click **OK** to apply the settings.
8. Close **Personalization** window when done.

Log Off from Current User Account

Introduction to the Logging off from a User Account

Since the interface of Microsoft Windows 8 operating system is quite new and is specifically designed for touchscreen computers, sometimes it might be challenging for new users to log off from their accounts once they are done with their work.

How to Log off from a Current User Account?

In order to log off from are currently logged on user account on a Windows 8 computer, steps given below must be followed:

1. On the desktop screen, hover mouse to the bottom right corner of the window.
2. From the displayed options, click **Start**.
3. On the **Start** screen, click the name of the currently logged on user account from the top left corner.
4. From the displayed options, click **Sign out**.

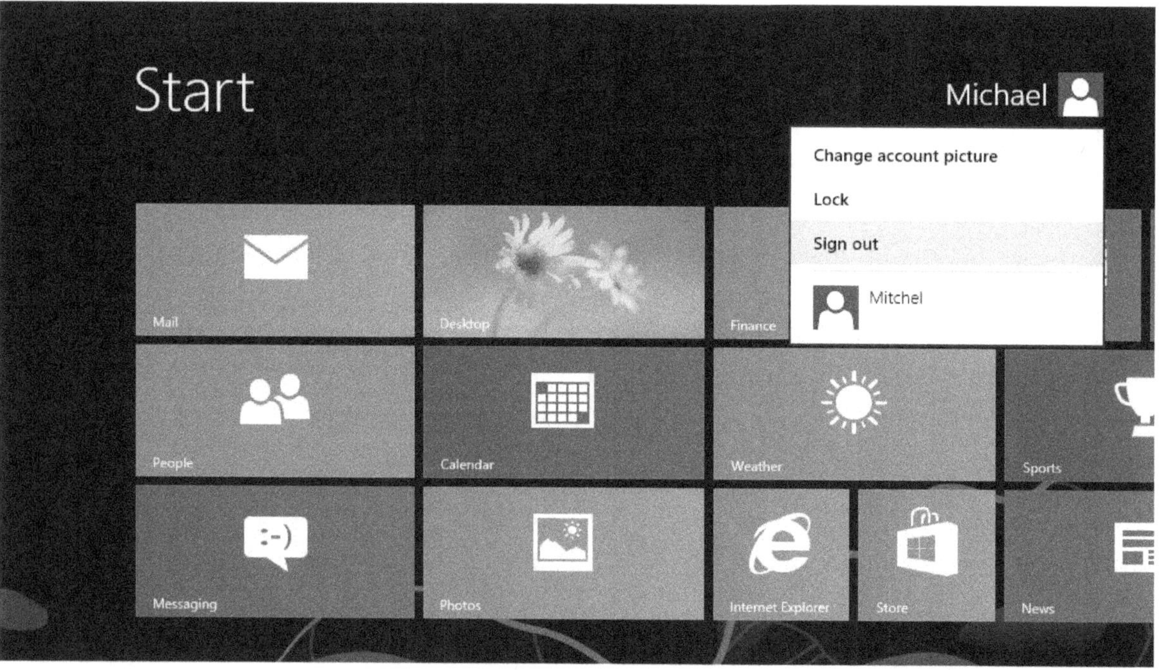

Rename a Computer

Introduction to Renaming a Computer

When Microsoft Windows 8 is installed, the installation process allows administrators to specify a name to the computer. Administrators can specify any desired name to Windows 8 computer at that time, as long as the specified name is unique in the network. In home computer once a computer name is specified, it is unlikely that administrators would need to rename it. On the other hand, when Windows 8 is installed on a computer that is used in production environments and is required to be connected to other computers in the network, administrators might need to change the computer name according to the naming convention used in the organization.

Administrators in production environments might also want to rename the computer before adding it to the domain in order to make the computer become identifiable by more sensible name according to the naming convention used in the client/server network architecture.

How to Rename a Computer?

In order to rename a Microsoft Windows 8 computer, steps given below must be followed:

1. Log on to Microsoft Windows 8 computer with administrator account.
2. From the **Start** screen, click **Desktop** tile.
3. On the desktop window, click **File Explorer** icon from the taskbar.
4. On the opened **Libraries** window, right-click **Computer** from the left pane.
5. From the displayed context menu, click **Properties**.
6. On the opened **System** window, click **Change settings** under the **Computer name, domain, and workgroup settings** section.
7. On the opened **System Properties** box, make sure that **Computer Name** tab is selected and click **Change** button.
8. On the **Computer Name/Domain Changes** box, in the **Computer name** field type the new computer name.

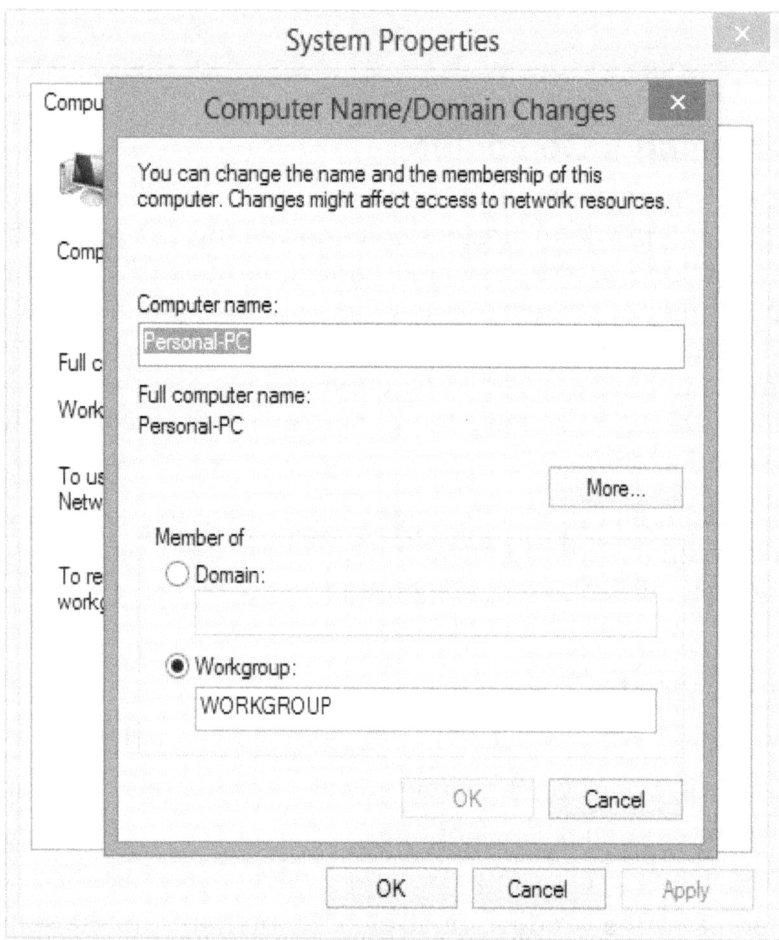

9. Click **OK** when done and on the displayed information box, click **OK**.
10. Back on **System Properties** box, click **Close**.
11. On the displayed box, click **Restart Now** button to restart the computer.

Switch to Another User Account

Introduction to Switching User Accounts

Microsoft Windows 8 also allows fast user switching feature that enables multiple users to log on to their accounts simultaneously, i.e. without logging off from any account. Because of fast user switching feature, users can keep their files and applications open and can hand over the computer system to another user who can then log on to another account using different credentials. This eliminates the requirement of closing down the applications when another user logs on to the system, and reopening them when the first user logs back again.

In Microsoft Windows 8, switching from one user to another is simpler as compared to the earlier versions of Microsoft operating systems.

How to Switch to Another User Account?

In order to switch to another user account in Microsoft Windows 8, steps given below must be followed:

1. While logged on using one user account, on the desktop screen hover mouse to the bottom right corner of the window.
2. From the displayed options, click **Start**.
3. On the **Start** screen, click the name of the currently logged on user account from the top left corner.
4. From the displayed options, click the name of the other user.

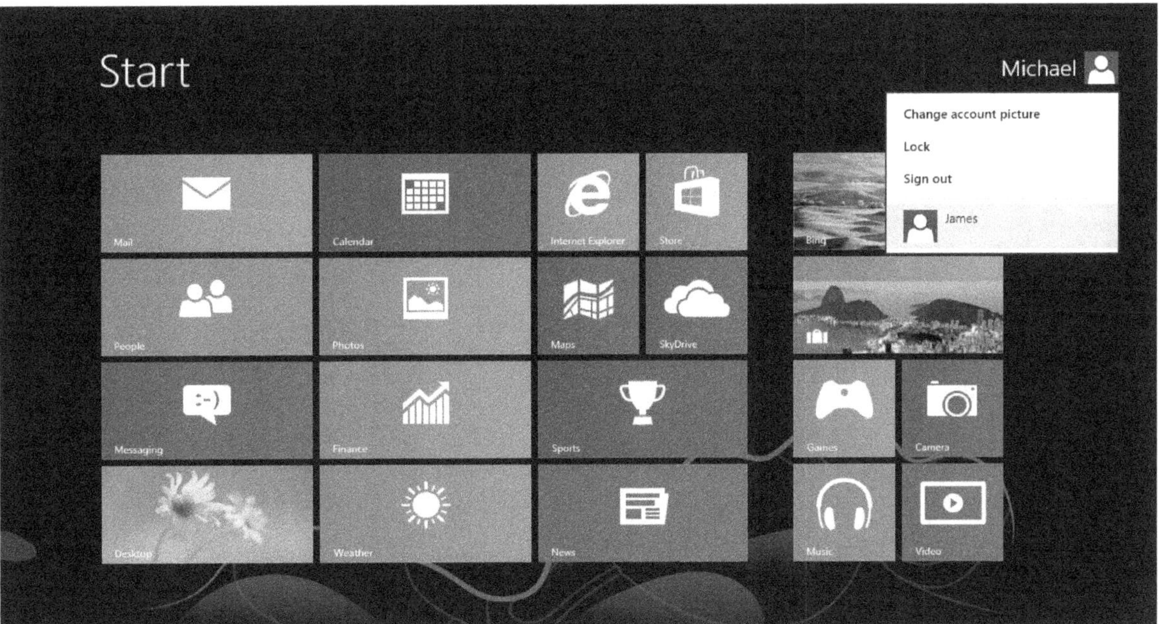

5. On the displayed logon box, type the password for the selected user and press **Enter** key to log on to the account without logging off from the previous one.

Change Account Picture

Introduction to Changing Account Picture

Account pictures in Microsoft Windows 8 can be used to identify a user account. In other words they can serve the purpose of an avatar for the user accounts that reside in the computer. In pre-Windows 8 operating systems, account pictures were automatically assigned to every user account that was created. Whereas Windows 8 does not assign any account picture during the creation of user account and users must manually do so using their own credentials.

Assigning and/or changing account picture is a user specific task and users can change only their own account pictures. This further means that one user account cannot change or assign the account picture for any other user account.

How to Change Account Picture

In order to change account picture for a user account in Microsoft Windows 8, steps given below must be followed:

1. Log on to Microsoft Windows 8 computer with the account for which account picture that is to be changed.
2. On the **Start** screen, click the name of the logged on user account from the top right corner.
3. From the displayed options, click **Change account picture**.
4. On the **PC settings** window, make sure that **Personalize** category is selected in the left.
5. From the right, click **Browse** to browse for and locate an image to set as the account picture. Alternatively, **Camera** icon under **Create an account picture** section can also be clicked to use device's integrated camera to capture a snap and use it as the account picture.

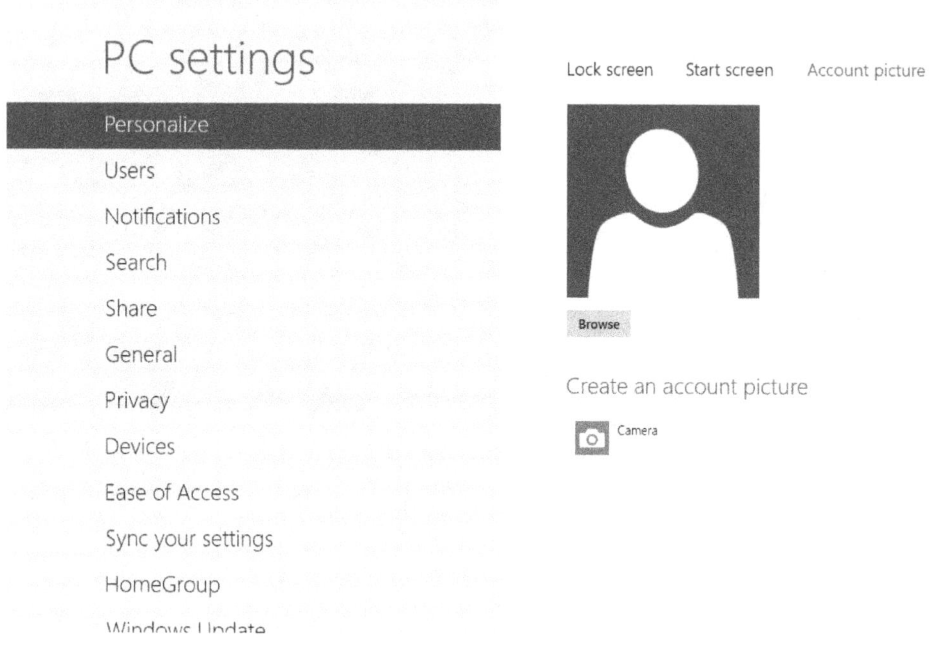

6. After clicking **Browse** button, from the opened window, navigate and locate the desired image file.
7. Click to select the located picture and click **Choose image** button to set the selected image as the account picture.

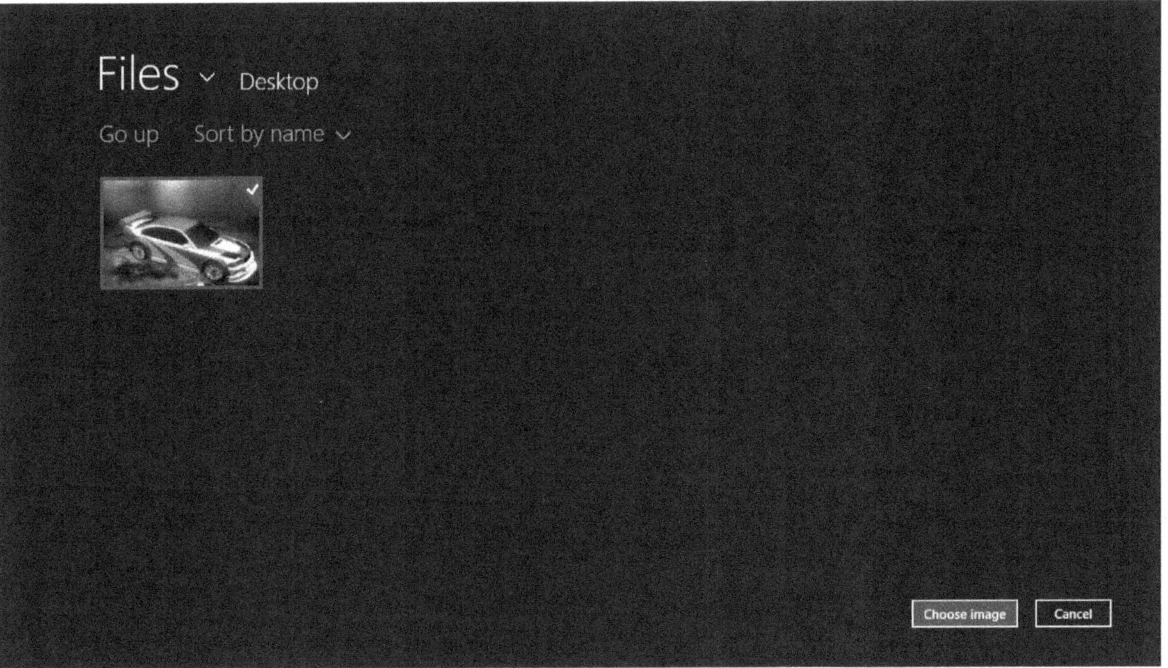

Restart/Shutdown a Computer

Introduction to Restarting/Shutting Down a Computer

Because of the new interface in Microsoft Windows 8, sometimes it might be challenging for users to find the 'Shutdown' or 'Restart' option while using the operating system. Although users can use the command prompt to restart or shut down the computer using the appropriate commands, not every user is expected to be familiar with the shut down and restart commands.

The background process of restarting and shutting down a computer is identical to that used in earlier versions of Microsoft Windows, however due to the changed the interface users might get confused while initiating the process.

How to Restart/Shutdown a Computer?

In order to restart/shutdown of Microsoft Windows 8 computer, steps given below must be followed:

1. On the desktop screen, hover mouse to the bottom right corner of the window.
2. From the displayed options, click **Settings**.
3. From the **Settings** pane, click the **Power** button.
4. From the displayed options, click **Shut down** or **Restart** to shut down or restart the computer respectively.

View Microsoft Windows 8 Product ID

Introduction to Product ID

Product ID is a unique number that is automatically generated during the installation of any operating system, including Microsoft Windows 8.

When Microsoft Windows 8 is installed on a computer, the installation process of the operating system collects information of all the hardware devices connected to the computer. During the installation process, when the product key of the operating system is provided, Windows 8 uses the collected information of the hardware devices and the product key to generate a unique product ID that is displayed at the bottom of the 'System' window.

The generated product ID can be used to get help from the Microsoft technical support team. Since the product ID is unique and is required while requesting for technical support from Microsoft, it is strongly recommended that it must be noted down and kept in a safe place.

Where to Find the Product ID in Microsoft Windows 8?

In order to view the unique product ID in Microsoft Windows eight, steps given below must be followed:

1. Log on to Microsoft Windows 8 computer with any account.
2. From the **Start** screen, click **Desktop** tile.
3. On the desktop screen, click **File Explorer** icon from the taskbar.
4. On the opened **Libraries** window, right-click **Computer** from the left pane.
5. From the context menu, click **Properties**.
6. On the opened **System** window, product ID can be found under the **Windows activation** section.

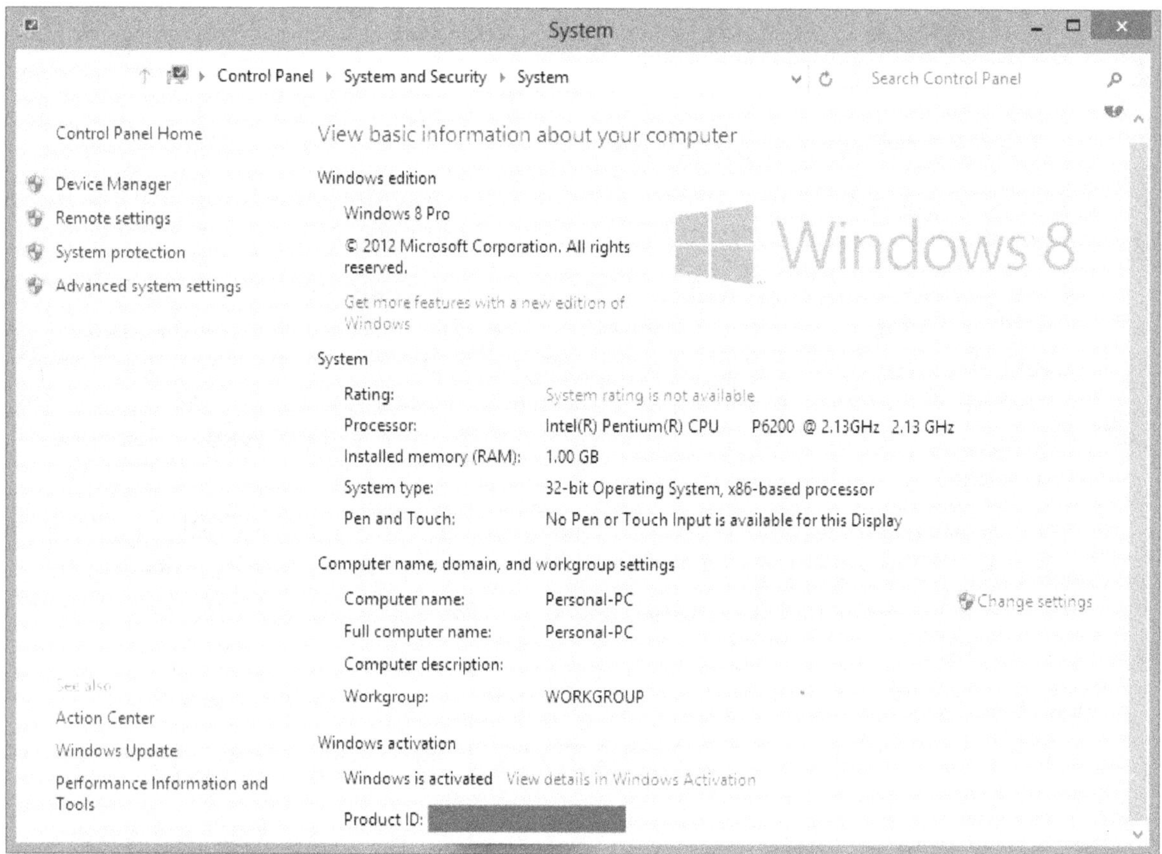

7. Close **System** window when done.

Enable or Disable Startup Sound

Introduction to Sounds and Sound Schemes

When Microsoft Windows 8 is installed on a computer, a default sound scheme is also automatically configured. Sound scheme notifies users about various events that take place in a computer by playing a notification sound. As per the sound scheme, different notifications play different sounds that help users identify the type of event that occurred. For example, when the Recycle Bin is emptied, Windows 8 plays 'Windows Recycle' sound that helps users know that the Recycle Bin has been successfully emptied. Sound scheme that is by default configured during the installation of Microsoft Windows 8 operating system can be customized as per users' individual preferences.

In pre-Windows 8 operating systems, the default configuration played a startup sound every time Windows used to boot. Moreover, those operating systems also allowed users to modify the startup sounds according to their personal choices. On the other hand, in Microsoft Windows 8, no sound is played when the computer start. In case users want the operating system to play a startup sound, they must enable the feature manually.

How to Enable Startup Sound in Microsoft Windows 8?

In order to enable startup Sound in Microsoft Windows 8, steps given below must be followed:

1. Log on to Microsoft Windows 8 computer with any account.
2. From the **Start** screen, click **Desktop** tile.
3. On the desktop screen, right-click anywhere.
4. From the context menu, click **Personalize**.
5. From the bottom of the **Personalization** window, click **Sounds**.
6. On the opened **Sound** box, make sure that **Sounds** tab is selected.
7. From below the **Program Events** list, check **Play Windows Startup sound** checkbox.

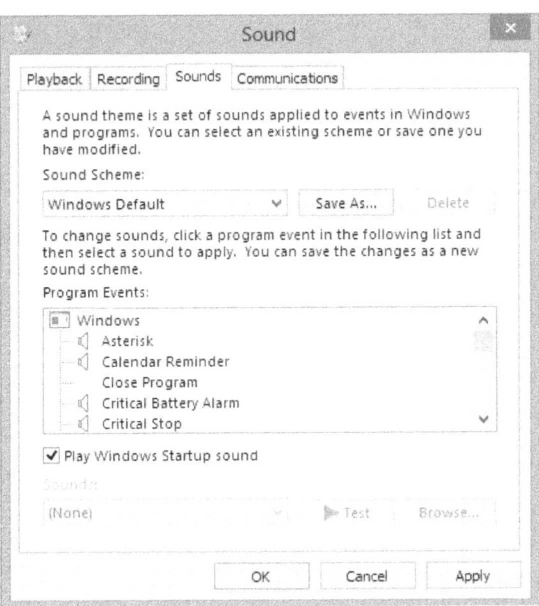

8. Click **OK** to enable Windows Startup sound.

To disable Windows startup sound, steps 1 to 8 can be followed, while unchecking the **Play Windows Startup sound** checkbox when on step 7.

Use Windows Narrator

Introduction to Windows Narrator

Windows Narrator is a built-in program integrated in Microsoft Windows 8 operating system. This program, when initialized, narrates every text that is displayed on the screen. Under normal conditions, and when Windows 8 is used by normal people, Windows Narrator is not required to be initialized. Whereas it might be difficult for physically challenged people, especially with weak eyesight, to use the operating system as comfortably as normal people do. Therefore, such users can initialize Windows Narrator so that they can hear the text that is displayed on the computer screens in order to identify the contents.

Apart from narrating the text that is displayed on a computer screen, Windows Narrator in Microsoft Windows 8 narrates the key presses and mouse movements as well. With the help of this feature, physically challenged users can provide inputs and give commands to the computer easily without looking at the monitors.

Initializing and using Windows Narrator is a user specific task that does not require any elevated privileges. In other words, even a standard user account can initialize and use Windows Narrator to operate Windows with comfort.

How to Initialize Windows Narrator?

In order to initialize Windows Narrator in Microsoft Windows 8, steps given below must be followed:

1. Log on to Microsoft Windows 8 computer with any account.
2. From the **Start** screen, click **Desktop** tile.
3. On the desktop screen, right-click anywhere.
4. From the context menu, click **Personalize**.
5. On the **Personalization** window, from the bottom of the left pane, click **Ease of Access Center**.
6. On the **Ease of Access Center** window, click **Start Narrator** to start Windows Narrator.

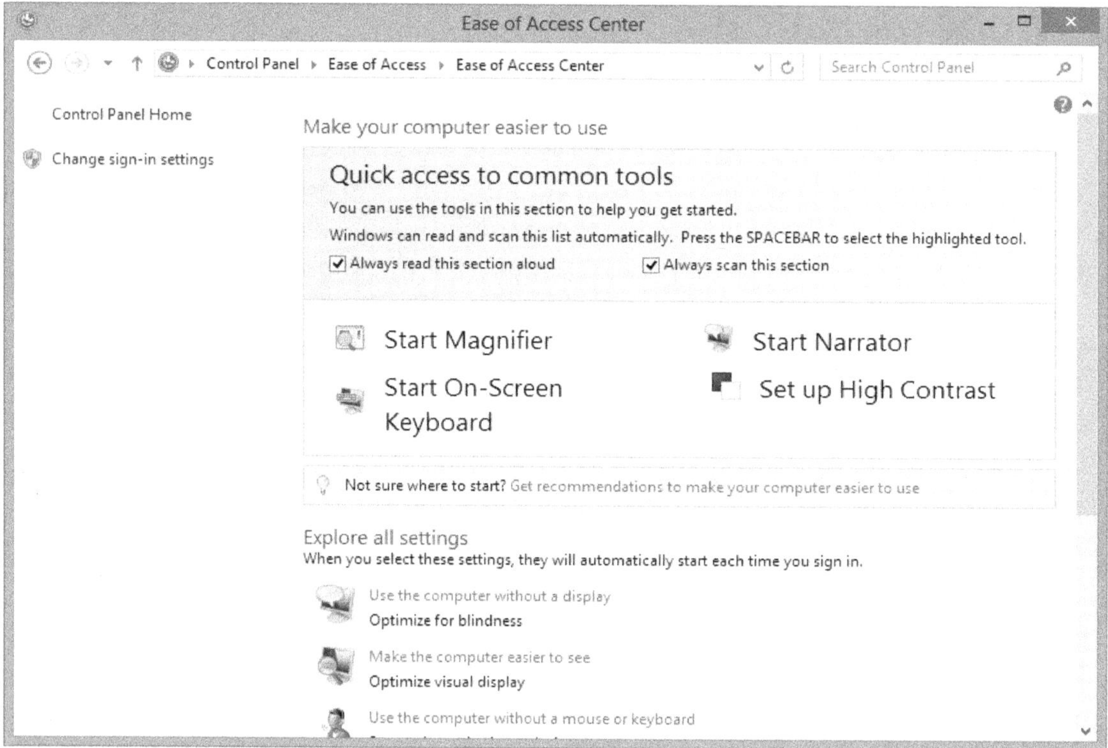

7. To exit **Windows Narrator**, click **Exit** on the **Narrator Settings** window.

Customize 'Send to' Menu

Introduction to 'Send to' Menu

While working on Microsoft Windows 8, it is likely that users might connect additional storage media in order to transfer data from the local hard disk drives of the computers to the connected devices. Additional storage devices that users generally connect to the computers are USB flash drives, external hard disk drives, etc. When such devices are connected to the computers, in order to transfer data from the local hard disk drives to the connected devices, users copy data from the source locations and paste the copied data at the destination locations. This is quite simple and straightforward method to transfer data from one location to another. However there is another option that many users use to transfer data, but there are many of them who are still not aware of this.

The other option that users may use to transfer data from local hard disk drives to any additionally connected storage media is by right-clicking the target object, and hovering mouse to the 'Send to' option from the context menu. Once they do so, a submenu appears that displays various destination locations where the data can be transferred. Additionally connected storage media is also displayed in the same submenu, and users can click the desired media to initiate the data transfer process.

Although 'Send to' menu consists of almost all main destination locations where users or administrators of Windows 8 computer are likely to transfer data, the menu can still be customized and the destination locations can be added or removed as desired.

How to Customize 'Send to' Menu?

In order to customize 'Send to' menu, steps given below must be followed:

1. Log on to Microsoft Windows 8 computer with administrator account.
2. From the **Start** screen, click **Desktop** tile.
3. On the desktop screen, click **File Explorer** icon from the taskbar.
4. From the opened **Libraries** window, navigate to locate the destination that is to be added to the 'Send to' menu.
5. Once located, right-click the destination location and click **Create Shortcut** from the displayed context menu.
6. Once the shortcut is created, cut the shortcut file and paste it in **C:\Users\<user-name>\AppData\Roaming\Microsoft\Windows\SendTo** folder.

   ***Note**: 'C:' in the above path is the system drive where Windows 8 has been installed. Drive letter may vary if Windows 8 is installed on multi-boot environment. In that case 'C:' must be replaced with the drive letter of the system drive. <username> represents the name of the user account for which the 'Send to' menu is modified. 'Users' folder contains the folders with the names of the user accounts that are created in Windows 8 operating system.*

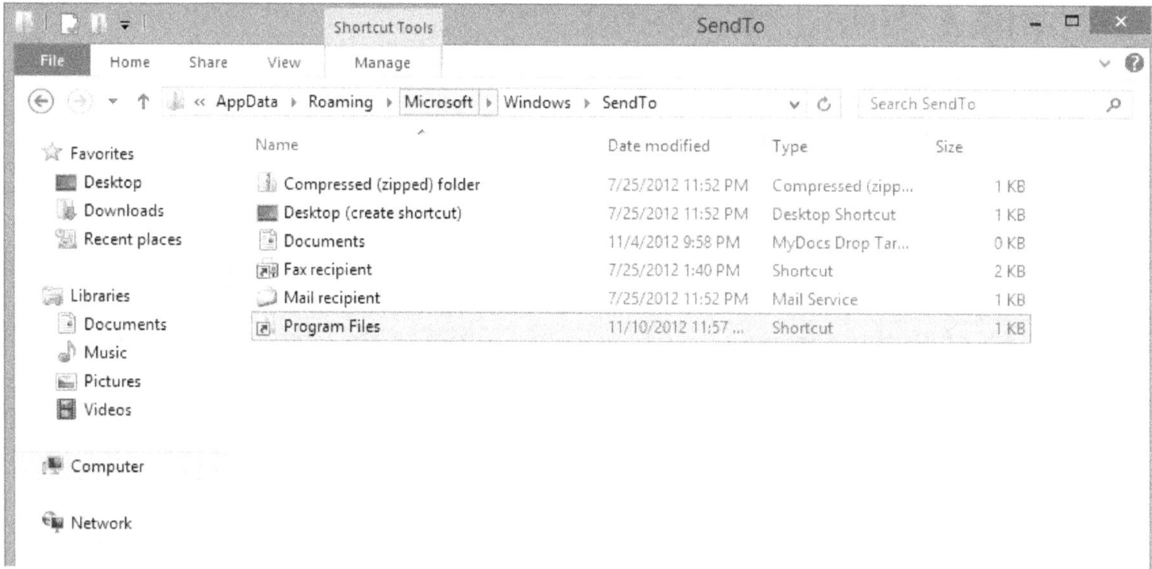

7. Log on to the computer with the user account whose 'Send to' menu has been modified to view the added location in the menu.

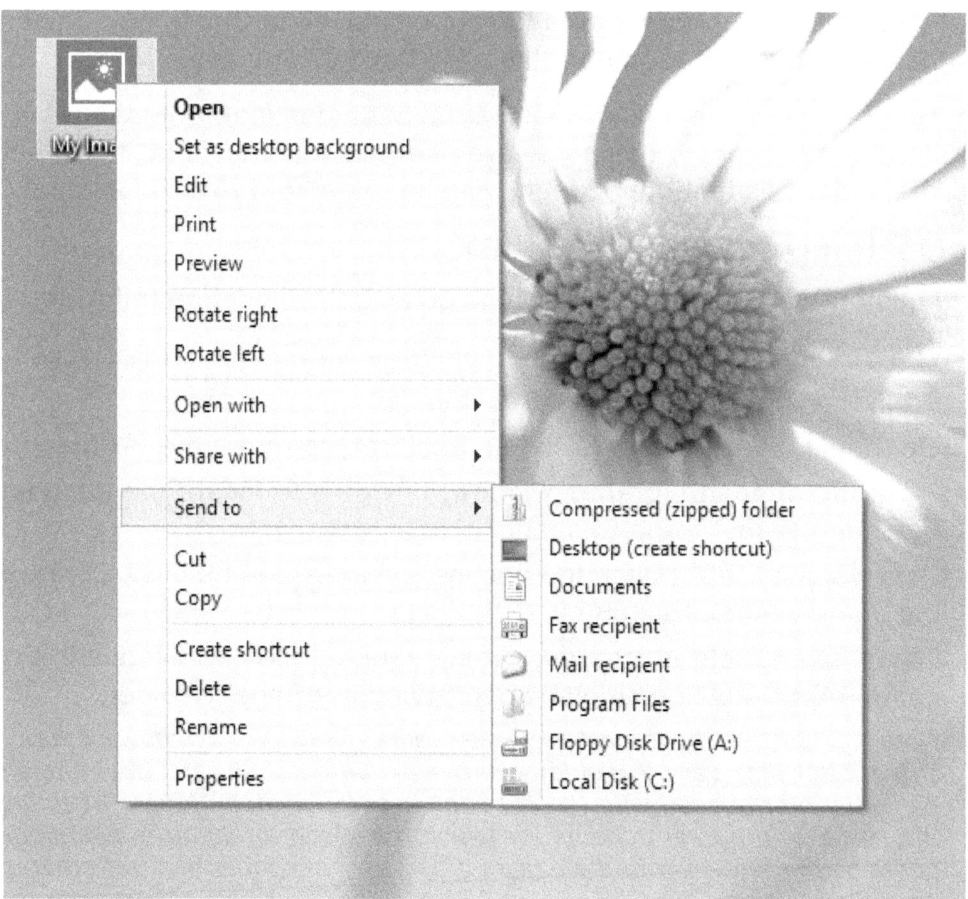

Display Hidden Locations of 'Send to' Menu

Introduction to 'Send to' Menu Locations

In Microsoft Windows 8, when any object is right-clicked and the mouse is hovered to 'Send to' option from the displayed context menu, the submenu that appears consists of some default destination locations where the object can be sent. The default locations that are displayed include any connected removable drive, Desktop (create shortcut), optical media drives, etc. These default locations are the most common destination locations where users are expected to transfer data while using Windows 8 computer in their regular day to day lives.

As mentioned in previous chapter, although default destination locations can be added or removed from the 'Send to' menu, some hidden destination locations are also available in the menu but are not visible by default. In other words, even if users do not customize the 'Send to' menu, they can still transfer data to the hidden destination locations by making them visible in the 'Send to' menus of the objects' context menus.

How to View and Transfer Data to the Hidden 'Send to' Destination Locations?

In order to view and transfer data to the hidden 'Send to' locations, the steps given below must be followed:

1. Log on to Microsoft Windows 8 computer with administrator account.
2. From the **Start** screen, click **Desktop** tile.
3. On the desktop screen, click **File Explorer** icon from the taskbar.
4. From the opened **Libraries** window, navigate to locate the target object that is to be sent to the hidden location in the 'Send to' menu.
5. Once located, click to select the object and press and hold **Shift** key.
6. While pressing **Shift** key down, right-click the selected object.
7. From the displayed context menu, go to **Send to** option to view additional destination locations in the displayed submenu.

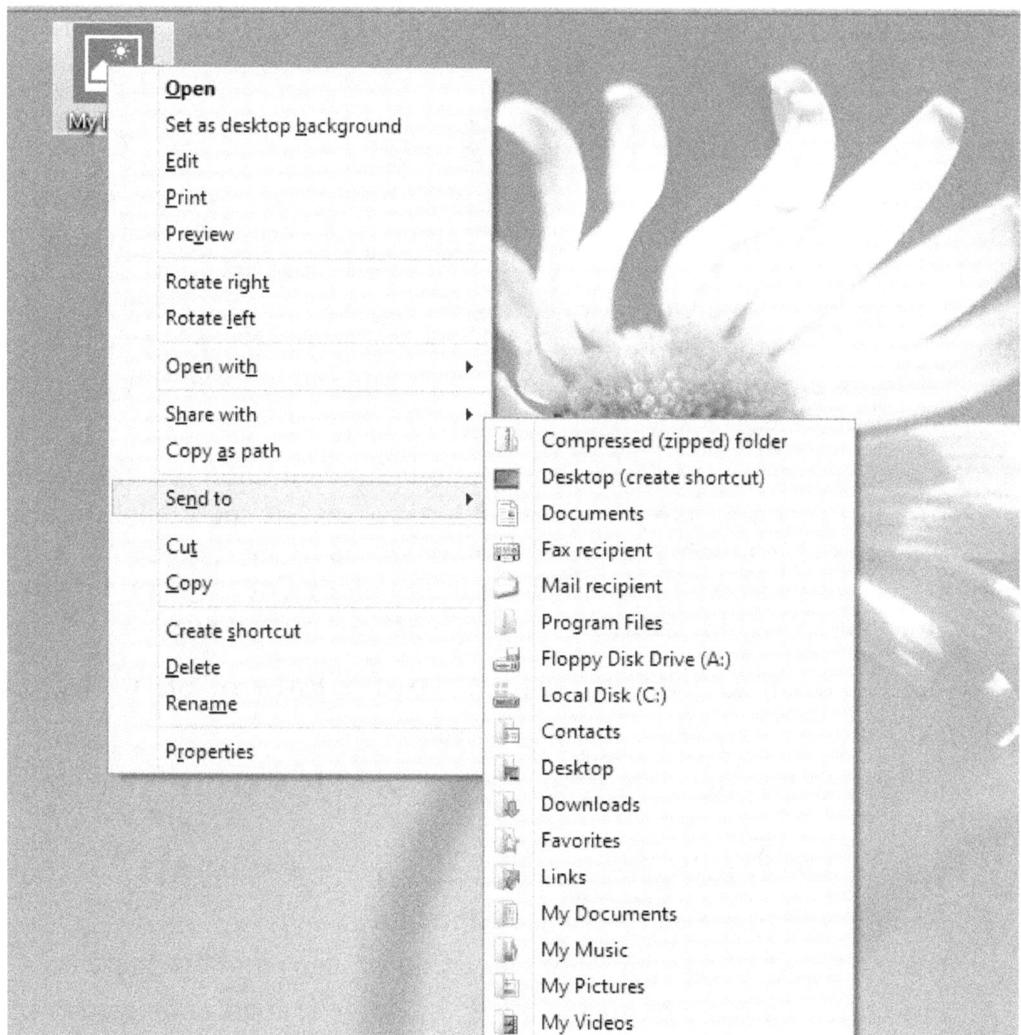

8. Click the desired destination from the submenu to send the selected object to that location.

Use Character Map

Introduction to Character Map

Character Map is a built-in tool in Microsoft Windows 8 that allows users to find and type special characters that are not normally present on the keyboard. Special characters that users may want to type can be a heart shape, a smiley face, some special bullets, etc. With the help of Character Map, users can locate special shapes of their choices and can either copy them to the clipboard, or can view their keystroke codes right end of the status bar of the Character Map interface. The codes can then be typed in the text editor interface using the keyboard to make the corresponding special character.

Users can also select different fonts which make Character Map display various types of symbols related to the selected font.

How to Use Character Map?

In order to copy a symbol to the clipboard or view its code using Character Map in Microsoft Windows 8, steps given below must be followed:

1. Log on to Microsoft Windows 8 computer with any account.
2. From the **Start** screen, click **Desktop** tile.
3. On the desktop window, open any text editor (e.g. MS Word).
4. Hover mouse to the bottom right corner of the window.
5. From the displayed options, click **Search**.
6. On the opened **Apps** window, click **Character Map** from the **Windows Accessories** category.
7. On the **Character Map**'s opened interface, from the displayed symbols, click to select the one that is to be inserted into the text editor.

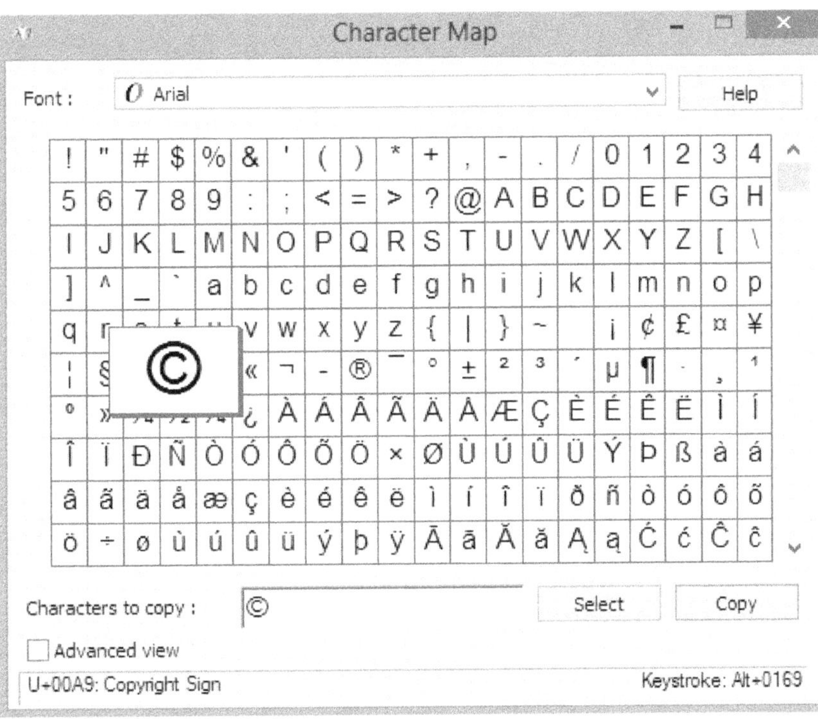

8. Click Select button and then click Copy button to copy the symbol to the clipboard. Alternatively, its corresponding keystroke code can also be viewed from the right side of status bar of the **Character Map**.
9. Make the text editor interface active and paste the copied symbol. Alternatively, keyboard can also be used to type the corresponding keystroke codes to insert the selected symbol into the text editor.
10. Close **Character Map** when done.

Pin Run Command to the Taskbar

Introduction to Run Command

In all Microsoft Windows operating systems Run command box is always available that helps users to execute the commands instantaneously. Many users avoid opening the installed applications by navigating through the various options in Windows. They rather prefer typing the names of the applications in the Run command box in order to initiate them. For example if users want to initiate Calculator in Microsoft Windows, they can initiate the Run command box and can type 'Calc' command and can press 'Enter' key to open the application. Same process (but different commands) can be followed to initiate Notepad, WordPad, Microsoft Word, etc.

In Microsoft Windows Vista and Windows 7 operating systems, Start menu also had a Search box that was available at the bottom of the menu. With the presence of the Search box, requirement of Run command box was almost eliminated. In these operating systems, users could type the names of the desired programs right in the Search box and could press 'Enter' key to open any installed application. Although the initialization of the applications was quite easy with the help of Search box, Run command box still has an added advantage that the Search box doesn't have. When a command is typed in the Run command box, the typed command is saved in the buffer and can be executed multiple times just by selecting it from the list of commands displayed in the Run command box. On the other hand, Search box does not buffer the commands. This means that every time users want to initiate a program, they are required to type the entire command in the Search box.

Because of the modified user interface of Microsoft Windows 8, for many users it might become a challenging task to locate Run command. Therefore it is recommended that the command should be pinned to the taskbar so that it can be accessed easily and instantaneously.

How to Pin Run Command to the Taskbar

In order to pin Run command to the taskbar, steps given below must be followed:

1. Log on to Microsoft Windows 8 computer with the account on which Run command box is to be placed in the taskbar.
2. From the **Start** screen, click **Desktop** tile.
3. On the desktop screen, right-click anywhere and from the context menu, go to **New**.
4. From the displayed submenu, click **Shortcut**.
5. On the opened **Create Shortcut** window, in the **Type the location for the item** field type **C:\Windows\explorer.exe shell:::{2559a1f3-21d7-11d4-bdaf-00c04f60b9f0}** and click **Next.**

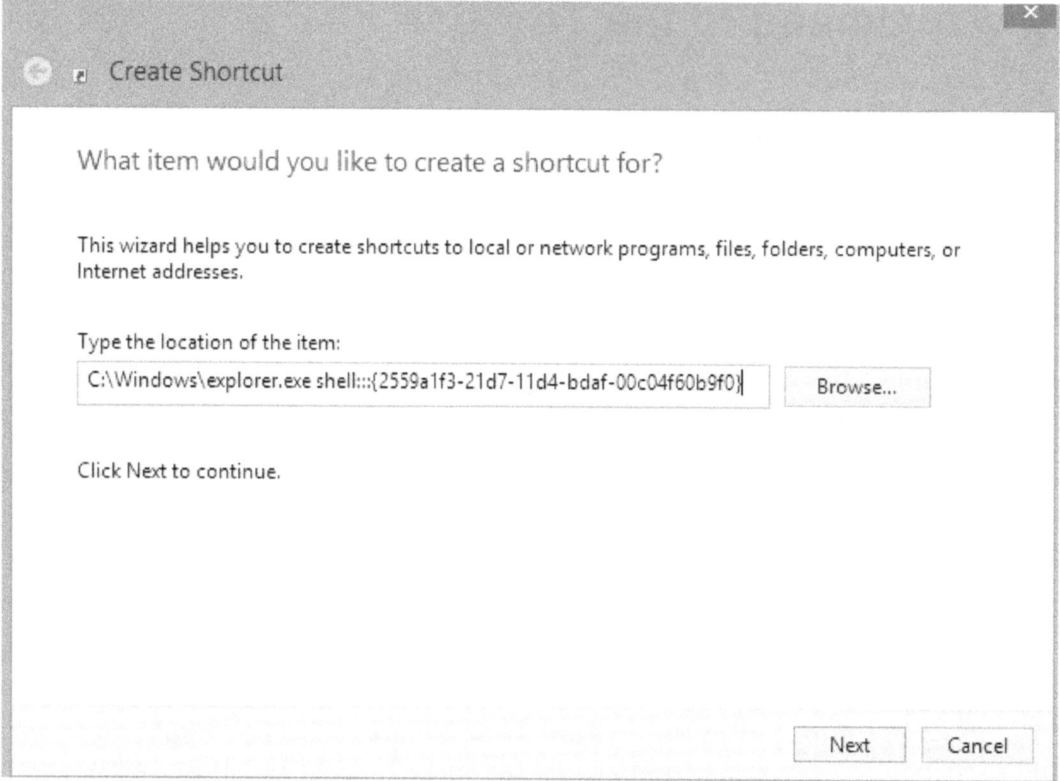

6. On the next window, specify a name for the shortcut (e.g. Run) in the **Type a name for this shortcut** field and click **Finish**.
7. Once done, back on the desktop screen, drag the created shortcut to the task-bar.
8. To open the **Run** command box, click the dragged shortcut from the taskbar.

Add Sticky Notes to the Desktop

Introduction to Gadgets

With the release of Microsoft Windows Vista, the concept of gadgets was also introduced. Gadgets are small programs that are integrated with the operating system and are automatically installed along with the installation of the OS. In Microsoft Windows Vista, some gadgets were automatically displayed right after the successful completion of the installation process of the operating system. In order to display the gadgets on the desktop screens in Windows Vista, another built-in application named Sidebar was also required to be initialized. Because of this, Microsoft Windows Vista used to consume additional resources and was considered more resource intensive as compared to Microsoft Windows 7. In Windows 7, the gadgets were not displayed by default, and when users added gadgets on the desktop screen, no sidebar was required. This remarkably reduced consumption of the resources and also allowed users to place the gadgets anywhere on the desktop screens.

However, because of new Metro UI Start screen in Microsoft Windows 8, that allows apps to be accessed instantaneously, Gadgets platform has been removed from the operating system.

Introduction to Sticky Notes

Sticky Notes is an app which when initiated, provides a small text editor interface right on the desktop screen and allows users to note down important information easily. For example if a user is attending a telephone call and requires to note down a dictation or a telephone number, Sticky Notes app becomes a handy tool in such situation.

Earlier, Sticky Notes was considered a gadget that was automatically installed along with the installation of Windows operating systems, and was by default displayed on Windows Vista desktop screen. In Microsoft Windows 8, since Gadgets platform has been removed, Sticky Notes can be accessed from Apps screen.

How to Add Sticky Notes on the Desktop Screen?

In order to add Sticky Notes on the desktop screen, steps given below must be followed:

1. Log on to Windows 8 computer with the account on which Sticky Notes is to be added to the desktop.
2. From the **Start** screen, click **Desktop** tile.
3. On the desktop screen, hover mouse to the bottom right corner of the window.
4. From the displayed options, click **Search**.
5. On the opened **Apps** window, locate **Sticky Notes** under **Windows Accessories** category.

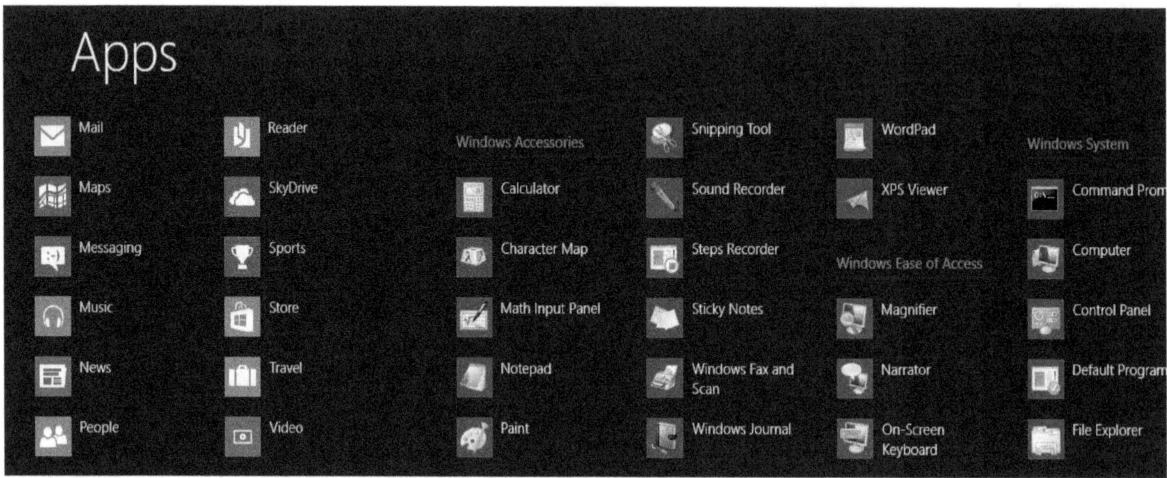

6. Once located, click **Sticky Notes** to place it on the desktop.
7. Click inside the sticky note to start typing.

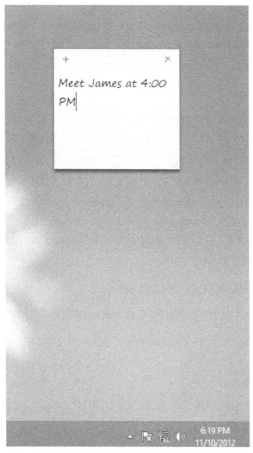

8. To add another instance, click plus sign (+) on the top left corner of an existing sticky note.

Configure Laptop PC's Reaction When Its Lid Is Closed

Introduction to Laptop PCs' Lids' Reactions

When an operating system is installed on a laptop computer, several laptop specific functions and features are also installed along with the OS. These additional functions and features help users customize their laptop PC settings according to their personal preferences and choices. For example when Microsoft Windows 8 is installed on a desktop computer, a default power scheme is automatically configured and set. The default power scheme allows users to customize the power plan settings so that the computer can provide optimum results. Whereas when Windows 8 is installed on a laptop PC, apart from the default power plan settings and options, the power scheme also provides additional laptop specific power option. These laptop specific power options allow users to configure the laptops for both the situations, i.e. when they are running on batteries and when they are plugged in to the direct power supply.

Similarly Windows 8 running on a laptop also provides additional laptop's lid related features that allow users to configure the reaction of the laptop PC when its lid is closed while it is powered on. With the help of available options, users can make the laptop go to sleep mode, hibernate, shut down or do nothing when its lid is closed.

How to Configure Laptop's Reaction When Its Lid Is Closed?

In order to configure Microsoft Windows 8 laptop's reaction when its lid is closed, steps given below must be followed:

1. Log on to Microsoft Windows 8 computer with any account.
2. From the **Start** screen, click **Desktop** tile.
3. From the desktop screen, hover mouse to the bottom right corner of the window.
4. From the displayed options, click **Settings**.
5. On the **Settings** pane, click **Control Panel**.
6. On the **Control Panel** window, click **System and Security** category.
7. On the opened **System and Security** window, right-click **Power Options** category.
8. On the **Power Options** window, click **Choose what closing the lid does** option from the left pane.
9. On the **System Settings** window, under the **Power and sleep buttons and lid settings** section, choose the appropriate reaction of the lid when closed from the **When I close the lid** drop-down lists under both **On battery** and **Plugged in** columns.

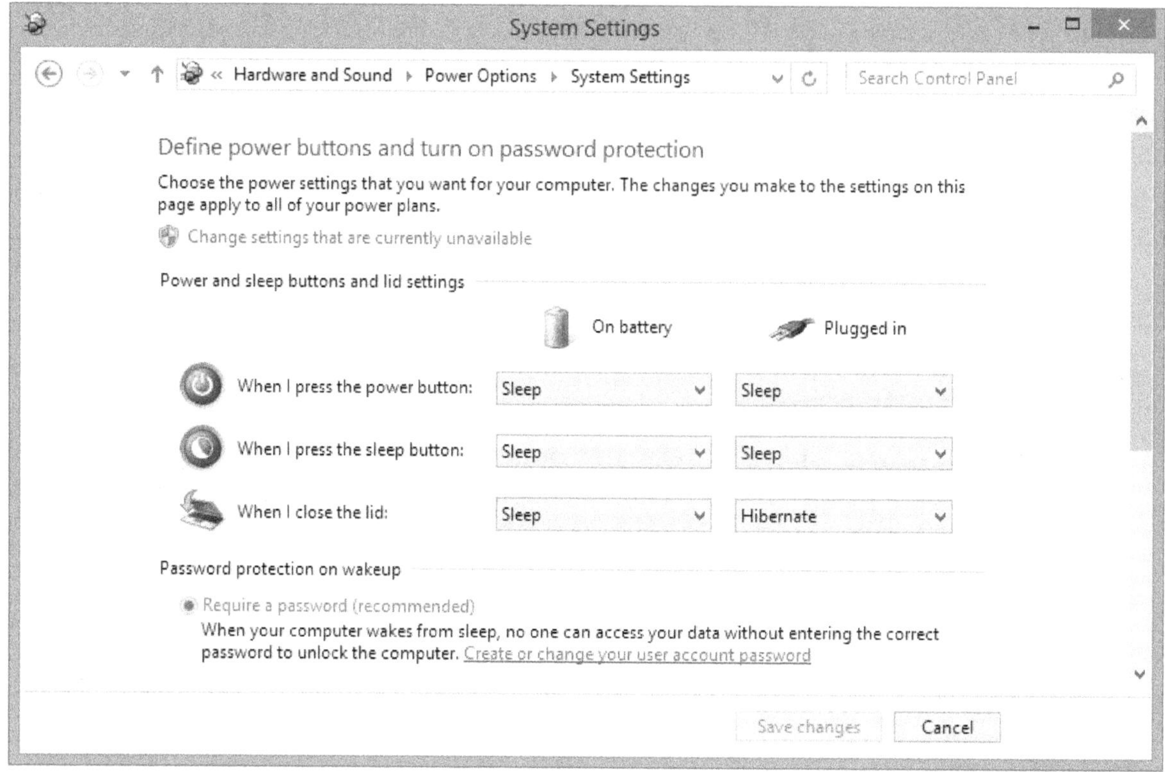

10. Click **Save changes** when done.

Add Administrative Tools to Start Screen

Introduction to Administrative Tools and Its Location

Administrative Tools is a container that consists of several advanced Windows features that can be used to customize the operating system as per the needs. In pre-Windows 8 operating systems, the OS had a Start menu that can be opened by clicking the Start button (in Microsoft Windows XP or below) or the Start orb (in Microsoft Windows Vista and Windows 7). In these operating systems, Administrative Tools was not by default added to the Start menu, and if it was required to be accessed quite frequently, users were required to pin Administrative Tools to the Start menu manually.

Since in Microsoft Windows 8 the Start menu has been replaced by the Metro UI Start screen, it has become a bit challenging for the new users to locate the frequently used options. Moreover, because of the unavailability of the Start menu, it is also not possible for the users to pin Administrative Tools manually. However things can still become easier by pinning Administrative Tools feature to the Start screen to get instantaneous access.

Pinning Administrative Tools to the Start screen is a user specific task and can be performed without elevated privileges. However administrative credentials might still be required to initiate and work on the tools available in the Administrative Tools. This is because the options available in Administrative Tools are mostly used by the administrators to perform administrative tasks on the computers.

How to Pin Administrative Tools to the Start Screen?

In order to pin Administrative Tools to the Start screen in Microsoft Windows 8, steps given below must be followed:

1. Log on to Microsoft Windows 8 computer with the account on which **Administrative Tools** is to be placed in the Start screen.
2. From the **Start** screen, click **Desktop** tile.
3. From the desktop screen, hover mouse to the bottom right corner of the window.
4. From the displayed options, click **Settings**.
5. On the **Settings** pane, click **Control Panel**.
6. On the **Control Panel** window, click **System and Security** category.
7. On the opened **System and Security** window, right-click **Administrative Tools** category.
8. From the displayed context menu, click **Pin to Start**.

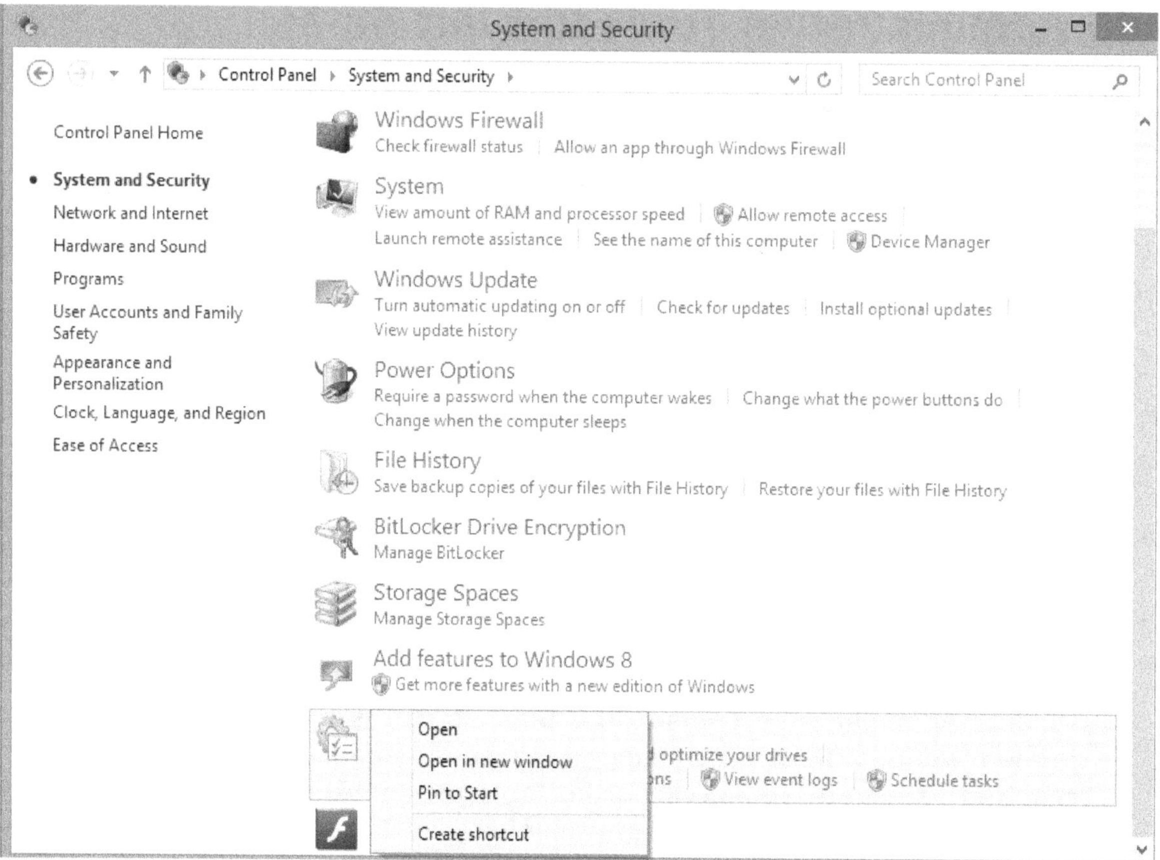

To remove **Administrative Tools** from the **Start** screen, hover mouse to the bottom left corner of the window and click the popped up **Start** screen icon. On the **Start** screen, right-click **Administrative Tools** and from the advanced options displayed at the bottom of the screen, click **Unpin from Start**.

Note: *In almost all Microsoft-based network operating systems, like Windows Server 2003 and Windows Server 2008, Administrative Tools are by default available in the Start menu, and therefore no manual configuration is required.*

Set Default Landing Folder

Introduction to Landing Folder

When users log on to Windows 8 computer and on the desktop window they click the File Explorer icon from the taskbar, Libraries window opens. Libraries window contains logged on user's profile specific containers where the user might have stored data. The containers that Libraries window displays are Documents, Music, Pictures and Videos.

Unlike Microsoft Windows XP, in which My Computer icon was by default available on the desktop, Windows 8 only has the Recycle Bin icon on the desktop screen as default profile settings. This default profile settings for Windows 8 might sometimes confuse users if they want to open Computer window while using the operating system. Although they have an option to place Computer icon on the desktop window, some users might still want the File Explorer icon to open Computer window when it is clicked.

Windows 8 allows users to change the default landing folder from Libraries to Computer window. This process is user specific and must be done on every user account that resides in Microsoft Windows 8 computer.

How to Change Landing Folder from Libraries to Computer?

In order to change the Libraries landing folder to Computer window, steps given below must be followed:

1. Log on to Microsoft Windows 8 computer with any account.
2. From the **Start** screen, click **Desktop** tile.
3. Right-click the **File Explorer** icon from the taskbar.
4. From the displayed options, right-click **File Explorer**.
5. From the context menu, click **Properties**.

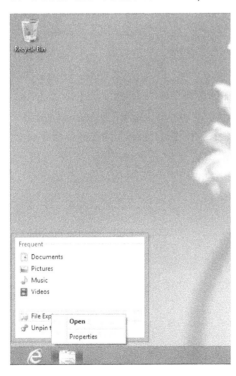

6. On the **File Explorer Properties** box, make sure that **Shortcut** tab is selected.
7. In the **Target** field, note down the current path and save it at a secured location for future use.
8. Once done, replace the entire path in the **Target** field with **%windir%\explorer.exe /root,::{20D04FE0-3AEA-1069-A2D8-08002B30309D}**.

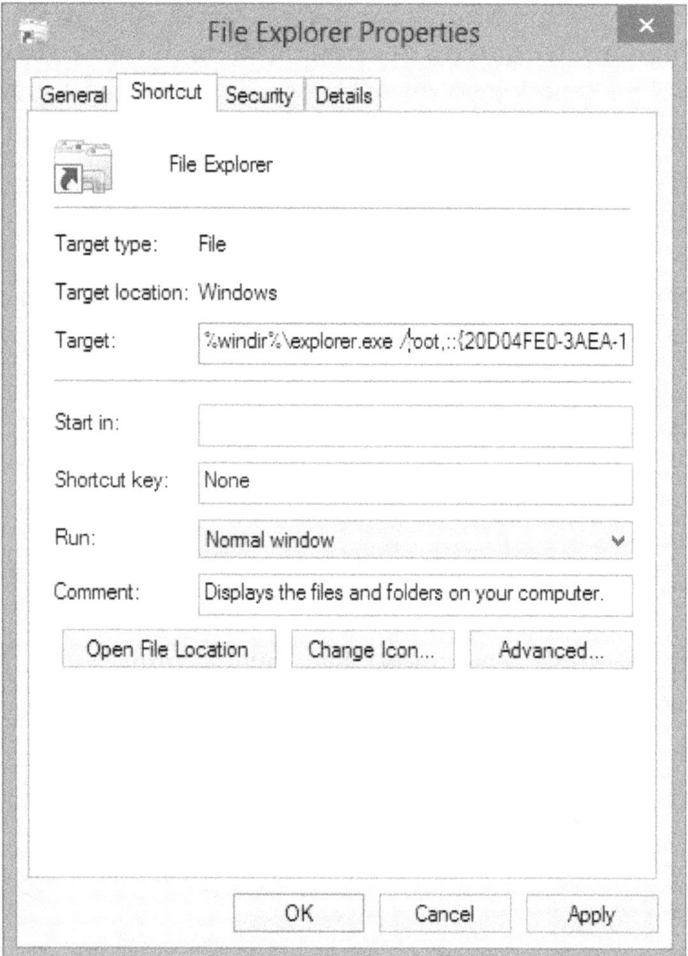

9. Click **OK** to save the changes.
10. Click **File Explorer** icon to get **Computer** the window.

To get back Libraries window as the landing folder when File Explorer icon is clicked, follow steps from 1 to 9, while replacing the current text in the **Target** field with the one that was noted in step 7.

Remove Touch Keyboard from the Taskbar

Introduction to Touch Keyboard

Since Microsoft Windows 8 has been designed to be mostly used on the devices that have touch screens, by default Touch Keyboard is displayed in the taskbar near the notification area. When This Touch Keyboard is tapped on the touchscreen monitor, a virtual keyboard appears on the screen. Users can touch the virtual keys displayed on the virtual keyboard to type.

While using any device that has touchscreen, this Touch Keyboard tool serves quite good to the end-users. However users who use normal laptop computers or desktop PCs might not appreciate to have an additional tool displayed on the taskbar, and may want to remove it.

How to Remove Touch Keyboard from the Taskbar?

In order to remove Touch Remote from Microsoft Windows 8 taskbar, steps given below must be followed:

1. Log on to Microsoft Windows 8 computer with any account.
2. From the **Start** screen, click **Desktop** tile.
3. On the desktop screen, right-click the taskbar.
4. From the displayed context menu, go to **Toolbars** option.
5. From the displayed submenu, click to uncheck **Touch Keyboard**.

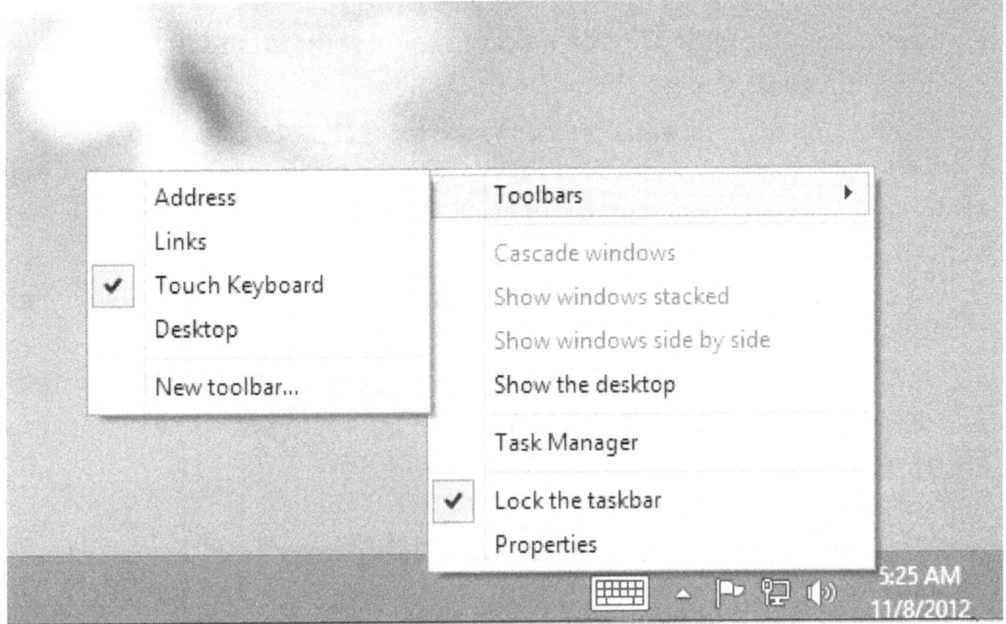

To get the **Touch Keyboard** back, steps 1 to 5 can be followed. Clicking the **Touch Keyboard** option from the **Toolbars** submenu works as a toggle system which when click for the first time disables the virtual keyboard, and clicking it again re-enables it.

Change Computer's Owner Name

Introduction to Computers' Owner Names

When Microsoft Windows 8 is installed on bare metal machine, i.e. a fresh install is performed, the installation process requests the installers to define a user name, which then is automatically added to the Administrators group. Since the user that is created during the installation of the operating system is added to the Administrators group, it gets unrestricted privileges on the computer. Moreover, since this user is the first account on the computer that holds elevated privileges, the operating system automatically registers its name as the owner of the computer. The name of the owner of the computer can be seen by typing WINVER command in the Run command box and hitting Enter key. As it is not recommended to erase Windows and reinstall the operating system every now and then, owner's name of the computer remains unchanged, until a fresh copy of Windows is installed on the computer.

When a used PC is purchased in which Windows is already installed, the previous owners name can be seen by typing WINVER command in the Run command box. In home environments this situation doesn't matter much, whereas when a used PC is bought in a production environment, the new owner might want to change the owner's name and replace it with the name of the administrator or the current organization.

How to Change Owner's Name of a Computer?

In order to change owner's name on a Microsoft Windows 8 computer, steps given below must be followed:

1. Log on to Microsoft Windows 8 computer with administrator account.
2. From the **Start** screen, click **Desktop** tile.
3. On the desktop screen, press **Windows** + **R** keys simultaneously to initiate **Run** command box.
4. In the opened **Run** command box, type **REGEDIT** command and press **Enter** key.
5. On the displayed **User Account Control** confirmation box, click **Yes** to grant the consent to open **Registry Editor**.
6. On the opened **Registry Editor** window, from the left pane, locate and select
7. **HKEY_LOCAL_MACHINE\SOFTWARE\Microsoft\Windows NT\CurrentVersion**.
8. Once **CurrentVersion** is selected in the left pane, from the right pane double-click **RegisteredOwner** string.
9. In the opened **Edit String** box, in the **Value data** field, replace the current owner name with the new one.

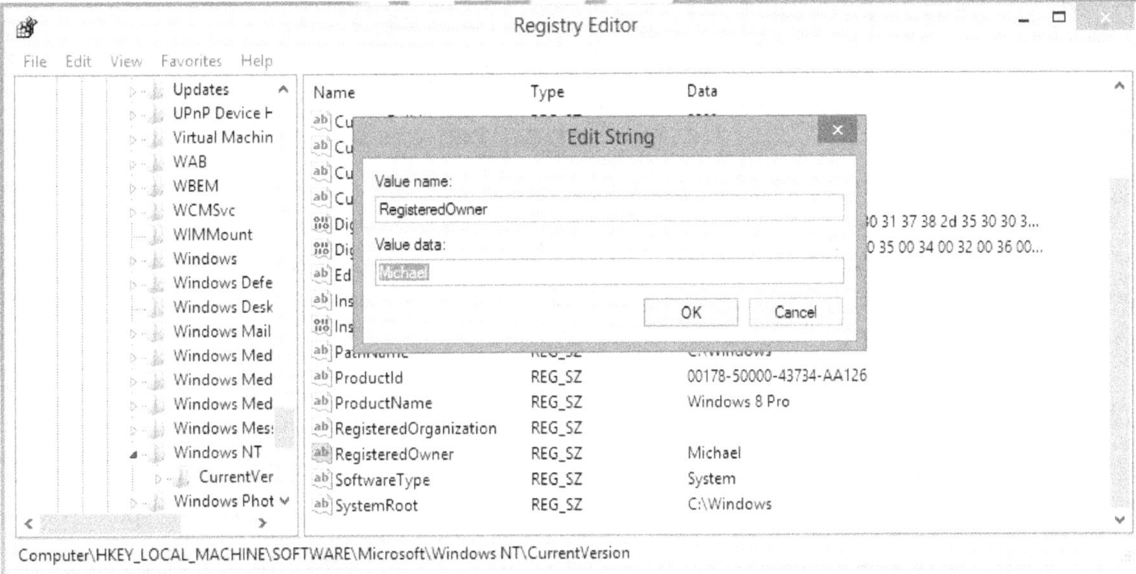

10. Once done, click **OK**.
11. Close the **Registry Editor** window and restart the computer.

Change Registered Organization Name

Introduction to Registered Organization Name

When a fresh copy of Microsoft Windows 8 is installed on a computer, the name of the organization that is specified during the installation becomes permanent and remains intact till the operating system is removed and reinstalled. When a used PC is purchased, the name of the previous organization can be seen by typing WINVER command in the Run command box and pressing Enter key.

As mentioned in previous lesson, in homes the names of previous organizations to which the computers were registered never matter much. Whereas in production environments it becomes essential for the administrators to change previous registered organization names and replace them with the current organizations' names.

Modifying the registered organization name on a Windows 8 computer requires elevated privileges and therefore administrator credentials must be used to perform the task.

How to Change Registered Organization Name?

In order to change registered organization name in Microsoft Windows 8, steps given below must be followed:

1. Log on to Microsoft Windows 8 computer with administrator account.
2. From the **Start** screen, click **Desktop** tile.
3. On the desktop screen, press **Windows** + **R** keys simultaneously to initiate **Run** command box.
4. In the opened **Run** command box, type **REGEDIT** command and press **Enter** key.
5. On the displayed **User Account Control** confirmation box, click **Yes** to grant the consent to open **Registry Editor**.
6. On the opened **Registry Editor** window, from the left pane, locate and select
7. **HKEY_LOCAL_MACHINE\SOFTWARE\Microsoft\Windows NT\CurrentVersion**.
8. Once **CurrentVersion** is selected in the left pane, from the right pane double-click **RegisteredOrganization** string.
9. In the opened **Edit String** box, in the **Value data** field, replace the current organization name with the new one.

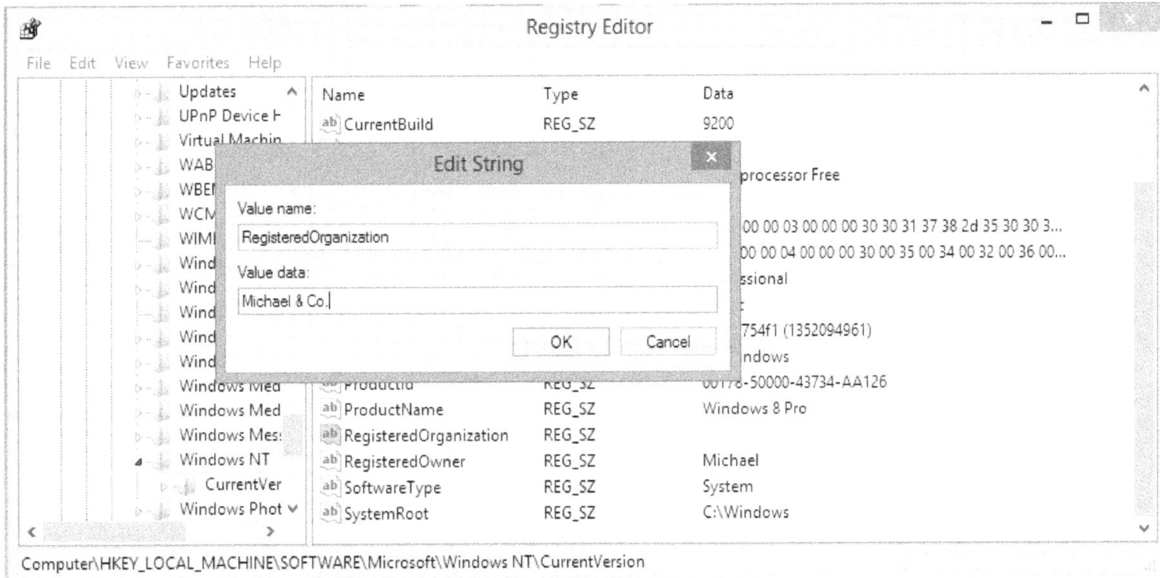

10. Once done, click **OK**.
11. Close the **Registry Editor** window and restart the computer.

Keep NumLock On When Windows Starts

Introduction to the NumLock Status

When Windows 8 is installed on a computer, the default state of the NumLock is set to off. This means that in order to type numbers using the NumPad, users must press the Num-Lock key on their keyboards to turn it on. Sometimes this default configuration doesn't harm at all as users can easily press the NumLock key if they want to type the numbers. Although it is unlikely that normal users would frequently use the NumPad to type the numbers and many laptops do not have NumPads as well, people who belong to accounting domain, or any other domain where numerical digits are frequently used, it becomes easier for them to use NumPads while typing the numbers.

One disadvantage of having the default state of the NumLock off is that if the password of a user account contains numerical characters, the characters could not be typed until the NumLock key is pressed to enable the NumPad. Many times users start using the Num-Pad to type the numerical characters while providing their passwords without noticing the state of the NumLock. Because of this, they type wrong passwords and get confused.

In order to avoid confusions and awkward situations, administrators can configure Windows 8 and make the default state of the NumLock set to on.

How to Keep NumLock On When Windows Starts?

In order to configure Microsoft Windows 8 to keep the NumLock on every time the operating system starts, steps given below must be followed:

1. Log on to Microsoft Windows 8 computer with administrator account.
2. From the **Start** screen, click **Desktop** tile.
3. On the desktop screen, press **Windows** + **R** keys simultaneously to initiate **Run** command box.
4. In the opened **Run** command box, type **REGEDIT** command and press **Enter** key.
5. On the displayed **User Account Control** confirmation box, click **Yes** to grant the consent to open **Registry Editor**.
6. On the opened **Registry Editor** window, from the left pane, locate and select
7. **HKEY_USERS\.DEFAULT\Control Panel\Keyboard**.
8. Once **Keyboard** is selected in the left pane, from the right pane double-click **InitialKeyboardIndicators** string.
9. In the opened **Edit String** box, in the **Value data** field, replace the current value with the **2**.

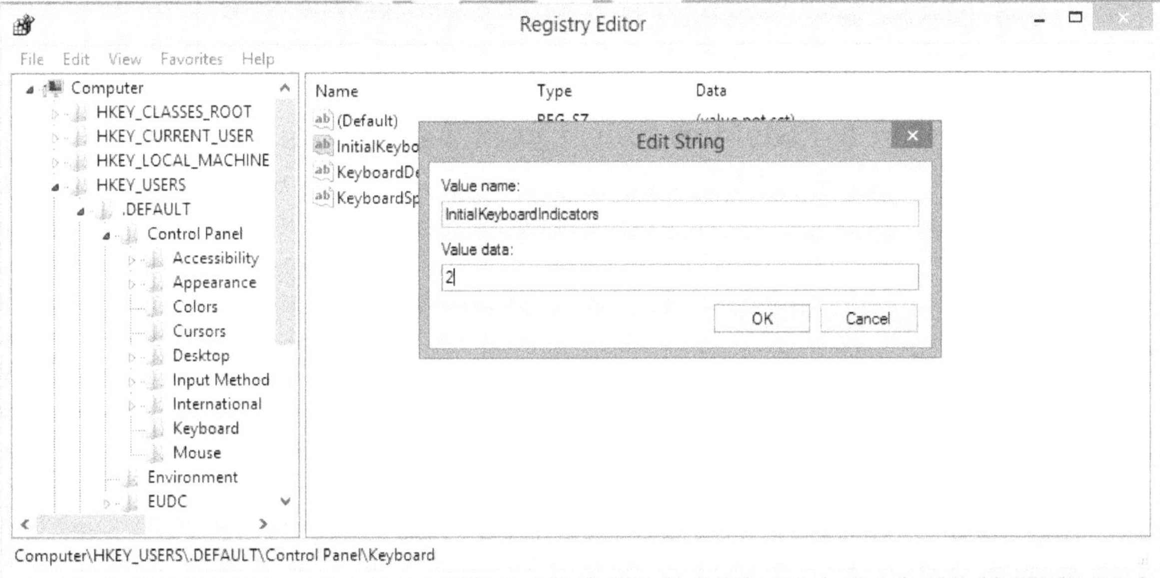

10. Once done, click **OK**.
11. Close the **Registry Editor** window and restart the computer.

Manage Desktop Icon Label Text Appearance

Introduction to Desktop Icon Label Text Appearance

In earlier versions of Microsoft Windows, for example Microsoft Windows XP, the label texts of the desktop icons were not as sharp as they are in Microsoft Windows Vista and above operating systems. The additional feature that makes the texts sharper and clearly visible in latest versions of Microsoft operating systems is known as Drop Shadow. Drop Shadow adds a shadow effect on the icon label texts which makes them clearly visible and more readable.

By default the Drop Shadow feature is enabled in all latest versions of operating systems, and it is recommended that the state of the feature must be left intact to experience clear visibility of the texts. However the feature can be disabled if a CRT monitor is attached to the computer, or if the contrast of the desktop wallpaper is not compatible with the default settings.

How to Disable Drop Shadow?

In order to disable Drop Shadow feature in Microsoft Windows 8, steps given below must be followed:

1. Log on to Microsoft Windows 8 computer with the account on which Drop Shadow feature is to be disabled.
2. From the **Start** screen, click **Desktop** tile.
3. On the desktop screen, click **File Explorer** icon from the taskbar.
4. On the opened **Libraries** window, right-click **Computer** from the left pane.
5. From the displayed context menu, click **Properties**.
6. On the opened **System** window, click **Advanced system settings** from the left pane.
7. On the **System Properties** box, make sure that **Advanced** tab is selected.
8. Under the **Performance** section, click **Settings** button.
9. On the **Performance Options** box, make sure that **Visual Effects** tab is selected.
10. From the available radio buttons, click to select **Custom**.
11. From the displayed list of options, uncheck the **Use drop shadows for icon labels on the desktop** checkbox available at the bottom of the list.

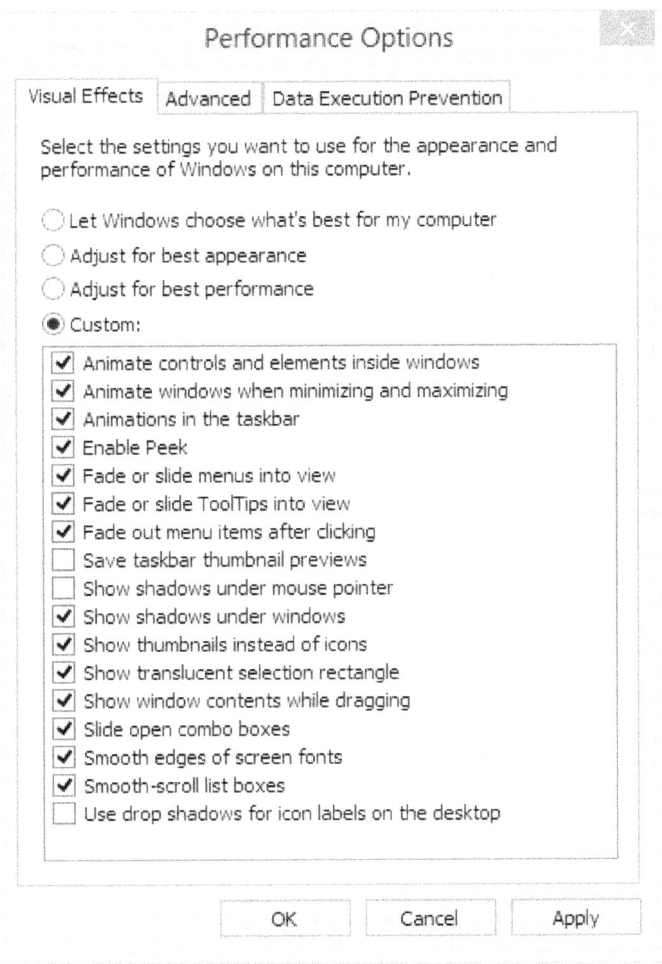

12. Click **OK** when done.
13. Back on the **System Properties** box, click **OK** again.
14. Log off from the user account and log back on to experience the modified settings.

In order to re-enable Drop Shadow feature, steps 1 to 14 must be followed, while checking the **Use drop shadows for icon labels on the desktop** checkbox when on step 11.

Disable Media Features

Introduction to Media Features

When Microsoft Windows 8 is installed on a computer, one media feature named Windows Media Player is automatically installed along with the installation of the operating system. For home users Media Features might be quite useful as no third-party application is required to be installed in order to play media files. On the other hand, when Windows 8 is installed on a computer that is used in production environment, administrators may want to remove the Media Features from the operating system so that the employees cannot use the media programs during office hours and in the official premises.

Although standard user accounts can be restricted from accessing Windows Media Player by various methods, making the program globally unavailable is the easiest way to prevent the misuse of the computers used in production environments.

Removing Media Features from Windows 8 computer is an administrative task and therefore elevated privileges are required to complete the process successfully.

How to Remove Media Features?

In order to remove Media Features from Microsoft Windows 8 computer, steps given below must be followed:

1. Log on to Microsoft Windows 8 computer with administrator account.
2. From the **Start** screen, click **Desktop** tile.
3. On the desktop screen, hover mouse to the bottom right corner of the window.
4. From the displayed options, click **Settings**.
5. On the **Settings** pane, click **Control Panel**.
6. On the opened **Control Panel** window, click **Programs** category.
7. On the **Programs** window, click **Turn Windows features on or off** option under the **Programs and Features** category.
8. On the opened **Windows Features** box, uncheck **Media Features** checkbox.
9. On the opened information box, click **Yes** button to continue removal of the **Media Features**.

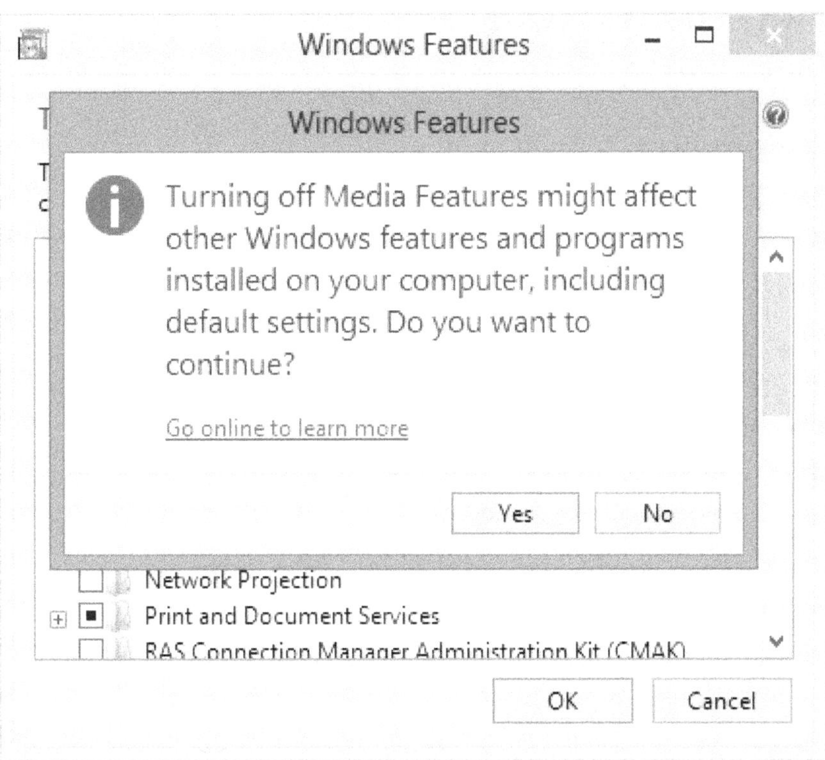

10. Click **OK** and wait till the feature is removed from the computer.
11. Once completed, click **Close** button on the opened box.

To make **Media Features** available again, steps 1 to 11 can be followed, while checking **Media Features** checkbox when on step 8.

Adjust Speed of the Slideshow

Introduction to Slideshow

In Microsoft Windows 8, when multiple images are stored in a folder, the operating system allows users to view all the images by initiating the slideshow. The slideshow that is capable of displaying the images is a built-in feature in Microsoft Windows 8 and can be initiated without installing any additional or third-party application such as Microsoft PowerPoint. Although the built-in slideshow feature does not provide as much configuration options as any dedicated presentation application does, the transition speed of the slideshow can still be adjusted as per users' conveniences.

The speed of the slideshow can be set to any of the three available options in Windows 8. The three options are:

- Slide Show Speed - Slow
- Slide Show Speed - Medium
- Slide Show Speed - Fast

In case users want to customize the speed of the slideshow more granularly, other presentation applications, such as Microsoft PowerPoint, must be installed.

How to Adjust Speed of Sideshow?

In order to adjust speed of the slideshow in Microsoft Windows 8, steps given below must be followed:

1. Log on to Microsoft Windows 8 computer with the account on which the slideshow is to be run with the modified speed.
2. From the **Start** screen, click **Desktop** tile.
3. From the desktop screen, click **File Explorer** icon from the taskbar.
4. On the opened **Libraries** window, navigate to the destination folder where image files are saved.
5. Once located, click **Manage** from the menu bar at the top.
6. From the displayed options in the ribbon, click **Slideshow** from the **View** category.
7. Once the slideshow is initiated, right-click the running show and from the context menu, select the desired slide show speed.

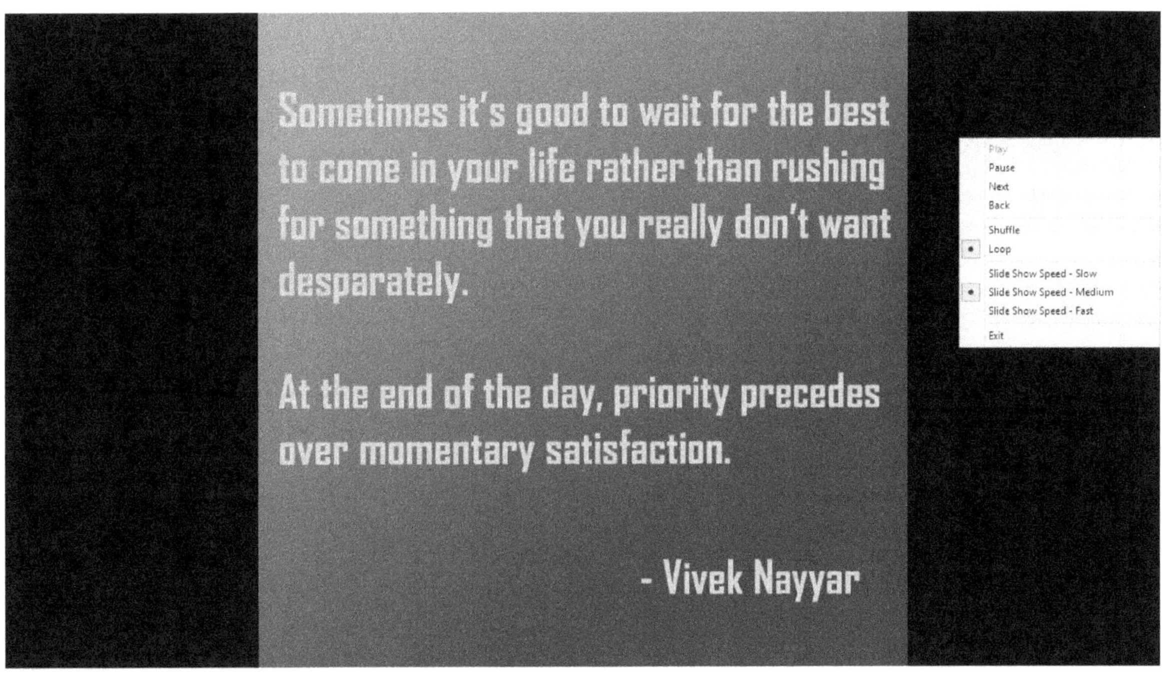

8. To exit the slide show, press **Esc** key on the keyboard.

Configure Pointing Devices

Introduction to Pointing Devices

Since the release of the very first Graphical User Interface-based operating system, i.e. Microsoft Windows 95, pointing devices, such as the Mouse, are mostly used by end users in order to work on the operating systems easily and quickly. Unlike Command Line Interface, where users were required to type the entire command to perform a task, Graphical User Interface (GUI) allows users to use their pointing devices to locate the target objects just with the movement of their hands. Moreover, in order to perform certain tasks on the selected objects, users just need to click the buttons available on the pointing devices. For example if an object is to be deleted from the computer, it can be right-clicked and 'Delete' option can be selected from the displayed context menu.

When Windows is used under normal conditions, the default pointing device settings that are automatically configured during the installation of the operating system are best and provide optimum user experience. Complications may occur when a user is left-hander and finds it challenging to use the pointing device (the Mouse) with the default settings. Sometimes physically challenged users might also find it complicated to use the mouse as it might be hard for them to double-click the mouse buttons quickly to open a folder or a file, or to initialize an application.

Considering the above challenges, Microsoft Windows 8 allows users to configure the pointing devices and customize the default settings according to their individual preferences. Since it is expected that Windows 8 would be installed on the laptop PCs, the operating system allows users to configure the settings of the pointing devices for both TouchPad and Mouse.

How to Customize Pointing Device Settings?

In order to customize pointing device settings in Microsoft Windows 8, steps given below must be followed:

1. Log on to Microsoft Windows 8 computer with the account on which the mouse buttons are to be switched.
2. From the **Start** screen, click **Desktop** tile.
3. On the desktop screen, over mouse to the bottom right corner of the window.
4. From the displayed options, click **Settings**.
5. On the **Settings** pane, click **Control Panel**.
6. On the **Control Panel** window, click **Hardware and Sound** category.
7. On the **Hardware and Sound** window, click **Mouse** from the **Devices and Printers** category.
8. On the **Mouse Properties** box, make sure that **Buttons** tab is selected.
9. Under the **Button configuration** section, check **Switch primary and secondary buttons** checkbox.

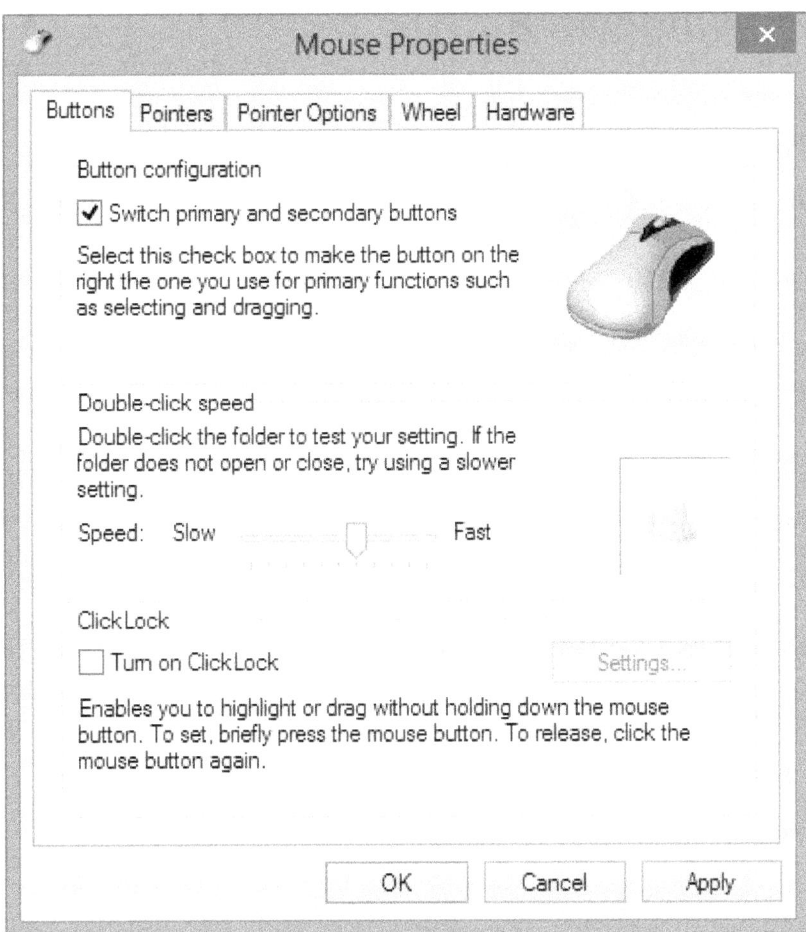

10. Once checked, right-click **OK** button. (**OK** button can be pressed only by right-clicking on it because as soon as the above mentioned checkbox is checked, the configuration is applied instantaneously).

To get the default mouse settings back, follow steps 1 to 10 while unchecking the **Switch primary and secondary buttons** checkbox when on step 9. (Left-click can be used to click **OK** button in this case.)

Note: *Above mentioned steps are same for both Mouse and the Touchpad (laptop PCs). In order to customize the settings for any particular device, users must select the device type from the available device list.*

Activate Microsoft Windows 8

Introduction to Windows 8 Activation

When a laptop PC is purchased from a vendor, it is likely that it would have Microsoft Windows 8 already installed in it. Since vendors nowadays purchase Windows license keys in bulk, the installed Windows 8 operating system on the purchased laptop PC is likely to be activated by Original Equipment Manufacturer (OEM). Whereas when Windows 8 is separately purchased either online or from a retail shop, the purchased copy of the operating system must be activated manually in order to use the OS for unlimited time duration.

Although a trial version of Microsoft Windows 8 can be downloaded from Microsoft's official website, the system becomes unusable once the trial period of the operating system expires. In this situation, a genuinely purchased product key of Windows 8 must be used to activate the OS.

Apart from using the operating system for a limited period of time, another benefit of activating the installed copy of Windows 8 is that the users can get latest updates from Microsoft and can also avail technical support that Microsoft support team provides.

How to Activate an Installed Copy of Microsoft Windows 8?

In order to activate an installed copy of Microsoft Windows 8, steps given below must be followed:

1. Make sure that the computer is connected to an active Internet connection.
2. Log on to Microsoft Windows 8 computer with administrator account.
3. From the **Start** screen, click **Desktop** tile.
4. On the desktop screen, click **File Explorer** icon from the taskbar.
5. On the **Libraries** window, right-click **Computer** from the left pane.
6. From the context menu, click **Properties**.
7. On the **System** window, under the **Windows activation** section click the **View details in Windows activation** option.
8. On the **Windows Activation** screen, click appropriate activation button (to activate Windows online or to buy an activation key).

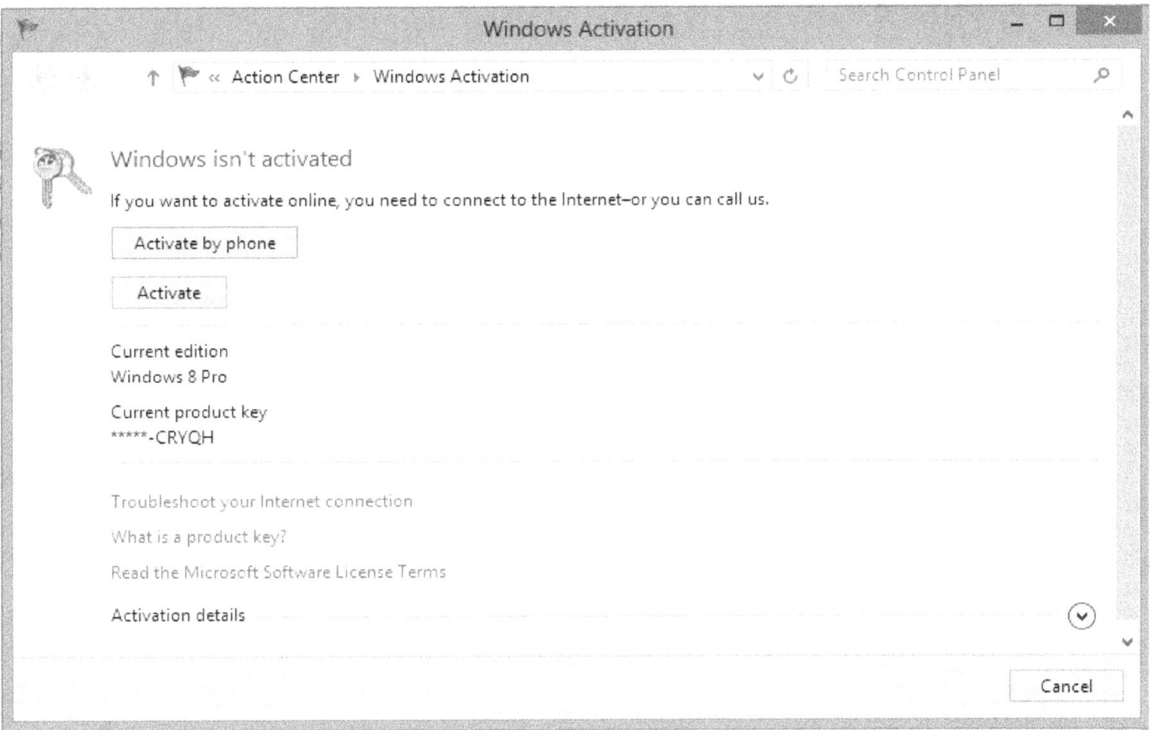

9. Follow on-screen instruction to activate Windows thereafter.

Reduce the Size of the Taskbar Icons

Introduction to Taskbar Icons

In Microsoft Windows operating systems, the taskbar is by default located at the bottom of the desktop screen, and is configured to remain always on top of all the windows that users open. Every time any application, a file or a folder is opened by a user, its icon is displayed in the taskbar. With the help of displayed icons, it becomes easier for the users to identify the opened objects, and the icons also allow users to switch between the objects easily by clicking on them.

By default the size of the icons displayed in the taskbar is large for better visibility, but if required, the size can be decreased in order to get more space on the desktop screen. When the size of the icons in the taskbar is reduced, the size of entire taskbar also decreases, hence making additional room to work on the desktop and any application that users open.

How to Reduce Size of the Taskbar Icons?

In order to reduce size of the taskbar icons in Microsoft Windows 8, steps given below must be followed:

1. Log on to Microsoft Windows 8 computer with the user account for which the size of the taskbar icons are to be reduced.
2. From the **Start** screen, click **Desktop** tile.
3. On the desktop screen, right-click the taskbar and from the context menu click **Properties**.
4. On the opened **Taskbar Properties** box, make sure that **Taskbar** tab is selected.
5. Once on the **Taskbar** tab, check **Use small taskbar buttons** checkbox.

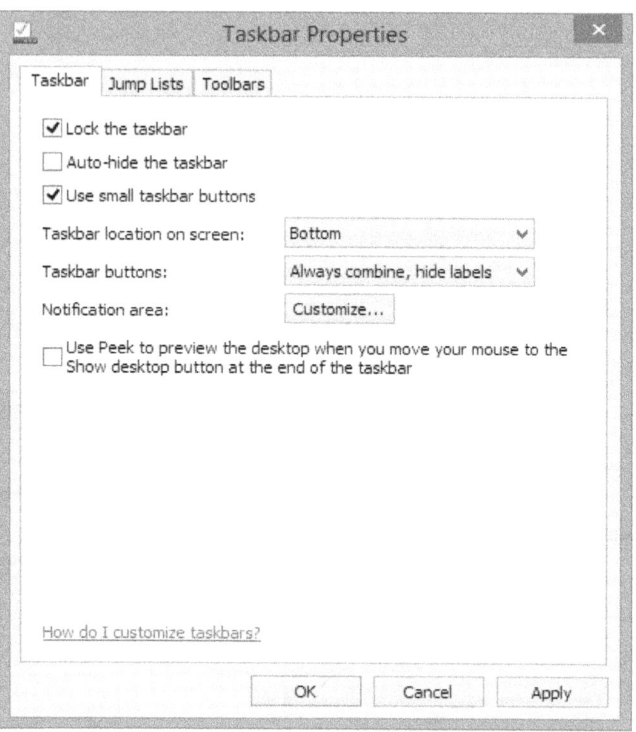

6. Click **OK** when done.

To set the size of the taskbar icons back to their normal size, steps 1 to 6 must be followed, while unchecking **Use small taskbar buttons** checkbox when on step 5.

Configure Immediate File Deletion

Introduction to File Deletion

When a file or folder is no longer required, users mostly delete it from the computer. In order to delete an object from a computer, the object must be right-clicked and 'Delete' option must be selected from the displayed context menu. Alternatively the 'Delete' or 'Del' button on the keyboard can also be pressed after selecting the unwanted object to remove it from the computer.

When a user attempts to delete an object, in order to prevent accidental deletion, Windows displays a confirmation box prompting the user to confirm the deletion of the object. Moreover, in order to prevent accidental data loss, by default Windows does not remove the deleted object permanently from the hard disk drive. Instead, the deleted object is sent to the Recycle Bin, from where it can be restored if required. In case the object is removed from the Recycle Bin as well, it becomes permanently unavailable.

Although, it is strongly recommended that the default deletion settings must be left intact and the deleted files should be sent to the Recycle Bin before they can be removed from the computer permanently, for testing purposes the feature can be disabled and the OS can be configured to remove the files permanently from the computer, without sending them to the Recycle Bin.

How to Remove Files Permanently from the Computer without Sending Them to the Recycle Bin?

1. Log on to Microsoft Windows 8 computer with the user account on which immediate file deletion is to be configured.
2. From the **Start** screen, click **Desktop** tile.
3. On the desktop screen, right-click the **Recycle Bin**.
4. From the displayed context menu, click **Properties**.
5. On the **Recycle Bin** Properties box, from the displayed list, make sure that the drive (volume), for which immediate file deletion is to be configured is selected.
6. Under the **Settings for selected location** section, click to select **Don't move files to the Recycle Bin. Remove files immediately when deleted** radio button.

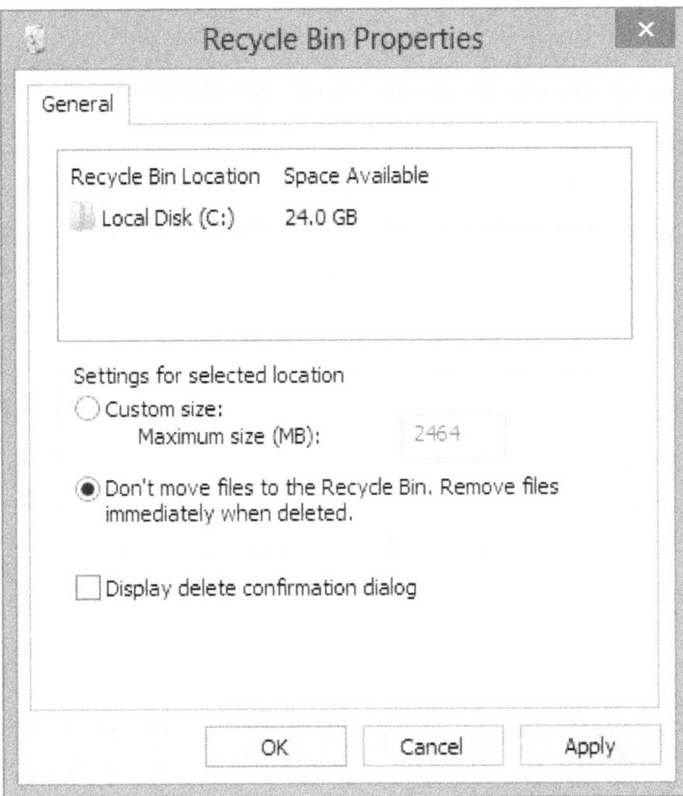

7. Click **OK** when done.

Connect to the Projector

Introduction to the Connection to the Projector

When Microsoft Windows 8 is installed and used in production environments, it is quite likely that it would be used for presentations in seminars and other official meetings as well. As it is well-known that the presentations are mostly played on the computers, but in order to increase the visibility of the displayed contents for the crowd, a projector is required.

Since a projector is a device that receives inputs from the desktop computers or laptop PCs and gives the outputs on any flat surface (a wall or a whiteboard), it must be connected and configured appropriately to the computers.

When the projector is connected to a computer, there are various options that Windows provides according to which the display can be projected on the flat surface only, on the flat surface and displayed on the computer screen as well, can be seen on the computer monitor only, etc.

How to Connect a Projector?

In order to connect a projector to Windows 8 computer and configure the required outputs, steps given below must be followed:

1. Log on to Microsoft Windows 8 computer with any account.
2. Make sure that the projector is connected to the computer and its appropriate driver is installed.
3. Also ensure that the projector is powered on.
4. From the **Start** screen, click **Desktop** tile.
5. On the desktop screen, press **Windows** + **P** keys together.
6. From the **Second screen** pane that appears in the right, click **Duplicate** option to display the contents of current monitor on the projector as well.

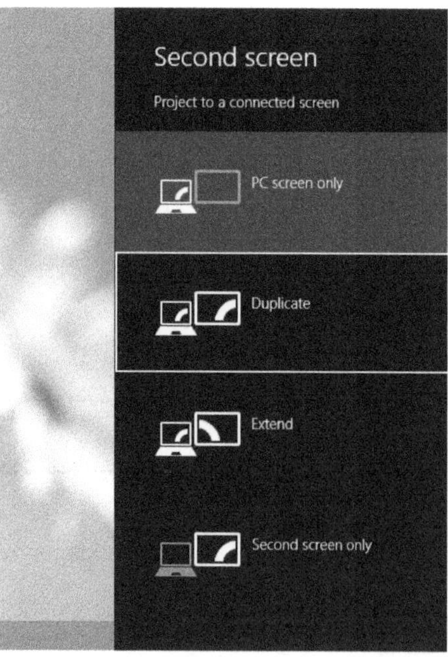

Prevent Themes from Changing Icons

Introduction to the Themes

When Microsoft operating system is installed, users might want to change the appearance of the interface in order to make the Windows look more attractive. To modify the ambience, users install and use different themes that automatically change the color schemes and the desktop wallpapers according to their predefined preferences. Moreover, by default the installed themes also modify the default icons of the objects (e.g. Computer, Recycle Bin, etc.) to make them look different than usual.

For many home users this change in the ambience and the modified icons might be quite interesting and they might want to keep the changed settings intact. Whereas, some home users may find it difficult to identify the changed icons that have been modified because of the preferences of the installed theme. When this is the case, users can configure Windows 8 so that the default icons remain intact even after a new theme is installed on the computer.

How to Prevent Themes from Changing Icons?

In order to prevent installed themes from changing icons in Microsoft Windows 8, steps given below must be followed:

1. Log on to Microsoft Windows 8 computer with any account.
2. From the **Start** screen, click **Desktop** tile.
3. On the desktop screen, right-click anywhere.
4. From the displayed context menu, click **Personalize**.
5. On the **Personalization** window, click **Change desktop icons** from the left pane.
6. On the **Desktop Icons Settings** box, uncheck **Allow themes to change desktop icons** checkbox.

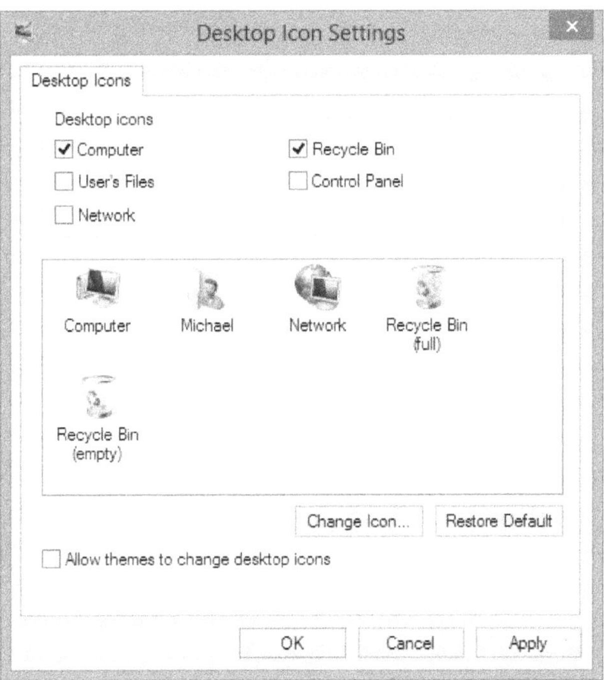

7. Click OK to apply the changes.

To allow the installed themes to change the icons, steps 1 to 7 can be followed, while checking **Allow themes to change desktop icons** checkbox when on step 6.

Increase the Size of Every Object

Introduction to the Object Sizes

When Microsoft Windows 8 is installed, the default size of all the objects and icons that the computer has is set to provide the optimum performance and most appropriate display to the users. In earlier versions of Windows, such as Microsoft Windows XP or earlier, the operating systems allowed users to increase or decrease the size of the objects, texts, icons, etc. individually. Unlike earlier operating systems, in Microsoft Windows 8, size of all the objects can be increased by 25% or 50% with the help of a few mouse clicks. When size of all the objects is increased, the entire ambience of the interface also increases, hence providing better visibility to the normal, and especially to the physically challenged users who have visibility problems.

Apart from the benefits of increasing the size of all the objects, the customization also has some negative effects. Because of the increased objects' sizes, the desktop screen and other opened windows and applications look overpopulated, and sometimes because of this, it becomes hard for the users to locate any particular object.

How to Increase Size of Every Object?

In order to increase size of every object in Microsoft Windows 8, steps given below must be followed:

1. Log on to Microsoft Windows 8 computer with any account.
2. From the **Start** screen, click **Desktop** tile.
3. On the desktop screen, right-click anywhere.
4. From the displayed context menu, click **Personalize**.
5. On the **Personalization** window, click **Display** from the bottom of the left pane.
6. On the **Display** window, click to select the appropriate radio button as desired under **Change the size of all items** section.

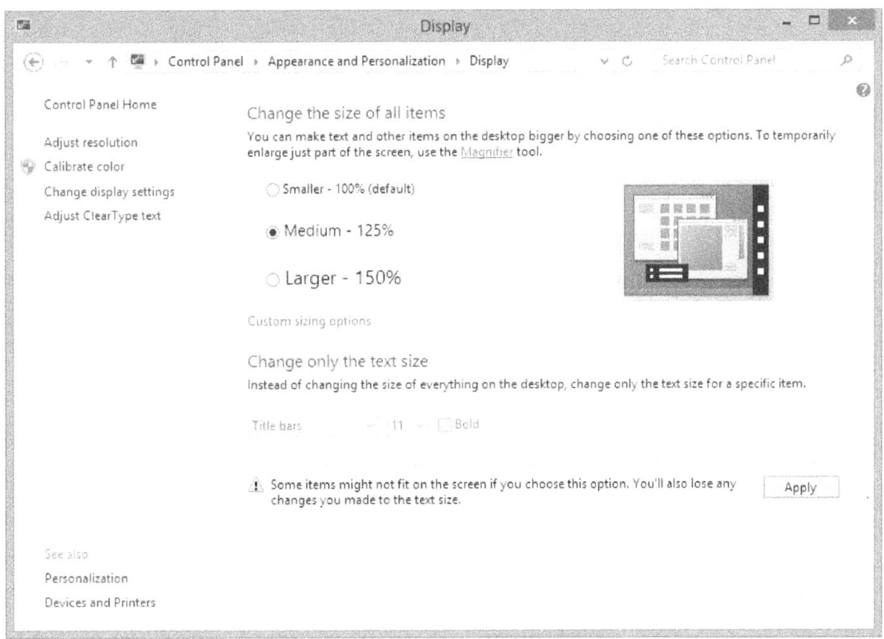

7. Click **Apply** to apply the changes.
8. Close **Display** window when done.

Enable Screen Savers

Introduction to Screen Savers

There is a misconception behind enabling screen savers, according to which the screen savers are enabled to prevent any opened information from getting exposed to any unauthorized person. According to this misconception, when timeout duration is set to start the screensaver, the display of the screen saver hides the exposed information, hence preventing the sensitive data from getting revealed to unauthorized/untrusted users.

However, the fact is, in Microsoft Windows screen savers are enabled to increase the lives of the monitors. It is mostly seen that built-in screen savers have dark backgrounds and at least one light colored moving object that wanders around on the entire monitor screens. Technical reason behind such graphic display is that the transistors in TFT monitors, liquids in LCD monitors and the electron beams in CRT monitors do not affect the areas where the dark colored background image is displayed. In other words, the thin film transistors do not emit lights, liquids do not glow, and the electron beams do not fall on the areas where the dark background is to be displayed, hence giving the affected areas some rest for a while. The only area on the desktop screen that gets affected is where the colored object is displayed.

Since the colored object keeps on moving around on the monitor screens, the areas which display colored object at one instance become inactive at the other when the object is moved to another location. This gives the lighted areas some rest for a short period, hence increasing the lives of the output units (monitors) in the long run.

How to Enable Screen Savers?

In order to enable screen savers in Microsoft Windows 8, steps given below must be followed:

1. Log on to Microsoft Windows 8 computer with any account.
2. From the **Start** screen, click **Desktop** tile.
3. On the desktop screen, right-click anywhere.
4. From the displayed context menu, click **Personalize**.
5. From the bottom of **Personalization** window, click **Screen Saver**.
6. On the **Screen Saver Settings** box, choose the appropriate screen saver from the **Screen saver** drop-down list.

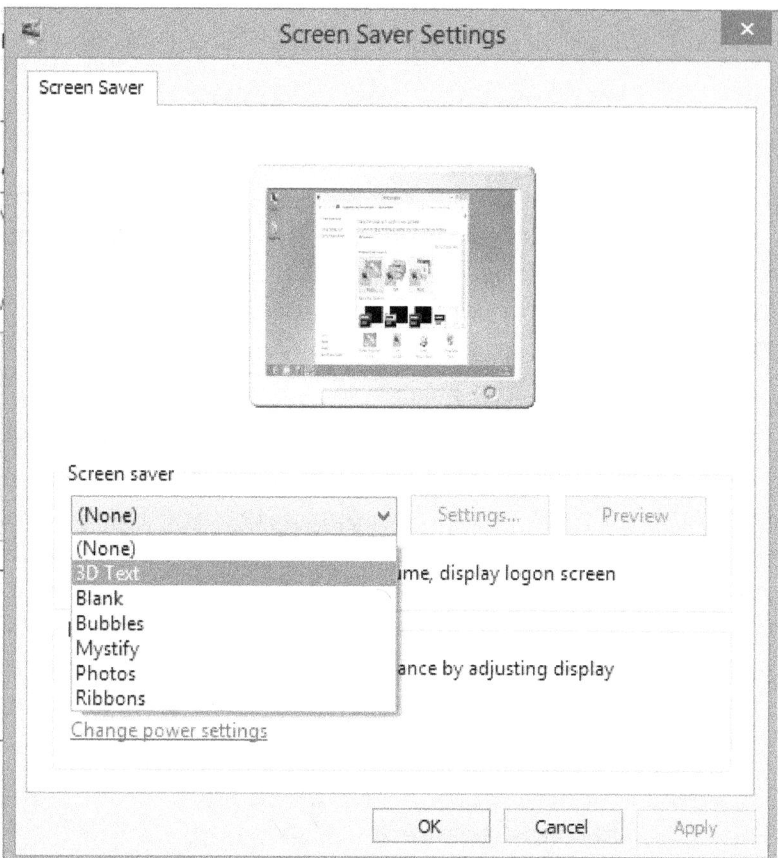

7. In the **Wait** field, specify the timeout limit (in minutes) after which Windows starts the screen saver.
8. Click **OK** to apply the changes.

Automatically Change Desktop Wallpapers

Introduction to the Desktop Wallpapers

When an operating system is installed, the desktop screen has default wallpaper that is automatically set according to the default user profile that is created during the installation. In production environments administrators might want to force the logos of the organizations to be used as the default wallpapers on the computers. In order to do so, they configure the group policy settings either on every computer individually (in a workgroup network setups) or apply a domain wide group policy (in client/server network setups).

Situations might differ when an operating system is installed on home computers. In homes, users might want to change the desktop wallpapers on a regular basis in order to change the ambience of the computer display. Users can change the desktop wallpapers manually, and in earlier versions of Windows, such as Microsoft Windows XP, they used to install third-party applications such as Webshots that used to change the wallpapers automatically according to the specified time intervals.

Microsoft Windows 8 provides a built-in feature that automatically changes the desktop wallpapers as per user-defined time interval. Because of this built-in feature, the requirement of any third-party wallpaper cycling application is completely eliminated, which remarkably reduces resource consumption, such as memory and processing.

How to Change Desktop Wallpapers Automatically?

In order to change desktop wallpapers automatically in Microsoft Windows 8, steps given below must be followed:

1. Log on to Microsoft Windows 8 computer with any account.
2. From the **Start** screen, click **Desktop** tile.
3. On the desktop screen, right-click anywhere.
4. From the displayed context menu, click **Personalize**.
5. From the bottom of **Personalization** window, click **Desktop Background**.
6. On the **Desktop Background** window, from the displayed images, click to select the ones that are to be used when cycled during automatic wallpaper changes. (Multiple images can be selected by checking the checkbox displayed at the top left corner of every image when the mouse is hovered on it.)
7. From the enabled **Change picture every** drop-down list, select the desired time interval to cycle the images.

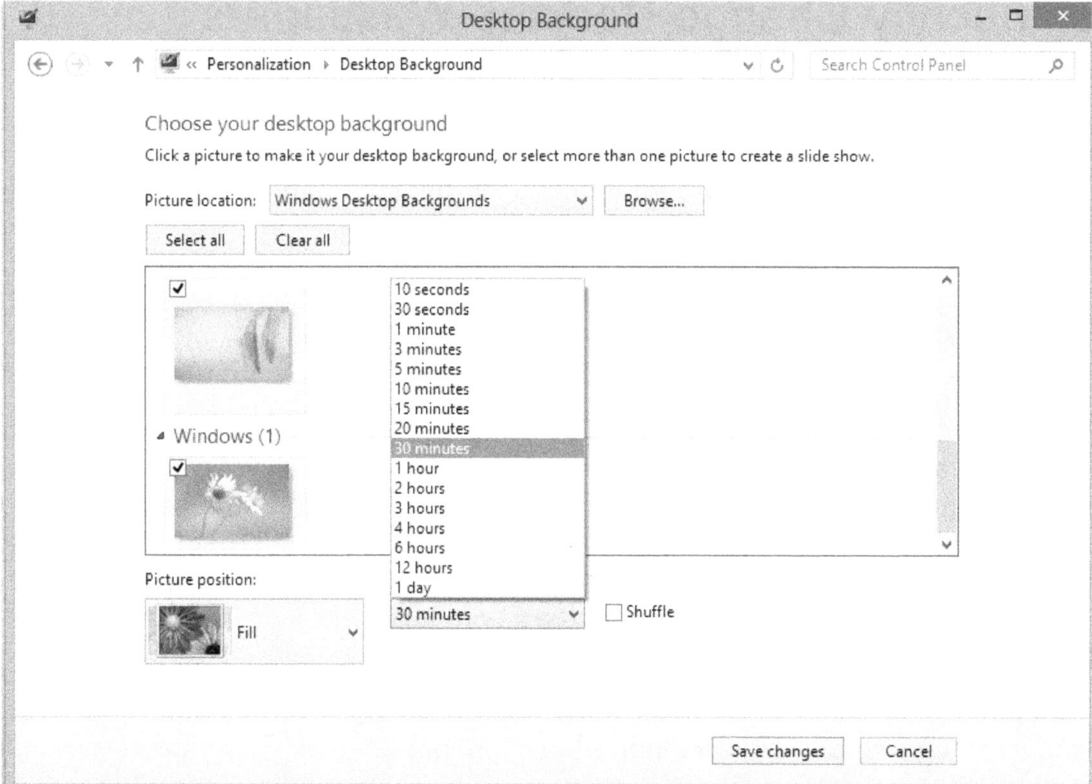

8. Click **Save changes** button to apply the settings.
9. Close **Personalization** window.

Configure Text Display

Introduction to ClearType Text

In earlier days, most PCs had CRT monitors connected to them that were unable to display the objects and texts on the screens as clearly as the TFT and/or LCD monitors nowadays do. Because of the limitations of the CRT monitors, it was recommended that the ClearType text feature should be disabled in order to experience better visibility of the texts. Since most computer systems nowadays have either TFT or LCD monitors connected to them, the ClearType text feature should be turned on and properly configured to get the clear and sharp texts on the computer screens in order to increase their readability.

Configuration of the ClearType text is the Next-Next-Finish process, however the options that users choose while configuring the feature totally depend on their individual choices and preferences.

How to Configure ClearType Text?

In order to configure ClearType text in Microsoft Windows 8, steps given below must be followed:

1. Log on to Microsoft Windows 8 computer with any account.
2. From the **Start** screen, click **Desktop** tile.
3. On the desktop screen, right-click anywhere.
4. From the displayed context menu, click **Personalize**.
5. On the **Personalization** window, click **Display** from the bottom of the left pane.
6. On the **Display** window, click **Adjust ClearType text** from the left pane.
7. On the **ClearType Text Tuner** window, make sure that **Turn on ClearType** checkbox is checked.
8. Click **Next** to proceed.
9. On the next window, click to select the box with most clearly visible text and click **Next**.

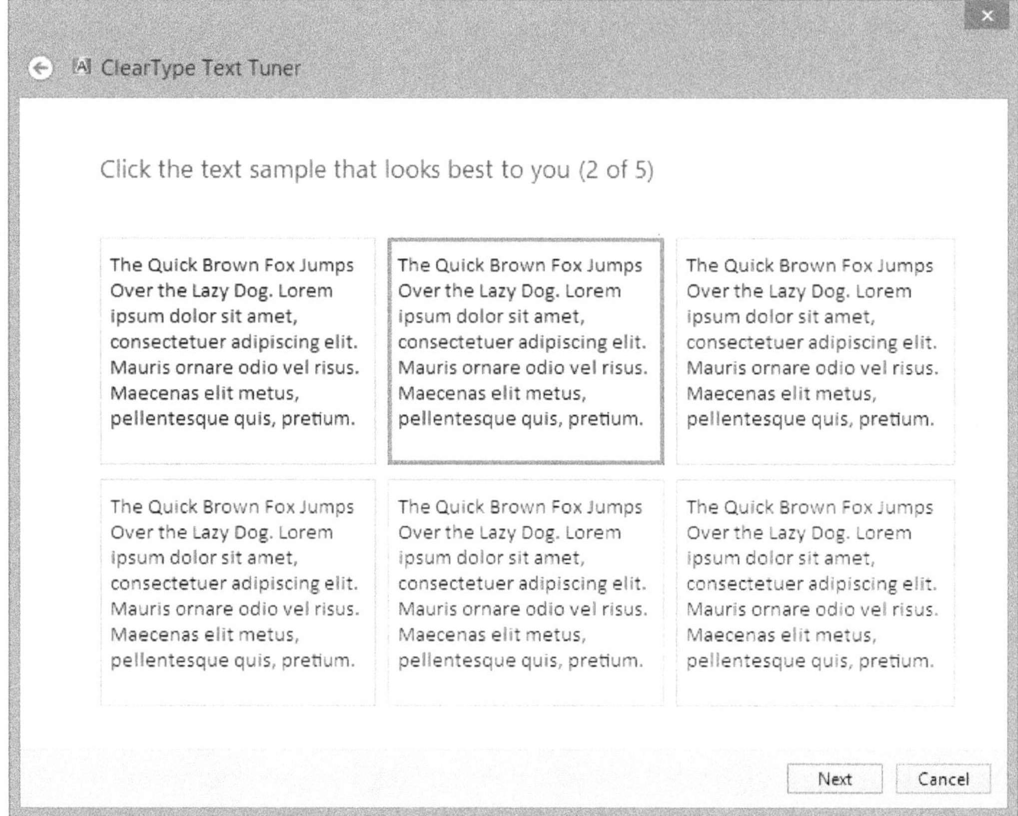

10. Repeat step 9 on all the windows that follow thereafter.
11. On the last **You have finished tuning the text for your monito**r window, click **Finish**.
12. Close **Display** window when done.

Change Desktop Wallpaper

Introduction to Desktop Wallpaper

Wallpaper is a background image that is displayed on the desktop screen when any application or window is not opened. When Microsoft Windows 8 is installed on a computer, default wallpaper is automatically set by the operating system.

In production environments, most administrators configure the group policy settings to enforce the logos of the organizations to be used as the desktop wallpapers on all the computers. On the other hand, home users might find it boring to use the same desktop background for several days. In order to avoid such boring situations, users keep on changing the desktop wallpapers on a regular basis. Many users also install some third-party applications that automatically cycle desktop wallpapers as per the predefined time intervals. Microsoft Windows 8 has a built-in feature that eliminates the requirement of third-party applications to change the wallpapers automatically.

How to Change Desktop Wallpaper Manually?

In order to change the desktop wallpapers manually in Microsoft Windows 8, steps given below must be followed:

1. Log on to Microsoft Windows 8 computer with any account.
2. From the **Start** screen, click **Desktop** tile.
3. On the desktop screen, right-click anywhere.
4. From the displayed context menu, click **Personalize**.
5. From the bottom of **Personalization** window, click **Desktop Background**.
6. On the **Desktop Background** window, from the available images, click to select the desired picture.

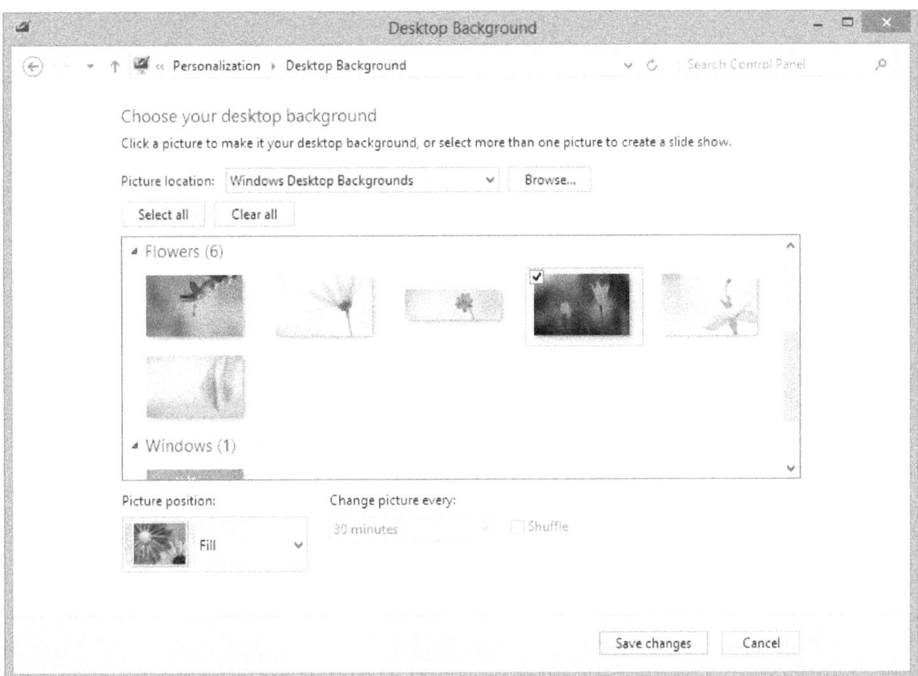

7. Click **Save changes** button to set the selected picture as the desktop wallpaper.

Capture Screenshot

Introduction to Capturing a Screenshot

In legacy versions of operating systems, such as Microsoft Windows XP or earlier, if users wanted to capture screenshots, they used to install either any third-party application which came along with the price tag, or they used to use 'Print Screen' key on their keyboards that captured the image of all the objects that were displayed on the computer screens. Screenshots captured using 'Print Screen' key required further editing and cropping in order to get the exact image as required by the users.

Microsoft Windows 8 has a built-in feature named 'Snipping Tool' that allows users to capture screenshots just with a single mouse click. Because of the 'Snipping Tool', requirement of any third-party application is eliminated, and the 'Print Screen' button is no longer used to capture the images. Moreover, with the help of 'Snipping Tool', the precise images of the desired areas of the compute screen and/or interfaces can be captured just with one or two mouse clicks.

How to Capture a Screenshot?

In order to capture a screenshot using 'Snipping Tool' in Microsoft Windows 8, steps given below must be followed:

1. Log on to Microsoft Windows 8 computer with any account.
2. From the **Start** screen, click **Desktop** tile.
3. From the desktop screen, hover mouse to the bottom right corner of the window.
4. From the displayed options, click **Search**.
5. From the **Apps** window, locate and click **Snipping Tool** under **Windows Accessories** category.
6. Once the **Snipping Tool** is initiated, click **New** button on the opened interface.

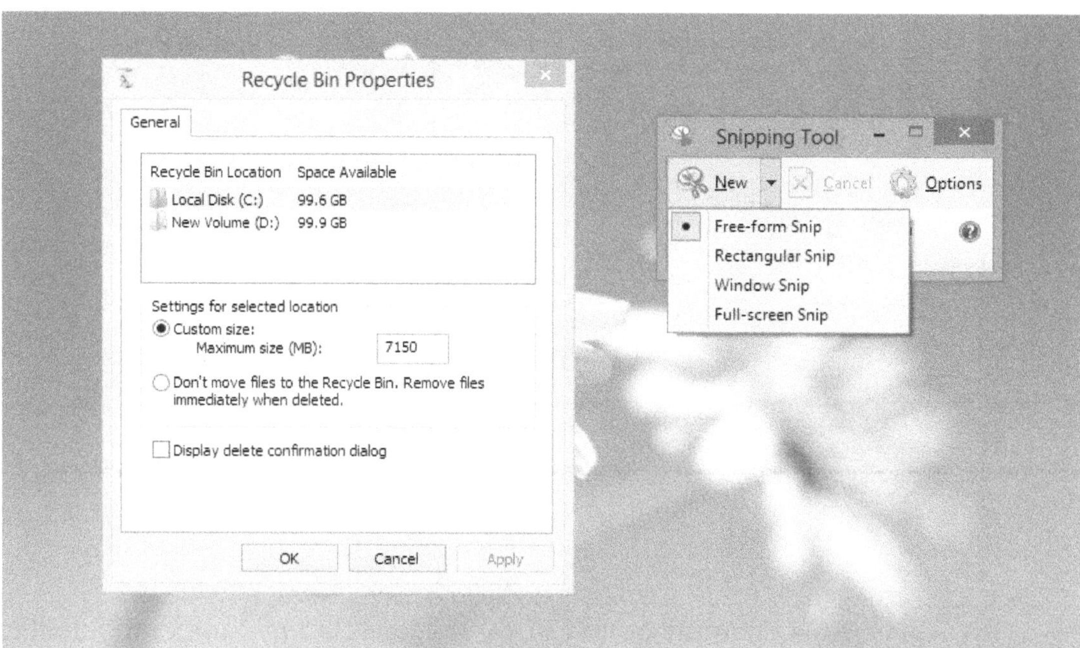

7. Left-click and drag mouse across the area of the screen, snapshot of which is required.
8. Release the mouse button when done.
9. From the displayed options in the standard toolbar, click **Save** icon (floppy icon) to save the captured image at the desired location.

Note: *Other snapshot capturing options can be selected by clicking the down facing triangle button available in the right to the* ***New*** *button on the* ***Snipping Tool****'s interface.*

Disable/Enable Aero Peek to Preview Desktop

Introduction to Aero Peek Preview

In Microsoft Windows 8 operating system, there is an Aero Peek button available at the bottom right corner of the desktop screen (at the right end of the taskbar). Aero Peek button, when clicked, allows users to switch back to the desktop screen instantaneously. In other words, Aero Peek button has replaced the Show Desktop button that was available in earlier versions of Microsoft operating systems, such as Microsoft Windows XP.

When Aero Peek button is clicked, all the opened windows and applications are minimized in a single go, hence exposing the desktop screen to the users.

Another advantage that the Aero Peek button provides is that when users hover mouse on the button, a preview of the desktop screen is displayed on the monitor. This eliminates the requirement of clicking the button and minimizing all the opened applications and windows to view the desktop screen.

How to Disable Aero Peek Preview?

Although it is not recommended to disable the Aero Peek Preview feature in Microsoft Windows 8, if users want, they can follow the steps given below to do so for testing purposes:

1. Log on to Microsoft Windows 8 computer with any account.
2. From the **Start** screen, click **Desktop** tile.
3. From the desktop screen, right-click the taskbar.
4. From the displayed context menu, click **Properties**.
5. On the **Taskbar Properties** box, make sure that **Taskbar** tab is selected.
6. Uncheck **Use peek to preview the desktop when you move your mouse to the Show Desktop button at the end of the taskbar** checkbox.

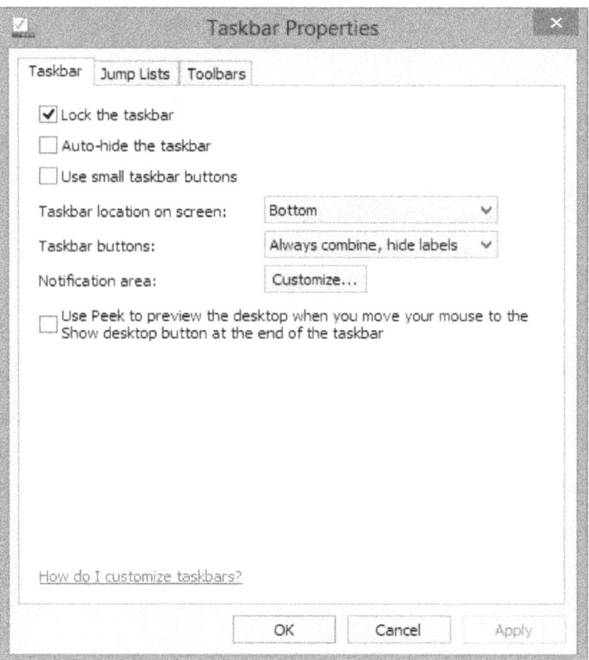

7. Click **OK** to apply the changes.

To re-enable Aero Peek Preview feature, steps 1 to 7 can be followed, while checking the **Use peek to preview the desktop when you move your mouse to the Show Desktop button at the end of the taskbar** checkbox when on step 6.

Disable Thumbnail Previews

Introduction to Thumbnail Previews

In Microsoft Windows 8, when image files are stored in a folder, by default the operating system displays their icons as the thumbnails. A thumbnail is a small preview of the picture that is displayed in the window, even when the image file is not opened. This default configuration makes it easier for the users to locate their desired images without opening the files.

Since this default setting eases users' tasks, it is recommended that the configuration should not be modified. However in some situations, users might not want the operating system to display the preview of the images because of security reasons. In such cases, they might want to disable the thumbnail preview so that the sensitive information may not get exposed to unknown people.

How to Disable Thumbnail Previews?

In order to disable thumbnail previews in Microsoft Windows 8, steps given below must be followed:

1. Log on to Microsoft Windows 8 computer with any account.
2. From the **Start** screen, click **Desktop** tile.
3. On the desktop screen, click **File Explorer** icon from the taskbar.
4. On the opened **Libraries** window, click **View** from the menu bar.
5. Click **Options** from the displayed tools in the **View** ribbon.
6. On the **Folder Options** box, go to **View** tab.
7. From the displayed options in the **Advanced settings** list, check **Always show icons, never thumbnails** checkbox.

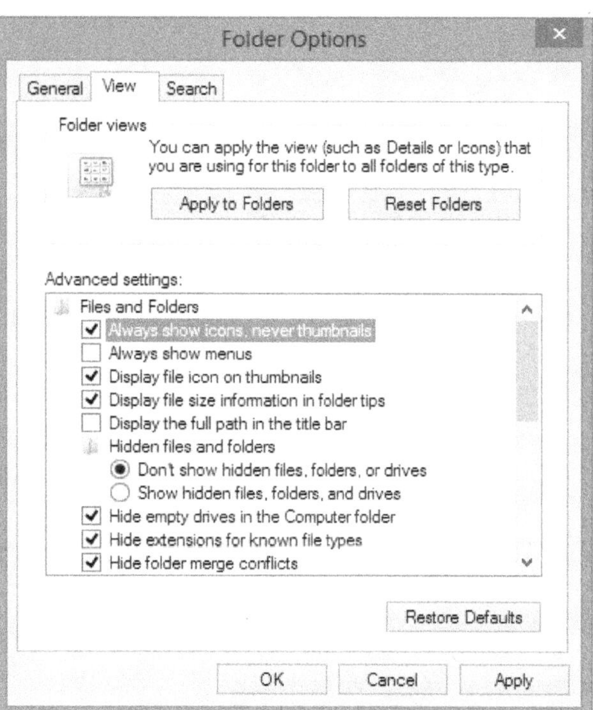

8. Click **OK** to apply the settings.

To re-enable thumbnail previews, steps 1 to 8 can be followed, while unchecking Always show icons, never thumbnails checkbox when on step 7.

Increase or Decrease Mouse Pointer Speed

Introduction to Mouse Pointer Speed

As per Microsoft Windows 8's default configuration, the speed of the mouse pointer is set to medium so that it becomes easier for the users to control the mouse while working on Windows. The default pointer speed is configured so keeping mouse handling speed of majority of users in mind. However there might be cases when expert level users use the computer and find the mouse pointer speed quite slow. There might also be cases when users are quite new to the operating system and are not able to control the mouse when it is set to its default configuration. In such situations it might be helpful to increase or decrease the speed of the mouse pointer as per users' conveniences.

How to Increase or Decrease Mouse Pointer Speed?

In order to increase or decrease mouse pointer speed in Microsoft Windows 8, steps given below must be followed:

1. Log on to Microsoft Windows 8 computer with any account.
2. From the **Start** screen, click **Desktop** tile.
3. On the desktop screen, hover mouse to the bottom right corner of the window.
4. From the displayed options, click **Settings**.
5. From the **Settings** pane, click **Control Panel**.
6. On the **Control Panel** window, click **Hardware and Sound** category.
7. On the **Hardware and Sound** window, click **Mouse** option under the **Devices and Printers** category.
8. On the **Mouse Properties** box, go to **Pointers Options** tab.
9. Under the **Motion** section, move the slider to the right or left to increase or decrease the mouse pointer speed respectively.

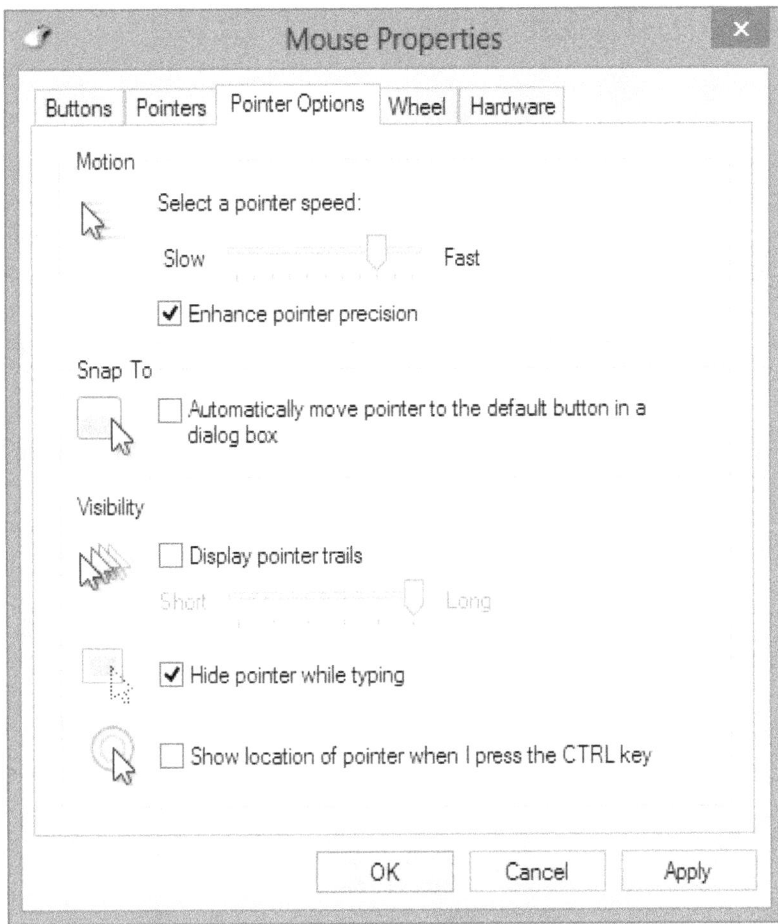

10. Click **OK** to apply the changes.
11. Close **Hardware and Sound** window when done.

Manage Mouse Double-Click Speed

Introduction to Mouse Double-Click Speed

Just like mouse pointer speed, by default the double-click speed of the mouse is also set to medium in Microsoft Windows 8. The double-click speed of the mouse is the time interval between the two consecutive mouse left-clicks. The shorter the time interval between the two consecutive mouse clicks is, the more is the double-click speed of the mouse. In other words the specified time interval between the two consecutive mouse clicks is inversely proportional to the mouse double-click speed.

For normal users, the default mouse double-click settings is perfect and should not be modified. Whereas, when users are new to Windows, it might be helpful to decrease the mouse double-click speed. Mouse double-click speed can be decreased by moving the horizontal slider to the left that increases the time interval between the two consecutive mouse clicks. In the same way, for experienced users it would be a time-saving configurations if the mouse double-click speed is increased, i.e. the time interval between the two consecutive mouse clicks is decreased by moving the horizontal slider to the right.

How to Increase or Decrease Mouse Double-Click Speed?

In order to increase or decrease mouse double-click speed in Microsoft Windows 8, steps given below must be followed:

1. Log on to Microsoft Windows 8 computer with any account.
2. From the **Start** screen, click **Desktop** tile.
3. On the desktop screen, hover mouse to the bottom right corner of the window.
4. From the displayed options, click **Settings**.
5. From the **Settings** pane, click **Control Panel**.
6. On the **Control Panel** window, click **Hardware and Sound** category.
7. On the **Hardware and Sound** window, click **Mouse** option under the **Devices and Printers** category.
8. On the **Mouse Properties** box, make sure that **Buttons** tab is selected.
9. Under the **Double-click speed** section, move the **Speed** slider to the right or left to increase or decrease the mouse double-click speed respectively. (Double-click speed can be tested by double-clicking the folder icon available at the right of the **Speed** slider under the **Double-click speed** section.)

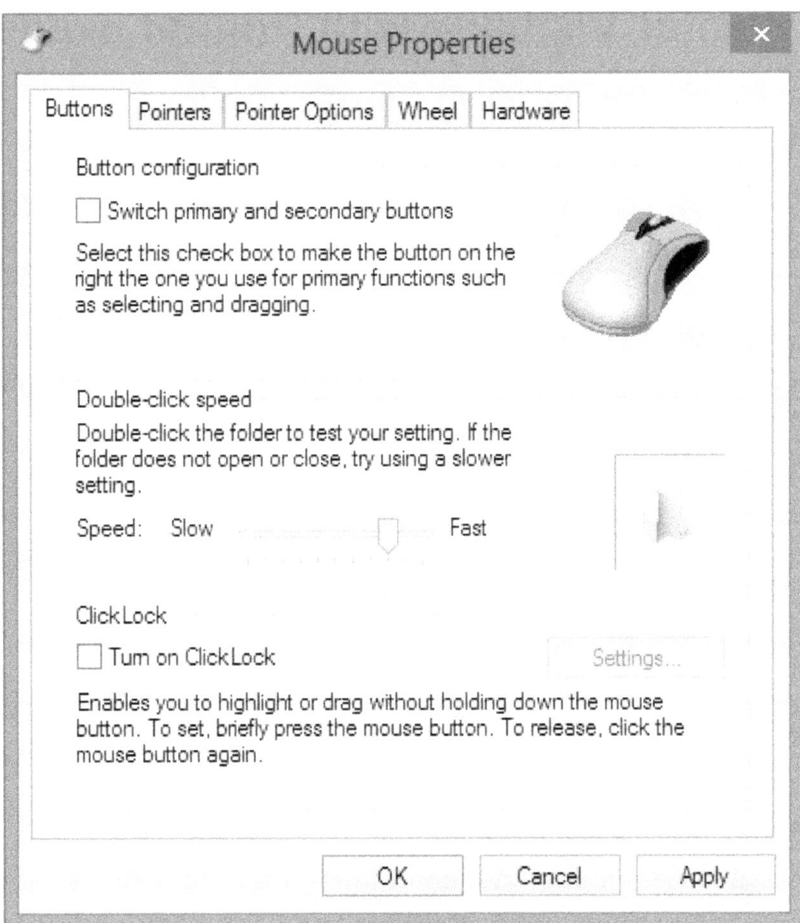

10. Click **OK** to apply the changes.
11. Close **Hardware and Sound** window when done.

Increase Mouse Pointer Visibility with Pointer Trails

Introduction to Pointer Trails

When Microsoft Windows 8 is installed, a default mouse pointer is used to point, select or initialize or open an application or window respectively. The default mouse pointer is represented by a white arrow facing the north-west direction. For people with normal eyesight, the default shape and size of the mouse pointer works perfectly well and does not require any modifications. Whereas people who suffer from visibility problems, it might be challenging for them to locate the mouse pointer, especially when it is moved around in the computer with speed.

In order to increase the visibility of the mouse pointer to help such people, Microsoft Windows 8 allows users to add pointer trail to the mouse pointer. When a pointer trail is added to the mouse pointer, its movement can be noticed quite easily and the pointer can be located without any trouble, even if it is moved quite fast.

How to Add a Pointer Trail to the Mouse Pointer?

In order to add a pointer trail to the mouse pointer in Microsoft Windows 8, steps given below must be followed:

1. Log on to Microsoft Windows 8 computer with any account.
2. From the **Start** screen, click **Desktop** tile.
3. On the desktop screen, hover mouse to the bottom right corner of the window.
4. From the displayed options, click **Settings**.
5. From the **Settings** pane, click **Control Panel**.
6. On the **Control Panel** window, click **Hardware and Sound** category.
7. On the **Hardware and Sound** window, click **Mouse** option under the **Devices and Printers** category.
8. On the **Mouse Properties** box, go to **Pointers Options** tab.
9. Under the **Visibility** section, check the **Display pointer trails** checkbox.

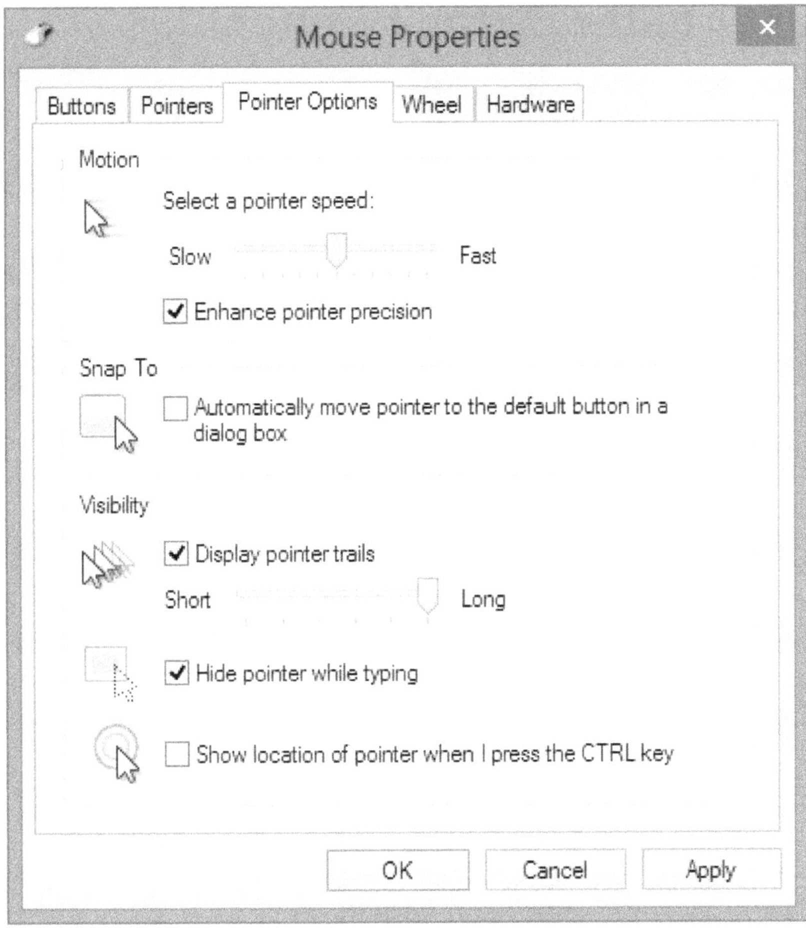

10. Click **OK** to apply the changes.
11. Close **Hardware and Sound** window when done.

To remove the pointer trail from the mouse pointer, steps 1 to 11 can be followed, while unchecking the **Display pointer trails** checkbox when on step 9.

Move Mouse Pointer to the Default Button

Introduction to the Default Button

In Microsoft Windows 8, when users perform any task, many times a dialogue box appears in response to the triggered event. The displayed dialogue box mostly consists of a few buttons, and the users are expected to click any one button in order to allow the computer to initiate or complete the desired task. Microsoft Windows is designed in such a way that every time a dialogue box appears, it has a default button that the operating system expects to be clicked by the users. The default button is highlighted by a thin dotted outline that wraps the button.

Many times the dotted outline that wraps the default button cannot be seen by the users. As the result, users might sometimes click the wrong button, hence giving inappropriate command to the computer accidentally.

Microsoft understands this and therefore it allows users to configure the mouse pointer so that it is automatically moved to the default button that Windows expects the users to click. Configuring the mouse to move its pointer to the default button every time a dialogue box appears is a user specific task and no elevated privileges are required.

How to Configure the Mouse to Move Its Pointer Automatically to the Default Button?

In order to configure the mouse to move its pointer automatically to the default button in Microsoft Windows 8, steps given below must be followed:

1. Log on to Microsoft Windows 8 computer with any account.
2. From the **Start** screen, click **Desktop** tile.
3. On the desktop screen, hover mouse to the bottom right corner of the window.
4. From the displayed options, click **Settings**.
5. From the **Settings** pane, click **Control Panel**.
6. On the **Control Panel** window, click **Hardware and Sound** category.
7. On the **Hardware and Sound** window, click **Mouse** option under the **Devices and Printers** category.
8. On the **Mouse Properties** box, go to **Pointers Options** tab.
9. Under the **Snap To** section, check the **Automatically move pointer to the default button in a dialog box** checkbox.

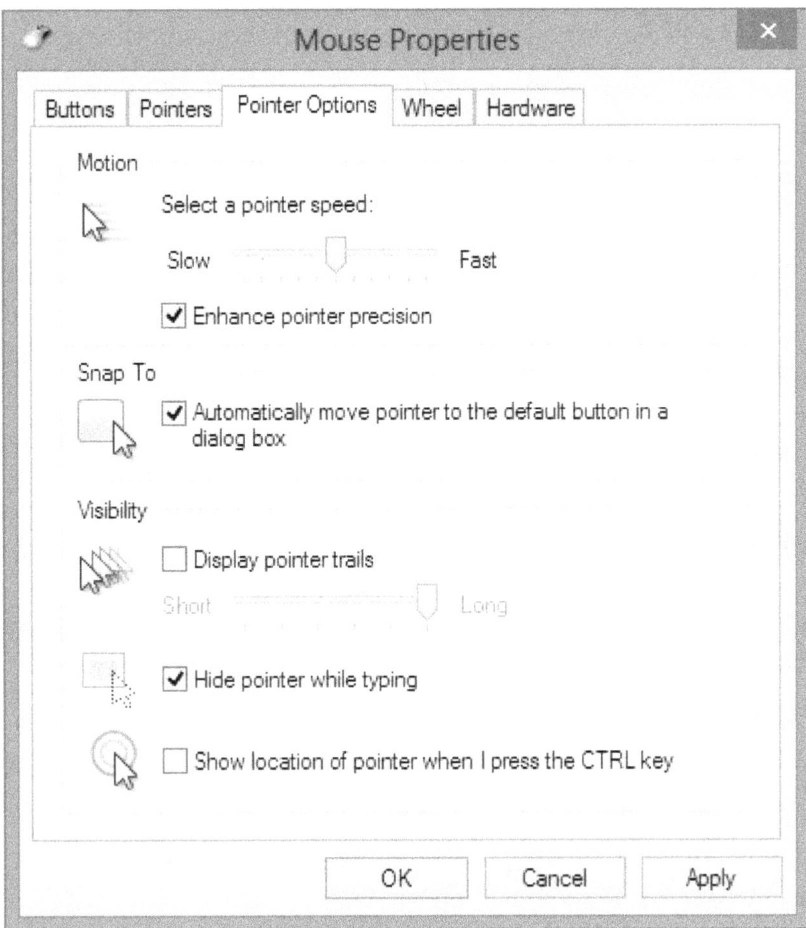

10. Click **OK** to apply the changes.
11. Close **Hardware and Sound** window when done.

To revert back the mouse to its default configuration, steps 1 to 11 can be followed, while unchecking **Automatically move pointer to the default button in a dialog box** checkbox when on step 9.

Change Mouse Pointers

Introduction to Mouse Pointers

According to the default mouse configuration in Microsoft Windows 8, the default mouse pointer is a white arrow that faces the north-west direction. When Windows 8 is working in the background, a rotating blue circle appears to the right of the pointer, and when the operating system is busy, mouse pointer turns into a rotating blue circle. These default icons of the mouse pointer are considered ideal for almost all Windows-based environments. However there might be times when users (especially home users) might want to modify the icons of the mouse pointers, just for a change.

When third-party themes are installed on a computer, they automatically change the mouse pointers as well. Moreover, Windows 8 also provides some built-in mouse pointer icons that users can use to configure the settings as in which condition what mouse pointer icon will be used by the Windows. Apart from the third-party themes and the Windows built-in mouse pointer icons, there are a few third-party applications that also allow users to create, customize and animate the mouse pointers.

How to Change Mouse Pointers?

In order to change mouse pointers and use Windows 8 built-in pointer icons, steps given below must be followed:

1. Log on to Microsoft Windows 8 computer with any account.
2. From the **Start** screen, click **Desktop** tile.
3. On the desktop screen, hover mouse to the bottom right corner of the window.
4. From the displayed options, click **Settings**.
5. From the **Settings** pane, click **Control Panel**.
6. On the **Control Panel** window, click **Hardware and Sound** category.
7. On the **Hardware and Sound** window, click **Mouse** option under the **Devices and Printers** category.
8. On the **Mouse Properties** box, go to **Pointers** tab.
9. From the available arrow types in the **Customize** list, click to select the one that is to be changed.

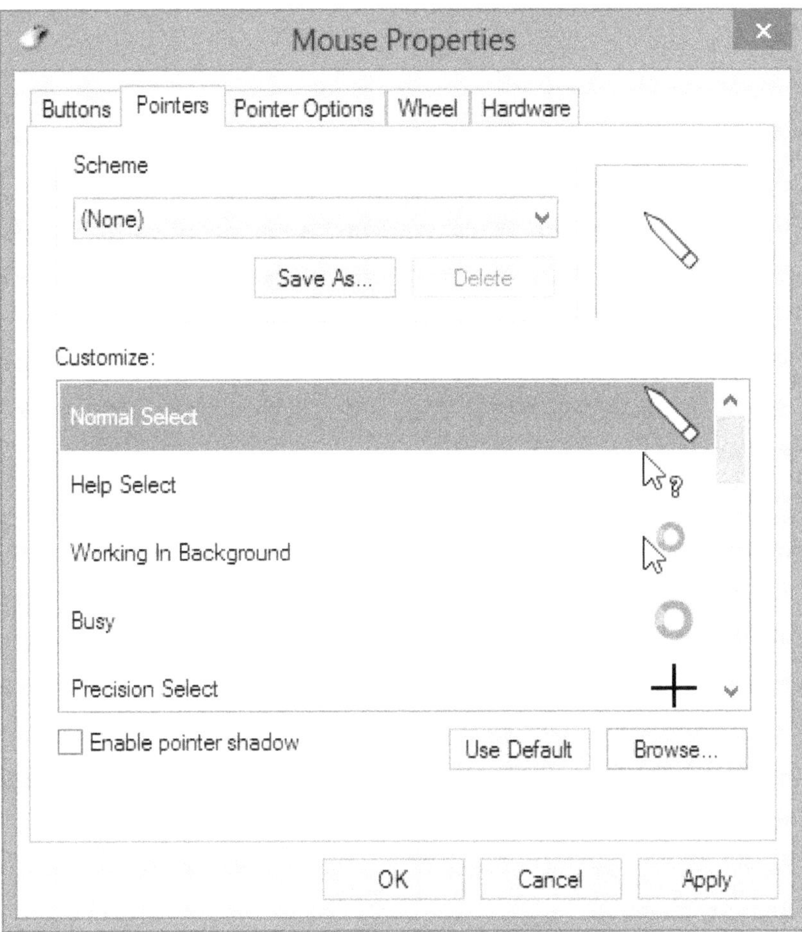

10. Once selected, click **Browse** button to choose the desired arrow type.
11. Click **OK** to apply the changes.
12. Close **Hardware and Sound** window when done.

To set mouse pointer settings back to the default configuration, follow the steps from 1 to 8 and click **Use Default** button. Click **OK** and close the **Hardware and Sound** window.

Enable Mouse Keys

Introduction to Mouse Keys

With all versions of GUI-based Microsoft operating systems, a pointing device, such as mouse, is required in order to work on the OS comfortably. In these operating systems, keyboards are only used when users want to type the texts or specify the passwords while logging on. Users nowadays have become quite habitual of using the mouse, and they find it difficult to navigate and wander around in Windows with the keyboards.

Using a mouse, and getting used to it while working with Windows doesn't harm at all till everything is working fine. Complications may occur when the mouse fails to work, and users are forced to use the keyboards in order to operate the Windows. Since most users do not know the keyboard shortcuts, it might be challenging for them to work on Windows in the absence of mouse.

In order to overcome this complication, Microsoft Windows 8 allows its users to enable Mouse Keys that configures the keyboard settings in such a way that the arrow keys of the num pad can be used to move the mouse pointer, as if the users are using the real mouse.

Although using the num pad of the keyboard as mouse might make the movement of the mouse pointer slower as compared to the speed of movement when the real mouse is used, it still makes the tasks quite easier for the users when the mouse is not available.

How to Enable Mouse Keys?

In order to enable Mouse Keys in Microsoft Windows 8, steps given below must be followed:

1. Log on to Microsoft Windows 8 computer with any account.
2. From the **Start** screen, click **Desktop** tile.
3. On the desktop screen, right-click anywhere and from the context menu, click **Personalize**.
4. On the **Personalization** window, click **Ease of Access Center** from the bottom of the left pane.
5. On the **Ease of Access Center** the window, under **Explore all settings** section, click **Make the mouse easier to use**.
6. On the opened window, under the **Control the mouse with the keyboard** section, check **Turn on Mouse Keys** checkbox.

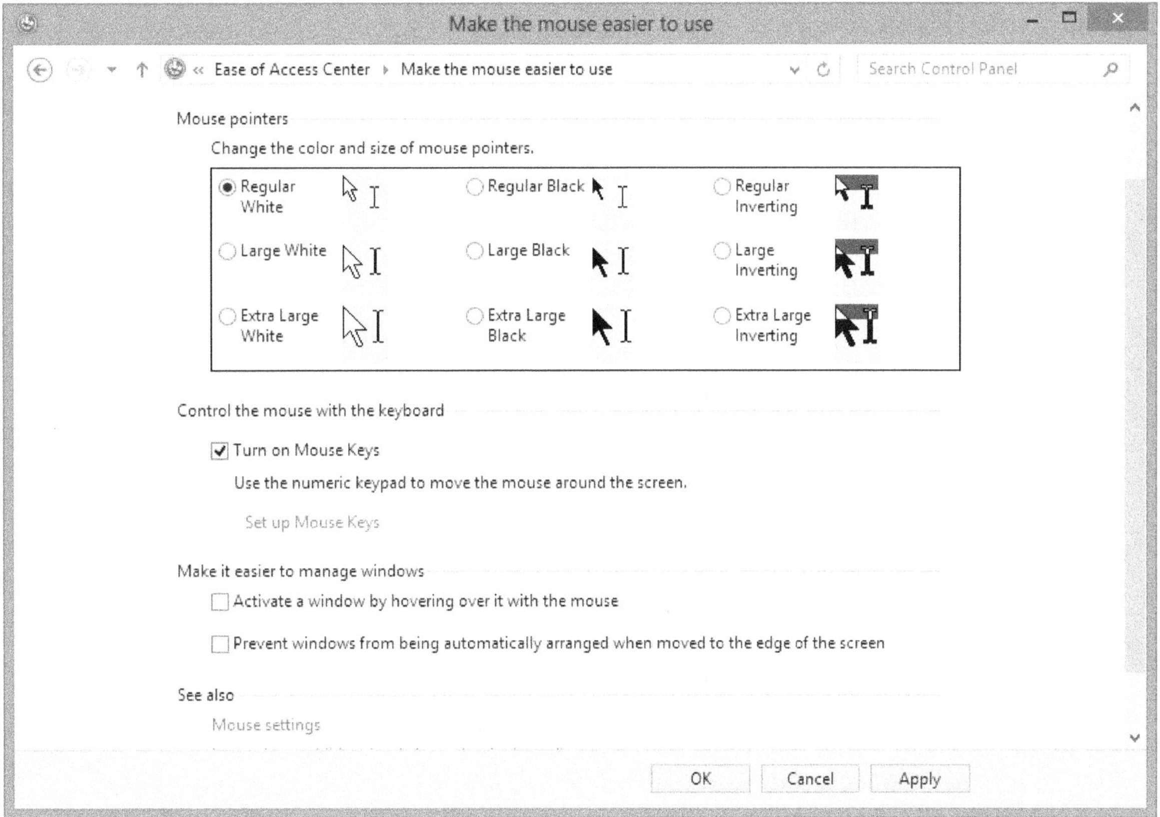

7. Click **OK** to apply the changes.
8. Close **Ease of Access Center** window when done.

To disable the **Mouse Keys** feature, steps 1 to 8 can be followed, while unchecking **Turn on Mouse Keys** checkbox when on step 6.

Enable ClickLock

Introduction to ClickLock

ClickLock is a feature in Microsoft Windows 8 that allows users to drag and drop objects from one place to another without pressing and holding down the mouse button continuously. In other words, when ClickLock is enabled, users can left-click the desired object once and can release the mouse button. This selects the object. Users can then drag the mouse to the destination location, where they want to move the selected object, and can left-click the mouse button again to move the object to the selected location.

This feature is useful for the users who are not well versed with the Windows and find it difficult to use the mouse. If ClickLock feature is kept disabled for such users, they might start dragging their desired objects, but may drop them somewhere else by releasing the mouse button accidently, hence placing the object at a different location unwantedly. Therefore in order to avoid such situations, ClickLock must be turned on for the new and/ or slow (physically challenged) users.

How to Enable ClickLock?

In order to enable ClickLock in Microsoft Windows 8, steps given below must be followed:

1. Log on to Microsoft Windows 8 computer with any account.
2. From the **Start** screen, click **Desktop** tile.
3. On the desktop screen, hover mouse to the bottom right corner of the window.
4. From the displayed options, click **Settings**.
5. From the **Settings** pane, click **Control Panel**.
6. On the **Control Panel** window, click **Hardware and Sound** category.
7. On the **Hardware and Sound** window, click **Mouse** option under the **Devices and Printers** category.
8. On the **Mouse Properties** box, make sure that **Buttons** tab is selected.
9. Under the **ClickLock** section, check **Turn on ClickLock** checkbox.

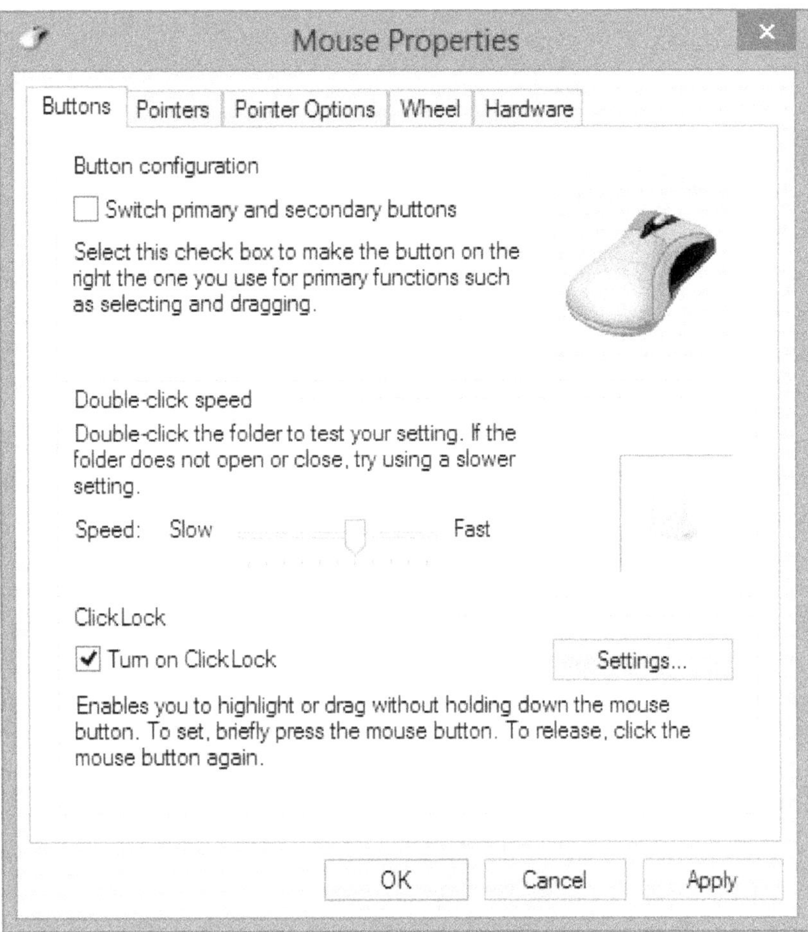

10. Click **OK** to apply the changes.
11. Close **Hardware and Sound** window when done.

To disable **ClickLock** feature, steps 1 to 11 can be followed, while unchecking **Turn on ClickLock** checkbox when on step 9.

Enable Filter Keys

Introduction to Filter Keys

When Microsoft Windows 8 is used by either new or physically challenged users, it is quite likely that they might press a single key multiple times, hence repeatedly typing the same character several times. Although this is a human error, computer does not understand this and therefore it expects the keystrokes as the input given by the user. Single character can be typed multiple times even when a key is pressed down and held for long duration accidently or intentionally.

Because of the above mentioned errors, it might be challenging for the users to complete their work in time and with comfort. Therefore in order to avoid such situations, Microsoft Windows 8 allows users to enable Filter Keys that ignores the same values that the computer receives because of repeated keystrokes. Moreover, the default Filter Keys settings can also be modified and the time interval between the two consecutive keystrokes of the same the key can be changed before which Windows 8 ignores the identical input values. For example if the time interval between the two consecutive keystrokes is set to 0.5 seconds, Windows 8 does not type the character again if the same key is pressed before 0.5 seconds.

How to Enable Filter Keys?

In order to enable Filter Keys in Microsoft Windows 8, steps given below must be followed:

1. Log on to Microsoft Windows 8 computer with any account.
2. From the **Start** screen, click **Desktop** tile.
3. On the desktop screen, right-click anywhere and from the context menu click **Personalize**.
4. On the **Personalization** window, click **Ease of Access Center** from the bottom of the left pane.
5. On the **Ease of Access Center** window, under **Explore all settings** section, click **Make the keyboard easier to use**.
6. On the opened window, under the **Make it easier to type** section, check **Turn on Filter Keys** checkbox.

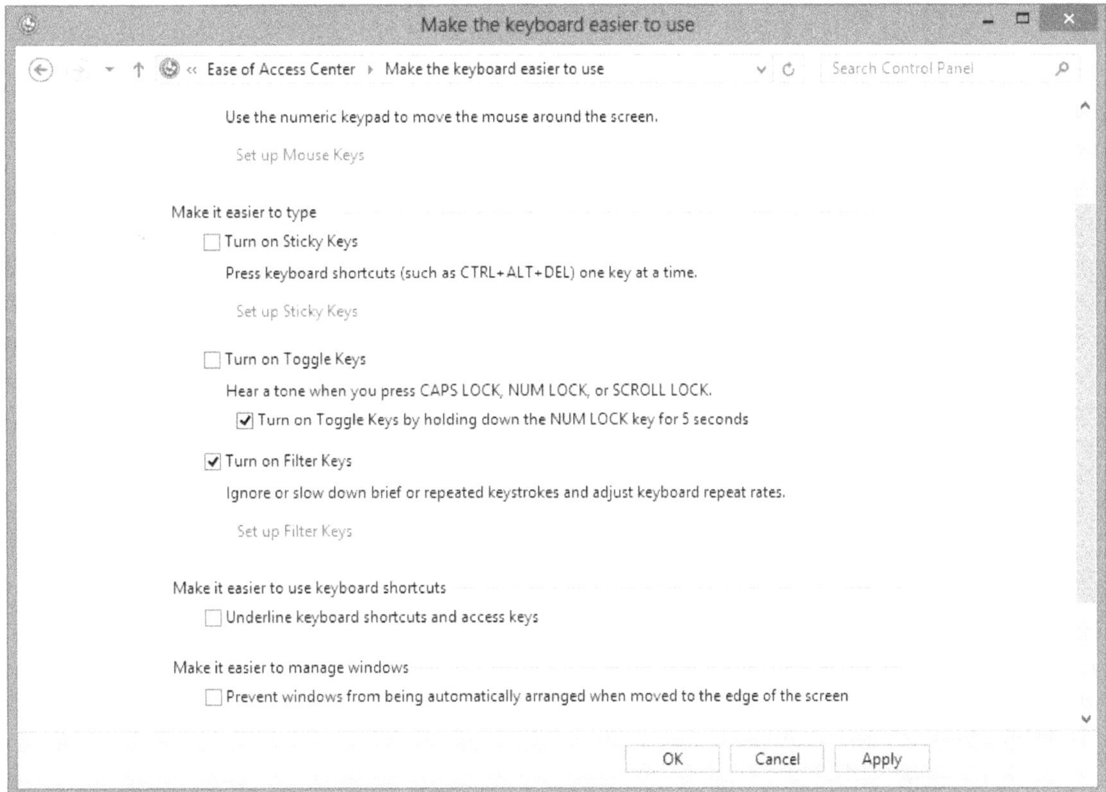

7. Click **OK** to apply the changes.
8. Close **Ease of Access Center** window when done.

To disable the **Filter Keys** feature, steps 1 to 8 can be followed, while unchecking **Turn on Filter Keys** checkbox when on step 6.

Enable Toggle Keys Notification Sounds

Introduction to Toggle Key Notification Sounds

When Microsoft Windows 8 is used with its default settings, no notification sounds are heard when any toggle key is pressed. Toggle Keys in a computer are the ones that enable a particular feature, and disable them when pressed again. The three main toggle keys that users mostly use while working with Windows are Caps Lock, Num Lock and Scroll Lock. As mentioned above, when any of these toggle keys are pressed, by default no notification sound is heard. Because of this, users are unable to notice the current states of these toggle keys, hence mistyping the data unintentionally and unwantedly.

In order to avoid these situations, Microsoft Windows 8 allows users to enable notification sounds for the toggle keys. When notification sounds are enabled, every time a toggle key is pressed, the computer makes a sound that notifies the users that a toggle key is pressed.

How to Enable Toggle Keys Notification Sounds?

In order to enable toggle keys notification sounds in Microsoft Windows 8, steps given below must be followed:

1. Log on to Microsoft Windows 8 computer with any account.
2. From the **Start** screen, click **Desktop** tile.
3. On the desktop screen, right-click anywhere and from the context menu, click **Personalize**.
4. On the **Personalization** window, click **Ease of Access Center** from the bottom of the left pane.
5. On the **Ease of Access Center** window, under **Explore all settings** section, click **Make the keyboard easier to use**.
6. On the opened window, under the **Make it easier to type** section, check **Turn on Toggle Keys** checkbox.

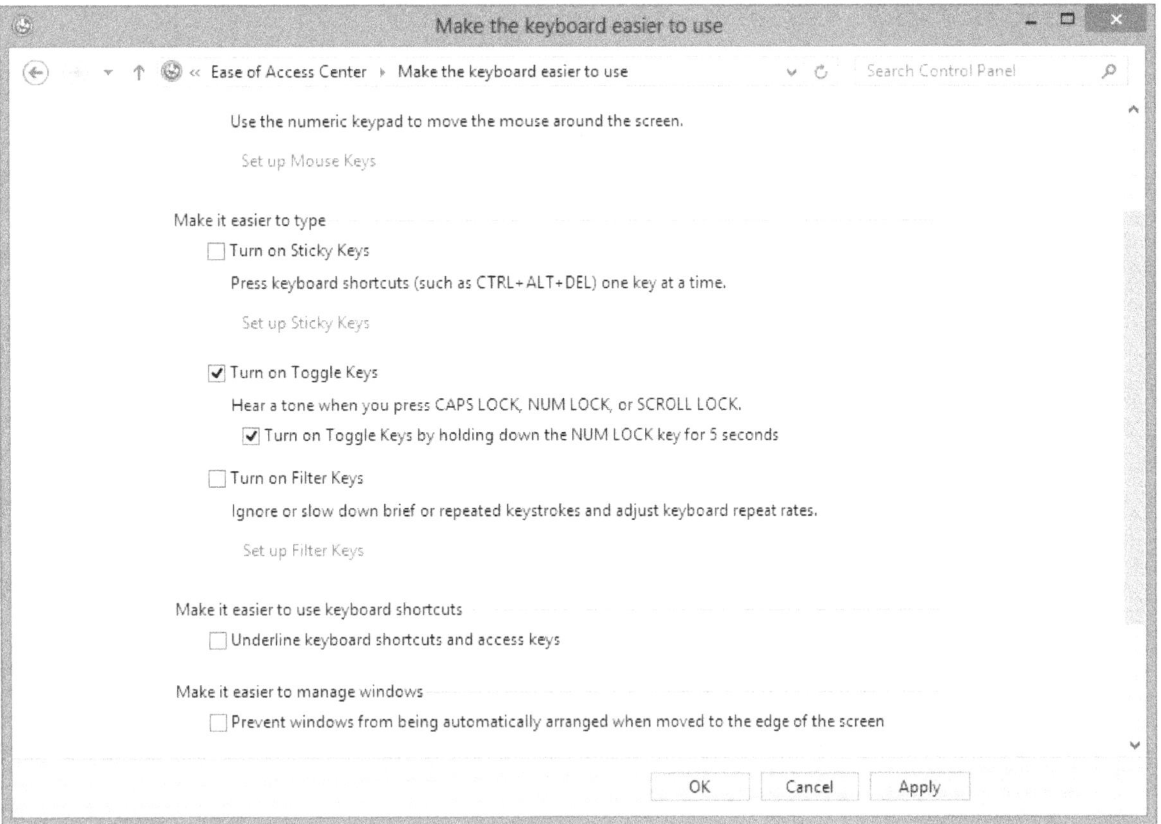

7. Click **OK** to apply the changes.
8. Close **Ease of Access Center** window when done.

To disable the **Toggle Keys** feature, steps 1 to 8 can be followed, while unchecking **Turn on Toggle Keys** checkbox when on step 6.

Enable Sticky Keys

Introduction to Sticky Keys

While working with Windows 8 operating systems, users might want to use some shortcut keys to save their time. In order to use shortcut keys, in almost all cases users are required to press multiple keys simultaneously at the same time. An example of a shortcut key is 'Ctrl + S'. When these two keys are pressed simultaneously, the current opened document gets saved. If the user is trying to save the document for the very first time after creating it, the Saved As box gets initiated.

For normal users, this method of using the shortcut keys is quite useful and time-saving, whereas for physically challenged users, it might be challenging to use the shortcut keys with the default configuration of Microsoft Windows 8.

In order to make things easier for physically challenged users, Microsoft Windows 8 allows them to enable Sticky Keys. When Sticky Keys are enabled, the requirement of pressing multiple keys simultaneously is eliminated, and users can press one key at a time, even if a shortcut key is used. For example, after enabling Sticky Keys, if users want to use 'Ctrl + S' shortcut key, they can press 'Ctrl' and release the key, and then they can press and release the 'S' key to save the opened document.

How to Enable Sticky Keys?

In order to enable Sticky Keys in Microsoft Windows 8, steps given below must be followed:

1. Log on to Microsoft Windows 8 computer with any account.
2. From the **Start** screen, click **Desktop** tile.
3. On the desktop screen, right-click anywhere and from the context menu, click **Personalize**.
4. On the **Personalization** window, click **Ease of Access Center** from the bottom of the left pane.
5. On the **Ease of Access Center** the window, under **Explore all settings** section, click **Make the keyboard easier to use**.
6. On the opened window, under the **Make it easier to type** section, check **Turn on Sticky Keys** checkbox.

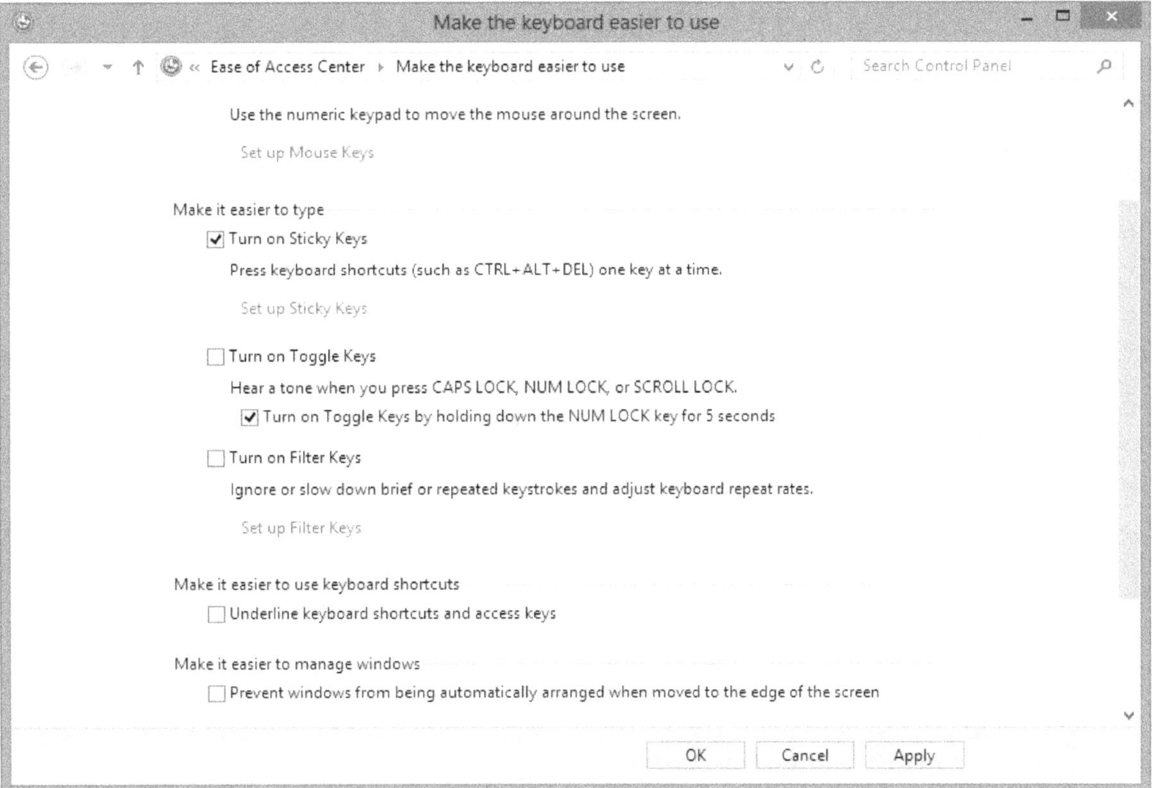

7. Click **OK** to apply the changes.
8. Close **Ease of Access Center** window when done.

To disable the **Sticky Keys** feature, steps 1 to 8 can be followed, while unchecking **Turn on Sticky Keys** checkbox when on step 6.

Disable Sticky Keys Popup Dialog Box

Introduction to Sticky Keys Popup Dialog Box

In Microsoft Windows 8, when the Shift key is pressed for five times repeatedly, Sticky Keys feature automatically gets enabled. While getting enabled, a dialog box is displayed on the computer screen informing the users about the initialization of the Sticky Keys feature.

Under normal conditions, this default configuration is quite appropriate when users want to enable Sticky Keys feature with ease and instantaneously. This configuration eliminates the requirements of manually going to the Sticky Keys option in order to enable the feature.

However this configuration might not be appreciated by most game lovers. The reason behind this is that while playing games, they might need to press the Shift key several times. If this configuration is enabled, every time users repeatedly press the Shift keys on their keyboards, games windows might get minimized and the Sticky Keys popup dialog box might appear on the monitors, hence disturbing the users. Therefore to play PC games in peace, most users prefer disabling this feature on their computers.

How to Disable Sticky Keys Popup Dialogue Box?

In order to disable Sticky Keys popup dialog box in Microsoft Windows 8, steps given below must be followed:

1. Log on to Microsoft Windows 8 computer with any account.
2. From the **Start** screen, click **Desktop** tile.
3. On the desktop screen, right-click anywhere and from the context menu, click **Personalize**.
4. On the **Personalization** window, click **Ease of Access Center** from the bottom of the left pane.
5. On the **Ease of Access Center** the window, under **Explore all settings** section, click **Make the keyboard easier to use**.
6. On the opened window, from the **Make it easier to type** section, under **Turn on Sticky Keys** checkbox click **Set up Sticky Keys**.
7. On the **Set up Sticky Keys** box, under **Keyboard shortcut** section, uncheck **Turn on Sticky Keys when SHIFT is pressed five times** checkbox.

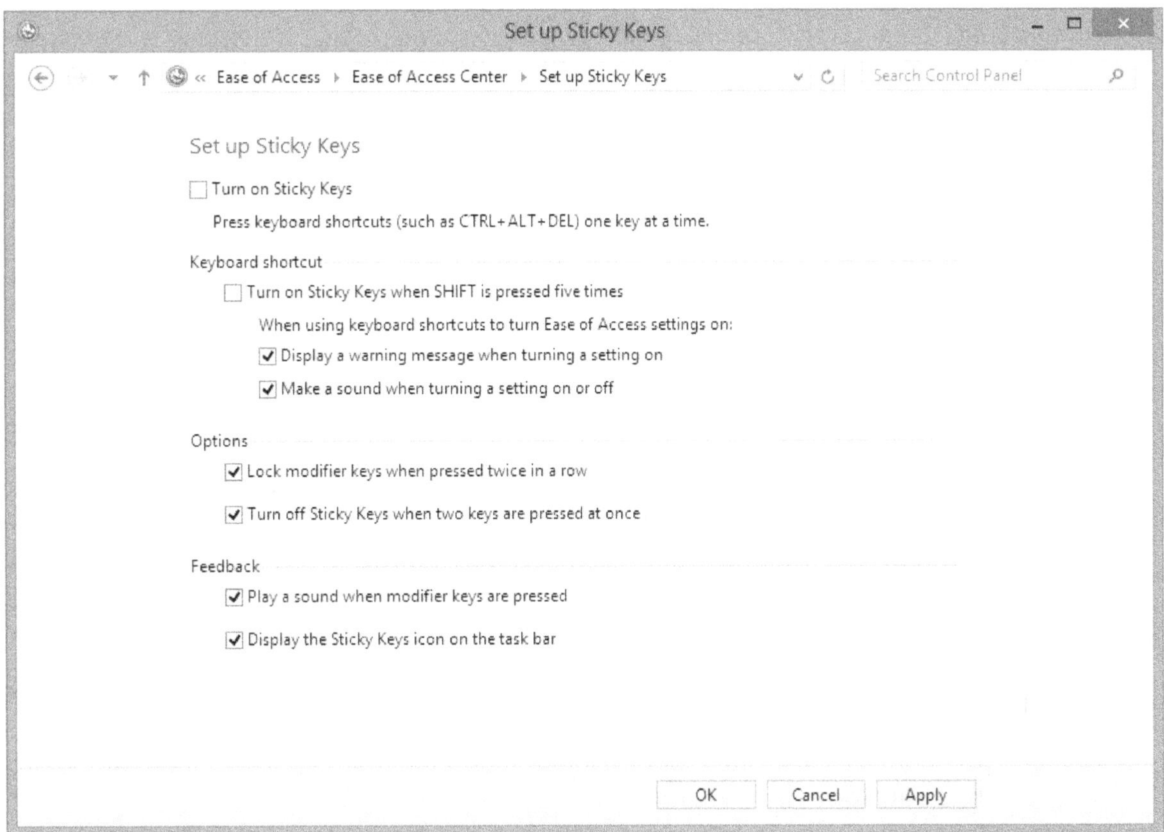

8. Click **OK** to apply the changes and back on the previous window, click **OK** again.
9. Close **Ease of Access Center** window when done.

To re-enable the **Sticky Keys** popup dialog box, steps 1 to 9 can be followed, while checking the **Turn on Sticky Keys when SHIFT is pressed five times** checkbox when on step 7.

Change the Taskbar Location

Introduction to Taskbar Location

In Microsoft Windows, the taskbar is by default located at the bottom of the screen, and is by default configured to remain on the top of all the opened windows and applications. According to the display resolution of the computer, in most cases the default configuration and the location of the taskbar is quite appropriate which requires no modifications. Whereas in some situations, especially when the interface of an application is quite space consuming, it might be a good idea to change the taskbar's location in order to work on the opened application without getting some of its options hidden behind the taskbar.

How to Change the Taskbar Location?

Although the taskbar can be unlocked and mouse can be used to drag and drop it to the desired location, steps given below can be followed to select a definite location of the taskbar with ease:

1. Log on to Microsoft Windows 8 computer with any account.
2. From the **Start** screen, click **Desktop** tile.
3. On the desktop screen, right-click the taskbar.
4. From the displayed context menu, click **Properties**.
5. On the **Taskbar Properties** box, make sure that **Taskbar** tab is selected.
6. Choose the desired taskbar location from the **Taskbar location on screen** drop-down list.

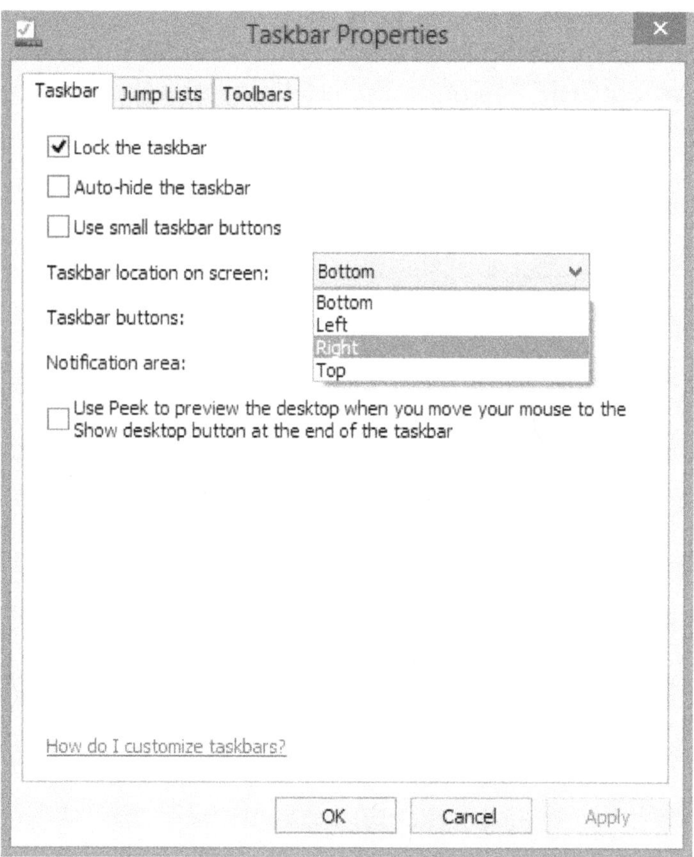

7. Click **OK** to apply the changes.

Note: *Taskbar location can also be changed manually by dragging and dropping the taskbar to the desired area of the desktop screen. However in order to change the location manually, taskbar must be unlocked. To learn how to unlock the taskbar, refer to 'Make the Taskbar Adjustable' lesson in this chapter.*

Hide the Taskbar Automatically

Introduction to the Auto-hide Feature

In Microsoft Windows 8, and all other versions of Microsoft Windows, by default the taskbar is configured to remain on top of all the opened applications and windows. This allows users to switch between the windows and the applications quite easily. This default configuration also allows users to access other available applications, icons of which are available on the taskbar.

Under normal situations, this configuration is quite appropriate and no modifications are required. However if an application has large interface and requires more than available space on the monitor, it is recommended that the taskbar should be configured to get hidden automatically when the mouse pointer is not at the bottom of the window.

When auto-hide for the taskbar is enabled, the taskbar remains hidden until the mouse is moved at the bottom of the window. As soon as users move the mouse pointer to the bottom of the screen, the taskbar automatically gets visible, and as soon as the mouse pointer is moved away from the bottom, the taskbar again gets hidden.

How to Enable Auto-hide for the Taskbar?

In order to enable auto-hide for the taskbar in Microsoft Windows 8, steps given below must be followed:

1. Log on to Microsoft Windows 8 computer with any account.
2. From the **Start** screen, click **Desktop** tile.
3. On the desktop screen, right-click the taskbar.
4. From the displayed context menu, click **Properties**.
5. On the **Taskbar Properties** box, make sure that **Taskbar** tab is selected.
6. Check **Auto-hide the taskbar** checkbox.

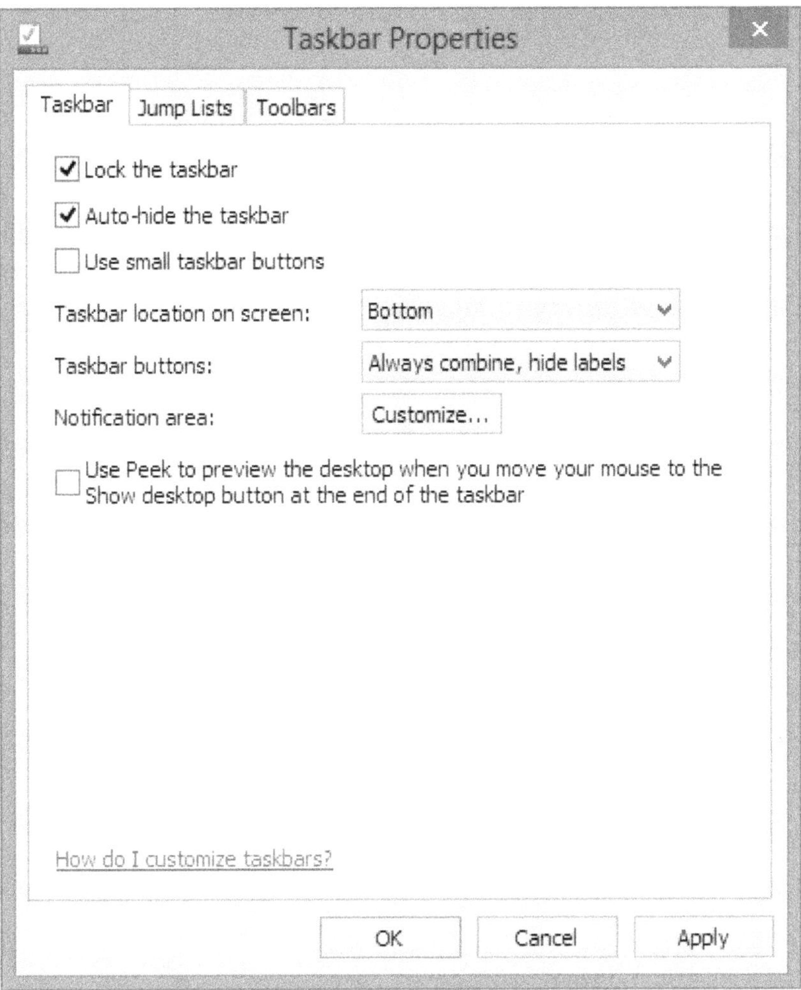

7. Click **OK** to apply the changes.

To disable auto-hide for the taskbar, steps 1 to 7 can be followed, while unchecking **Auto-hide the taskbar** checkbox when on step 6.

Make the Taskbar Adjustable

Introduction to the Taskbar Lock

In Microsoft Windows operating systems, by default the taskbar is locked. This prevents users from changing the size of the taskbar accidentally. Moreover, a locked taskbar cannot be moved to a different location by dragging and dropping. Nonetheless the location of the locked taskbar can still be changed by going to the taskbar properties and selecting the desired taskbar location from the 'Taskbar location on screen' drop-down list.

To protect Windows from accidental change in the interface, the default configuration should be left unchanged. However if users want to change the default size of the taskbar in order to view all the opened applications and windows, the taskbar must be unlocked. After unlocking, users can change its size by dragging the handles that appear when the mouse is moved to the edge of the taskbar. Once the modifications have been made, the taskbar should be locked back again.

How to Unlock the Taskbar?

In order to unlock the taskbar, steps given below must be followed:

1. Log on to Microsoft Windows 8 computer with any account.
2. From the **Start** screen, click **Desktop** tile.
3. On the desktop screen, right-click the taskbar.
4. From the displayed context menu, click **Properties**.
5. On the **Taskbar Properties** box, make sure that **Taskbar** tab is selected.
6. Uncheck **Lock the taskbar** checkbox.

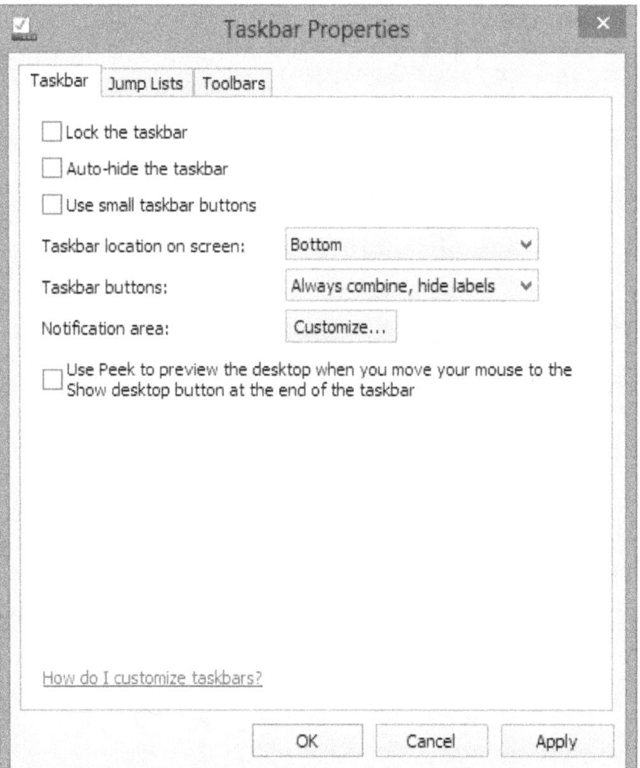

7. Click **OK** to apply the changes.

To lock the taskbar again, steps 1 to 7 can be followed, while checking **Lock the taskbar** checkbox when on step 6.

View the Labels of the Opened Applications

Introduction to the Labels of the Opened Applications

In Microsoft Windows 7 and Windows 8 operating systems, the opened applications and windows that are displayed in the taskbar are by default combined into the groups, hence making the labels of the entities invisible. In other words, when the applications or windows are opened, only the icons are displayed in the taskbar, and users are required to identify them through their icons only. For experienced users, the default configuration is quite appropriate and does not require modifications as they can easily identify the opened applications by their icons. Whereas, for users who are new to the Windows platform, or are new to the computer field altogether, identifying the entities by their icons might be a challenging task.

In order to overcome this situation, it is recommended that the labels of the opened entities should be made visible to the users.

How to View Labels of the Opened Applications and Windows?

In order to view the labels of the opened applications and windows in Microsoft Windows 8, steps given below must be followed:

1. Log on to Microsoft Windows 8 computer with any account.
2. From the **Start** screen, click **Desktop** tile.
3. On the desktop screen, right-click the taskbar.
4. From the displayed context menu, click **Properties**.
5. On the **Taskbar Properties** box, make sure that **Taskbar** tab is selected.
6. From the **Taskbar buttons** drop-down list, select **Never combine** option.

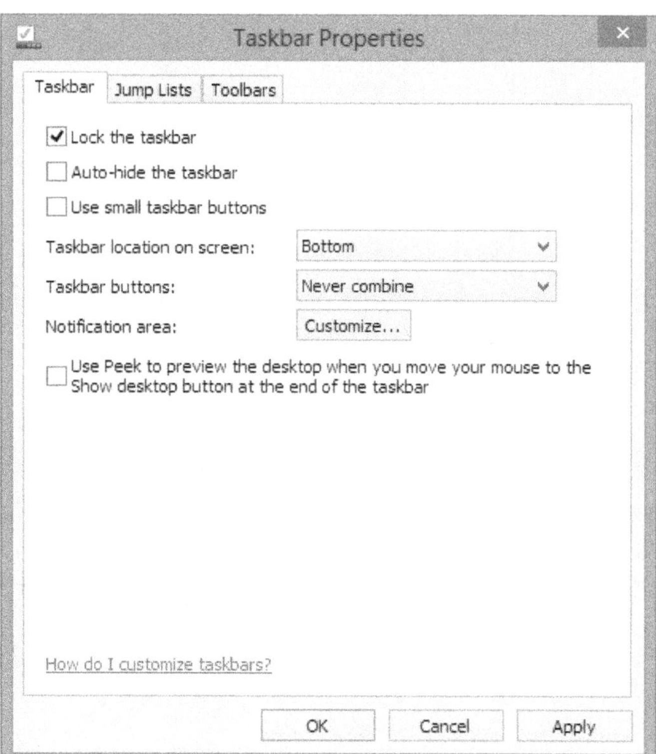

7. Click **OK** to apply the changes.

To set the taskbar settings back to default, steps 1 to 7 can be followed, while selecting **Always combine, hide labels** when on step 6.

Place the Desktop Icon on the Taskbar

Introduction to the Desktop Icon

In Microsoft Windows operating systems, the desktop screen consists of all the important icons and shortcuts that are frequently used by the users. Also, it is quite likely that while working with Windows, users might open several windows and applications at the same time, hence making it hard to reach back to the desktop screens easily. Although users can click the Aero Peek button that is available at the right end of the taskbar to go to the desktop instantaneously, doing so minimizes all the windows and applications and users must search for the previously active window or application once they are done working on the desktop.

A better solution to make things easier for the users is to place the desktop icon right on the taskbar. When the desktop icon is placed on the taskbar, it displays all the objects that are available on the desktop when clicked. This practice remarkably saves users' time and allows them to access the desired object with ease and instantaneously.

How to Place the Desktop Icon on the Taskbar?

In order to place the desktop icon on the taskbar in Microsoft Windows 8, steps given below must be followed:

1. Log on to Microsoft Windows 8 computer with any account.
2. From the **Start** screen, click **Desktop** tile.
3. On the desktop screen, right-click the taskbar.
4. From the context menu, go to **Toolbars** option.
5. From the displayed submenu, click **Desktop**.

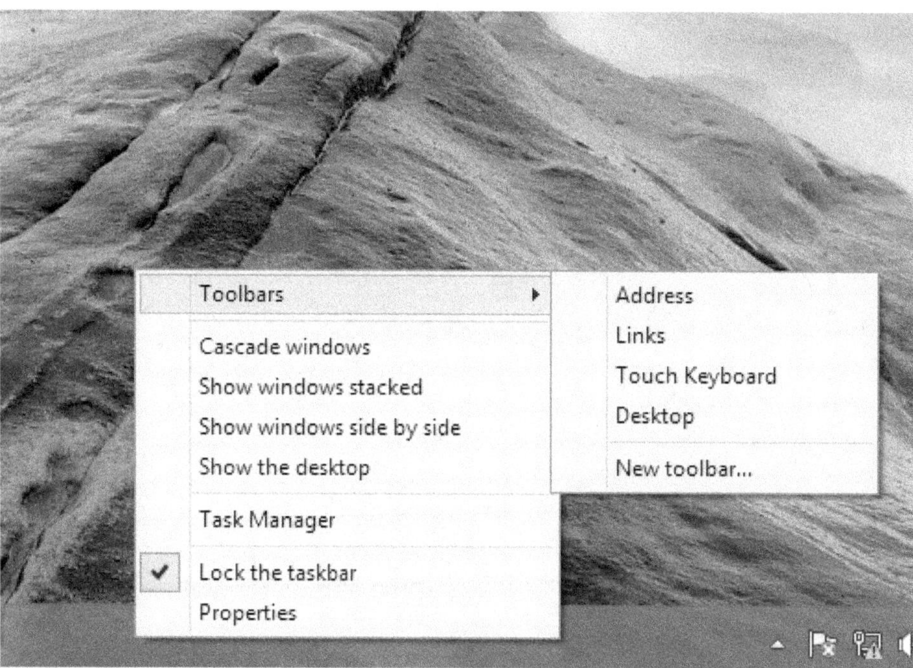

To remove the desktop icon from the taskbar, steps 1 to 5 can be followed, while clicking the **Desktop** option again when on step 5.

Place the Recycle Bin on the Taskbar

Introduction to the Recycle Bin Icon

By default the Recycle Bin icon is placed on the desktop in all Microsoft Windows operating systems. This default setting is considered most appropriate as it has been this way since the birth of GUI-based Microsoft operating systems. However sometimes users might want to clear the desktop screens and might want to remove the Recycle Bin icon from the desktop as well. By all means they can do so, but it is strongly recommended that they place the Recycle Bin icon somewhere else before removing it from the desktop screen. Best option in this regard can be to place the Recycle Bin icon on the taskbar.

How to Place the Recycle Bin on the Taskbar?

In order to place the Recycle Bin on the taskbar in Microsoft Windows 8, steps given below must be followed:

1. Log on to Microsoft Windows 8 computer with any account.
2. From the **Start** screen, click **Desktop** tile.
3. On the desktop screen, right-click anywhere.
4. From the context menu, go to **New**.
5. From the displayed submenu, click **Shortcut**.
6. On the **Create Shortcut** window, type **%SystemRoot%\explorer.exe shell:RecycleBinFolder** in the **Type the location for the item** field.

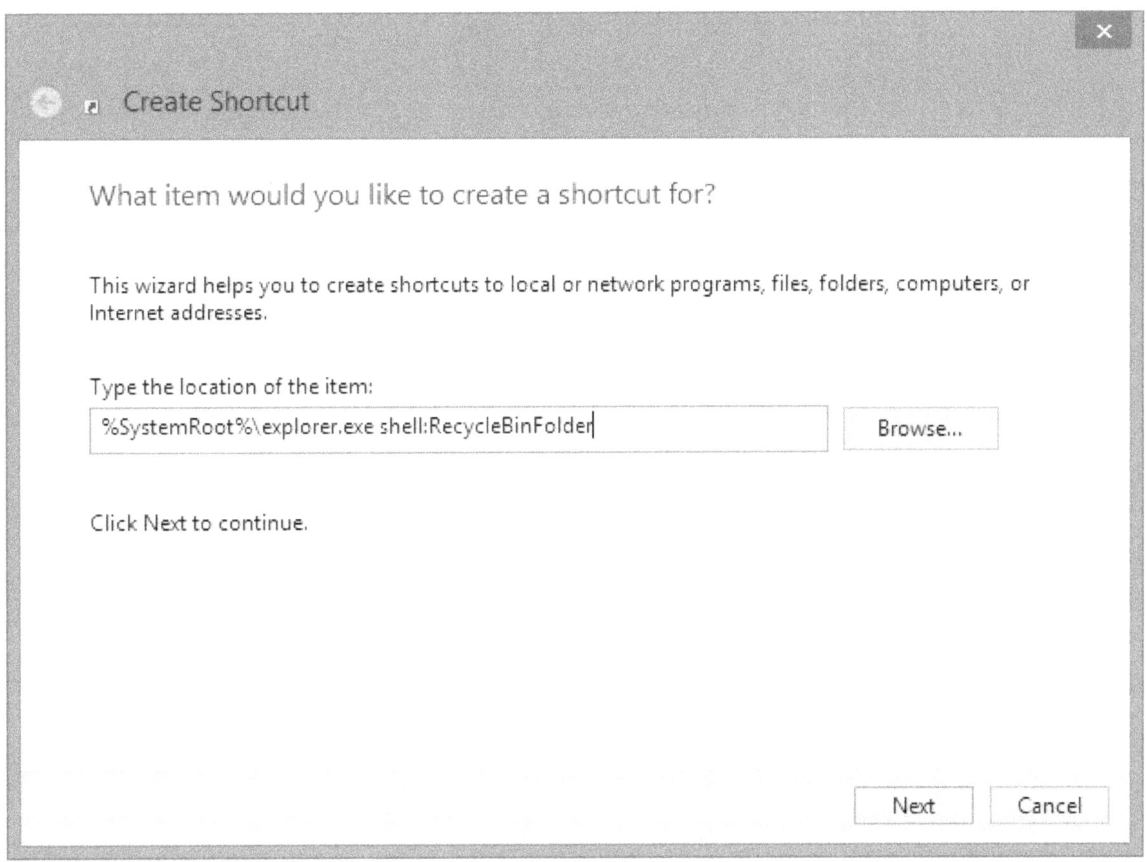

7. Click **Next** button to continue.
8. In the available field on the next window, specify a name for the new shortcut. (Most appropriate name could be Recycle Bin.)
9. Click **Finish** when done.
10. Drag the newly created shortcut from the desktop screen to the taskbar. Optionally, the icon for the shortcut can also be changed before dragging by going to its properties box and clicking **Change Icon** button from the **Shortcut** tab.

To remove the **Recycle Bin** from the taskbar, right-click the icon in the taskbar and from the displayed options, click **Unpin this program from taskbar**.

Make the Taskbar Work as Windows Vista

Introduction to Windows Vista's Taskbar

The taskbar in Windows Vista used to work quite dynamically. When users opened a few applications or windows, Windows Vista's taskbar used to display their icons along with their label names. When the taskbar was overpopulated with excess of opened applications and/or windows, it used to group the labels of applications/windows of similar types, hence displaying only their icons. This default configuration of the taskbar in Windows Vista helped users identify the opened entities with their label names as well as by their icons.

In Microsoft Windows 8, by default icons of all the opened applications and windows are grouped together, irrespective of the availability of the space in the taskbar. This default configuration of the operating system can be changed and Windows 8 taskbar can also be configured to work as that of Microsoft Windows Vista.

How to Make the Taskbar Work as That of Windows Vista?

In order to make Microsoft Windows 8 taskbar to work the same way the taskbar of Windows Vista does, steps given below must be followed:

1. Log on to Microsoft Windows 8 computer with any account.
2. From the **Start** screen, click **Desktop** tile.
3. On the desktop screen, right-click the taskbar.
4. From the displayed context menu, click **Properties**.
5. On the **Taskbar Properties** box, make sure that **Taskbar** tab is selected.
6. From the **Taskbar buttons** drop-down list, select **Combine when taskbar is full** option.

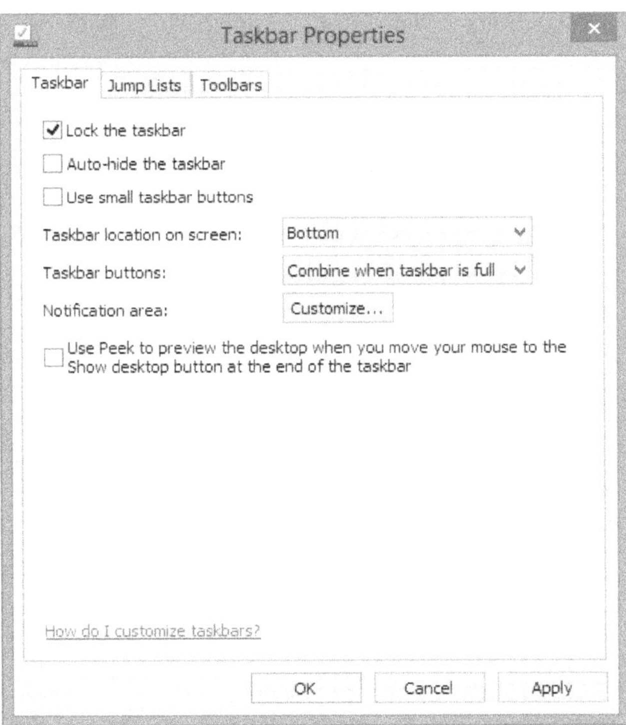

7. Click **OK** to apply the changes.

To set the taskbar settings back to default, steps 1 to 7 can be followed, while selecting **Always combine, hide labels** option when on step 6.

Show Full DOS Path in the Title Bar

Introduction to the Full DOS Path

When users navigate and look for any object in Microsoft Windows 8, in the background the DOS commands are executed, that help them locate the desired object. In earlier versions of Windows operating systems, like Microsoft Windows XP, the entire DOS path was displayed in the address bar of the located window. Whereas the interface has been changed with the release of Microsoft Windows Vista and the modified interface is now carried forward to Windows 8 as well. Because of the modifications in the interface, no DOS path is now displayed in the address bar of the opened window. Although if users want they can click inside the address bar window in order to view the DOS path, the process still requires user interaction, which might not be appreciated by many users.

In order to make things easier, users can configure their profiles so that the full DOS path to the located folder is displayed on the title bar of the opened window.

How to Display Full DOS Path in the Title Bar?

In order to display the full DOS path on the title bar of the opened window, steps given below must be followed:

1. Log on to Microsoft Windows 8 computer with any account.
2. From the **Start** screen, click **Desktop** tile.
3. On the desktop screen, click **File Explorer** icon from the taskbar.
4. On the opened **Libraries** window, click **View** from the menu bar.
5. Click **Options** from the icons displayed in the ribbon.
6. On the **Folder Options** box, go to **View** tab.
7. From the **Advanced settings** list, check **Display the full path in the title bar** checkbox.

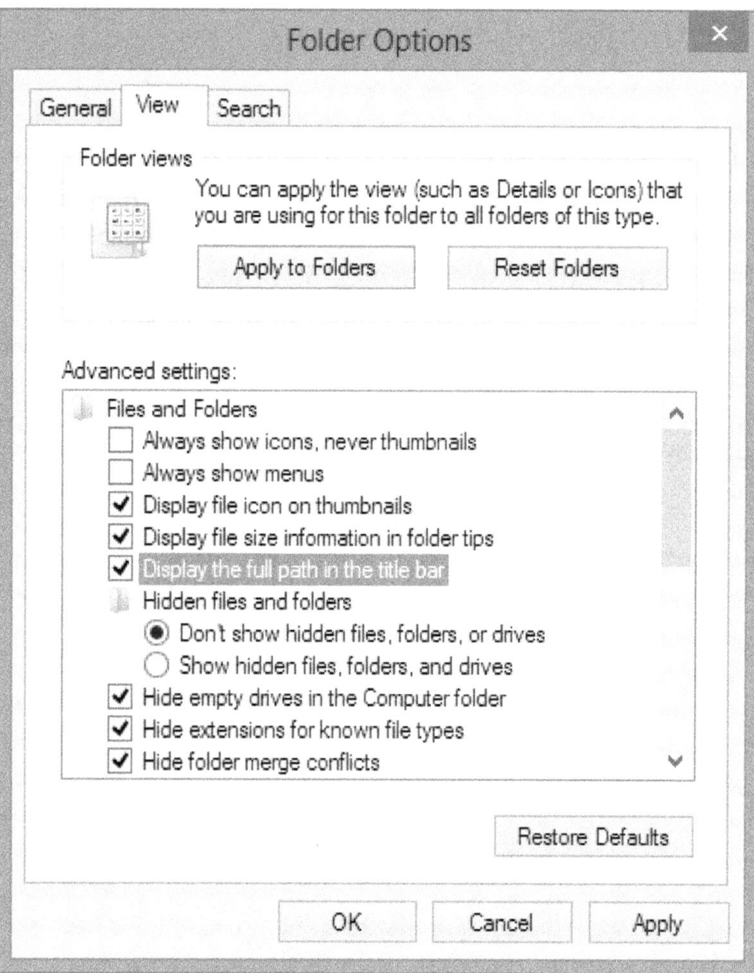

8. Click **OK** to apply the changes.

To set the configuration back to default, steps 1 to 8 can be followed, while unchecking **Display the full path in the title bar** checkbox when on step 7.

Uninstall/Modify/Repair a Program

Introduction to Uninstalling, Modifying or Repairing a Program

While using Microsoft Windows 8, it is likely that users might install several Microsoft or non-Microsoft-based applications in order to ease their tasks. Also, from home users it is expected that they might install games on their computers for entertainment purposes. Moreover many users might also install third-party media players to play the movies and audio files on their computers.

As users install the applications, it is likely that they might also want to uninstall them in case they are no longer required. Apart from uninstalling the applications, if the programs start performing obnoxiously, users might also want to repair them in order to make them work properly. There might also be cases when users might want modify the installed applications to add or remove certain features as per their requirements.

Uninstalling, modifying or repairing installed applications totally depend on the nature of the programs. For example when Microsoft Office is installed, users can initiate the repairing process for the package in case it starts behaving abnormally. Moreover, users can also modify the package and add or remove the built-in features as per their requirements. In case MS Office package is not required at all, users can also remove the entire application altogether.

How to Uninstall, Modify or Repair an Application?

In order to uninstall, modify or repair an application in Microsoft Windows 8, steps given below must be followed:

1. Log on to Microsoft Windows 8 computer with administrator account.
2. From the **Start** screen, click **Desktop** tile.
3. On the desktop screen, hover mouse to the bottom right corner of the window.
4. From the displayed options, click **Settings**.
5. On the **Settings** pane, click **Control Panel**.
6. On the **Control Panel** window, click **Uninstall a program** option under **Programs** category.
7. On the opened **Programs and Features** window, from the displayed list, click to select the application that is to be removed, modified or repaired.

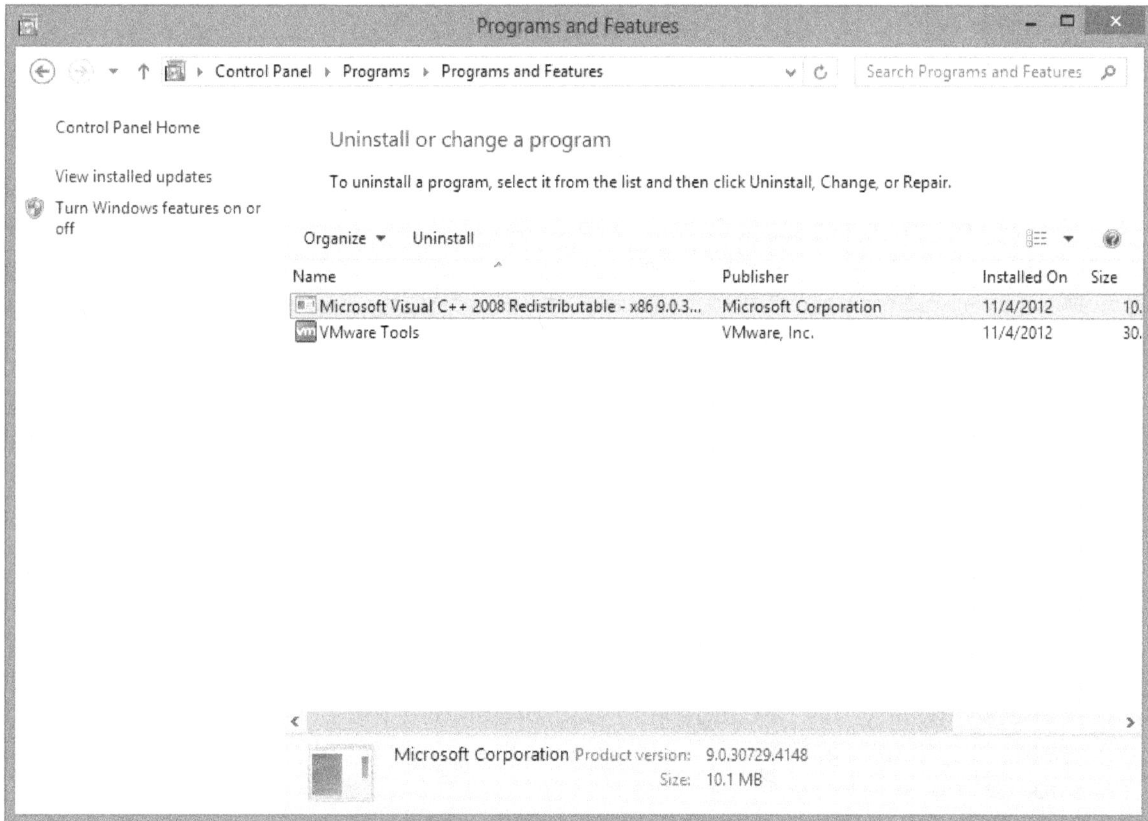

8. Once selected, click the appropriate option available at the top of the list.
9. Follow on-screen instructions thereafter. (Steps may vary while removing/modifying/repairing different application.)
10. Once done, close **Programs and Features** window.

Rename the Recycle Bin

Introduction to Renaming the Recycle Bin

Microsoft Windows 8 also allows users to rename the Recycle Bin if users want to do so. Although it is not at all recommended, and neither does it make any sense to rename the Recycle Bin under any circumstances, users can still go for it for testing purposes, or if they want to confuse other users who share the same computer and access the same user account.

Since Recycle Bin is available for all users and is displayed in all user profiles, renaming it is a user specific task and no elevated privileges are required to do so.

How to Rename the Recycle Bin?

In order to rename the Recycle Bin in Microsoft Windows 8, steps given below must be followed:

1. Log on to Microsoft Windows 8 computer with any account.
2. From the **Start** screen, click **Desktop** tile.
3. On the desktop screen, right-click **Recycle Bin** icon.
4. From the displayed context menu, click **Rename**.

5. In the editable label text field, specify a new name for the **Recycle Bin**.
6. Press **Enter** key when done.

Enable the Delete Confirmation Dialog Box

Introduction to the Delete Confirmation Dialog Box

While working with Microsoft Windows operating systems, users keep adding or deleting files on the computers. When users add files, they occupy some space in the hard disk drive, and when the stored files are deleted, the disk space is freed up.

In pre-Windows 8 versions of Microsoft operating systems, when users used to delete any object from the computer, a confirmation dialog box was displayed that asked users to confirm the deletion process. The dialog box that appeared ensured that the deletion process was initialized on purpose, and the data was being deleted accidentally. In other words, the confirmation box made sure that no accidental deletion occurred due to human errors.

Unlike earlier versions of Windows, the delete confirmation box has been disabled by default in Microsoft Windows 8. Microsoft configured Windows 8 in this way in order to save users decent amount of time that they otherwise used to spend in earlier versions while taking Yes button on the delete confirmation box. Since most of the times users delete objects on purpose, Microsoft considered the delete confirmation box as an obstacle and a time taking process while removing the objects. Since accidental data loss is still prevented as the deleted objects are moved to the Recycle Bin instead of getting removed community from the hard disk drive, removing delete confirmation box from Microsoft Windows 8 is an optimistic approach in order to save users time and energy.

Even though by default delete confirmation box has been removed from Windows 8, it still allows users to enable it in case they feel uncomfortable while deleting the objects in the absence of the confirmation box.

How to Enable Delete Confirmation Box?

In order to enable delete confirmation box in Microsoft Windows 8, steps given below must be followed:

1. Log on to Microsoft Windows 8 computer with any account.
2. From the **Start** screen, click **Desktop** tile.
3. On the desktop screen, right-click **Recycle Bin** icon.
4. From the displayed context menu, click **Properties**.
5. On the **Recycle Bin Properties** box, check **Display delete confirmation dialog** checkbox.

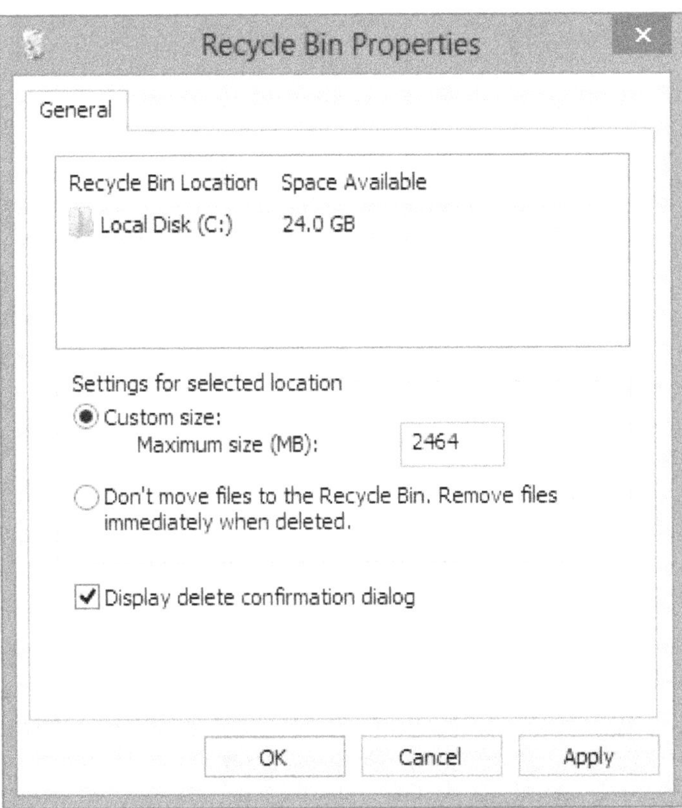

6. Click **OK** to apply the changes.

To disable the delete confirmation box again, steps 1 to 6 can be followed, while unchecking **Display delete confirmation dialog** checkbox when on step 5.

Change Recycle Bin Capacity

Introduction to Recycle Bin Capacity

Recycle Bin capacity is the total size of the deleted files that the Recycle Bin can hold before deleting them permanently from the hard disk drive. As everyone knows, every time a file is deleted, it is sent to the Recycle Bin from where it can be restored if the deletion was made in error. If the total size of the deleted file is larger than the storage capacity of the Recycle Bin, Windows deletes the file permanently from the hard disk drive, without sending it to the Recycle Bin.

In Microsoft Windows 8, by default the maximum Recycle Bin capacity is 10% of the total space of a drive (volume). For example if total size of C: is 100 GB, the maximum capacity of Recycle Bin for C: would be 10 GB. This means that when a file that is smaller than 10 GB is deleted, it is sent to the Recycle Bin, whereas if the file is larger than 10 GB in size, it is deleted permanently from the hard disk drive.

Under normal circumstances, in both homes and production environments the default Recycle Bin capacity is considered sufficient enough and should not be modified. However sometimes administrators may want to increase the total capacity of the Recycle Bin in order to store the deleted files that are huge in size. Since all the volumes in the hard disk drives are not expected to be of same size, Recycle Bin capacity must be modified for every available volume individually.

How to Modify the Default Recycle Bin Capacity?

In order to change the default maximum Recycle Bin capacity in Microsoft Windows 8, steps given below must be followed:

1. Log on to Microsoft Windows 8 computer with administrator account.
2. From the **Start** screen, click **Desktop** tile.
3. On the desktop screen, right-click **Recycle Bin** icon.
4. From the displayed context menu, click **Properties**.
5. On the **Recycle Bin Properties** box, from the displayed drive list, click to select the drive for which **Recycle Bin** capacity is to be modified.
6. Once selected, ensure that **Custom size** radio button under the **Settings for selected location** section is selected.
7. In the **Maximum size (MB)** field, specify the new storage capacity in megabytes for the selected drive.
8. Click **OK** to apply the changes.

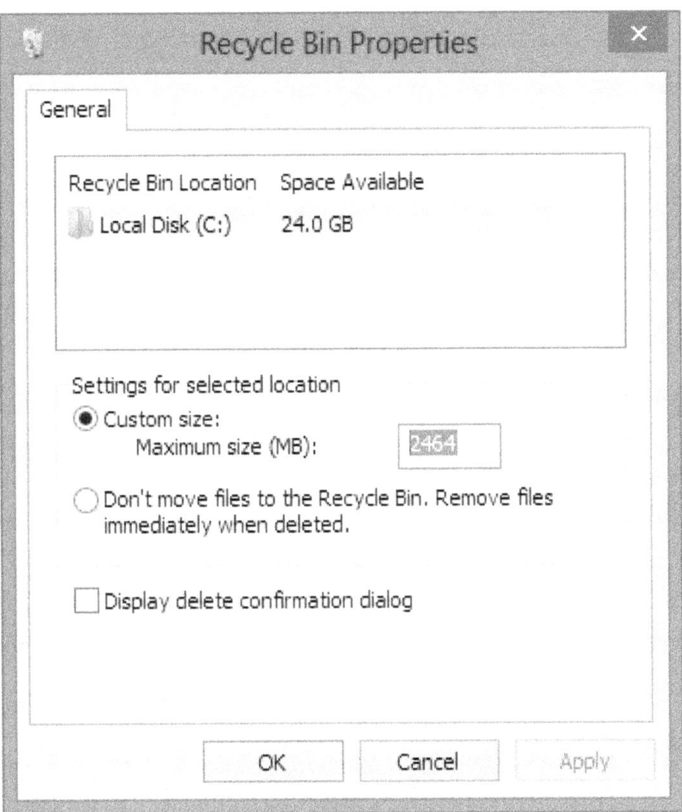
Recycle Bin Properties
General
Recycle Bin Location
Space Available
Local Disk (C:)
24.0 GB
Settings for selected location
Custom size:
Maximum size (MB):
2464
Don't move files to the Recycle Bin. Remove files immediately when deleted.
Display delete confirmation dialog
OK
Cancel
Apply

Add New Fonts

Introduction to Fonts

Fonts are the files that contain character sets of specific shapes and sizes. When Microsoft Windows 8 is installed, some default fonts are also installed along with the operating system automatically. It is because of the fonts that the texts are displayed on the computer. Even the label of the icons and other generally seen texts on the computer screen are visible only because of the presence of the fonts.

As mentioned above, although along with the installation of Microsoft Windows 8, several types of fonts are automatically installed, if users want they can download other fonts from the Internet and can install them on the computers to get the character sets of different shapes and sizes. Installing new fonts help users format the texts in different styles when working on the files.

Generally TrueType Font (.TTF) files are used as the font files in Microsoft Windows which can be downloaded directly from the Internet. Font files can be extracted from the installation media of any application in which they exist.

How to Add a New Font?

In order to add a new font in Microsoft Windows 8, steps given below must be followed:

1. Log on to Microsoft Windows 8 computer with administrator account.
2. From the **Start** screen, click **Desktop** tile.
3. On the desktop screen, click **File Explorer** icon from the taskbar.
4. From the **Libraries** window, navigate and locate the target font file that is to be installed.
5. Right-click the located font (.TTF) file, and from the displayed context menu, click **Install**.

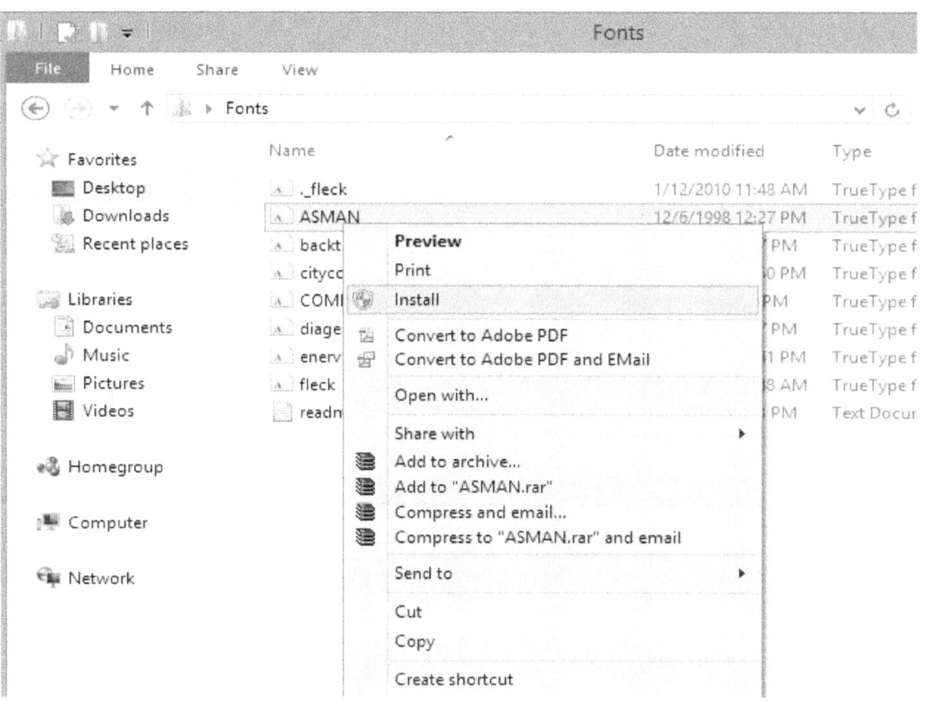

In order to delete an installed font from Windows 8 computer, steps given below must be followed:

1. Log on to Microsoft Windows 8 computer with administrator account.
2. From the **Start** screen, click **Desktop** tile.
3. On the desktop screen, hover mouse to the bottom right corner of the window.
4. From the displayed options, click **Settings**.
5. On the **Settings** pane, click **Control Panel**.
6. From the **Control Panel** window, click **Appearance and Personalization** category.
7. From the **Appearance and Personalization** window, click **Fonts**.
8. In the **Fonts** window, right-click the font that is to be deleted.
9. From the context menu, click **Delete**.

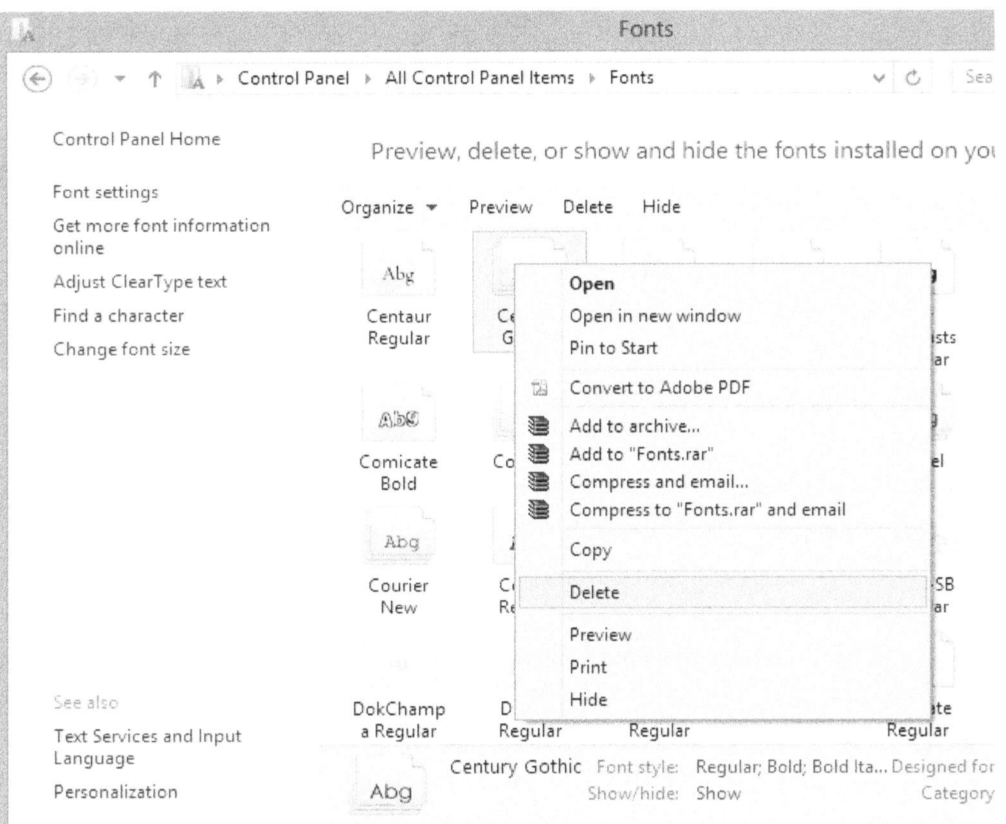

10. On the **Delete Font** box, click **Yes** button to confirm the deletion.
11. Close **Fonts** window when done.

Burn ISO Image on an Optical Media

Introduction to ISO Images

ISO images are the files with .ISO extensions and they work as the containers to store multiple scattered files so that they can be transferred from one location to another as a single entity and with minimum chances of data loss.

ISO images can be created using several ISO image applications that can be downloaded from the Internet. Same applications can be used to extract or burn the ISO files at different locations or on the CDs/DVDs respectively.

The reason why the ISO images are accepted and appreciated by majority of users worldwide is that if the images are created from any bootable media, the ISO images also become bootable. When the bootable ISO images are burned on the CDs/DVDs, the produced optical media also become bootable.

Because of the popularity of the ISO images worldwide, even Microsoft Windows 8 now supports ISO files and allows users to burn them on the optical media without using any third-party application.

How to Burn an ISO Image?

In order to burn an ISO image on an optical media in Microsoft Windows 8, steps given below must be followed:

1. Log on to Microsoft Windows 8 computer with the account that has burning privileges.
2. From the **Start** screen, click **Desktop** tile.
3. On the desktop screen, click **File Explorer** icon from the taskbar.
4. From the opened **Libraries** window, navigate and locate the .ISO image that is to be burned on a disc.
5. Right-click the target disc image file, and from the context menu, click **Burn disc image**.
6. On the **Windows Disc Image Burner** box, select the appropriate burner from the **Disc burner** drop-down list.

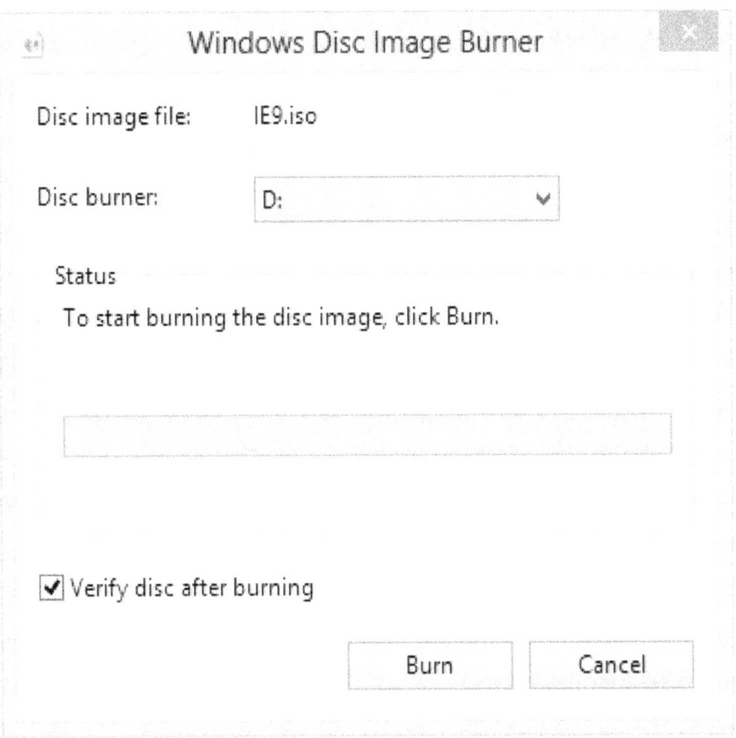

7. To be on the safer side, check **Verify disc after burning** checkbox. (Optional)
8. Click **Burn** to start the image burning process.

Record DOS Command Outputs in a File

Introduction to Recording DOS Command Outputs in a File

When DOS commands are typed in the command prompt, the results are displayed in the same window instantaneously. As more commands are typed in the same command prompt, previously displayed results keep scrolling up. This makes it difficult for the users to locate previously displayed results. Moreover, if CLS command this typed in the DOS window, all displayed information is removed in order to clear the screen, hence erasing all the results as well. If users want to get the results back, they are needed to type the commands again, which might be quite tedious and irritating task sometimes.

In order to avoid such situations, it is advisable to save the DOS results in the files so that they can be accessed whenever they are required, without having users to type the commands in the DOS window.

Another advantage of recording the outputs in the files is that users can maintain the records of the outputs can use them for future references, especially when tracking the status of the data stored on the computers.

How to Record the DOS Command Outputs in a File?

In order to record DOS command outputs in a file in Microsoft Windows 8, steps given below must be followed:

1. Log on to Microsoft Windows 8 computer with any account.
2. From the **Start** screen, click **Desktop** tile.
3. On the desktop screen, hover mouse to the bottom right corner of the window.
4. From the displayed options, click **Search**.
5. On the opened **Apps** window, locate and click **Command Prompt** under **Windows Accessories** category.
6. On the opened command window, type any printed-result oriented command (e.g. IPCONFIG) followed by **|** (pipe sign) and **CLIP** command to copy the results to the clipboard. (**E.g. IPCONFIG | CLIP**)

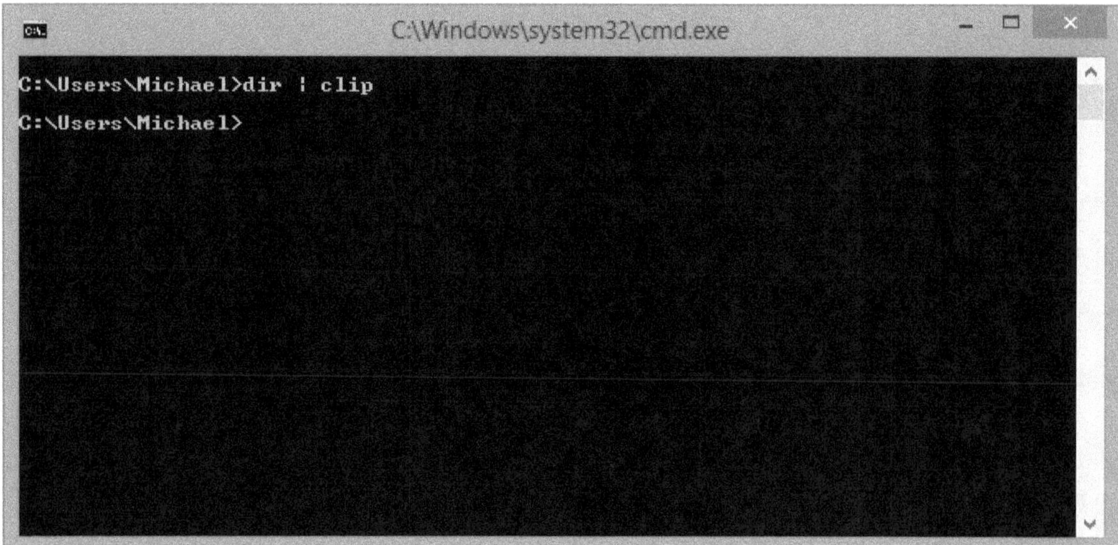

7. Once done, open any text editor such as MS Word and press **Ctrl** + **V** keys simultaneously to paste the contents of the clipboard (results of the given DOS command) in the text editor.

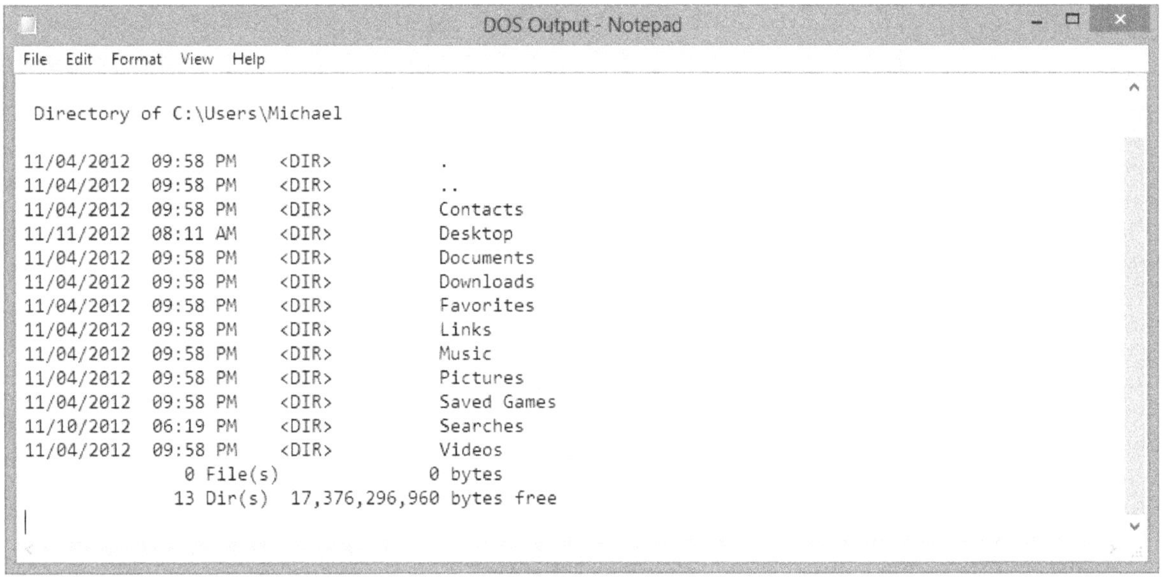

DOS Output - Notepad

File Edit Format View Help

```
 Directory of C:\Users\Michael

11/04/2012  09:58 PM    <DIR>          .
11/04/2012  09:58 PM    <DIR>          ..
11/04/2012  09:58 PM    <DIR>          Contacts
11/11/2012  08:11 AM    <DIR>          Desktop
11/04/2012  09:58 PM    <DIR>          Documents
11/04/2012  09:58 PM    <DIR>          Downloads
11/04/2012  09:58 PM    <DIR>          Favorites
11/04/2012  09:58 PM    <DIR>          Links
11/04/2012  09:58 PM    <DIR>          Music
11/04/2012  09:58 PM    <DIR>          Pictures
11/04/2012  09:58 PM    <DIR>          Saved Games
11/10/2012  06:19 PM    <DIR>          Searches
11/04/2012  09:58 PM    <DIR>          Videos
               0 File(s)              0 bytes
              13 Dir(s)  17,376,296,960 bytes free
```

8. Save the text editor file for future references.

Rename Multiple Files Simultaneously

Introduction to Renaming the Files Simultaneously

Nowadays computers have large storage areas and therefore users prefer storing their sensitive and private information on them. When users store large amount of data on the computers, many times the data files are of same types. For example if a business organization deals in documentations, it is likely that all the information will be stored in various .DOC files. Likewise, a photo studio might have large quantity of image files that the administration might want to store in order to maintain records. In such cases, the most challenging task for the operators is to rename the files according to the specified naming conventions defined by the management or administrators.

Since it may take quite a long time to rename each file individually, in order to make things easier for the users, Microsoft Windows 8 allows them to rename multiple files in a single go. With the help of the following method, users can rename 10, 100, or even 1000 files within seconds. However appropriate naming conventions must be used according to which files are to be renamed.

How to Rename Multiple Files Simultaneously?

In order to rename multiple files simultaneously in Microsoft Windows 8, steps given below must be followed:

1. Log on to Microsoft Windows 8 computer with any account.
2. From the **Start** screen, click **Desktop** tile.
3. On the desktop screen, click **File Explorer** icon from the taskbar.
4. From the opened **Libraries** window, navigate and locate the folder where several images are stored.
5. Once inside the folder, press **Ctrl** + **A** keys simultaneously to select all files.
6. Right-click the first file, and from the context menu, click **Rename**.
7. In the editable label text field, type a new name for the first file. (E.g. My Images)

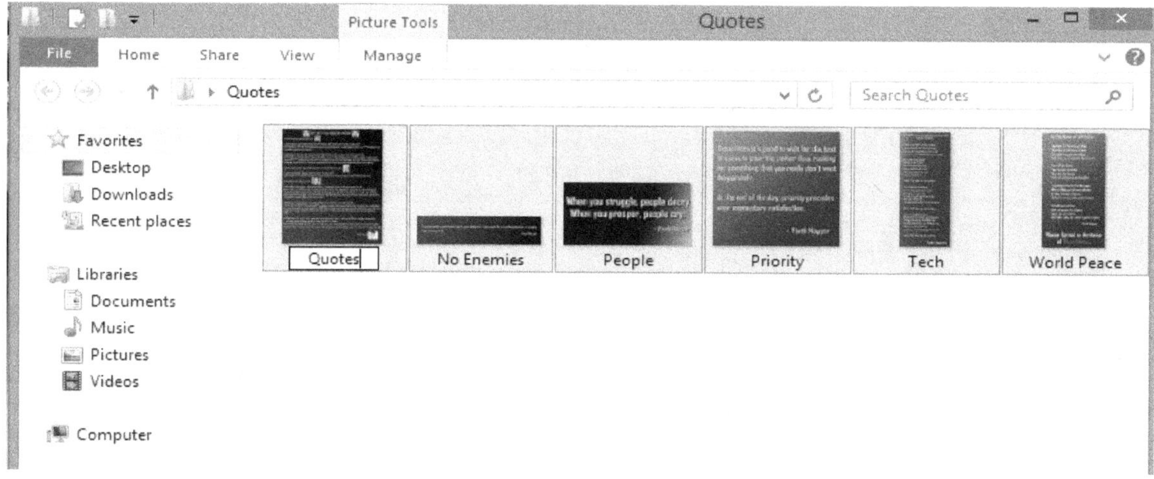

8. Press **Enter** key to rename all the selected files simultaneously as per the naming convention. (E.g. My Images (1), My Images (2), and so on.)

View Full DOS Path of a Folder in the Address Bar

Introduction to Full DOS Path in the Address Bar

In earlier versions of Microsoft operating systems, such as Microsoft Windows XP, the entire DOS path of any opened folder was displayed in the address bar of the window. With the release of Windows Vista, Microsoft has changed the interface of Windows Explorer. Because of the modified interface, the complete and proper DOS path for a folder is not displayed in the address bar when its window is opened.

In Microsoft Windows 8, the address bar displays the root folder, the parent folder and the sub-folder that has been opened by the user. But the entire chain of the folders and subfolders is separated by the ▶ symbol. This means that the proper DOS path is still not displayed by default.

How to Display Full DOS Path of a Folder in the Address Bar?

In order to display full and proper DOS path of a folder in the address bar in Microsoft Windows 8, steps given below must be followed:

1. Log on to Microsoft Windows 8 computer with any account.
2. From the **Start** screen, click **Desktop** tile.
3. On the desktop screen, click **File Explorer** icon from the taskbar.
4. From the opened **Libraries** window, navigate and locate the folder for which full DOS path is to be viewed in the address bar.
5. Once inside the target folder, in the address bar, click to the right of the folder name to change the new path display convention to the legacy DOS path.

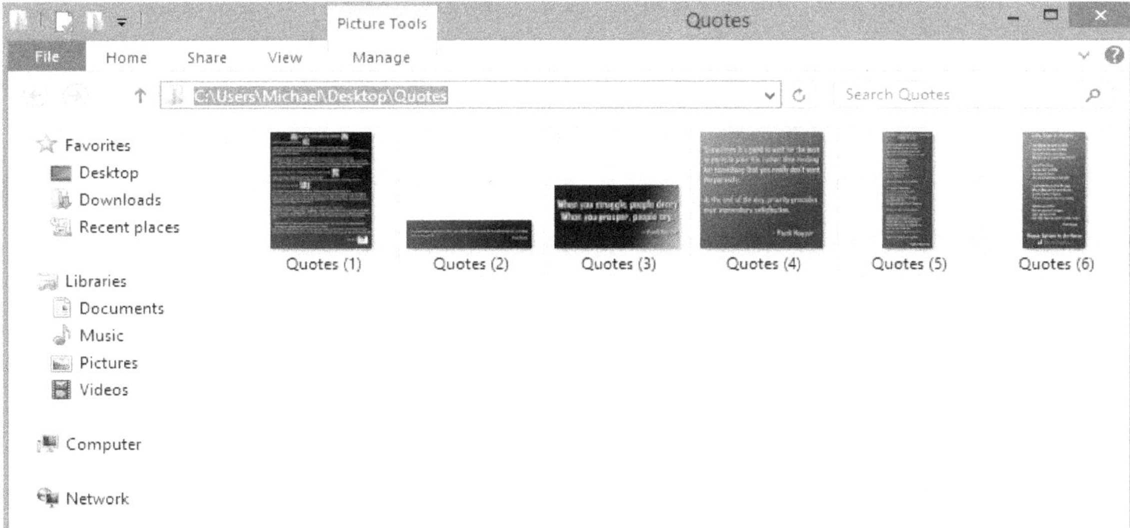

6. Close the opened window when done.

Make Hidden Control Panel Features Visible

Introduction to the Hidden Control Panel Features

When Microsoft Windows 8 is installed, it displays the most common features that, according to Microsoft, users usually use while working with the operating system. Only the commonly known features are displayed in order to make Windows 8 a complete user-friendly and easy-to-use operating system that can be operated even by a layman. However there are majority of people who love to play around with the operating systems and in order to do so they need to get access to the features that are not easily and by default visible to the normal users.

Taking the above discussion to the next level, Control Panel in Microsoft Windows 8 also displays only the features that Microsoft thinks are mostly used by the users. For security reasons, and to make the operating system user-friendly, the Control Panel does not display advanced features that are available in the OS and can be used to customize Windows more granularly.

How to Make Hidden Control Panel Features Visible?

In order to make hidden Control Panel features visible in Microsoft Windows 8, steps given below must be followed:

1. Log on to Microsoft Windows 8 computer with any account.
2. From the **Start** screen, click **Desktop** tile.
3. On the desktop screen, right-click anywhere.
4. From the context menu, go to **New**.
5. From the displayed submenu, click **Folder**.
6. Rename the folder with the desired name followed by **.{ED7BA470-8E54-465E-825C-99712043E01C}**. (E.g. **CP_GodMode.{ED7BA470-8E54-465E-825C-99712043E01C}**)

7. Press **Enter** key when done.
8. Double-click the created folder to view all features (including the hidden ones) of the **Control Panel**.

Manage Window Navigation Sounds

Introduction to Window Navigation Sounds

In pre-Windows 8 operating systems, while navigating the Windows, users used to hear a sound that notified them about the navigation start. For example when users double-clicked a folder to open, a notification sound was heard. Moreover, if they moved forward or go back to the previous folders, the same notification sound was heard as well.

Although in Microsoft Windows 8 the navigation sound is disabled by default, it can be manually enabled so that home users can be notified about the successful navigation. On the other hand, in production environments, administrators or users might not want the computers to play the navigation sounds in order to avoid disturbances caused to other users or to keep the navigation secret. In such situations, it is advisable to disable navigation sounds.

How to Enable/Disable Window Navigation Sounds?

In order to enable/disable window navigation sounds in Microsoft Windows 8, steps given below must be followed:

1. Log on to Microsoft Windows 8 computer with any account.
2. From the **Start** screen, click **Desktop** tile.
3. On the desktop screen, right-click anywhere.
4. From the context menu, click **Personalize**.
5. From the bottom of the **Personalization** window, click **Sounds**.
6. On the opened **Sound** box, make sure that **Sounds** tab is selected.
7. From the **Program Events** list, under the **File Explorer** category, click to select **Start Navigation**.
8. Once selected, choose **Windows Navigation Start** from the **Sounds** drop-down list.

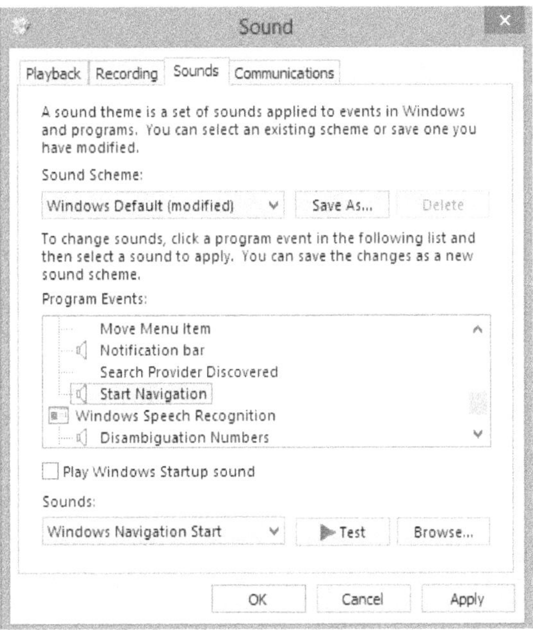

9. Click **OK** to enable navigation sounds.
10. Close **Personalization** window when done.

To disable navigation sounds, steps 1 to 10 can be followed, while selecting **(None)** from the **Sounds** drop-down list when on step 8.

Install Internet Information Services (IIS)

Introduction to Internet Information Services (IIS)

Internet Information Services (IIS) are the services which, when installed, allow the operating system to work as a web server. With the help of IIS, users can host a website, provided they have obtained a public static IP address from their respective ISPs. Even if the users have not obtained the public static IP address, they can still install and configure IIS for testing purposes and in lab environments.

When IIS is installed and configured on any network operating system, such as Windows Server 2003, Windows Server 2008 or Windows Server 2012, one server can host multiple websites provided each hosted website has been assigned with a different port number. On the other hand, when IIS is installed and configured on a client operating system, such as Microsoft Windows XP, Windows Vista, Windows 7 or Windows 8, one computer can host only one website at a time.

How to Install Internet Information Services (IIS)?

Configuring the Internet Information Services (IIS) is beyond the scope of this section, but it order to install the services on a Windows 8 computer, steps given below must be followed:

1. Log on to Microsoft Windows 8 computer with administrator account.
2. From the **Start** screen, click **Desktop** tile.
3. On the desktop screen, hover mouse to the bottom right corner of the window.
4. From the displayed options, click **Settings**.
5. From the **Settings** pane, click **Control Panel**.
6. On the **Control Panel** window, click **Programs** category.
7. On the **Programs** window, click **Turn Windows features on or off** option from the **Programs and Features** category.
8. On the opened **Windows Features** box, from the displayed list, check the **Internet Information Service** checkbox.

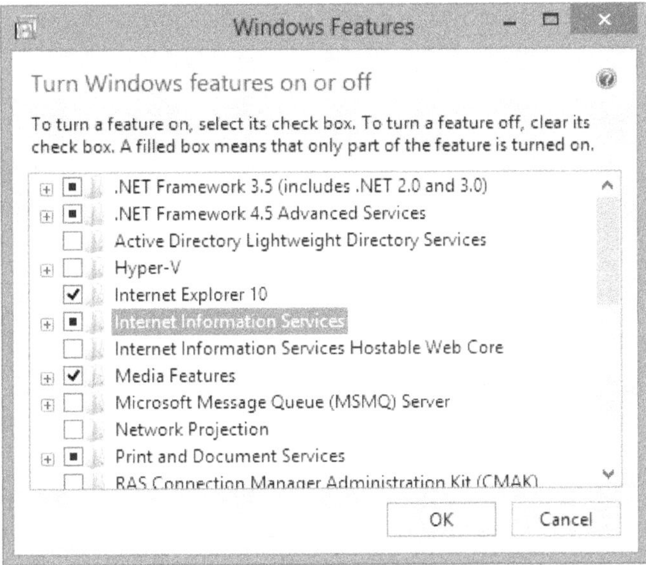

9. Click **OK** to install IIS on the computer.
10. On the opened box, click **Restart now** button to restart the computer.

To remove IIS from the computer, steps 1 to 10 can be followed, while unchecking **Internet Information Service** checkbox when on step 8.

Abort Shutdown Process

Introduction to Aborting the Shutdown Process

While using Microsoft Windows, many times users initiate the shutdown process but after the shutdown command has been executed, they realize that there was still some pending task that was required to be completed. In these cases, users are unwantedly required to wait till the entire shutdown process completes before they can start the computer again to finish their pending work.

Users can overcome these awkward situations by creating a shortcut button and placing it on the desktop screens. The created shortcut button prevents the computer from getting shutdown by aborting the executed shutdown command.

Although users can manually type the command that works in the background when the shortcut button to abort the shutdown command is double-clicked, problem in doing so is that if the users are slow in typing, the computer might shutdown before they type and execute the command. On the other hand, double-clicking a button on the desktop is comparatively simple and time-saving task that can be performed even by the new users.

How to Abort the Shutdown Process?

In order to abort the shutdown process in Microsoft Windows 8, steps given below must be followed:

1. Log on to Microsoft Windows 8 computer with any account.
2. From the **Start** screen, click **Desktop** tile.
3. On the desktop screen, hover mouse to the bottom right corner of the window.
4. From the displayed options, click **Search**.
5. From the **App** window, locate and click **Command Prompt** from **Windows Accessories** category.
6. In the opened command window, type **SHUTDOWN -a** command and press **Enter** key to abort the shutdown process.

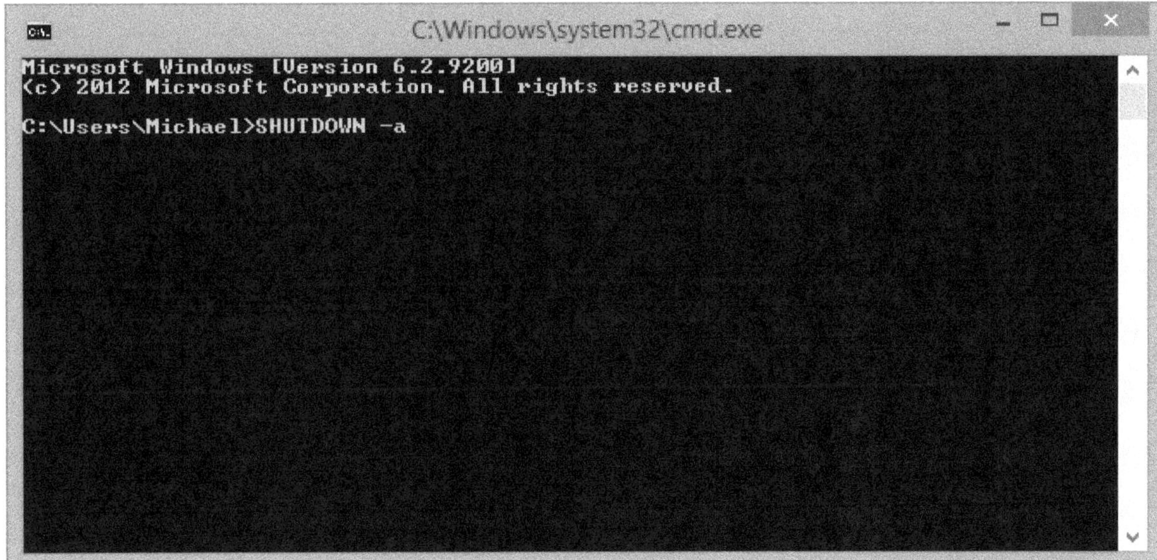

Note: *Since the shutdown command is executed too fast, in order to expedite the aborting shutdown process, users may create a new shortcut file by right-clicking on the desktop and going to* ***New > Shortcut****.* ***SHUTDOWN -a*** *command can be typed in the* ***Type the location of the item*** *field. Once the shortcut file is created, shutdown process can be aborted just by double-clicking the created shortcut file.*

Hide Unnecessary Icons to Shrink Notification Area

Introduction to Notification Area

In all Microsoft windows operating systems, system tray is also referred to as the notification area because it displays all Windows related notifications. Since the notification area consists of many active applications that run in the background, or the programs that users manually initiate, it sometimes becomes overpopulated and covers large area in the taskbar. Many icons that the notification area has are just there to allow users to get instant access to their corresponding features/applications. For example, the speaker icon that is always available in the notification area helps users adjust the sound volume and other basic audio related configurations. However it is quite unlikely that this feature would be used in production environments. In such cases, administrators can hide the speaker icon from the notification area in order to reduce its size and make some room in the taskbar for the icons of the active applications that users may initiate.

How to Hide Unnecessary Icons in the Notification Area?

In order to hide unnecessary icons to reduce the size of the notification area in Microsoft Windows 8, steps given below must be followed:

1. Log on to Microsoft Windows 8 computer with any account.
2. From the **Start** screen, click **Desktop** tile.
3. On the desktop screen, right-click the taskbar.
4. From the context menu, click **Properties**.
5. On the **Taskbar Properties** box, make sure that **Taskbar** tab is selected.
6. Click **Customize** option opposite to **Notification area** label.
7. From the **Notification Area Icons** window, select **Hide icon and notifications** from the drop-down lists of the unwanted notification area icons. Alternatively, **Only show notifications** option can also be selected from the drop-down list to view only the notifications, and hide the icons.

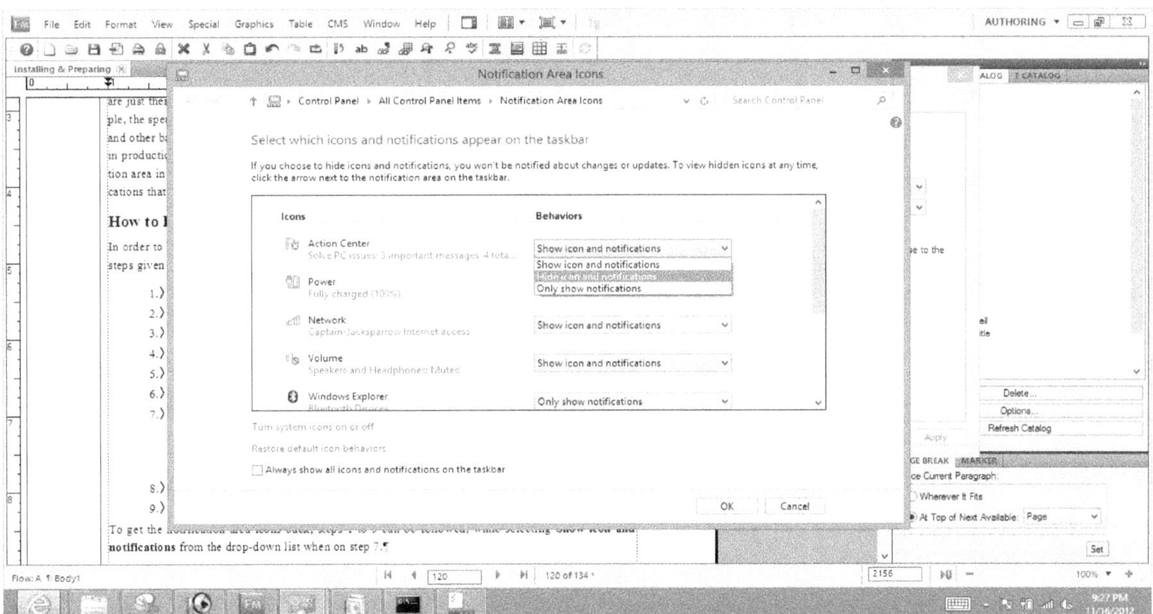

8. Click **OK** to apply the changes.
9. Back on **Taskbar Properties** box, click **OK** again.

To get the notification area icons back, steps 1 to 9 can be followed, while selecting **Show icon and notifications** from the drop-down list when on step 7.

Manage Operating System Timeout Duration

Introduction to Operating System Timeout Duration

When two or more operating systems are installed on a computer, a list of all the installed operating systems is displayed to the users every time the computer starts. From the displayed list, users can select any of the available operating system in order to work on it.

The list of operating systems that is displayed to the users is visible to the users for just 30 seconds. This duration of 30 seconds is technically known as the timeout duration for the operating systems. When the list is displayed, the 30 seconds countdown starts and users must select the operating systems of their choices before the timeout counter reaches 0. In case users fail to do so, the default operating system is automatically selected and the boot process for the automatically selected OS is initiated.

Although the default timeout duration for the operating systems is best in most scenarios, users can modify the duration if they think that the default available time is not sufficient for them.

How to Increase or Decrease Operating System Timeout Duration?

In order to increase or decrease operating system timeout duration in Microsoft Windows 8, steps given below must be followed:

1. Log on to Microsoft Windows 8 computer with administrator account.
2. From the **Start** screen, click **Desktop** tile.
3. On the desktop screen, press **Windows** + **R** Keys Simultaneously to Initiate **Run** command box.
4. In the **Run** command box, type **MSCONFIG** command and press **Enter** key.
5. From the **System Configuration** box, go to **Boot** tab.
6. In the available **Timeout** field, specify the operating system's timeout duration in seconds.

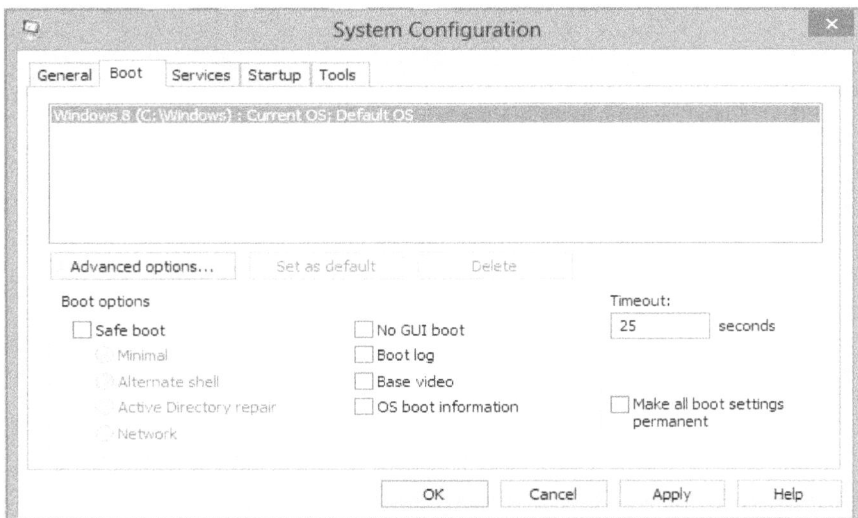

7. Click **OK** to apply the changes.
8. On the displayed box, click **Restart** button to restart the computer.

Enable Quick Launch Toolbar

Introduction to Quick Launch Toolbar

In legacy versions of Microsoft operating systems, such as Windows XP, the taskbar had Quick Launch toolbar that was available at the bottom-left end of the screen, on the right side of the Start buttons. In latest operating systems, such as Microsoft Windows 7 and Windows 8, the Quick Launch toolbars have been removed, and the OS now allow users to pin frequently used applications in the taskbars as required. Also, a few basic built-in programs are already pinned to the taskbars in order to allow users get instant access to them. Example of one such built-in application is Internet Explorer.

Since unavailability of Quick Launch toolbar might not be appreciated by many users, Microsoft Windows 8 allows Quick Launch toolbar to be added manually to the taskbar, in case it is required.

How to Enable Quick Launch Toolbar?

In order to enable Quick Launch toolbar in Microsoft Windows 8, steps given below must be followed:

1. Log on to Microsoft Windows 8 computer with any account.
2. From the **Start** screen, click **Desktop** tile.
3. On the desktop screen, right-click the taskbar.
4. From the context menu, go to **Toolbars**.
5. From the displayed submenu, click **New toolbar**.
6. On the opened **New Toolbar - Choose a folder** box, type **%userprofile%\App-Data\Roaming\Microsoft\Internet Explorer\Quick Launch** in the **Folder** field.

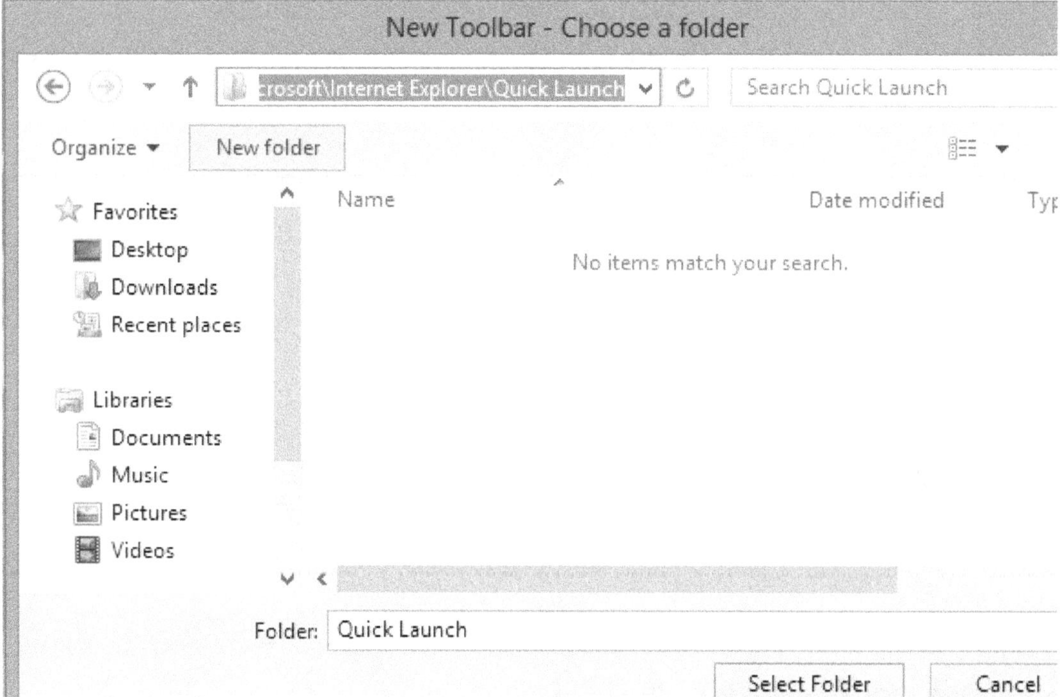

7. Click **Select Folder** button to place the **Quick Launch** toolbar near the notification area in the right end of the taskbar.
8. Right-click the **Quick Launch** toolbar and from the context menu, click to uncheck **Show Text** and **Show title** options.
9. Right-click the taskbar and click to uncheck **Lock the taskbar**.
10. Drag the **Quick Launch** toolbar to adjust its position as desired.
11. Right-click the taskbar again and click to check **Lock the taskbar**.

To remove the **Quick Launch** toolbar from the taskbar, unlock the taskbar, right-click the **Quick Launch** toolbar and from the context menu, click **Close toolbar**. Lock the taskbar again when done.

Open Command Prompt for Folder Location

Introduction to the Command Prompt for a Folder Location

In Microsoft Windows 8, when the command prompt is initiated, in order to go to any particular folder, users must type the entire path of the target location. For example if a folder named ABC resides inside another folder named AB, and AB resides inside A which is in C:, in order to go to the ABC folder through command prompt, users must type the 'CD' command followed by name of the parent folder in which the subfolder resides. Sometimes users might not remember the exact hierarchy of the folders, and therefore they use the 'DIR' command in order to view the list of subfolders that the parent folder contains.

Although the above mentioned method is not incorrect, it is still a time taking process and requires a decent typing speed. Also, because of the complexities involved in the process, many times the above mentioned method might not be appreciated by the new users.

Therefore in order to make things easier for the users, Microsoft Windows 8 allows them to open the command prompt for the target folders instantaneously and without typing the lengthy commands.

How to Open Command Prompt for a Folder Location?

In order to open command prompt for a folder location in Microsoft Windows 8, steps given below must be followed:

1. Log on to Microsoft Windows 8 computer with any account.
2. From the **Start** screen, click **Desktop** tile.
3. On the desktop screen, click **File Explorer** icon from the taskbar.
4. From the opened **Libraries** window, navigate and locate the folder for which command prompt is to be opened.
5. Click to select the target folder and press and hold down **Shift** key.
6. While pressing and holding down the **Shift** key, right-click the target folder.
7. From the displayed context menu, click **Open command window here** to open the command window for the selected folder.

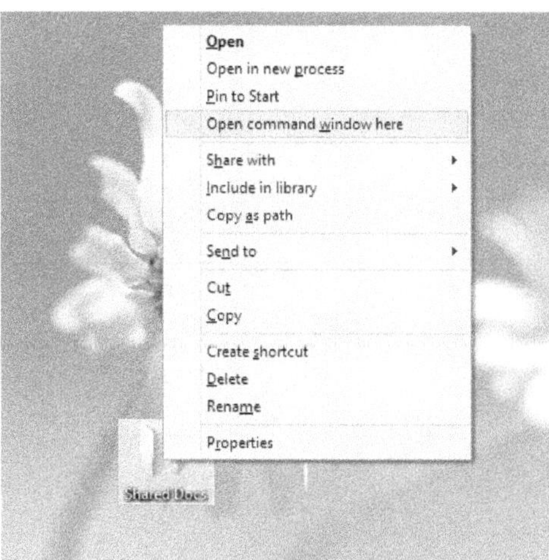

Add Control Panel to the Start Screen

Introduction to the Start Screen

With the release of Microsoft Windows 8, a new Metro UI is also introduced. Metro UI has replaced the Start menu that was available in Windows 7 and earlier versions of Microsoft operating systems.

When the Start menu was available in the operating systems, the menu also contained a link to the Control Panel that allowed users to access the Control Panel window instantaneously. Whereas in Microsoft Windows 8, since no Start menu is available, it might become challenging for the users to access the Control Panel, especially if they are new to the computer field itself.

In order to overcome these situations, users can pin the Control Panel to the Start screen, from where it can be accessed instantaneously and without troubles.

How to Add Control Panel to the Start Screen?

In order to add Control Panel to the Start screen in Microsoft Windows 8, steps given below must be followed:

1. Log on to Microsoft Windows 8 computer with any account.
2. From the **Start** screen, click **Desktop** tile.
3. On the desktop screen, hover mouse to the bottom right corner of the window.
4. From the displayed options, click **Search**.
5. From the **App** window, locate and right-click **Control Panel** from **Windows Accessories** category.
6. From the advanced options displayed at the bottom of the window, click **Pin to Start** to pin the **Control Panel** to the **Start** screen.

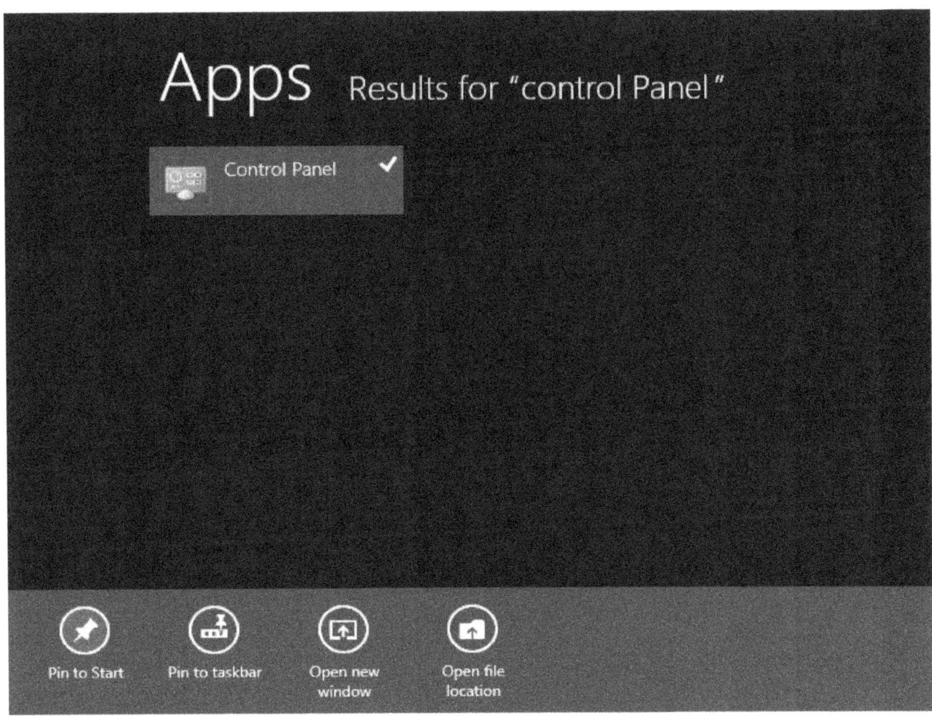

To remove the **Control Panel** from the **Start** screen, users must go to the **Start** screen and right-click **Control Panel**. From the advanced options displayed at the bottom of the window, users must click **Unpin from Start**.

Place Videos Link in the Start Screen

Introduction to the Videos Container

Since Microsoft has removed the Start menu from Windows 8 and has replaced it with the Metro UI Start screen, links for many containers are not available in the Metro UI window. The most frequently visited containers in Microsoft operating systems are Pictures, Videos, Music, etc.

In Microsoft Windows 7 and in earlier versions of the operating systems, Start menu never contained the Videos container. Same is the case with Microsoft Windows 8 as well. Because of this, whenever users want to access their favorite videos that are stored in Videos folder, they must go to the desktop and click the Windows Explorer icon that is available on the taskbar. From the opened Libraries window, they can then click to select the Videos container that is available in the navigation pane in the left.

In order to make Videos folder easily accessible, users can pin the container to the Start screen.

How to Pin the Videos Container to the Start screen?

In order to pin the Videos container to the Start screen in Microsoft Windows 8, steps given below must be followed:

1. Log on to Microsoft Windows 8 computer with any account.
2. From the **Start** screen, click **Desktop** tile.
3. On the desktop screen, click **File Explorer** icon from the taskbar.
4. On the opened **Libraries** window, right-click **Videos** from the **Libraries** container in the left pane.
5. From the displayed context menu, click **Pin to Start**.

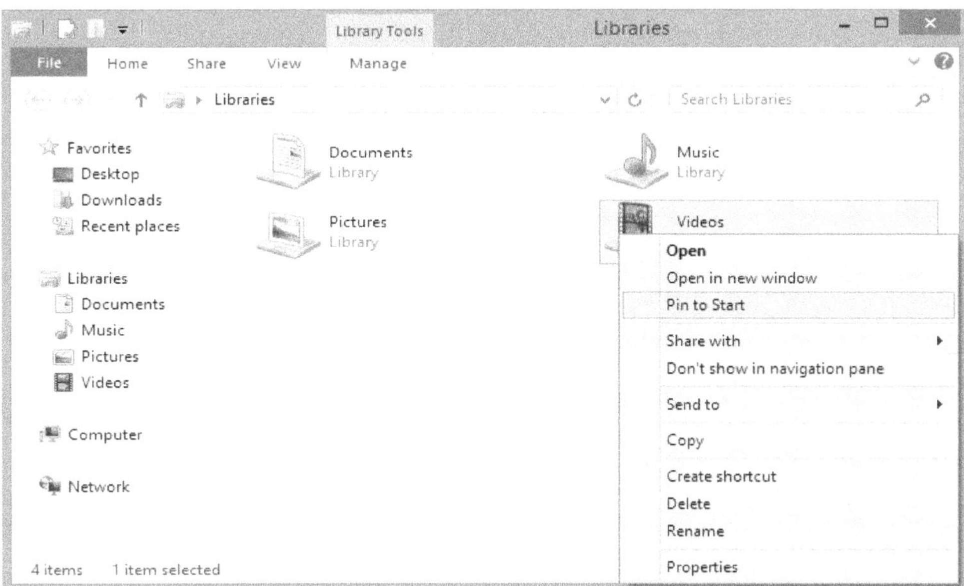

To remove the **Videos** container from the **Start** screen, users must go to the **Start** screen, right-click **Videos** and from the advanced options displayed at the bottom of the window, they must click **Unpin from Start**.

Open Files/Folders with Single-Click

Introduction to Single-Click Option

When Windows 8 is installed, as per the default configurations, users must double-click files or folders in order to open them. In case they want to select any file or folder, they must click on them just once. Using computers with this configuration might be easy for experienced users, however things might be challenging for the ones who are new to the Windows or are fresher in computer field. Such users might find it difficult to double-click the objects, and they might also get confused as when they are needed to single-click an object and when the object is required to be double-clicked.

To make things easier for such users, Microsoft Windows 8 can be configured so that the files or the folders can be opened when they are single-clicked, and can be selected when the mouse pointer is hovered on them.

How to Open Files/Folders with Single-Click?

In order to configure Microsoft Windows 8 to open files/folders with a single-click, steps given below must be followed:

1. Log on to Microsoft Windows 8 computer with any account.
2. From the **Start** screen, click **Desktop** tile.
3. On the desktop screen, click **File Explorer** icon from the taskbar.
4. On the opened **Libraries** window, click **View** from the menu bar.
5. Click **Options** from the displayed **View** ribbon.
6. On the **Folder Options** box, make sure that **General** tab is selected.
7. Under the **Click items as follows** section, click to select **Single-click to open an item (point to select)** radio button.

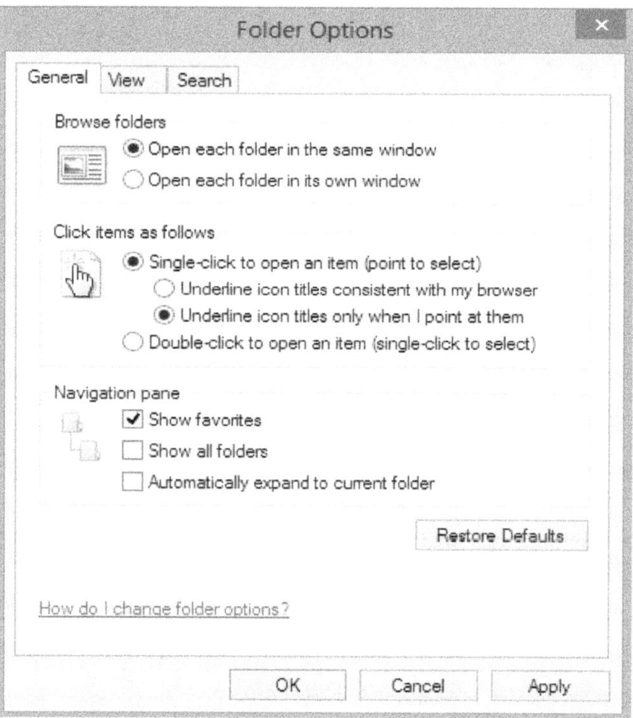

8. Click **OK** to apply the changes.
9. Close **Libraries** window when done.

To revert Windows back to its normal configuration, steps 1 to 9 can be followed, while selecting **Double-click to open an item (single-click to select)** radio button when on step 7.

Assign a Shortcut Key to Open an Application

Introduction to the Shortcut Keys

Shortcut keys are the combination of keys which, when pressed simultaneously, initiate the corresponding applications.

Mostly shortcut keys include combination of 'Ctrl', 'Alt' and/or 'Shift' keys along with any other character key that has been assigned for the target application.

Microsoft Windows 8 also allows users to assign shortcut keys to any application of their choices. By assigning the shortcut keys to the applications, the applications can be initialized instantaneously.

While assigning shortcut keys to the applications manually, users must press the 'Ctrl' key when specifying the key combination. When the 'Ctrl' key is pressed while specifying the key combination, Windows automatically uses 'Alt' key. Users are then required to define a unique character key to complete the shortcut key assignment for the target application.

Once a shortcut keys assigned, the target application can be initialized by pressing the assigned shortcut keys simultaneously.

How to Assign Shortcut Keys for an Application?

In order to assign shortcut keys to open an application in Microsoft Windows 8, steps given below must be followed:

1. Log on to Microsoft Windows 8 computer with any account.
2. From the **Start** screen, click **Desktop** tile.
3. On the desktop screen, right-click the shortcut icon of the application for which a shortcut key is to be assigned.
4. From the context menu, click **Properties**.
5. On the applications properties box, make sure that **Shortcut** tab is selected.
6. Click to place the cursor in the **Shortcut** key field.
7. Press and hold down **Ctrl** key and press a unique character from the keyboard to specify it as the shortcut key for the selected application.

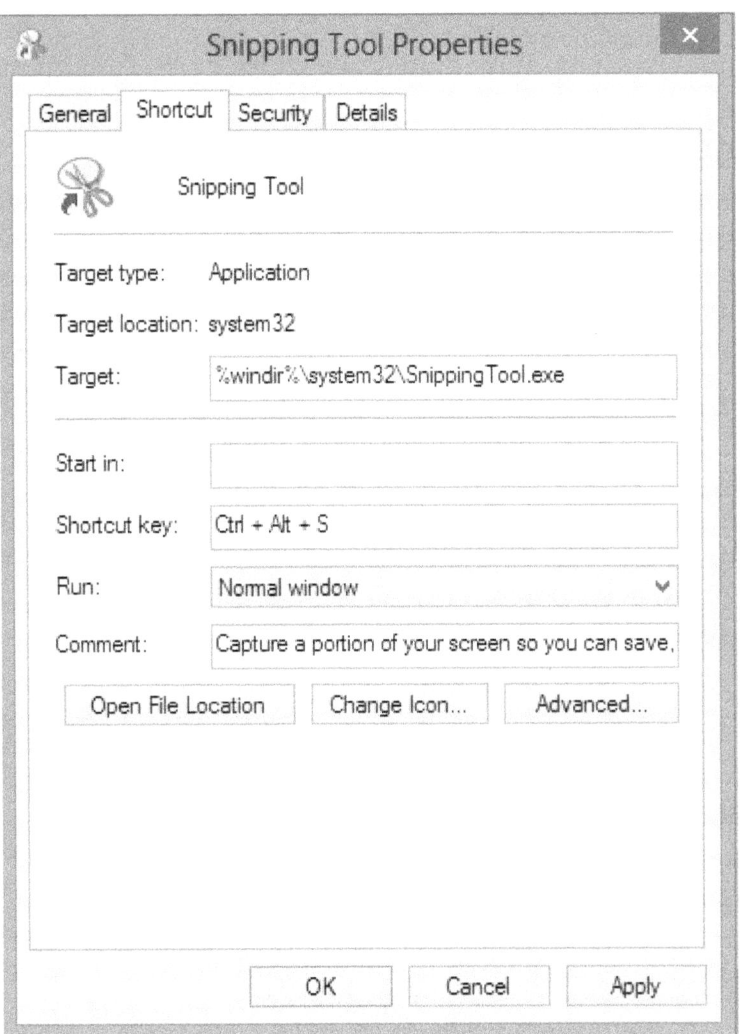

8. Click **OK** to apply the changes.

To remove the assigned shortcut keys, steps 1 to 9 can be followed, while pressing **Back-space** key (instead of **Ctrl** and unique keys) when on step 7.

Note: *When* ***Ctrl*** *key is pressed while assigning a shortcut key,* ***Alt*** *key is automatically added to form a complete combination. Therefore, in order to open the application using the assigned shortcut key,* ***Ctrl+Alt+****(chosen unique character key) must be pressed simultaneously on the keyboard.*

Calculate Mortgage

Introduction to Mortgage Calculation

In today's busy and expense life, it is quite likely that most users pay mortgages on a regular basis. Also, there might be many of them who might be planning to buy new houses and pay the amounts in the forms of mortgages. In order to calculate accurate mortgages, many times users rely on third-party applications, or they go through a special calculation process which might be time-consuming.

Microsoft Windows 8 helps such users by allowing them calculate their mortgages with the help of Calculator, which is a built-in program in the operating system itself.

How to Calculate Mortgage?

In order to calculate mortgage using built-in Calculator in Microsoft Windows 8, steps given below must be followed:

1. Log on to Microsoft Windows 8 computer with any account.
2. From the **Start** screen, click **Search** tile.
3. From the **Apps** window, locate and click **Calculator** from the **Windows Accessories** category.
4. On the **Calculator** interface, click **View** from the menu bar.
5. From the displayed list, go to **Worksheets**.
6. From the submenu, click **Mortgage**.

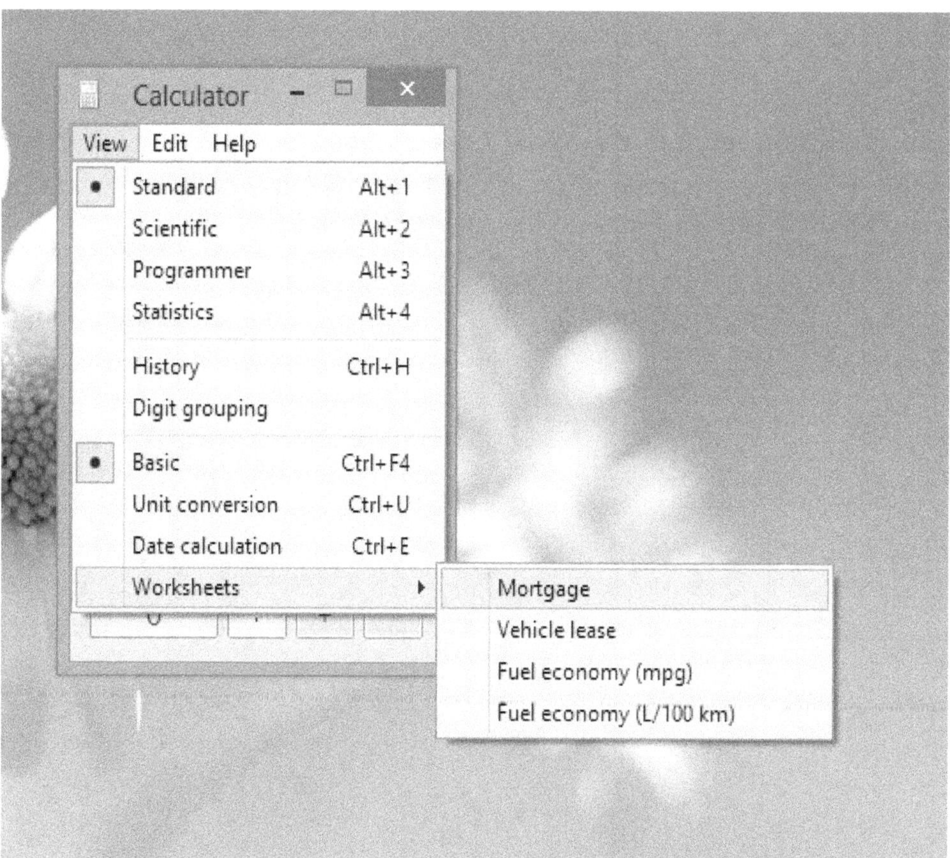

7. Mortgage can be calculated by populating the fields with the appropriate values in the extended calculator interface in left section.

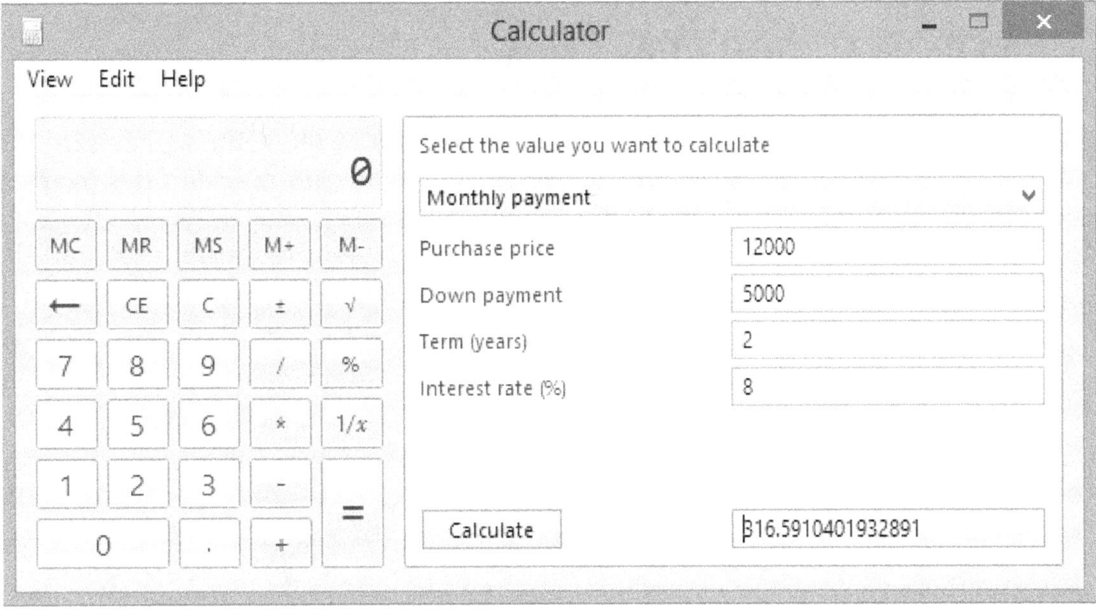

Opening .DOCX Files without Microsoft Office Package

Introduction to .DOCX File Types

From Microsoft Office 97 to Microsoft Office 2003, the Word files that the packages allowed users to create had .DOC extensions. Since MS Office package is developed by Microsoft itself, WordPad also supported .DOC files and the files that were created using the built-in WordPad program had .DOC extensions as well. This means that irrespective of the text editor used to create a document file, users were able to read the contents of the file using either MS Word or the WordPad.

When Microsoft Office 2007 was released, the default extension that the document files started having was .DOCX. Even Microsoft Office 2010 uses .DOCX extension for its Word files. The .DOCX files can be read only when Microsoft Office 2007 or Microsoft Office 2010 is used to open the files. In case users want the files to become backward compatible (files which can be read using earlier versions of Microsoft Office, such as Microsoft Office 2003 or earlier), they must save the files in the Compatibility Mode.

Irrespective of above mentioned limitations, Microsoft Windows 8 allows users to read the .DOCX files even if Microsoft Office 2007/2010 is not installed on a computer.

How to Read .DOCX Files without Microsoft Office 2007/2010?

In order to read .DOCX files without Microsoft Office 2007/2010, steps given below must be followed:

1. Log on to Microsoft Windows 8 using any account.
2. Make sure that MS Office 2007/2010 package is not installed.
3. From the **Start** screen, click **Desktop** tile.
4. On the desktop screen, click **File Explorer** icon from the taskbar.
5. From the **Libraries** window, navigate and locate the .DOCX file that is to be opened.
6. Right-click the target file.
7. From the context menu, click **Open with**.
8. On **How do you want to open this file** box, click **Keep using WordPad** to open the selected file.

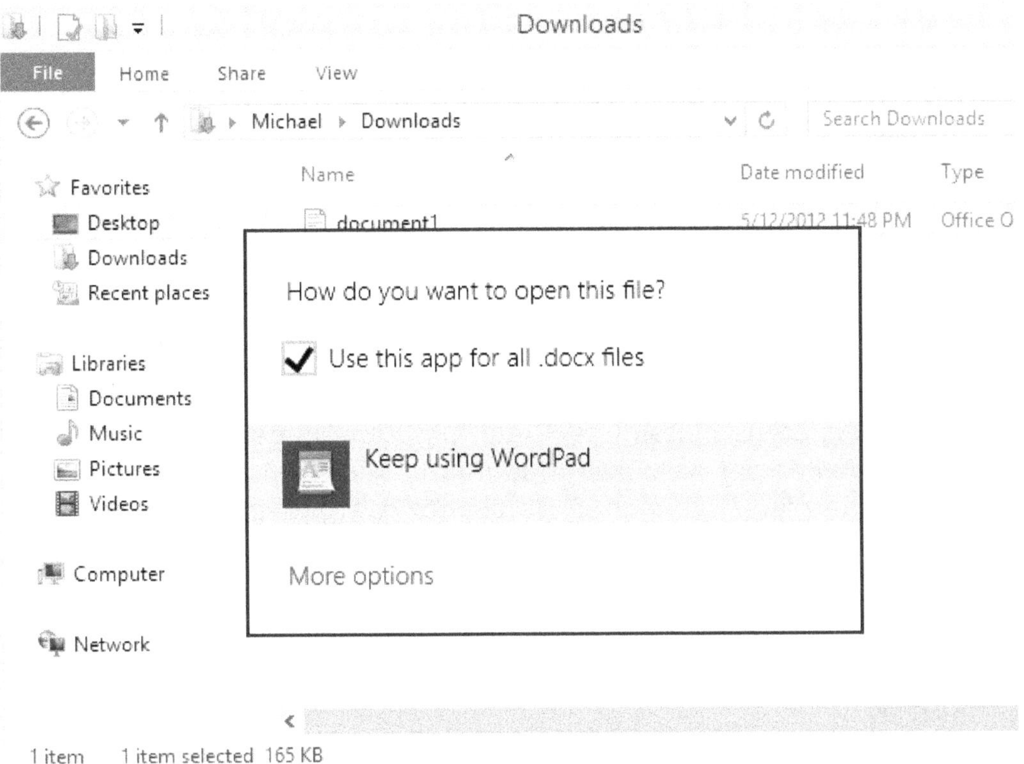

Note: *In case* ***Keep using WordPad*** *option is not available,* ***WordPad.EXE*** *file must be manually located by clicking* ***Look for another app on this PC*** *option from the bottom of the box.* ***WordPad.EXE*** *can be found in* ***C:\Program Files (x86)\Windows NT\Accessories*** *and* ***C:\Program Files\Windows NT\Accessories (in x64 operating systems)*** *and* ***C:\Program Files\Windows NT\Accessories (in x86 operating systems)****.*

Use Built-In Calculator as a Unit Converter

Introduction to Unit Conversion

Almost all users, irrespective of the domain they belong to, need to convert the digits from one unit to another in order to have accurate measurements to best fit their requirements. While working on computers, many times users look for third-party conversion applications that might be either quite expensive, or are inefficient to fulfill the needs of the users.

In order to help users in these situations, Microsoft Windows 8 allows them to convert the units with the help of the built-in Calculator program. In earlier versions of Microsoft Windows, Calculator was not as efficient as it is in Microsoft Windows 8, and the feature of unit conversion the latest version of Calculator has, provides an additional advantage to the program.

How to Convert Units Using Built-In Calculator?

In order to convert units using built-in Calculator in Microsoft Windows 8, steps given below must be followed:

1. Log on to Microsoft Windows 8 computer with any account.
2. From the **Start** screen, click **Search** tile.
3. From the **Apps** window, locate and click **Calculator** from the **Windows Accessories** category.
4. On the **Calculator** interface, click **View** from the menu bar.
5. From the displayed list, click **Unit Conversion**.
6. Units can be converted by populating the appropriate fields in the extended interface to the right.

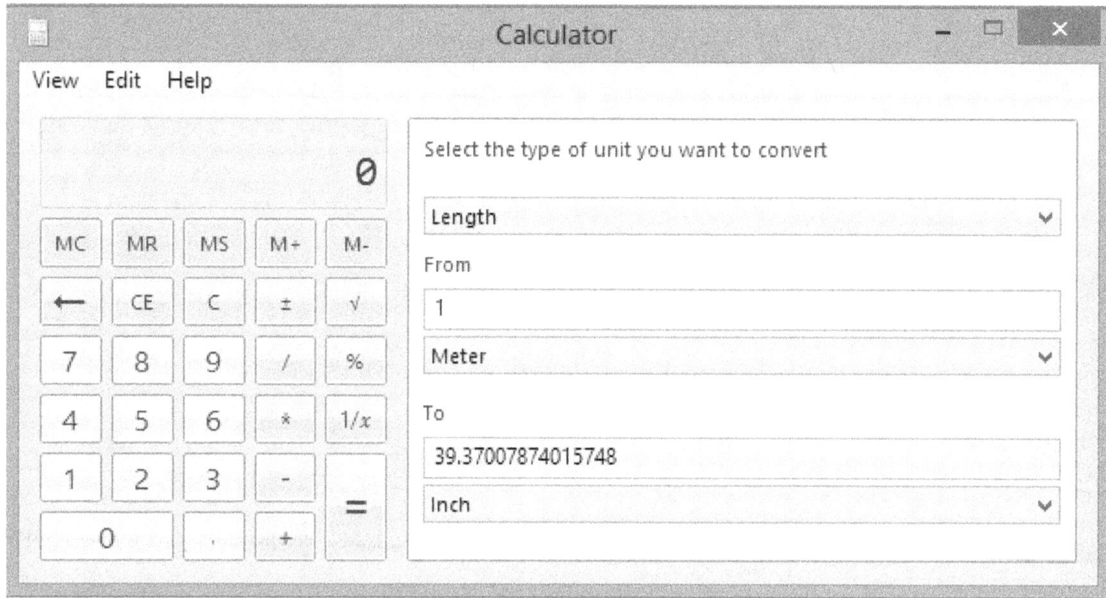

Initiate Internet Surfing without Opening the Web Browser

Introduction to Web Browser and Internet Surfing

In order to surf the Internet, the very first requirement is that the computer must have an active Internet connection. The next important entity that the PC must have in order to allow users surf the Internet is an efficient web browser.

All Microsoft operating systems ship along with a default built-in web browser named Internet Explorer that automatically gets installed along with the OS. Internet Explorer allows users to surf the Internet without installing any third-party web browser. Nonetheless, Internet Explorer must be opened before users can type the URL addresses of the desired websites while surfing the web.

Microsoft Windows 8 allows users to initiate Internet surfing without opening any web browser. All they need to do is that they need to add the address bar in the taskbar.

How to Initiate Internet Surfing without Opening the Web Browser?

In order to initiate Internet surfing without opening any web browser in Microsoft Windows 8, steps given below must be followed:

1. Log on to Microsoft Windows 8 computer with any account.
2. From the **Start** screen, click **Desktop** tile.
3. On the desktop screen, right-click the taskbar.
4. From the context menu, go to **Toolbars**.
5. From the displayed submenu, click **Address**.

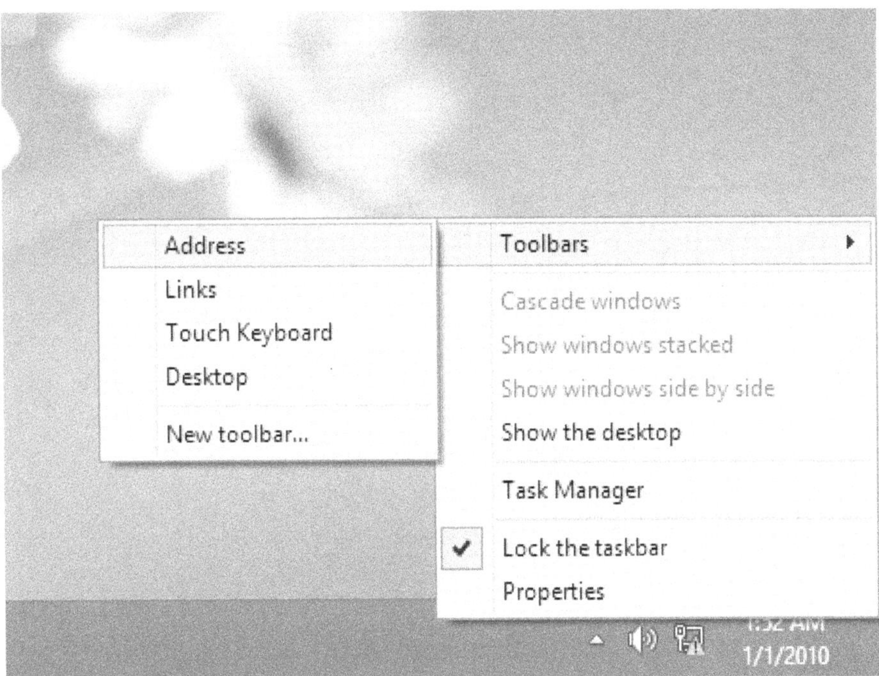

6. A website can be opened by typing its URL in the **Address** toolbar available in the taskbar, and pressing **Enter** key.

To remove **Address** toolbar from the taskbar, unlock the taskbar, right-click **Address** toolbar and from the context menu and click **Close** toolbar.

Note: *When address of the desired website is typed in the address bar and* ***Enter*** *key is pressed,* ***Internet Explorer*** *automatically gets initialized and the website is then displayed in the opened web browser.*

Change the Default Save Location

Introduction to the Default Save Location

While using Microsoft Windows 8, when users create a file of any type and try to save it for the very first time, the default location that the operating system suggests is the 'Documents' folder. The 'Documents' folder is a profile specific container that is automatically created when a user logs on to the computer for the first time. This further means that every user profile has a different 'Documents' folder, and when a user saves a file in the default suggested location, the saved file can be accessed only by the user who has created the file, or by the user who has access to the account of the file creator.

Since it is recommended that home users should not save their important files in the C: drive and the 'Documents' folder is located in C:, users are required to manually browse for and locate the destination where they want to save the files.

In order to eliminate the above mentioned additional overhead, Microsoft Windows 8 allows users to change the default save location to any other destination where they want the documents to be saved by default.

How to Change the Default Save Location?

In order to change the default save location in Microsoft Windows 8, steps given below must be followed:

1. Log on to Microsoft Windows 8 computer with any account.
2. From the **Start** screen, click **Desktop** tile.
3. On the desktop screen, click **File Explorer** icon from the taskbar.
4. On the opened **Libraries** window, right-click **Documents** under the **Libraries** container from the left pane.
5. From the context menu, click **Properties**.
6. On the **Documents Properties** box, click **Add** button.
7. From the **Include Folder in Documents** box, browse for and locate the desired destination location where the documents should be suggested to be saved by default.
8. Select the located folder and click **Include folder** button.
9. Back on the **Documents Properties** window, click to select the added location from the **Library locations** list.
10. Click **Set save location** button to set the added location as the default save location.

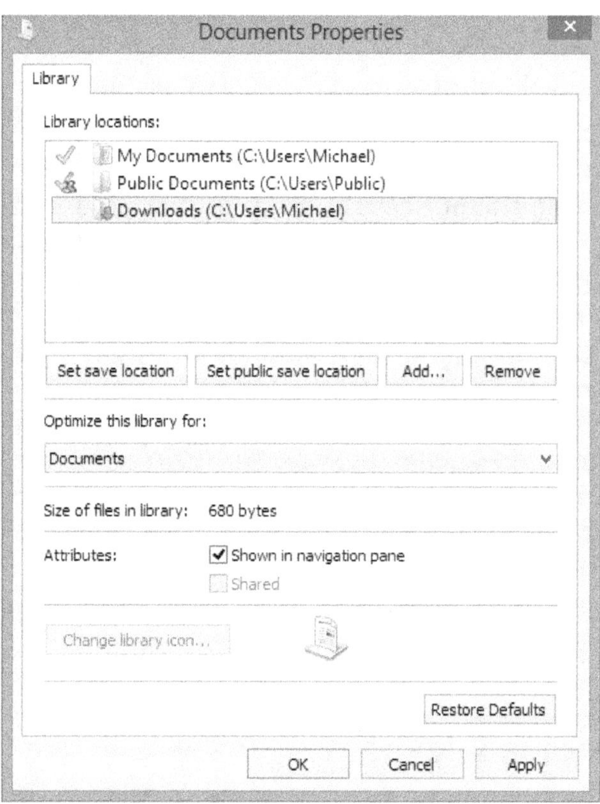

11. Right-click the added location, and from the context menu, click **Move up** option.

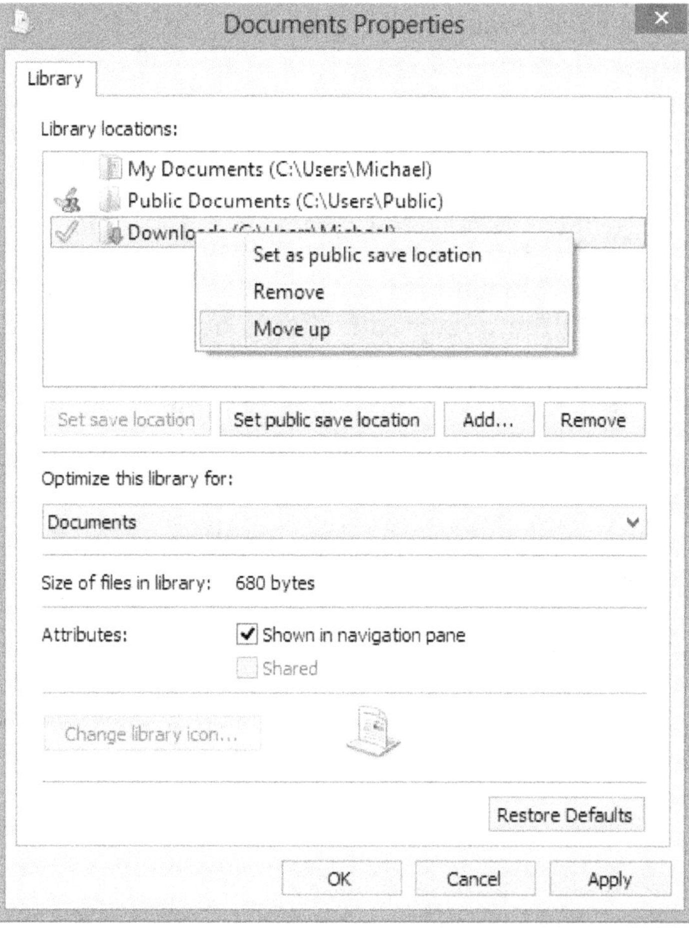

12. Repeat steps 11 till the added location gets on top of the list.
13. Click **OK** to apply the changes.
14. Close **Libraries** window when done.

CHAPTER 2:

WINDOWS UPDATE

Manage Automatic Updates

Introduction to Automatic Updates

When Microsoft operating system is installed on a computer, the installed copy of the operating system contains the files that were created while developing the OS. If the operating system is installed after a few months of its official release, it is quite likely that the newer versions of some of the files have been released by Microsoft and are available on Microsoft update server.

Even after the final release of the operating system, Microsoft keeps on working on the files of the OS and it also adds new files as well. All the updated and new files that Microsoft creates are uploaded to the Microsoft update server from where they can be downloaded by all the users of the operating systems who have genuinely purchased the copy of Windows.

How the Updates are Downloaded and Installed?

After installing the operating system on a computer, as soon as the computer is connected to the Internet, Microsoft Windows communicates with the Microsoft update server, where it looks for the latest patches or updates that might have been released by Microsoft. In case new updates or patches are found, as per the default configuration of the operating system, the updates and/or patches are automatically downloaded and installed on the Windows.

Microsoft Windows 8 allows users to control the way the operating system downloads and installs the updates. As mentioned above, the default configuration in almost all Microsoft operating systems, (including Microsoft Windows 8) is that as soon as the updates are found on Microsoft update server, Windows downloads them and installs them automatically.

In most production environments and homes, this default configuration might not be appropriate because of various security and efficiency reasons. Therefore in order to make the computer perform efficiently and reduce bandwidth consumption, most home users modify this default configuration as per their personal preferences.

The available options while choosing Windows updates are:

- **Install updates automatically (recommended)** - This option is selected by default. When Windows is configured on this option, all available updates are automatically downloaded and installed on the computer.
- **Download updates but let me choose whether to install them** - When this option is selected, all available updates are automatically downloaded from Microsoft update server. However, administrators must manually install the updates individually.
- **Check for updates but let me choose whether to download and install them** - When this option is selected, administrators are notified about the available updates. After being notified, administrators can download and install the desired updates as per their requirements.

- **Never check for updates (not recommended)** - When this option is selected, Windows never checks for updates. Since no updates are checked and detected, administrators are never notified about them, hence leaving Windows 8 un-updated.

Role of Windows Server Update Services

As far as automatic updates in production environments are concerned, if a network setup has several computers running Microsoft Windows operating systems, administrators prefer configuring Windows Server Update Services (WSUS) server in the network. With the help of WSUS server, administrators can download latest patches and updates from Microsoft update server for all the computers right on the WSUS server. Once all the latest patches and updates are downloaded on the WSUS server, the WSUS server then distributes the updates and patches to all the computers that are connected to the local area network. This eliminates the requirement of downloading updates for all the computers individually from the Microsoft update server, hence remarkably saving a decent amount of Internet bandwidth.

How to Manage Automatic Updates?

In order to manage automatic updates in Microsoft Windows 8, steps given below must be followed:

1. Log on to Microsoft Windows 8 computer with the administrator account.
2. On the **Start** screen, click the **Desktop** tile.
3. On the desktop screen, hover mouse to the bottom right corner of the window.
4. From the displayed options, click **Settings**.
5. From the **Settings** pane in the right, click **Control Panel**.
6. On the opened **Control Panel** window, click **System and Security** category.
7. On the **System and Security** window, click **Windows Updates** from the displayed list.
8. On the **Windows Updates** window, click **Change settings** from the left pane.
9. On the **Changed Settings** window, choose the appropriate update option from the **Important updates** drop-down list.

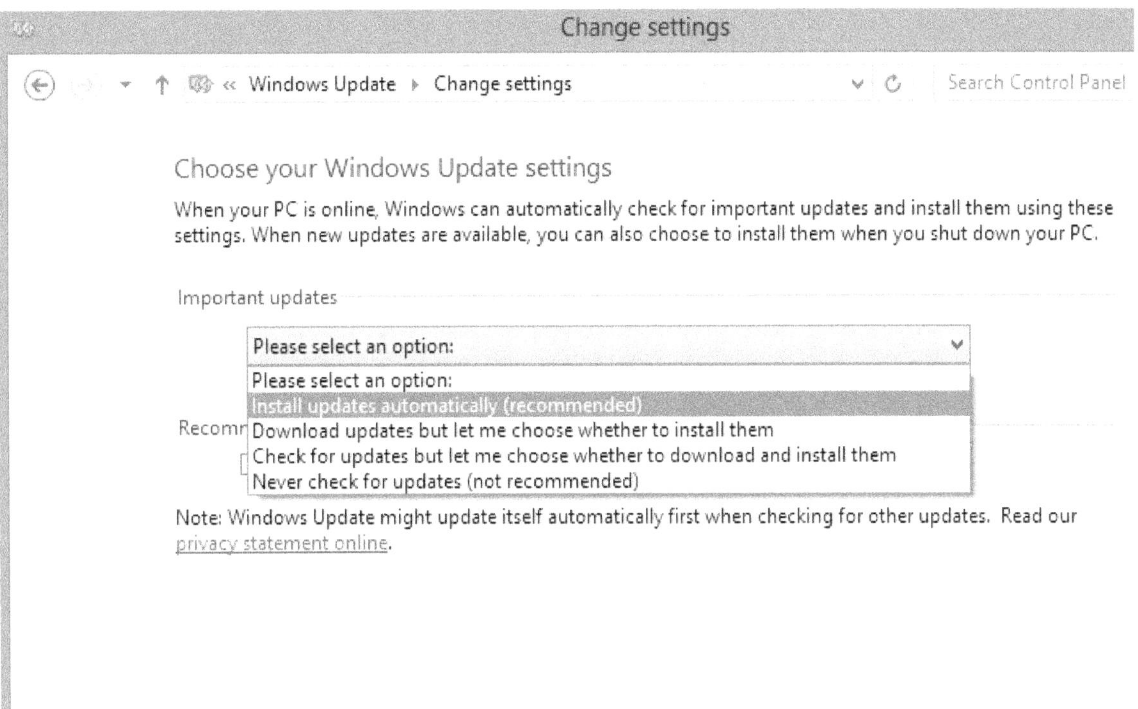

10. Once done, click **OK** button to save the changed settings.
11. Close all the opened windows and restart the computer to allow the settings to take effect.

CHAPTER 3:

OPTIMIZATION

Increase Virtual Memory

Introduction to Virtual Memory

In Microsoft Windows 98 and earlier operating systems, virtual memory was a reserved space in the system drives of the computers, and was used to hold inactive applications temporarily when the physical memory (RAM) was full.

How Virtual Memory Works

When users initiate an application, the instance occupies some space in the physical memory, from where its threads are sent to the microprocessor for processing. When multiple applications are initiated, each application consumes some space in the memory. Because of this, sometimes entire space in the physical memory is consumed leaving no room for any other application. When this situation comes and users try to initiate a new program, the very first inactive program that the physical memory contains is transferred to the virtual memory.

When the inactive program that was transferred to the virtual memory is required to be accessed by the users, the program is transferred back to the physical memory and in order to make room in the physical memory to accommodate the application, the next inactive program from the physical memory is transferred to the virtual memory. This process is technically known as 'file swapping'.

Modifications in Virtual Memory

With the release of Microsoft Windows 2000 and in all later versions of operating systems, the concept of Page File is implemented. A Page File is automatically created when any post Windows 98 operating system is installed. Page File is by default stored in the system drive, where Windows has been installed and is named as 'pagefile.sys'.

In post Windows 98 operating systems, Page File replaces the virtual memory. This means that unlike pre-Windows 2000 operating systems where a specific amount of hard disk space was reserved for the virtual memory, in Windows 2000 and above, the Page File contains the swapped files. Benefit of using Page File is that the files are divided into multiple parts (technically known as the pages) before they are transferred to the Page File. This ensures that only the amount of physical memory that is required to store a newly initiated application is freed up by transferring only the pages that consume the required amount of space in the physical memory. For example if a new process or application that a user has initiated requires 20 MB of space in the physical memory and all previous applications in the RAM are more than 20 MB in size, file of the first inactive application will be divided into pages and only the 20 MB of pages will be transferred to the Page File. This memory management process is technically known as Paging.

Although all operating systems use the concept of paging quite optimally, sometimes even the Page File gets fully consumed, hence degrading the system's performance. In such situations, users must close some unwanted applications, or they can restart their computers to solve the issue. Another option that users might go for can be that they can increase the size of the Page File so that it can store more data and allow the operating system to function more smoothly.

The size of the Page File expands dynamically, i.e. as the pages are transferred to the Page File, its size increases accordingly. The minimum size of the Page File is 1.5 times of the total physical memory and can be increased up to 4 times. For example if a computer has 1 GB of the physical memory (RAM), the default and minimum size of the Page File would be 1.5 GB which can be increased up to 4 GB.

How to Increase the Virtual Memory (Page File)?

Although virtual memory is automatically managed by Microsoft Windows 8 and automatic management provides optimum results, if administrators want to increase the size of the page file manually, steps given below must be followed:

1. Log on to Microsoft Windows 8 computer with the administrator account.
2. On the **Start** screen, click **Desktop** tile.
3. On the desktop screen, click **File Explorer** icon from the taskbar.
4. On the opened **Libraries** window, right-click **Computer** from the left pane.
5. From the displayed context menu, click **Properties**.
6. On the **System** window, click **Advanced system settings** from the left pane.
7. On the **System Properties** box, make sure that **Advanced** tab is selected.
8. Under the **Performance** section, click **Settings** button.
9. On the **Performance Options** box, go to the **Advanced** tab.
10. Click **Change** button under **Virtual memory** section.
11. On the **Virtual Memory** box, uncheck **Automatically manage paging file size for all drives** checkbox.
12. Once unchecked, click to select enabled **Custom size** radio button.
13. Populate the **Initial size (MB)** and **Maximum size (MB)** fields with appropriate values according to the size of the physical memory installed on the computer.

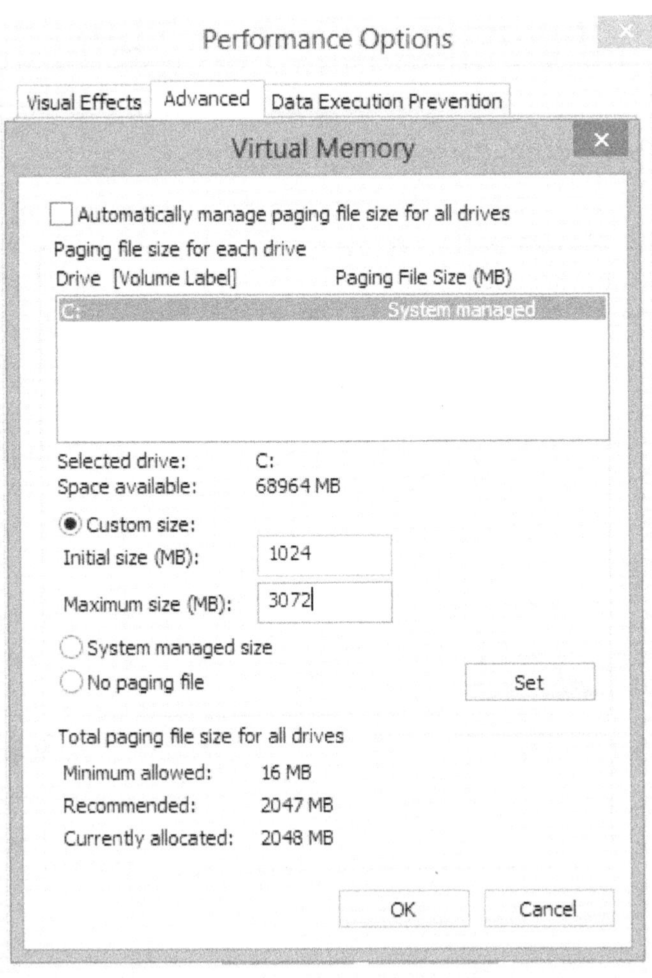

14. Click **Set** button to confirm the provided values, and click **OK** to save the chances.
15. Once done, close all the opened boxes and windows.
16. Restart the computer.

Manage Application Window State When It Starts

Introduction to the State of Window or Application

When an application is initialized, by default the window of its interface is in maximized state. This default configuration allows users to work on the application without making any additional move. Users can minimize the opened window if they want to work on any other application. When they need the minimized application back, they can restore the window to its normal state.

In most cases and under normal circumstances, this default configuration is quite useful and should not be modified. However there might be cases when users might want to initiate an application but want it to run in the background. This means that users do not want to work on the interface, and because of this they are required to minimize the opened interface of the application.

Tasks can be made simpler in such situations by configuring the default state of the target application. Users can configure to keep the state of the window of the opened application minimized every time it is initiated.

How to Manage the State of the Window of the Opened Application?

In order to manage the state of the window of an opened application in Microsoft Windows 8, steps given below must be followed:

1. Log on to Microsoft Windows 8 computer with any account.
2. On the **Start** screen, click **Desktop** tile.
3. From the desktop screen, navigate and locate the shortcut icon of the application whose startup window state is to be configured.
4. Once located, right-click the icon and from the displayed context menu, click **Properties**.
5. On the application's properties box, make sure that the **Shortcut** tab is selected.
6. On the **Shortcut** tab, choose the appropriate window state of the selected application as desired from the **Run** drop-down list. (**Normal window**, **Minimized** or **Maximized**)

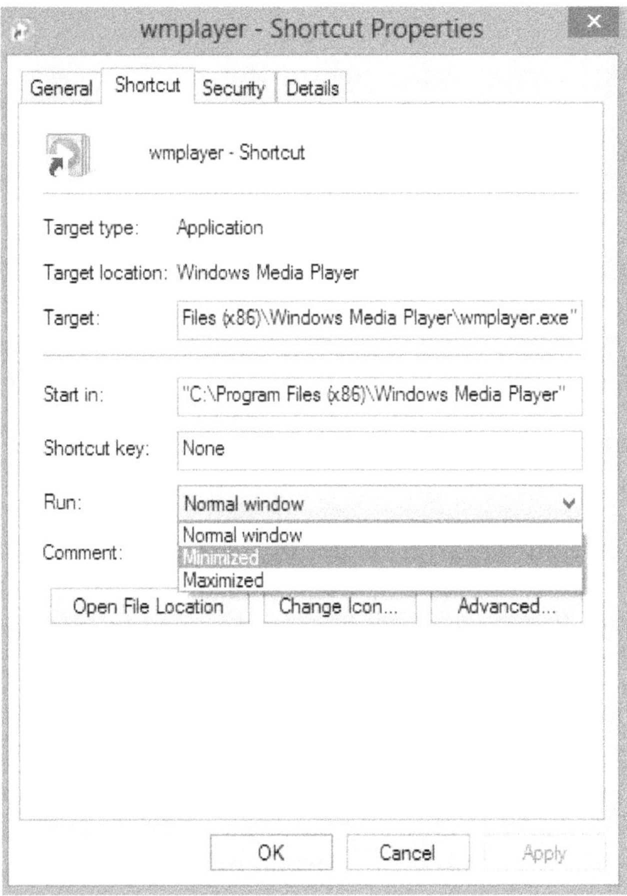

7. Click **OK** when done.
8. Double-click the shortcut icon of the application to verify the modified settings.

Run Legacy Applications

Introduction to Legacy Applications

As soon as a new operating system is officially released, people rush for it. In homes users install the latest version of the operating systems without considering the compatibility issues that they might face while using the earlier versions of third-party or Microsoft-based applications. In other words when a new operating system is installed, it is quite likely that the earlier versions of the applications might not be compatible with the latest OS. This might prevent users from working on their files, and the existing data that used the earlier version of the application might also become inaccessible. Whenever home users face such situation, they contact the vendors from where they are purchased their computers and request for technical support.

In production environments, wise administrators consider all aspects and the impact that the new version of the operating system might make if it is installed on the computers. Administrators also consider about the compatibility issues that users might face while using older versions of the applications on the new OS.

In order to solve such issues in homes and in production environments, Microsoft Windows 8 allows users to run the earlier versions of applications in the compatibility mode. When an application is initiated in compatibility mode, irrespective of the current version of the operating system on which it is installed, it considers that the version of the operating system is the one that was specified while enabling the compatibility mode.

How to Run Legacy Versions of Applications?

In order to run legacy versions of applications in Microsoft Windows 8, steps given below must be followed:

1. Log on to Microsoft Windows 8 computer with any account.
2. On the **Start** screen, click **Desktop** tile.
3. On the desktop screen, click **File Explorer** icon from the taskbar.
4. From the opened **Libraries** window, navigate and locate the executable file of the application that is to be run in compatibility mode.
5. Once located, right-click the executable file and from the context menu click **Properties**.
6. On the application's properties box, go to the **Compatibility** tab.
7. Under the **Compatibility mode** section, check **Run this program in compatibility mode for** checkbox.
8. From the enabled drop-down list, choose the desired version of legacy operating system to make the application run in the selected OS's compatibility mode.

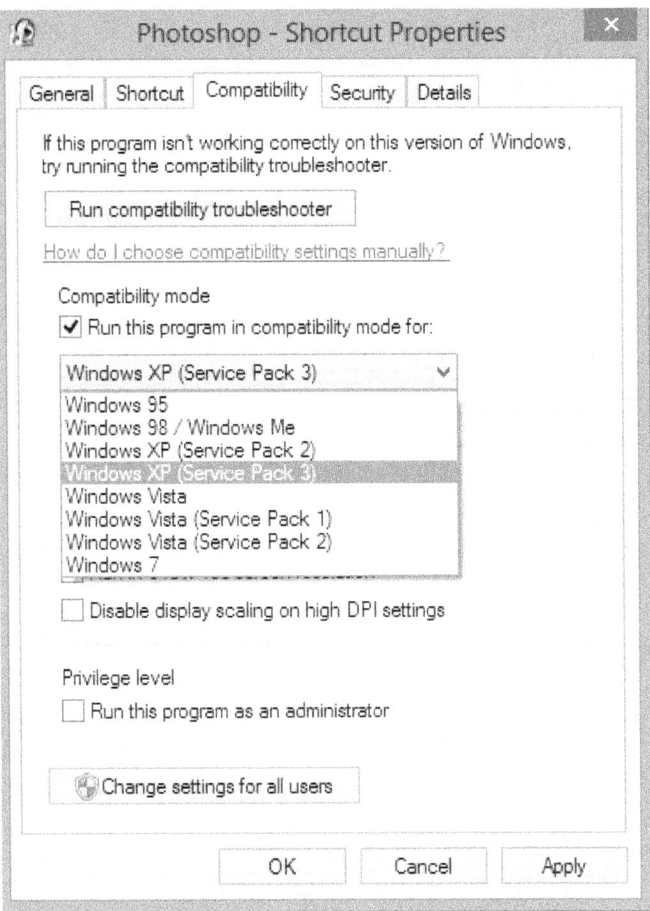

9. Click **OK** to save the modified settings.
10. Double-click the executable file of the application to run in the selected OS's compatibility mode.

Disable Legacy File Creation

Introduction to Legacy Files

In earlier days, especially when MS-DOS was mostly used, the files that users used to create could have maximum of 8 characters in their names and the extensions of the files could contain maximum of 3 characters. The file names and the extensions of the files were separated by a '.' (Dot), also known as (a.k.a.) a 'Period'. This naming convention was technically called 8.3.

Latest applications that users mostly install on their computers are capable of creating the files that can have more than 8 characters in their names and more than 3 characters in their extensions. However, in order to make the latest versions of Windows backward compatible, operating systems still support 8.3 naming conventions and if any older application creates a file using 8.3 naming convention, the file can be read by the latest operating systems.

In Microsoft Windows 8, 8.3 naming convention is enabled by default which consumes a decent amount of processing unnecessarily. Therefore if users are sure that no legacy application has been installed on the computer, and all the earlier versions of the software programs have been upgraded and have been made compatible with Microsoft Windows 8, it is recommended that the 8.3 naming conventions should be disabled.

How to Disable 8.3 Naming Convention?

In order to disable 8.3 naming convention in Microsoft Windows 8, steps given below must be followed:

1. Log on to Microsoft Windows 8 computer with administrator account.
2. On the **Start** screen, hover mouse to the bottom right corner of the screen.
3. From the displayed options, click **Search**.
4. On the **Apps** window, scroll horizontally and locate **Command Prompt**.
5. Once located, right-click the **Command Prompt** icon.
6. From the displayed advanced options at the bottom of the screen, click **Run as administrator**.
7. On the displayed User Account Control confirmation box, click **Yes** to provide the consent to open the command prompt with elevated privileges.
8. On the opened command line interface, type **FSUTIL BEHAVIOR SET DISABLE8DOT3 1** command and press **Enter** key to disable Legacy file creation.

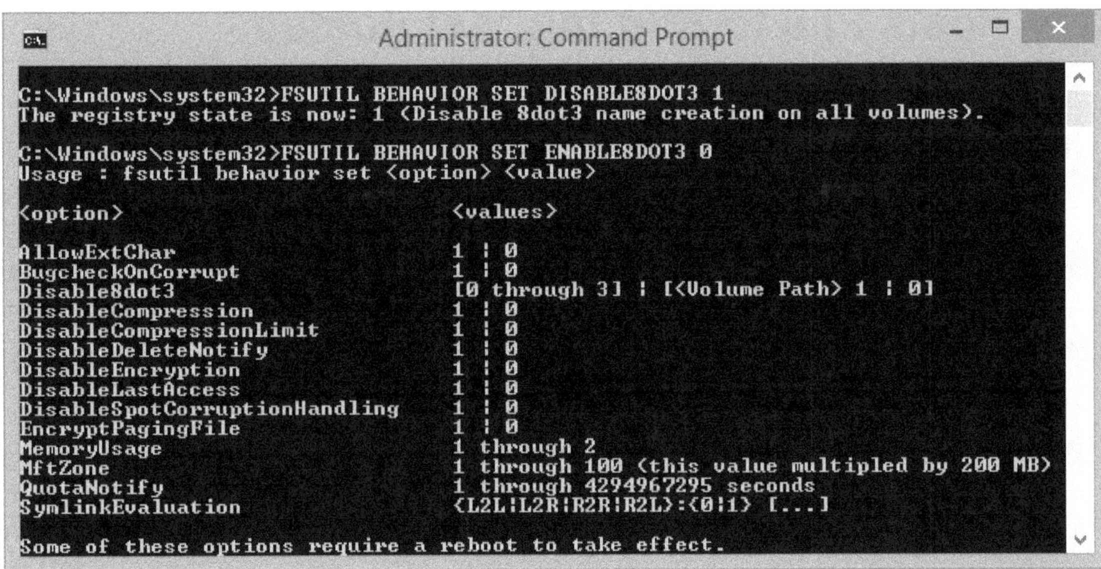

Administrator: Command Prompt
C:\Windows\system32>FSUTIL BEHAVIOR SET DISABLE8DOT3 1
The registry state is now: 1 (Disable 8dot3 name creation on all volumes).
C:\Windows\system32>FSUTIL BEHAVIOR SET ENABLE8DOT3 0
Usage : fsutil behavior set <option> <value>
<option> <values>
AllowExtChar 1 ¦ 0
BugcheckOnCorrupt 1 ¦ 0
Disable8dot3 [0 through 3] ¦ [<Volume Path> 1 ¦ 0]
DisableCompression 1 ¦ 0
DisableCompressionLimit 1 ¦ 0
DisableDeleteNotify 1 ¦ 0
DisableEncryption 1 ¦ 0
DisableLastAccess 1 ¦ 0
DisableSpotCorruptionHandling 1 ¦ 0
EncryptPagingFile 1 ¦ 0
MemoryUsage 1 through 2
MftZone 1 through 100 (this value multipled by 200 MB)
QuotaNotify 1 through 4294967295 seconds
SymlinkEvaluation <L2L¦L2R¦R2R¦R2L>:<0¦1> [...]
Some of these options require a reboot to take effect.

To re-enable 8.3 naming convention, steps 1 to 8 must be followed and the command must be replaced with **FSUTIL BEHAVIOR SET DISABLE8DOT3 0** in step 8.

Modify Hosts File to Run Internet Faster

Introduction to the Hosts File

A Hosts file is located in the system drive. Every time a user types the address of a website in the address bar of the web browser, the computer initiates a query, and the query is sent to the Hosts file to look for the IP address of the requested website. In case the IP address is not available in the Hosts while, the query is then forwarded to the DNS server, which then replies back with the IP address of the searched website.

Role of DNS Server

When a home computer is connected to the Internet, the computer receives the address of the DNS server from its corresponding ISP. On the other hand, in production environments administrators configure internal DNS servers that receive queries from the local clients and forward them to the DNS servers of the ISPs. In either case, the DNS servers of the ISPs play a major role in the process of resolving the URLs of the websites to their respective IP addresses.

Although the above process works quite fine in most network setups, users can still expedite the process by manually specifying the IP addresses of the frequently visited websites in the Hosts file.

How to Add the IP Addresses of the Frequently Visited Websites to the Hosts File?

In order to and the IP addresses of the frequently visited websites to the Hosts file, steps given below must be followed:

1. Log on to Windows 8 computer with administrator account.
2. On the **Start** screen, click **Desktop** tile.
3. On the desktop screen, click **File Explorer** icon from the taskbar.
4. On the opened **Libraries** window, expand **Computer** from the left pane.
5. From the displayed list, click to select the system drive (C: in most cases).
6. In the details pane in the right, navigate to **Windows\System32\Drivers\etc** folder.
7. In the **etc** folder, right-click **hosts** file and from the context menu, click **Open with** option.
8. From the displayed list of options, click **Notepad**
9. Once the **hosts** file is opened, go to the bottom of the file and specify the IP address and the URL of the website separated by a tab.

hosts - Notepad

File Edit Format View Help

```
# Copyright (c) 1993-2009 Microsoft Corp.
#
# This is a sample HOSTS file used by Microsoft TCP/IP for Windows.
#
# This file contains the mappings of IP addresses to host names. Each
# entry should be kept on an individual line. The IP address should
# be placed in the first column followed by the corresponding host name.
# The IP address and the host name should be separated by at least one
# space.
#
# Additionally, comments (such as these) may be inserted on individual
# lines or following the machine name denoted by a '#' symbol.
#
# For example:
#
#      102.54.94.97     rhino.acme.com          # source server
#       38.25.63.10     x.acme.com              # x client host
#       192.168.5.14    Mywebsite.com

# localhost name resolution is handled within DNS itself.
#       127.0.0.1       localhost
#       ::1             localhost
```

10. Finally save the changes and close the file.
11. If required, restart the computer.

To remove the added IP addresses from the **hosts** file, steps 1 to 11 can be followed and unwanted entry can be deleted while on step 9.

Enable File/Folder Level Compression

Introduction to Compression

Compression is a process in which the total size of an object is reduced before it is saved in the storage media (for example a hard disk drive). There are several third-party compression applications available in the market with the help of which users compress their data and store the scattered files/folders in a single compressed file. An example of such application is WinRAR.

Although third-party compression applications provide some extended features, they come with the price tags which might not be appreciated by many users. In order to make things easier and cheaper for the users, Microsoft Windows 8 has its own built-in file/folder level compression feature that users can enable to compress the objects. File/folder level compression means that even a single file or a folder containing multiple files can be compressed, without disturbing any other file or folder that may reside on the same volume or in a common parent folder. For example if folder AB contains two sub-folders naming A and B, the entire A folder can be compressed irrespective of the contents it may have. The compression process of folder A does not affect folder B that resides in the AB parent folder.

Apart from the default compression feature that can be enabled at file or folder level, Windows 8 also allows users to create a compressed folder which works as a container to hold multiple files and compresses them when they are added to it.

Drawbacks of Enabling Compression

When users enable file or folder compression, Windows takes some time and consumes some processing to compress the objects. When users try to access the compressed objects, Windows decompresses them before it allows users to work on them. Once users are done working and they try to save the files, the operating system compresses them again before it finally saves the changes and closes the files. This entire the compression and decompression process might take some time before the files are actually opened and saved. The time taken to compress and decompress the files is transparent to the users and is almost negligible.

Prerequisites to Enable Compression

File/Folder level compression can be enabled only on the volumes that have NTFS file system. If FAT 32 file system is used to format a volume, compression cannot be enabled on it whatsoever. In order to enable compression on such volume, it must be converted to NTFS, or the entire volume must be reformatted using NTFS file system.

How to Enable Compression on a Folder?

In order to enable compression are on a folder in Microsoft Windows 8, steps given below must be followed:

1. Log on to Microsoft Windows 8 computer with the account, folder of which is to be compressed.
2. On the **Start** screen, click **Desktop** tile.
3. On the desktop screen, click **File Explorer** icon from the taskbar.

4. From the opened **Libraries** window, navigate and locate the folder that is to be compressed.
5. Once the folder is located, right-click the folder and from the context menu, click **Properties**.
6. On the opened folder's properties box, make sure that the **General** tab is selected and click **Advanced** button.
7. On the **Advanced Attributes** box, under **Compress or Encrypt attributes** section, check the **Compress contents to save disk space** checkbox.

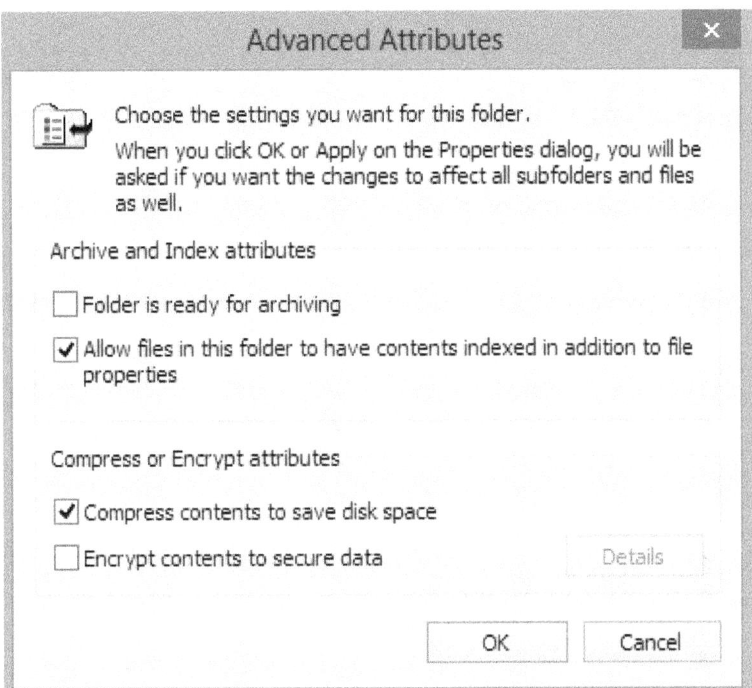

8. Click **OK** and back on the folder's properties box, click **OK** again.
9. On the **Confirm Attribute Changes** box, make sure that **Apply changes to this folder, subfolders and files** radio button is selected and click **OK** to start the compression process.

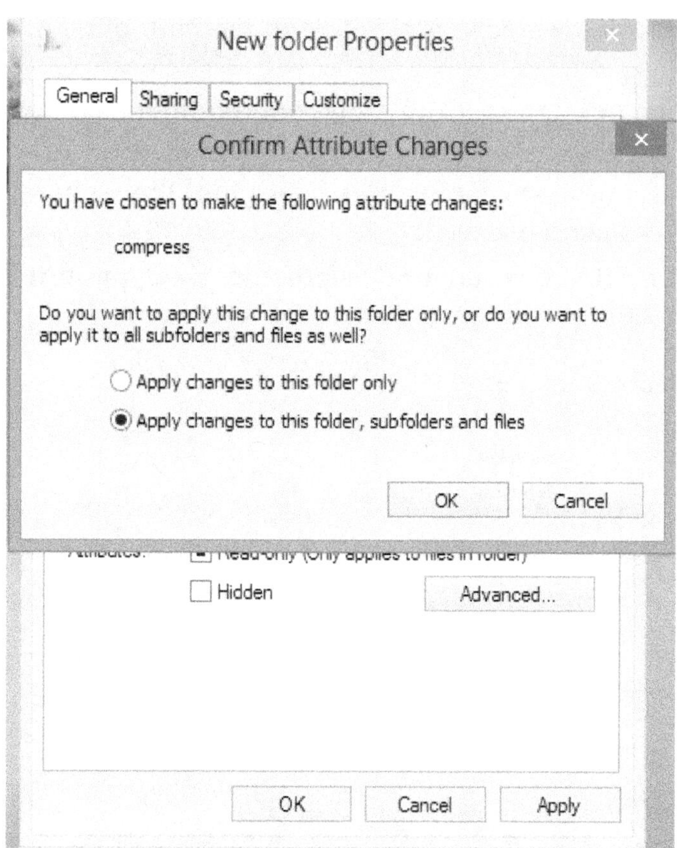

To disable compression, steps 1 to 9 can be followed, while unchecking the **Compress contents to save disk space** checkbox in step 7.

Sort Files According to Modification Dates

Introduction to File Sorting

File sorting is a process in which the files can be arranged (sorted) as per the given criteria. For example files can be sorted by their names, by their types (extensions), by their sizes, etc. File sorting makes it easier for the users to locate the desired files easily and quickly. File sorting becomes important when there are several files stored in a container, and users want to search a specific file or some specific file types.

When a file is created on a Windows 8 computer its time of creation is added to its properties. Each time the file is accessed and or modified, its last access/modification date and time is automatically added to its properties as well. This information can be viewed by right clicking the file and the clicking the 'Properties' option from the displayed context menu. The information mentioned above is permanent and cannot be modified manually, hence eliminating the chances of forgery or frauds.

Microsoft Windows 8 allows users to arrange (sort) the files in the order of the dates when they were last modified. Users might want to sort the files in this order to monitor the objects and/or locate the cause of the troubles that they might be facing. By sorting the files as per their modification dates, users can easily locate the cause of the errors or can find the culprit individual.

How to Sort Files as per Their Modification Dates?

In order to sort files as per the modification dates, steps given below must be followed:

1. Log on to Microsoft Windows 8 computer.
2. On the **Start** screen, click **Desktop** tile.
3. From the desktop screen, navigate and locate the folder, contents of which are to be sorted as per their modification dates.
4. Once located, double-click the folder to enter into it.
5. Right-click anywhere in the folder (make sure that no object is selected while right-clicking), and from the displayed context menu go to **Sort by**.
6. From the displayed submenu, click **More**.
7. On the opened **Choose Details** box, check **Date modified** checkbox and click **OK**

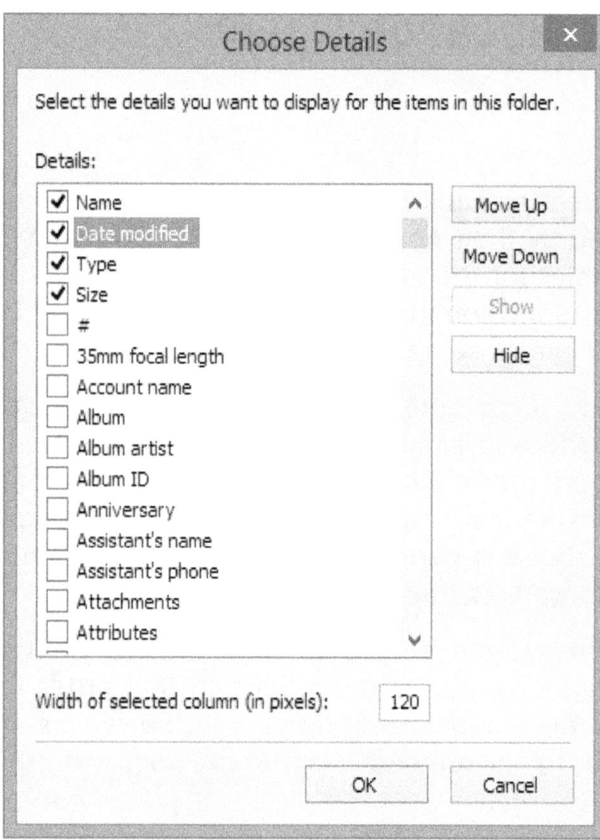

8. Back on the opened folder window, follow steps 1 to 6 but select the displayed **Date modified** option in the **Sort by** submenu to sort the objects of the container as per their modification dates.

To view files by the default sort order, steps 1 to 6 can be followed while selecting **Name** from the **Sort by** submenu in step 6.

Add Locations for Indexing

Introduction to Indexing and Quick Search

In Microsoft Windows 8, indexing is a feature that expedites the process of file searching. With the help of indexing, users can locate the files in real time, which means that the names of matched files start appearing on the screens as the users type the names. For example if a user wants to search a file named 'Music', as soon as 'M' and then 'Mu' is typed, the files with the matching characters in their names are displayed on the screen.

By default only 'Offline Files' folder, 'Start Menu' folder, 'User's folder (excluding 'App-Data' folders for all users) are indexed, and quick search is enabled on them only. In order to enable quick search on other locations, where users frequently look for the files, they must add those locations for indexing as well.

How to Add Locations for Indexing?

In order to add locations for indexing manually in Microsoft Windows 8, steps given below must be followed:

1. Log on to Microsoft Windows 8 computer.
2. On the **Start** screen, hover mouse to the bottom right corner of the screen.
3. From the displayed options click **Search**.
4. On the opened **Apps** window, in the **Search** pane in the right, type **Indexing Options** in the available field.

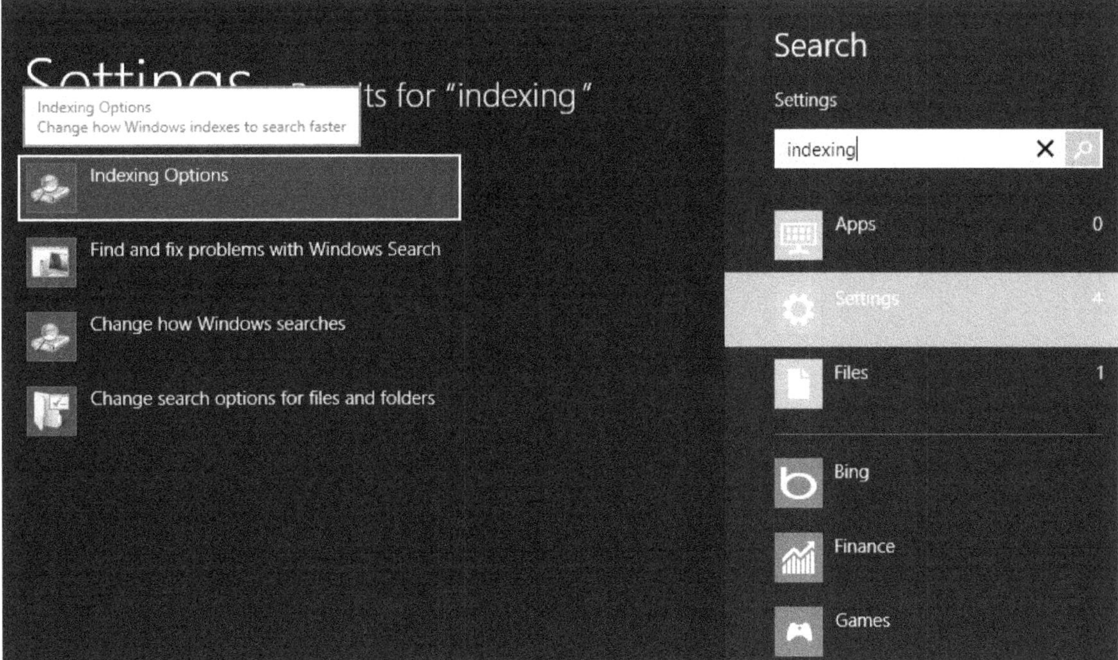

5. Click **Settings** category below the text field, where **Indexing Options** command was typed.
6. From the **Settings** window in the left, click **Indexing Options**.
7. On the opened **Indexing Options** box, click **Modify** button.

8. On the **Indexed Locations** box, from the **Change selected locations** list, check the checkboxes of the locations that are to be added for indexing.

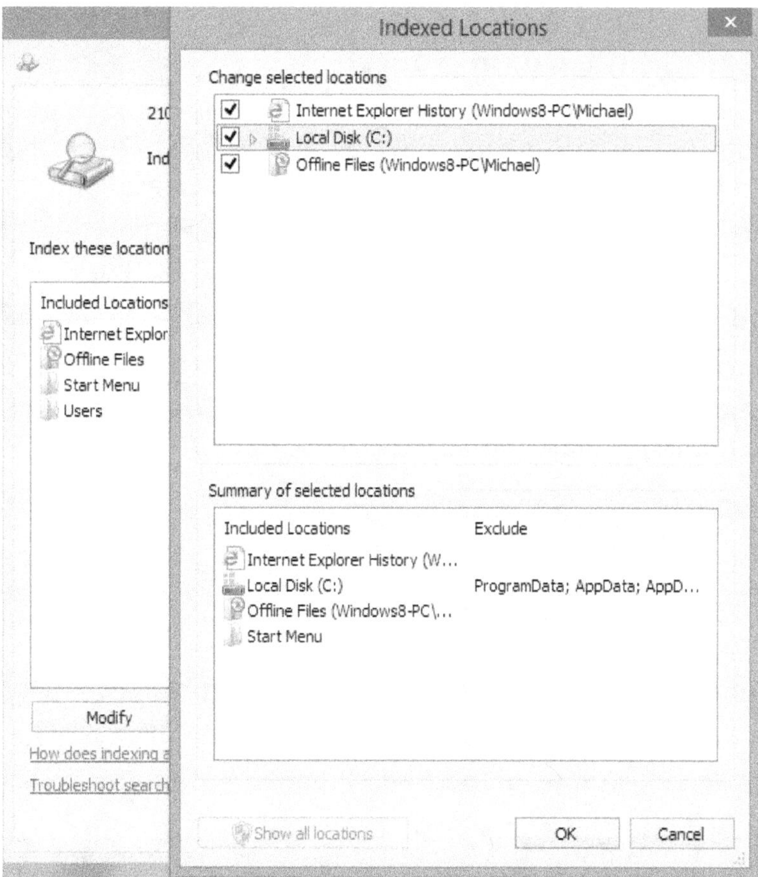

9. Click **OK** when done.
10. Back on the **Indexing Options** box, click **Close**.

To remove the added indexed location, steps 1 to 10 can be followed while unchecking the checkboxes of the locations that are to be removed from the list in step 8.

Delete Themes

Introduction to the Themes

While using Microsoft Windows, many times users install third-party themes in order to change the ambience of the operating system. Microsoft Windows 8 also has some built-in themes which can be enabled in order to experience different set of Windows sounds, different wallpaper, etc.

When Windows theme is applied on the operating system, it also allows users to customize its settings by changing the wallpapers and/or modifying the sound schemes. When this is done, a custom theme is created and added under My Themes list. When users frequently change the settings of the themes, multiple themes are added under My Themes list, hence overpopulating the category. In such situations, users might want to remove the unwanted themes in order to make the list look less populated and tidy.

How to Delete Themes?

In order to delete themes from Microsoft Windows 8 computer, steps given below must be followed:

1. Log on to Microsoft Windows 8 computer with the user account from which a theme is to be deleted.
2. From the **Start** screen, click **Desktop** tile.
3. On the desktop screen right-click anywhere, and from the displayed context menu, click **Personalize**.
4. On the **Personalization** window, make sure that the theme that is to be deleted is not currently applied to the computer.
5. Once assured, right-click the unwanted theme from the **My Themes** list and click **Delete theme** to remove the theme from the computer.

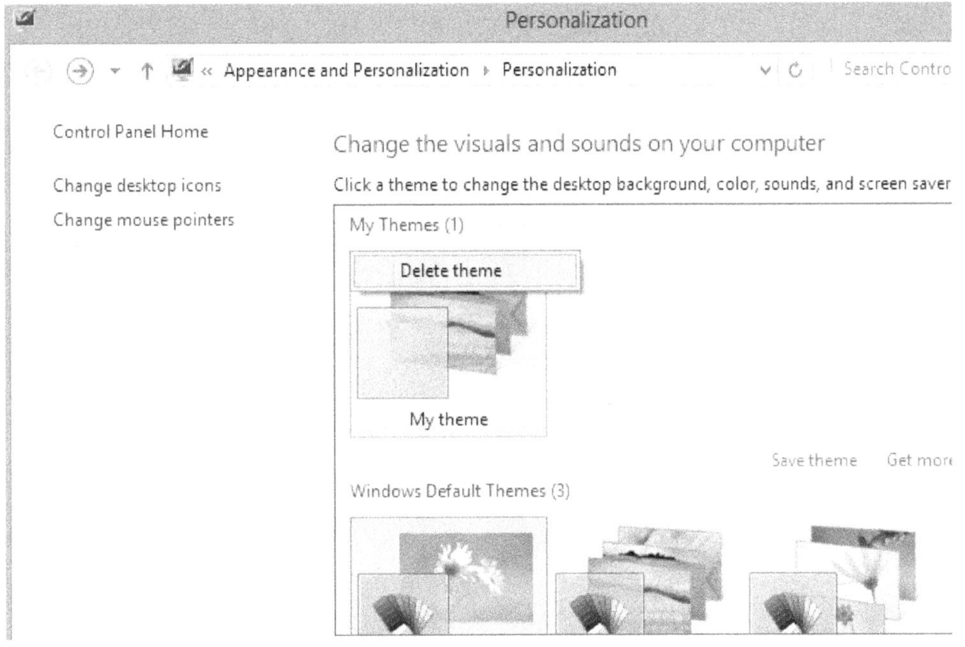

6. Close **Personalization** window when done.

Keep/Delete User Profiles When Deleting Accounts

Introduction to User Profiles

When a new user account is created and the user logs on to the computer for the very first time, a user profile for that user is created. The created user profile contains account specific desktop icons, wallpaper, and folders like Documents, Music, Videos, etc. Every time a user logs on to the computer and creates and saves the files to the default locations, the created and saved files become the part of the profile.

In home environments when a new user account for a family member is created and its profile is generated, it is very unlikely that the account will be deleted. On the other hand, in production environments, because employees are hired and fired on a regular basis, their respective accounts are also added and deleted quite frequently.

As mentioned above, although in homes it is unlikely that the user accounts would be deleted, and even if such situation comes, it is recommended that the users' personal data should also be removed in order to free some disk space, and prevent the data from getting exposed to everyone. However cases may be different in production environments where administrators are required to take appropriate step in order to protect the data from getting accidentally deleted while deleting the user accounts.

Microsoft Windows 8 allows administrators to keep the users' files even if the user accounts have been deleted. This eliminates the chances of losing the data that the users have saved while they used to use the accounts.

How to Keep/Delete User Profiles and Data While Deleting User Accounts?

In order to keep/delete user profiles and data while deleting user accounts in Microsoft Windows 8, steps given below must be followed:

1. Log on to Microsoft Windows 8 computer with the administrator account and make sure that the user account that is to be deleted is not logged on.
2. From the **Start** screen, click **Desktop** tile.
3. On the desktop screen, hover mouse to the bottom right corner of the window.
4. From the displayed options, click **Settings**.
5. On the **Settings** pane, click **Control Panel**.
6. On the **Control Panel** window, click **User Accounts and Family Safety** category.
7. On the **User Accounts and Family Safety** window, under the **User Accounts** category, click **Remove user accounts**.

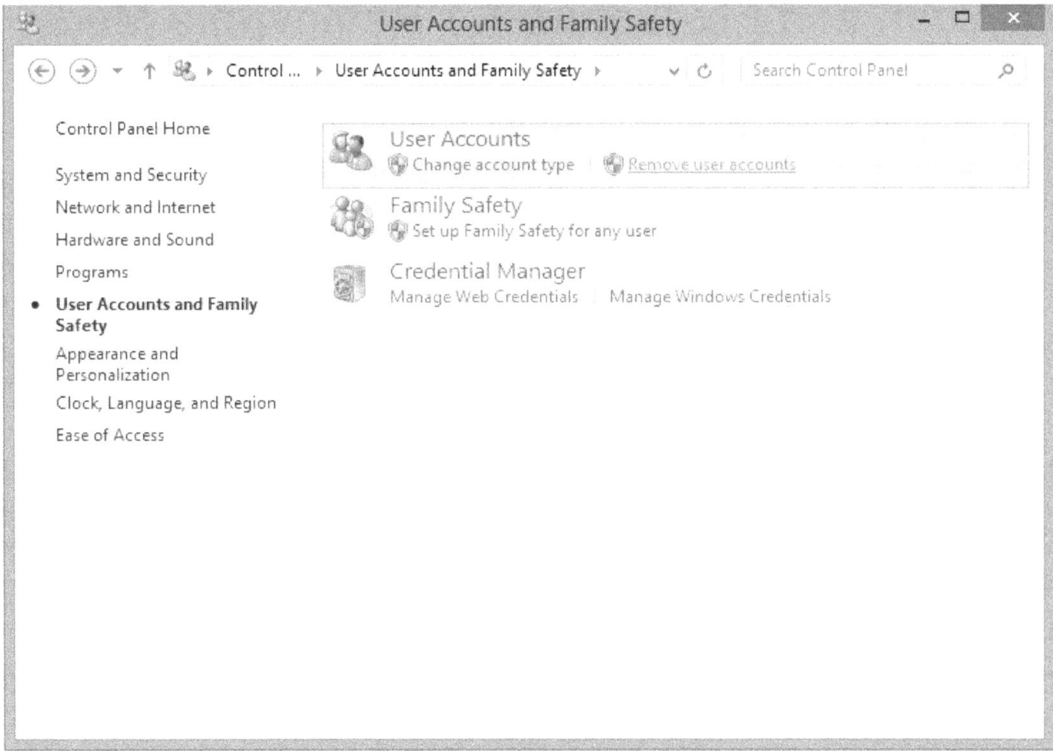

8. On the **Manage Accounts** window, from the displayed list of available user accounts, click the account that is to be deleted.
9. On the **Change an Account** window, click **Delete the account** from the available options in the left.
10. On the **Delete Account** window, click **Delete Files** or **Keep Files** button to remove or keep the profile and the data of the user account that is being deleted.

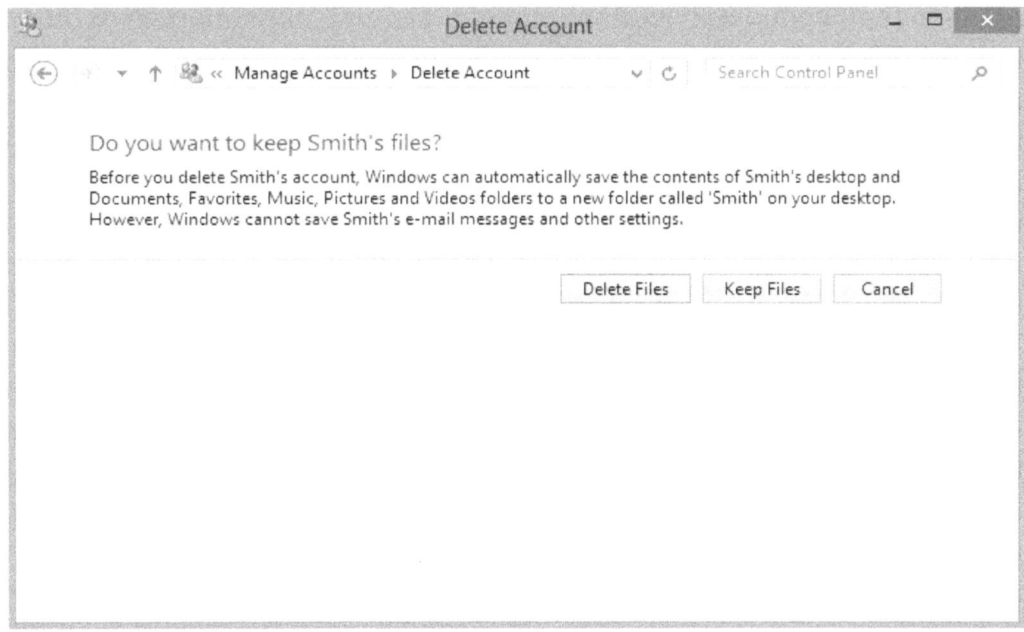

11. On the **Confirm Deletion** window, click **Delete Account** button to delete the selected account.
12. Close all the opened windows.

Disable Scan and Fix feature for Removable Media

Introduction to Scan and Fix Feature

In Microsoft Windows 8, every time a removable media, such as a USB drive, is connected to the computer, a message box appears asking whether the user wants to perform a quick can on the inserted drive and fix any known errors that the Windows may detect. From security point of view, this built-in function is quite helpful as it protects the computers from accidental data loss because of improper file system of the media. However it might be annoying for the users who already know that the media that they have connected to the computer is error free.

When users are always sure that every removable media that they would connect to the computer would be error free, they can disable the default Scan and Fix feature from the operating system. By disabling the feature, they can also save their decent amount of time, which they would have otherwise spent while closing the opened box every time the media was connected to the computer.

How to Disable Scan and Fix Feature for Removable Media?

In order to disable Scan and Fix feature for removable media in Microsoft Windows 8, steps given below must be followed:

1. Log on to Microsoft Windows 8 computer with the administrator account.
2. From the **Start** screen, click **Desktop** tile.
3. On the desktop screen, press **Windows** + **R** keys simultaneously to initiate the **Run** command box.
4. In the **Run** command box, type **SERVICES.MSC** command and press **Enter** key.
5. On the opened **Services** snap-in, double-click **Shell Hardware Detection** service.
6. On the opened properties box, click **Stop** button to stop the running service.

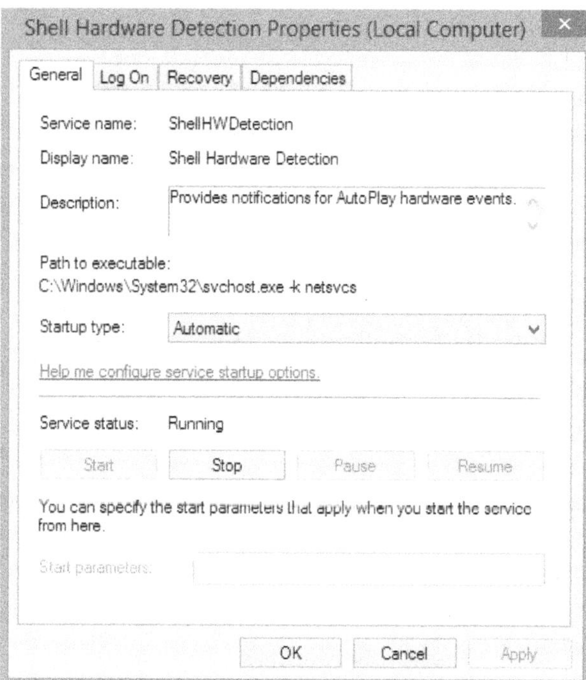

7. From the **Startup type** drop-down list, select **Disabled** option.

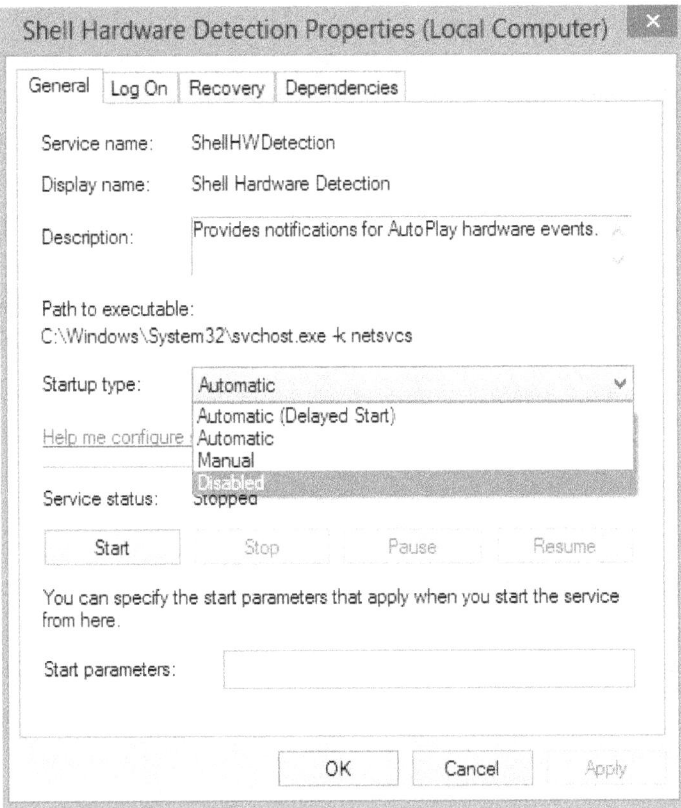

8. Click **OK** to save the changes.

To re-enable the feature, follow steps 1 to 5 and choose **Automatic** option from the **Startup type** drop-down list and click **Apply**. Once done, click **Start** button to start the service.

Manage OS in Dual-Boot Environments

Introduction to Dual-Boot Environments

Dual-boot environments are when multiple operating systems are installed on a single computer. When more than one operating systems are installed, users are displayed with a list of OS from which they must choose the one on which they want to work. The list of available operating systems is by default displayed for 30 seconds. As soon as the list appears on the computer screens, a countdown starts and users must select the operating system of their choices before the countdown reaches 0. If users fail to do so, the default operating system is automatically selected and its boot process is initiated.

In most cases, the default countdown duration, i.e. 30 seconds, is quite appropriate and does not need modifications either at homes or in production environments. However if administrators want they can increase or decrease the default countdown duration as per their personal choices and/or for testing purposes.

How to Manage Microsoft Windows 8 in Dual-Boot Environments?

In order to manage Microsoft Windows 8 in dual-boot environments, steps given below must be followed:

1. Log on to Microsoft Windows 8 computer with the administrator account.
2. From the **Start** screen, click **Desktop** tile.
3. Once on the desktop screen, click **File Explorer** icon from the taskbar.
4. On the opened **Libraries** window, from the left pane, right-click **Computer**.
5. From the displayed context menu, click **Properties**.
6. On the opened **System Properties** box, make sure that **Advanced** tab is selected.
7. On the **Advanced** tab, under **Startup and Recovery** section, click **Settings**.
8. On **Startup and Recovery** box, from the **Default operating system** drop-down list, choose the desired operating system to set as default. (Dual-boot environment)
9. Ensure that **Time to display the list of operating systems** checkbox is checked and specify the desired timeout duration after which the default operating system will be automatically selected.

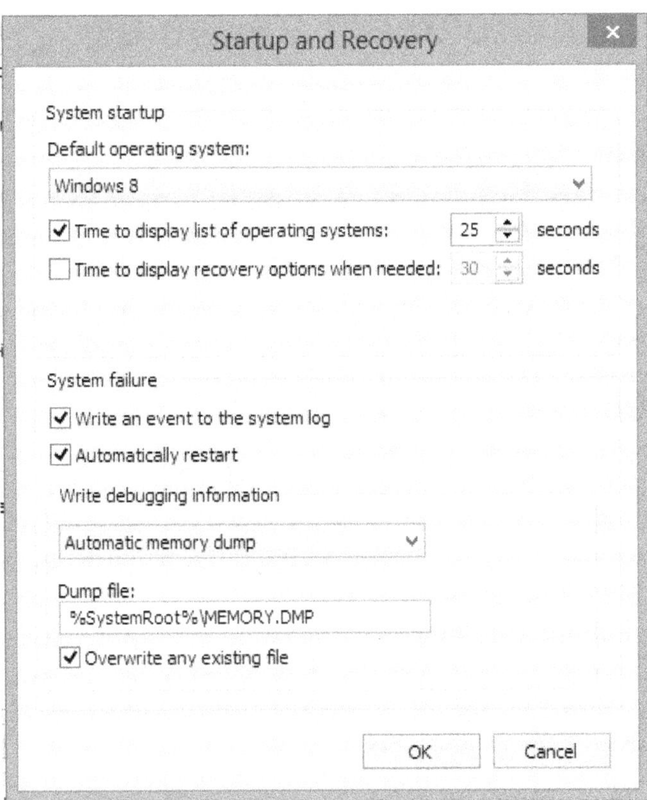

10. Click **OK** button to save the changes, and back on **System Properties** box click **OK** button again.
11. Close **System** window and restart the computer to allow the changes to take effect.

Specify System Specific Environment Variables

Introduction to Environment Variables

Environment variables help users initiate certain tasks and/or applications by typing the specific keywords assigned to them. When the assigned keywords are typed in the Run command box, Windows look for the typed characters in the environment variables. Once their corresponding applications or tasks are located, Windows initiates them accordingly.

Types of Environment Variables

There are two types of environment variables in Microsoft Windows 8:

- **User Specific Environment Variables** - These environment variables are only effective and can be used when the user account for which the variables have been specified is logged on.
- **System Specific Environment Variables** - These environment variables are globally effective, irrespective of the logged on user. Most administrators modify the system specific environment variables in order to make the keywords effective on the entire computer and for every user.

How System Specific Environment Variables Work?

When a user types a name of a program, such as 'Notepad', in the Run command box, Windows searches for the typed word in all the locations that are specified in the system variable named 'Path'. 'Path' is the system variable in which all the system locations are added. The system locations that the 'Path' system variable has include C:\Windows, C:\Program Files, etc.

In case users want to initiate a program or batch file that resides at a separate location, they must add the location to the 'Path' system variable.

How to Specify System Specific Environment Variables?

In order to specify system specific environment variables in Microsoft Windows 8, steps given below must be followed:

1. Log on to Microsoft Windows 8 computer with the administrator account.
2. From the **Start** screen, click **Desktop** tile.
3. Once on the desktop screen, click **File Explorer** icon from the taskbar.
4. On the opened **Libraries** window, from the left pane, right-click **Computer**.
5. From the displayed context menu, click **Properties**.
6. On the opened **System Properties** box, make sure that **Advanced** tab is selected.
7. On the **Advanced** tab, click **Environment Variables** button.
8. On the **Environment Variables** box, from the **System variables** list, double-click **Path** system variable.

9. On the **Edit System Variable** box, in the **Variables value** field, at the end of the specified locations, add a **;** (semicolon) followed by the path for the location where the application or batch file is saved.

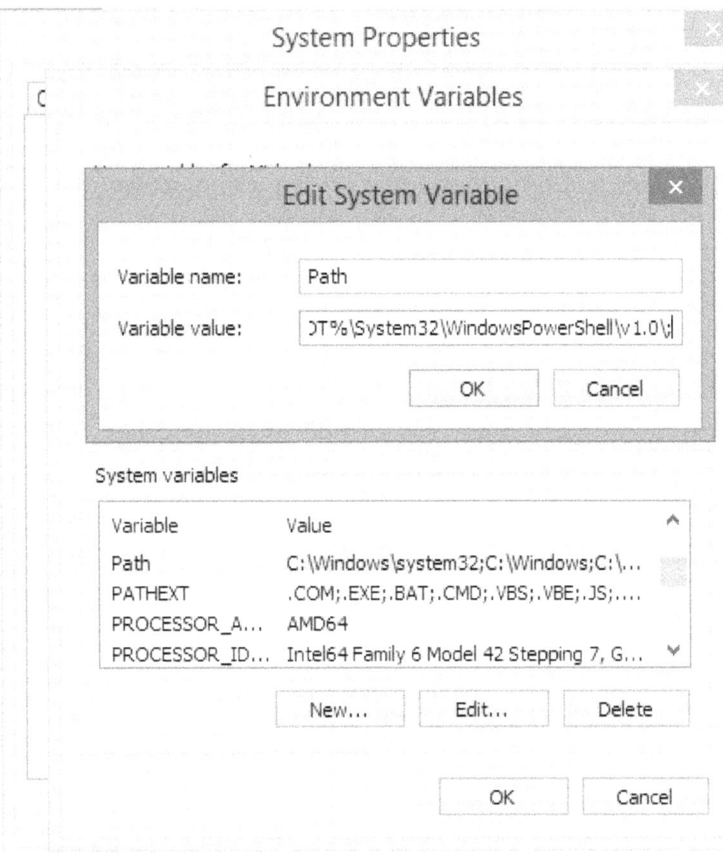

10. Once done, click **OK** button to save the changes.
11. Close all opened boxes and Windows and if required, restart the computer to allow the changes to take effect.

To remove system specific environment variables, steps 1 to 11 can be followed, while removing the desired location from the **Path** system variable when on step 9.

Re-Gain Reduced Audio Volume

Introduction to Audio Volume Reduction

In Microsoft Windows 8, the volume mixer can be used to manage the volume controls for the audio output by all applications individually. For example if a Windows 8 computer has VLC Media Player and Winamp installed on it, when both the applications are initialized simultaneously and the media files are added to the applications to run at the same time, volume for each of the active applications can be adjusted individually.

Because of this reason, when a new application that produces sounds as output is installed on the computer, it takes an exclusive control over the volume. In such cases it is quite possible that the volume settings of the new application automatically decreases the sound output, hence making users experience reduced sound volume. When this happens, the master volume bar in the volume mixer is still at its full. This unwanted configuration might confuse several users as they can see that the volume is set to maximum, but they still experience reduced volume output.

In order to get back the original sound volume, users must configure Windows 8 to keep the sound volume settings intact if a new audio oriented application is installed and initialized.

How to Get the Original Sound Volume Back?

In order to get the original sound volume back (full volume), steps given below must be followed:

1. Log on to Microsoft Windows 8 computer with the user account on which the above discussed sound settings are to be configured.
2. From the **Start** screen, click **Desktop** tile.
3. On the desktop screen, right-click the speaker icon from the system tray at the bottom right corner of the window.
4. From the displayed context menu, click **Playback devices**.
5. On the opened **Sound** box, go to the **Communications** tab.
6. From the available radio buttons, click to select the one that represents **Do nothing**.

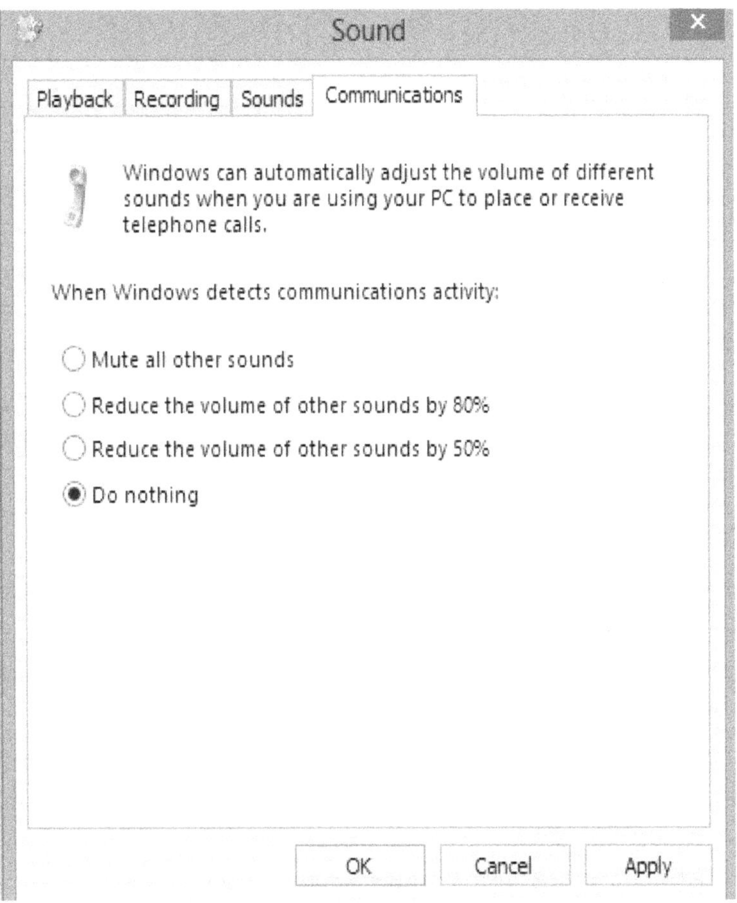

7. Click **OK** when done.

To set sound volume settings in Microsoft Windows 8 back to the default configuration, steps 1 to 7 can be followed, while selecting **Reduce the volume of other sounds by 80%** radio button when on step 6.

Adjust Volume Mixer for Individual Applications

Introduction to the Volume Mixer in Windows 8

In Microsoft Windows 8, volume mixer allows users to manage the volumes of the sound outputs on per application basis. For example if multiple applications that produce sound outputs are initialized simultaneously, sound volume of each initiated application can be managed (increased or decreased) individually.

This helps users prioritize the applications from which they want the sound outputs to be heard clearly (by increasing the sound volume), and which applications they want to produce the sounds that could be heard as if they were played in the background (by decreasing the sound volume).

How to Adjust Volume Mixer for Individual Applications?

In order to adjust volume mixer for individual applications in Microsoft Windows 8, steps given below must be followed:

1. Log on to Microsoft Windows 8 computer with the account on which the sound volume for an individual application is to be adjusted.
2. From the **Start** screen, click **Desktop** tile.
3. On the desktop screen, click the speaker icon from the system tray at the bottom right corner of the window.
4. From the bottom of the displayed volume slider, click **Mixer**.
5. On the opened **Volume Mixer** box, move the slider of the desired sound application up or down to increase or decrease its volume respectively.

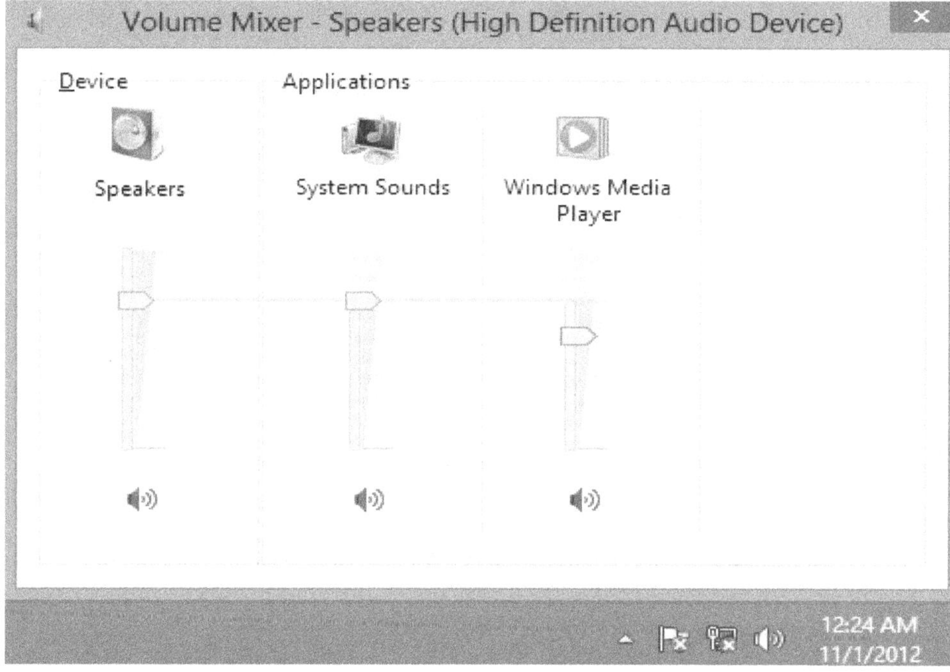

Note: Volume slider for a particular application can be identified by the application's logo that is displayed at the top of the slider.

6. Once done, close the **Volume Mixer** box.

Disable Windows Defender

Introduction to Windows Defender

Windows Defender is a built-in program in Microsoft Windows 8 that prevents the computer from getting infected with malware and unwanted malicious scripts. Although the operating system has a built-in firewall that protects the computer from intrusion and other external threats, Windows Defender adds an additional layer of security to the operating system, irrespective of the third-party or built-in security measures that administrators have applied on the computers.

Windows Defender works as real-time protection tool, which means that it runs in the background and monitors the traffic. As soon as it detects a malicious script order malware, it takes appropriate action as specified in its configuration.

Nowadays almost all antivirus applications are have a built-in firewall, and sometimes administrators install even more sophisticated security oriented applications that provide quite promising features. When these highly efficient security oriented applications are installed, administrators mostly disable the Windows Defender in order to reduce the consumption of processing and memory.

How to Disable Windows Defender?

In order to disable Windows Defender in Microsoft Windows 8, steps given below must be followed:

1. Log on to Microsoft Windows 8 computer with the administrator account.
2. From the **Start** screen, click **Desktop** tile.
3. On the desktop screen, press **Windows** + **R** keys simultaneously to initiate the **Run** command box.
4. In the **Run** command box, type **SERVICES.MSC** command and press **Enter** key.
5. On the opened **Services** snap-in, double-click **Windows Defender Service**.
6. On the opened properties box of the **Windows Defender Service**, click **Stop** button.

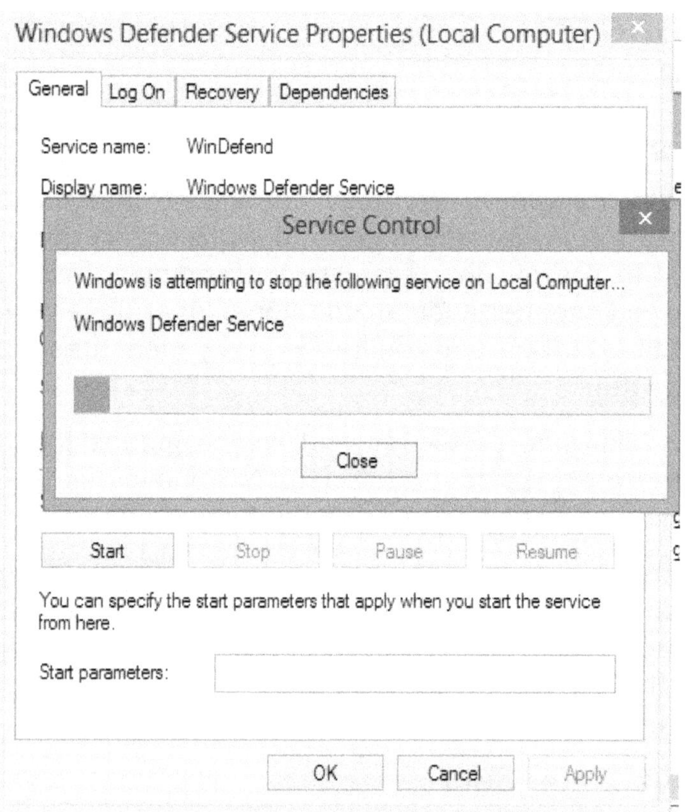

7. From the **Startup type** drop-down list, choose **Disabled** option and click **OK** to permanently disable the service and close the properties box.

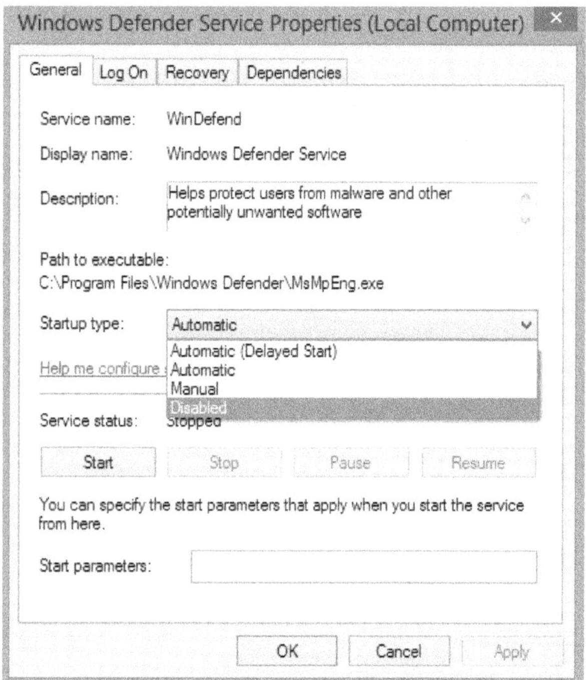

8. If required, restart the computer to allow the changes to take effect.

To re-enable Windows Defender, follow steps from 1 to 5 and from the **Startup type** drop-down list, select **Automatic** option and click **Apply** button. Once done, click the **Start** button to start **Windows Defender Service**.

Enable and Configure Windows Speech Recognition

Introduction to Windows Speech Recognition

Windows Speech Recognition is a built-in feature in Microsoft Windows 8 that allows users to control the entire operating system through their voices. In order to use Windows Speech Recognition in Windows 8, users must enable and configure the feature.

Configuring Windows Speech Recognition means that after enabling the feature, users must speak a couple of words into the microphone in order to make Windows adapt the voices of the speakers and recognize the way they pronounce the words. During the configuration process, Windows Speech Recognition also determines and adapts the accent that users use while speaking.

Although there are some third-party speech recognition applications available in the market that provide several promising features and are developed precisely to solve the purpose, they also come along with the price tags which might not be appreciated by many users. With the help of built-in Windows Speech Recognition, users can now control their computers with their voices without paying additional amounts.

How to Enable and Configure Windows Speech Recognition?

In order to enable and configure Windows Speech Recognition in Microsoft Windows 8, steps given below must be followed:

1. Log on to Microsoft Windows 8 computer with any account.
2. On the **Start** screen, hover mouse to the bottom right corner of the window.
3. From the displayed options, click **Search**.
4. On the opened **Apps** window, click W**indows Speech Recognition** from **Windows Ease of Access** category.
5. On **Welcome to Speech Recognition** box, click **Next**.
6. On **What type of microphone is Microphone (High Definition Audio Device)?** page, click to select the appropriate radio button according the type of microphone connected to the computer.

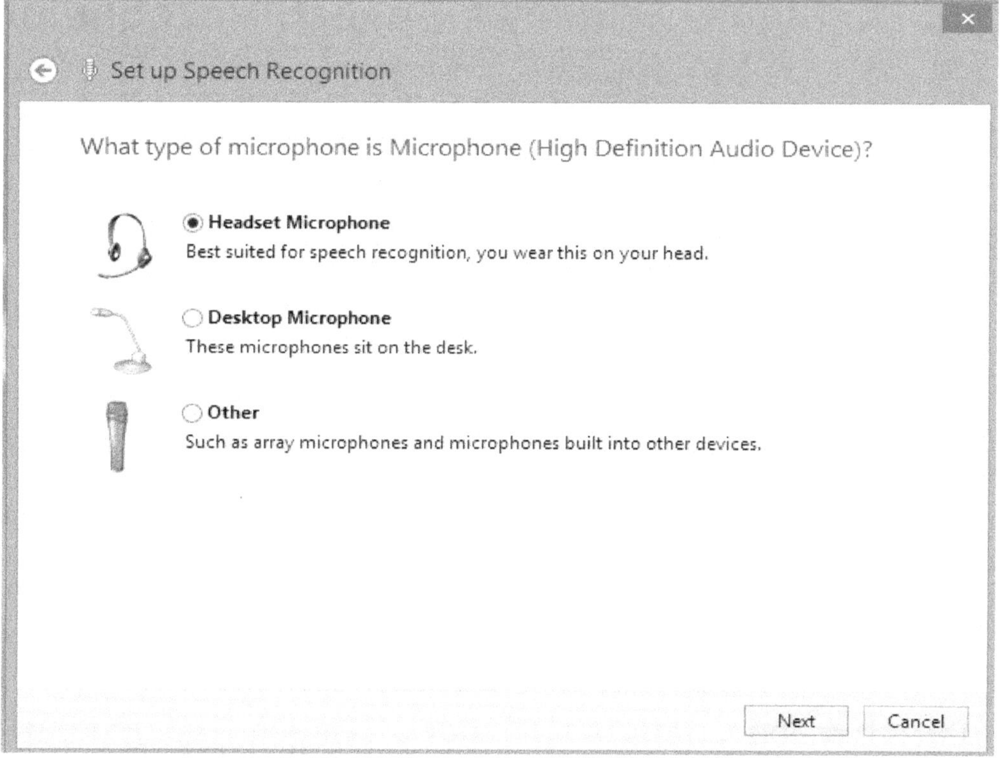

7. Click **Next** to continue.
8. On **Set up your microphone** window, click **Next**. (Make sure that the microphone is at the correct distance and position from the speaker's mouth and is properly connected).
9. On **Adjust the volume of microphone (High Definition Audio Device)** window, speak the displayed text into the microphone.

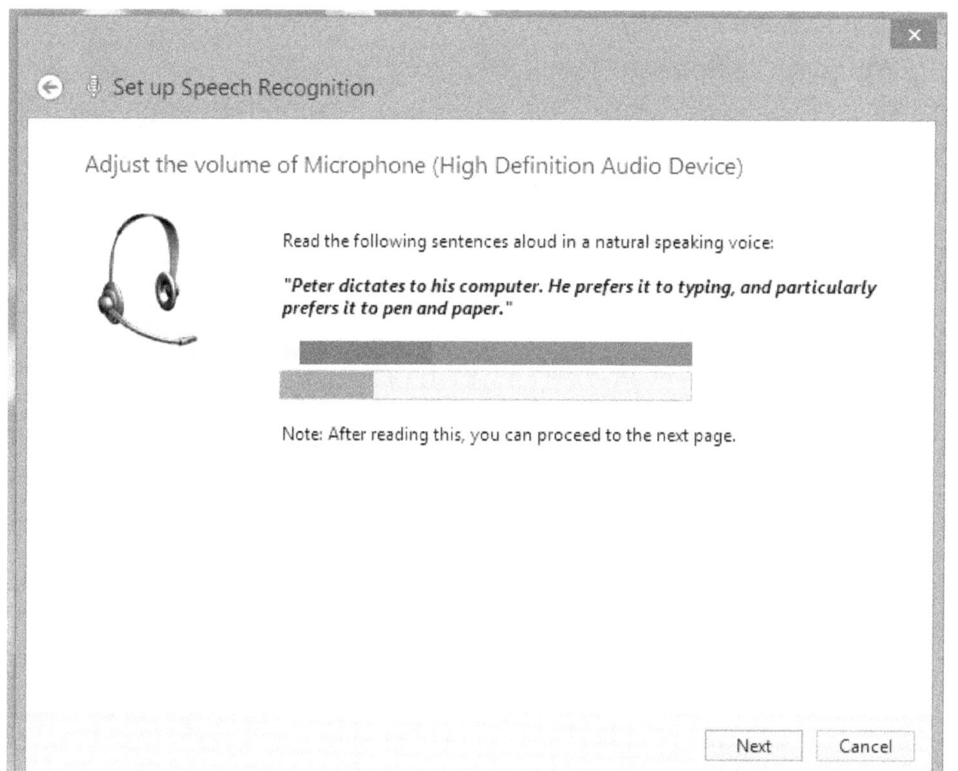

10. Once done and the button gets enabled, click **Next**.
11. On **Your microphone is now set up** window, click **Next**.
12. On **Improve speech recognition accuracy** window, click to select the desired radio button and click **Next** to proceed.

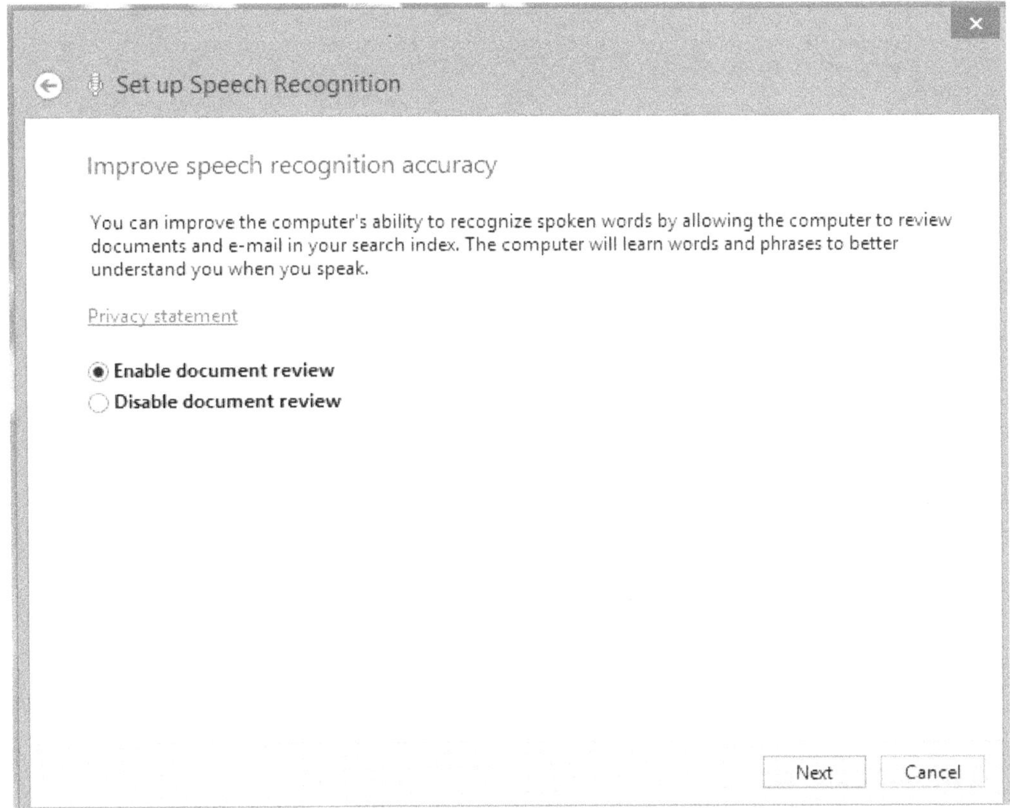

13. On **Choose an activation mode** window, click to select the desired radio button to control Windows Speech Recognition manually or through voice.
14. Click **Next** to proceed.
15. On **Print the Speech Reference Card** window, click **Next**.
16. On **Run Speech Recognition every time I start the computer** window, ensure that **Run Speech Recognition at startup** checkbox is checked and click **Next**.
17. On **You can now control this computer by voice** window, click **Start Tutorial** button to begin tutorial and allow Windows to adapt the voice of the speaker. Alternatively **Skip Tutorial** button (clicked for this demonstration) can also be clicked to continue without going through the tutorial.

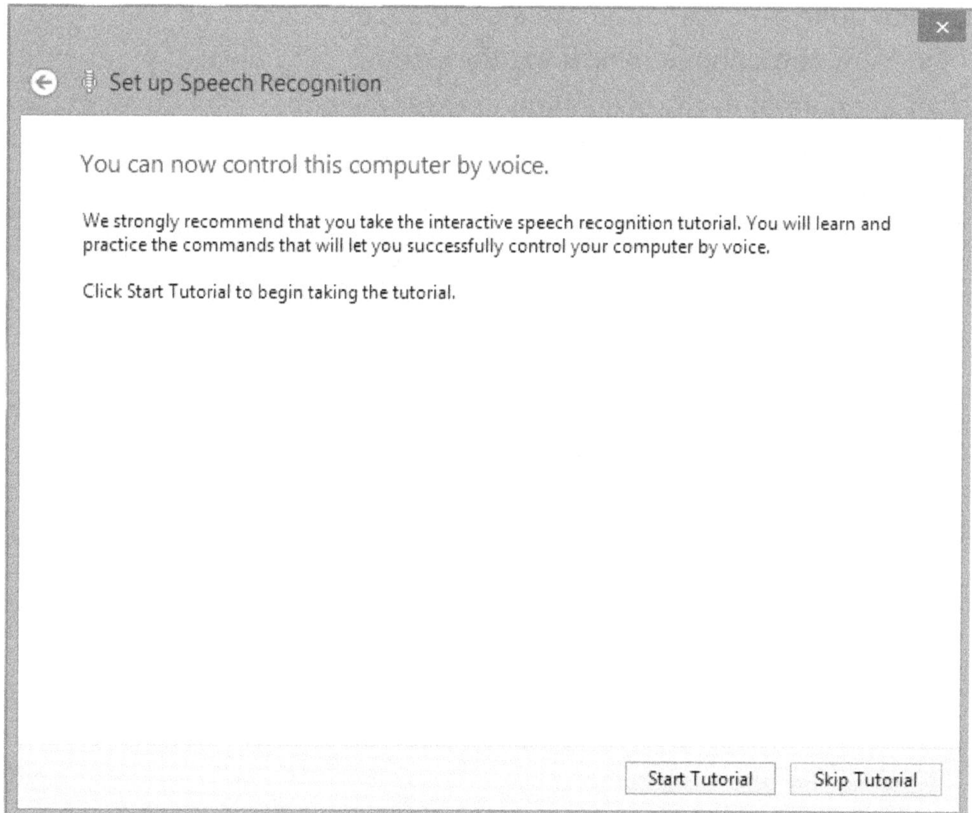

18. Start using Windows Speech Recognition when done.

Enable ReadyBoost to Improve Performance

Introduction to ReadyBoost

ReadyBoost is a feature that was introduced with the release of Microsoft Windows Vista. It was also available with Windows 7 and now it is in Windows 8 as well. ReadyBoost can be enabled by connecting a USB flash drive or any other portable storage media to the computer, as long as the media is larger than 256 MB in size.

When administrators connect a USB Flash Drive to a Windows 8 computer, Windows displays an AutoPlay box prompting users to click or tap the appropriate option from the available list. Administrators can then choose ReadyBoost option to improve system performance. ReadyBoost tab is also included in the USB drive's properties box, and administrators can configure ReadyBoost settings from their as well.

On the ReadyBoost tab, the three available options are:

- **Do not use this device** - When this radio button is selected, the ReadyBoost feature is not enabled on the selected drive.
- **Dedicate this device to ReadyBoost** - When this radio button is selected, Windows 8 reserves the total space of the USB drive for ReadyBoost. The drive must not be used in this case.
- **Use this device** – When this radio button is selected, the available slider can be moved left or right to decrease or increase the reserved space of the drive for ReadyBoost respectively. By default the slider is set to use the full space of the volume.

When a specific amount of space in a USB flash drive is reserved for ReadyBoost, although the remaining space of that drive can be used for data storage, this practice is not recommended at all in order prevent accidental data loss.

How ReadyBoost Works?

When ReadyBoost is enabled, Windows 8 stores the cached copy of the data in the portable storage media and not in the physical memory (RAM). Because of this, the physical memory does not get over populated, hence gives Windows 8 enough room to work freely and efficiently.

How to Enable ReadyBoost?

In order to enable ReadyBoost on a USB flash drive in Microsoft Windows 8, steps given below must be followed:

1. Log on to Microsoft Windows 8 computer with administrator account.
2. From the **Start** screen, click **Desktop** tile.
3. On the desktop window, click **File Explorer** icon from the taskbar.
4. On the opened **Libraries** window, click **Computer** from the left pane.
5. On the **Computer** window, right-click the icon of the USB flash drive on which ReadyBoost is to be enabled.

   Note: *For security reasons, make sure that the drive contains no important data in it.*
6. From the context menu, click **Properties**.

7. From the drive's properties box, go to **ReadyBoost** tab.
8. From the available radio buttons, click to select the desired one.

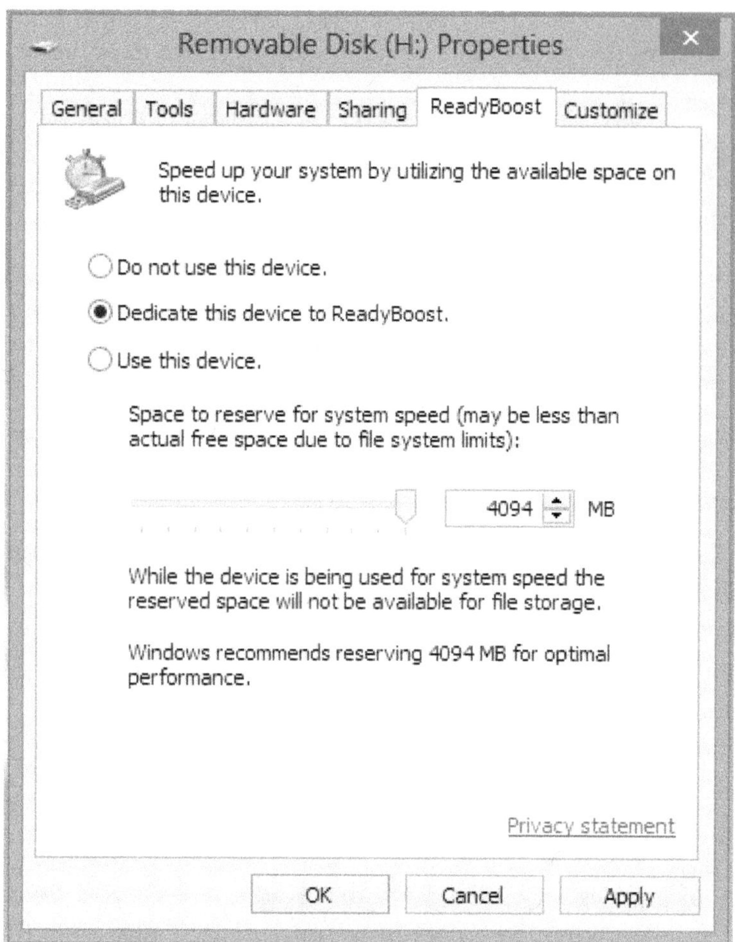

9. Click **OK** to enable ReadyBoost on the USB flash drive.

CHAPTER 4:

MICROSOFT ACCOUNTS, WINDOWS STORE & APPS

Create a Microsoft Account

Introduction to Microsoft Account

Microsoft account is a Windows Live account that can be used to log on to Windows 8 computer. Microsoft account creation process requires an active Internet connection. Microsoft account can be created either using any existing e-mail address or using e-mail created on any public domain, or a new e-mail account can be created using the same wizard. Once Microsoft account is created, Windows 8 allows users to log on to the computer using that account. Since Microsoft account is created using an e-mail address, or a new e-mail address is created, it can be used to log on to any Windows 8 computer that can be anywhere around the globe, as long as it has access to an active Internet connection. Moreover, the same Microsoft account can be used to log on to Mail, People or Messaging apps. The same Microsoft account can also be used to download and install various apps from Windows Store. While installing paid apps from Windows Store, the same Microsoft account can be used to add payment method in order to pay for the apps.

Although the installation process of Windows 8 operating system allows administrators to create a Microsoft account, users can do so even after the installation is successfully complete. However in order to create a Microsoft account after the installation process, users must log on to the computer using any local account. Once Microsoft account creation process is completed successfully using a local Windows 8 account, the local account automatically gets converted and Windows 8 allows users to log on to the computer using Microsoft account only.

How to Create Microsoft Account?

In order to create a Microsoft account in Microsoft Windows 8, steps given below must be followed:

1. Log on to Microsoft Windows 8 computer with any account.
2. Ensure that the computer is connected to an active Internet connection.
3. From the **Start** screen, hover mouse to the bottom right corner of the window.
4. From the displayed options, click **Settings**.
5. From the **Settings** pane, click **Change PC settings**.
6. On the opened **PC settings** window, click to select **Users** from the left.
7. From the right, click **Switch to a Microsoft account**.

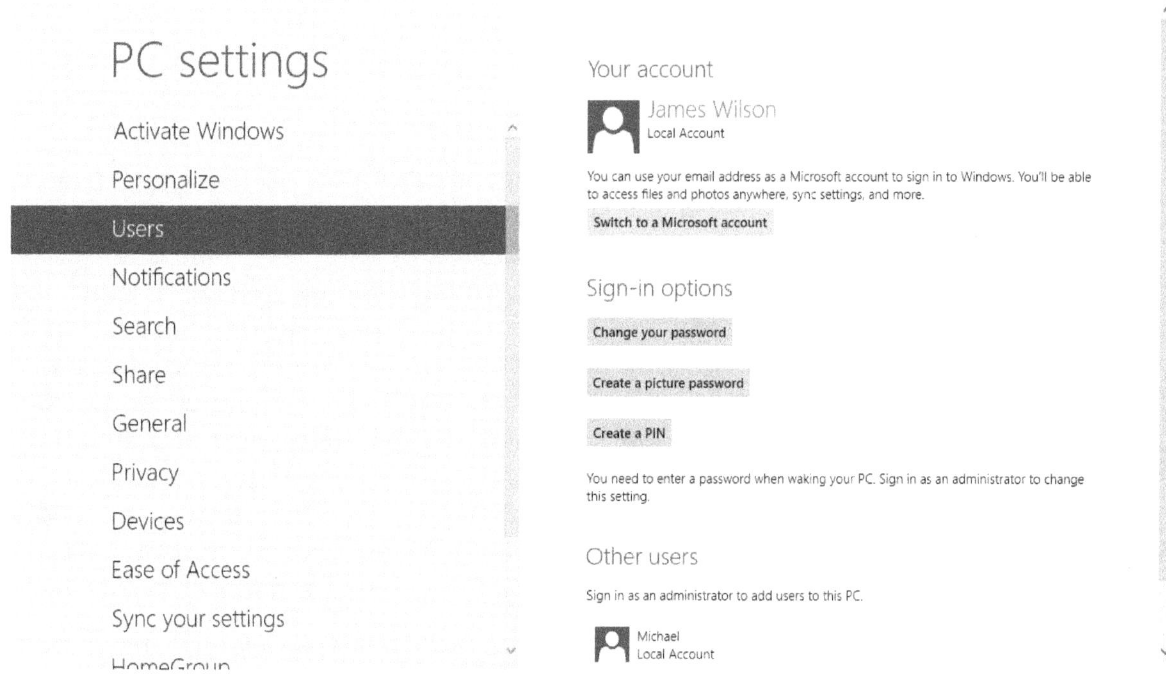

8. On the opened window, type the password for the currently logged on user account.

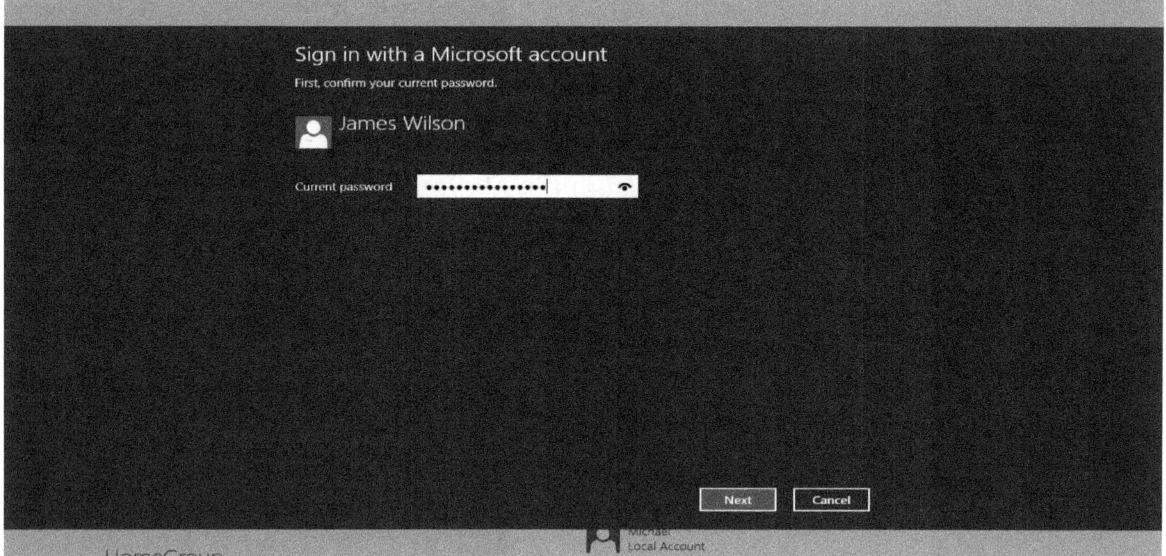

9. Click **Next** to proceed.
10. From the bottom of the next window, click **Sign up for a new email address** option.

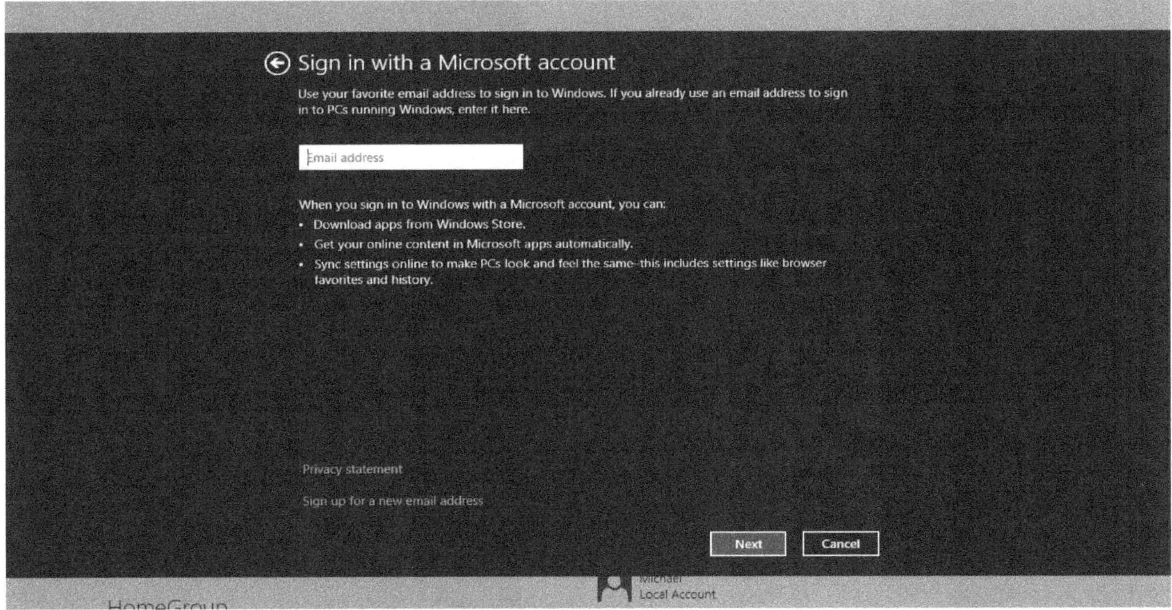

11. On the **Sign up for a new email address** window, populate the available fields with the appropriate values.

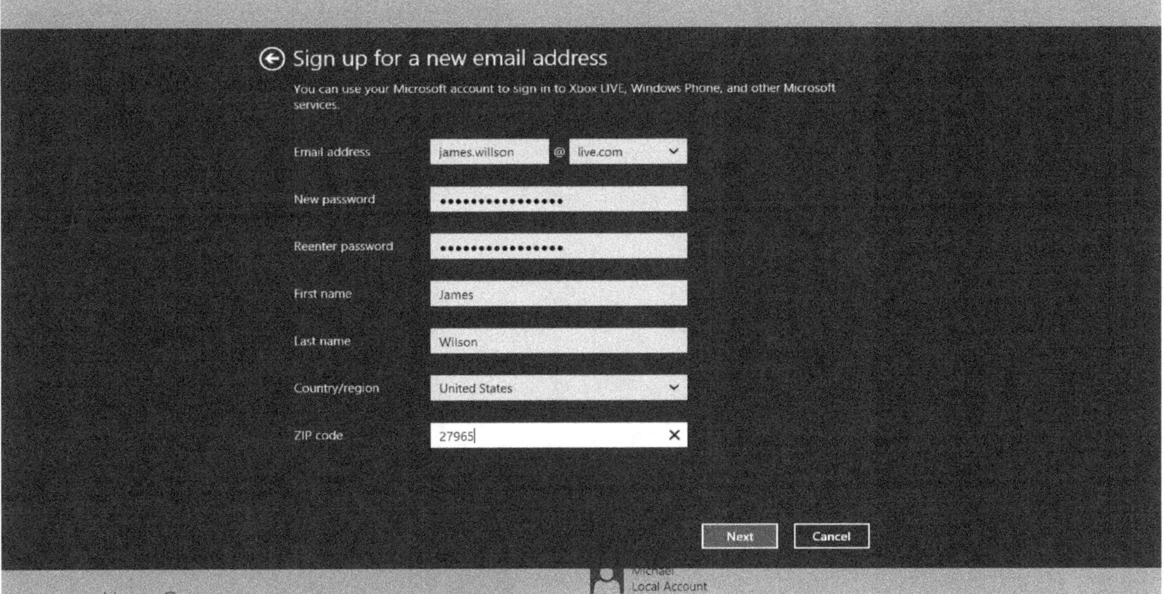

12. Click **Next** button to continue.
13. On **Add security info** window, populate the available fields with the appropriate values.

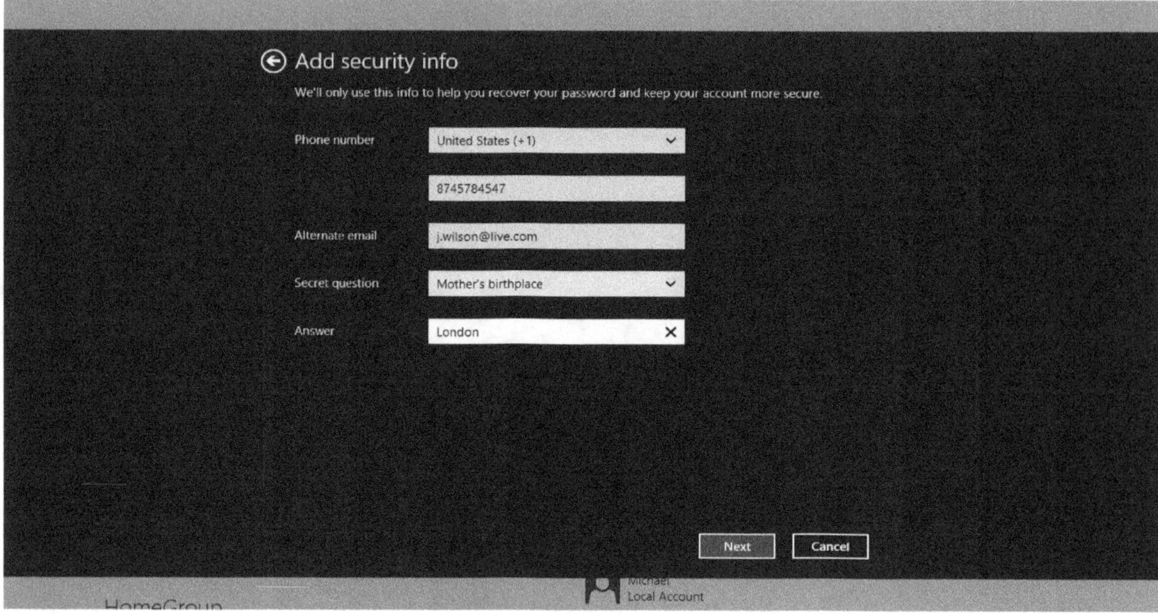

14. Click **Next** to continue.
15. On the **Finish up** window, provide appropriate information and click **Next**.

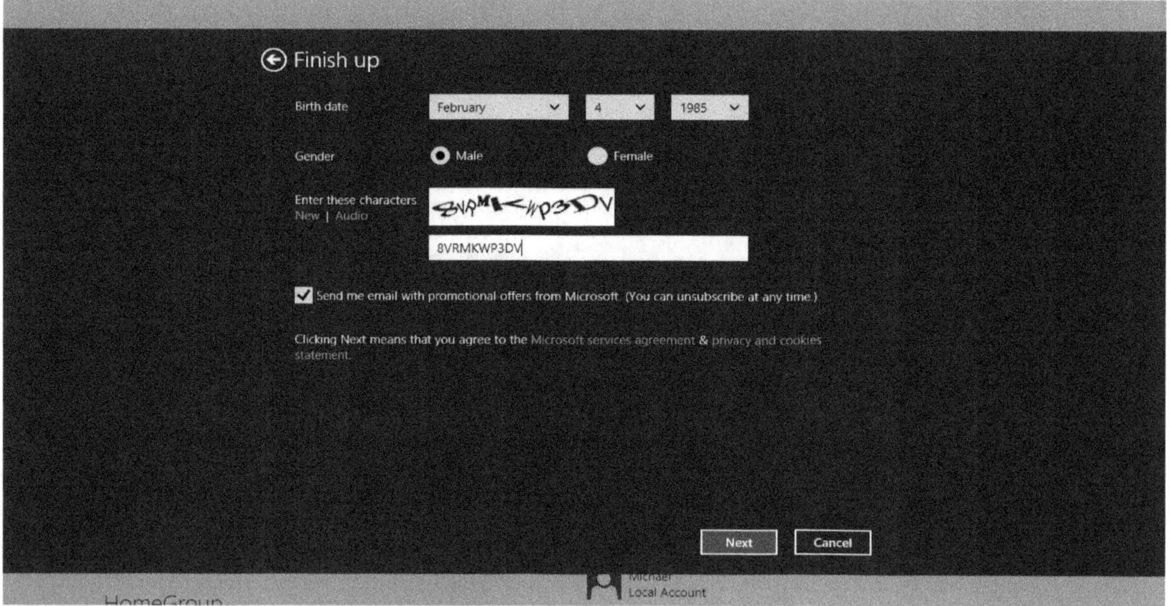

16. On the next window, click **Finish** to log on to the computer using newly created Microsoft account.

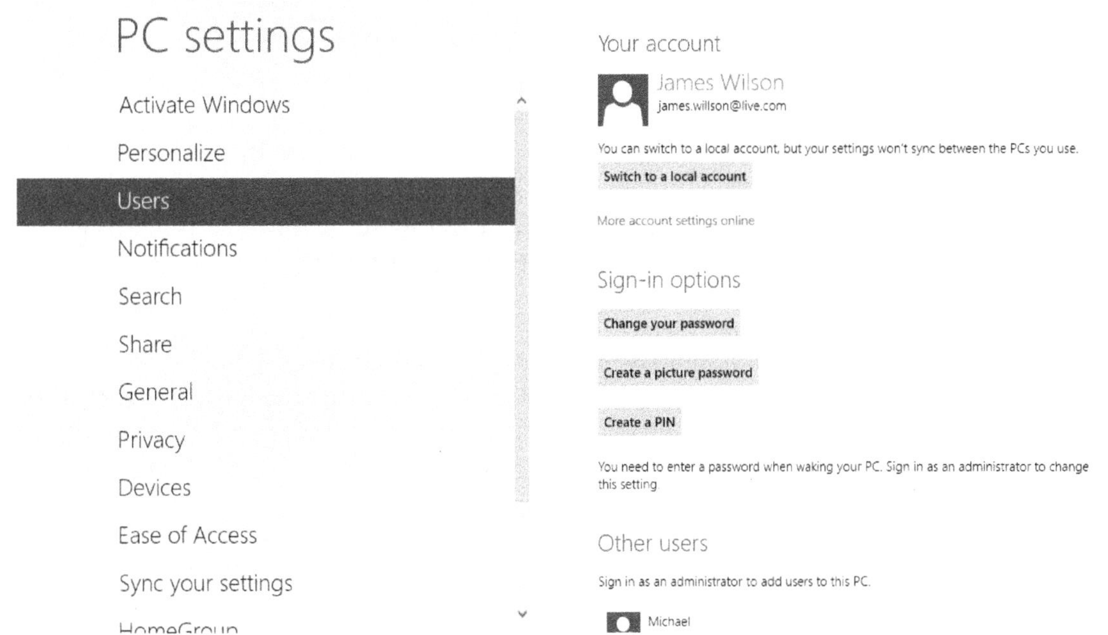
PC settings
Activate Windows
Personalize
Users
Notifications
Search
Share
General
Privacy
Devices
Ease of Access
Sync your settings
Your account
James Wilson
james.willson@live.com
You can switch to a local account, but your settings won't sync between the PCs you use.
Switch to a local account
More account settings online
Sign-in options
Change your password
Create a picture password
Create a PIN
You need to enter a password when waking your PC. Sign in as an administrator to change this setting
Other users
Sign in as an administrator to add users to this PC.
Michael

Add Payment Method to Windows Store

Introduction to Payment Method

With the release of Microsoft Windows 8, Microsoft has introduced Windows Store as well. Windows Store is an online marketplace from where several apps can be downloaded and installed either for free, or by paying for them if they are the paid apps. In order to install paid apps, users can pay the amount either by credit cards or through their PayPal account.

Whatever payment method users choose, it must be added to the Windows Store before purchases can be made using that method. For security reasons, every time users try to install a paid app from the Windows Store, they are required to provide their Microsoft account password. However Windows 8 remembers the payment method that users have added.

It is recommended that the payment method and the Microsoft accounts password should not be used on any public computer that is used and accessed by several people.

How to Add Payment Method to Windows Store?

In order to add payment method to Windows Store in Microsoft Windows 8, steps given below must be followed:

1. Log on to Microsoft Windows 8 computer with any account.
2. From the **Start** screen, click **Store** tile.
3. On the **Store** screen, hover mouse to the bottom right corner of the window.
4. From the displayed options, click **Settings**.
5. From the **Settings** pane, click **Your account**.
6. On the **Your account** window, click **Sign in** button.
7. On the displayed **Add your Microsoft account** box, provide the Microsoft account's credentials. Alternatively, a new Microsoft account can also be created by clicking **Sign up for Microsoft account** link.
8. Once signed in, click **Add payment method** button.

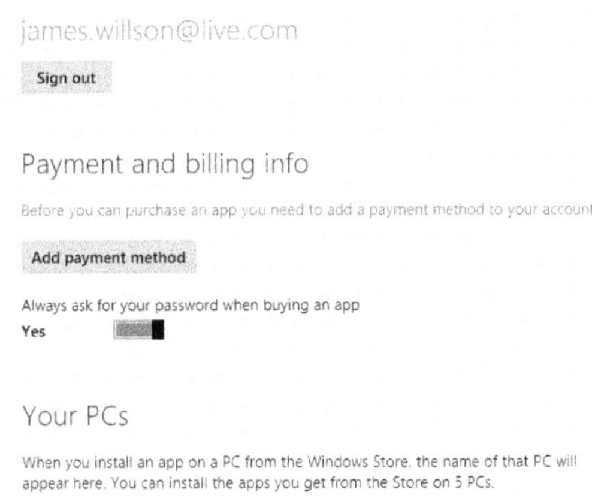

9. On **Payment and billing** window, provide appropriate information.

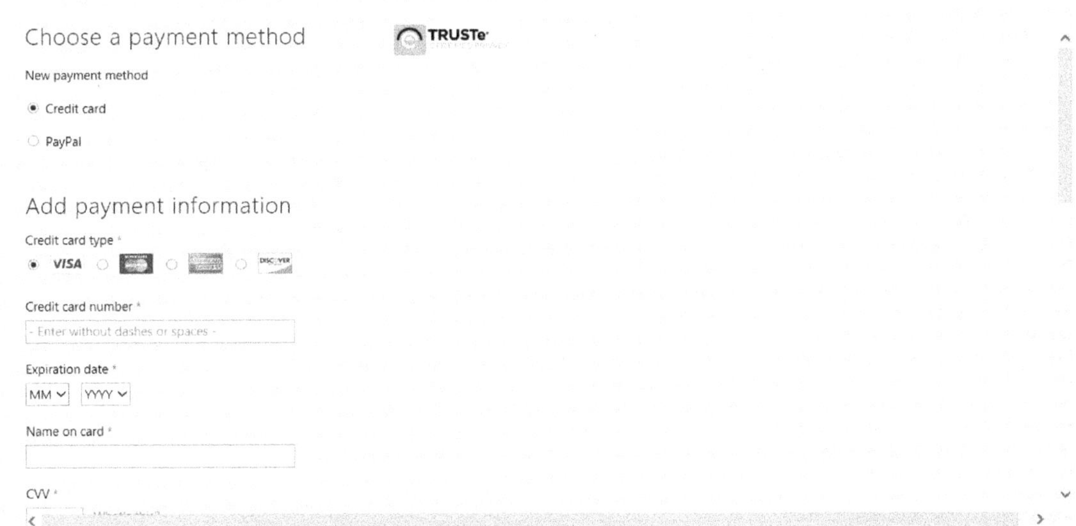

10. Click **Submit** to add the payment method.

Download Apps from Windows Store

Introduction to Apps and Windows Store

Unlike earlier versions of Microsoft Windows, Windows 8 allows administrators and home users to download various apps right from Windows Store. Windows Store is an online marketplace for Windows 8 users that contains various free and paid apps which can be downloaded and installed on PCs and mobile phones. In order to download and install apps from Windows Store, Microsoft account must be used. Microsoft account can be created during Windows 8 installation, using PC settings window or Windows 8 allows users to create one as soon as they try to download and install any app from the Windows Store. If users already have a Microsoft account, they must provide appropriate credentials in the box displayed before the app's downloading and installation process starts.

Providing Microsoft accounts credential's is a one-time process and the logon box is displayed for the first time users try to install any app from Windows Store. Once the credentials are provided, Windows 8 remembers them and uses the same credentials every time the user tries to download a free app from Windows Store. However Windows 8 request for the password every time users try to download any paid app from the store. Moreover, appropriate payment method must also be specified before downloading any paid app from Windows Store. If the payment method is not specified, the app's page automatically redirects the user to the 'Payment and billing' page in case a paid app is being downloaded for the first time on the computer. Payment method is required to be specified for the first time only, and Windows 8 remembers it for next the purchases. Nonetheless, before downloading a paid app, Windows 8 still prompts users for the Microsoft account password to authenticate the account.

Downloading and installing app from Windows Store is a user specific task and even standard user (non-administrative) accounts can install the apps using their credentials.

How to Download Apps from Windows Store?

In order to download an app form Windows Store, steps given below must be followed:

1. Log on to Microsoft Windows 8 computer with administrator account.
2. From the **Start** screen, click **Store** tile.
3. On the **Store** screen, click to select the desired app that is to be installed.
4. On the opened screen, click **Install** or **Buy** button to start downloading and installing the free or paid app respectively.

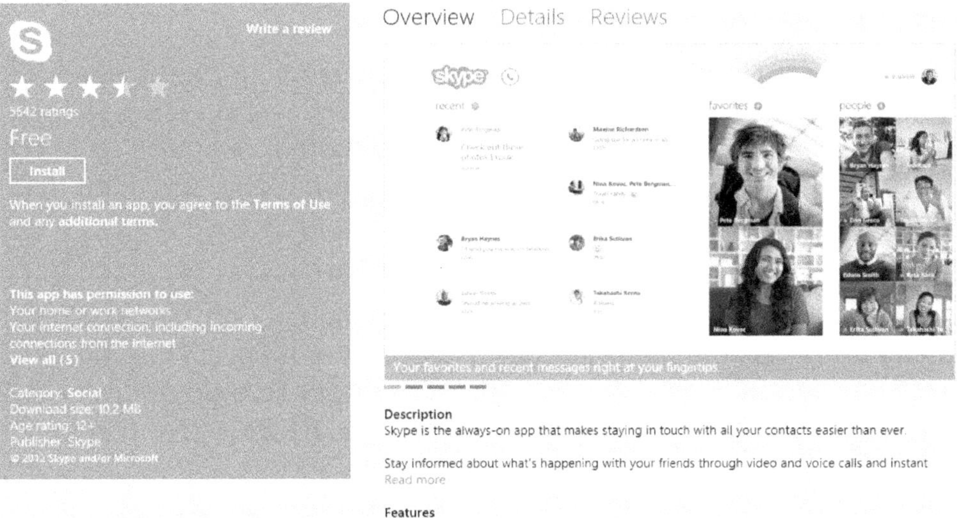

Note: *If Windows Store is being used to download an app for the first time, Microsoft account's credentials must be provided.*

5. Installed app can be executed from the **Start** screen.

Use SkyDrive

Introduction to SkyDrive

SkyDrive is a cloud service hosted by Microsoft. It allows users to store data (typically documents, images and media files) on the online data storage area that Microsoft hosts. The benefit of using SkyDrive is that the data that is stored in SkyDrive can be accessed from any PC, Tab, Smartphone, etc. around the globe, provided that device has access to the Internet and the SkyDrive app is installed on it.

SkyDrive can be used by any user who has Microsoft account, and every user gets 7 GB of free online storage space. The storage capacity on the SkyDrive can be increased by paying a few extra dollars. At the time of this writing, 25 GB of online storage in SkyDrive can be added by paying just $ 10, 50 GB of online storage in the SkyDrive can be added by paying $ 25, and 100 GB of the storage in the SkyDrive can be added by paying $ 50.

Although Windows Essential 2012 suite can be downloaded and installed to get various advanced features that SkyDrive provides, the built-in SkyDrive app that is displayed as a tile in the Start screen can serve the purpose well for home users.

When SkyDrive is initialized to be used for the first time, Windows 8 prompts users to either provide the credentials of an existing Microsoft account, or create a new one by clicking on the available link. After using the Microsoft's account to connect to the SkyDrive, users can upload their personal information. When users use separate computer or a device, they can access their data from the SkyDrive by logging to the Microsoft account and opening the SkyDrive app. Users can download the uploaded files from the online SkyDrive space.

How to Upload Documents or Images to the SkyDrive?

In order to upload documents or images to the SkyDrive, steps given below must be followed:

1. Log on to Microsoft Windows 8 computer with any account.
2. From the **Start** screen, click **SkyDrive** tile.
3. When prompted, provide the credentials for the Microsoft account.
4. On the opened window, click any container to upload the data of its corresponding category to the SkyDrive. (E.g. Pictures or Documents for images or document files respectively).
5. On the next window, right-click anywhere and from the displayed options at the bottom of the screen, click **Upload**.

Pictures on James's SkyDrive 0 items

This folder is empty. Choose Upload and pick some files, and you'll be able to access the files from anywhere.

6. From the opened window, browse for and locate the file that is to be uploaded.
7. Click to select the located file and click **Added to SkyDrive** button to upload the selected file to the SkyDrive online storage.

To download an uploaded file from the SkyDrive, follow the steps from 1 to 5, while right-clicking the desired file and clicking the **Download** button from the displayed options at the bottom left corner of the screen.

Pictures on James's SkyDrive 1 item

Use People and Messaging Apps

Introduction to People and Messaging Apps

People and Messaging are the two different apps that are displayed as tiles in the Start screen of Windows 8 operating system. Both the tiles, when accessed, allow users to connect to their friends online. When People tile is clicked, after providing Microsoft account's credentials, the app allows users to connect to various social networking sites like Facebook, LinkedIn, Twitter, etc. Likewise, when Messaging tile is clicked, after providing Microsoft account's credentials, the app allows users to communicate with their friends who are using the same app. Moreover Messaging app can also be connected to the Facebook account, which then allows users to communicate with Facebook friends as well.

How to Use People and Messaging Apps?

In order to use People and Messaging apps in Microsoft Windows 8, steps given below must be followed:

1. Log on to Microsoft Windows 8 computer with any account.
2. From the **Start** screen, click **People** or **Messaging** tile.
3. When prompted, provide Microsoft account's credentials, or create a new account.
4. Once signed in using Microsoft account, on the opened interface, click **Connected to** option from the top right corner of the screen.

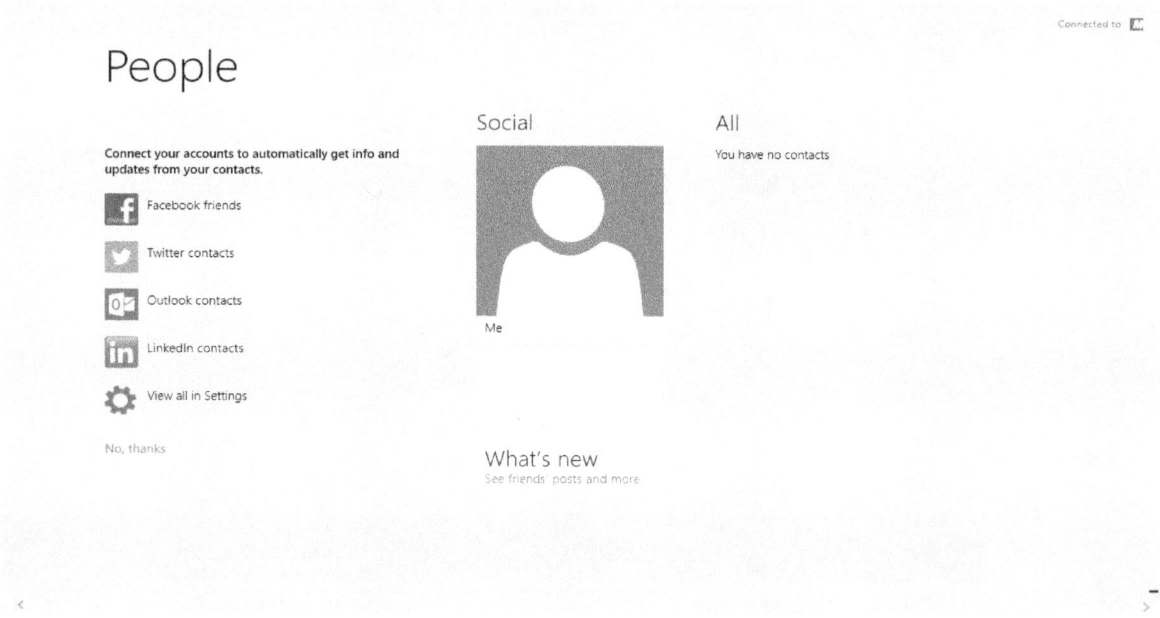

5. On the displayed **Accounts** pane in the right, click **Add an account** to add a new social networking account to communicate with friends.

Using Mail App

Introduction to Mail App

Mail is a built-in app in Microsoft Windows 8 computer that eliminates the requirement of having any third-party e-mail client application. Once Mail app is configured appropriately, all e-mail messages can be received and replied back using the app itself. In order to access Mail app for the first time, Microsoft account is required. Once users sign in to the Mail app using the Microsoft account, other e-mail accounts can also be added to eliminate the requirement of opening separate web browser tabs to access different mail accounts.

How to Use Mail App?

In order to use Mail app in Microsoft Windows 8, steps given below must be followed:

1. Log on to Microsoft Windows 8 computer with any account.
2. From the **Start** screen, click **Mail** tile.
3. On the **Add your Microsoft account** box, provide the credentials of Microsoft account, or create a new one.
4. Click **Save** to allow Windows 8 to remember the credentials for future use.
5. All emails can be viewed on the opened interface.

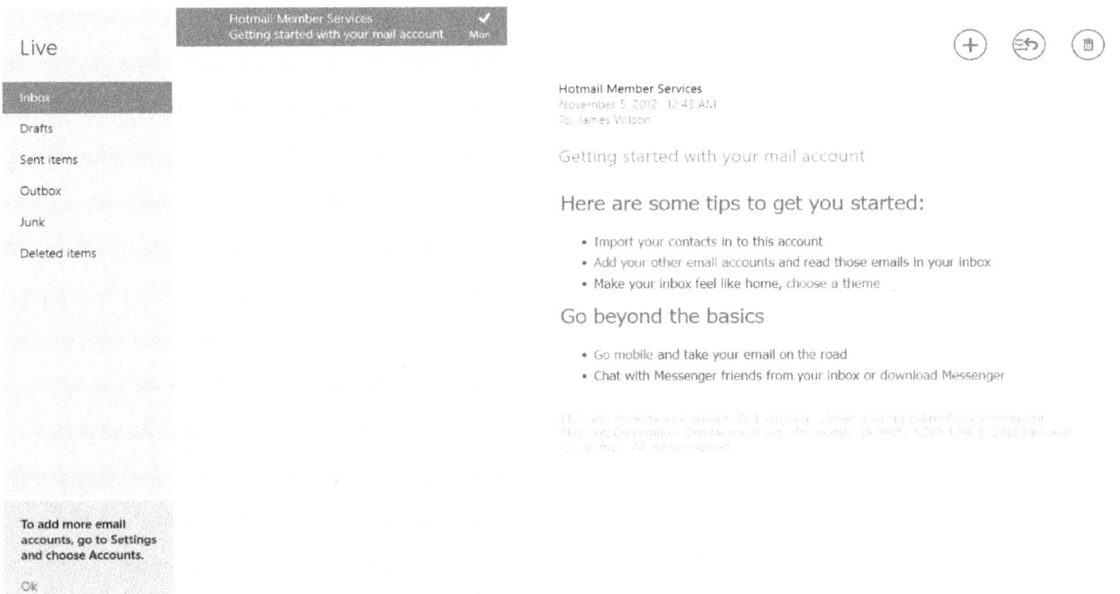

To add a new email account, follow the steps from 1 to 5 and:

1. Hover mouse to the bottom right corner of the window.
2. From the displayed options, click **Settings**.
3. On the **Settings** pane, click **Accounts**.
4. On the **Accounts** pane in the left, click **Add an account** option.
5. From the available options, click the desired email service provider and follow on-screen instructions to setup the account.

To delete an added account (Microsoft account in this case), while being on Mail app's interface, hover mouse to the bottom right corner of the screen and click **Settings** and then click **Accounts**. From the **Accounts** pane, click **Live** and from the bottom of the **Live** pane in the left, click **Remove all accounts** button. **Remove all accounts** button must be pressed two times to remove the account.

Note: *Once Microsoft account is removed from the Mail app, all the other added accounts are also removed automatically.*

Sign out from Windows Store

Introduction to Signing out from Windows Store

In order to download and install any free or paid app from Windows Store, Microsoft account's credentials must be used When Microsoft account's credentials are provided in Windows Store, Windows 8 remembers those credentials for future use. For home users this configuration is quite helpful and time-saving, whereas it might not be appropriate from the security point of view as Windows Store also contains user's payment method and other personal information.

Considering security of users' personal information and payment details, Windows 8 allows them to sign out from the Windows Store if required.

How to Sign out from Microsoft Account in Windows Store?

In order to sign out from Microsoft account in Windows Store, steps given below must be followed:

1. Log on to Windows 8 computer using the account on which Microsoft account has been used to sign in to Windows Store.
2. From the **Start** screen, click **Store** tile.
3. From the **Store** window, hover mouse to the bottom right corner of the screen.
4. From the displayed options, click **Settings**.
5. From the **Settings** pane, click **Your account**.
6. On the **Your account** window, click **Sign out** button to sign out from **Windows Store**.

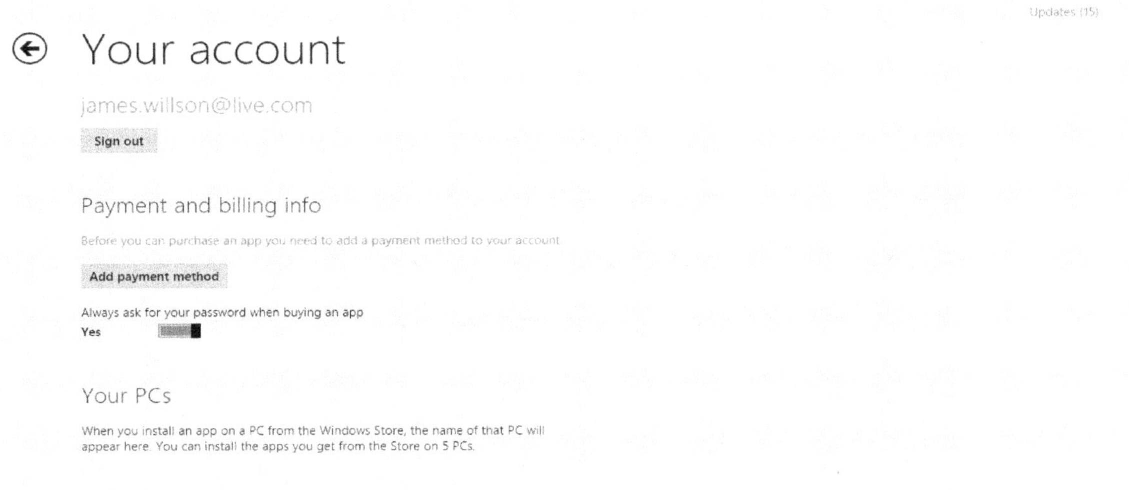

Switch Back from Microsoft Account to Local Account

Introduction to Switching Back from Microsoft Account

when local account is used to create/switch to the Microsoft account to log on to Windows 8 computer, the local account automatically gets converted to the Microsoft account, and allows users to log on to the computer using Microsoft account only. Since logging on to Windows 8 computer using Microsoft account requires active Internet connection, this method of logging on might not be appreciated by many users. In such cases users may want to switch back to the local Windows 8 account and may want to log on locally on the computer every time they want to use it. When users switch back to a local account, the account remains same however a new password is required. The process is somewhat like creating a new local user account.

How to Switch to a Local Account?

In order to switch to local account in Microsoft Windows 8, steps given below must be followed:

1. Make sure that the Windows 8 computer is connected to active Internet connection.
2. Log on to the computer using Microsoft account.
3. From the **Start** screen, over mouse to the bottom right corner of the window.
4. From the displayed options, click **Settings**.
5. From the bottom of the **Settings** pane, click **Change PC settings**.
6. On the **PC settings** window, click to select **Users** from the left.
7. From the right, click **Switch to a local account**.
8. On the next window, provide the password for the currently logged on Microsoft account.

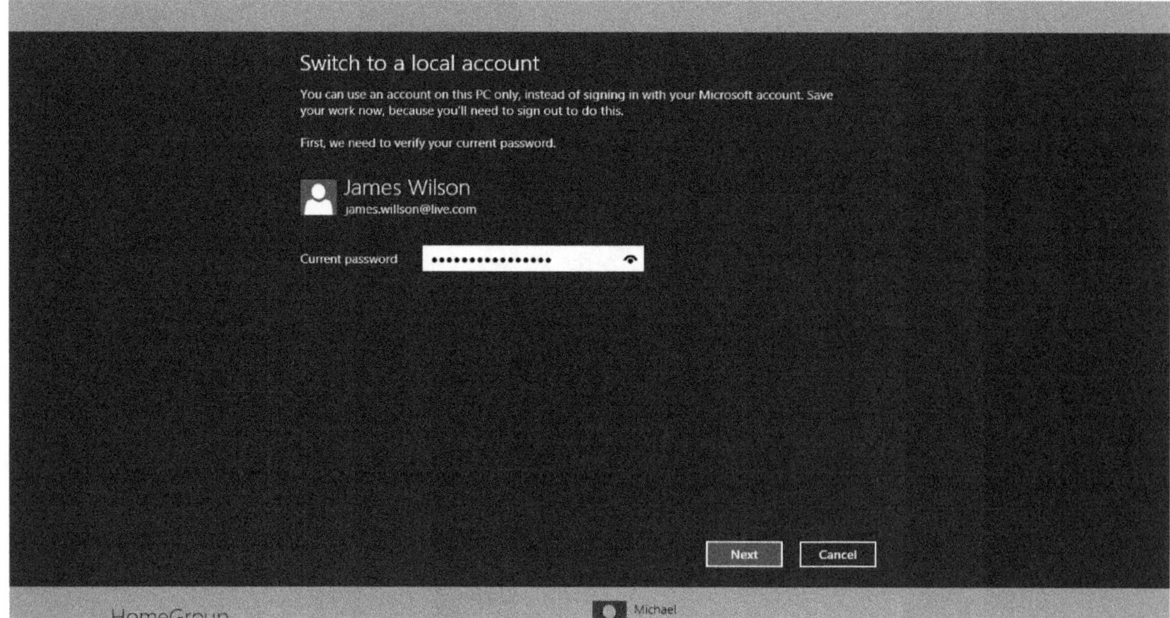

9. Click **Next** to proceed.
10. On the next window, populate the available fields with desired values and click **Next**.

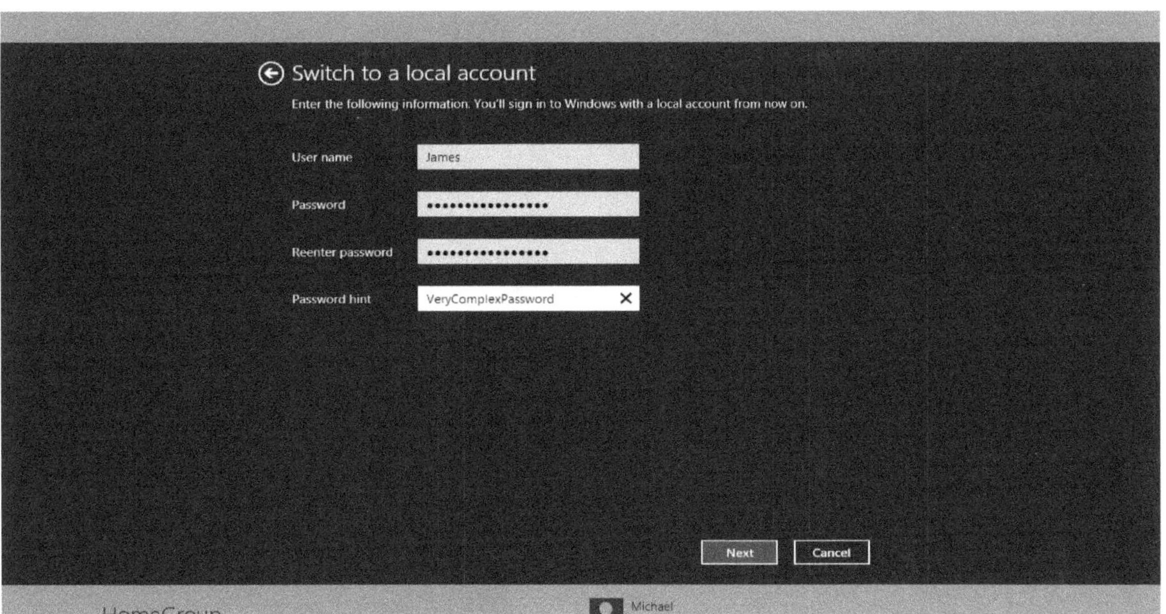

11. On the next window, click **Sign out and finish** button.

CHAPTER 5:

POWER OPTIONS

Configure Power Button

Introduction to the Power Button

Every computer system, a desktop computer or a laptop PC, on which Microsoft Windows 8 is installed has a power button which, when pressed, automatically initiates the shut-down process and shuts down the system.

Many times users might not want the computers to be shutdown when they might be in the middle of working on some files and want to leave the computers for a short period of time. In such situations, users mostly hibernate their computers or put them to the sleep mode.

Hibernating the computers or putting them to the sleep mode manually might be time taking process as compared to pressing the power button to shut down the computers. In order to save time, users can configure the power button on their computer systems so that when the button is pressed, the computers may get hibernated or go to the sleep mode. The power button can also be configured to do nothing at all when pressed.

How to Configure the Power Button?

In order to configure the power button in Microsoft Windows 8, steps given below must be followed:

1. Log on to Microsoft Windows 8 computer with the user account for which the power button is to be configured.
2. From the **Start** screen, click **Desktop** tile.
3. On the desktop screen, hover mouse to the bottom right corner of the window.
4. From the displayed options, click **Settings**.
5. On the **Settings** pane, click **Control Panel**.
6. On the opened **Control Panel** window, click **System and Security** category.
7. On the **System and Security** window, click **Power Options**.
8. On the **Power Options** window, click **Choose what the power button does** option from the left pane.
9. On the **System Settings** window, under the **Power button settings** section, choose the desired option from the **When I press the power button** drop-down list.

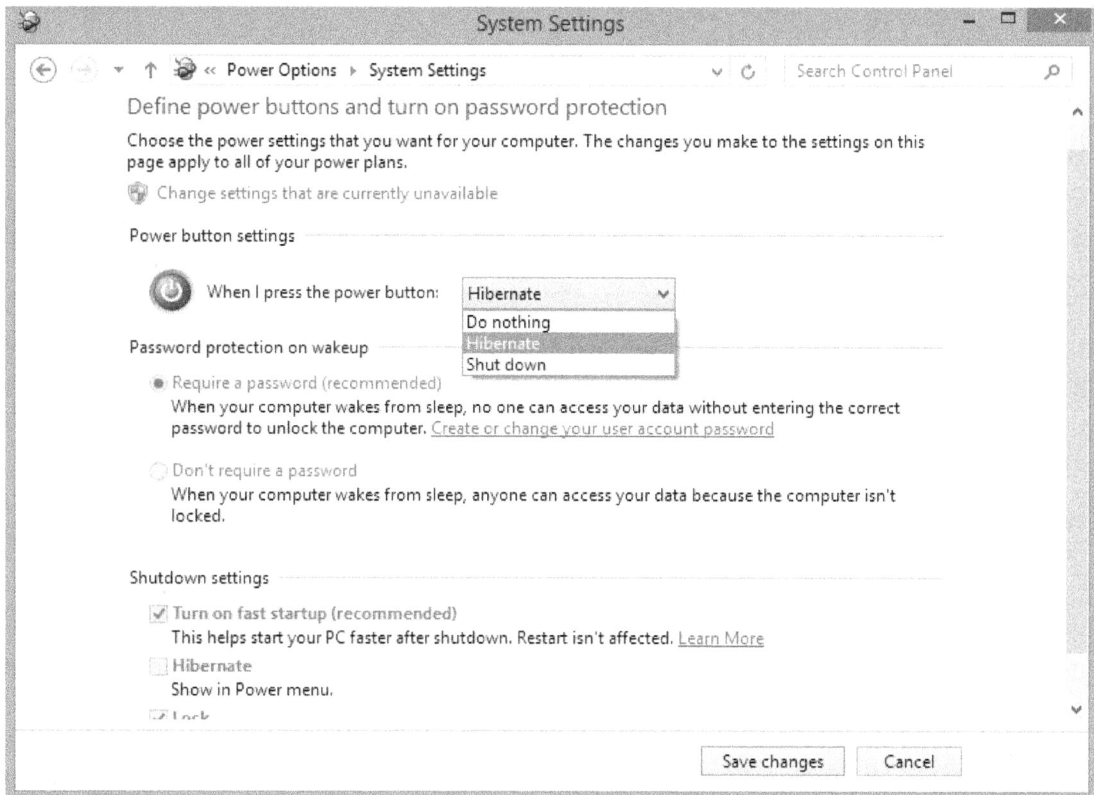

10. Once done, click **Save changes** button to save the changes.

Enable Hibernate Option

Introduction to Hibernate Option

Hibernate is a feature that has been used in Windows since quite a while. When a computer is put to Hibernate, the entire state of the current system (including opened windows and running processes) is halted and the computer is powered off. Hibernate is slightly different than Sleep mode in a way that in Sleep mode the computer is not completely powered off but remains in standby mode. When a computer is sent to Sleep mode, it wakes up and resumes its previous state only when it has been plugged in to the constant power supply. If a laptop PC runs out of battery or the desktop computer is removed from the power supply, the computer gets powered off at all its state is lost. Next time when the computer is switched on, it initiates the boot process right from the start. On the other hand when a computer is sent to Hibernate mode, the current state of the system gets paused and the computer shuts down (it can be plugged off from the direct power supply, or the battery of the laptop PC can be removed). Although, when a computer is sent to Hibernate mode it is powered off, no system hardware must be modified (e.g. RAM or other hardware devices) during that period. If hardware components of the system are modified while the computer is powered off during Hibernate mode, the computer displays error notification and initializes the boot process from the scratch when it is powered on.

In previous versions of Microsoft Windows, Hibernate option was easily visible to the users, whereas in Windows 8, the option is by default not displayed. Hibernate feature can be enabled quite easily in Windows 8 using administrative credentials. This means that enabling Hibernate feature is a global task, which when enabled using administrator account, gets enabled for all other accounts on the computer.

How to Enable Hibernate Option?

In order to enable Hibernate option in Microsoft Windows 8, steps given below must be followed:

1. Log on to Microsoft Windows 8 computer with administrator account.
2. From the **Start** screen, click **Desktop** tile.
3. From the desktop screen, hover mouse to the bottom right corner of the window.
4. From the displayed options, click **Settings**.
5. From the **Settings** pane, click **Control Panel**.
6. On the **Control Panel** window, click **System and Security**.
7. On the **System and Security** window click **Power Options**.
8. On the **Power Options** window, click **Choose what the power button does** option from the left pane.
9. On the **System Settings** window, click **Change settings that are currently unavailable** option.
10. From the enabled **Shutdown settings** section, check the **Hibernate** checkbox.

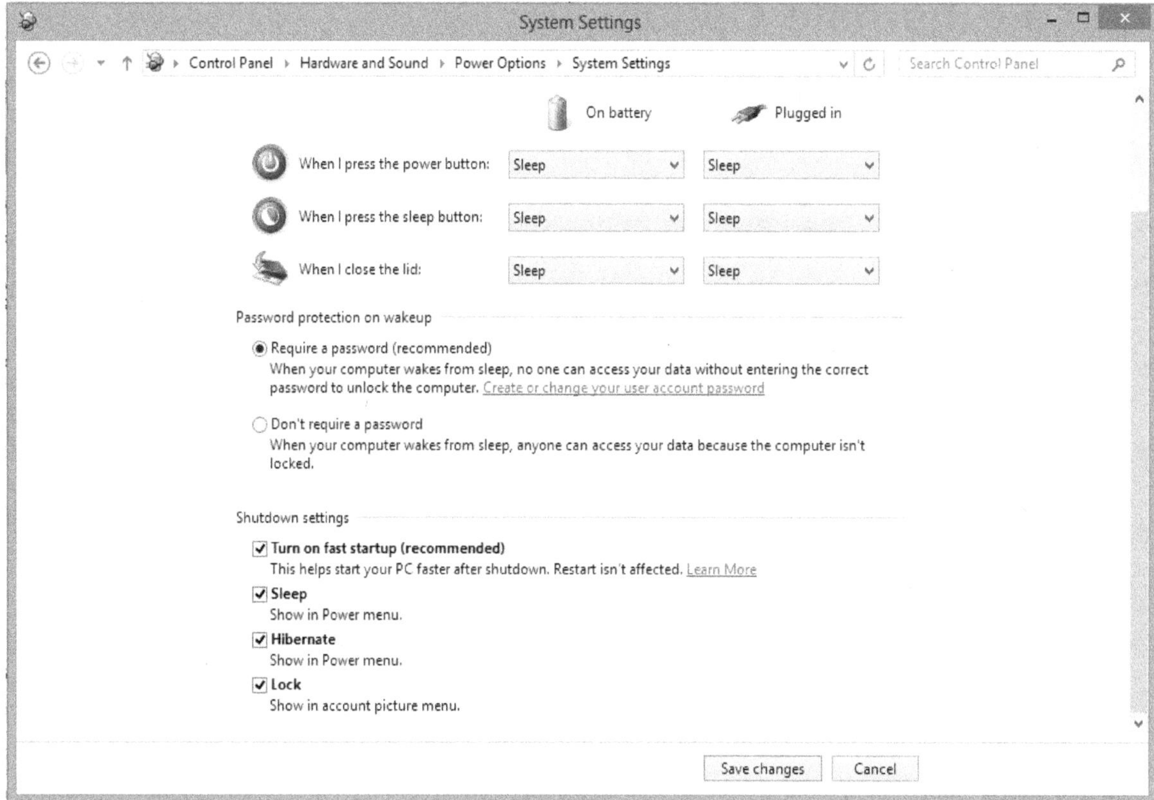

11. Click **Save changes** button when done.

Manage Power Plan (for Laptop Computers)

Introduction to the Power Plan in Laptop Computers

When Microsoft Windows 8 is installed on a laptop computer, few other options become available to the users. With the help of these additional options, the operating system can be configured to adjust the brightness of the display when the laptop is running on batteries or when it is plugged in to the direct power supply.

The default Balanced (Recommended) power plan that is automatically set when Windows 8 is installed on a laptop computer dims the brightness of the display after 2 min, turns off the display completely after 5 min, and puts the computer to sleep mode after 10 min if it detects no user interaction while running on batteries. On the other hand when the computer is connected to the direct power supply, the above mentioned time duration changes to 5 min, 10 min and 30 min respectively.

Under normal circumstances, the above mentioned settings provide optimum performance and require no modifications. However users can still customize the settings according to their personal preferences if required.

How to Modify Power Plans Settings for Laptop PCs?

In order to modify power plans settings for laptop computers, steps given below must be followed:

1. Log on to Microsoft Windows 8 computer with the user account for which the power button is to be configured.
2. From the **Start** screen, click **Desktop** tile.
3. On the desktop screen, hover mouse to the bottom right corner of the window.
4. From the displayed options, click **Settings**.
5. On the **Settings** pane, click **Control Panel**.
6. On the opened **Control Panel** window, click **System and Security** category.
7. On the **System and Security** window, click **Power Options**.
8. On the **Power Options** window, click **Change plan settings** for the desired power plan.
9. On the **Edit Plan Settings** window, choose the appropriate options from the available drop-down lists under both **On battery** and **Plugged in** categoies.Optionally, **Change advanced power settings** option can also be clicked to make appropriate changes to the selected power plan more granularly.

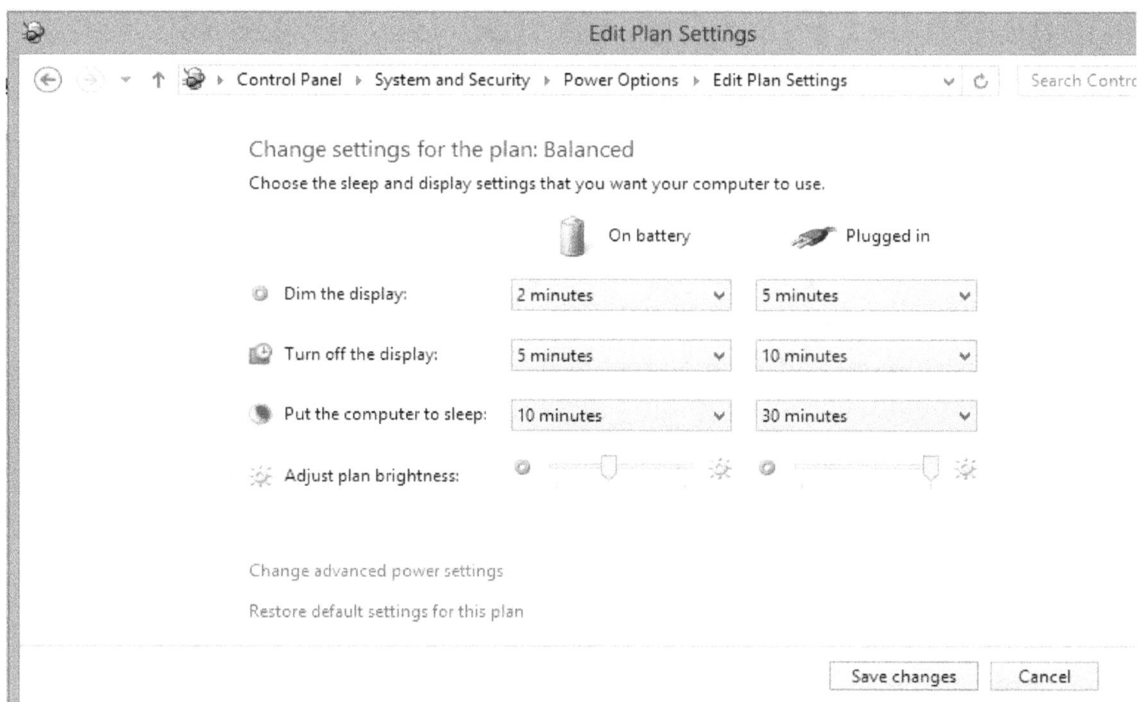

10. Click **Save changes** button when done.

Create a Custom Power Plan

Introduction to Power Plans

When Microsoft Windows 8 is installed on a computer, especially on a laptop PC, a default power plan is automatically created and set to be used. The default power plan contains the settings to provide optimum performance by adjusting brightness of the monitor, setting the dim timeout duration, setting the sleep timeout duration, setting the display turn off duration, etc.

In laptop PCs, Microsoft Windows 8 allows users to configure two types of settings in a power plan:

- **On battery** - This power plan comes into effect when a laptop starts running on batteries, i.e. it is unplugged from the direct power source. The 'On battery' settings configured in the power plan have dimmed display and shorter timeout durations of the options as compared to the settings configured for 'Plugged in'. This is done in order to provide more battery backup by adjusting the settings for reduced battery consumption.
- **Plugged in** - This power plan comes into effect when a laptop PC is directly connected to the power supply while in use. Since the laptop PC is directly connected to the power source, according to the settings configured in the power plan, the display settings and the sleep mode settings are configured to provide the brighter display and delayed sleep timeout respectively.

It is strongly recommended that in order to increase the lives of the batteries, laptop PCs must be disconnected from direct power supply once they are fully charged. If users strictly follow the recommendations, they can modify the 'On battery' settings of the power plan as per their individual choices, i.e. to get brighter display, delayed sleep timeout duration, etc. Moreover, modified settings can be saved as a new custom power plan that contains user defined power scheme.

How to Create a Custom Power Plan?

In order to create a custom power plan in Microsoft Windows 8, steps given below must be followed:

1. Log on to Microsoft Windows 8 computer with the user account for which the power button is to be configured.
2. From the **Start** screen, click **Desktop** tile.
3. On the desktop screen, hover mouse to the bottom right corner of the window.
4. From the displayed options, click **Settings**.
5. On the **Settings** pane, click **Control Panel**.
6. On the opened **Control Panel** window, click **System and Security** category.
7. On the **System and Security** window, click **Power Options**.
8. On the **Power Options** window, click **Create a power plan** option from the left pane.
9. On the **Create a Power Plan** window, click to select any of the available radio button to use its settings as the base configuration for the new power plan.

10. In the **Plan name** field, specify a name for the new power plan and click **Next**.

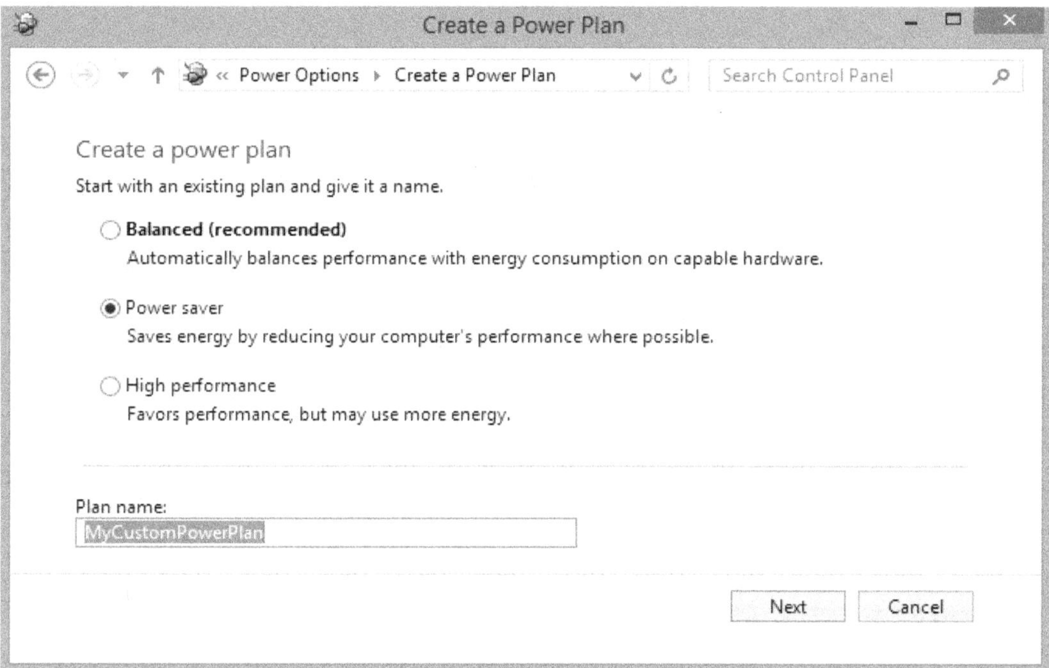

11. On the next window, choose the appropriate options from the available drop-down lists as desired.

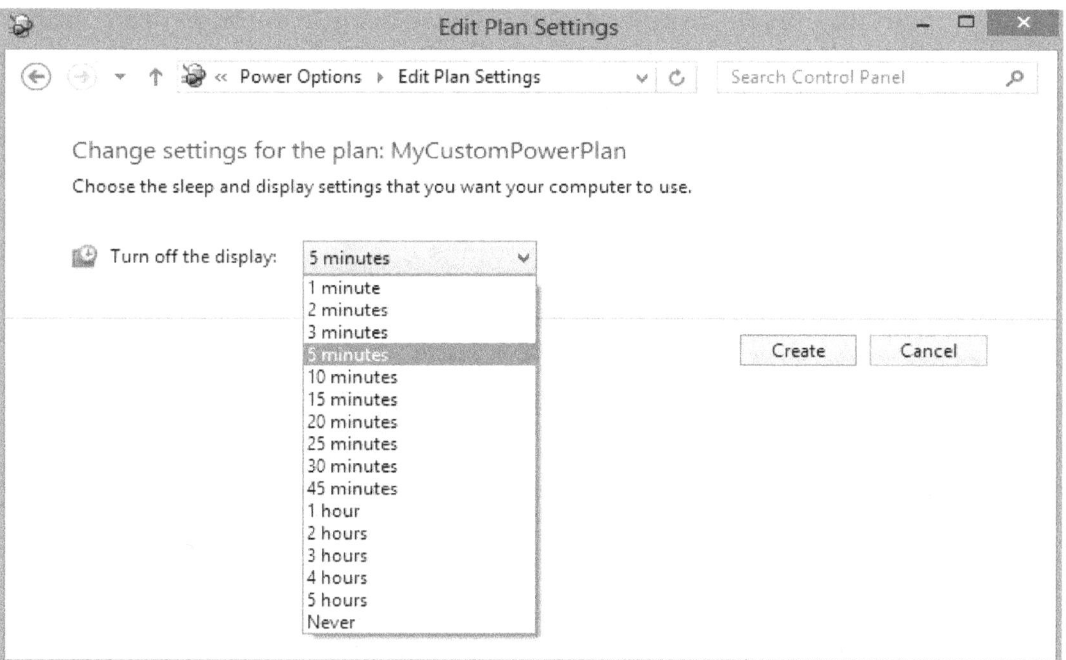

12. Once done, click **Create** button to create a new power plan with the specified settings.

Note: *Settings for the new power plan can be configured more granularly by modifying the power plan after it has been created successfully. To learn how to modify an existing power plan, previous lesson can be referred.*

Prevent Computers from Entering Sleep Mode

Introduction to Sleep Mode

As per Microsoft Windows 8's default configuration, when the operating system does not detect any user interaction for a certain amount of time, it automatically puts the computer to sleep mode. When the computer is in the sleep mode, all background services and processes stop working. Only the hard disk drive remains active and the opened applications remain in the memory. This makes the computers consume minimal power, hence saving some electricity when connected to the power supply or decreasing battery consumption while running on batteries.

Although users can bring the system out from the sleep mode by pressing the power button, the process still takes some time which might not be acceptable and/or appreciated by most users. Therefore in order to save time, users can prevent computers from entering the sleep mode.

How to Prevent Computers from Entering the Sleep Mode?

In order to prevent computers from entering the sleep mode in Microsoft Windows 8, steps given below must be followed:

1. Log on to Microsoft Windows 8 computer with the user account for which the power button is to be configured.
2. From the **Start** screen, click **Desktop** tile.
3. On the desktop screen, hover mouse to the bottom right corner of the window.
4. From the displayed options, click **Settings**.
5. On the **Settings** pane, click **Control Panel**.
6. On the opened **Control Panel** window, click **System and Security** category.
7. On the **System and Security** window, click **Power Options**.
8. On the **Power Options** window, click **Change plan settings** option for the currently applied power plan.
9. On the **Edit Plan Settings** window, from the **Put the computer to sleep** drop-down list, select **Never** option. (If Windows 8 is installed on a laptop computer, **Never** option must be selected from the drop-down lists under both **On battery** and **Plugged in** categories.)

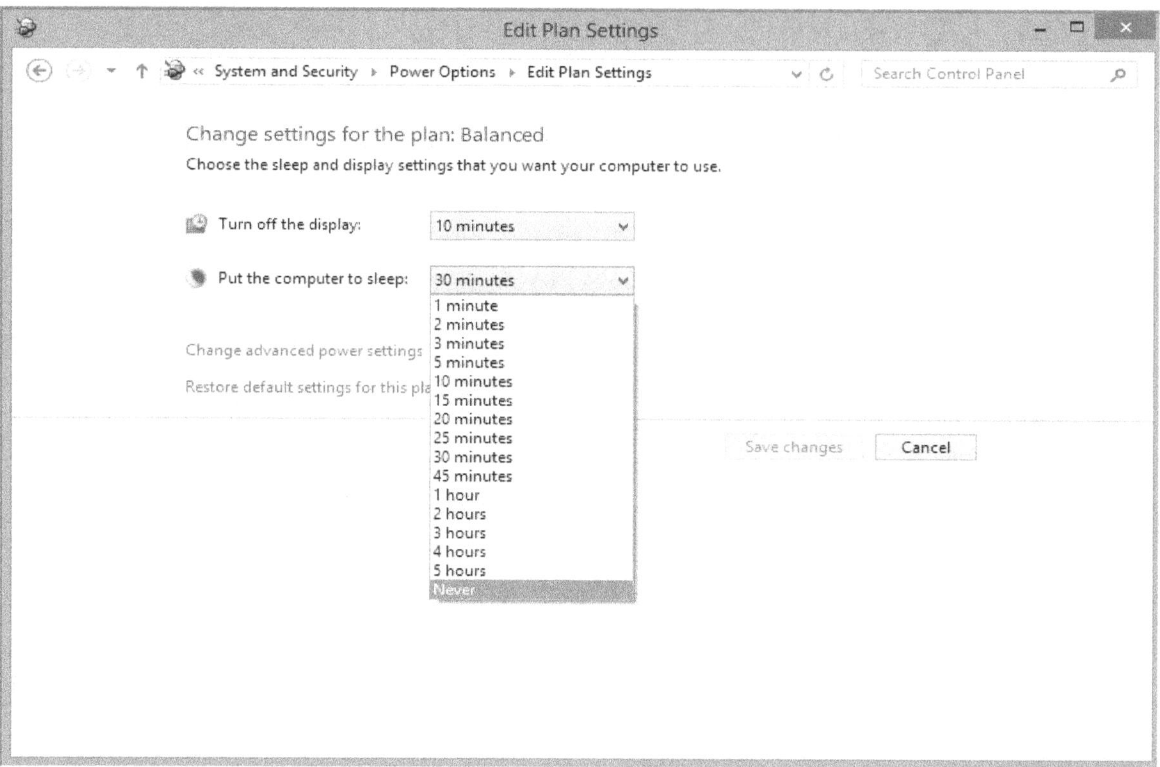

10. Once done, click **Save** changes button to save the modified settings.

To set the computer back to the default configuration, steps 1 to 10 can be followed, while selecting **30 minutes** option when on step 9.

Disable Password Requirement on Wakeup

Introduction to the Password Requirement on System Wakeup

When Microsoft Windows 8 is brought back from the sleep mode, as per the default configuration, it requests for the password of the user that was logged on to the computer before it was sent to sleep mode.

In production environments this default configuration is highly appreciated as it prevents sensitive data from getting exposed to the unwanted users. On the other hand, in homes this default nature of the operating system might be annoying for many users.

Since in homes, it is not expected that the computers would contain sensitive information, users can prevent the operating system from requesting for the password every time it comes out of the sleep mode.

How to Disable Password Requirement on System Wakeup?

In order to prevent the operating system from requesting for the password every time it comes out of the sleep mode, steps given below must be followed:

1. Log on to Microsoft Windows 8 computer with the user account for which the power button is to be configured.
2. From the **Start** screen, click **Desktop** tile.
3. On the desktop screen, hover mouse to the bottom right corner of the window.
4. From the displayed options, click **Settings**.
5. On the **Settings** pane, click **Control Panel**.
6. On the opened **Control Panel** window, click **System and Security** category.
7. On the **System and Security** window, click **Power Options**.
8. On the **Power Options** window, click **Require a password on wakeup** option from the left pane.
9. On the **System Settings** window, click **Change settings that are currently unavailable** option.
10. Under the **Password protection on wakeup** section, click to select **Don't require a password** radio button.

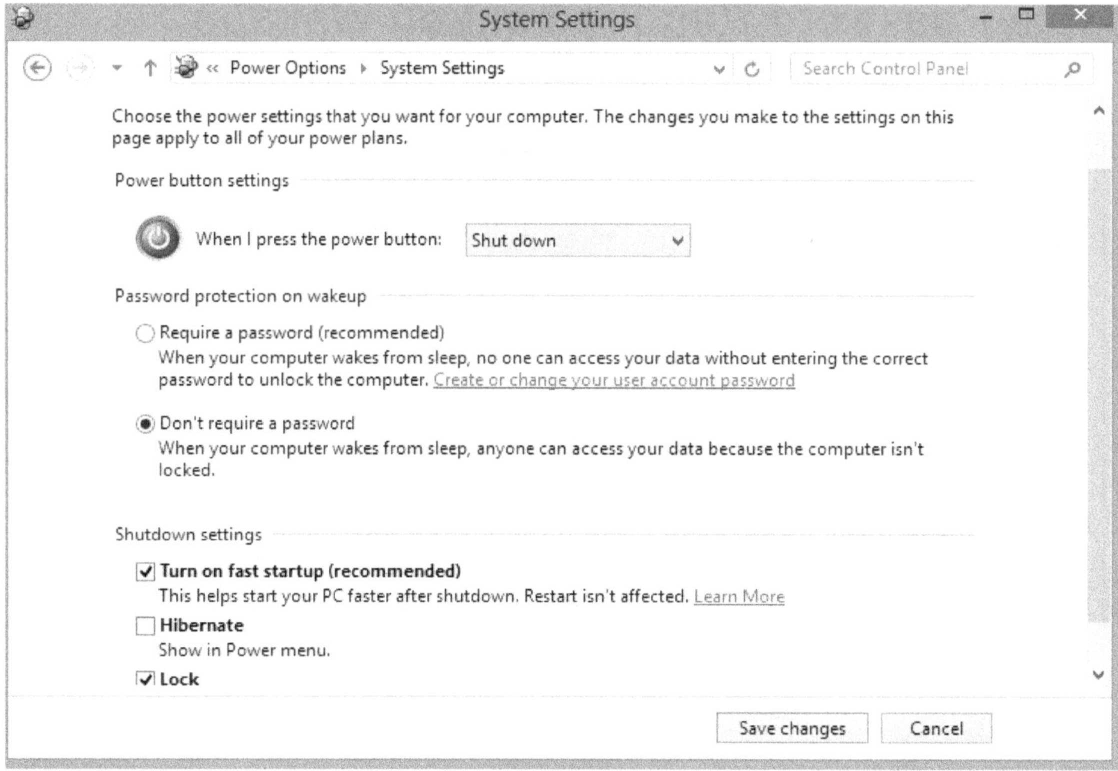

11. Click **Save changes** when done.

To set Windows back to its default configuration, steps 1 to 11 can be followed, while selecting **Require password (recommended)** radio button when on step 10.

CHAPTER 6:

MANAGE USERS & GROUPS

Create a New User Account

Introduction to New User Accounts

When Microsoft Windows 8 is installed, the installation process allows the administrators to create a user account so that they can log on to the computer using the created account. The user account that administrators create during the installation is automatically added to the Administrators group, and therefore it gets unrestricted privileges on the computer. Although a built-in Administrator account is automatically created during Windows installation, the account is kept disabled by default. The reason behind keeping the built-in Administrator account disabled by default is that the account has unrestricted privileges on the computer and no limitations of User Account Control are applicable on it. On the other hand, the user account that is created manually during the installation of Windows receives the User Account Control confirmation box every time the user tries to perform an administrative task.

Apart from the user account that is created during the installation, Windows 8 also allows administrators to create other user accounts. Additional user accounts are required when a computer is shared among multiple users. When additional user accounts are created by default they are added to the Users group and have limited and restricted privileges to the computer. If administrators want to grant unrestricted privileges to the account, they must add the new user to the Administrators group.

Irrespective of the method that administrators follow to create a user account, and irrespective of the type of user account they create, every time a user tries to perform an administrative task, User Account Control confirmation box is displayed.

How to Create a New User Account?

As mentioned above, in Microsoft Windows 8 user accounts can be created from Computer Management snap-in and through Control Panel, both the methods are discussed below:

User Account Creation from Computer Management

1. Log on to Microsoft Windows 8 computer with administrator account.
2. From the **Start** screen, click **Desktop** tile.
3. Once on the desktop screen, click **File Explorer** icon from the taskbar.
4. On the opened **Libraries** window, from the left pane, right-click **Computer**.
5. From the displayed context menu, click **Manage**.
6. On the opened **Computer Management** snap-in, under the **System Tools** category from the left pane, expand **Local Users and Groups**.
7. From the expanded list, right-click **Users** container.
8. From the displayed context menu, click **New User**.
9. On the **New User** box, populate **User name**, **Full name**, **Description**, **Password** and **Confirm password** fields with appropriate values as desired.

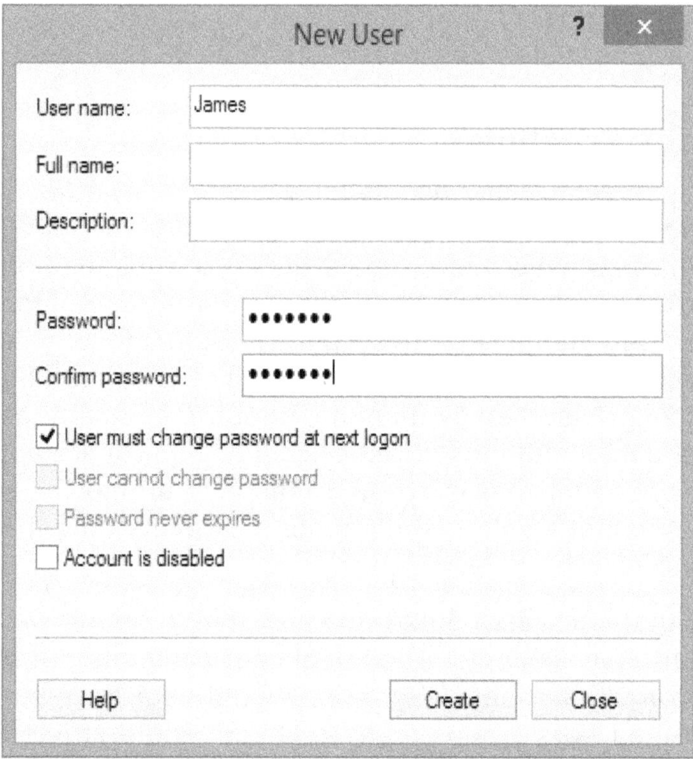

10. Click **Create** button to create the new user account.

User Account Creation from Control Panel

1. Log on to Microsoft Windows 8 computer with administrator account.
2. From the **Start** screen, click **Desktop** tile.
3. From the desktop screen, hover mouse to the bottom right corner of the window.
4. From the displayed options, click **Settings**.
5. From the **Settings** pane, click **Control Panel**.
6. On the opened **Control Panel** window, click **User Accounts and Family Safety** category.
7. On the **User Accounts and Family Safety** window, click **User Accounts** category.
8. On **User Accounts** window, click **Manage another account**.

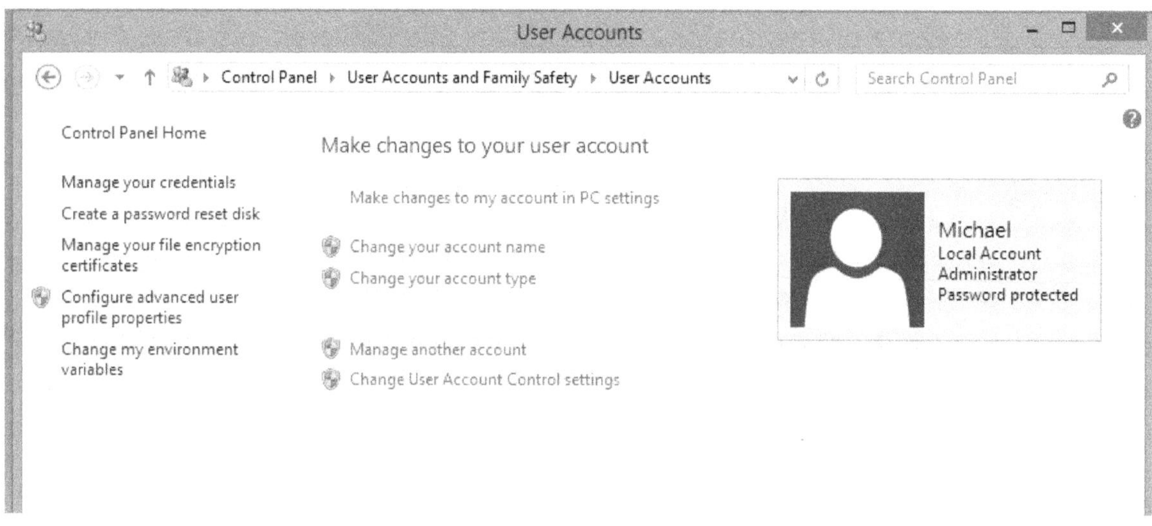

9. On **Manage Accounts** window, click **Add a new user in PC settings**.
10. On the opened **PC settings** window, ensure that **Users** category from the left section is selected.
11. From the right section, under **Other users** category, click **Add a user**.

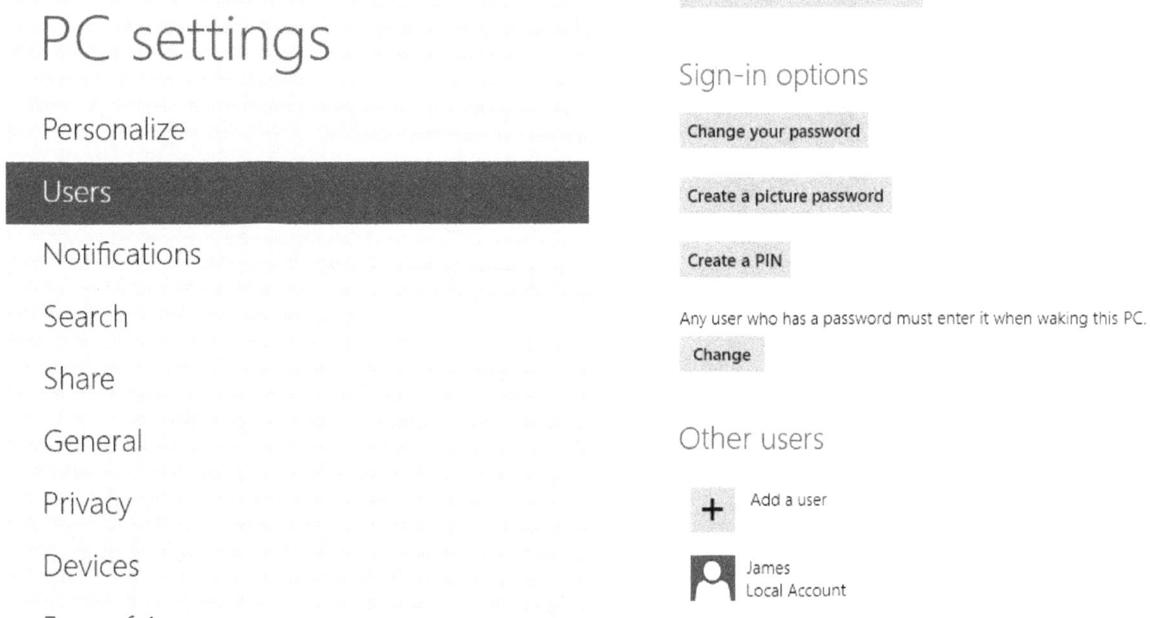

12. From the bottom of **Add a user** window, click **Sign in without a Microsoft account**.

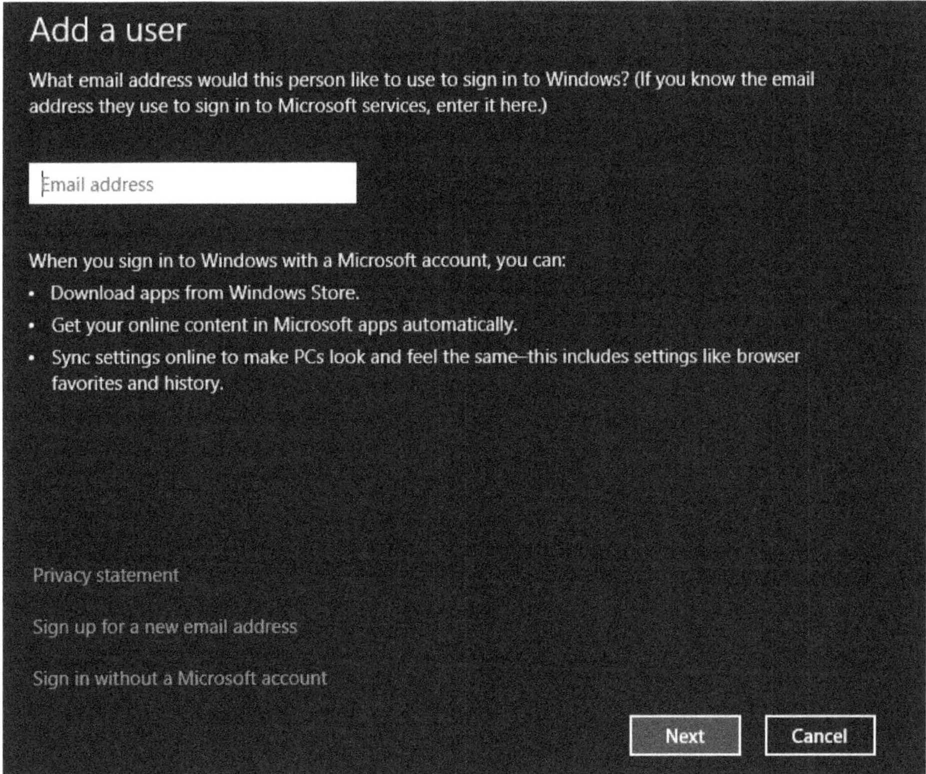

13. On the next window that appears, click **Local account** button to create a local user account on Windows 8. Alternatively, **Microsoft account** button can also be clicked to create a new Microsoft account.

14. On the next window, populate the fields with appropriate values and click **Next**.

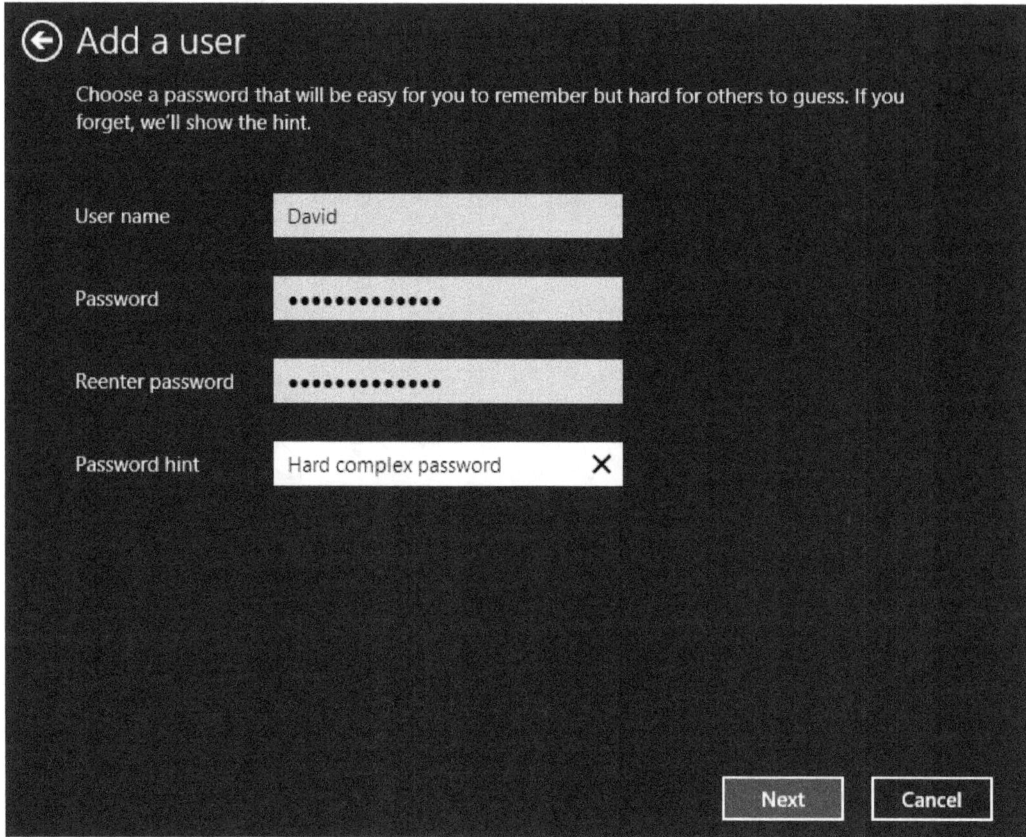

15. On the next window, click **Finish** to finalize the creation process.

Add/Remove Multiple User Accounts

Introduction to Bulk Creation and Removal of User Accounts

When Windows 8 is installed in homes, a very few user accounts are required to be created. The number of user accounts that home users create depend on the number of members that family may have. It is expected that a nuclear family has up to 4 members in it, and if it is the joint family, it may have up to 6-8 members. Keeping these numbers in mind, creating 4-8 user accounts on a computer is not a tough job and can be done quite easily. On the other hand, when Windows 8 is installed on a computer that is used in production environment where more than 20 users are expected to share the same computer, it might be a challenging task to create that many user accounts individually. Therefore in order to save time, administrators mostly create multiple user accounts in a single go by creating the batch files.

What Are Batch Files?

Batch files are like other normal text files created using any text editor, for example Notepad or Microsoft Word, but have .BAT extension. A batch file contains multiple commands that administrators want to execute as a single batch and in one session. To execute the commands that a batch file contains, the batch file must be double-clicked either normally or using elevated privileges (by right clicking the batch file and clicking 'Run as administrator' option from the context menu). The commands that a batch file contains are executed in the order they are typed in the batch file. For example if the first command in the batch file is 'MD C:\AB' and the second command is 'MD C:\CD', when the batch file is executed, the folder named 'AB' will be created before the 'CD' folder.

How to Add/Remove Multiple User Accounts?

In order to add/remove multiple user accounts with the help of batch file, steps given below must be followed:

1. Log on to Microsoft Windows 8 computer with administrator account.
2. From the **Start** screen, click **Desktop** tile.
3. On the desktop screen, hover mouse to the bottom right corner of the window.
4. From the displayed options, click **Search**.
5. From the **Apps** window, locate and click **Notepad**.
6. In the notepad, use **NET USER <USERNAME> <PASSWORD> /ADD** syntax to define command line for a new user creation, where **NET USER** is the command, <**USERNAME**> is the logon name of the new user account that is to be created, <**PASSWORD**> is the password specified for the new user account and **/ADD** is the parameter for the **NET USER** command specifying that a new user account is to be added. For example **NET USER USER001 4XFHIOP /ADD**.
7. Once done, click **File** menu in the Notepad and click **Save As**.
8. On the opened **Save As** box, in the **File name** field, specify a filename followed by **.BAT** extension. Make sure that the entire filename along with its extension is wrapped within double quotes. For example **"Create User.BAT"**.

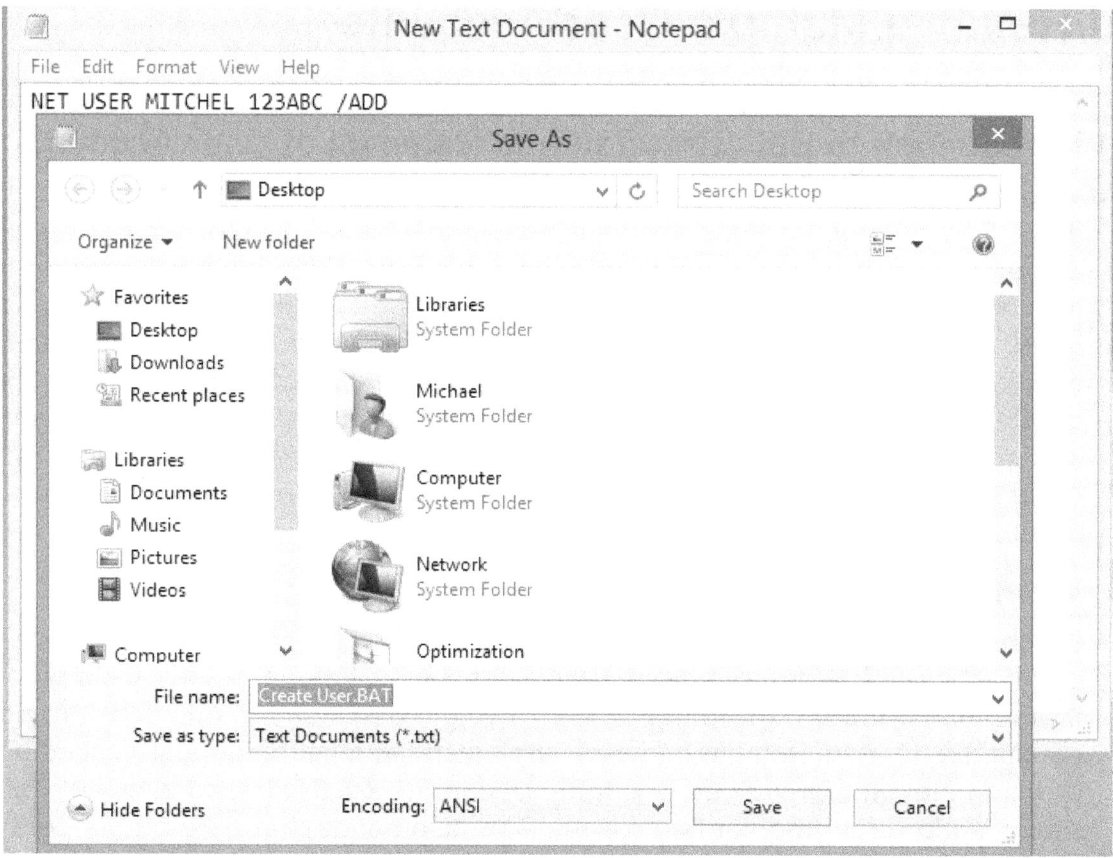

9. Click **Save** button when done.
10. Once saved, double-click the batch file to create a new user account as specified in the file.

Note: *Multiple user accounts can be created in a single go by using the batch file. The above discussed syntax must be used for each user account that is to be created. For example if five accounts are to be created with the help of batch file, the above syntax must be typed five times in the file, specifying different usernames and passwords in each command.*

Disable a User Account

Introduction to Disabling a User Account

In Microsoft Windows 8, when a new user account is created, it is enabled by default. This means that any person who knows the username and the password of the user account can log on to the computer without troubles.

Although new user accounts are created to be used by the users, in some cases a user might be on a business tour or on a long vacation and is not expected to log on the computer. In such situations, it is advisable to disable the user account so that it cannot be used or hack attempts could be made on it.

How to Disable a User Account?

In order to disable a user account in Microsoft Windows 8, steps given below must be followed:

1. Log on to Microsoft Windows 8 computer with administrator account.
2. From the **Start** screen, click **Desktop** tile.
3. Once on the desktop screen, click **File Explorer** icon from the taskbar.
4. On the opened **Libraries** window, from the left pane, right-click **Computer**.
5. From the displayed context menu, click **Manage**.
6. On the opened **Computer Management** snap-in, under the **System Tools** category from the left pane, expand **Local Users and Groups**.
7. From the expanded list, click **Users** container.
8. From the right pane, right-click the user account that is to be disabled.
9. From the context menu, click **Properties**.
10. On the user's properties box, check the **Account is disabled** checkbox.

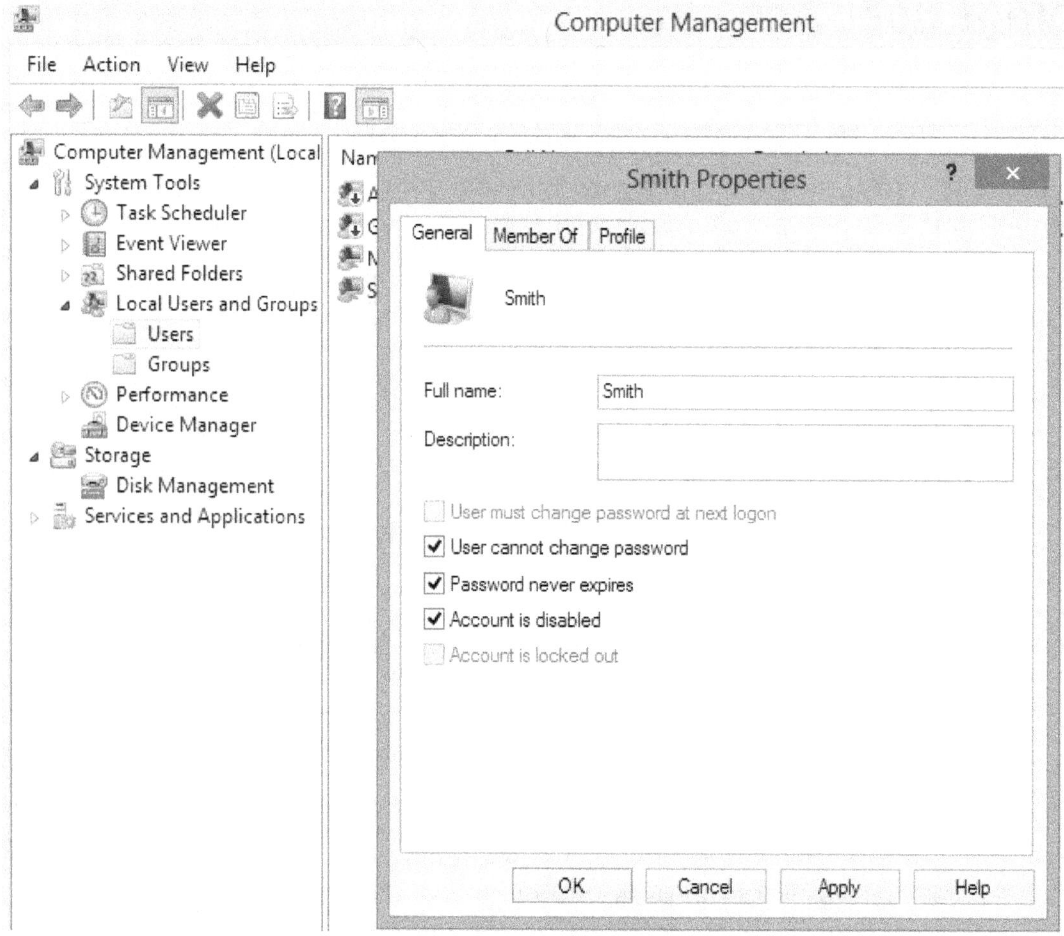

11. Click **OK** to disable the selected user account.

To re-enable a disabled user account, steps 1 to 11 can be followed, while unchecking the **Account is disabled** checkbox when on step 10.

Change Passwords

Introduction to Changing the Passwords

Security in computer field is incomplete if no passwords are specified. Even in Microsoft Windows 8, when a user account is created, the operating system strongly recommends to specify a complex password in order to protect the data from any unauthorized access.

Once a user account is created and a password is defined for the account, it is recommended that the password should be changed on a regular basis. This prevents unauthorized users from accessing the data even if they manage to know the passwords anyhow.

When a user account is created on a computer and the password for the user account is defined, the default password age is 42 days after which it expires. The operating system starts prompting the user to change the password for the account five days prior to the expiration of the password, and displays an interface from where the user can change the password. If the user does not change the password when prompted, the logon attempt is denied after password age expires.

How to Change the Password?

In order to change password for the user account in Microsoft Windows 8, steps given below must be followed:

Change Password as Administrator

1. Log on to Microsoft Windows 8 computer with administrator account.
2. From the **Start** screen, click **Desktop** tile.
3. Once on the desktop screen, click **File Explorer** icon from the taskbar.
4. On the opened **Libraries** window, from the left pane, right-click **Computer**.
5. From the displayed context menu, click **Manage**.
6. On the opened **Computer Management** snap-in, under the **System Tools** category from the left pane, expand **Local Users and Groups**.
7. From the expanded list, click **Users** container.
8. From the right pane, right-click the user account whose password is to be changed.
9. From the context menu, click **Set Password**.
10. On the opened warning box, click **Proceed** button.
11. On the next box, type the new password in **New password** and **Confirm password** fields.

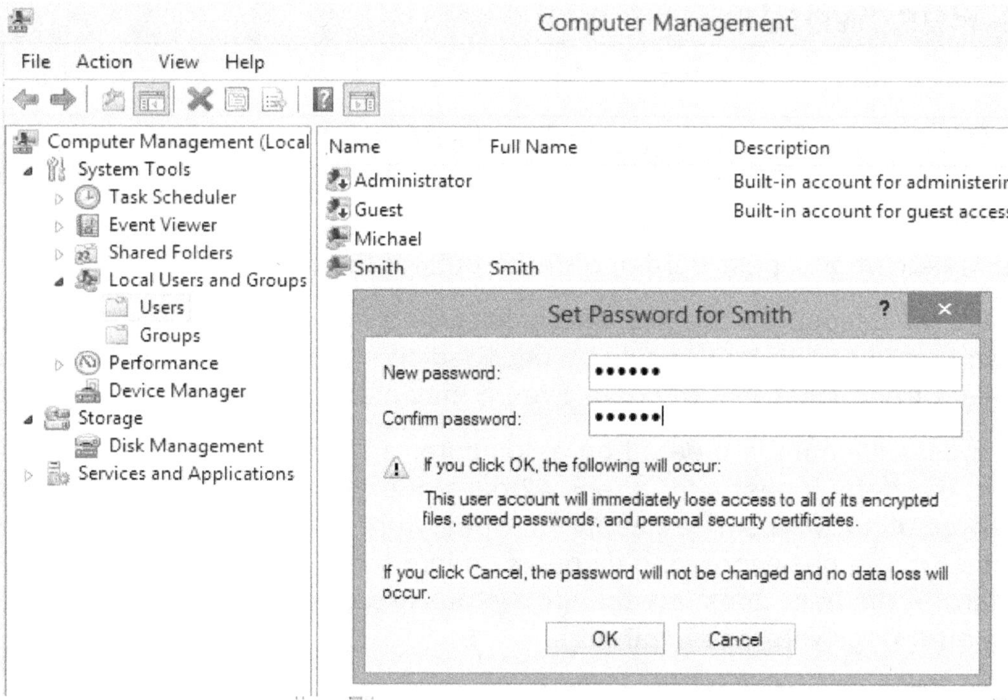

12. Click **OK** to set the new password.

Change Password as User

1. Log on to Microsoft Windows 8 computer with the user account password of which is to be changed.
2. From the **Start** screen, click **Desktop** tile.
3. On the desktop screen, hover mouse to the bottom right corner of the window.
4. From the displayed options, click **Settings**.
5. From the **Settings** pane, click **Change PC settings**.
6. On the **PC Settings** window, click to select **Users**.
7. On **Your account** window, under **Sign-in options** section, click **Change your password**.

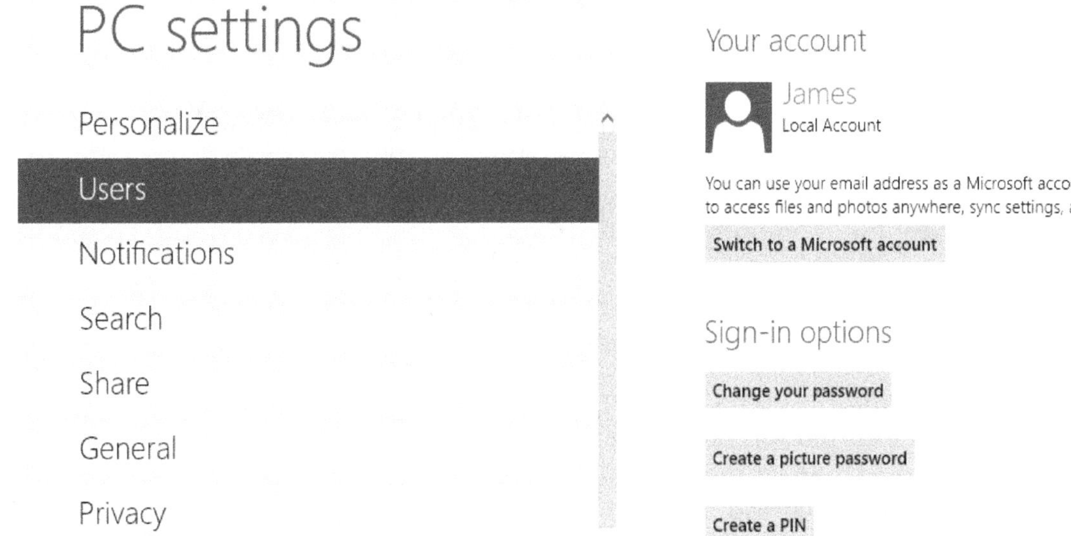

8. On **Change your password** window, type the current password in the **Current password** field and click **Next**.
9. On the next window, populate **New password**, **Reenter password** and **Password hint** fields with the appropriate values as desired and click **Next**.
10. On the next window that appears, click **Finish** to complete the process.
11. Log off from the current user account and log back in using the new password.

Note: *In order to allow a user to change password,* ***User cannot change password*** *checkbox must be unchecked in the user's properties box in* ***Local Users and Groups*** *snap-in.*

Restrict Users from Changing the Passwords

Introduction to Restriction of Changing the Passwords

In Microsoft Windows 8, when new user accounts are created from Computer Management snap-in, as per the default configuration, users must change their passwords when they logon to the computer for the very first time. This default configuration can be changed by unchecking the 'User must change password at next logon' checkbox. When the checkbox is unchecked, the two other checkboxes get enabled that allow administrators to control the password expiration and the way the users handle their passwords.

In homes, no security resections are required as the computers are not expected to contain sensitive information. Moreover, since computers in homes are accessed only by the family members, allowing or restricting users from changing the passwords becomes meaningless. However things differ when a computer is used in production environments. Although it is recommended that the passwords should be changed on a regular basis, many administrators might not want the users to change their passwords on their own.

How to Prevent Users from Changing Their Passwords?

In order to prevent users from changing their passwords in Microsoft Windows 8, steps given below must be followed:

1. Log on to Microsoft Windows 8 computer with administrator account.
2. From the **Start** screen, click **Desktop** tile.
3. Once on the desktop screen, click **File Explorer** icon from the taskbar.
4. On the opened **Libraries** window, from the left pane, right-click **Computer**.
5. From the displayed context menu, click **Manage**.
6. On the opened **Computer Management** snap-in, under the **System Tools** category from the left pane, expand **Local Users and Groups**.
7. From the expanded list, click **Users** container.
8. From the right pane, right-click the user account that is to be disabled.
9. From the context menu, click **Properties**.
10. On the user's properties box, make sure that **General** tab is selected.
11. On the **General** tab, uncheck **User must change password at next logon** checkbox.
12. Once done, check **User cannot change password** checkbox.

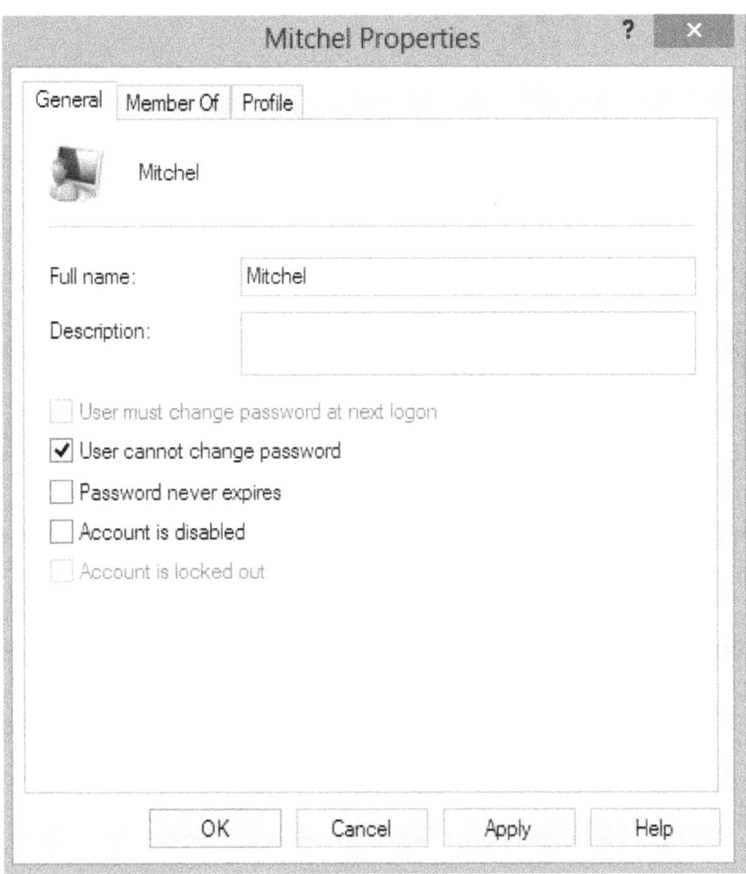

13. Click **OK** to prevent the selected user from changing the password.

To allow users to change their passwords, steps 1 to 13 can be followed, while unchecking the **User cannot change password** checkbox when on step 12.

Creating Password Reset Disk

Introduction to the Password Reset Disk

A password reset disk is a storage media that is used to reset the password of the user accounts in case users forget them. Creating a password reset disk is a user specific task and no administrative interaction or interference is required to complete the creation process. In order to create a password reset disk, a USB flash drive is required. Once a password reset disk created, it is recommended that the USB drive must be kept in a safe place so that it can be prevented from any unauthorized access.

How Password Reset Disk Works?

When a password reset disks is created, a timestamp is also added to the disk. The timestamp is the time and the date at which the password reset disks was created. When users forget their passwords, and they type the wrong passwords while logging on to the computer, the operating system suggests them to use the password reset disk to reset their passwords. When the password reset disks is connected to the computer, in the background, Windows checks for the timestamp in the reset disk with the timestamp stored in the Windows. When the two timestamps match, Windows asks users to specify the new password.

Only one password reset disk can be created for a user at a time. After creating one password reset disk, if a user creates another disk, the previously created reset disk automatically becomes invalid, and only the latest reset disk can be used to reset the password. The reason behind this is that when a second password reset disk is created, Windows updates its timestamp and adds the same timestamp to the new password reset disk. When the user connects the old password reset disk to reset the password, the timestamp does not match and therefore Windows denies the password reset request.

How to Create a Password Reset Disk?

In order to create a password reset disk in Microsoft Windows 8, steps given below must be followed:

1. Log on to Microsoft Windows 8 computer with any account.
2. Make sure that a blank floppy disk is inserted in the available floppy disk drive.
3. From the **Start** screen, click **Desktop** tile.
4. On the desktop window, hover mouse to the bottom right corner of the screen.
5. From the displayed options, click **Settings**.
6. On the **Settings** pane, click **Control Panel**.
7. On the **Control Panel** window, click **User Accounts and Family Safety** category.
8. On the **User Accounts and Family Safety** window, click **User Accounts** category.
9. On the **User Accounts** window, click **Create a password rest disk** from the left pane.
10. On **Welcome to the Forgotten Password Wizard** box, click **Next**.

11. On **Create a Password Reset Disk** box, make sure that **Floppy Disk Drive (A:)** option is selected in the **I want to create a password key disk in the following drive** drop-down list and click **Next**.

12. On the **Current User Account Password** window, type the current password for the logged on user account in the available field.

13. Click **Next** to proceed.
14. On **Creating Password Reset Disk** box, wait till the creation process completes successfully and click **Next** when done.

15. On **Completing the Forgotten Password Wizard** box, click **Finish**.

Set Curfew

Introduction to Curfew

Setting curfew in Microsoft Windows 8 is a process in which administrators can specify the time at which users can log on to the computers using their credentials. In case users try to logon at the time that is not specified by the administrators, they receive an error message and their logon attempts fail.

In earlier days, logon time restriction was only possible in the network operating systems, such as Microsoft Windows Server 2003, and that too when they were promoted as the domain controllers. Moreover, logon time restriction was only applicable on the domain user accounts.

With the release of Microsoft Windows Vista and above operating systems (including Microsoft Windows 8), even the client operating systems can now be configured to prevent local user accounts from logging on to the computers after or before certain hours. For example if parents want that their kids should not be able to logon to the computers before 2 PM in the afternoon and after 10 PM the night from Monday to Friday, they can configure the Windows accordingly.

Curfew can be set only on standard user (non-administrator) account. Windows 8 does not allow one administrator of a computer to set curfew restrictions for other administrator accounts of the computer.

How to Set Curfew?

In order to set curfew Microsoft Windows 8, steps given below must be followed:

1. Log on to Microsoft Windows 8 computer with administrator account.
2. From the **Start** screen, click **Desktop** tile.
3. On the desktop screen, hover mouse to the bottom right corner of the window.
4. From the displayed options, click **Settings**.
5. On the **Settings** pane, click **Control Panel**.
6. On the **Control Panel** window, click **Set up Family Safety for any user** option available under **User Accounts and Family Safety** category.
7. On the **Family Safety** window, click the user account for which curfew is to be set.
8. On the **User Settings** window, click to select **On, enforce current settings** radio button under **Family Safety** section.
9. Click **Time limits** option available under the **Windows settings** section.

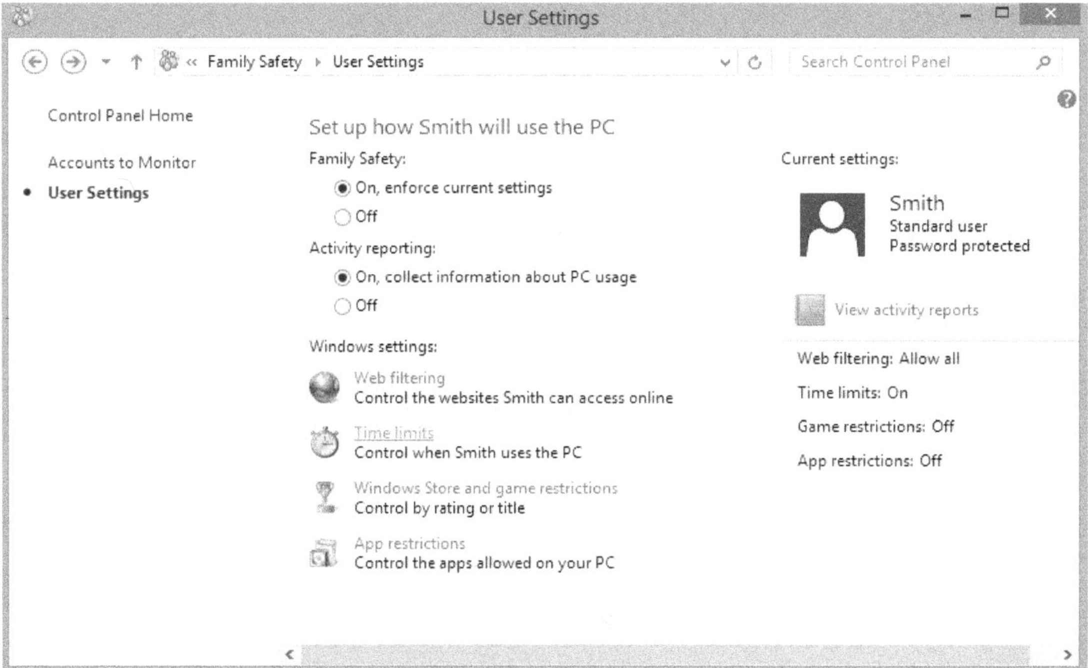

10..On the **Time Limits** window, click **Set curfew** option under the **Set the time of day <username> can use the PC** section.

11. On the next window, click to select **<username> can only use the PC during the time ranges I allow** radio button.

12. On the displayed graph, click and drag the mouse over the squares representing the hours when the selected user is to be allowed to log on to the PC. Dragging the mouse horizontally specifies the logon hours of the day and dragging it vertically specifies the days of the week.

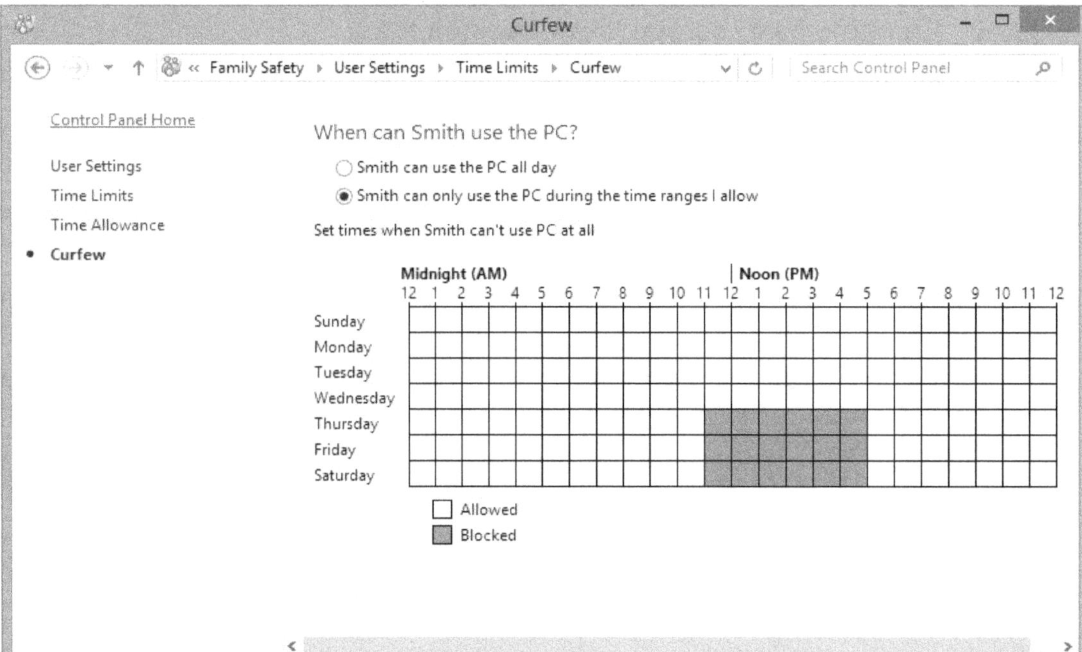

Note: *Hours when the selected user is allowed to log on to the PC is displayed in blue color, whereas the hours when the user account is restricted from using the computer is displayed in white color in the graph.*

Specify Time Allowance for User Account

Introduction to Time Allowance

Time Allowance is a new feature introduced in Microsoft Windows 8. Time Allowance allows administrators to configure the total amount of time for which a user can use the PC in a day. This means that when a standard user (non-administrator) account is configured accordingly, user can use the PC for the specified hours only. For example if the administrators have specified that user 'A' can use Windows 8 computer only for three hours every day, user 'A' will be allowed to log on to the computer only for three hours in every 24 hours, irrespective of the hour of the day. This further means that user 'A' can use the PC for one hour in the morning, one are in the afternoon and one are in the evening. Once time allowance period of user 'A' (three hours in this example) is over, the user cannot log on to the computer whatsoever.

Moreover, while specifying logon time allowance, administrators can specify separate hours for weekdays and weekends. Windows 8 counts the weekdays from Mondays to Fridays of every week, and Saturdays and Sundays of every week as the weekends. Specific log on time allowance can be configured more granularly on per weekday and/or weekend basis by clicking the down buttons at the left of 'Weekdays' and 'Weekend' categories.

Time Allowance can be configured only on standard user (non-administrator) account. Windows 8 does not allow one administrator of a computer to set Time Allowance restrictions for other administrator accounts of the computer.

How to Specify Time Allowance?

In order to specify time allowance in Microsoft Windows 8, steps given below must be followed:

1. Log on to Microsoft Windows 8 computer with administrator account.
2. From the **Start** screen, click **Desktop** tile.
3. On the desktop screen, hover mouse to the bottom right corner of the window.
4. From the displayed options, click **Settings**.
5. On the **Settings** pane, click **Control Panel**.
6. On the **Control Panel** window, click **Set up Family Safety for any user** option available under **User Accounts and Family Safety** category.
7. On the **Family Safety** window, click the name of the user account on which time allowance is to be applied.
8. On the **User Settings** window, click to select **On, enforce current settings** radio button.
9. Click **Time limits** option from the **Windows settings** section.
10. On the **Time Limits** window, click **Set time allowance** option under the **Set the number of hours <username> can use the PC per day** section.

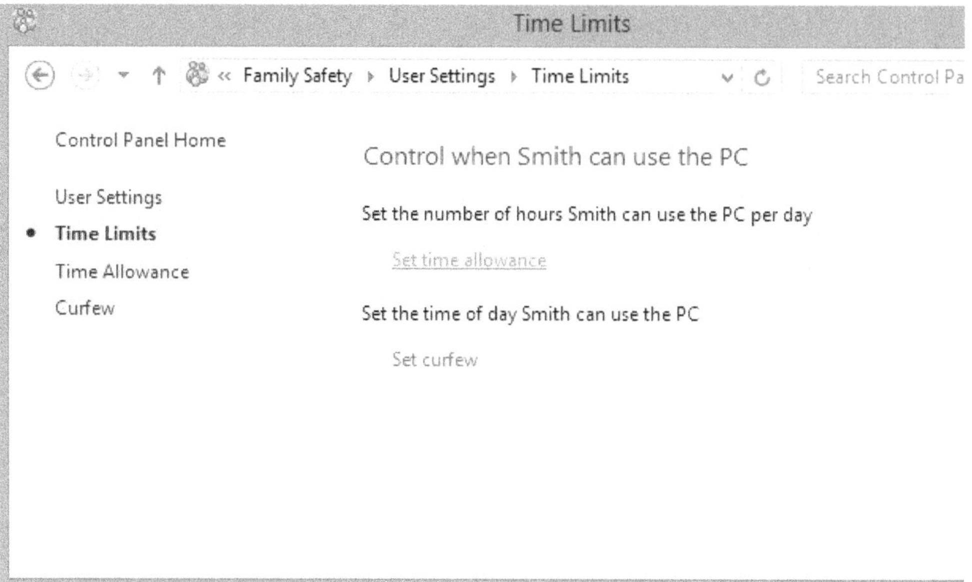

11. On the next window, click to select **<username> can only use the PC for the amount of time I allow** radio button.
12. On the displayed **Weekdays** and **Weekend** fields, specify the amount of time in hours and minutes when the selected user can use the computer. Optionally down button available at the left to **Weekdays** and **Weekend** can also be clicked to specify time allowance for the selected user on per day of the weekday and/or weekend basis.

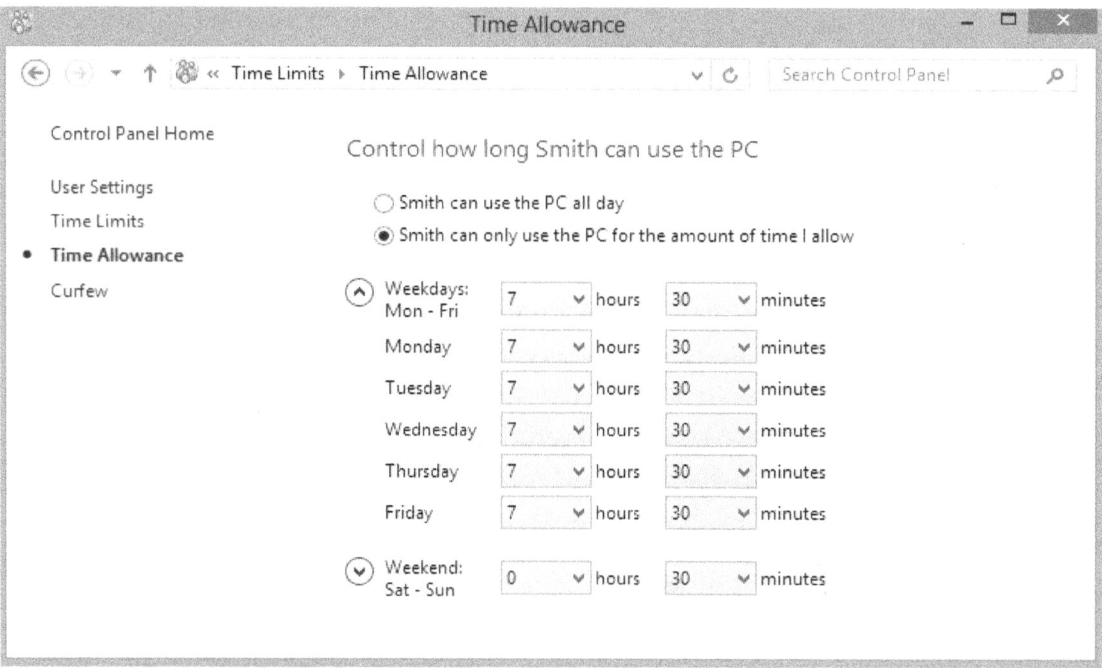

13. Once done, close all the opened windows.

Enable Automatic User Logon

Introduction to Automatic User Logon

In earlier versions of Windows, for example in Windows 98, users were logged on to their accounts as soon as the computers started. In Microsoft Windows 2000, the installation process used to ask the installers if they wanted to allow the administrator account to log on to the computers without requesting for the password. If the installers allowed the administrator account to log on to the computers without requesting for the password, as soon as they used to start the computers, they were automatically logged on to their accounts and their desktop screens were displayed. On the other hand, in post Windows 2000 operating systems, including Microsoft Windows 8, users are required to provide their passwords in order to log on to their accounts.

The installation process of Microsoft Windows 8 allows the installers to create a user account that is automatically added to the Administrators group and gets unrestricted privileges on the computer. The installation process also recommends that the created user account must be protected by a strong password. In case no password is specified to the account, the user is automatically logged on to the computer as soon as the operating system boots. When multiple accounts are created on Windows 8, a logon screen is displayed, from where users can select an account to log on.

As mentioned above, if there is only one user account available in Windows 8 and is protected with the password, users are required to provide the password before they can log on to the Windows. However if users want, they can bypass this step by enabling auto logon from the registry.

When auto logon is enabled, irrespective of the number of user accounts Windows 8 may have, and irrespective of the passwords user accounts may be protected with, the account name that was specified while enabling the auto logon automatically logs on to the computer as soon as Windows starts.

How to Enable Automatic User Logon?

In order to enable automatic user logon in Microsoft Windows 8, steps given below must be followed:

1. Log on to Microsoft Windows 8 computer with administrator account.
2. From the **Start** screen, click **Desktop** tile.
3. Once on the desktop screen, press **Windows** + **R** keys simultaneously to initiate **Run** command box.
4. In the **Run** command box, type **REGEDIT** command and press **Enter** key.
5. On the **User Account Control** confirmation box, click **Yes** button to provide the consent to open **Registry Editor**.
6. On the opened **Registry Editor**, from the left pane, locate **HKEY_LOCAL_MACHINE\SOFTWARE\Microsoft\Windows NT\CurrentVersion\Winlogon**.
7. Keeping **Winlogon** selected in the left pane, right-click **AutoAdminLogon** from the right pane.

8. From the displayed context menu, click **Modify**.
9. On the opened **Edit String** box, under **Value data** field, replace the default value **0** with **1** and click **OK** button to close the box.

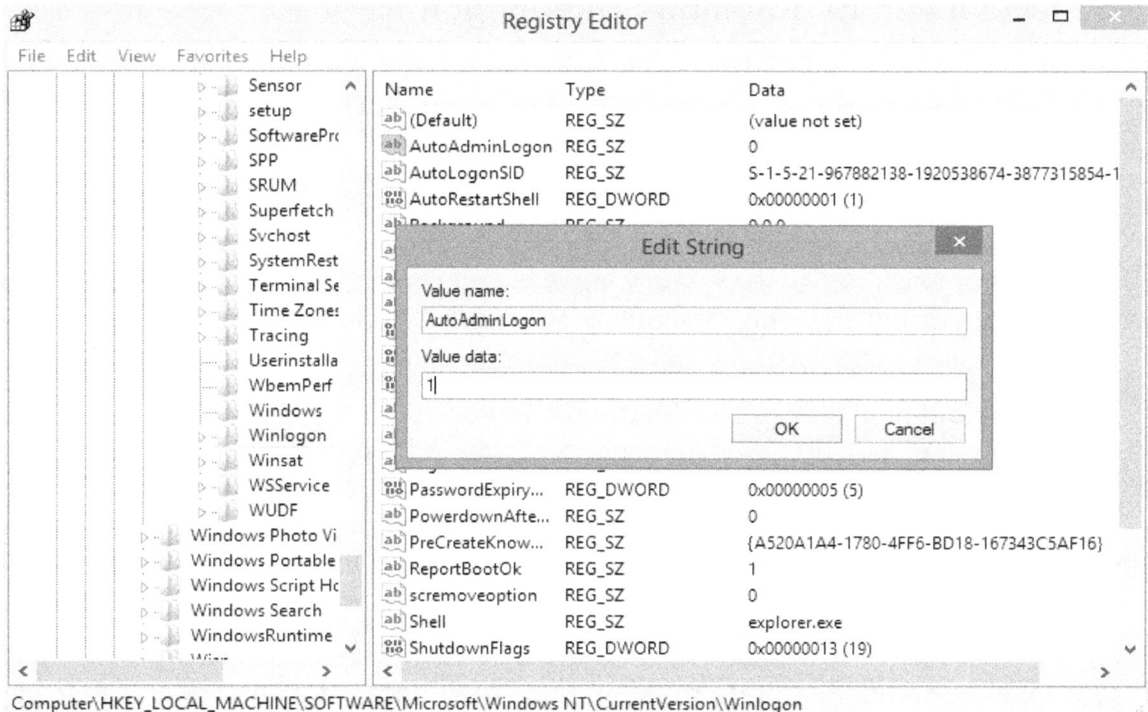

10. Being on the same interface, double-click **DefaultUserName** string from the right pane.
11. On the opened **Edit String** box, in the **Value data** field, type the logon name of the user account that is to be logged on automatically when the computer starts.

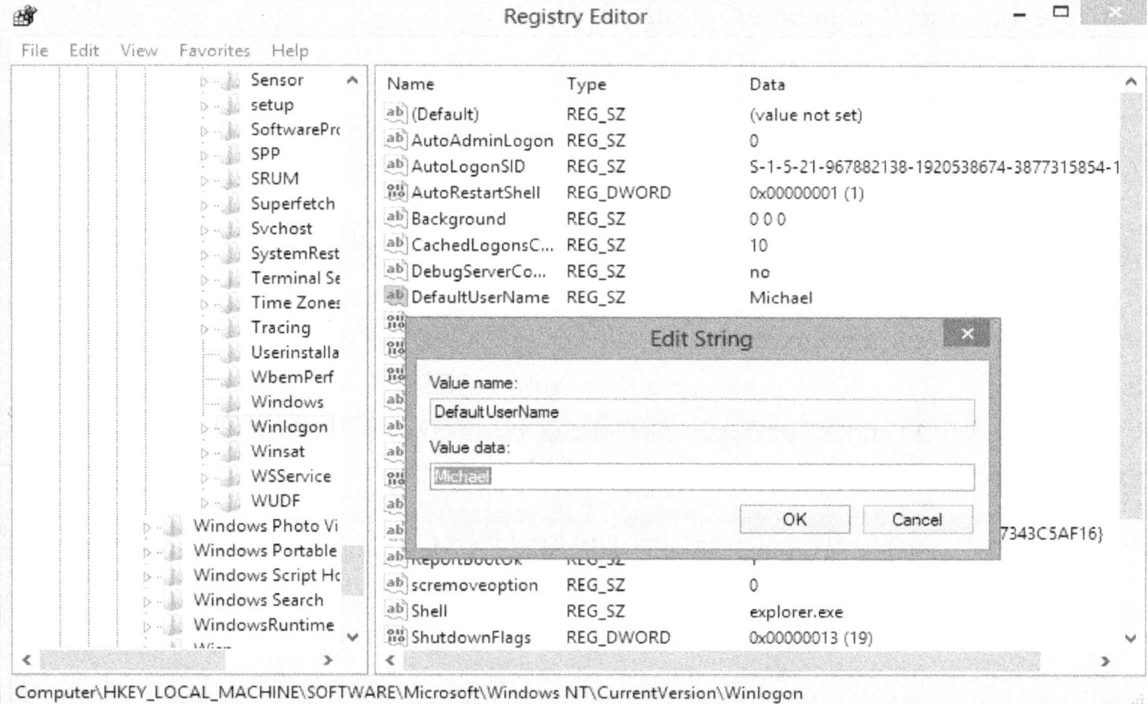

12. Click **OK** when done to close the box.
13. Right-click anywhere on the same interface in the right pane.
14. From the displayed context menu, go to **New** and from the displayed submenu, click **String Value**.
15. Rename the newly created string as **DefaultPassword** and double-click the renamed string.
16. On the **Edit String** box, in the **Value data** field, type the password for the user account for which automatic logon is to be enabled.
17. Click **OK** to save the changes.
18. Finally close the **Registry Editor** and restart the computer to allow the changes to take effect.

To disable automatic user logon, steps 1 to 9 can be followed, while replacing 1 in the Value Data field with 0 and clicking **OK** when done. Once the modifications are done, restart the computer to allow the changes to take effect.

Disconnect Other Logged on Users

Introduction to Other Logged on Users

With the release of Microsoft Windows XP, the concept of fast user switching was also introduced in the operating systems. Because of fast user switching, users are allowed to logon to other accounts on the same computers (if they have appropriate credentials) without logging off from the currently logged on account.

Fast user switching eliminates the requirement of closing all the opened applications and files before another user logs on to the computer. For example if user A is working on a computer and have opened several files at the time, and at the same time B enters the room and requests to use the PC for a short while because of some urgent work. In such case, user A needs not to close the files that were opened. Instead, fast user switching can be used to allow B to logon to his account without logging off from the A account.

Disadvantages of Fast User Switching

One disadvantage of fast user switching is that after users have completed their tasks, it is quite likely that they might forget to log off from their accounts, which might reduce the system performance. When this is the case, the administrator of Windows 8 computer can terminate the sessions of other logged on users, hence enforcing them to log off from the computer.

How to Disconnect Other Logged on Users?

In order to disconnect other logged on users from Microsoft Windows 8, steps given below must be followed:

1. Log on to Microsoft Windows 8 computer with administrator account.
2. From the **Start** screen, click **Desktop** tile.
3. From the desktop screen, right-click the taskbar.
4. From the displayed context menu, click **Task Manager**.
5. From the bottom of the **Task Manager** window, click **More details**.
6. From the displayed expanded options, go to **Users** tab.
7. From the displayed logged on users' list, right-click the one that is to be logged off forcefully.
8. From the context menu, click **Sign off**.

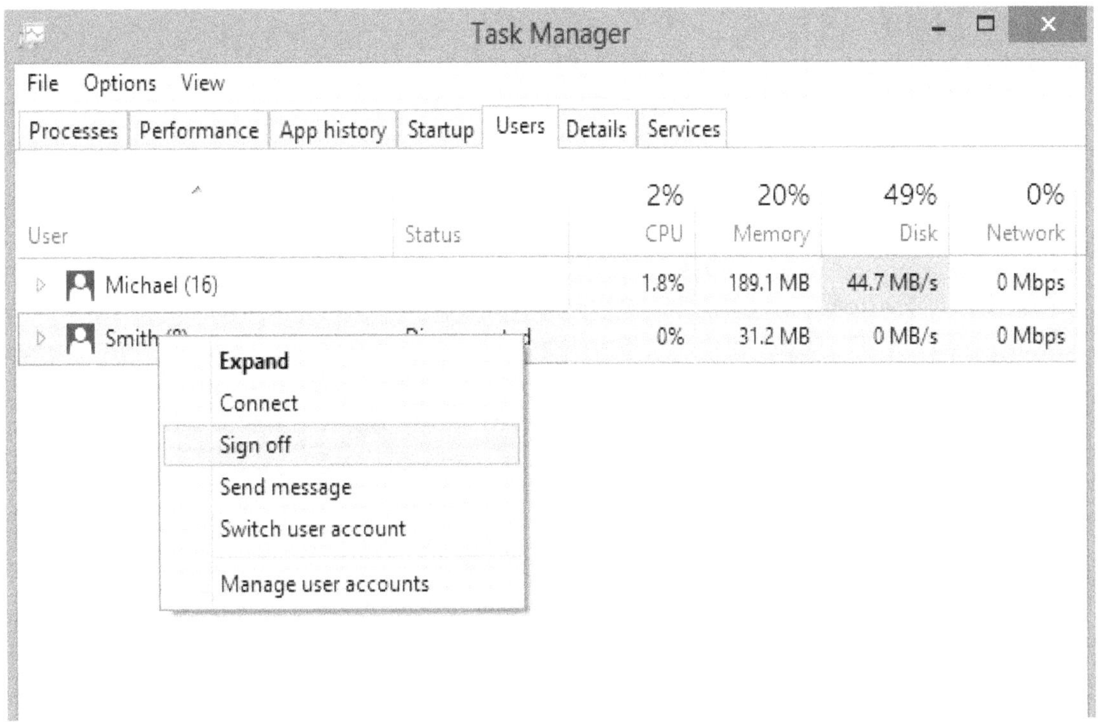

9. On the displayed confirmation box, click **Sign out user** button to forcefully log off the selected user.
10. Close the **Task Manager** box when done.

Create a New Group

Introduction to Groups

In Microsoft Windows 8, 'Groups' work as the containers that hold multiple user accounts in them. When administrators want to set NTFS or shared permissions on multiple user accounts, instead of setting the permissions on each user account individually, they create a new 'Group' and add all user accounts in it. Once all the accounts are added to the 'Group', all NTFS and shared permissions can be assigned to that 'Group'. NTFS or shared permissions assigned for a 'Group' on an object are always inherited by the child objects that the parent object contains, until administrators block inheritance on them individually.

Types of Groups

There are three types of groups in Microsoft Windows 8. The types of 'Groups' are:

- **Built-In Groups** - These 'Groups' are automatically created when Microsoft Windows 8 is installed on a computer. All built-in 'Groups' have different level of permissions and privileges by default set on them. Every time administrators add a new user account to any of the built-in 'Group', the user account gets all the permissions and privileges that the 'Group' by default has. Examples of built-in 'Groups' are 'Administrators', 'Backup Operators', 'Users', 'Power Users', 'Guests', etc.
- **System Groups** - Like built-in 'Groups', system 'Groups' are also automatically created along with the installation of Microsoft Windows 8 operating system. The only difference between built-in 'Groups' and the system 'Groups' is that in system 'Groups' the user accounts are automatically added as soon as the accounts are created and cannot be deleted manually. Moreover user accounts cannot even be added manually to any of the available system 'Groups'. Examples of system 'Groups' are 'Everyone', 'Authenticated Users', etc.
- **Manually Created Groups** - As the name says, these 'Groups' are the ones that administrators create manually on the computer as per their preferences and requirements. Administrators can set NTFS and share permissions on manually created 'Groups' and can add as many user accounts in them as they want.

Note: *One user account can be a member of multiple 'Groups' at the same time. In this situation, all the NTFS permissions that are set on all the 'Groups' are added and the effective permissions that the user account finally receives are the most privileged permissions on a particular object. For example if user 'A' is a member of 'G1' and 'G2' 'Groups' and on the folder named 'Important' 'G1' and 'G2' have 'Read' and 'Write' permissions respectively, user 'A's' effective permissions in this situation would be 'Read' + 'Write'.*

How to Create a Group?

In order to create a 'Group' in Microsoft Windows 8, steps given below must be followed:

1. Log on to Microsoft Windows 8 computer with administrator account.
2. From the **Start** screen, click **Desktop** tile.
3. Once on the desktop screen, click **File Explorer** icon from the taskbar.

4. On the opened **Libraries** window, from the left pane, right-click **Computer**.
5. From the displayed context menu, click **Manage**.
6. On the opened **Computer Management** snap-in, under the **System Tools** category from the left pane, expand **Local Users and Groups**.
7. From the expanded list, right-click **Groups** container.
8. From the displayed context menu, click **New Group**.
9. On the opened **New Group** box, specify a unique name for the 'Group' in **Group name** field.

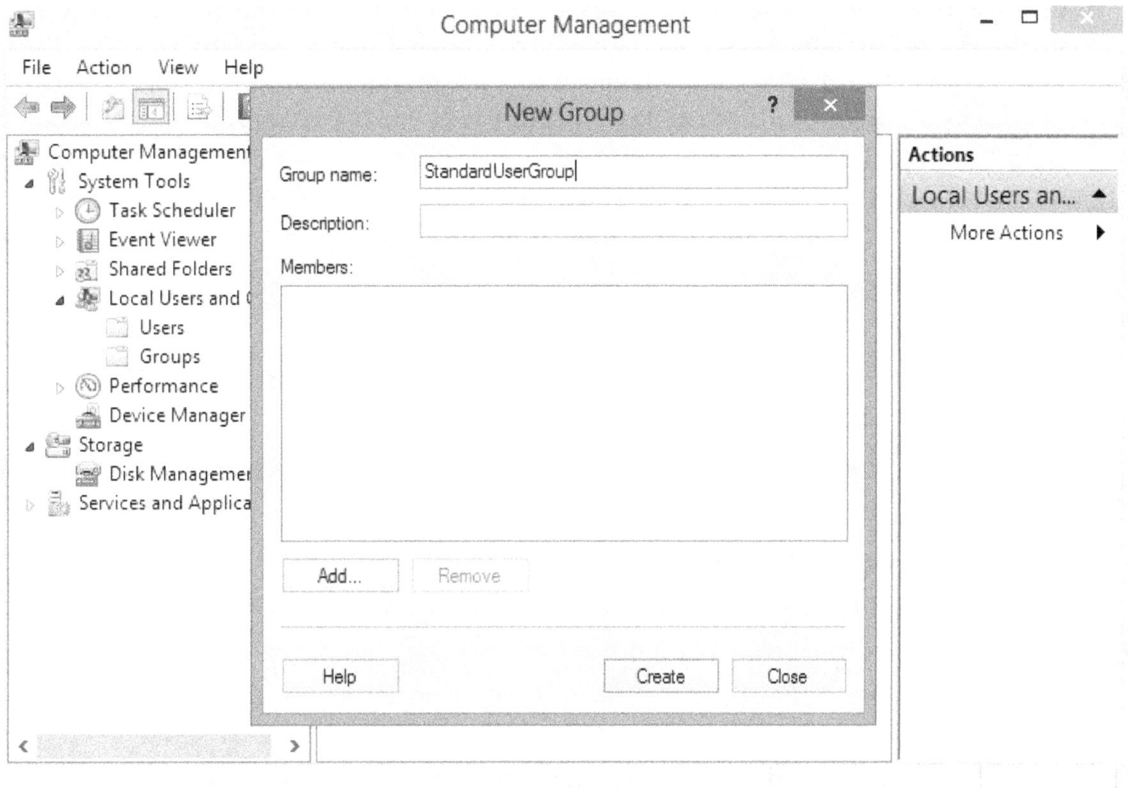

10. In the **Description** field, type a brief description about the 'Group'. (Optional)
11. Click **Create** button to create the 'Group'.

Add a User to Group

Introduction to Adding a User to a Group

In Microsoft Windows 8, after creating a new user account, administrators may want to add the account to at least one 'Group' so that it may get appropriate privileges and permissions on the objects, to work on which it was created.

Administrators may want to add multiple user accounts to a 'Group' to reduce their administrative overheads and make it easier for them to set NTFS and shared permissions on a particular object. In case the user accounts are not added to the 'Group', and identical level of NTFS and share permissions are to be set on multiple user accounts at the same time, administrators must set the permissions on each account individually. On the other hand, when all the user accounts are added to a 'Group', administrators can set NTFS and shared permissions on the 'Group' just once. This saves administrators' decent amount of time which they can utilize focusing on some other important aspects of the network.

How to Add a User to a Group?

In order to add a user account to a 'Group' in Microsoft Windows 8, steps given below must be followed:

1. Log on to Microsoft Windows 8 computer with administrator account.
2. From the **Start** screen, click **Desktop** tile.
3. Once on the desktop screen, click **File Explorer** icon from the taskbar.
4. On the opened **Libraries** window, from the left pane, right-click **Computer**.
5. From the displayed context menu, click **Manage**.
6. On the opened **Computer Management** snap-in, under the **System Tools** category from the left pane, expand **Local Users and Groups**.
7. From the expanded list, click to select the **Groups** container.
8. From the right pane, right-click the 'Group' to which a user account is to be added.
9. From the context menu, click **Properties**.
10. On the opened 'Group's' properties box, click **Add** button.
11. On the **Select Users** box, type the name of the user account in the **Enter the object names to select** field.

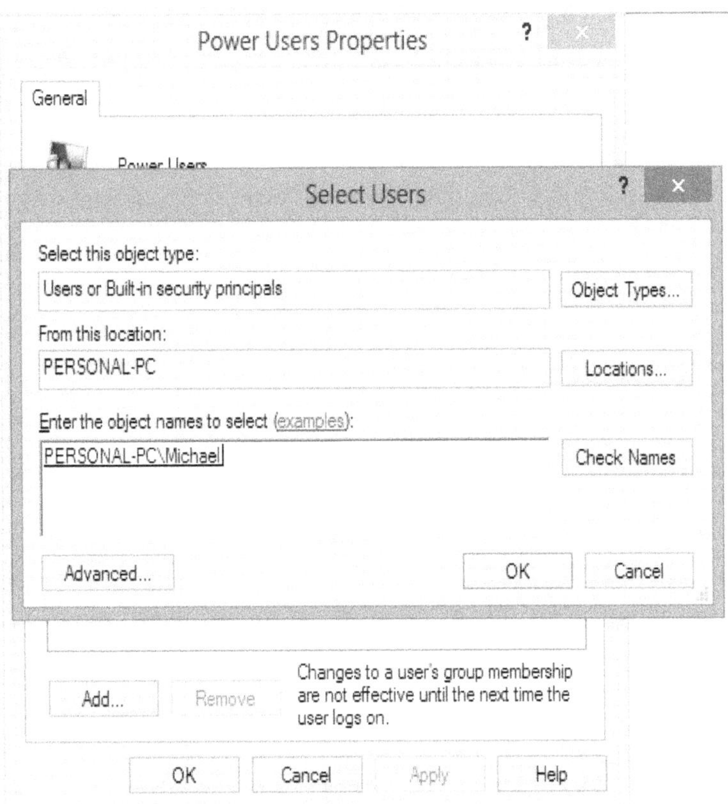

12. Click **Advanced** button to verify the typed user name.
13. Once verified, click **OK**.
14. Back on 'Group's' properties box, click **OK** to add the selected user to the 'Group'.

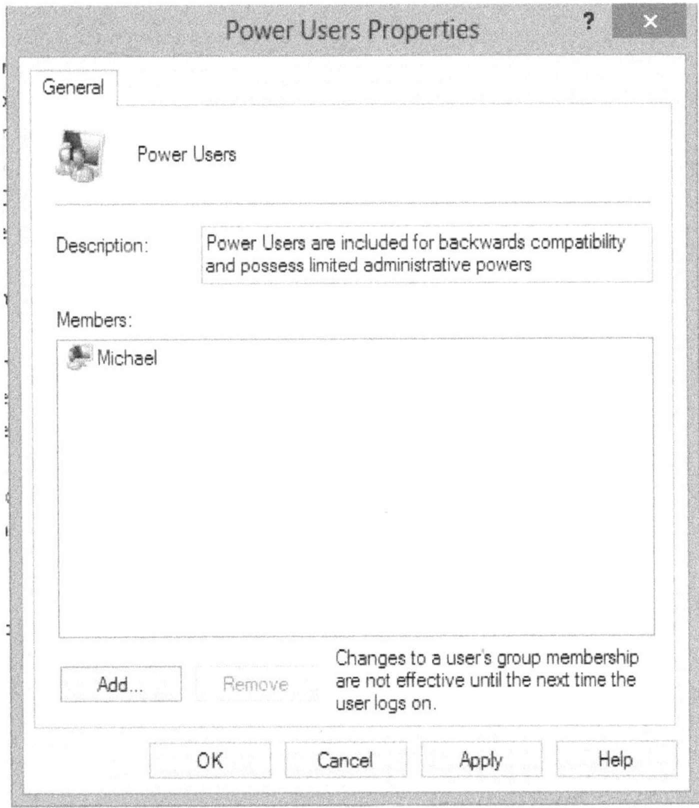

CHAPTER 7:

MANAGE HARDWARE DEVICES

How to Find Missing Drivers for Hardware

Introduction to Missing Device Drivers

When Microsoft Windows 8 is installed on a computer, because of its own driver database, it automatically installs the drivers for almost all commonly used hardware devices. If there are some additional devices attached to the computers, such as a TV tuner card, graphics card, etc., users must install their drivers through the driver discs that is provided along with the devices when they are purchased. In most laptop computers, the operating system is already installed when it is purchased and the vendors strongly recommend that the restoration disc should be created as soon as the laptop is bought.

The above mentioned scenario is the most ideal one and if the proper guidelines are followed, everything would work absolutely fine. However, while working on the computers in the real world, things might not be as easy as they seem to be. Sometimes after installing the device drivers once on the computers, users may misplace their installation discs, and it is quite likely that after users have purchased the laptop computers, they would not have created the restoration discs at all. When this happens, and Windows is reinstalled on a computer after erasing the older copy of the operating system, it is likely that not all the device drivers would be automatically installed. When the drivers of the devices are not installed, the devices are displayed with a yellow question mark in the 'Device Manager' under the 'Other devices' category.

For non-technical users, it might be a challenging task to identify the exact device driver that they must download in order to make the device work properly. Fortunately Microsoft Windows 8 allows users to detect the device IDs, drivers of which are not installed. Once the IDs of the devices are found, users can search for the drivers on the basis of the found device IDs and can download the exact drivers for the devices.

How to Find the Device IDs?

In order to find the IDs of the devices whose drivers are missing, steps given below must be foilowed:

1. Log on to Microsoft Windows 8 computer.
2. From the **Start** screen, click **Desktop** tile.
3. On the desktop screen, press **Windows** + **R** keys simultaneously to initiate **Run** command box.
4. In the **Run** command box, type **MSINFO32** command and press **Enter** key.
5. On the opened **System Information** window, expand **Components** category from the left pane.
6. From the expanded list, click to select **Problem Devices** to get the IDs of all the unknown devices in the right pane.

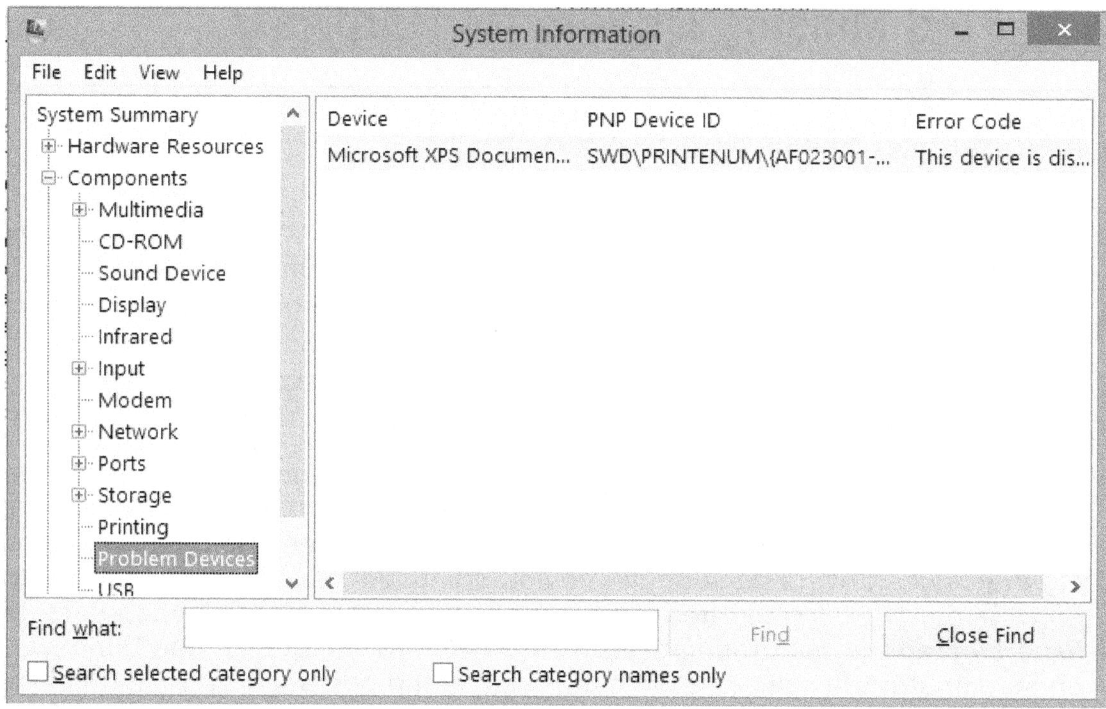

7. Close the **System Information** window when done.

Scan for Newly Attached Hardware Device

Introduction to New Hardware Device Scanning

When a new hardware device is connected to a Windows 8 computer, the operating system automatically initiates the scanning process and detects the connected device. Once the device is detected, Windows 8 searches for its appropriate driver in its driver database. If the appropriate driver for the connected device is found, Windows 8 automatically installs the driver and displays a message in the notification area informing that the device driver has been successfully installed, and the device is ready to use. An example can be a USB pen drive. When a USB drive is connected to the computer for the first time, Windows 8 automatically detects and installs its driver automatically.

As mentioned above, although Microsoft Windows 8 detects and installs drivers for almost all plug and play devices, there might still be times when the operating system fails to initiate the device scanning process. In such situations, users can manually make the computer scan for the newly connected device.

Note: *When scanning process is initiated, the operating system detects both plug and play and non-plug and play devices. The drivers for almost all plug and play devices are automatically installed once the devices are detected and the appropriate drivers are found in the driver database of the OS. On the other hand if Windows 8 detects non-plug and play devices, it puts them under the 'Other devices' category in the 'Device Manager'. Users can refer 'How to Find Missing Drivers for Hardware' of this chapter to know how to find the device IDs and can download the missing drivers for the non-plug and play devices.*

How to Scan for Newly Attached Devices?

In order to scan for newly attached devices in Microsoft Windows 8, steps given below must be followed:

1. Log on to Microsoft Windows 8 computer.
2. From the **Start** screen, click **Desktop** tile.
3. On the desktop screen, click **File Explorer** icon from the taskbar.
4. On the opened **Libraries** window, right-click **Computer** from the left pane.
5. From the displayed context menu, click **Manage**.
6. On the **Computer Management** snap-in, under **System Tools** category from the left pane, click to select **Device Manager**.
7. From the right pane, right-click the name of the computer at the top of the list.
8. From the displayed context menu, click **Scan for hardware changes** option to scan for any newly installed hardware device.

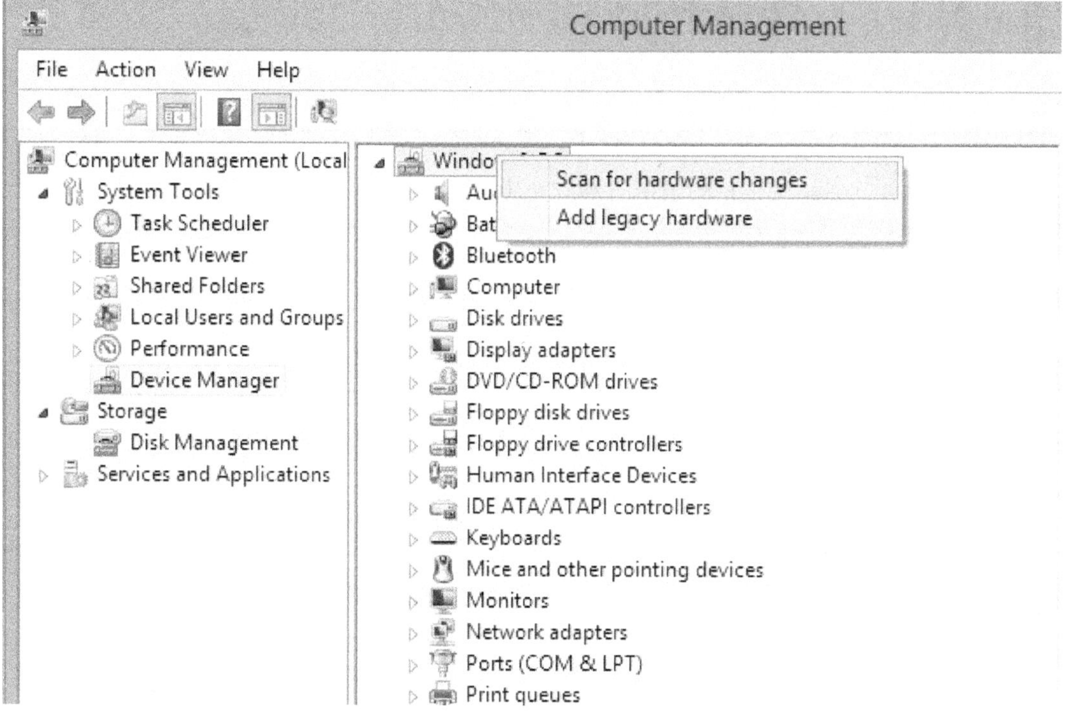

9. Close **Computer Management** snap-in when done.

Update Device Drivers

Introduction to the Latest Device Drivers

When a new hardware device is purchased, its driver installation disc is also provided along with it. With the help of driver installation disc, users can install the driver of the device after it is connected to the computer.

In almost all cases, the vendors of devices keep on working on the driver files and update the versions of the drivers on a regular basis. Users, at their end, are recommended to visit the official websites of the vendors regularly and download and install the latest drivers for their devices. This helps users to stay up to date with the device drivers and experience more efficient performance of the attached devices.

Note: *In some cases latest device driver for a device might not be compatible with the version of operating system that is installed on a computer. When this happens, the device may not work as smoothly as it used to work when the older version of driver was installed. Sometimes the device may even stop working at all. In such situation, older version of the device driver must be re-installed in order to make the device start working again.*

How to Update Device Drivers?

In order to update device drivers in Microsoft Windows 8, steps given below must be followed:

1. Log on to Microsoft Windows 8 computer.
2. From the **Start** screen, click **Desktop** tile.
3. On the desktop screen, click **File Explorer** icon from the taskbar.
4. On the opened **Libraries** window, right-click **Computer** from the left pane.
5. From the displayed context menu, click **Manage**.
6. On the **Computer Management** snap-in, under **System Tools** category from the left pane, click to select **Device Manager**.
7. From the displayed list in right pane, expand the category of the devices, driver of which is to be updated.
8. Right-click the target device from the expanded list and from the displayed context menu, click **Update Drive Software** option.

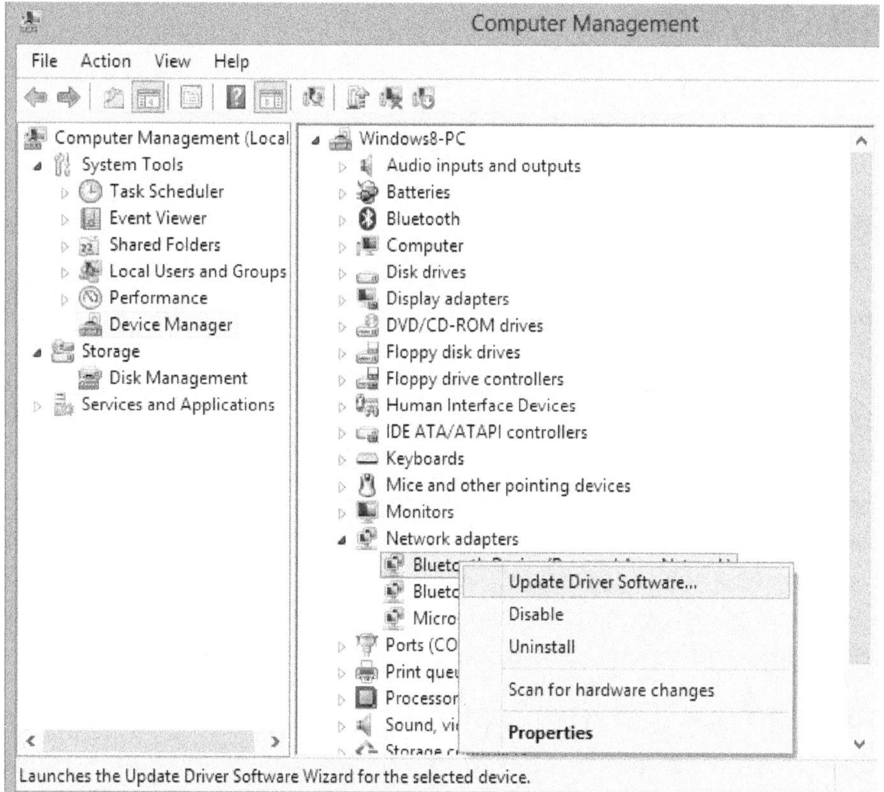

9. On the opened box, click **Search automatically for updated driver software** option to automatically search for updated drivers for the selected device in the local hard disk drive and on the Internet. Alternatively **Browse my computer for drive software** option can also be clicked to locate and install the updated driver from the local hard disk drive manually.

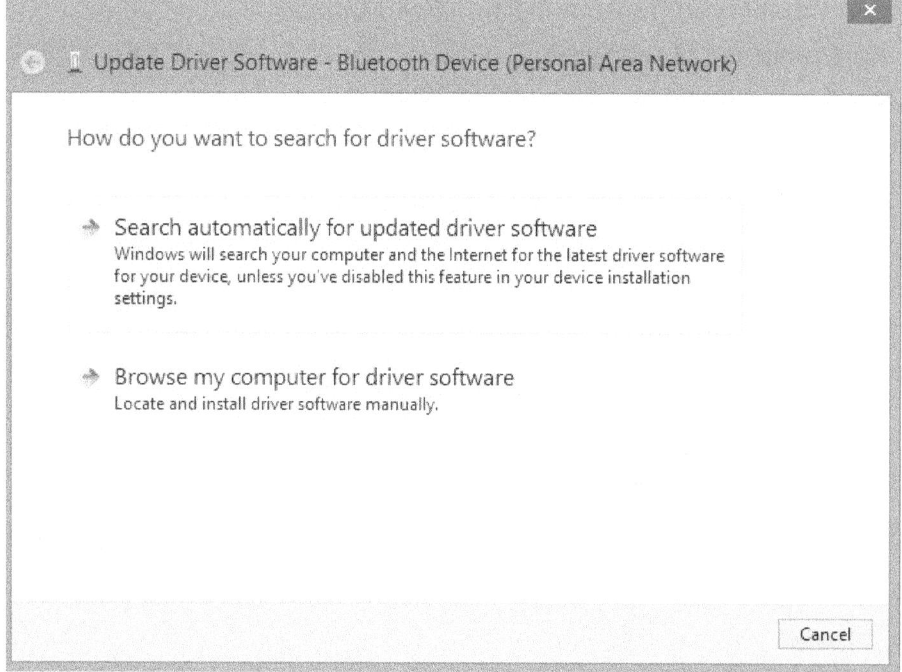

10. Once the new driver software for the selected device is successfully installed, restart the computer.

Verify Devices and Their Drivers

Introduction to the Devices and Their Installed Drivers

Many non-technical users may not be able to detect the devices that their computers may have, and many times they are not even aware of the types of devices and their drivers that their computer systems contain. Users may only come to know about the devices and their drivers when the devices stop functioning. Normally non-technical users need not to know such complexities because they might belong to a different domain. However some users might still be interested in understanding the way their computers work and what types of devices and their drivers are required that make their computers function flawlessly. Users can easily know about the devices and their drivers that their computer systems may have.

How to Verify the Devices and Their Drivers?

In order to verify the devices and their drivers that the computer system may have, steps given below must be followed:

1. Log on to Microsoft Windows 8 computer.
2. From the **Start** screen, click **Desktop** tile.
3. On the desktop screen, click **File Explorer** icon from the taskbar.
4. On the opened **Libraries** window, right-click **Computer** from the left pane.
5. From the displayed context menu, click **Manage**.
6. On the **Computer Management** snap-in, under **System Tools** category from the left pane, click to select **Device Manager**.
7. In the right pane, expand the category of the devices to view the installed driver for a specific device.
8. To view driver details of a particular hardware device, expand the category of the devices from the displayed list in right pane.
9. Right-click the target device from the expanded list and from the displayed context menu, click **Properties**.
10. On the opened properties box, go to **Driver** tab.
11. Click **Driver Details** button and on the **Driver Files Details** box, view the details of the installed driver for the selected device along with the name of the driver file and its location.

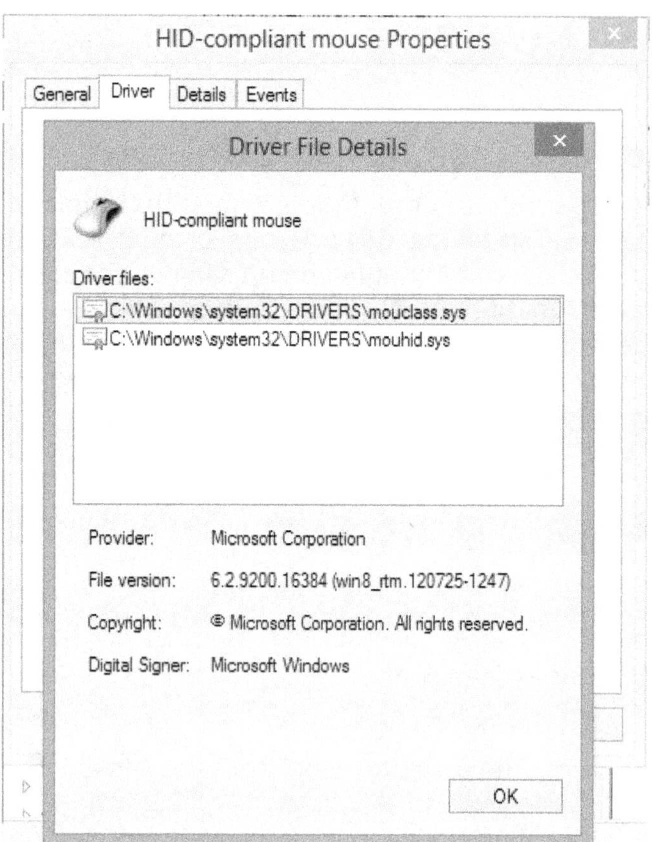

.***Note:*** *Devices whose drivers are not installed are displayed in* ***Other devices*** *category in the right pane of the* ***Device Manager****.*

Check Which Graphic Card Is Installed

Introduction to the Installed Graphic Card Verification

Nowadays almost all desktop computers and the laptop PCs have decent graphic cards installed in them. Graphic cards that computer systems may have can work only when their appropriate drivers are installed. In desktop computers, after the users have installed the drivers for their graphic cards, they may misplace their installation discs, and in the cases of laptop PCs, users might forget to create restoration discs altogether. When this is the case, it becomes hard for the users to detect the type of graphic card that is installed on their computers, and which drivers are required to make the device work efficiently.

To overcome the above mentioned problems, users are recommended to verify the type of graphic cards that the computer systems have and download the appropriate drivers for the cards in advance.

How to Check the Installed Graphic Card?

In order to check the installed graphic card on a Microsoft Windows 8 computer, steps given below must be followed:

1. Log on to Microsoft Windows 8 computer with administrator account.
2. From the **Start** screen, click **Desktop** tile.
3. On the desktop screen right-click anywhere and from the context menu, click **Screen resolution**.
4. On the opened **Screen Resolution** window, click **Advanced settings**.
5. On the opened box, make sure that **Adapter** tab is selected.
6. Installed graphic card can be seen under **Adapter Type** section. Detailed information about the adapter can be found under **Adapter Information** section on the **Adapter** tab itself.

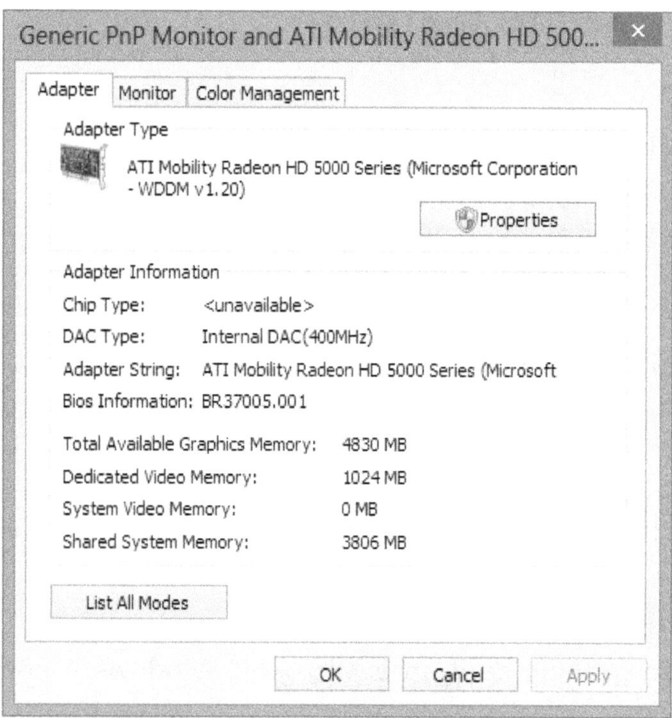

7. Further and more granular information about the driver can be found by clicking on **Properties** button and going to **Driver** tab and clicking **Driver Details** button on the opened properties box.

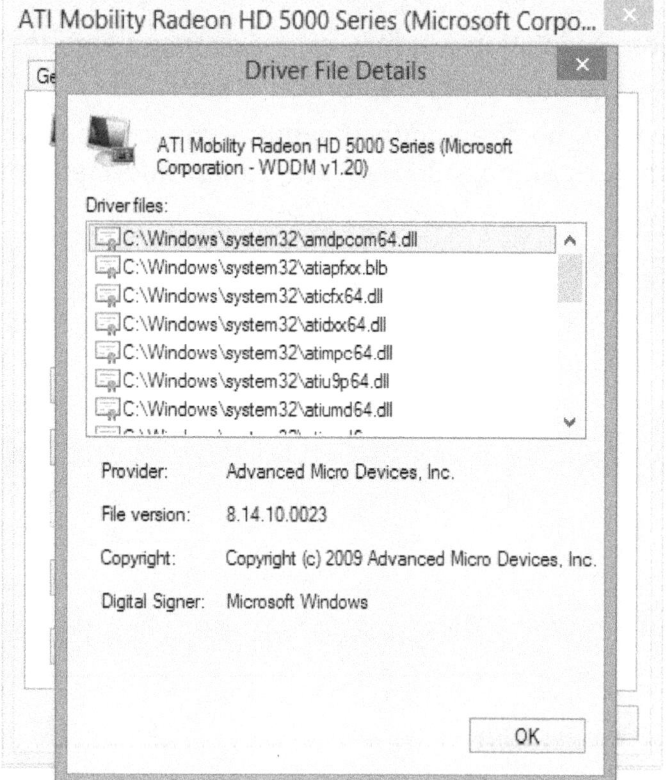

Uninstall a Device Driver

Introduction to Uninstalling a Device Driver

Once a device is connected to the computer and its driver is installed, the device starts working and users can experience its flawless performance. Although users purchase the devices and install them on the computers because they really need them, there might still be situations when they might want to uninstall the drivers for their devices. One scenario can be that they might want to install a different version of driver for the device (mostly older version). Another scenario can be that they might not want the device to be available on the computer for use.

Uninstalling a device driver is an administrative task and elevated privileges are required to complete the process successfully.

How to Uninstall a Device Driver?

In order to uninstall a device driver from a Microsoft Windows 8 computer, steps given below must be followed:

1. Log on to Microsoft Windows 8 computer with administrator account.
2. From the **Start** screeN, click **Desktop** tile.
3. On the desktop screen, click **File Explorer** icon from the taskbar.
4. On the opened **Libraries** window, right-click **Computer** from the left pane.
5. From the displayed context menu, click **Manage**.
6. On the **Computer Management** snap-in, under **System Tools** category from the left pane, click to select **Device Manager**.
7. In the right pane, expand the category of the devices to uninstall the installed driver for a specific device.
8. Right-click the target device from the expanded list and from the displayed context menu, click **Uninstall**.

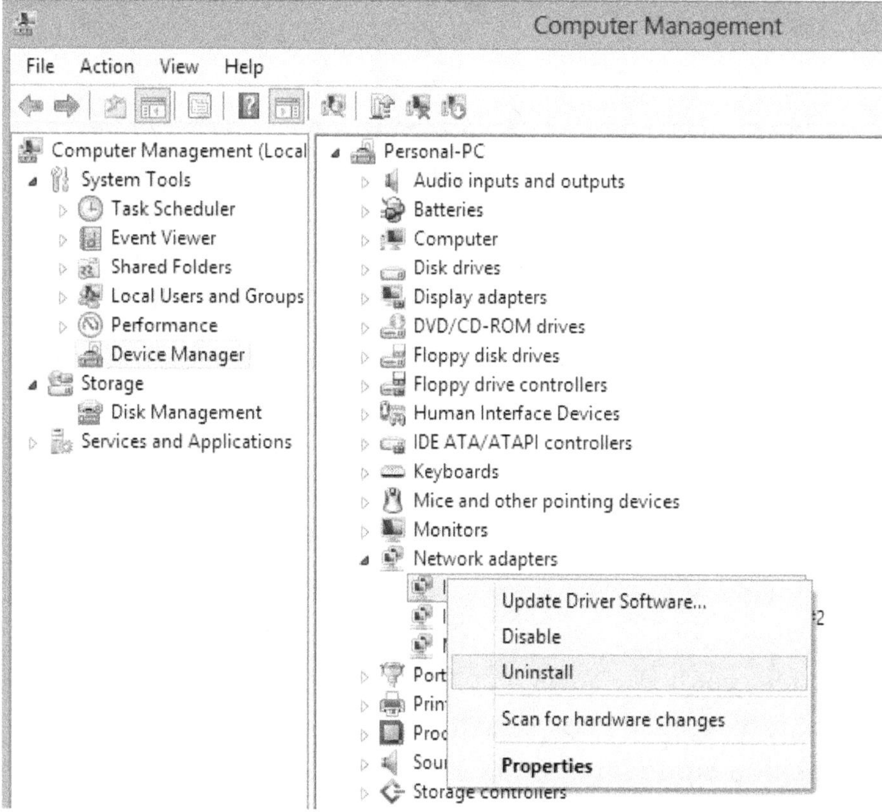

9. On the displayed confirmation box, click **Yes** to confirm and start the driver uninstallation process.
10. Restart the computer when done.

Disable Hardware Devices

Introduction to Disabling Hardware Devices

Disabling hardware devices means that making the devices unavailable on a temporary basis. Users might want to disable hardware devices if they find that the devices are being misused or they are not required for some time.

Although drivers for the unwanted devices can also be uninstalled in order to make the devices unavailable, it might not be a practical step to take when the devices are expected to be made available to the users after a short period of time. Moreover uninstallation and installation of the device drivers also require some additional administrative overhead which might not be appreciated by most administrators.

Home users may also want to disable some hardware devices in order to prevent other family members, especially the kids, from using the devices. An example can be that parents might not want their kids to use CD/DVD drives during their exam times.

How to Disable Hardware Devices?

In order to disable hardware devices in Microsoft Windows 8, steps given below must be followed:

1. Log on to Microsoft Windows 8 computer with administrator account.
2. From the **Start** screen, click **Desktop** tile.
3. On the desktop screen, click **File Explorer** icon from the taskbar.
4. On the opened **Libraries** window, right-click **Computer** from the left pane.
5. From the displayed context menu, click **Manage**.
6. On the **Computer Management** snap-in, under **System Tools** category from the left pane, click to select **Device Manager**.
7. In the right pane, expand the category of the devices to disable a specific device.
8. Right-click the target device from the expanded list and from the displayed context menu, click **Disable**.

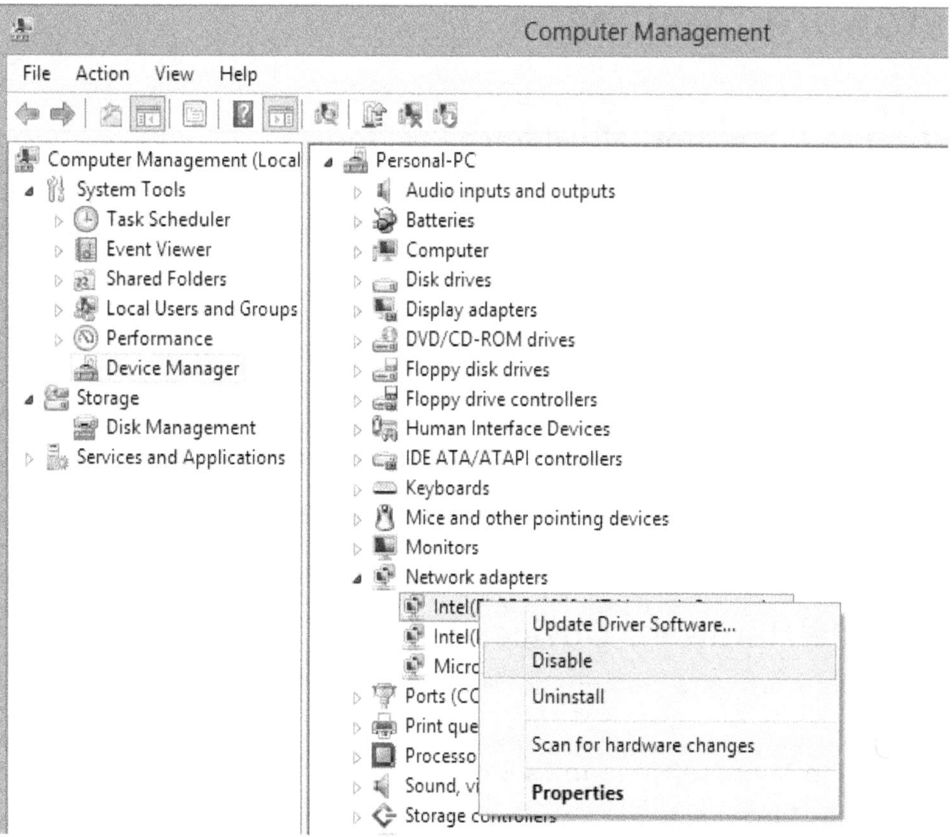

9. On the displayed confirmation box, click **Yes** to disable the device.

To re-enable a disabled device, steps 1 to 8 can be followed, while clicking Enable when on step 8.

CHAPTER 8:

MANAGE PRINTERS

Install a Virtual Printer

Introduction to Virtual Printers

It is likely that almost all home users who use computers nowadays also use at least one printer. It is also quite obvious that the printers are always required in production environments. Considering these scenarios and situations, many times it might not be required to install a virtual printer on a Windows 8 computer. But things might differ in cases where users might not have physical printers connected to the computers but some applications that they might be working on might require a printer connected to the systems. Moreover there might also be situations when some applications might want a specific type of printer to be connected to the computers, which might not be possible for the users to buy, before the applications can function efficiently. In such situations, it becomes essential for the users to install virtual printers in order to make the demanding applications feel that their requirements for the printers are fulfilled.

A virtual printer is nothing but the printer driver that administrators install on the computer without physically connecting the printer. When the driver of an unavailable printer is installed, the printer icon is displayed in the 'Devices and Printers' window. All commands that users normally send to the physically available printers are also accepted by the virtual printers. However the virtual printers obviously do not produce the physical printed pages.

How to Install a Virtual Printer?

In order to install a virtual printer on a Microsoft Windows 8 computer, steps given below must be followed:

1. Log on to Microsoft Windows 8 computer.
2. From the **Start** screen, click **Desktop** tile.
3. On the desktop screen, hover mouse to the bottom right corner of the window.
4. From the displayed options, click **Settings**.
5. On the **Settings** pane, click **Control Panel**.
6. From the **Control Panel** window, click **Hardware and Sound** category.
7. On **Hardware and Sound** window, click **Devices and Printers**.
8. On the **Devices and Printers** window, click **Add a printer** button below the standard toolbar.
9. From the bottom of the **Add Printer** window, click **The printer that I want isn't listed** option.
10. From the next window that appears, click to select **Add a local printer or network printer with manual settings** radio button.

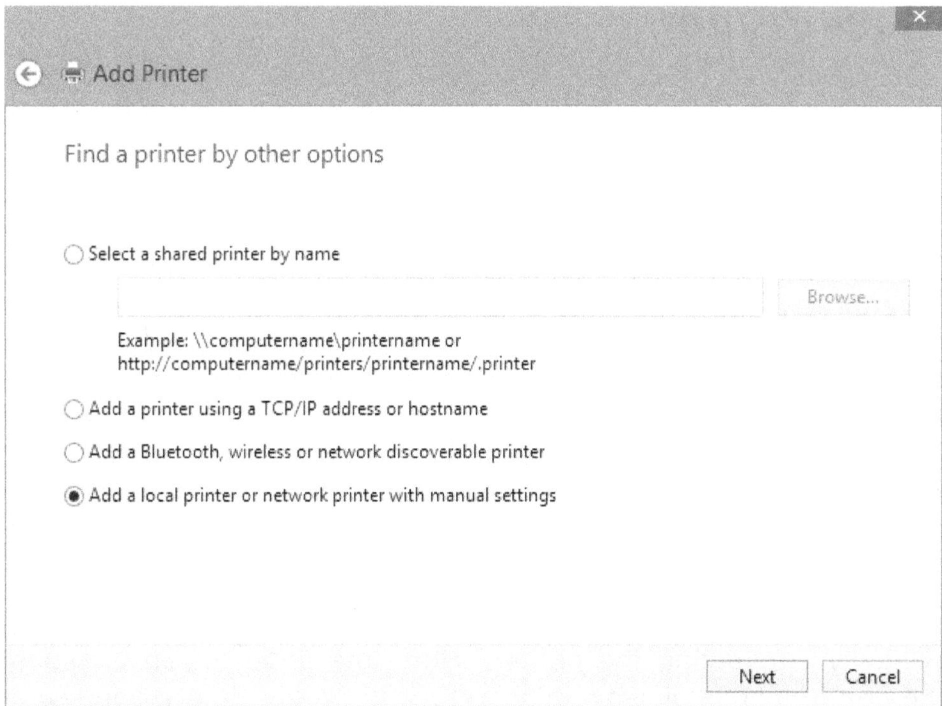

11. Click **Next** button to continue.
12. On **Choose a printer port** page, make sure that **Use an existing port** radio button is selected and click **Next**.
13. On **Install the printer driver** page, click to select the desired printer manufacturer from the **Manufacturer** list in the left.
14. From the **Printers** list in the right, click to select the desired printer model of the selected manufacturer.

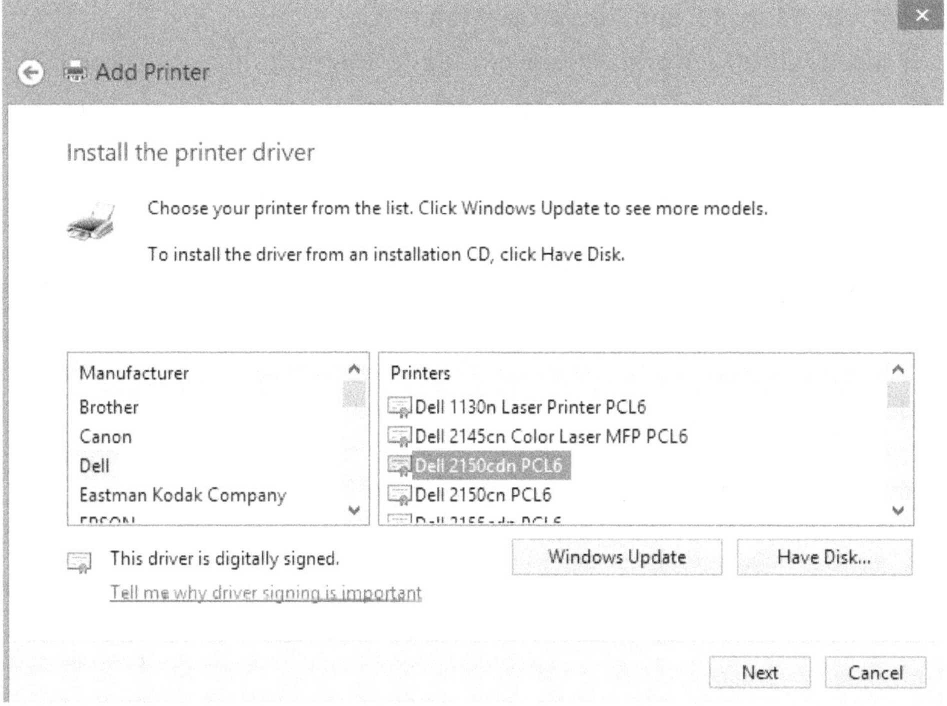

15. Click **Next** button to proceed.

16. On **Type a printer name** page, type the name for the printer as desired in the **Printer name** field and click **Next**.
17. On the **Printer Sharing** page, choose any of the available radio buttons to enable or disable printer sharing as required and click **Next**.
18. On the next page, ensure that **Set as the default printer** checkbox is checked in case the virtual printer is to be set as default. Alternatively the checkbox can also be unchecked if any other physical printer is installed on the computer and is set as default.
19. Click **Finish** button to start the printer driver (virtual printer) installation process.
20. Once done, close all the opened windows and boxes.

To remove an installed virtual printer, steps 1 to 8 can be followed, while right-clicking the unwanted printer from the **Printers** category and clicking **Remove device** from the displayed context menu when on step 8. Make sure to click **Yes** button on any confirmation box that appears.

Manage Printer Availability

Introduction to Printer Availability

When a printer is installed on a Microsoft Windows 8 computer, it is available for 24 hours of the day and for 7 days a week. This default configuration is mostly left intact and is not modified in both homes and production environments.

Sometimes there might be cases when administrators might want to limit the hours when the printer might be available for the users and accept the print commands from them. When the printer availability is configured, the printers only become available during the hours that the administrators specify. For example if administrators want that the printers must be available to the users between 9 AM in the morning till 5 PM in the evening, the printers would not accept the print commands beyond the specified hours. Administrators might want to take this step when they feel that the printers are being misused by the employees in the organizations, or by other family members in homes.

How to Manage Printer Availability?

In order to manage printer availability in Microsoft Windows 8, steps given below must be followed:

1. Log on to Microsoft Windows 8 computer.
2. From the **Start** screen, click **Desktop** tile.
3. On the desktop screen, hover mouse to the bottom right corner of the window.
4. From the displayed options, click **Settings**.
5. On the **Settings** pane, click **Control Panel**.
6. From the **Control Panel** window, click **Hardware and Sound** category.
7. On **Hardware and Sound** window, click **Devices and Printers**.
8. On the **Devices and Printers** window, right-click the printer from the **Printers** category whose availability is to be configured.
9. From the displayed context menu, click **Printer properties**.
10. On the opened properties box, go to **Advanced** tab and click **Available from** radio button.
11. In the available fields, specify the time duration between which the printer would accept the print commands from the users.

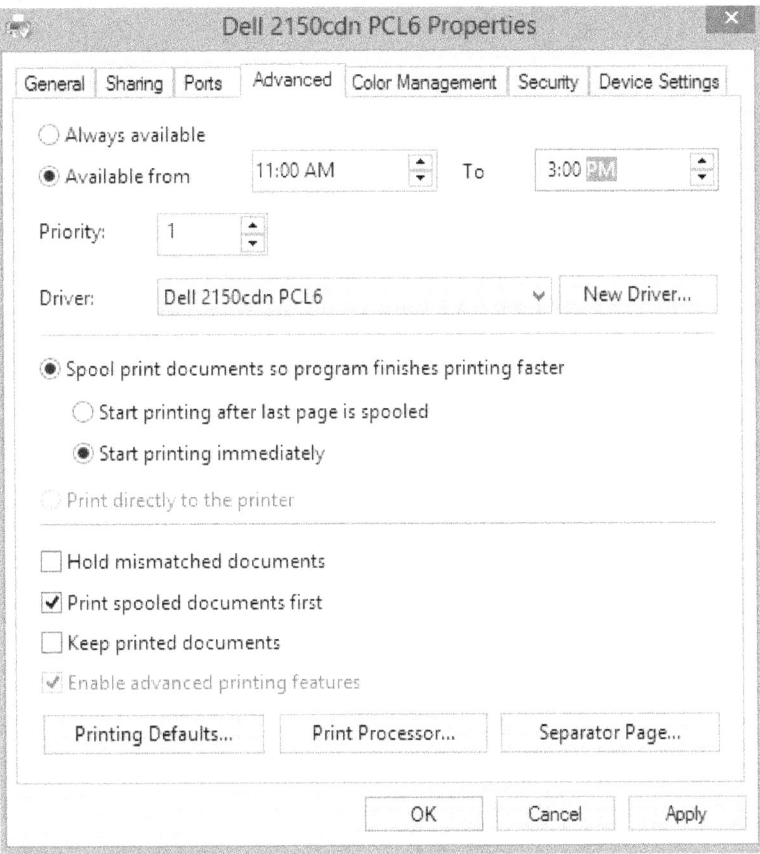

12. Click **OK** when done.

To make the printer available for 24 hours a day and for 7 days a week, steps 1 to 10 can be followed, while selecting **Always available** radio button when on step 10. Finally click **OK** when done.

Share a Locally Installed Printer

Introduction to Printer Sharing

When a printer is locally installed on a Microsoft Windows 8 computer, it is available for all local users who log on to the computer interactively. When a printer is installed on a home computer, it is not required to be shared as it is expected that homes have limited number of computers and removable storage media (USB flash drives) are used to transfer data from any other computer to the one where printer is installed.

Situations differ when a printer is installed in a production environment where several computers are connected to each other. In these scenarios it is practically impossible for all users in the organization to access the computer locally on which the printer is installed. In such cases, it becomes essential for the administrators to share a locally installed printer so that it can be made available to all the users in the network.

Note: *Although it is not required to share a printer in home networks, users can still do it if needed.*

How to Share a Locally Installed Printer?

In order to share a locally installed printer in Microsoft Windows 8, steps given below must be followed:

1. Log on to Microsoft Windows 8 computer.
2. From the **Start** screen, click **Desktop** tile.
3. On the desktop screen, hover mouse to the bottom right corner of the window.
4. From the displayed options, click **Settings**.
5. On the **Settings** pane, click **Control Panel**.
6. From the **Control Panel** window, click **Hardware and Sound** category.
7. On **Hardware and Sound** window, click **Devices and Printers**.
8. On the **Devices and Printers** window, right-click the printer from the **Printers** category that is to be shared.
9. From the displayed context menu, click **Printer properties**.
10. On the opened properties box, go to **Sharing** tab.
11. On the **Sharing** tab, check **Share this printer** checkbox.

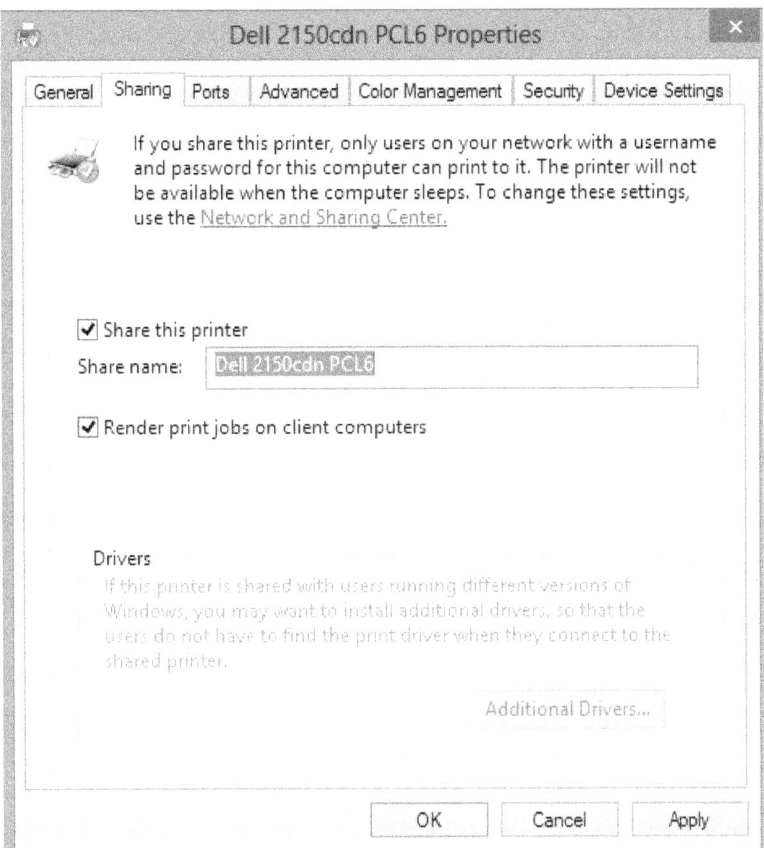

12. In the **Share name** field, specify a user-friendly share name for the printer. (Optional)
13. Click **OK** to share the printer.

To un-share a shared printer, steps 1 to 11 can be followed, while unchecking **Share this printer** checkbox when on step 11. Finally click **OK** when done.

Manage Printer Security

Introduction to Printer Security

When a printer is installed on Microsoft Windows 8 computer, it is available for all local users. By default all standard users (non-administrators) are allowed to send the print commands to the printers, and are also allowed to manage their own documents that are sent for printing. Managing documents means that standard users can cancel their print commands that they have sent to the printers. This further means that standard users cannot cancel the print commands that other users have sent to the printers. On the other hand, administrators of Microsoft Windows 8 computer can manage any document, manage the printers, grant or revoke print permissions to and from the users respectively, etc.

Apart from the default security configurations, administrators can manually modify the NTFS permissions in order to limit the accessibility of the printers. Administrators can also set the NTFS permissions for other users who might access the printers via network (applicable only when the printers are shared).

How to Manage Printer Security?

In order to manage printer security using NTFS permissions, steps given below must be followed:

1. Log on to Microsoft Windows 8 computer.
2. From the **Start** screen, click **Desktop** tile.
3. On the desktop screen, hover mouse to the bottom right corner of the window.
4. From the displayed options, click **Settings**.
5. On the **Settings** pane, click **Control Panel**.
6. From the **Control Panel** window, click **Hardware and Sound** category.
7. On **Hardware and Sound** window, click **Devices and Printers**.
8. On the **Devices and Printers** window, right-click the printer from the **Printers** category on which NTFS permissions are to be set.
9. From the displayed context menu, click **Printer properties**.
10. On the opened properties box, go to **Security** tab.
11. On the **Security** tab, click **Add** button to add a new user account or group to set NTFS permissions for the printer. To remove a user account or group from the list, select the unwanted object (user or group) and click **Remove** button. Make sure to click **Yes** on any confirmation box that appears.

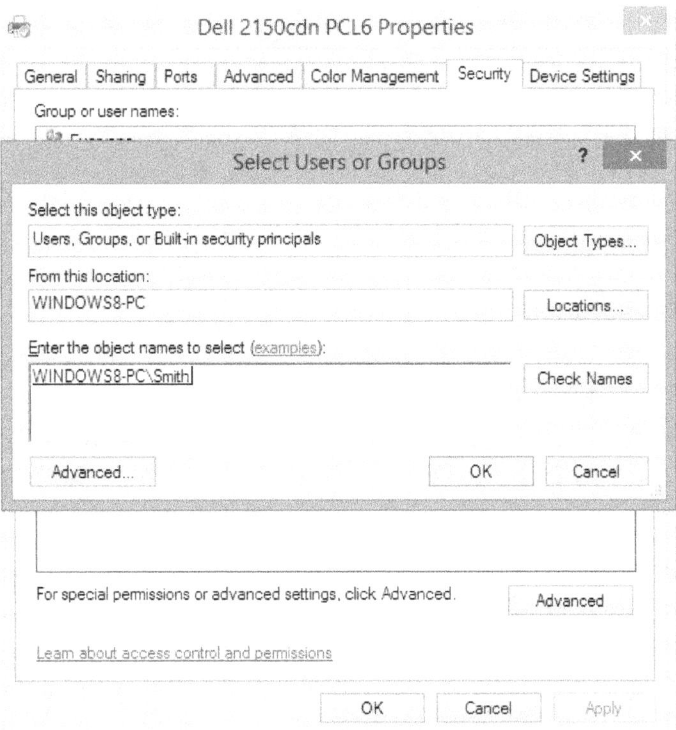

12. Once the appropriate object is selected in the group or user names list, desired NTFS permissions for the selected object can be set from the **Permissions for <user or group name>** list.

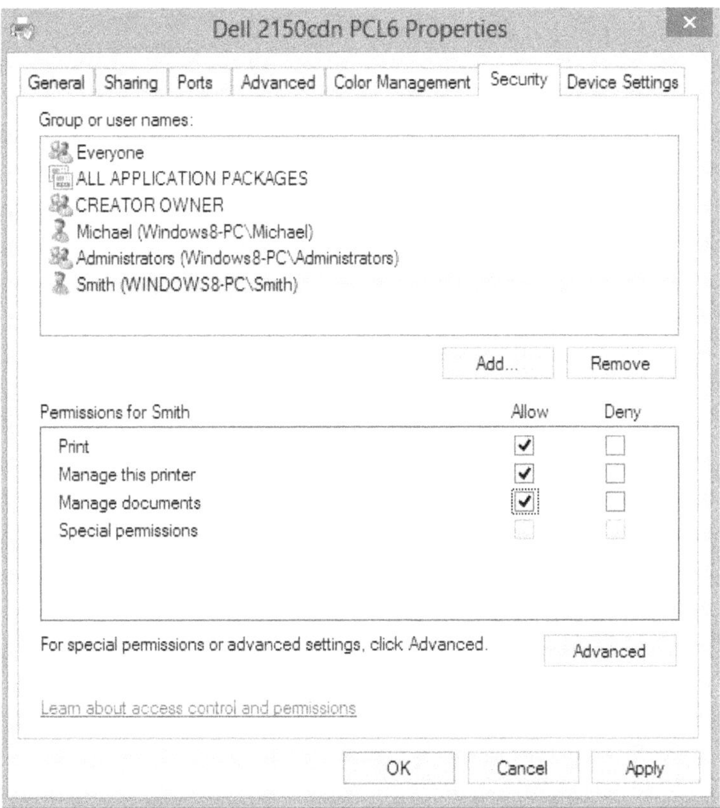

13. Click **OK** when done to apply the modified NTFS permissions on the configured object(s).

Enable Printer Pooling

Introduction to Printer Pooling

Printer pooling is a process in which multiple printers are connected to the network and work like a single entity. When printer pooling is enabled, all the printers that are added to the printer pool are displayed as a single unit to the users, hence making the complexities of printer pooling completely transparent to them.

After printer pooling is enabled, when the first user sends a print command, the first printer in the print pool receives the command and initiates the printing process. In the meanwhile if the second user sends the command to the printer, and the first printer is busy, the second available printer in the print pool receives the command and starts printing.

As mentioned above, a printer pool is displayed as a single unit to the users and therefore only one printer icon is visible to them. This prevents users from getting confused, and allows them to work with the printers quite easily.

Requirements and Recommendations While Enabling Printer Pooling

Requirements:

All the printers that administrators plan to add to the printer pool must be of same vendor and of the same model. In case the vendors or the models of the printers vary, printer pooling could not be enabled, or the printers from different vendors or of different models could not be added to the printer pool.

Recommendations:

It is recommended that all printers that are added to the print pool must be kept together, and if possible, in the same room. The reason behind this is that since the entire printer pooling configuration remains transparent to the users, when they send the print commands, they never know which printer has accepted the command and has initiated the printing process. If the printers are kept at different locations, it might be quite tedious for the users to search for the printer that has printed their documents.

How to Enable Printer Pooling?

In order to enable printer pooling in Microsoft Windows 8, make sure that two or more printers on which pooling is to be enabled are from same manufacturer and of same model. Also ensure that the correct drivers for the printers are installed on different printer ports (LPT1, LPT2, etc.) in the computer. Once the mentioned prerequisites are met, steps given below must be followed:

1. Log on to Microsoft Windows 8 computer.
2. From the **Start** screen, click **Desktop** tile.
3. On the desktop screen, hover mouse to the bottom right corner of the window.
4. From the displayed options, click **Settings**.
5. On the **Settings** pane, click **Control Panel**.
6. From the **Control Panel** window, click **Hardware and Sound** category.
7. On **Hardware and Sound** window, click **Devices and Printers**.

8. On the **Devices and Printers** window, right-click the printer from the **Printers** category on which printer pooling is to be configured.
9. From the displayed context menu, click **Printer properties**.
10. On the opened properties box, go to **Ports** tab.
11. From the bottom of the tab, check **Enable printer pooling** checkbox.
12. From the displayed port list, check all the checkboxes on which the printers that are to be pooled are installed.

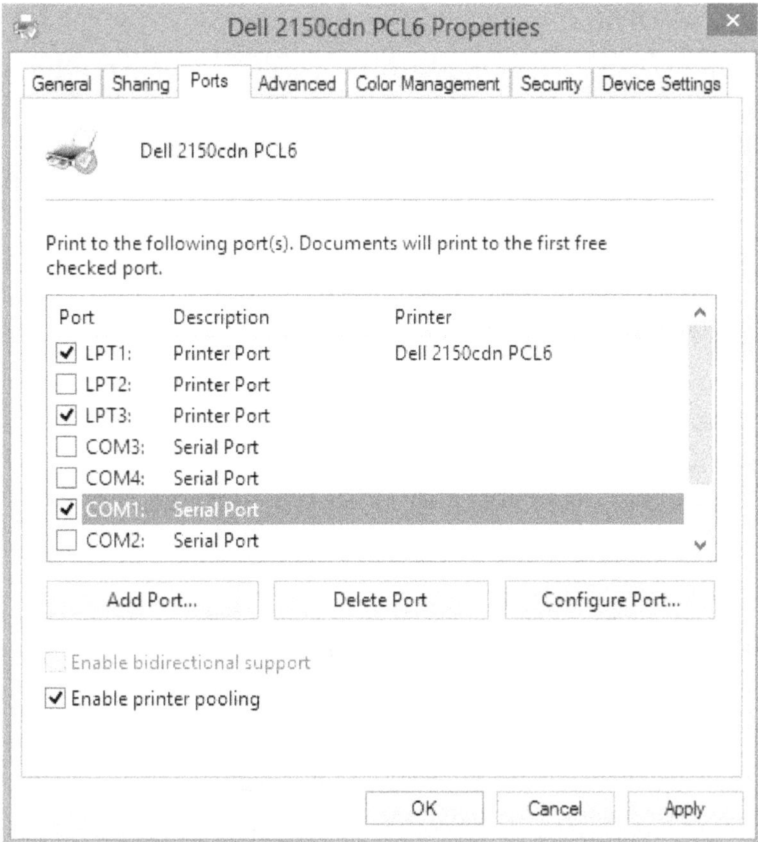

13. Click **OK** when done.
14. Repeat steps 1 to 13 for all the printers that must be added to the printer pool.

To remove a printer from the printer pool, steps 1 to 13 can be followed, while unchecking the checkbox representing the unwanted printer when on step 12.

Disable Printer Spooling

Introduction to Printer Spooling

When a printer is installed on Microsoft Windows 8 computer, by default printer spooling is enabled. Printer spooling can be thought of as a buffer or a cache memory for the printer that stores the contents of the document that are to be printed.

How Printer Spooling Works?

When a user sends the print command to the printer, by default the printer starts printing as soon as the first page of the document is spooled. While the printer prints the page, other pages of the document are spooled in the background. This default configuration can be changed and administrators can make the printer spool the entire document before it starts printing the contents.

Once the entire document is spooled, users can close the document.

Effects of Disabling Printer Spooling

When printer spooling is disabled, the printer starts printing a document as soon as it receives the print command. The drawback of disabling printer spooling is that the document that is sent to the printer to be printed must be kept opened till all its pages are printed. If users close the document in the middle of the printing process, the print process also stops.

How to Disable Printer Spooling?

Although it is not recommended to disable printer spooling, for testing purposes, in lab environments or to expedite the printing process, administrators can do so by following the steps given below:

1. Log on to Microsoft Windows 8 computer.
2. From the **Start** screen, click **Desktop** tile.
3. On the desktop screen, press **Windows** + **R** keys simultaneously to initiate **Run** command box.
4. In the **Run** command box, type **SERVICES.MSC** command and press **Enter** key.
5. On the **Services** window, double-click **Print Spooler** service.
6. On the **Print Spooler Properties** box, click **Stop** button.
7. From the **Startup type** drop-down list, select **Disabled**.

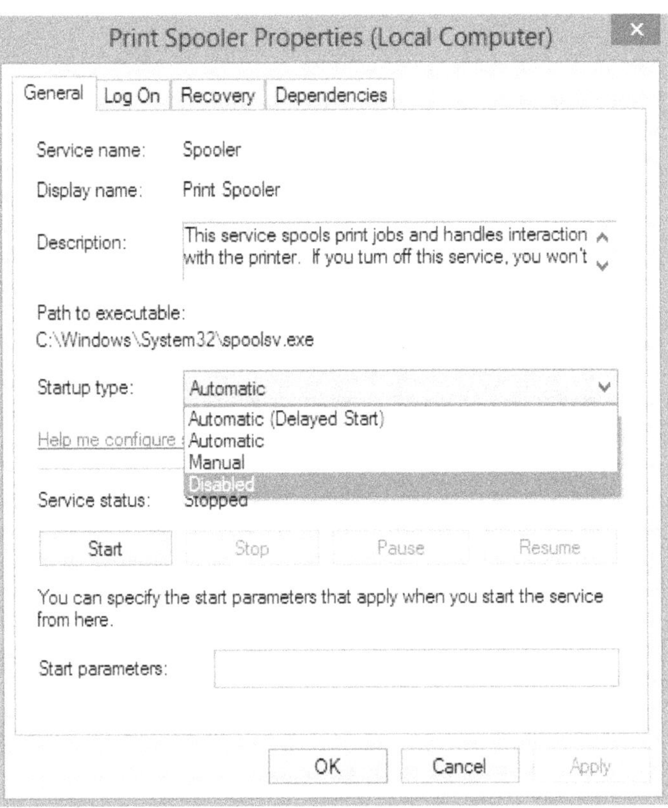

8. Click **OK** to disable printer spooling.

In order to re-enable the printer spooling in Microsoft Windows 8, follow steps 1 to 5, and on the **Print Spooler Properties** box, from the **Startup type** drop-down list, select **Automatic** and click **Apply** button. Click the enabled **Start** button to start the **Print Spooler** service.

CHAPTER 9:

MANAGE DISKS

Create Partitions

Introduction to Partitions

Partitions in a hard disk drive can be thought of as a big hall that has been divided into multiple smaller rooms. Just as all the rooms that have been created by dividing a big hall can be used for separate purposes, in the same way a blank hard disk drive can also be divided into multiple partitions and each partition can be used to store different data. When a new partition is created, the first available drive letter is automatically assigned to it. When the next partition is created, the next available drive letter is assigned to the next partition. For example when administrators create the first partition in the hard disk drive to install Windows, drive letter C: is automatically assigned to it. When another partition is created, D: is assigned to the partition.

Assignment of drive letters to the partitions in the hard disk drive start from C: because A: and B: are reserved for the floppy disk drives. When the first floppy disk drive is installed on the computer, drive letter A: is assigned to it, and when the second floppy disk drive is installed, drive letter B: is assigned to the second floppy disk drive automatically. Since floppy disk drives are no longer used these days and are not installed on the computers anymore, drive letters A: and B: are not displayed to the users while using Windows.

When a new computer system is purchased and a new hard disk drive is installed in it, the hard disk drive does not have any partition created in it. Partitions (sometimes also referred to as the volumes) are created during the installation of the Windows 8 operating system. When the partitions are created, each partition works as an individual hard disk drive. For example in a new hard disk drive if a user has created two partitions namely C: and D:, the created partitions can contain separate data. Moreover, each partition can be used to install a copy of operating system (one operating system on C: and the other OS on D:), hence making the computer dual-boot.

In homes many times users create multiple partitions in order to store different types of data in them. Whereas in production environments, administrators mostly allocate the total space of the hard disk drive to only one partition i.e. C: and install the operating system on it. Administrators do so in order to provide a decent amount of space on the system drive and to the operating systems to experience smooth and efficient performance even if heavy and resource intensive applications are installed on the computer. In order to store other data on the same computer, administrators install a separate hard disk drive and create multiple partitions in it.

Although Microsoft Windows 8 allows administrators to create partitions in the hard disk drive during the installation process, it is recommended that only C: must be created while installing Windows. If the total hard disk drive space is not allocated to C:, users can create other partitions in the hard disk drive after the successful installation of Windows 8.

How to Create a Partition?

In order to create a partition in Microsoft Windows 8, steps given below must be followed:

1. Log on to Microsoft Windows 8 computer.
2. From the **Start** screen, click **Desktop** tile.

3. On the desktop screen, click **File Explorer** icon from the taskbar.
4. On the opened **Libraries** window, right-click **Computer** from the left pane.
5. From the displayed context menu, click **Manage**.
6. On the **Computer Management** snap-in, under **Storage** category from the left pane, click to select **Disk Management**.
7. From the lower half section in the right pane, right-click the unallocated space from the hard disk drive where the new partition is to be created.
8. From the context menu, click **New Simple Volume**.

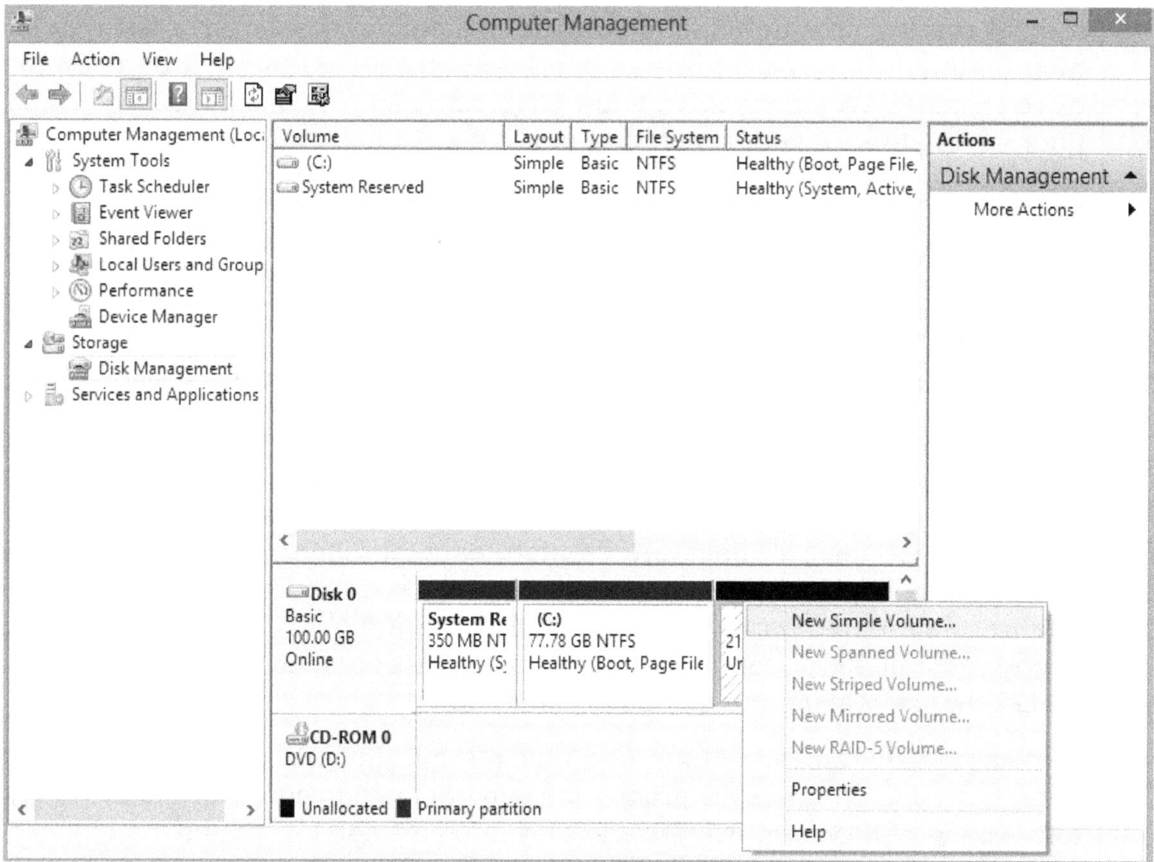

9. On the **Welcome to the New Simple Volume Wizard** page, click **Next**.
10. On the **Specify Volume Size** page, in the **Simple volume size in MB** field specify the size of the new partition (volume) in MB.

    Note: *Maximum size specified for the new partition (volume) must be less than or equal to the maximum available unallocated space in the hard disk drive.*
11. Click **Next** to proceed.
12. On **Assign Drive Letter or Path** page, leave everything as default and click **Next**.
13. On the **Format Partition** window, make sure that **Format this volume with the following settings** radio button is selected and **Perform a quick format** checkbox is checked.

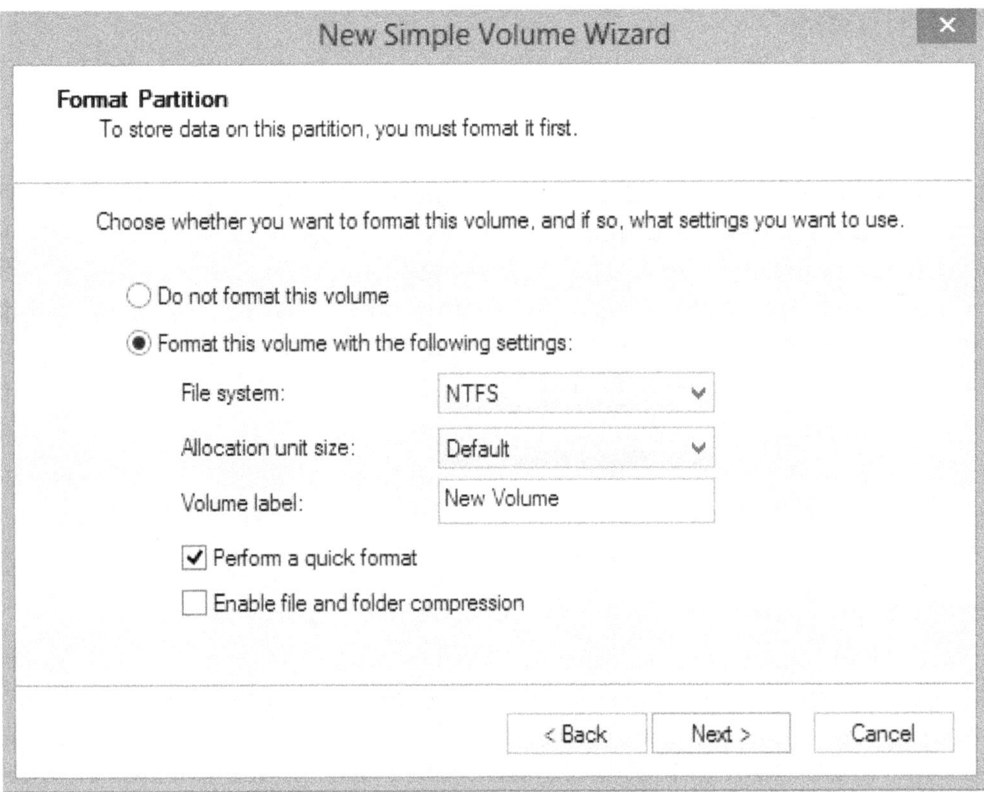

14. Click **Next** to proceed.
15. On **Completing the New Simple Volume Wizard** page, click **Finish** to create and format the new partition as per the defined specifications.

To delete a partition, follow the steps 1 to 6 and from the lower half section in the right pane, right-click the volume that is to be deleted and click **Delete Volume**. Make sure to click **Yes** on the displayed warning box.

Extend a Volume

Introduction to Extending a Volume

After Microsoft Windows 8 is installed on a computer, mostly in homes, users create multiple partitions on a single hard disk drive in order to save different types of data on them. Once a partition is created, users can store files in them. If users keep on storing files on a partition on a regular basis, the partition runs out of space, hence enforcing the users to either remove some data from the drive to make room for the new data, or install another hard disk drive to store the data in the new partition that they create on the new hard drive.

Microsoft Windows 8 eliminates the above mentioned situation by allowing administrators to extend the volumes (partitions) without deleting them. When a volume is extended, its disk space is increased, which allows users to store more data.

Challenges and Limitations While Extending a Partition

In order to extend a partition, the hard disk drive must have some unallocated disk space. The maximum amount of space that can be added to a partition for its extension is the total amount of unallocated disk space that a hard disk drive may have. For example if partition D: is of 50 GB and the total unallocated disk space on the hard disk drive is 25 GB, partition D: can be extended only up to 75 GB by adding the 25 GB of unallocated disk space to it.

In most situations the biggest challenge can be that the users have already allocated the entire disk space to the partitions that they have created after Windows installation, hence leaving no unallocated disk space to extend any other partition. To overcome this situation a different hard disk drive must be installed on the computer and both the disks must be converted to dynamic before using the unallocated disk space from the other hard disk drive to extend an existing partition.

How to Extend a Volume?

In order to extend a volume (partition) in a Microsoft Windows 8 computer, make sure that the hard disk drive whose partition is to be extended has unallocated space. After ensuring, steps given below must be followed:

1. Log on to Microsoft Windows 8 computer.
2. From the **Start** screen, click **Desktop** tile.
3. On the desktop screen, click **File Explorer** icon from the taskbar.
4. On the opened **Libraries** window, right-click **Computer** from the left pane.
5. From the displayed context menu, click **Manage**.
6. On the **Computer Management** snap-in, under **Storage** category from the left pane, click to select **Disk Management**.
7. From the lower half section in the right pane, right-click the volume that is to be extended.
8. From the context menu, click **Extend Volume**.
9. On **Welcome to the Extend Volume Wizard** page, click **Next**.

10. On the **Select Disks** page, make sure that the disk with unallocated space is displayed in the **Selected** list in the right.
11. In the **Select the amount of space in MB** field, specify the amount of space in megabytes that is to be added to the selected volume while extending.

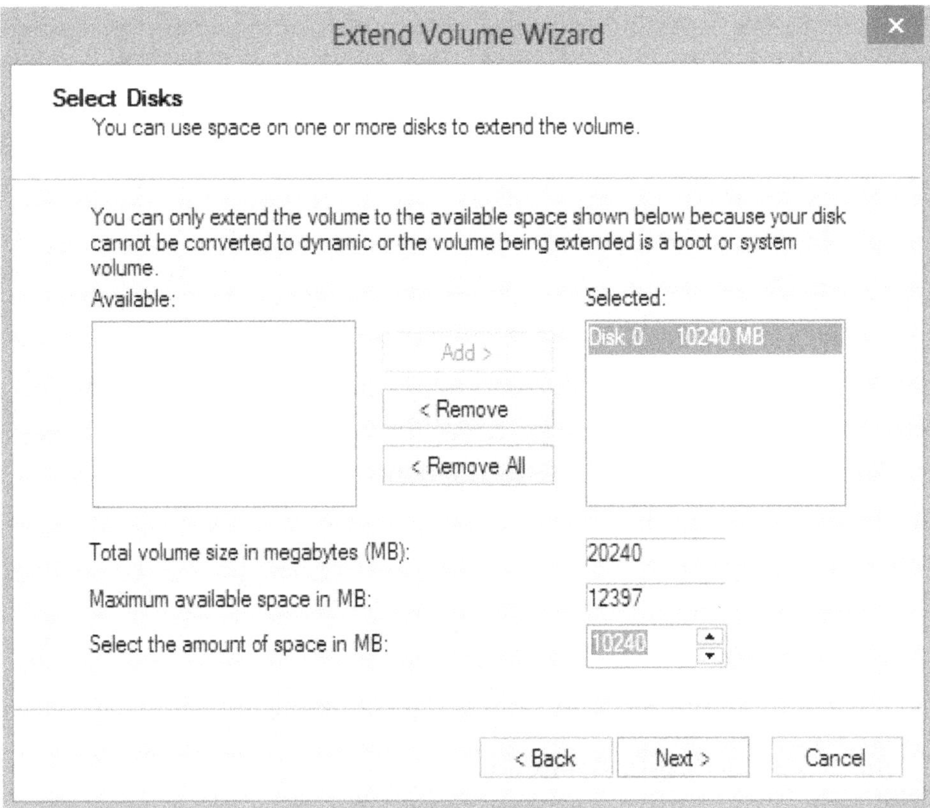

Note: *Maximum size specified to extend the existing partition (volume) must be less than or equal to the maximum available unallocated space in the hard disk drive.*

12. Click **Next** to proceed.
13. On **Completing the Extend Volume Wizard** page, click **Finish** to extend the selected volume.

Shrink a Volume

Introduction to Shrinking Volume

Shrinking volume means reducing the size of the partition in order to free some space on the hard disk drive. When a partition is shrunk, the actual size of the partition is decreased and the amount of space that is freed up because of shrinking becomes unallocated. This unallocated space can then be used to either create a new partition, or to extend any existing partition of the hard disk drive.

In Microsoft Windows 8, a partition can be shrunken only according to the free space that it may have. For example if a partition is of 100 GB in size and has 25 GB of free space in it, it can only be shrunken up to 75 GB, hence un-allocating 25 GB of the space.

Although all partitions in the hard disk drive can be shrunken as per the free space than they have, it is strongly recommended that the size system drive (the partition on which Windows is installed) must never be decreased in order to maintain the efficiency of the operating system.

How to Shrink a Volume?

In order to shrink a volume in Microsoft Windows 8, steps given below must be followed:

1. Log on to Microsoft Windows 8 computer.
2. From the **Start** screen, click **Desktop** tile.
3. On the desktop screen, click **File Explorer** icon from the taskbar.
4. On the opened **Libraries** window, right-click **Computer** from the left pane.
5. From the displayed context menu, click **Manage**.
6. On the **Computer Management** snap-in, under **Storage** category from the left pane, click to select **Disk Management**.
7. From the lower half section in the right pane, right-click the volume that is to be shrunken.
8. From the context menu, click **Shrink Volume**.
9. On the opened box, in the **Enter the amount of space to shrink in MB** field, specify the amount of space in megabytes that is to be subtracted from the selected volume.

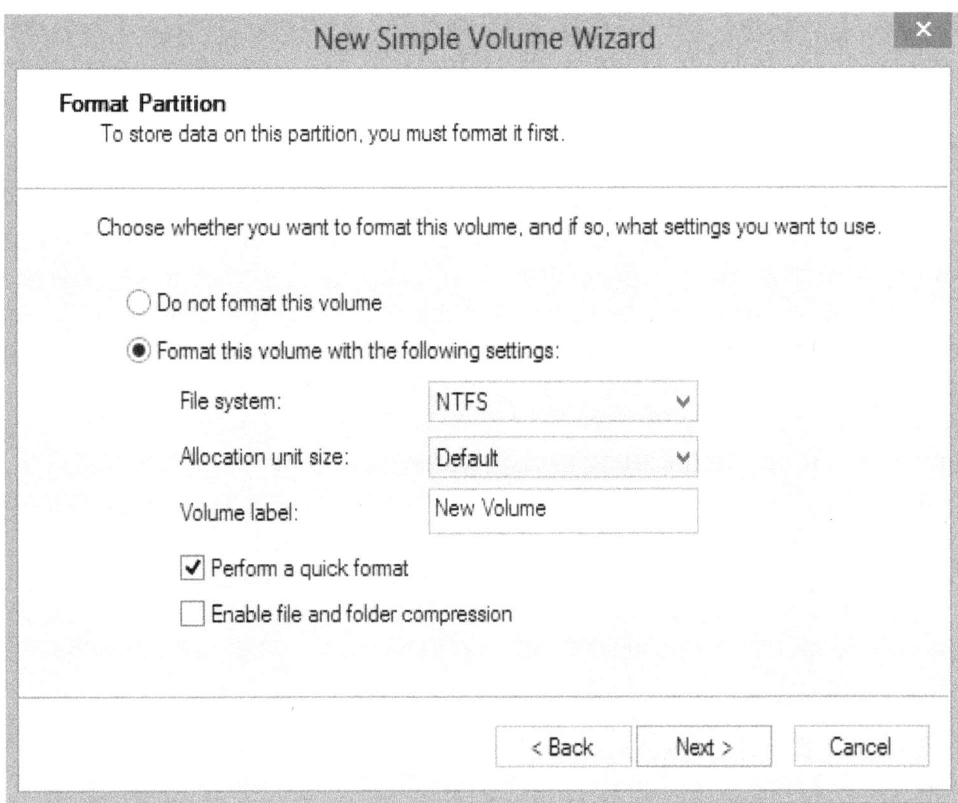

Note: *Maximum amount of space that can be subtracted from a volume must be smaller than the total free space available on that volume.*

10. Click **Shrink** button to shrink the volume.

Note: *Shrinking process may take some time depending on the amount of data stored in the volume.*

Change Drive Letter of Any Fixed/Removable Drive

Introduction to Changing the Drive Letters

When Microsoft Windows 8 is installed, the installation process allows users to create partitions by displaying an interface from where multiple partitions can be created. Since it is recommended that only one partition should be created (i.e. C:) while installing the Windows, and other partitions that administrators plan to have in the hard disk drive should be created after the installation process completes successfully, sequence of the drive letters that are assigned to the partitions might become inappropriate. For example if the recommendations are followed and only C: has been created during Windows 8 installation, as soon as the installation completes successfully, the CD/DVD drive is automatically assigned with the drive letter D:. When administrators create another partition in the hard disk drive, the next available drive letter is assigned to the newly created partition, i.e. E:. Same could be the case when a removable storage media is connected to the computer and Windows automatically assigns an improper drive letter to the media. For example, a connected storage media can be assigned with F: which might not be the last available drive letter.

While using computers in homes, this minute difference and irregular drive letter assignment to the partitions or removable drives might not be noticed by the users, but in production environments situations might differ. In the organizations, administrators might want the drive letters of the partitions in the hard disk drive to be displayed in a proper order and therefore they might want to change the assigned drive letters manually.

How to Change the Drive Letter Manually?

In order to change the drive letters manually in Microsoft Windows 8, steps given below must be followed:

1. Log on to Microsoft Windows 8 computer.
2. From the **Start** screen, click **Desktop** tile.
3. On the desktop screen, click **File Explorer** icon from the taskbar.
4. On the opened **Libraries** window, right-click **Computer** from the left pane.
5. From the displayed context menu, click **Manage**.
6. On the **Computer Management** snap-in, under **Storage** category from the left pane, click to select **Disk Management**.
7. From the lower half section in the right pane, right-click the volume whose driver letter is to be changed.
8. From the context menu, click **Change Drive Letter and Paths**.
9. On the opened box, make sure that the drive whose letter is to be changed is selected in the displayed list and click **Change**.
10. On the **Change Drive Letter or Path** box, ensure that **Assign the following drive letter** radio button is selected.
11. From the drive letters' drop-down list, choose the desired available drive letter to assign it to the selected drive.

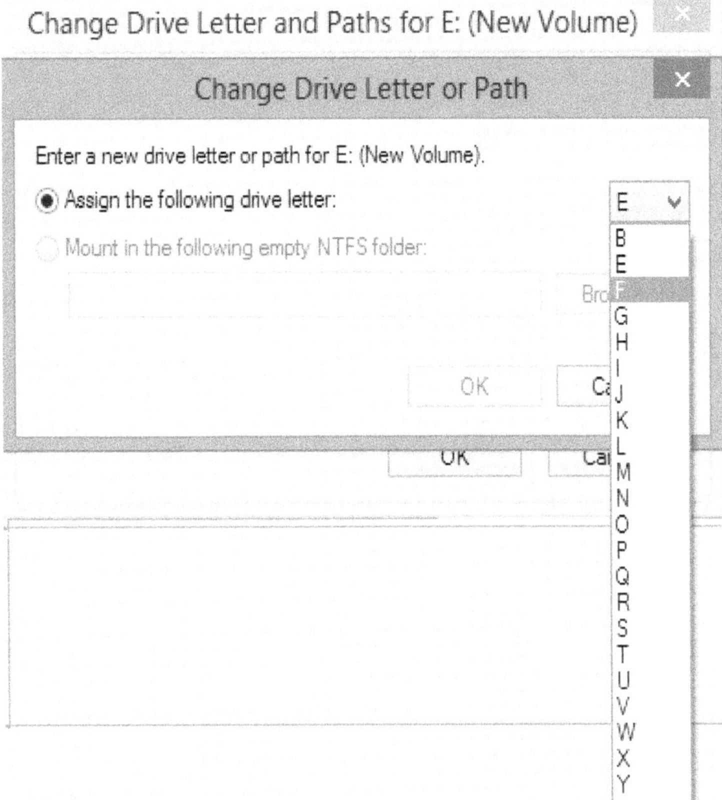

12. Click **OK** and on the displayed warning box, click **Yes** to confirm the changes.

Mount Partitions

Introduction to Mounting Partitions

While using Microsoft Windows 8 in production environments, many times the operating system runs out of the drive letters if users have mapped several network drives or have created multiple virtual image drives. Since every drive that is mapped or created on a computer is automatically assigned with a drive letter, when multiple drives are created, it is quite likely that all available drive letters are assigned to drives, hence leaving no drive letter for any other partition that administrators might create on a computer.

To overcome this situation, Microsoft Windows 8 allows administrators to mount any created partition on any folder that is created in an NTFS drive. In order to mount a partition on any folder, the folder must be blank and must not contain any other object in it.

When a partition is mounted on a folder, it is not assigned with any drive letter, but it can be identified by the name of the folder on which it has been mounted. After creating and mounting a partition on a folder, the partition can then be used as an individual drive which can contain multiple folders and files. If the icon of the partition is deleted from the folder on which it was mounted, the partition does not get deleted physically. Instead it becomes orphan and in order to reuse that partition, administrators must remount it on either the same folder or any other empty folder that resides in any other NTFS volume.

How to Mount a Partition on a Folder?

In order to mount an existing partition on a folder in Microsoft Windows 8, steps given below must be followed:

1. Log on to Microsoft Windows 8 computer.
2. From the **Start** screen, click **Desktop** tile.
3. On the desktop screen, click **File Explorer** icon from the taskbar.
4. From the opened **Libraries** window, navigate to the desired NTFS location and create a new folder.
5. Rename the newly created folder as per the used naming convention.
6. Once done, close the opened window and click **File Explorer** icon from the taskbar again to get back to the **Libraries** window.
7. On the **Libraries** window, right-click **Computer** from the left pane.
8. From the displayed context menu, click **Manage**.
9. On the **Computer Management** snap-in, under **Storage** category from the left pane, click to select **Disk Management**.
10. From the lower half section in the right pane, right-click the volume that is to be mounted on an NTFS folder.
11. From the context menu, click **Change Drive Letter and Paths**.
12. On the opened box, make sure that the drive that is to be mounted on an NTFS folder is selected in the displayed list and click **Add**.
13. On the **Add Drive Letter or Path** box, make sure that **Mount in the following empty NTFS folder** radio button is selected.

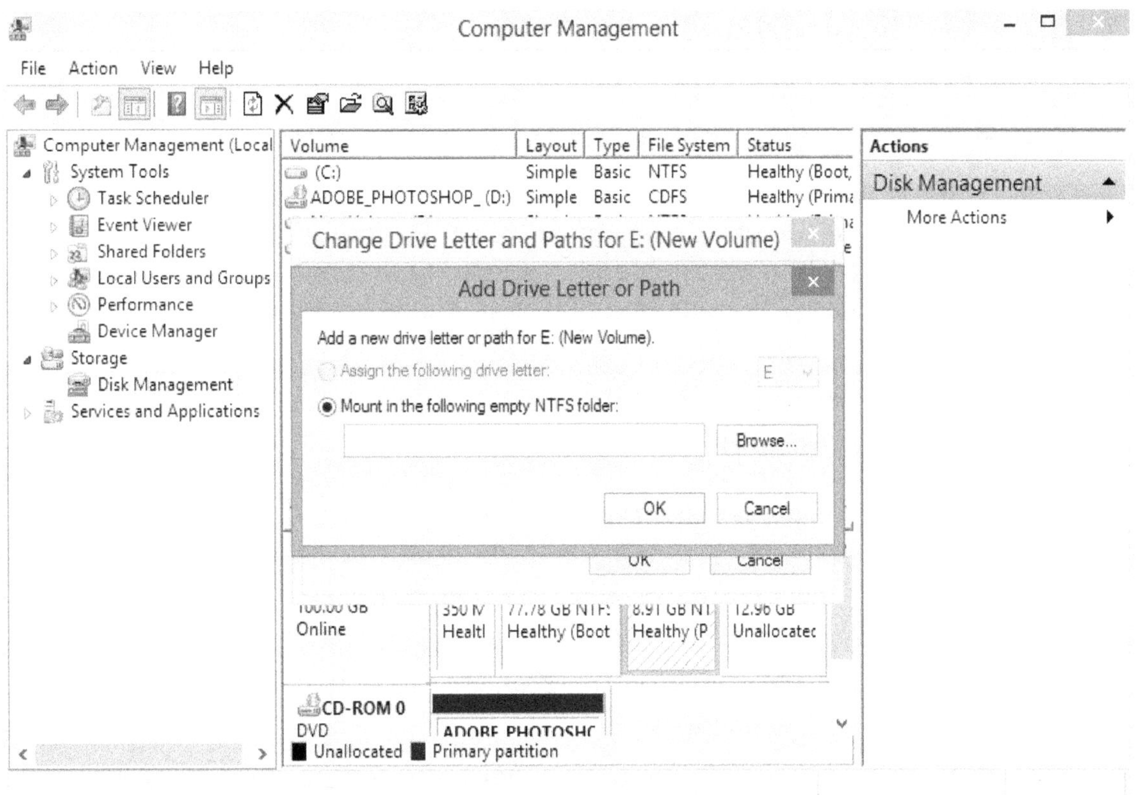

14. Click **Browse** button to browse for and locate the NTFS folder that was created and renamed in steps 4 and 5 respectively.
15. Back on the **Add Drive Letter or Path** box, click **OK** to mount the volume on the selected folder.

Note: *After mounting, optionally administrators can remove the drive letter assigned to the volume by selecting the drive letter from the list in* ***Add Drive Letter or Path*** *box and clicking* ***Remove*** *button. While removing the assigned drive letter, administrators must ensure that they click* ***Yes*** *on any warning box that appears.*

To un-mount a partition from an NTFS folder, follow the steps 1 to 10 and from the displayed list, click to select the folder from which the volume is to be un-mounted. After selecting the folder, click **Remove** button to un-mount the mounted volume. Make sure to click **Yes** on the warning box that appears.

Manage Disk Quota on Drives

Introduction to Disk Quota

Disk Quota is a feature in Microsoft Windows 8 that allows administrators to restrict the disk space usage for the users on per partition basis. For example administrators can enable disk quota on a partition and can specify that every user account that is created on the computer could only consume 10 GB of space on that partition.

Disk quota can be enabled and configured in two ways. When disk quota is enabled and quota limit is specified for the user accounts, by default Windows displays the warning message to the users if they exceed their quota limits. Windows does not restrict users from saving data on the partition. In order to prevent users from consuming the disk space after they have exceeded their quota limits, administrators must check the 'Deny disk space to users exceeding quota limit' checkbox to enable restriction. Moreover, apart from specifying a common quota limit for all users on a computer, administrators can also specify quota limits on per user basis.

Disk quota is only applicable on the standard user accounts, and it remains transparent for all administrator accounts of the computer.

In order to enable the disk quota on a partition, the partition must be formatted with the NTFS file system.

How to Enable Disk Quota?

In order to enable disk quota in Microsoft Windows 8, steps given below must be followed:

1. Log on to Microsoft Windows 8 computer.
2. From the **Start** screen, click **Desktop** tile.
3. On the desktop screen, click **File Explorer** icon from the taskbar.
4. From the opened **Libraries** window, navigate and locate the volume on which the disk quota is to be enabled.
5. Once the volume is located, right-click the target volume and from the context menu, click **Properties**.
6. On the opened properties box, go to **Quota** tab and click **Show Quota Settings** button.
7. On the opened box, check **Enable quota management** checkbox.
8. Check **Deny disk space to users exceeding quota limit** checkbox to prevent users from saving additional data once they have exceeded their quota limit.
9. To specify a common quota limit for all new user accounts, click to select **Limit disk space to** radio button.

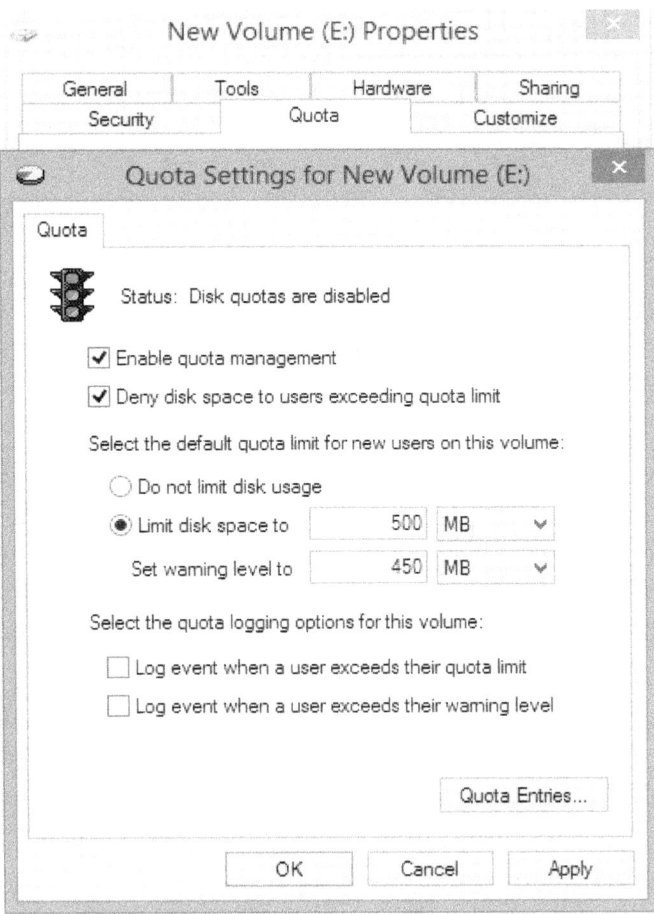

10. Specify the amount of disk space in the available field that is to be set as the quota limit.
11. From the available unit drop-down list, choose the appropriate unit to specify the limit. E.g. GB, TB, etc.
12. In the **Set warning level to** field, specify the limit of disk space usage after which the users should be notified about their limits.

    Note: *Amount of disk space usage set in warning field must be less than or equal to the amount specified while setting quota limit.*
13. Alternatively, **Quota Entries** button can also be clicked to configure quota limit on per user basis.
14. Once desired quota limit is set, click **OK**.
15. On the displayed warning box, click **OK** to apply the quota limits as configured.

Create and Use Virtual Hard Disks

Introduction to Virtual Hard Disks

Virtual hard disks are the files that have .VHD extension. Administrators can create virtual hard disk drives in Microsoft Windows 8 and attach them to the computer. When virtual hard disks are created and attached, they work exactly the way the physical hard disk drives work. The only difference between physical hard disk drives and the virtual hard disks is that the physical hard disks are installed physically on the computers whereas the virtual hard disk drives are just the files that a physical hard disk may contain.

Some other Microsoft-based virtualization applications, such as Microsoft Virtual PC and Microsoft Virtual Server use the virtual hard disk drives to install guest operating systems on them. These virtualization applications allow administrators to create virtual computers and attach the virtual hard disk drives to them. When this is done, virtual computers work exactly the way the physical computers work, with the difference that the virtual computers are the files that are stored in the physical hard disk drives (computer inside a computer).

When virtual hard disk drive is created and attached to a Microsoft Windows 8 computer, another operating system can be installed on it. If configured properly, a physical computer can be made dual boot where one operating system can be installed on the physical hard disk drive, and the virtual hard disk drive can contain the second OS.

Biggest advantage of installing an operating system on the virtual hard disk drive is that the .VHD file on which the operating system has been installed can be moved from one location to another easily and can be attached to any other computer, hence making the other computer dual boot without installing the operating system all over again.

How to Create and Attach a Virtual Hard Disk Drive?

In order to create and attach a virtual hard disk drive to Microsoft Windows 8 computer, steps given below must be followed:

1. Log on to Microsoft Windows 8 computer.
2. From the **Start** screen, click **Desktop** tile.
3. On the desktop screen, click **File Explorer** icon from the taskbar.
4. On the opened **Libraries** window, right-click **Computer** from the left pane.
5. From the displayed context menu, click **Manage**.
6. On the **Computer Management** snap-in, under **Storage** category from the left pane, click to select and then right-click **Disk Management**.
7. From the displayed context menu, click **Create VHD**.

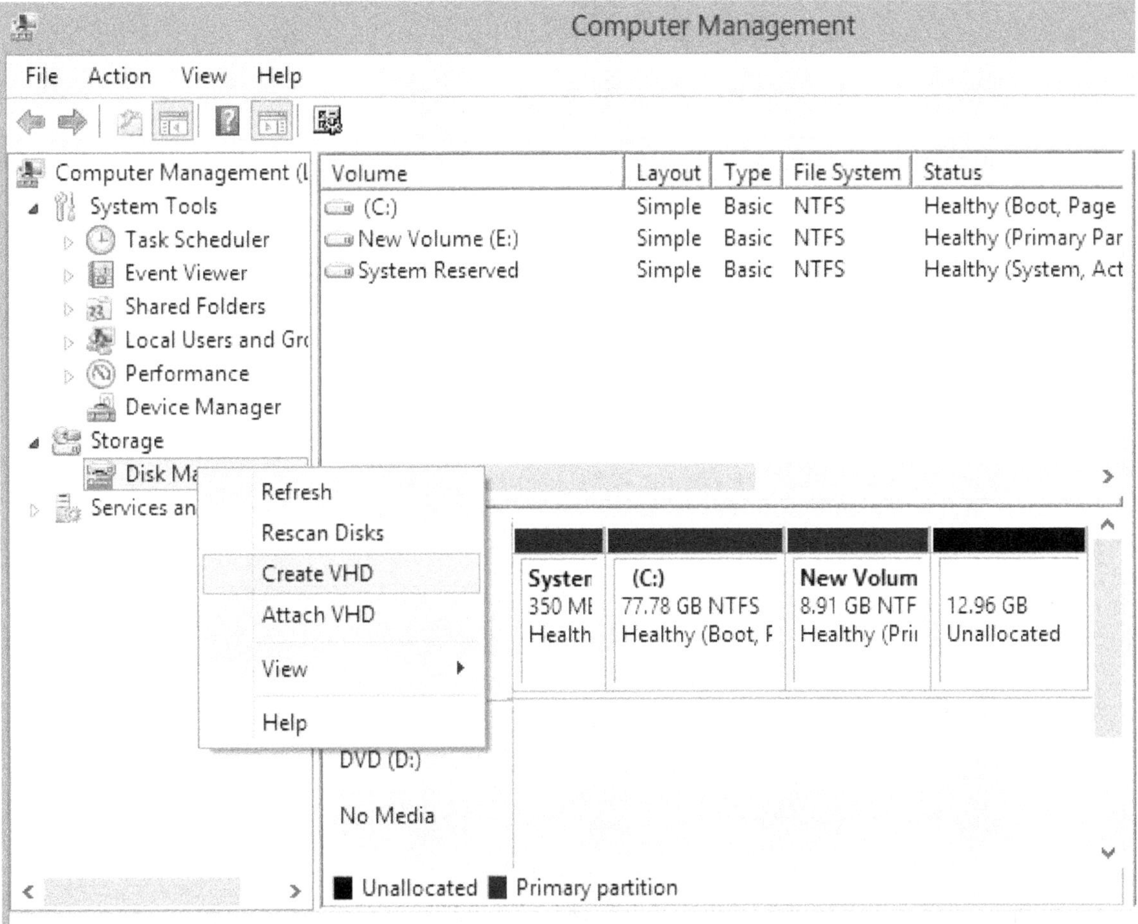

8. On **Create and Attach Virtual Hard Disk** box, click **Browse** button to browse for a location where the new virtual hard disk (VHD) file would be stored.
9. Specify the maximum size of the virtual hard disk in **Virtual hard disk** size field and choose the appropriate unit (MB, GB or TB) from the unit drop-down list.
10. If a fresh copy of Windows operating system is to be installed on the virtual hard disk drive, make sure that **Fixed size (recommended)** radio button under **Virtual hard disk type** section is selected. If the VHD is being created for any other purpose, administrators can click to select **Dynamically expanding** radio button.

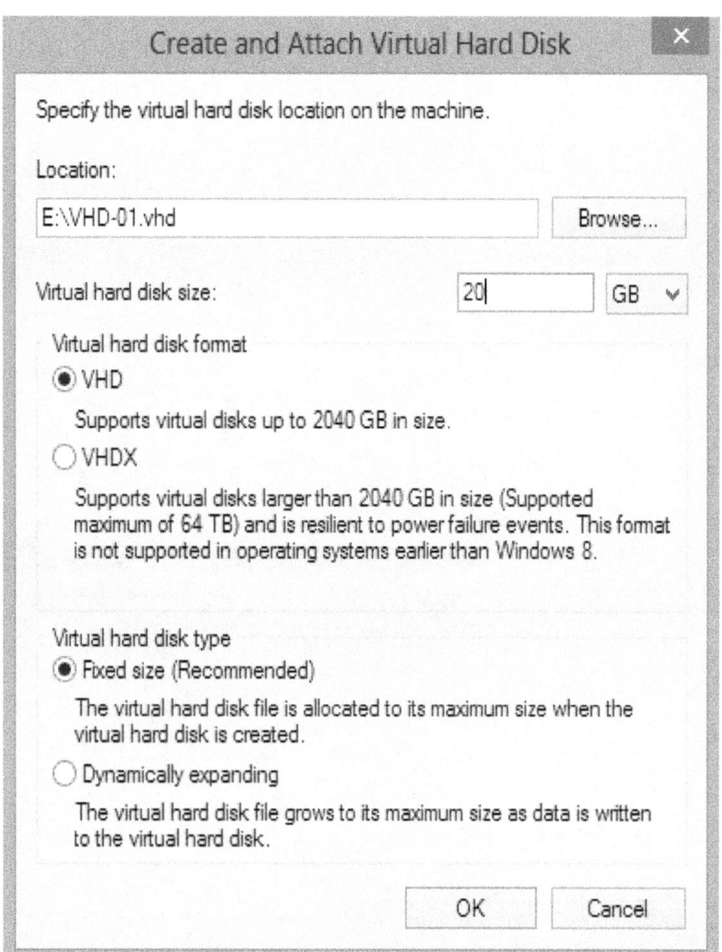

11. Leave everything else as default and click **OK** to create and automatically attach the created virtual hard disk drive to Windows 8 computer.

To detach an attached virtual hard disk drive, follow the steps 1 to 6 and when on step 6, instead of right-clicking, click to select Disk Management and from the right pane, right-click the name of virtual hard disk drive that is to be detached. After right-clicking, click **Detach VHD** and on the displayed box, click **OK** to detach the attached virtual hard disk file.

Attach an Existing Virtual Hard Disk Drive

Introduction to Attaching an Existing Virtual Hard Disk Drive

As mentioned in previous lesson, in Microsoft Windows 8, when a virtual hard disk is created using graphical user interface, the created virtual hard disk is automatically attached as well. Also, an attached virtual hard disk can also be detached by right-clicking the drive and clicking 'Detach VHD'.

Moreover, there might also be times when administrators of Windows 8 computer might want to attach an already created virtual hard disk. The task is quite simple when performed through graphical user interface. However it might sometimes be challenging for the home users and new administrators to attach an existing VHD through command line.

How to Attach an Existing Virtual Hard Disk Drive through Graphical User Interface (GUI)?

In order to attach an existing virtual hard disk through graphical user interface in Microsoft Windows 8, steps given below must be followed:

1. Log on to Microsoft Windows 8 computer.
2. From the **Start** screen, click **Desktop** tile.
3. On the desktop screen, click **File Explorer** icon from the taskbar.
4. On the opened **Libraries** window, right-click **Computer** from the left pane.
5. From the displayed context menu, click **Manage**.
6. On the **Computer Management** snap-in, under **Storage** category from the left pane, click to select and then right-click **Disk Management**.
7. From the displayed context menu, click **Attach VHD**.

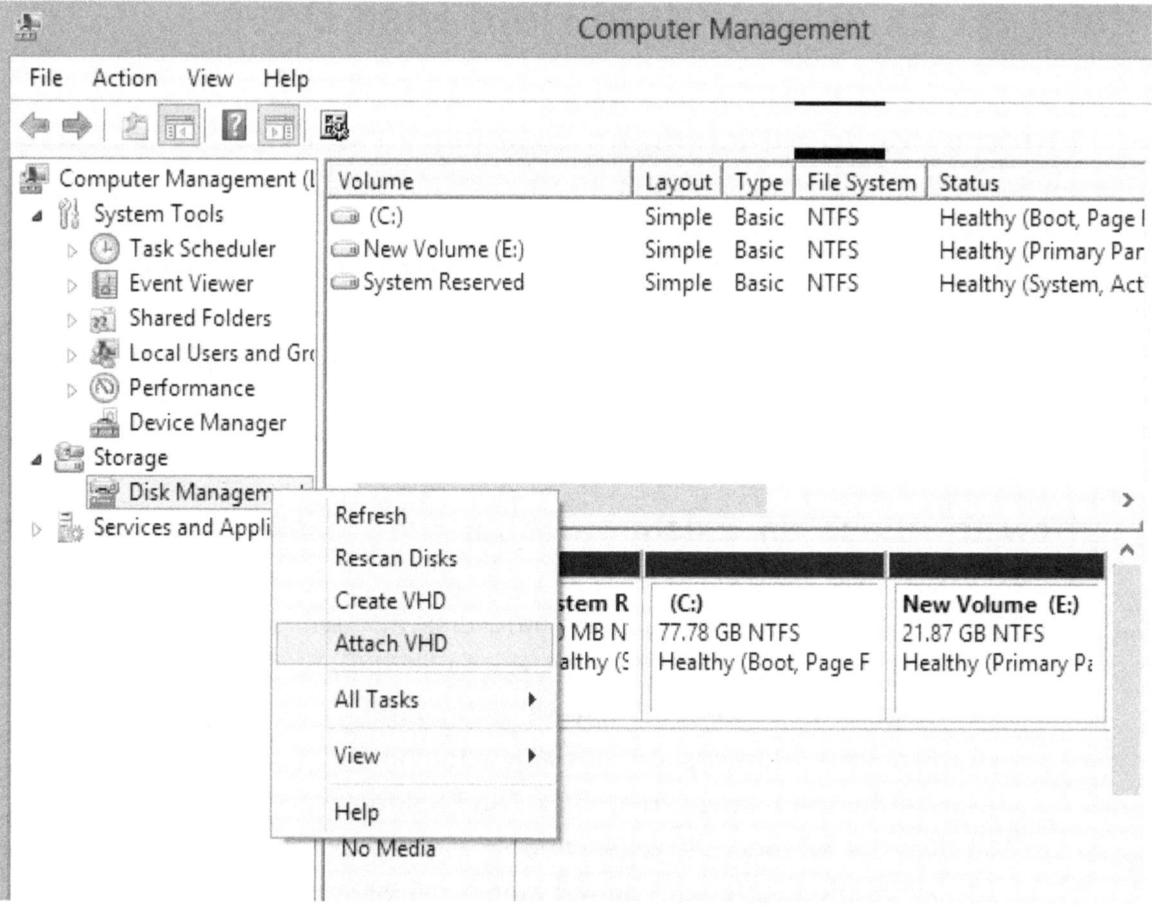

8. On **Attach a Virtual Hard Disk** box, click **Browse** button to browse for and locate an existing virtual hard disk.
9. Once done, click **OK** to attach the located virtual hard disk. Alternatively **Read-only** checkbox can also be checked before clicking **OK** button to attach the virtual hard disk in read-only mode.

Initialize an Attached Virtual Hard Disk

Introduction to Initializing an Attached Virtual Hard Disk

In Microsoft Windows 8, when a virtual or physical hard disk is installed, it must be initialized before administrators can create volumes in it and start storing data or install an operating system. The process of disk initialization is necessary only if a hard disk drive is already present the computer and an operating system is installed on it. In fact, disk initialization is the feature of Windows 8 operating system which automatically prompts administrators to initialize any additional virtual or physical hard disk drive that is attached to the computer.

Since the process of attaching a virtual hard disk drive to Windows 8 computer does not require system restart, the attached virtual hard disk drive is displayed in 'Disk Management' instantaneously. Once a virtual hard disk drive is attached, it is has a red arrow facing downwards displayed on its icon. The red arrow represents that the attached disk is unknown and must be initialized before it can be used on the computer.

How to Initialize an Attached Virtual Hard Disk?

In order to initialize an attached virtual hard disk in Microsoft Windows 8, steps given below must be followed:

1. Log on to Microsoft Windows 8 computer.
2. From the **Start** screen, click **Desktop** tile.
3. On the desktop screen, click **File Explorer** icon from the taskbar.
4. On the opened **Libraries** window, right-click **Computer** from the left pane.
5. From the displayed context menu, click **Manage**.
6. On the **Computer Management** snap-in, under **Storage** category from the left pane, click to select **Disk Management**.
7. From the lower half section in the right pane, right-click the attached virtual hard disk whose status is displayed as **Unknown**.
8. From the displayed context menu, click **Initialize Disk**.
9. On the **Initialize Disk** box, make sure that the virtual hard disk that is to be initialized is displayed in the **Select disks** list and the checkbox that represents the disk is checked.

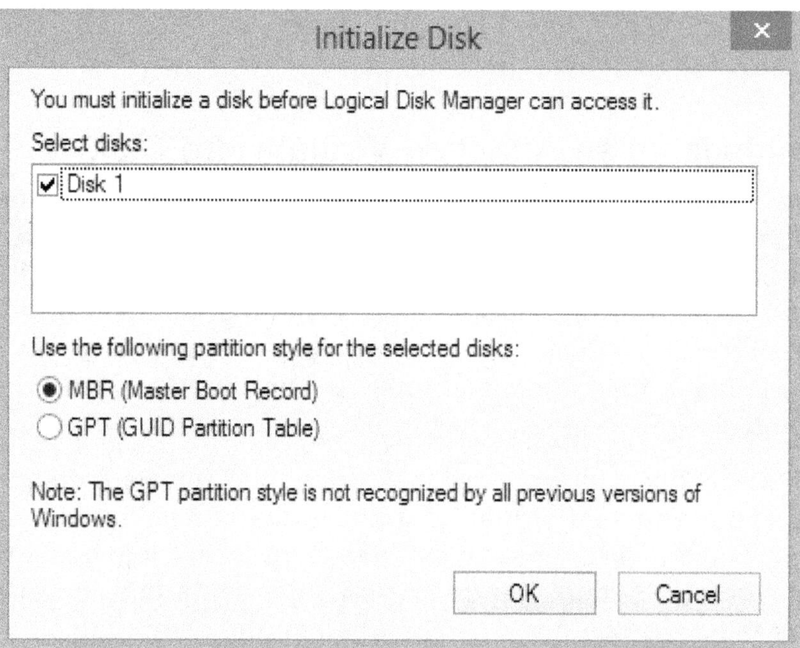

10. Leave everything else as default and click **OK** to initialize the attached virtual hard disk drive.

Note: *Initialization of a newly attached virtual hard disk drive is required even if the virtual hard disk was created earlier and was attached to another computer. In case a virtual hard disk was created, attached and detached from a computer, reattaching the virtual hard disk drive to the same computer does not require initialization.*

CHAPTER 10:
WINDOWS SECURITY

Hide or Unhide Files or Folders

Introduction to Hiding or Un-hiding Files or Folders

While using a computer system, it is quite obvious that users might want to prevent their sensitive information from getting exposed to unwanted people. In homes, parents might want to keep some files secret from their kids, and in production environments it becomes essential for the administrators to hide important files from getting displayed to everyone.

In order to make things easier, Microsoft Windows 8 allows its users to hide their files or the folders so that they are not displayed when the drive is accessed. Hiding or un-hiding files/folders is a user specific task and no elevated privileges are required to complete the process.

How to Hide or Unhide Files or Folders?

In order to hide or unhide files or folders in Microsoft Windows 8, steps given below must be followed:

1. Log on to Microsoft Windows 8 computer.
2. From the **Start** screen, click **Desktop** tile.
3. On the desktop screen, click **File Explorer** icon from the taskbar.
4. On the opened **Libraries** window, navigate and locate the file or folder that is to be hidden.
5. Once located, right click the object and from the context menu, click **Properties**.
6. On the opened properties box, make sure that **General** tab is selected and check **Hidden** checkbox from the **Attributes** section.

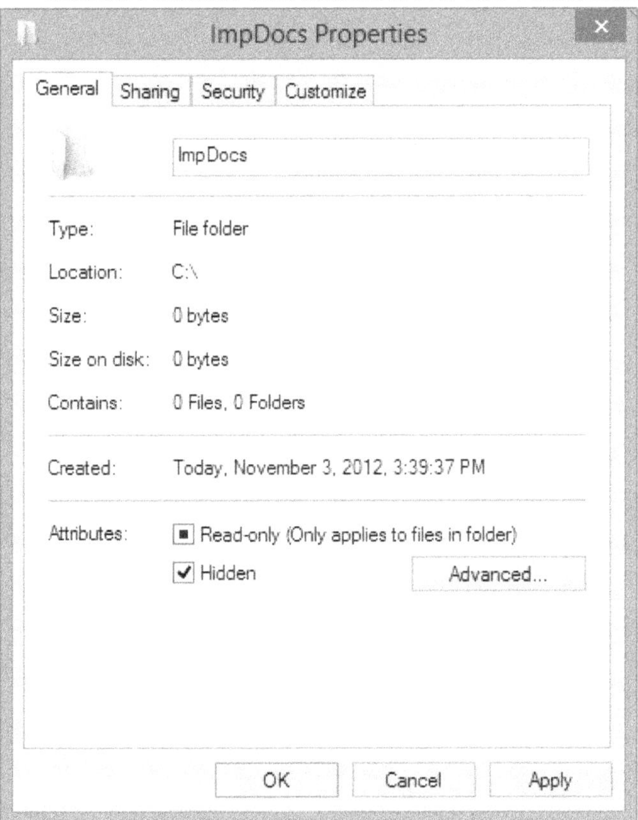

7. Click **OK** when done.

To unhide a hidden object, make sure that the operating system is configured to show hidden files, folders and drives (discussed in the next lesson) and follow the steps from 1 to 7 while unchecking the **Hidden** checkbox from the **Attributes** section when on step 6.

View Hidden Files and Folders

Introduction to Viewing Hidden Files and Folders

As mentioned in previous lesson, if users want to prevent some sensitive files from getting displayed, they must hide the files. In order to view and access the files, they can unhide the files. Biggest challenge while un-hiding files/folders is that since files are not displayed, their hidden attributes cannot be removed. In layman's language, a file cannot be unhidden if it is not displayed, and the file is not displayed because it is hidden.

In order to overcome above mentioned problem, Windows 8 allows users to view the hidden files and folders. When Windows 8 is configured to display hidden files and folders, hidden files and folders are displayed as semi-transparent objects.

How to View Hidden Files or Folders?

In order to view hidden files or folders in Microsoft Windows 8, steps given below must be followed:

1. Log on to Microsoft Windows 8 computer.
2. From the **Start** screen, click **Desktop** tile.
3. On the desktop screen, click **File Explorer** icon from the taskbar.
4. On the opened **Libraries** window, click View from the menu bar.
5. From the displayed options in the ribbon, click **Options**.
6. From the **Folder Options** box, go to **View** tab.
7. On the View, from the **Advanced settings** list, click to select **Show hidden files, folders, or drives** radio button.

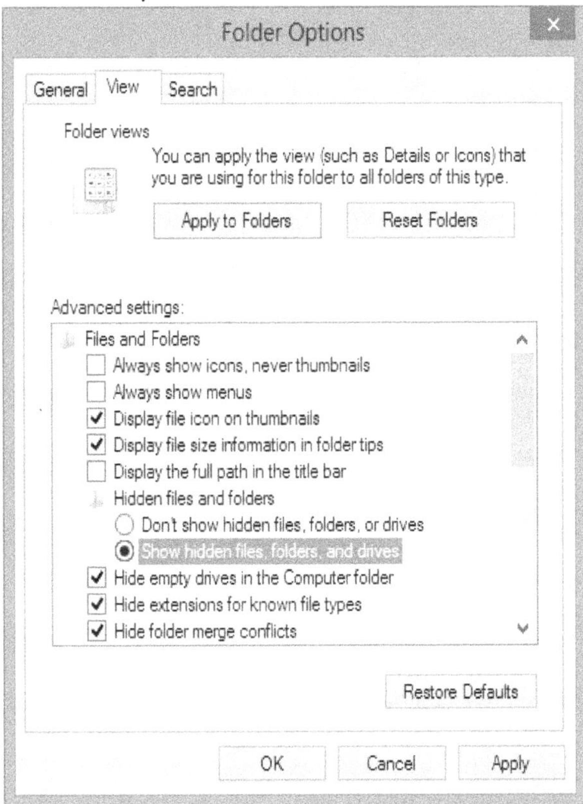

8. Click **OK** when done.

To set the operating system back to its default configuration, steps 1 to 8 can be followed while selecting **Don't show hidden files, folders or drives** radio button when on step 7.

Once hidden files or folders are displayed, their hidden attributes can be removed.

Set NTFS Permissions

Introduction to NTFS Permissions

After installing Microsoft Windows 8 on a computer, when partitions are created on the hard disk drive, created partitions can be formatted using NTFS file system that allows the administrators to set file or folder level NTFS permissions. With the help of NTFS permissions, access to the objects (files or folders) can be controlled, and only the authorized user accounts or groups can be allowed to gain access to the protected objects.

Generally, administrators of a computer are allowed to set NTFS permissions on user accounts or groups. However when a folder or a file is created by a standard user account, since the account becomes the creator owner of the object, the user who logs on to the account can set NTFS permissions for other user accounts or groups on that particular object. For example if 'A' is a standard (non-administrative) user on a computer and has created a folder named 'Important', since user 'A' is the creator of the folder, Windows considers 'A' as the owner of the object and allows to set NTFS permissions on the 'Important' folder and all the subfolders and files that it contains.

NTFS permissions have a slight difference when they are set on files and folders. While setting NTFS permissions on a folder, 'List folder contents' permission is available, whereas the same permission is not available while setting NTFS permissions on a file.

Types of NTFS Permissions

Mostly 6 types of NTFS permissions are available while setting security on a folder, and 5 types of permissions are available for file level security. The permissions and their details are as below:

- **Full control** - When a user account or a group is granted with this permission level, the account or all the accounts in the group get unrestricted privileges on the folder and its contents. Unrestricted permissions means that user/users can create subfolders and files in the folder, and can also modify the contents of the folder, subfolders or the files. Moreover the user account or the accounts in the group are also granted with the permission of setting the permissions for any other user account or group as well. For example if a user account 'A' has been granted with 'Full control' permission on folder 'Important', the account holder 'A' can set permissions for another user account 'B' on the folder.
- **Modify** - When a user or a group is granted with this level of permissions, the user or users get all the permissions that the account or group with 'Full control' permission gets. The only difference in 'Modify' permission level is that user/users cannot set NTFS permissions for any other user account or group. For example if a user account 'A' has been granted with 'Modify' permissions on folder 'Important', the account holder can only make modifications to the contents of the files or the objects in the folder. User 'A' cannot set permissions for the user 'B' on the folder, as it was the case with 'Full control' permission level.
- **Read & execute** - When a user or group is assigned with this level of permissions on a folder or file, user/users can read the contents of the folder or file and if the file is executable or the folder contains any executable file, they can initiate it as well.

- **List folder contents** - As mentioned earlier, this NTFS permission is only available when users assign permissions on a folder. When a user account or a group is granted with this level of permission, user/users can view the contents of the folder.
- **Read** - When this level of permission is assigned for a user or group, the account holder can read the contents of the file, or if the permission is assigned on a folder, the contents (files/subfolders) of the folder can be read as well.
- **Write** - When this NTFS permission is assigned for a user or group, the account holder can add contents to an existing file, or can add more files in the folder on which this level of permission is set.

Apart from above mentioned permission levels, another permission level is also available by the name of 'Special permissions'. By default 'Special permissions' permission level is disabled. The state of 'Special permissions' checkbox automatically changes when the object's NTFS permissions for a user or group are configured more granularly by clicking on 'Advanced' button that is available at the bottom of the interface.

While setting NTFS permissions, make sure that either Allow permission is set to the users or groups or window checkbox is checked at all. It is strongly recommended that Deny permission should not be set on any user or group to avoid unwanted restrictions as the consequences. When Allow permission is not set on any user or group, the commission is automatically set to Implicit Deny. On the other hand, when Deny permission is set on any user or group, the permission is set to Explicit Deny which takes precedence over all the Allow permissions that a user or group may receive because of being a member of any other group.

How to Set NTFS Permissions?

In order to set NTFS permissions on a file or folder in Microsoft Windows 8, steps given below must be followed:

1. Log on to Microsoft Windows 8 computer.
2. From the **Start** screen, click **Desktop** tile.
3. On the desktop screen, click **File Explorer** icon from the taskbar.
4. On the opened **Libraries** window, navigate and locate the file or folder on which NTFS permissions are to be set.
5. Once located, right click the target object and from the context menu, click **Properties**.
6. On the opened properties box, go to **Security** tab.
7. Click **Edit** button on the **Security** tab to add/remove the users or groups and to set the desired NTFS permissions for the users/groups on the selected object.

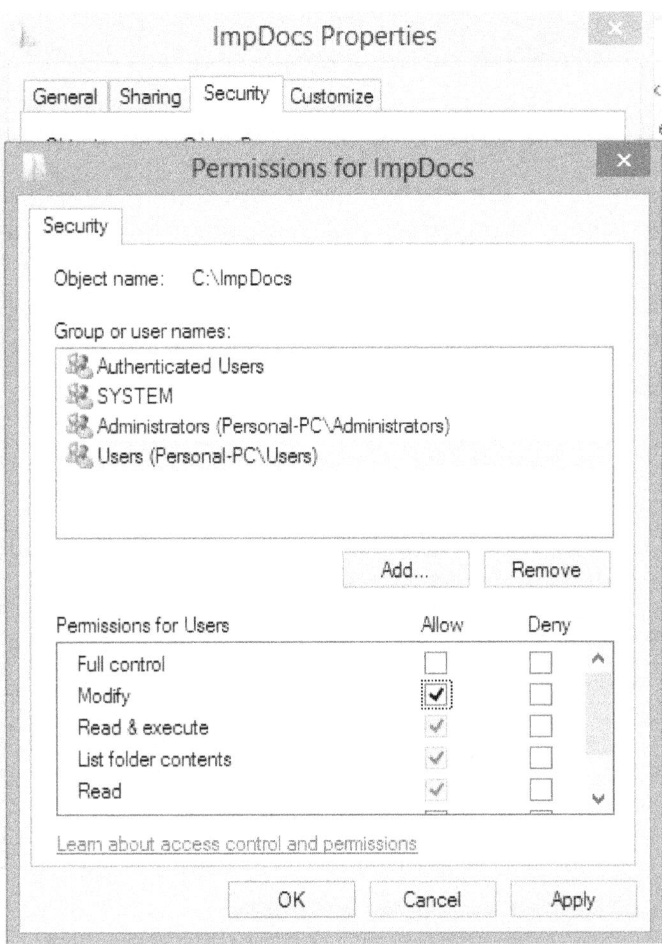

8. Once the appropriate NTFS permissions are set, click **OK** on all the properties boxes to apply the permissions.

View Effective NTFS Access

Introduction to Viewing Effective NTFS Access

When a partition is formatted with NTFS file system, it allows administrators to set NTFS permissions on files or folders that it contains. NTFS permissions can be set on the objects on per user or group basis. In most production environments, a user or group can be member of several other groups, and each group might have different levels of NTFS permissions on the files or folders. In such situations, it becomes quite challenging for the administrators to know the actual level of access a particular user or group has on a file or folder. For example administrators may not be able to know what level of NTFS permissions would be applicable on user 'A' if 'A' tries to access 'File-1' file, especially if 'A' is a member of 5 groups which have different level of NTFS permissions set on 'File-1'.

Fortunately Microsoft Windows 8 as a built-in feature using which administrators can view the level of access a user or group has on a particular object (file or folder).

How to View Effective NTFS Access?

In order to view effective NTFS access for a user or group, steps given below must be followed:

1. Log on to Microsoft Windows 8 computer.
2. From the **Start** screen, click **Desktop** tile.
3. On the desktop screen, click **File Explorer** icon from the taskbar.
4. On the opened **Libraries** window, navigate and locate the file or folder on which effective level access for a user or group is to be viewed.
5. Once located, right click the target object and from the context menu, click **Properties**.
6. On the opened properties box, go to **Security** tab.
7. From the bottom of the **Security** tab, check **Advanced** button.
8. On the opened box, go to the **Effective Access** tab.
9. Once on **Effective Access** tab, click **Select a user** option.
10. On the opened **Select User or Group** box, in the **Enter the object name to select** field, type the name of the user or group for whom effective level of access is to be viewed.
11. Click **Check Names** button to check and verify the name of the typed user or group.
12. Once verified, click **OK**.

    Note: *When a user or group is successfully verified, it's complete name is automatically underlined in the field. In case the typed username or group does not exist, an error message is displayed.*

13. Back on the advanced properties box, click **View effective access** button to view the effective level of NTFS access that the selected user or group has on the object.

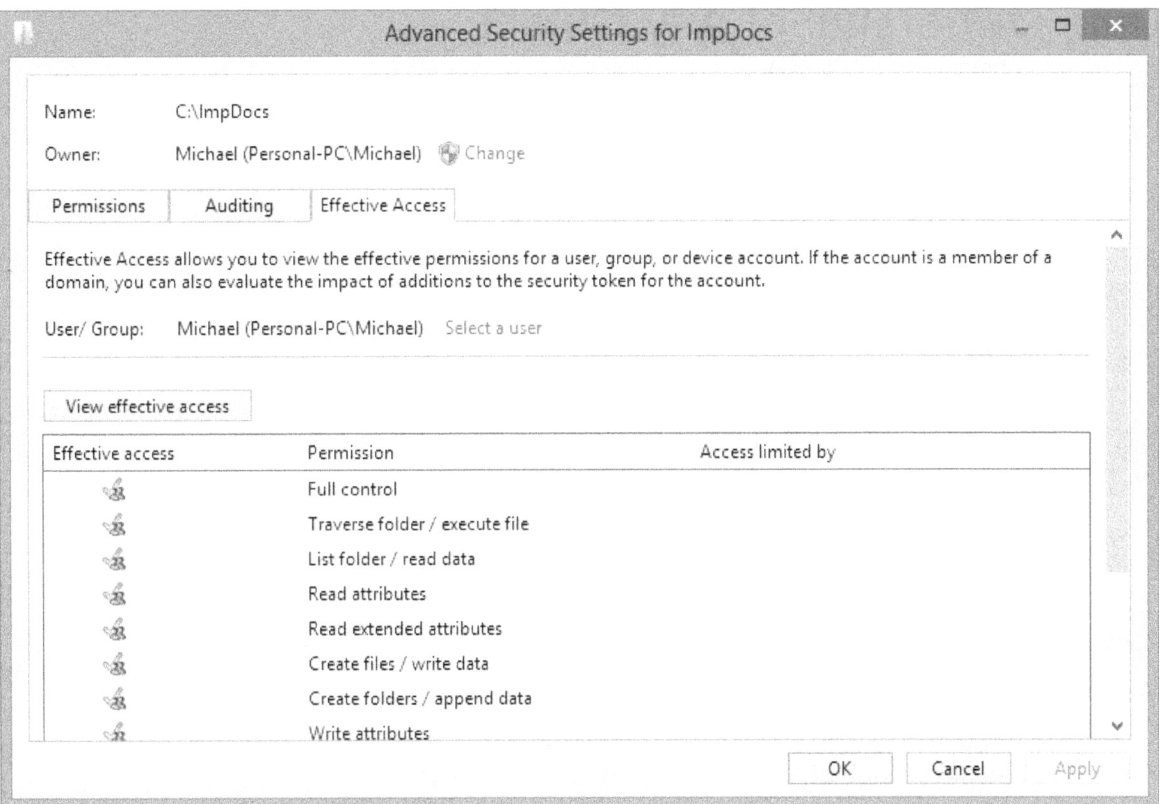

14. Close all the opened boxes and windows when done.

Take Ownership of Any Object

Introduction to Taking Ownership

Microsoft Windows 8 allows administrators of a computer to take ownership of any object on which they do not have permissions. Although administrators of a computer have unrestricted privileges on every object that reside on the computer, there might still be times when a user dealing with sensitive information has restricted access to classified contents, even for the administrators. As being professionals, administrators mostly do not interfere in such activities. However if because of any reason they still need to access the information, and the owner of the contents is not available, they can take ownership of that object.

Taking ownership is a forceful act which must be performed only in critical situations and in emergency. Once administrators have forcefully taken the ownership of an object, they can set NTFS permissions for other users on that object, and can even give the ownership of the object to any other user or group.

One of the biggest disadvantages while taking ownership of any object forcefully is that if the object is encrypted, it cannot be accessed by the new owner. In such case, the contents become permanently inaccessible. Therefore administrators must take utmost care while taking ownership, and must always confirm that the data is not encrypted. If the data is encrypted, they must decrypt it before taking the ownership of the object.

How to Take Ownership of an Object?

In order to take ownership of an object in Microsoft Windows 8, steps given below must be followed:

1. Log on to Microsoft Windows 8 computer with administrator account.
2. From the **Start** screen, click **Desktop** tile.
3. On the desktop screen, click **File Explorer** icon from the taskbar.
4. From the opened **Libraries** window, navigate and locate the object (file or folder) whose ownership is to be taken.
5. Right-click the located object, and from the context menu, click **Properties**.
6. From the object's properties box, go to **Security** tab.
7. Click **Advanced** button.
8. On the opened box, click **Change** option opposite to **Owner** label.
9. On **Select User or Group** box, type the name of the logged on administrator account in the **Enter the object name to select** field.
10. Click **Check Names** button to verify the typed name, and click **OK**.
11. Back on the previous box, check **Replace owner on subcontainers and objects** checkbox under the **Owner** label.

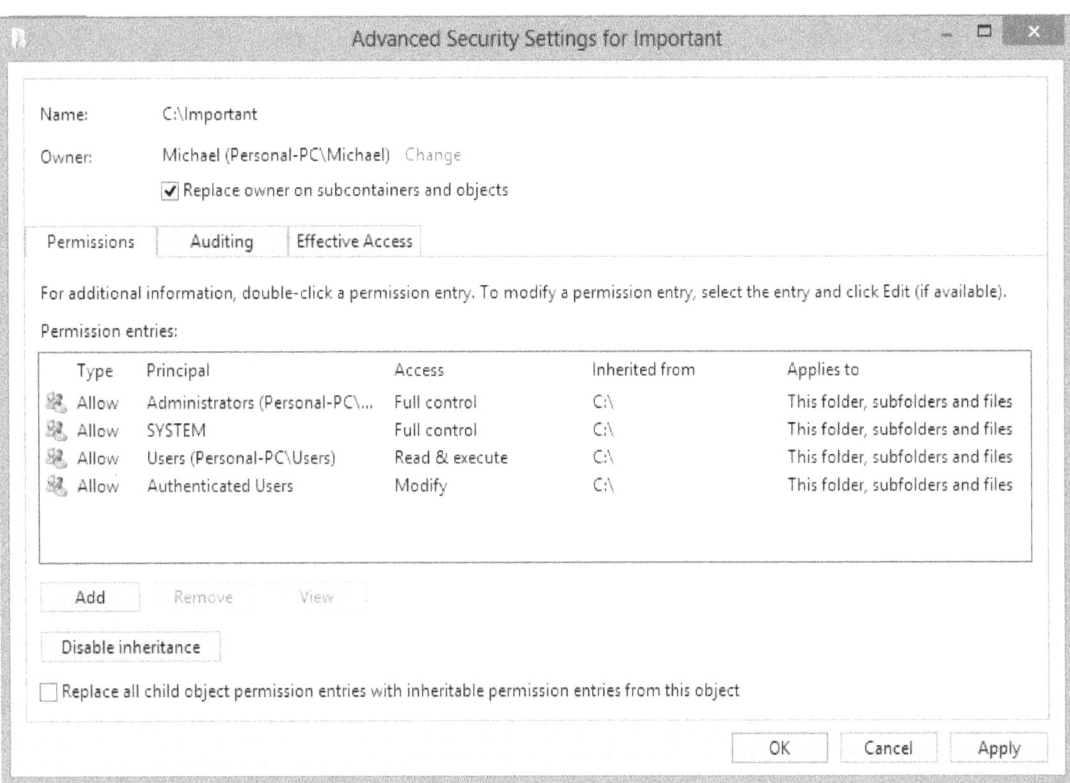

12. From the **Permission entries** list, click to select the user or group to which owner ship is to be given. (Typically the logged on user account or the group to which the logged on user belongs (Administrators)). Alternatively, **Add** button can also be clicked to add a new user or group to the list to grant ownership to the account or group.
13. Once done, click **OK**.
14. On the displayed **Windows Security** warning box, click **Yes** to continue.
15. Back on the object's properties box, click **OK**.
16. Once the object's properties box is closed, re-open it by right-clicking the object and clicking **Properties**.
17. On the object's properties box, go to **Security** tab to configure NTFS permissions as required.

Enable Object Access Auditing

Introduction to Object Access Auditing

In most production environments, it becomes essential for the administrators to keep track of the objects (files or folders) that contain sensitive information. Although administrators allow access to sensitive information only to authorized people and that too with the limited privileges, they must still keep a close eye on the users to prevent any misuse or mishandling of the files or folders.

In order to prevent users from misusing or mishandling files or folders that contain sensitive information, administrators must enable auditing on the objects. Object access auditing must be enabled individually on every object on which the administrators want to keep an eye. Auditing for the objects can be enabled for successful access and/or access failure events.

Once auditing is enabled, every time the object is accessed, a log is generated that can be viewed in the 'Event Viewer' that is available in 'Computer Management' snap-in.

Note: *Before enabling object access auditing on every object, the* ***'Audit object access'*** *policy must be enabled from the group policies.*

How to Enable Object Access Auditing on an Object (File or Folder)?

In order to enable object access auditing on an object (file or folder), steps given below must be followed:

1. Log on to Microsoft Windows 8 computer.
2. From the **Start** screen, click **Desktop** tile.
3. On the desktop screen, click **File Explorer** icon from the taskbar.
4. On the opened **Libraries** window, navigate and locate the file or folder on which auditing for a user or group is to be enabled.
5. Once located, right click the target object and from the context menu, click **Properties**.
6. On the opened properties box, go to **Security** tab.
7. From the bottom of the **Security** tab, check **Advanced** button.
8. On the opened box, go to the **Auditing** tab.
9. Once on **Auditing** tab, click **Add** button.
10. On the opened box, click Select a principal option opposite to Principal label.
11. On the opened **Select User or Group** box, in the **Enter the object name to select** field, type the name of the user or group from whom auditing is to be enabled.
12. Click **Check Names** button to verify the names.
13. Once verified, click **OK**.
14. Back on the previous box, from the **Type** drop-down list, choose the type of auditing that is to be applied on the object. (Success, Fail or All).

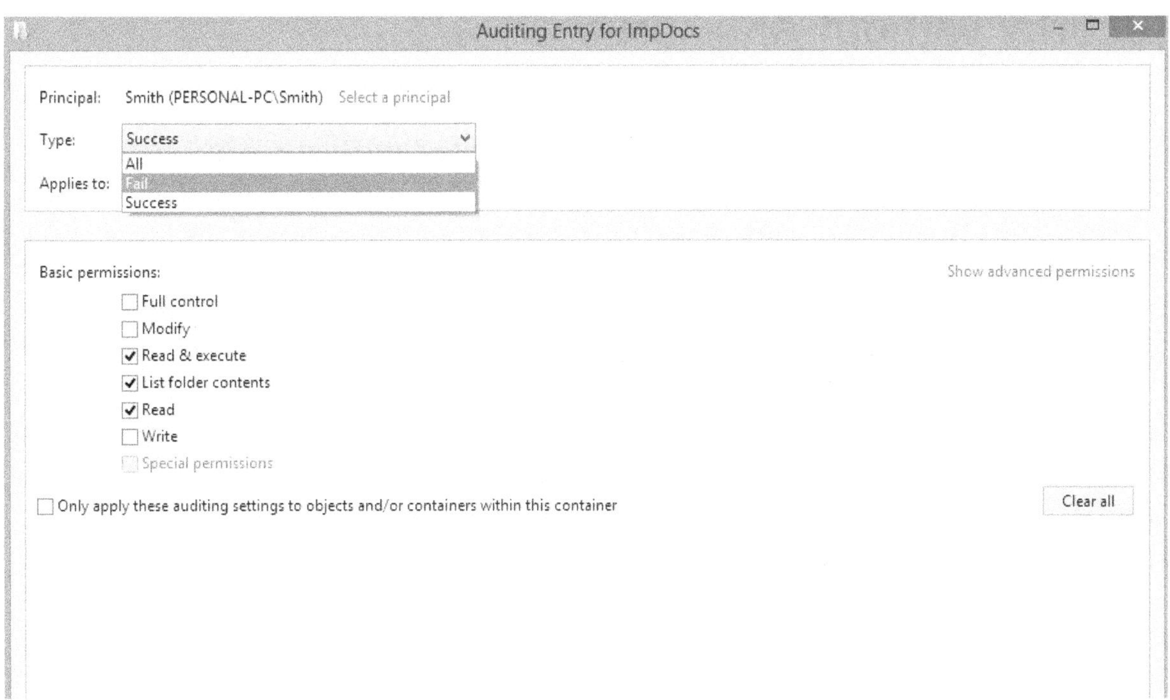

15. Under the **Basic permissions** section, check the checkboxes representing the level of permissions for which the auditing is to be enabled for the selected principal (user or group).
16. Click **OK** button and back on the previous box, click **OK** button again to apply the changes.
17. Back on object's properties box, click **OK**.

To disable object access auditing, follow the steps from 1 to 8 and on the **Auditing** tab, from the displayed users or groups in **Auditing entries** list, click to select the one for whom auditing is to be disabled and click **Remove**. Click **OK** to apply the changes.

Security without Anti-Virus

Introduction to Securing the Computer without Anti-Virus

Almost everywhere an anti-virus application is used to prevent computers from getting infected from the viruses. In production environments administrators install several third-party tools to prevent the networks from the virus attacks and intrusions. Since administrators are technically sound, they can handle the situation quite easily. Challenges might occur for home users when they want to protect their computers from the virus attacks. In order to do so they purchase expensive anti-virus software applications.

Computers can be protected from virus attacks even without installing antivirus applications, but taking just a few precautionary steps.

When an operating system is installed, the very first user that is created during the installation automatically becomes the member of Administrators group. Because of this, the user gets unrestricted privileges on the computer. When home users log on to the user account that was created during the installation, they can perform almost any task on the computer. When they connect to the Internet using the same credentials, the virus programs get into the system, and because the credentials of the logged on user have unrestricted privileges, viruses automatically get installed on the system drives. Most of the time this process remains transparent to the logged on user, hence allowing the virus application to infect the computer unknowingly.

In Microsoft Windows Vista and above operating systems (including Microsoft Windows 8) an additional layer of protection named User Account Control has been added. With the help of User Account Control, every time a logged on user tries to initiate an administrative task, a confirmation box is displayed, in which the user has to allow the program to access the system drive by click 'Yes' button.

Administrators for home computers, at their own ends, can add additional security to the operating systems by creating a standard user account and using that account for regular day-to-day uses. When a standard user account is logged on to the computer and the computer is connected to the Internet, even if a virus program manages to enter the system somehow, it does not get appropriate credentials to get automatically installed.

How to Create a Standard User Account?

*Lesson '**Create a New User Account**' from the chapter '**Manage Users and Groups**' can be referred to learn how to create a standard user account on a Microsoft Windows 8 computer.*

Enable File or Folder Level Encryption

Introduction to File or Folder Level Encryption

When a partition is formatted using NTFS file system, Microsoft Windows 8 allows users to encrypt their files or folders so that their sensitive information can be prevented from unauthorized access. When encryption is enabled on a file or folder, a certificate is automatically generated that contains encryption key and that encryption key is used to encrypt the files or folders. The generated certificate and the encryption key is user specific, which means that every user account on a computer has a different and unique encryption key. This further means that each user account on a computer can encrypt files or folders using its own encryption key, and which cannot be decrypted by any other user's key. When files or folders are encrypted, the entire process is technically called Encrypting File System (EFS).

When users try to access encrypted information, the operating system requests for the key to decrypt the data before it is made available to the users. While accessing the encrypted information, Windows uses the key of the currently logged on user account to decrypt the encrypted data. If the user who is trying to access encrypted information is the same who has encrypted the data, the encryption key matches and the data is decrypted using the key. In case any other user tries to access the data that has been encrypted by any other user, the encryption key does not match and therefore access to the encrypted information is denied for the user. This prevents data from being accessed by any unauthorized person.

For example if a Windows 8 computer has two user accounts namely A and B and A has encrypted file, B user would not be able to access the file that was encrypted by A. The reason behind this is that when A encrypted file, a certificate was automatically generated with a unique encryption key. The encryption key was then used to encrypt the data. When B logged on to the computer and tried to open the file that was encrypted by A, Windows requested for the key to decrypt the file. Since B was logged on, Windows tried to use the unique key that was contained in B's certificate to decrypt the information and failed. On the other hand, if A was logged on to the computer and had tried to access the files that was encrypted using A's credentials, Windows would have granted user A access to the file.

As soon as a file or folder is encrypted for the first time, Windows displays a message in the notification area suggesting the logged on user to back up the encryption key. This is a proactive approach that Windows suggests the user to take so that the encryption key can be restored in case the account's password is reset by the administrators, or because of any reason the encryption key is lost.

Note: *Files or folders can be either encrypted or compressed at a time. If a file is encrypted, it cannot be compressed and if a file is compressed, it cannot be encrypted. In order to encrypt a file, its compression must be removed, and to compress a file its description must be removed.*

How to Encrypt a File or Folder?

In order to encrypt a file or folder in Microsoft Windows 8, steps given below must be followed:

1. Log on to Microsoft Windows 8 computer.
2. From the **Start** screen, click **Desktop** tile.
3. On the desktop screen, click **File Explorer** icon from the taskbar.
4. On the opened **Libraries** window, navigate and locate the file or folder on which encryption is to be enabled.
5. Once located, right click the target object and from the context menu, click **Properties**.
6. On the objects properties box, make sure that **General** tab is selected and click **Advanced** button.
7. On the **Advanced Attributes** box, check **Encrypt contents to secure data** check-box from **Compress or Encrypt attribute**s section.

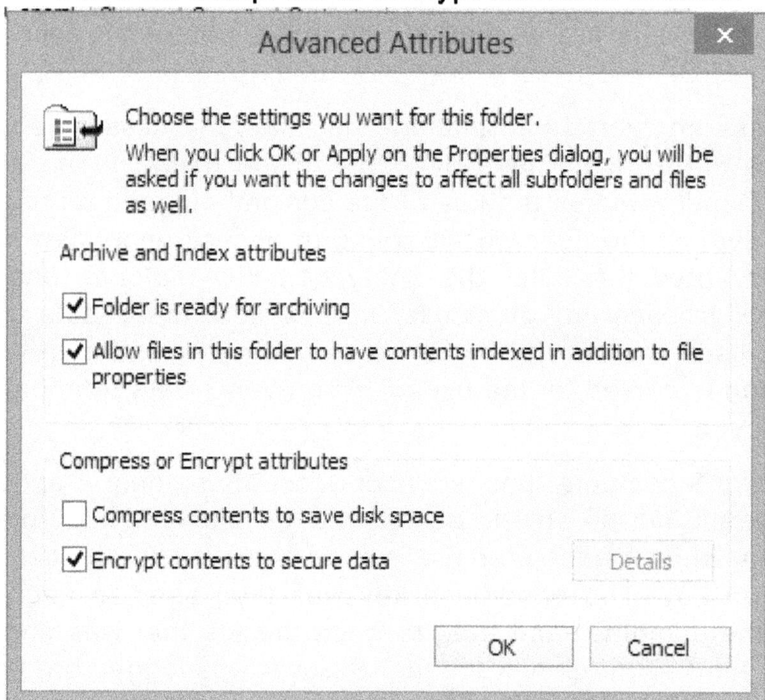

8. Click **OK** to continue.
9. Back on the objects properties box, click **OK** button.
10. On the **Confirm Attribute Changes** box, make sure that A**pply changes to this folder, subfolders and files** radio button is selected. (**Confirm Attribute Changes** box is displayed only when the encryption is enabled on a folder or a drive. The box does not appear when the encryption is enabled on a file.)

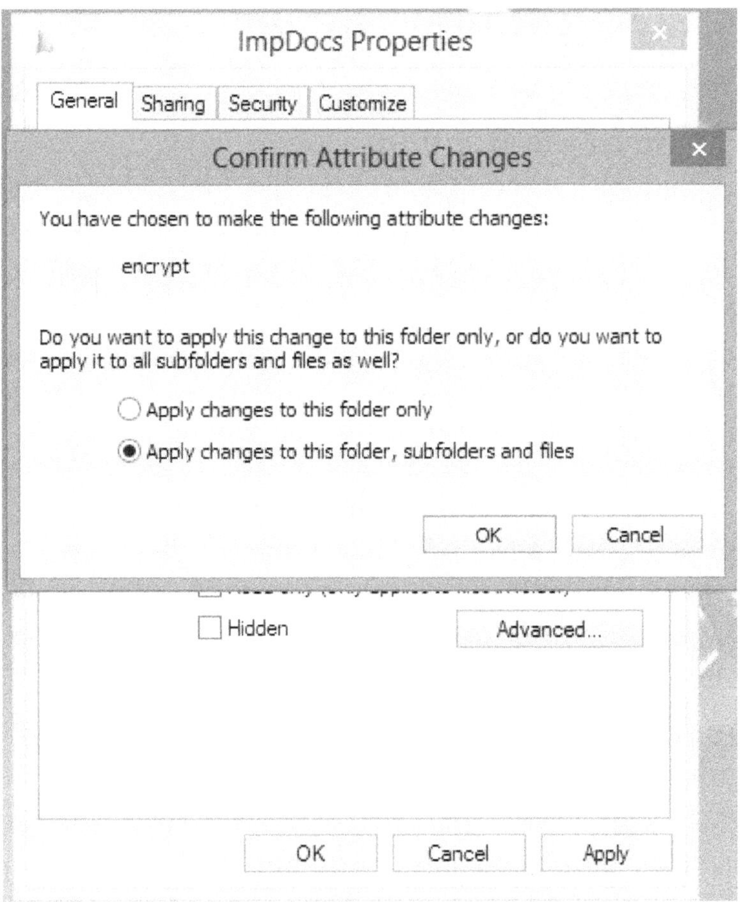

11. Click **OK** to encrypt the selected object.

To remove encryption from a file or folder, steps 1 to 11 can be followed, while unchecking **Encrypt contents to secure data** checkbox when on step 7.

Restrict Users from Playing Rated Games

Introduction to Rated Games Restriction

Microsoft Windows 8 has a built-in Parental Control feature that allows administrators of home computers to restrict other users from playing the games that have certain ratings. For example, with the help of Parent Control, parents can prevent their kids from playing the games that have adult ratings.

In most production environments, administrators use third-party applications to restrict users from accessing certain applications or games. Sometimes administrators also configure group policy settings in order to prevent users from opening specific applications. Since home users are not expected to be as technically sound as the administrators in production environments are, Parental Control feature allows them to control the accessibility of games without having in-depth technical knowledge.

When Parental Control is enabled on Microsoft Windows 8, it is only applicable on the standard user accounts. No administrator accounts are affected with the restrictions and limitations of Parental Control.

How to Restrict Users from Playing Rated Games?

In order to restrict users from playing rated games in Microsoft Windows 8, steps given below must be followed:

1. Log on to Microsoft Windows 8 computer with administrator account.
2. From the **Start** screen, click **Desktop** tile.
3. On the desktop screen, hover mouse to the bottom right corner of the window.
4. From the displayed options, click **Settings**.
5. On the **Settings** pane, click **Control Panel**.
6. From the opened **Control Panel** window, click **Set up Family Safety for any user** under the **User Accounts and Family Safety** category.
7. On the **Family Safety** window, click the standard user (non-administrator) account that is to be restricted from playing rated games.
8. On the **User Settings** window, under the **Family Safety** section, click to select **On, enforce current settings** radio button.
9. From the **Windows settings** section, click **Windows Store and game restrictions** option.
10. On the opened **Game and Windows Store Restrictions** window, click to select **<username> can only use games and Windows Store apps I allow** radio button.

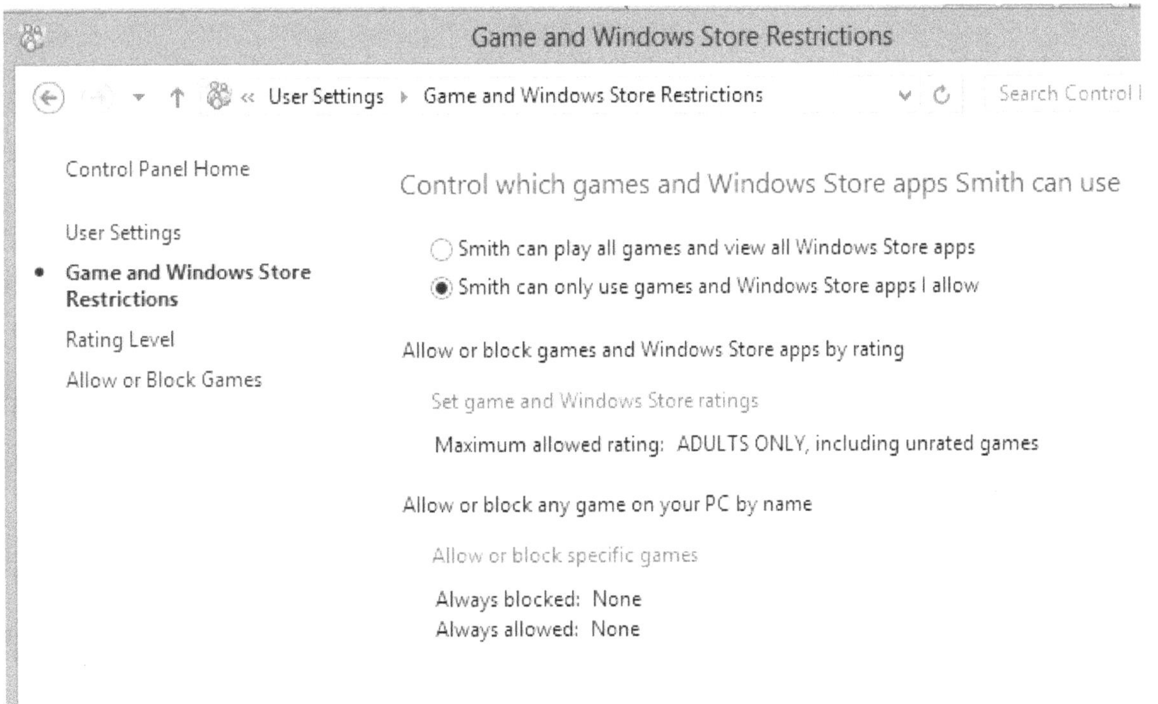

11. Under the **Allow or block games and Windows Store apps by rating** section, click **Set game and Windows Store ratings**.
12. On the **Rating Level** window, click to select the radio button representing the maximum level of allowed ratings for the selected user account. For example, when **Teens** radio button is selected, only the games and Windows Store apps that fall in the **Teens** or below category would be allowed for the user account.

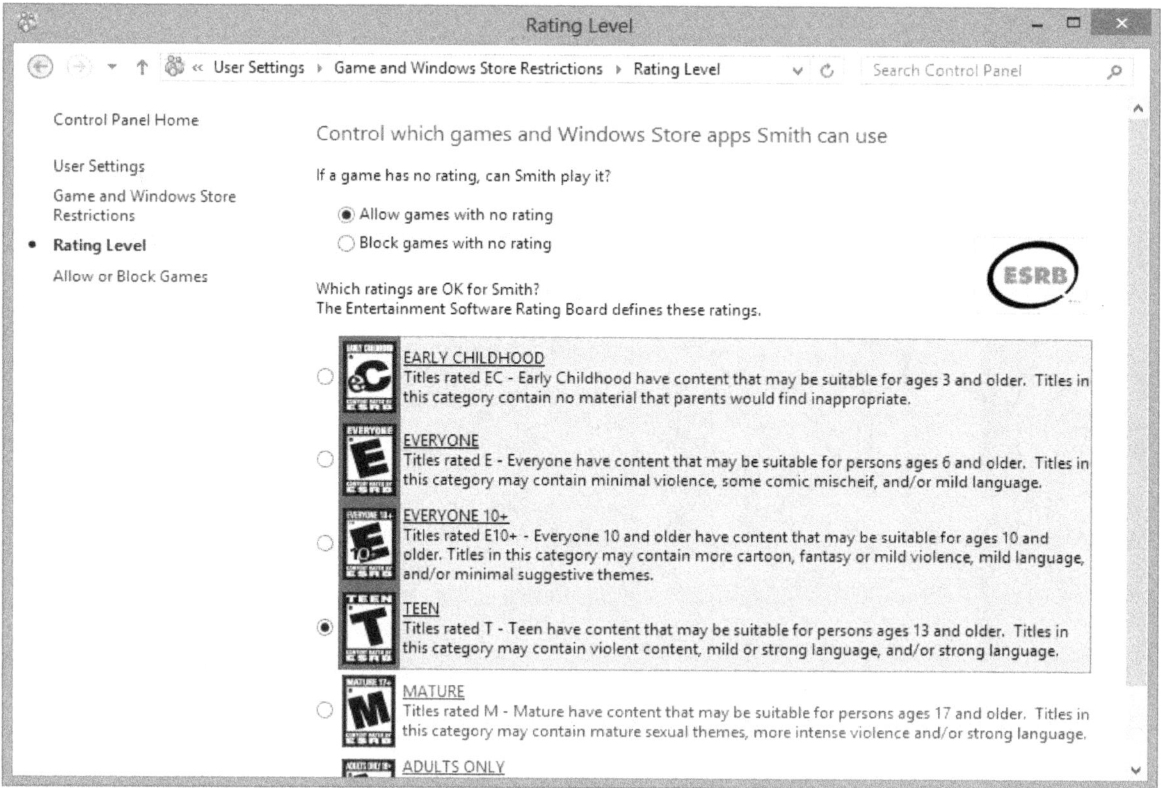

13. Close all the opened windows when done.

To remove the restriction, steps 1 to 8 can be followed, while selecting **Off** radio button under **Family Safety** section when on step 8.

Restrict Users from Using Certain Applications

Introduction to Application Usage Restriction

Parental Controls in Microsoft Windows 8 not only restricts users from playing rated games, but it also restricts users from accessing certain applications as well. As mentioned in previous lesson, administrator accounts remain unaffected from Parental Control restrictions and limitations and the restrictions are applied on standard user accounts only.

Parental Control restrictions can be applied on per user basis. This means that in order to prevent multiple users from accessing a particular application, restrictions must be applied for each user account individually.

How to Restrict Users from Using an Application?

In order to prevent users from using an application in Microsoft Windows 8, steps given below must be followed:

1. Log on to Microsoft Windows 8 computer with administrator account.
2. From the **Start** screen, click **Desktop** tile.
3. On the desktop screen, hover mouse to the bottom right corner of the window.
4. From the displayed options, click **Settings**.
5. On the **Settings** pane, click **Control Panel**.
6. From the opened **Control Panel** window, click **Set up Family Safety for any user** under the **User Accounts and Family Safety** category.
7. On the **Family Safety** window, click the standard user (non-administrator) account that is to be restricted from using applications.
8. On the **User Settings** window, under the **Family Safety** section, click to select **On, enforce current settings** radio button.
9. From the **Windows settings** section, click **App restrictions** option.
10. On the **App Restrictions** window, click to select **<username> can only use the apps I allow** radio button.

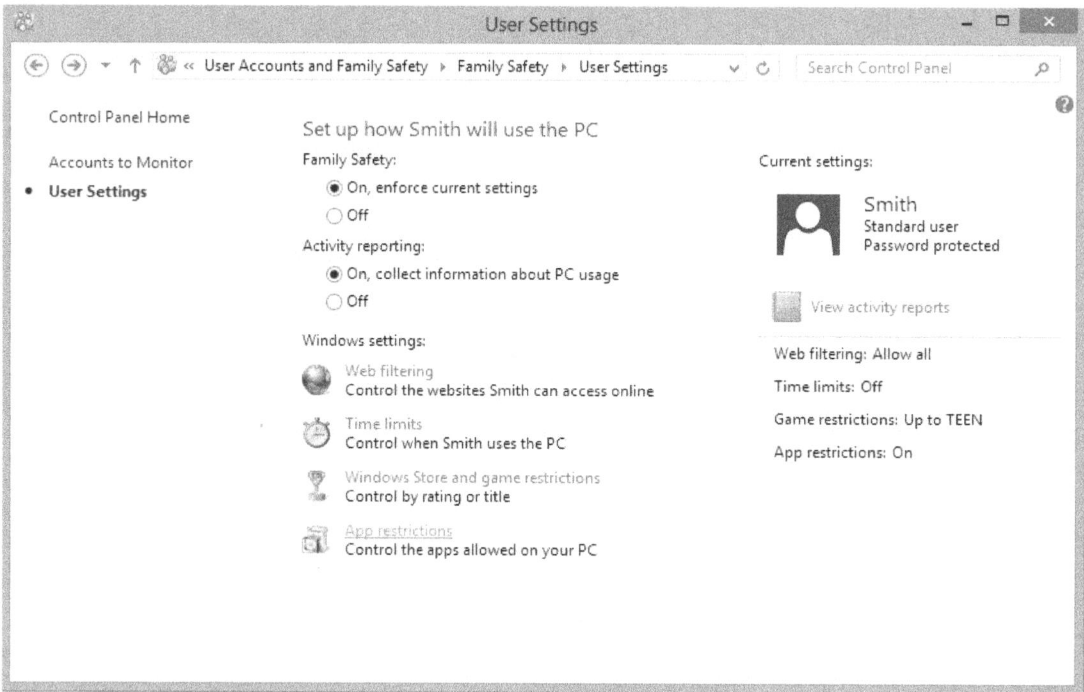

11. From the displayed list, check the checkboxes representing the apps that should to be available to the selected user.

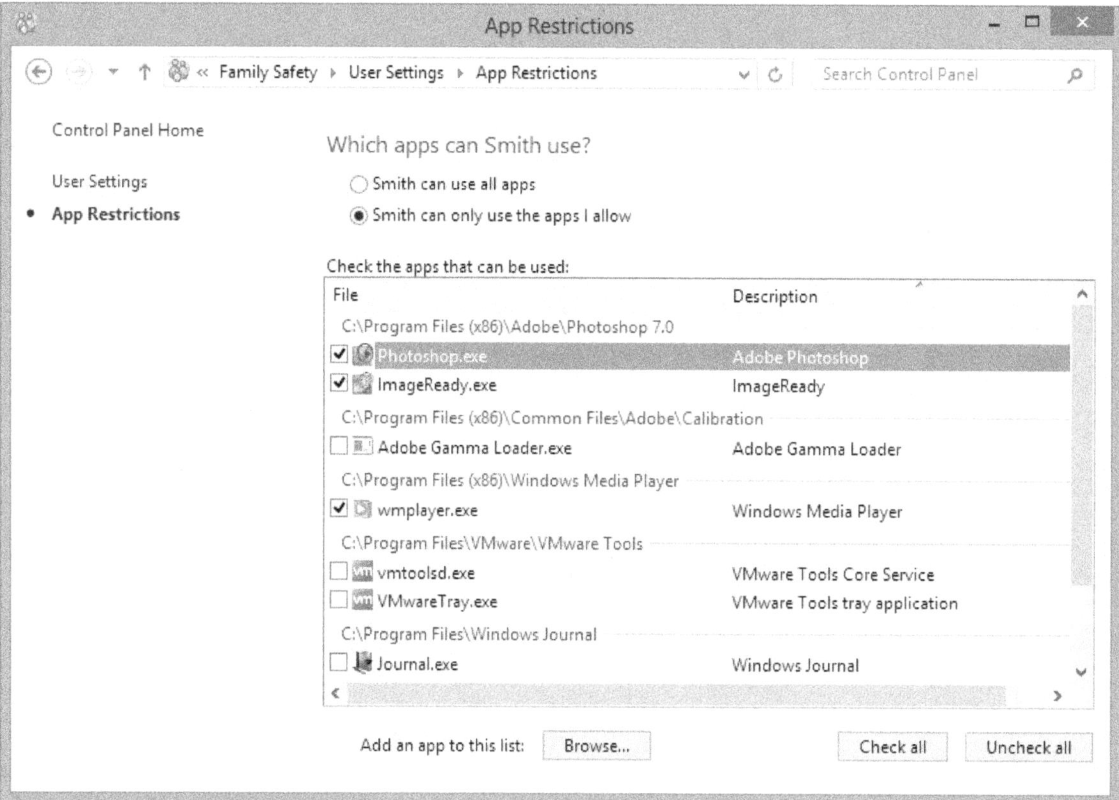

***Note:** If any app is not available in the displayed list, **Browse** button can be clicked to browse and add the missing app.*

To remove the restriction, steps 1 to 8 can be followed while selecting **Off** radio button under Family Safety section when on step 8.

Manage Data Execution Prevention (DEP)

Introduction to Data Execution Prevention (DEP)

Data Execution Prevention (DEP) is a built-in security feature in Microsoft Windows 8 that prevents malicious applications from getting loaded into the memory. Windows has its own criteria of identifying the malicious codes that an application may have, and once DEP detects malicious codes, it prevents them from getting loaded into the memory. This adds an extra layer of security to the operating system which prevents system files from getting corrupted. By default Data Execution Prevention feature is turned on in order to make the system secure.

Under normal conditions and in most home and production environments, users are not required to modify the Data Execution Prevention settings. However there might be times when users might install some third-party applications, codes of which are not recognized by the Windows. When this is the case, DEP takes them as the malicious codes and prevents them from getting loaded into the memory, hence not allowing the application to execute. In such scenarios, where the administrators know that the application is safe to run on a computer but it is still blocked by the DEP, they can configure Data Execution Prevention and make the feature oversee the applications, codes of which Windows cannot understand. Once the trusted applications are added to the Data Execution Prevention exception list, the programs can be executed flawlessly even if their codes are not recognized by the operating system.

How to Add Applications to Data Execution Prevention Exception List?

In order to add applications to the Data Execution Prevention exception list, steps given below must be followed:

1. Log on to Microsoft Windows 8 computer with administrator account.
2. From the **Start** screen, click **Desktop** tile.
3. Once on the desktop screen, click **File Explorer** icon from the taskbar.
4. On the opened **Libraries** window, right click **Computer** from the left pane.
5. From the displayed context menu, click **Properties**.
6. On the opened **System** window, click A**dvanced system settings** from the left pane.
7. On the opened **System Properties** box, you sure that **Advanced** tab is selected.
8. Under the **Performance** section, click **Settings** button.
9. On the opened **Performance Options** box, go to the **Data Execution Prevention** tab.
10. On the **Data Execution Prevention** tab, click to select **Turn on DEP for all programs and services except those I select** radio button.
11. Once done, click **Add** button to add the application that should not be monitored by DEP.

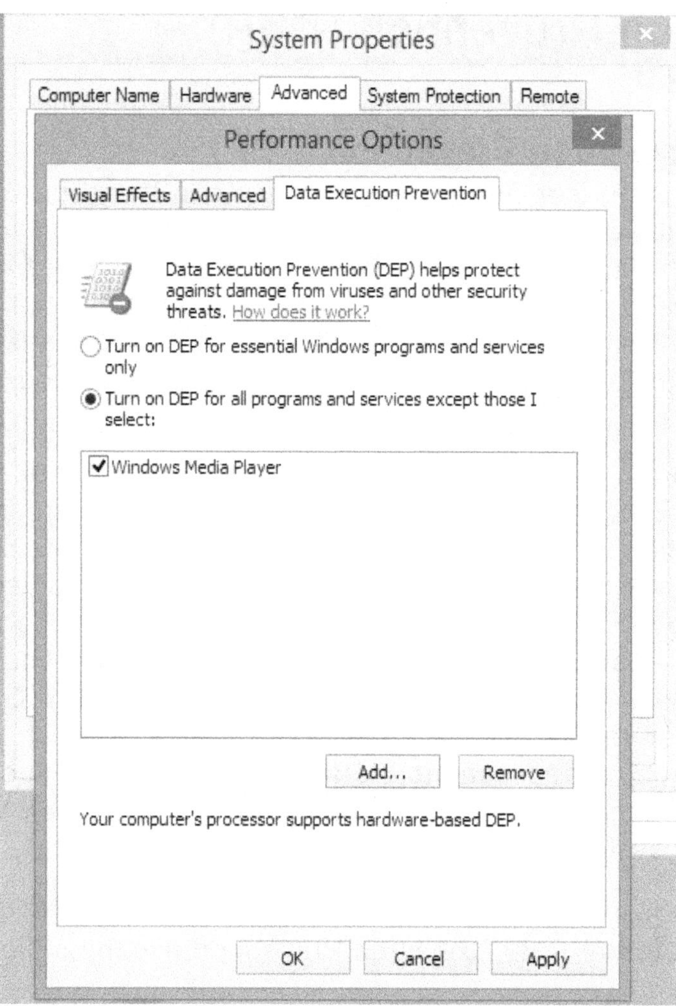

12. Click **OK** to save the changes.

To remove the applications from the Data Execution Prevention exception list, steps 1 to 9 can be followed and when on **Data Education Prevention** tab, the application that the administrators want to be monitored by DEP must be selected from the displayed list and **Remove** button must be clicked to remove the application from the list. **OK** button must be clicked to confirm the changes.

Encrypt Drives with BitLocker

Introduction to BitLocker Drive Encryption

BitLocker is a feature in Microsoft Windows 8 that allows administrators of a computer to encrypt the entire system drive. During the BitLocker Drive encryption process, an encryption key pair (set of two keys) is generated. The first key of the key pair is stored in the Trusted Platform Module (TPM) that is integrated in the motherboard, and the second key of the pair is displayed to the administrators. Administrators must note down the second key and keep it in a safe place in order to protect it from any unauthorized access.

After BitLocker Drive Encryption process successfully completes, when administrators try to start the computer, the computer requests for the second key of the key pair. When administrators type the second key of the key pair, it is then matched with the first key of the pair (that was stored in the TPM on the motherboard) to form a complete key pair. If the key provided by the administrators is correct, the complete key pair is then used to decrypt the encrypted system drive. On the other hand, when the key provided by the administrators is Incorrect, the drive becomes inaccessible. If the contents of the drive are tried to be extracted forcefully, the data that the drive contains gets permanently corrupted, hence preventing the contents to get exposed to any unauthorized person.

Although boot process is delayed when a system drive of a computer is encrypted with BitLocker, the introduced latency is almost negligible and remains transparent to the users.

Prerequisites to Enable BitLocker Drive Encryption

Before enabling BitLocker Drive Encryption, administrators must verify the presence of Trusted Platform Module (TPM) on the motherboards. In case the TPM is not present, administrators must configure Windows to enable BitLocker Drive Encryption without the TPM. This configuration can be done through the local group policies of the operating systems.

In case Windows 8 is configured to enable BitLocker Drive Encryption without TPM chip, a USB pen drive must be used to store the unlock key. After the system drive has been encrypted with BitLocker Drive Encryption, and the computer is started, the USB pen drive must be connected to the computer to allow the system to unlock the encrypted drive using the unlock key. In some cases, administrators can enable BitLocker drive encryption even without a USB flash drive. In such cases, they must manually provide the unlock key at the system start which then decrypts the encrypted drive.

How to Enable BitLocker Drive Encryption?

In order to enable BitLocker Drive Encryption on a Microsoft Windows 8 computer, steps given below must be followed:

1. Log on to Microsoft Windows 8 computer with administrator account.
2. From the **Start** screen, click **Desktop** tile.
3. On the desktop window, click **File Explorer** icon from the taskbar.
4. On the opened **Libraries** window, click **Computer** from the left pane.

5. On the opened **Computer** window, right-click the drive on which **BitLocker** drive encryption is to be enabled. (C: for this demonstration).
6. From the displayed context menu, click **Turn on BitLocker**.
7. Wait till **BitLocker** checks the selected drive.
8. On **Choose how to unlock your drive at startup** window click either **Insert a USB flash drive** or **Enter a password** option to proceed. (**Enter a password** option for this demonstration).

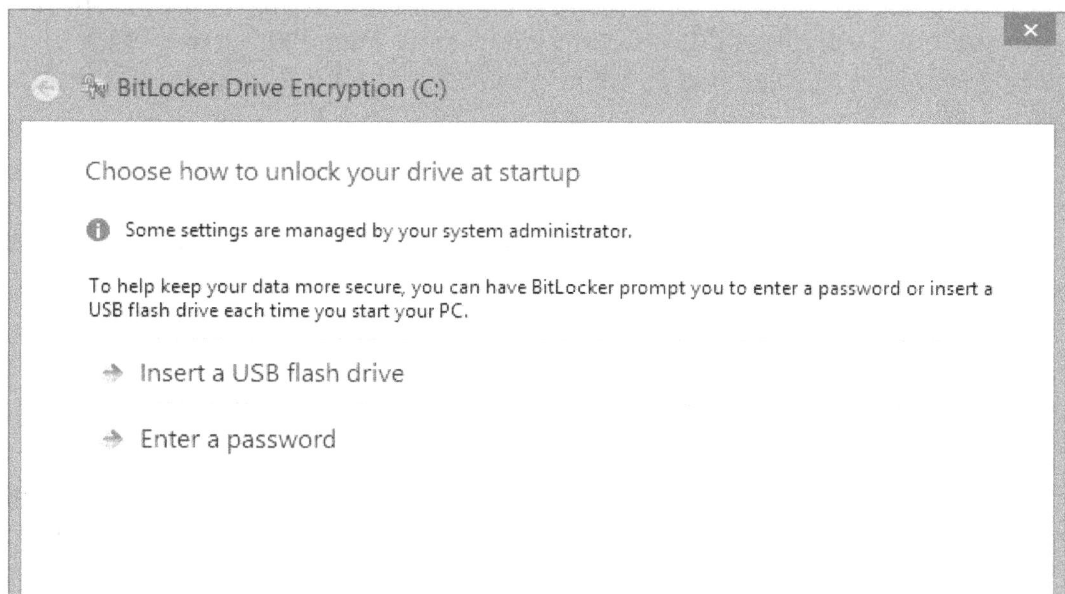

9. On **Create a password to unlock this drive** window, type and retype a strong password in the corresponding fields.

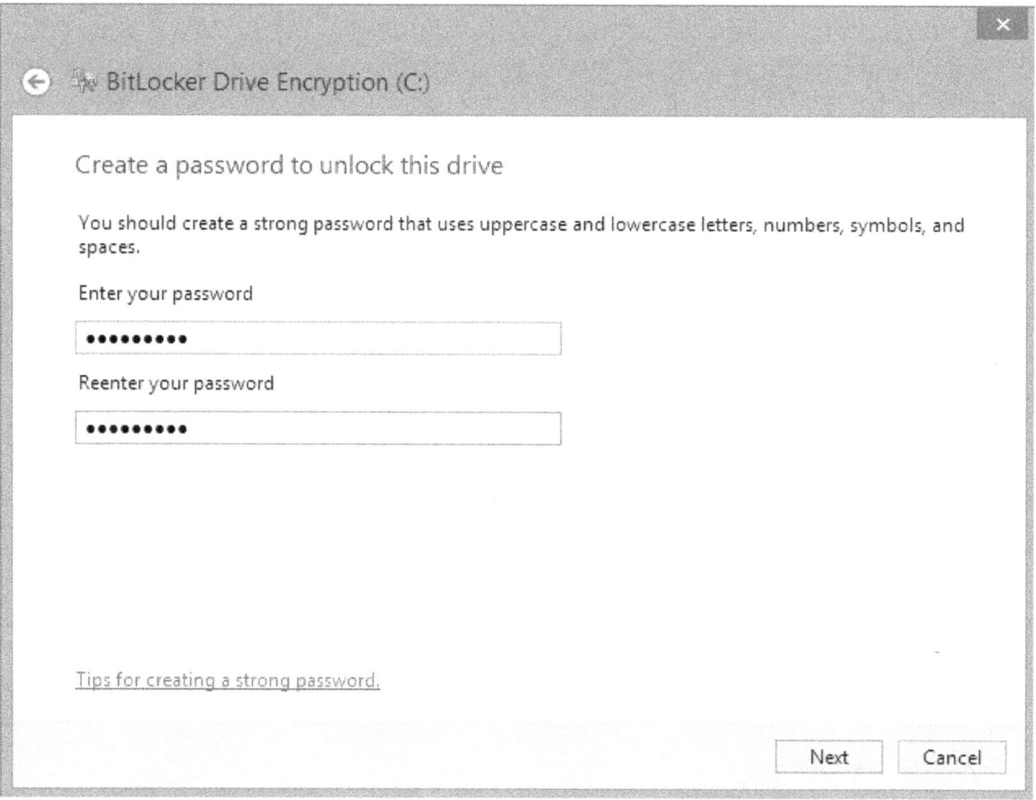

10. Click **Next** to proceed.
11. On **How do you want to back up your recovery key** window, click any of the available options as desired. (**Save to a file** option for this demonstration).

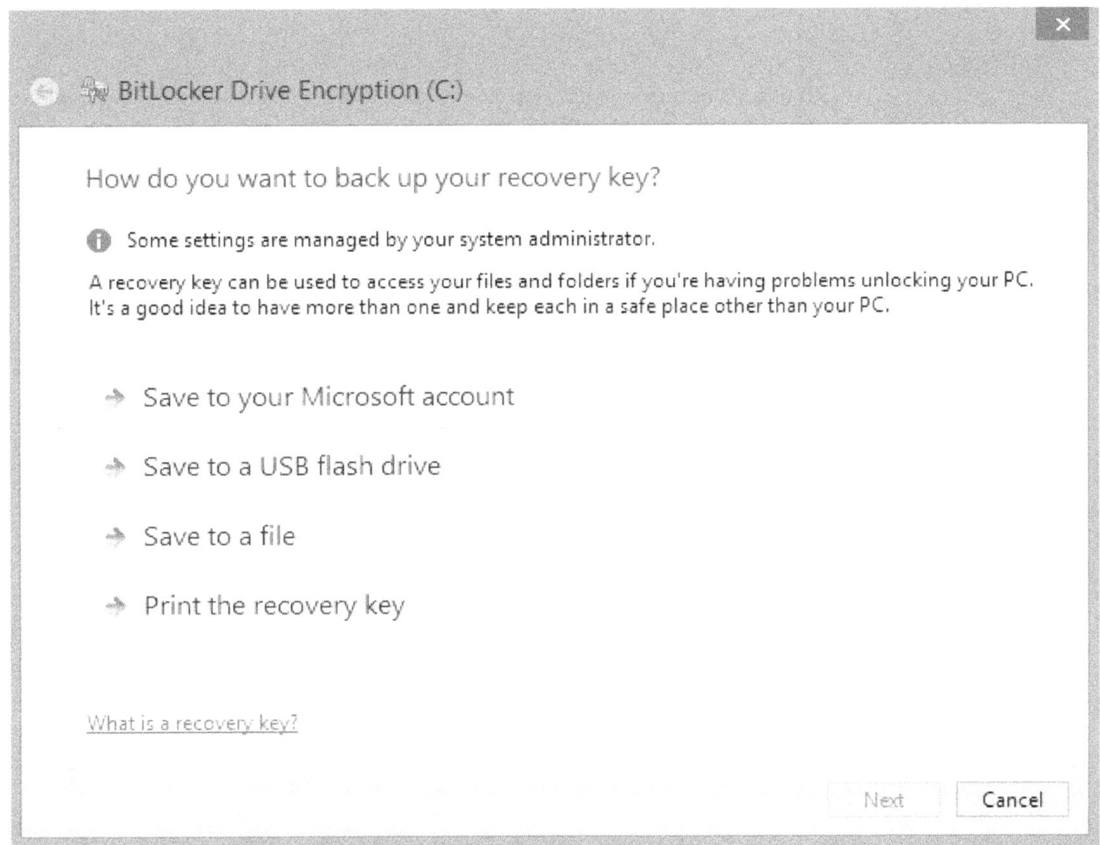

12. On the **Save BitLocker recovery key as** box, navigate and locate the destination location for the recovery file, specify the name of the file in the **File name** field, and click **Save**.
13. Back on the previous box, click **Next**.
14. On the **Choose how much of your drive to encrypt** window, leave the default radio button selected and click **Next**. Alternatively, **Encrypt entire drive (slower but best for PCs and drives already in use)** radio button can also be selected for maximum and efficient security before clicking **Next**.

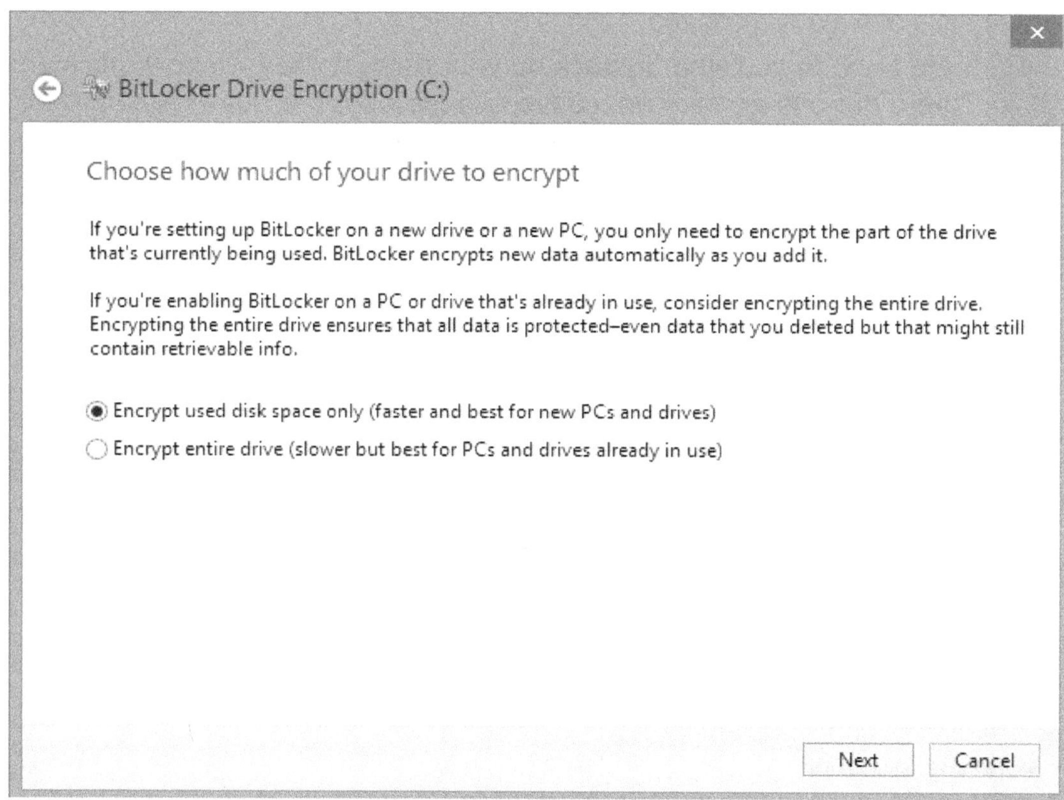

15. On **Are you ready to encrypt this drive** window, leave everything as default and click **Continue**.

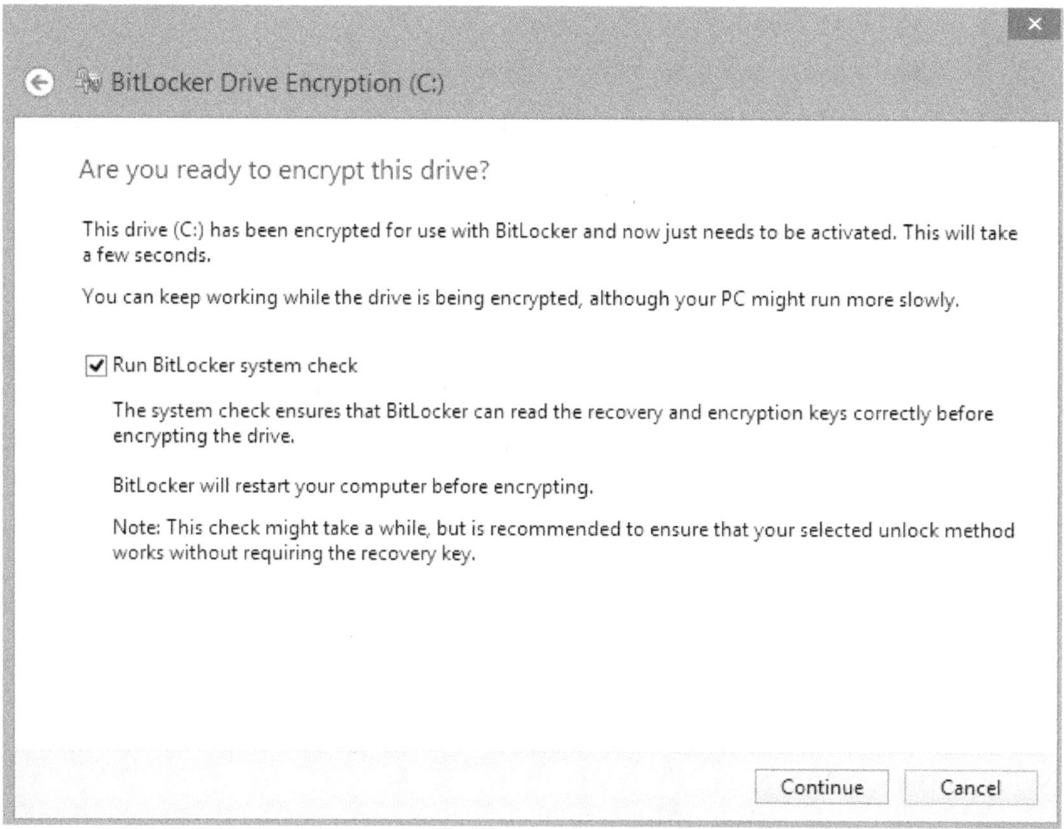

16. Remove any CD/DVD from the optical media drive and on the displayed box, click **Restart now** to restart the computer and continue the BitLocker drive encryption process.

17. After the restart, on the displayed screen, type the previously specified password in the **Enter the password to unlock this drive** field.

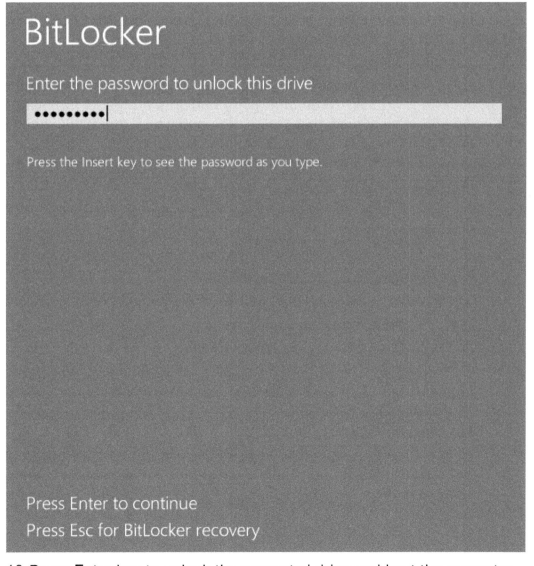

18. Press **Enter** key to unlock the encrypted drive and boot the computer.

Enable/Disable Windows Firewall

Introduction to Windows Firewall

Windows Firewall can be thought of as a gatekeeper that has been appointed to keep unwanted people out of the premises, and allow only the ones who have appropriate permissions to enter into the area.

Windows Firewall monitors all incoming and outgoing traffic on the computer. In Microsoft Windows 8, by default Windows Firewall blocks all incoming traffic and allows all outgoing packets. When administrators install a new application that requires either Internet or local area network access to communicate with other computers, a firewall rule is automatically generated in Windows Firewall and the application is allowed to establish connection to other computers and send or receive data from the network.

Many times some applications or services are by default blocked in Windows Firewall and therefore Windows prevents them from communicating with other computers on the network. In order to allow blocked applications and/or services, the applications and/or services must be added to the Windows Firewall exception list.

In most home and production environments, third-party antivirus programs are installed which also have built-in firewalls to protect the computers from intrusions apart from securing them from viruses. When third-party antivirus programs are installed on a Windows 8 computer, in most cases the installation process of the applications automatically disable Windows Firewall. If because of any reason, third-party antivirus programs fail to disable Windows Firewall, users must manually disable the feature.

How to Disable Built-In Windows Firewall?

In order to disable built-in Windows Firewall on a Microsoft Windows 8 computer, steps given below must be followed:

1. Log on to Microsoft Windows 8 computer with administrator account.
2. From the **Start** screen, click **Desktop** tile.
3. On the desktop screen, hover mouse to the bottom right corner of the window.
4. From the displayed options, click **Settings**.
5. On the **Settings** pane, click **Control Panel**.
6. On the opened **Control Panel** window, click **System and Security** category.
7. On the opened **System and Security** window, click **Windows Firewall**.
8. On the **Windows Firewall** window, click **Turn Windows Firewall on or off** option from the left pane.
9. On the **Customize Settings** window, click to select **Turn off Windows Firewall (not recommended)** radio buttons under both **Private network settings** and **Public network settings** sections.

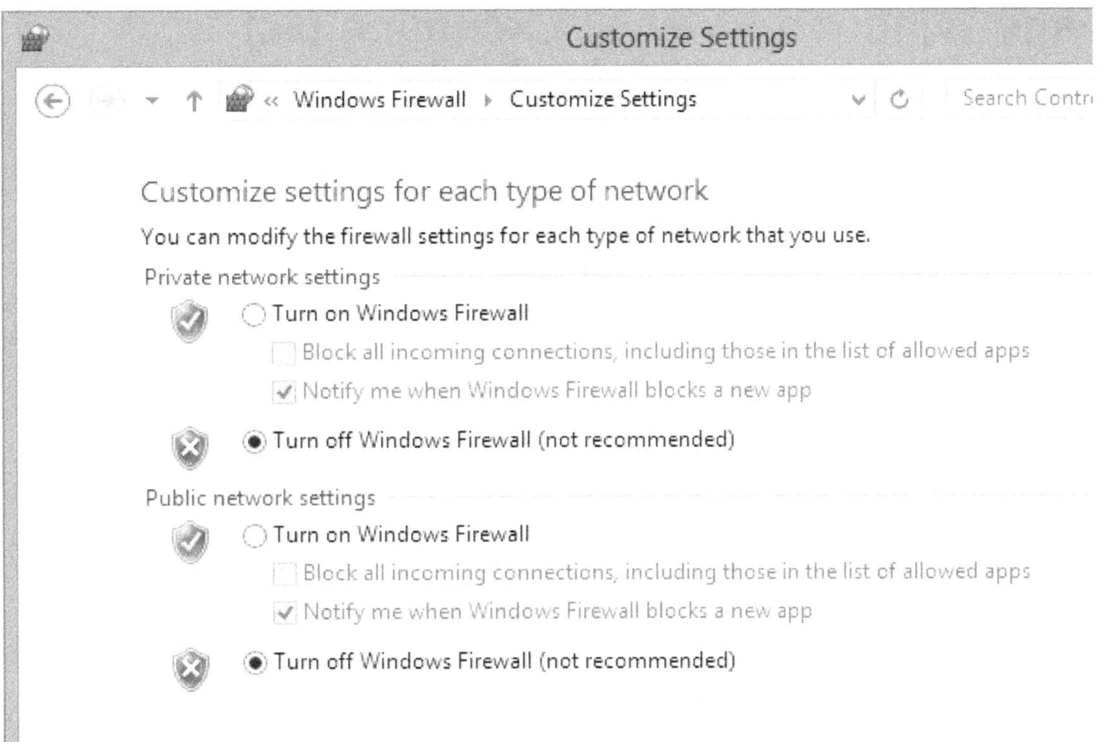

10. Click **OK** when done to save the changes.

To re-enable Windows Firewall, steps 1 to 10 can be followed, while selecting **Turn on Windows Firewall** radio buttons under both **Private network settings** and **Public network settings** sections when on step 9.

Manage Windows Firewall Exception List

Introduction to Windows Firewall Exception List

Windows Firewall exception list contains all applications, port numbers, protocols, etc. that administrators want to communicate with other computers on the local area network or on the Internet. As mentioned in previous lesson, by default Windows Firewall blocks all incoming packets and allows all outgoing traffic from Windows 8 computer if it is connected to the network. Since a complete communication of an application on a computer with other computers on the network includes both sending and receiving packets, it becomes essential for the administrators to add the application and the port number along with its corresponding protocol to the Windows Firewall exception list. This allows flawless communication between the applications installed on two computers that are connected to the network.

In case communication between two computers is to be restricted, the application and/or the corresponding port number must be removed from the Windows Firewall exception list.

How to Add/Remove Programs from Windows Firewall Exception List?

In order to add or remove programs from Windows Firewall exception list, steps given below must be followed:

1. Log on to Microsoft Windows 8 computer with administrator account.
2. From the **Start** screen, click **Desktop** tile.
3. On the desktop screen, hover mouse to the bottom right corner of the window.
4. From the displayed options, click **Settings**.
5. On the **Settings** pane, click **Control Panel**.
6. On the opened **Control Panel** window, click **System and Security** category.
7. On the opened **System and Security** window, click **Windows Firewall**.
8. On the **Windows Firewall** window, click **Allow an app or feature through Windows Firewall** option from the left pane.
9. On the **Allowed apps** window, from the **Allowed apps and features** list, check the checkboxes representing the apps and features that are to be allowed to communicate with other computers on the network or the Internet.

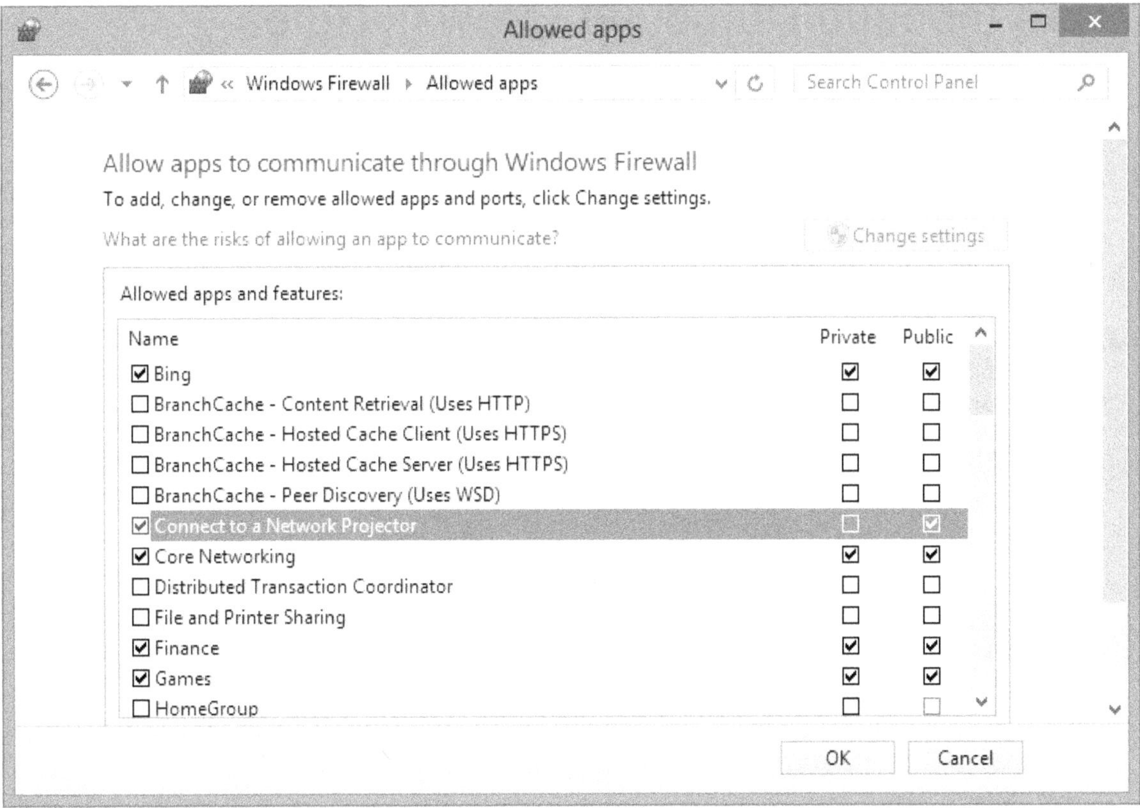

Note: *When a checkbox representing an app or feature is checked, it is added to the Windows Firewall exception list hence it is allowed to communicate with other computers on the local area network on the Internet. Unchecking the checkbox restricts the apps' or feature's communication with other computers on the LAN or the Internet. In case any app or feature is not available in the list,* ***Allow another app*** *button can be clicked to browse and add the missing object.*

10. Click **OK** to save the changes when done.

Create Inbound/Outbound Firewall Rules

Introduction to Inbound and Outbound Firewall Rules

When Microsoft Windows 8 is installed on a computer, Windows Firewall is by default enabled in order to protect the computer from intrusions and/or external threats. Default nature of Windows Firewall is that it monitors all incoming and outgoing packets. In addition to this, Windows Firewall always blocks the incoming packets and always allows the outgoing ones. Packets that arrive from the network into the system are technically called Inbound packets, whereas packets leaving the system to some other computer in the network or Internet are known as Outbound packets.

Every time administrators install a new application that needs to communicate with other computers on the network or Internet, Windows 8 automatically creates appropriate firewall rule for the installed application, and adds the program to the Windows Firewall exception list. In home computers and in small scale industries, where security is not a priority, Windows Firewall's default configuration needs not to be modified as it best serves the purpose. However situations may differ when Windows 8 is used in production environments, and administrators consider security of data at the first priority. In such cases, administrators can create inbound or outbound firewall rules separately to protect Windows 8 computer from intruders and external threats.

Although due to limited features and flexibilities, Windows Firewall in Windows 8 computer cannot be replaced with dedicated hardware or software firewall systems, it can still be used to add an additional and powerful layer of security to the computer.

Creating any inbound or outbound rule requires detailed knowledge about the port numbers, protocols, etc. Windows 8 allows administrators to create the following types of inbound or outbound rules:

- **Program** - When this type of rule is created, administrators can allow or block all the programs or a specific program to communicate with the local computer.
- **Port** - When this type of rule is created, administrators can allow or block packets filtered on the basis of port numbers and protocols (TCP or UDP). While allowing or blocking packets filtered on the basis of port numbers and protocols, administrators can allow or block all the local ports for specific protocol (TCP or UDP), or they can specify particular port numbers to allow or block using the protocols (TCP or UDP).
- **Predefined** - This option contains a predefined list of application layer protocols, programs, etc.). When this option is selected, administrators can choose any one of the available options from the **Predefined** drop-down list and can create a rule accordingly.
- **Custom** - Administrators can select this option when a custom rule is to be created. A custom rule can be created for a program, service, etc. Other granular options can also be configured while creating custom rule.

Once a firewall rule is created, it is automatically enabled and applied on the selected network types (Domain, Private or Public). Administrators can disable, delete or modify the rules as per their requirements.

Process of creating inbound and outbound firewall rules is identical, and to create any of the rules, elevated privileges are required.

How to Create a New Inbound or Outbound Firewall Rule?

In order to create a new inbound or outbound firewall rule, steps given below must be followed:

1. Log on to Microsoft Windows 8 computer with administrator account.
2. From the **Start** screen, click **Desktop** tile.
3. From the desktop window, hover mouse to the bottom right corner of the screen.
4. From the displayed options, click **Settings**.
5. From the **Settings** pane, click **Control Panel**.
6. On the **Control Panel** window, click **System and Security** category.
7. From the **System and Security** window, click **Windows Firewall**.
8. On the **Windows Firewall** window, click **Advanced settings** from the left pane.
9. On **Windows Firewall with Advanced Security** snap-in, click **Inbound Rules** or **Outbound Rules** from the console tree in the left. (Inbound Rules for this demonstration)

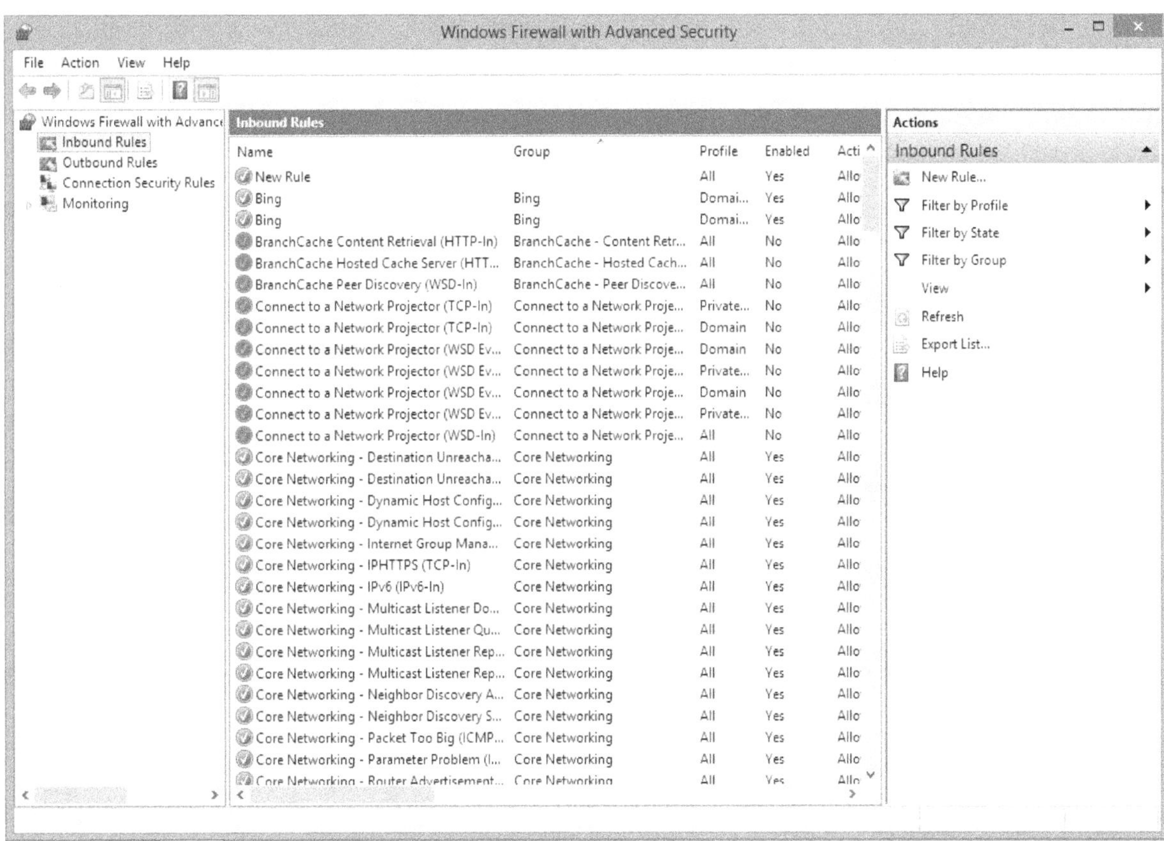

10. Once selected, click **New Rule** from the **Actions** pane in the right.
11. On the **New Inbound Rule Wizard** window, on the **Rule Type** page, click to select the appropriate radio button for which a new rule is to be created. (**Program** for this demonstration)

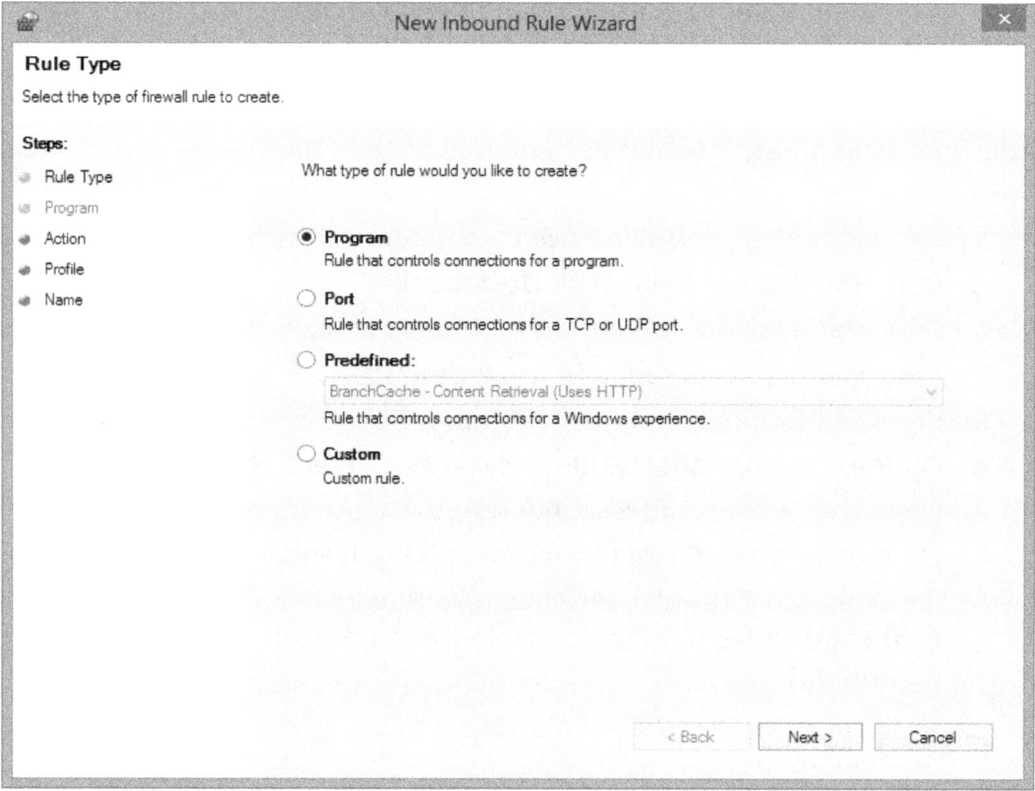

12. Click **Next** to continue.
13. From the **Program** page, click to select **This program path** radio button and click **Browse** button to browse for and locate the program for which the rule is to be created. Alternatively, **All programs** radio button can also be selected to create the rule for all the programs.

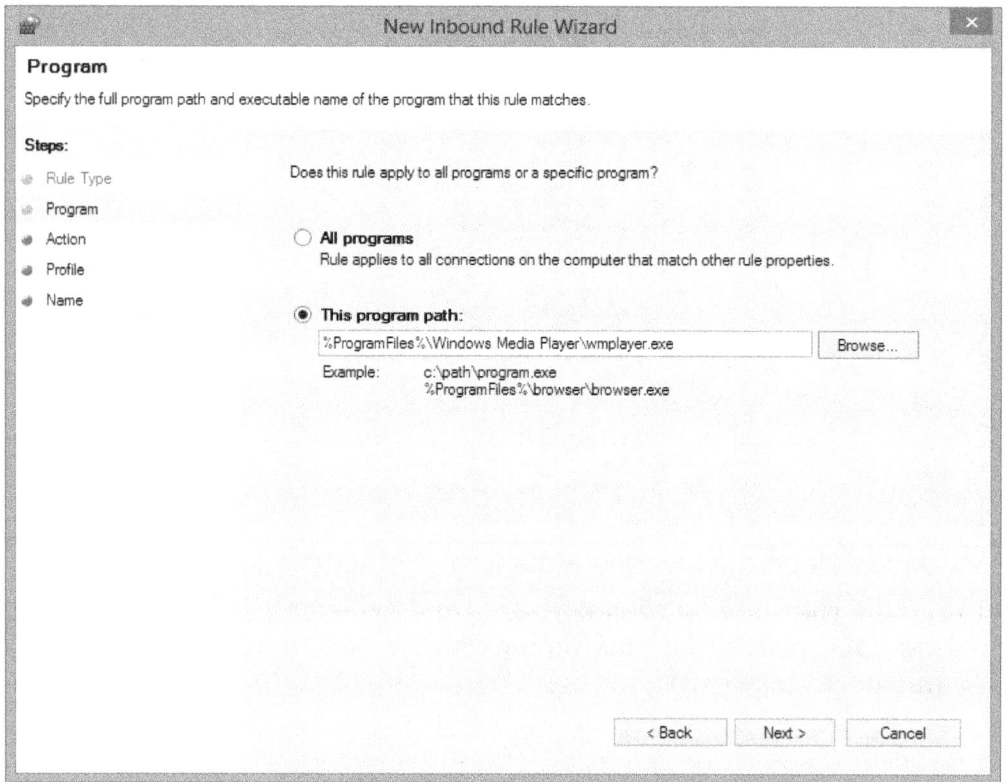

14. Click **Next** to proceed.
15. On the **Action** page, click to select **Allow the connection**, **Allow the connection if it is secure** or **Block the connection** radio button as desired.

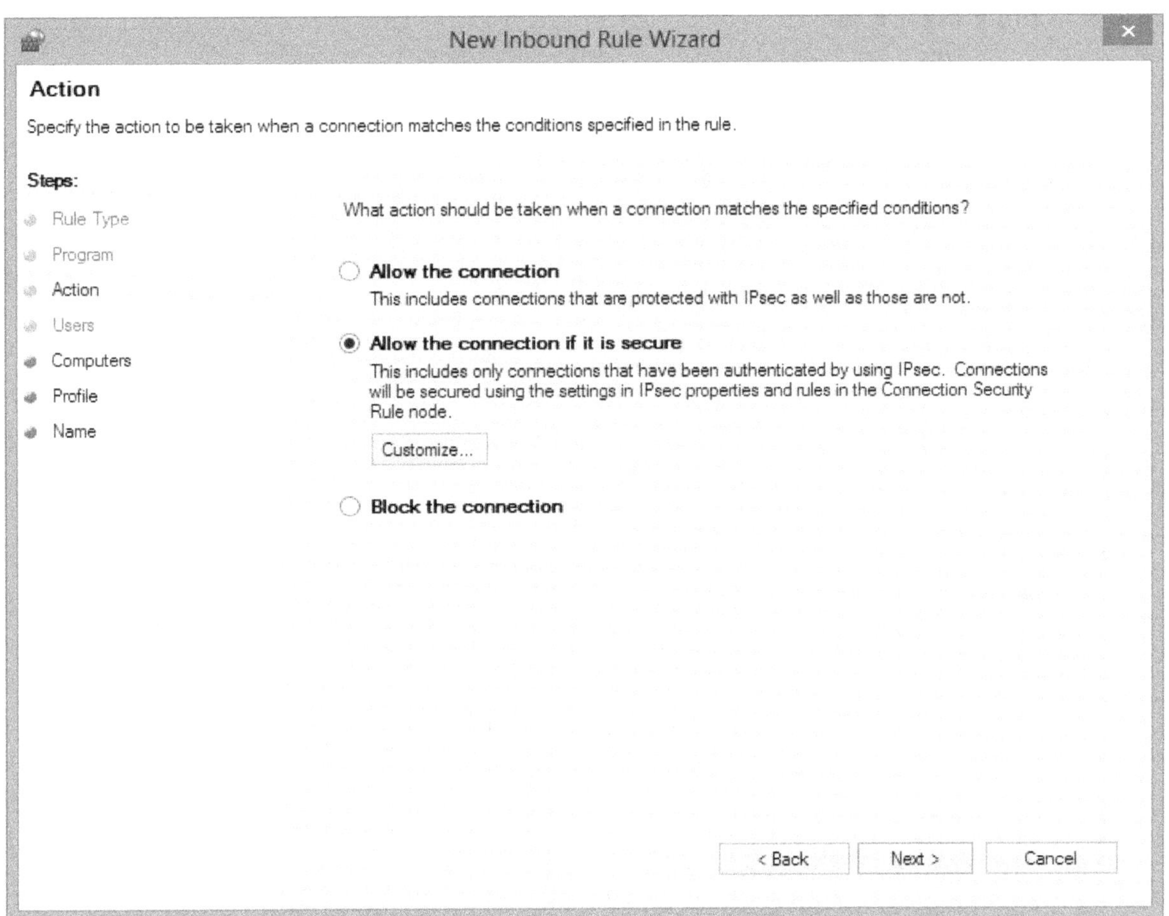

16. On the **Users** page, check **Authorized users** and **Exceptions** checkboxes to specify the users who can access the application remotely, and the ones the rule should not monitor respectively. Checkboxes can be left unchecked if no such permissions are to be granted to any user.

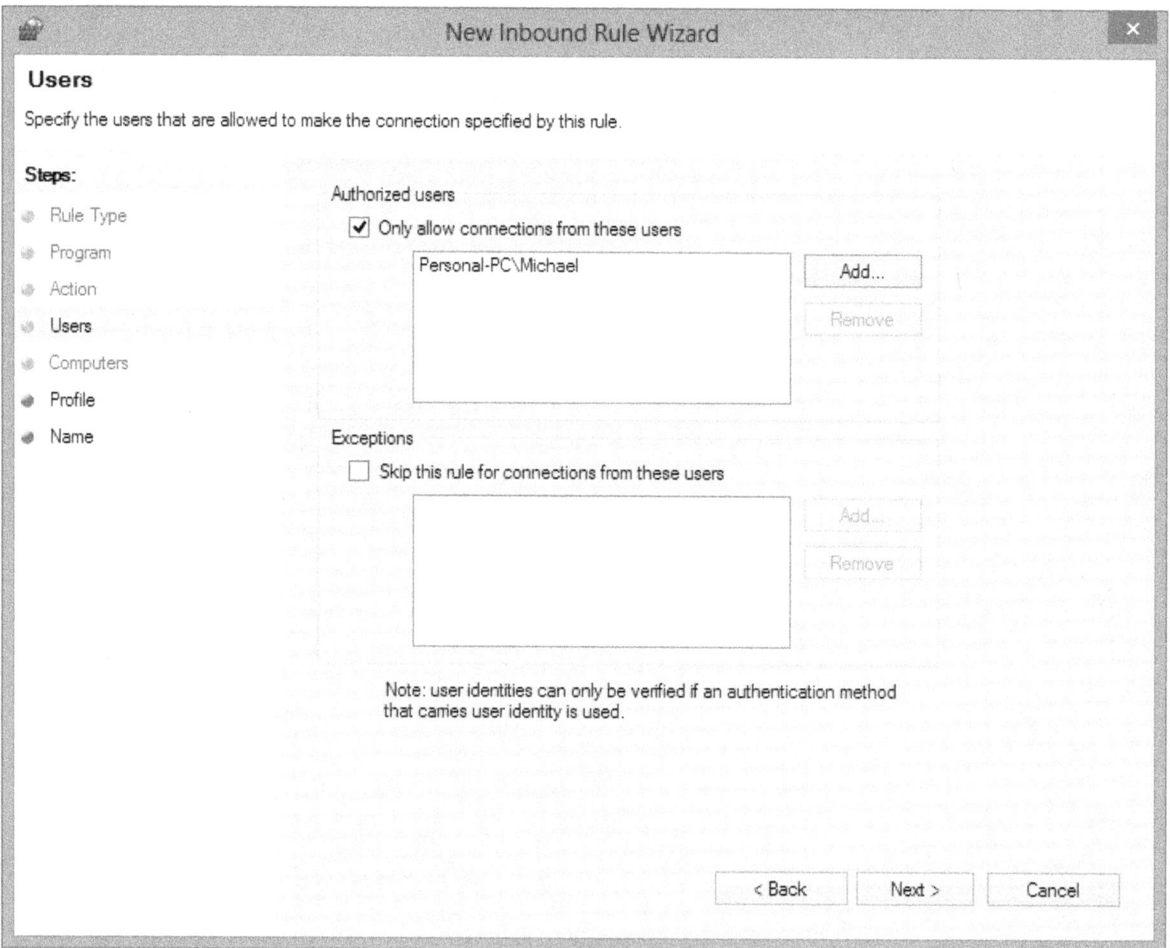

17. Click **Next** to proceed.
18. On the **Computers** page, check **Authorized computers** and **Exceptions** checkboxes to specify the computers from where the application can be accessed remotely, and the ones the rule should not monitor respectively. Checkboxes can be left unchecked if no such permissions are to be specified for any computer.
19. Click **Next** to proceed.
20. On the **Profile** page, check the checkboxes representing the network types on which the created rule would be applicable.

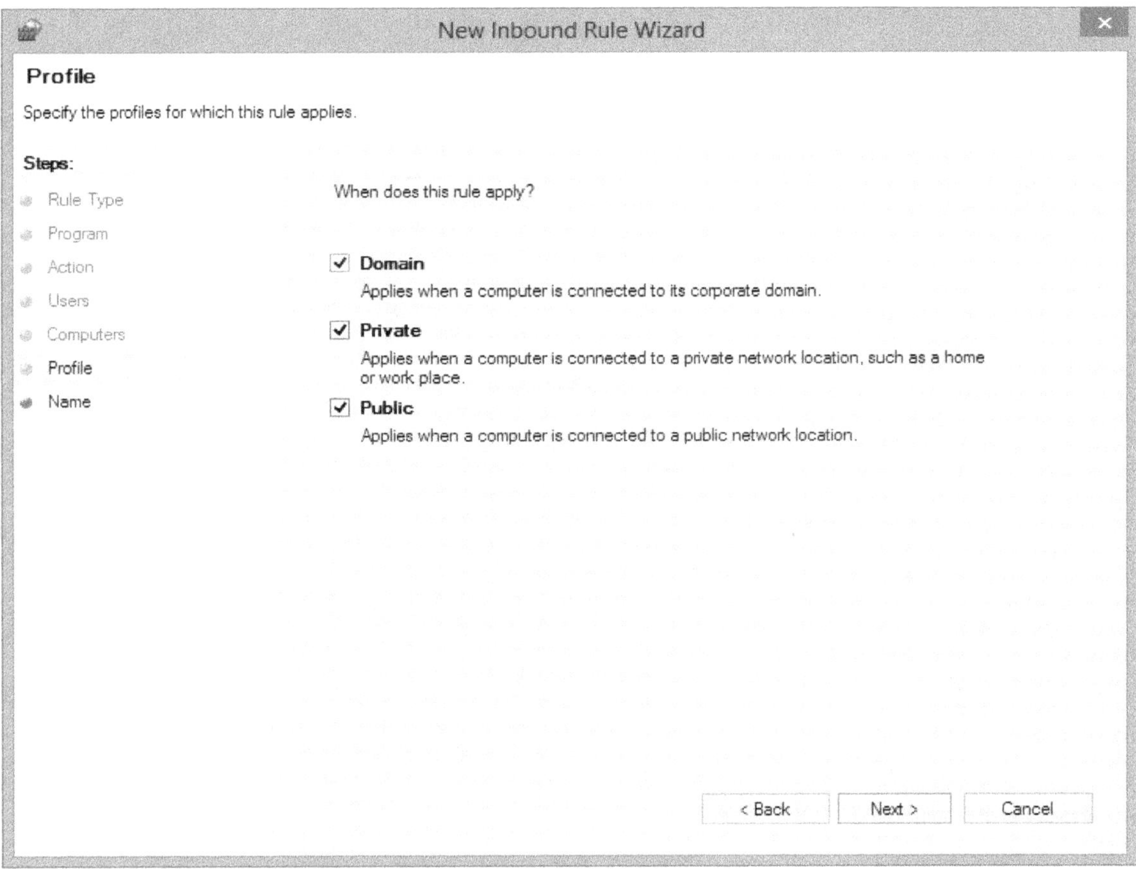

21. Click **Next** to proceed.
22. On the **Name** page, specify a new name for the created rule in the **Name** field.

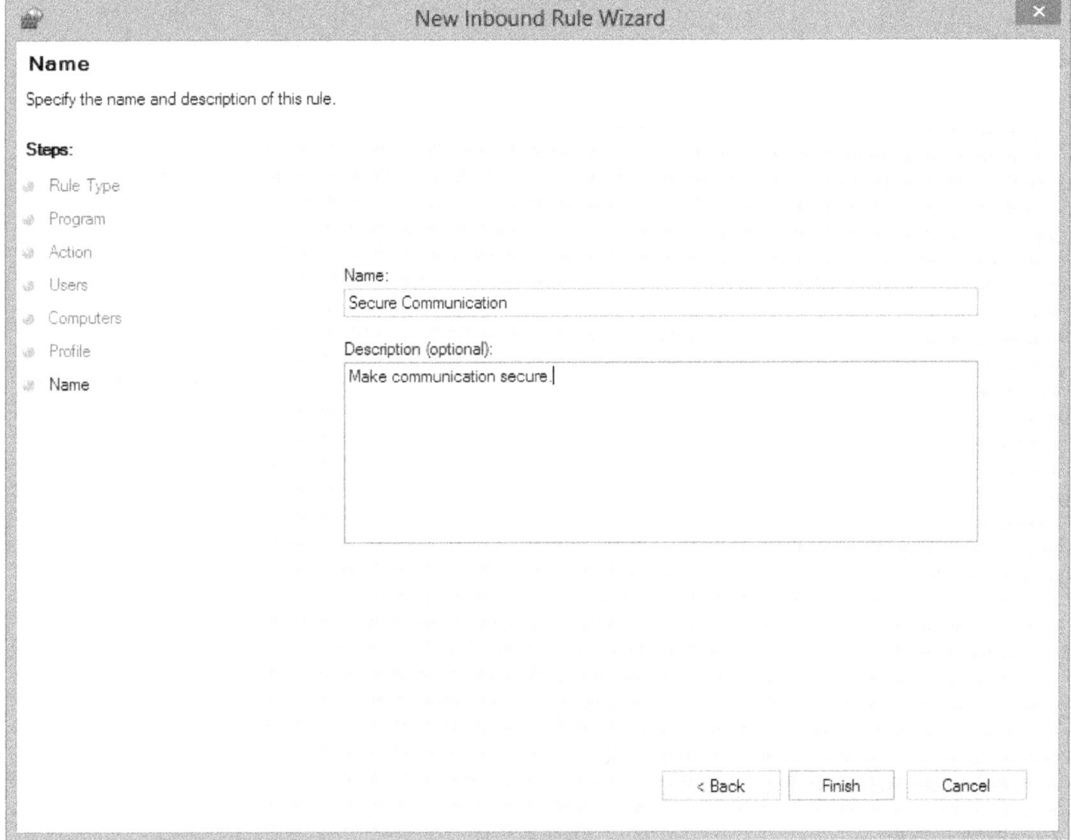

23. In the **Description** field, type a brief description about the rule. (Optional)
24. Click **Finish** button to create the rule.

Note: *Interface and boxes may change and/or steps may increase or decrease as per the selected program, ports, services, etc.*

CHAPTER 11:

NETWORK & SHARE

Assign a Static IP Address to an NIC

Introduction to IP Address

An IP address is a 32-bit decimal number which is divided into four octets and the octets are separated by '.' (Dot) a.k.a. 'Periods'. The decimal value of every octet starts from 0 and can go maximum up to 255. The four octets of an IP address are represented by A.B.C.D, where the decimal number of A indicates the class to which the IP address belongs.

An IP address is always accompanied with its corresponding subnet mask that specifies the number of computers that can be assigned with the same range of IP addresses in order to make them communicate with each other. Just like an IP address, subnet mask is also a 32-bit decimal number that is divided into four octets and octets are separated by the 'Periods'.

Example of an IP address along with its subnet mask is:

IP Address:192.168.0.1

Subnet Mask:255.255.255.0

Requirement of Assigning a Static IP Address

In most production environments where an organization has several computers, administrators generally install and configure DHCP servers that are responsible for assigning IP addresses automatically to all the client computers that have been configured to obtain the IP addresses automatically. When an IP address is assigned to a client computer automatically through a DHCP server, the IP address is known as a dynamic IP address.

On the other hand, static IP addresses are the ones that administrators manually assigned to the network interface cards installed on the computers. Administrators assign static IP addresses when there is no DHCP server available in the network. In most cases, administrators of home computers assign static IP addresses to the NICs as it is impractical to have a dedicated DHCP server in home networks.

Assigning a static IP address to an NIC is an administrative task and elevated privileges are required to complete the process successfully.

How to Assign a Static IP Address?

In order to assign a static IP address to an NIC in Microsoft Windows 8, steps given below must be followed:

1. Log on to Microsoft Windows 8 computer with the administrator account.
2. From the **Start** screen, click **Desktop** tile.
3. On the desktop screen, press **Windows** + **R** keys simultaneously to initiate **Run** command box.
4. In the **Run** command box, type **NCPA.CPL** command and press **Enter** key.
5. On the opened **Network Connections** window, right-click the NIC on which the static IP address is to be configured.
6. From the displayed context menu, click **Properties**.

7. On the opened properties box, make sure that **Networking** tab is selected.
8. From the **This connection uses the following items** list, double-click **Internet Protocol Version 4 (TCP/IPv4)**.
9. On the **Internet Protocol Version 4 (TCP/IPv4) Properties** box, click to select **Use the following IP address**.
10. In the enabled **IP address**, **Subnet mask** and **Default gateway** fields, provide the static IP address, its corresponding subnet mask and the default gateway respectively.

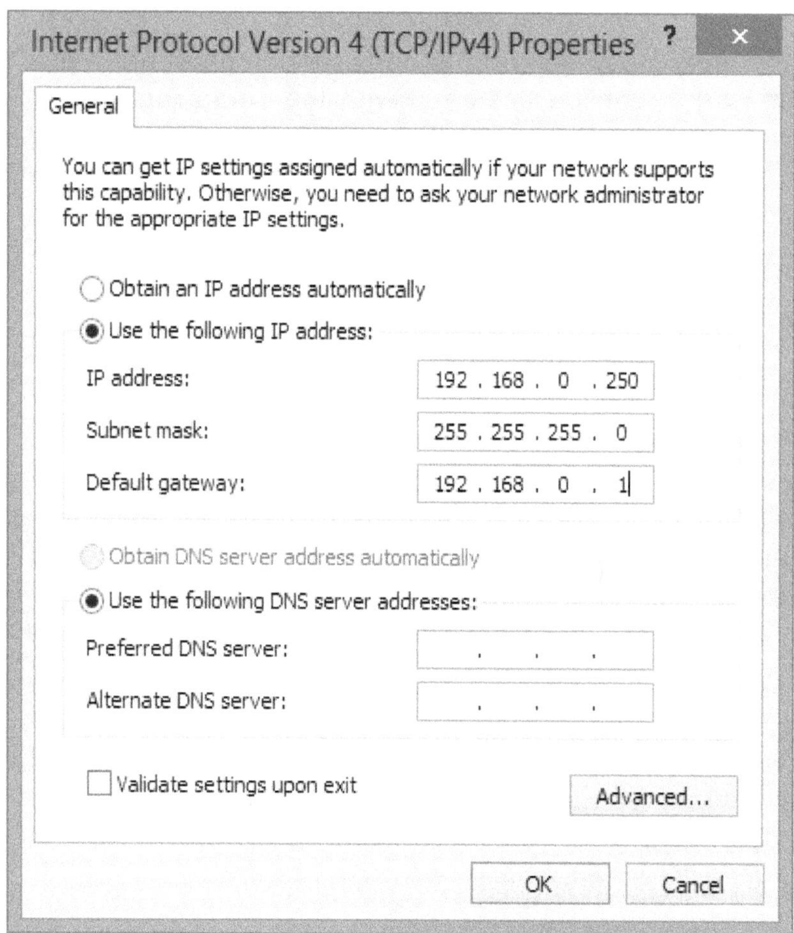

Note: *In most network scenarios, administrators also specify preferred and alternate DNS server address in the Preferred DNS server and Alternate DNS server fields respectively to allow the computer communicate with other computers that may reside on the same network, other networks or the Internet.*

11. Click **OK** to assign the provided static IP address to the computer.
12. Back on NIC's properties box, click **OK**.
13. From the displayed pane in the left, click to select appropriate option as desired. (Sharing can be allowed in home or work networks as they are considered secured and trustworthy.)

Assign Multiple IP Addresses to an NIC

Introduction to Multiple IP Addresses on a Single NIC

When an IP address is assigned to a computer, it can communicate with all the computers that have the same range of IP addresses assigned to them. When administrators want a computer to communicate with other computers that belong to some other IP address range, they mostly install another NIC and assign a separate IP address of the other range. This makes the computer communicate with the computers of two different networks at the same time.

Installing multiple NICs in a computer and assigning different range of IP addresses to them is a practical approach that most administrators take in production environments. In medium or large scale organizations it becomes essential to install multiple NICs to make a computer communicate with the computers that belong to different networks because to avoid bottlenecks on the NICs. On the other hand, in small scale organizations, administrators can provide multiple IP addresses on the same network interface card hence eliminating the requirement of purchasing a separate NIC for every IP address that they want to assign to the computer.

Note: *Assigning multiple IP addresses to an NIC may create bottlenecks (network congestions on the NICs that reduce performance and decrease transfer speed) if a computer is connected to the network with heavy network traffic. If the network traffic is quite heavy, in order to avoid bottlenecks, it is strongly recommended that multiple NICs must be installed and each NIC must be assigned with one IP address only.*

How to Assign Multiple IP Addresses to a Single NIC?

In order to assign multiple IP addresses to a single NIC in Microsoft Windows 8, steps given below must be followed:

1. Log on to Microsoft Windows 8 computer with the administrator account.
2. From the **Start** screen, click **Desktop** tile.
3. On the desktop screen, right-click the **Network** icon from the system tray at the bottom right corner of the window.
4. From the context menu, click **Open Network and Sharing Center**.
5. On the **Network and Sharing Center** window, click **Change adapter settings** from the left pane.
6. On the opened **Network Connections** window, right-click the NIC on which another IP address is to be configured.
7. From the displayed context menu, click **Properties**.
8. On the opened properties box, make sure that **Networking** tab is selected.
9. From the **This connection uses the following items** list, double-click **Internet Protocol Version 4 (TCP/IPv4)**.
10. On the **Internet Protocol Version 4 (TCP/IPv4) Properties** box, make sure that at least one static IP address is assigned.
11. Once verified, click **Advanced** button.

12. On the **Advanced TCP/IP Settings** box, make sure that **IP Settings** tab is selected.
13. Under the **IP addresses** section, click **Add** button.
14. On the **TCP/IP Address** box, specify another IP address and its corresponding subnet mask in the **IP address** and **Subnet mask** fields.

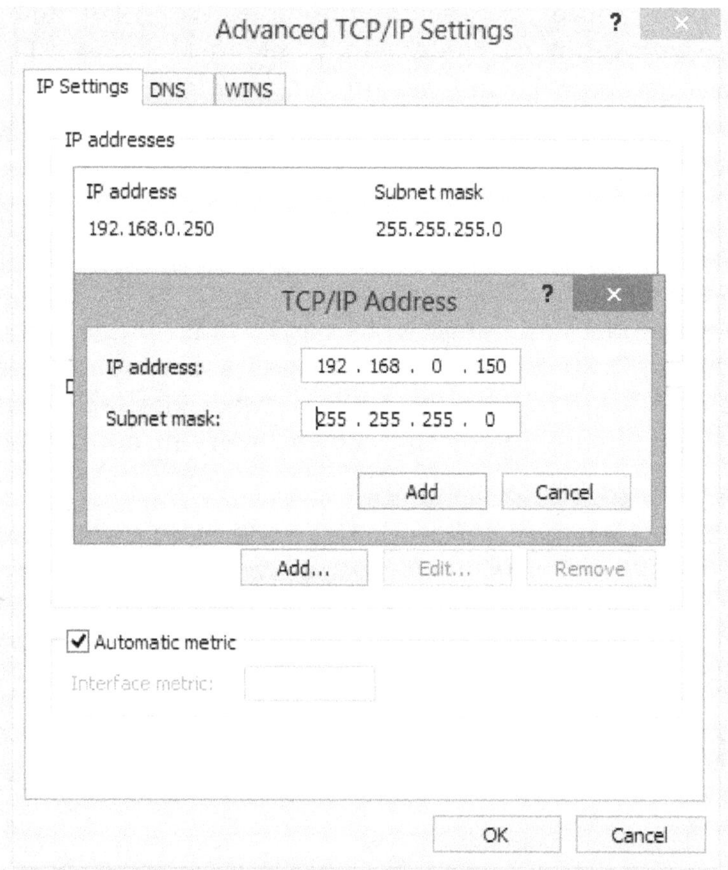

15. Click **Add** button when done.
16. Back on the **Advanced TCP/IP Settings** box, click **OK**.
17. Back on the **Internet Protocol Version 4 (TCP/IPv4) Properties** box, click **OK** to save the changes.
18. Back on NIC's properties box, click **OK**.

To remove an IP address from an NIC, steps 1 to 13 can be followed while selecting the unwanted IP address from the **IP addresses** list when on step 13 and clicking **Remove** button. **OK** button must be clicked on all the opened boxes to confirm the changes.

Assign More Than Two DNS Server Addresses

Introduction to DNS Servers

A DNS server is a dedicated computer that is responsible for resolving the names of the computers on the network or Internet to their corresponding IP addresses. In local area networks, the names of the computers can be simple to understand, whereas when a computer is connected to the Internet, users mostly type the URLs of websites. In order to allow communication between a computer and the server that hosts the requested website, a DNS server searches for the IP address of the webserver.

In production environments, administrators mostly install and configure an internal DNS server that receives the queries from the client computers and forwards them to the DNS server of the ISPs. On the other hand, in homes, since the computers are connected directly to the Internet modems, the queries are sent to the DNS servers of the ISPs without any requirement of having internal DNS servers.

Characteristics of a DNS Server

When a client computer tries to communicate with a computer or a website, the query is sent to the DNS server. DNS server, on its part, tries to resolve a query and replies back to the requesting client with the IP address of the requested computer or the website. In case the DNS server fails to resolve the query, it replies back with a negative response to the requesting computer.

Above mentioned is the scenario when only one DNS server address is assigned to an NIC of the computer. In order to eliminate such situations, most administrators install and configure multiple DNS servers in production networks. When multiple DNS server addresses are assigned to a computer, if the first DNS server fails to resolve a query, the query is transferred to the second available DNS server. If the second DNS server manages to resolve the IP address of the requested computer or the website, the DNS server replies back to the requesting client with the resolved IP address. In case even the second DNS server fails to resolve the query, the query is then transferred to the third DNS server, and so on.

How to Assign Multiple DNS Server Addresses?

The front and basic interface of IPv4 properties box allows administrators to provide only two DNS server addresses namely Preferred DNS server and Alternate DNS server. However as mentioned above, there might be times when administrators might want to assign multiple DNS server addresses to the computers. Microsoft Windows 8 allows the administrators to do so by following the steps given below:

1. Log on to Microsoft Windows 8 computer with the administrator account.
2. From the **Start** screen, click **Desktop** tile.
3. On the desktop screen, right-click the **Network** icon from the system tray at the bottom right corner of the window.
4. From the context menu, click **Open Network and Sharing Center**.
5. On the **Network and Sharing Center** window, click **Change adapter settings** from the left pane.

6. On the opened **Network Connections** window, right-click the NIC on which multiple DNS server addresses are to be configured.
7. From the displayed context menu, click **Properties**.
8. On the opened properties box, make sure that **Networking** tab is selected.
9. From the **This connection uses the following items** list, double-click **Internet Protocol Version 4 (TCP/IPv4)**.
10. On the **Internet Protocol Version 4 (TCP/IPv4) Properties** box, click **Advanced** button.
11. On the **Advanced TCP/IP Settings** box, go to the DNS tab.
12. Under the **DNS server addresses, in order of use** section, click **Add** button.
13. On the **TCP/IP DNS Server** box, specify another DNS server address in the **DNS server** field.

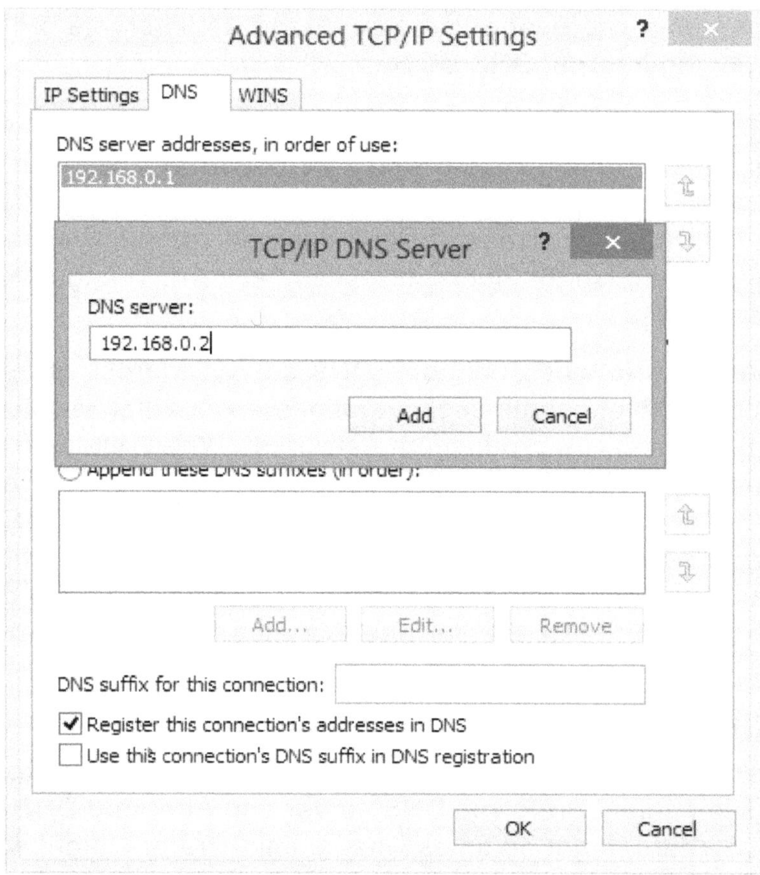

14. Click **Add** button when done.

    Note: *While on* ***Advanced TCP/IP Settings*** *box, steps 12 to 14 can be repeated each time a new DNS server address is to be added. Identical steps can be followed to remove an added DNS server by clicking* ***Remove*** *button after selecting the unwanted DNS server address from the list.*

15. Back on the **Advanced TCP/IP Settings** box, click **OK**.
16. Back on the **Internet Protocol Version 4 (TCP/IPv4) Properties** box, click **OK** to save the changes.
17. Back on NIC's properties box, click **OK**.

Find the Assigned IP Address

Introduction to the Interfaces to View the IP Addresses

When IP addresses assigned to multiple computers, it is quite likely that administrators may forget which IP address was assigned to which computer. This is mostly the case in production environments where a DHCP server has dynamically assigned IP addresses to the computers.

Even in homes, if a computer is connected to the Internet modem that is provided by the ISP, sometimes it might be challenging for the home users to know the IP address that has been assigned to the computers.

Microsoft Windows 8 helps users overcome the above situation by allowing them to view the IP addresses that have been assigned to their computers.

How to View an Assigned IP Address?

In order to view an assigned IP address to a Microsoft Windows 8 computer, steps given below must be followed:

1. Log on to Microsoft Windows 8 computer with any account.
2. From the **Start** screen, click **Desktop** tile.
3. On the desktop screen, press **Windows** + **R** keys simultaneously to initiate **Run** command box.
4. In the **Run** command box, type **CMD** command and press Enter key.
5. On the opened command prompt, type **IPCONFIG** command and press **Enter** key.

```
C:\Windows\system32\CMD.exe

Tunnel adapter isatap.{CFC889B4-4F31-48AC-AFC6-BFBD4CEC0DD0}:

   Media State . . . . . . . . . . . : Media disconnected
   Connection-specific DNS Suffix  . :

C:\Users\Michael>IPCONFIG

Windows IP Configuration


Ethernet adapter Ethernet:

   Connection-specific DNS Suffix  . :
   Link-local IPv6 Address . . . . . : fe80::71:76d3:1be6:23cc%12
   IPv4 Address. . . . . . . . . . . : 192.168.0.250
   Subnet Mask . . . . . . . . . . . : 255.255.255.0
   Default Gateway . . . . . . . . . : 192.168.0.1

Tunnel adapter isatap.{CFC889B4-4F31-48AC-AFC6-BFBD4CEC0DD0}:

   Media State . . . . . . . . . . . : Media disconnected
   Connection-specific DNS Suffix  . :

C:\Users\Michael>
```

6. The static or dynamic IP address, subnet mask and the default gateway will be displayed on the command window.

Note: *In case a computer has multiple LAN cards installed in it, users must know the NIC for which they want to view the IP address. When* ***IPCONFIG*** *command is executed, the command prompt displays the IP addresses, subnet masks and default gateways of all the LAN cards that are installed on the computer.*

Connect to a Wireless Network

Introduction to Wireless Network Connection

It is expected that Microsoft Windows 8 operating system will be mostly installed and used on laptops or tablet PCs. In this case, it becomes essential for the users to connect their Windows 8 computers to an available wireless network, as it is quite unlikely that they would ever connect their portable computers to a wired network connection.

In order to connect a Windows 8 computer to a wireless network, the wireless network must be available and must be within range. Moreover, appropriate authentication credentials must be provided while connecting the computer to the wireless connection, in case the security has been configured on the Wireless Access Point (WAP).

How to Connect to a Wireless Network?

In order to connect a Microsoft Windows 8 computer to a wireless network, steps given below must be followed:

1. Log on to Microsoft Windows 8 computer with administrator account.
2. From the **Start** screen, click **Desktop** tile.
3. Click the network icon in the notification area the bottom right corner.
4. In the opened **Networks** pane in the right, under the **Wi-Fi** category, click to select the desired wireless network from the available network list.
5. Once selected, click **Connect** and provide the pre-shared key in the displayed box.

To disconnect the computer from a wireless network, steps 1 to 5 can be followed, while clicking **Disconnect** button when on step 5.

Assign Static/Dynamic IP Address Using Batch File

Introduction to Assigning IP Addresses through Batch File

A batch file is a simple text file that contains multiple commands in it. The only difference between other text files and a batch file is that a batch file has.BAT extension. When a batch file is double-clicked, all the commands that it contains are executed automatically in the order in which they are specified in the file.

Since every task that users initiate in Microsoft Windows 8 executes a command in the background, users can also specify a static IP address to the computer using the command line. In order to make the tasks even simpler, most administrators create batch files which, when double-clicked, initiate a command that assigns a static IP address that is specified in the command that the batch file contains.

Apart from assigning a static IP address through batch file, the batch file can also be used to configure Microsoft Windows 8 computer to obtain IP address automatically from the DHCP server.

How to Assign Static/Dynamic IP Addresses through a Batch File?

In order to assign static IP address or to make Microsoft Windows 8 obtain an IP address automatically from a DHCP server, steps given below must be followed:

1. Log on to Microsoft Windows 8 computer with administrator account.
2. From the **Start** screen, click **Desktop** tile.
3. On the desktop screen, hover mouse to the bottom right corner of the window.
4. From the displayed options, click **Search**.
5. On the opened **Apps** screen, scroll and locate **Notepad**.
6. Once located, click the **Notepad**.
7. In the notepad workspace, type **NETSH INTERFACE IPV4 SET ADDRESS "Local Area Connection" STATIC 192.168.0.2 255.255.255.0 192.168.0.1** command.

   Note: *In the above command, IPV4 represents that the IP address version 4 will be configured, "Local Area Connection" represents the display name of the NIC. (Display name of the NIC can be changed manually. In case the display name of the NIC is changed, current display name must be specified in the batch file. If the correct NIC name is not specified while creating the batch file, the IP address will not be assigned to the computer.) STATIC represents that the specified IP address will be static in nature and 192.168.0.2, 255.255.255.0 and 192.168.0.1 numbers represent the IP address, subnet mask and the default gateway respectively that will be assigned to the computer.*

8. Once the command to specify static IP address is typed in the notepad, click **File** from the menu bar and from the displayed options, click **Save As**.
9. On the opened **Save As** box, in the **File name** field specify a filename followed by **.BAT** extension.
10. Make sure to wrap the filename along with its extension within double quotes. E.g. "ChangeIPAddress.BAT".

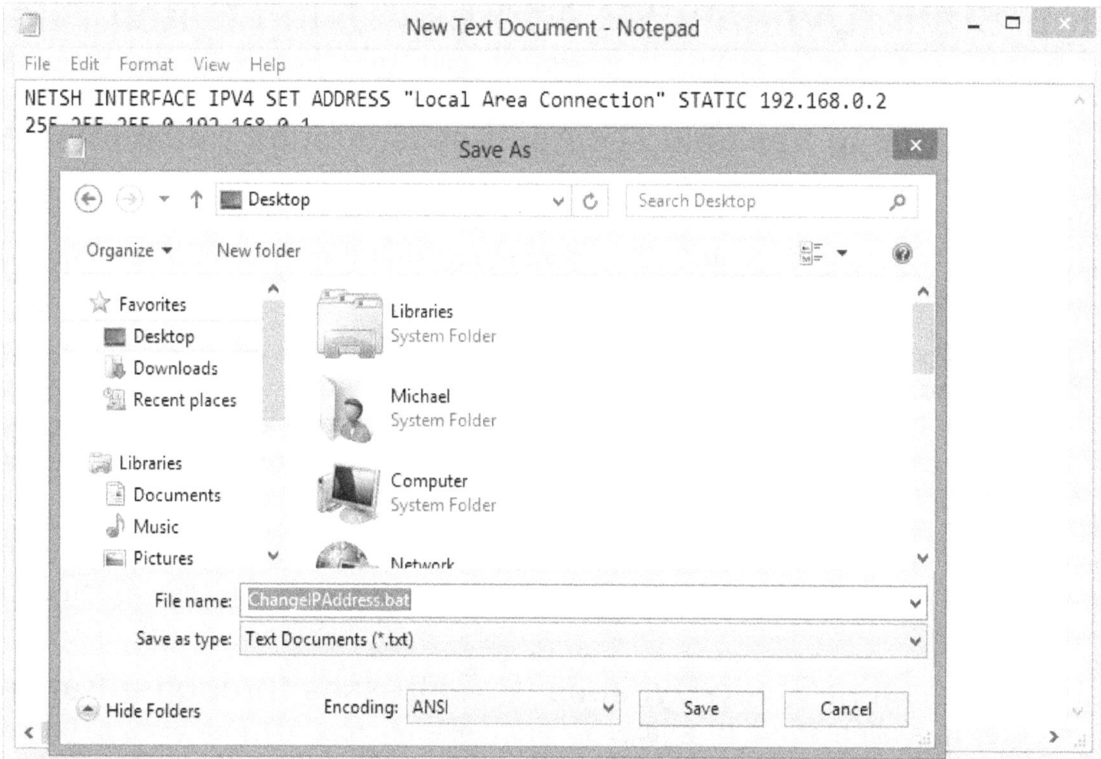

11. In order to set the static IP address using the created batch file, right-click the batch file and from the context menu, click **Run as administrator**.
12. On the displayed **User Account Control** confirmation box, click **Yes** button to provide the consent to execute batch file.

To configure the NIC to obtain an IP address automatically from a DHCP server, **NETSH INTERFACE IPV4 SET ADDRESS "Local Area Connection" SOURCE=DHCP** command must specified in the batch file.

Assign an Alternate IP Address to an NIC

Introduction to Alternate IP Address

When Microsoft Windows 8 is configured to obtain IP address automatically from a DHCP server, every time the computer starts, it sends a DHCP Discover packet to all the computers connected to the network. When the DHCP server receives the packet, it replies back with the IP address that is available in its address pool. When the client computer receives the offered IP address, it requests the DHCP server to assign the offered IP address. DHCP server, on its part, then finally assigns the requested IP address to the client computer. This complete communication is technically called DORA.

The above mentioned scenario works completely fine when the entire network is functioning properly. However there might be times when, because of any reason, DHCP server fails to reply back. When this happens, the client computer automatically assigns an IP address to itself. This automatic IP address assignment is possible because of a built-in feature named Automatic Private IP Addressing (APIPA) that Microsoft Windows 8 has. The IP address APIPA assigns to a computer belongs to class B and has the range of 169.254.0.0 with the subnet mask 255.255.0.0. Because of the IP addresses assigned by APIPA, all computers can communicate with each other since they have a common range of IP addresses.

Things might not be that easy every time. Since the IP addresses assigned by APIPA belong to entirely different range, the computers that have static IP addresses of different range cannot communicate with the ones that have APIPA assigned addresses. For example, if a domain controller in a network has a static IP address of 192.168.0.11, it cannot communicate with the computers that have IP addresses of 169.254.0.0 range. This prevents client computers (if they have APIPA assigned IP addresses) from logging on to the domain controller.

In order to avoid such situations, Microsoft Windows 8 allows administrators to assign an alternate IP address to the computers. Alternate IP address is automatically assigned to Windows 8 computer when it is configured to obtain the IP address from the DHCP server and the DHCP server fails to respond or is not available because of some reason. It is recommended that the alternate IP address that administrators assign to the computers must belong to the range of IP addresses that have been statically assigned to other computers in the network.

How to Assign an Alternate IP Address?

In order to assign an alternate IP address to a Microsoft Windows 8 computer, steps given below must be followed:

1. Log on to Microsoft Windows 8 computer with the administrator account.
2. From the **Start** screen, click **Desktop** tile.
3. On the desktop screen, right-click the **Network** icon from the system tray at the bottom right corner of the window.
4. From the context menu, click **Open Network and Sharing Center**.
5. On the **Network and Sharing Center** window, click **Change adapter settings** from the left pane.

6. On the opened **Network Connections** window, right-click the NIC on which an alternate IP address is to be configured.
7. From the displayed context menu, click **Properties**.
8. On the opened properties box, make sure that **Networking** tab is selected.
9. From the **This connection uses the following items** list, double-click **Internet Protocol Version 4 (TCP/IPv4)**.
10. On the **Internet Protocol Version 4 (TCP/IPv4) Properties** box, make sure that **Obtain an IP address automatically** radio button is selected.
11. Go to **Alternate Configuration** tab.
12. On the **Alternate Configuration** tab, click to select **User configured** radio button.
13. Populate the enabled fields with the appropriate values as desired, especially **IP address**, **Subnet mask**, **Default gateway**, **Preferred DNS server** and **Alternate DNS server**.

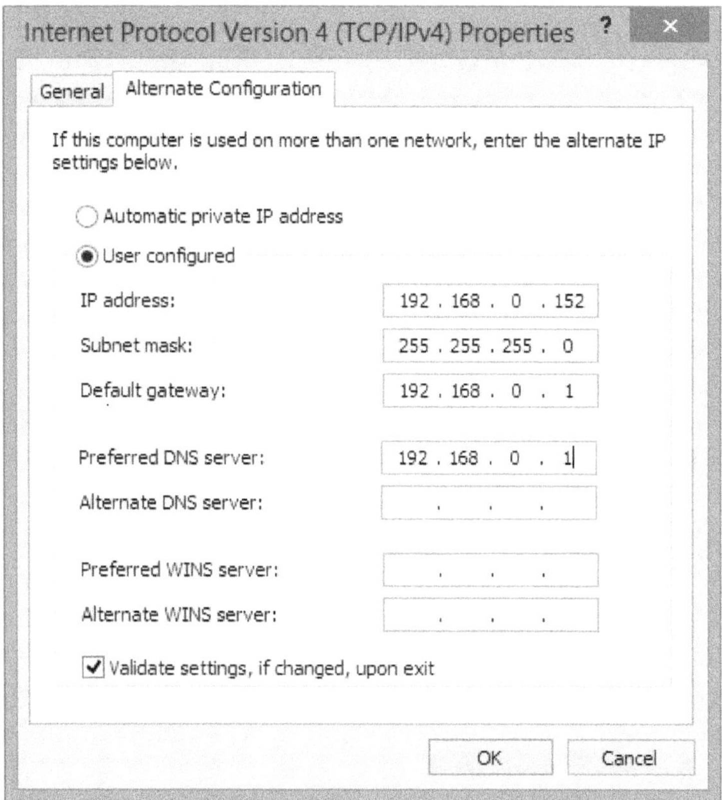

14. Once done, click **OK** to specify the alternate configurations to the computer.
15. Back on NIC's properties box, click **OK**.

To remove an assigned alternative IP address, steps 1 to 12 can be followed, while selecting Automatic private IP address radio button when on step 12. OK button on all the opened boxes must be clicked to save the changes.

Release and Renew IP Addresses

Introduction to Releasing and Renewing IP Addresses

When a DHCP server assigns a dynamic IP address to a computer, the IP address is assigned for a specific time duration. The time for which an IP address is assigned to a computer is technically known as the 'lease duration'. As per the default characteristics, when 50% of the lease duration of an IP address is lapsed, the client computer requests the DHCP server to renew the lease. When the DHCP server renews the lease duration, the IP address remains assigned to the client computer till 50% of the renewed duration is lapsed.

Sometimes when administrators change some configurations on the DHCP server, e.g. modifications in the IP addresses, etc., it becomes essential for them to re-assign new IP addresses to the client computers according to the range that they have configured in the DHCP server. To accomplish this task successfully, administrators must release the previous IP addresses that the DHCP server may have assigned earlier, and renew the addresses. When an IP address of a client computer is the renewed, it requests the DHCP server for a new IP address. If the DHCP server has an IP address available in its address pool, it assigns the address to the client computer.

How to Release and Renew an IP Address?

In order to release and renew and IP address in Microsoft Windows 8 computer, steps given below must be followed:

1. Log on to Microsoft Windows 8 computer with administrator account.
2. From the **Start** screen, click **Desktop** tile.
3. On the desktop screen, hover mouse to the bottom right corner of the window.
4. From the displayed options, click **Search**.
5. On the opened **Apps** screen, scroll and locate **Command Prompt**.
6. Once located, right-click **Command Prompt**.
7. From the advanced options displayed at the bottom of the window, click **Run as administrator**.
8. On the displayed **User Account Control** confirmation box, click **Yes** button to open the command prompt with elevated privileges.
9. On the opened command window, type **IPCONFIG /RELEASE** command and press **Enter** key to release the dynamic IP address automatically obtained from the DHCP server.

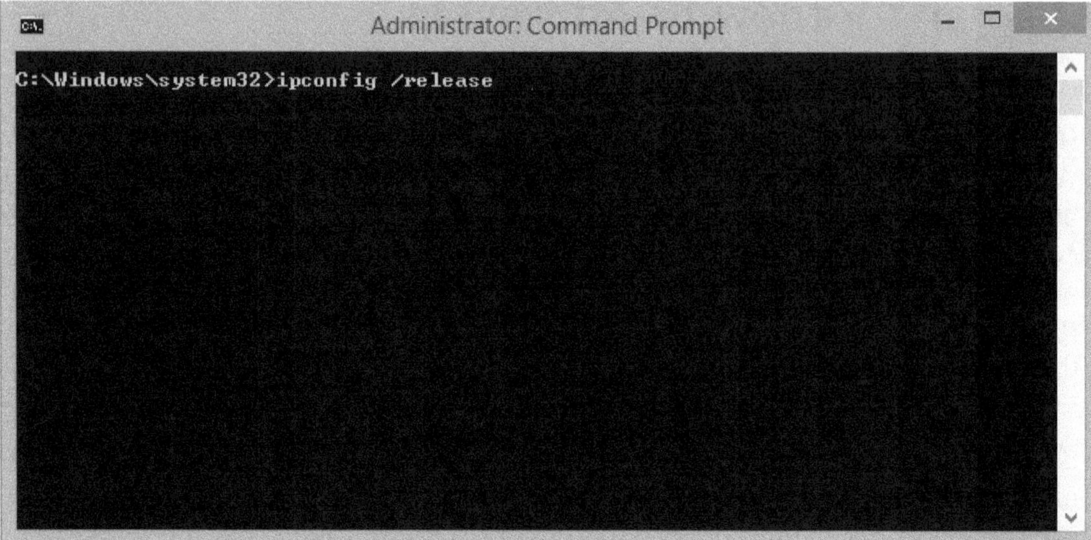

10. In order to renew the IP address, in the same command window, type **IPCONFIG /RENEW** command and press **Enter** key.

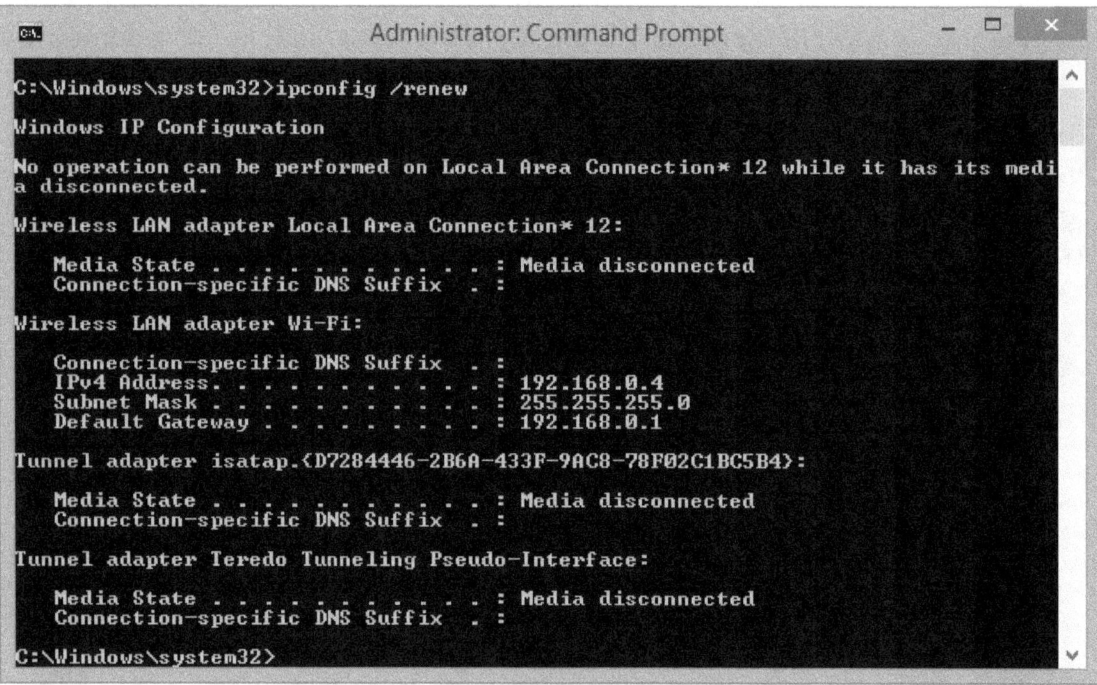

Manage Network Discovery/File and Printer Sharing

Introduction to Network Discovery and File and Printer Sharing**

Microsoft Windows 8 has a feature named Network Discovery which, when enabled, allows Windows 8 computer to discover other computers on the network and vice versa. By default Network Discovery is turned on as soon as the computer is connected to the network and administrators specify the network type as private.

File and Printer Sharing is a setting in Windows 8 operating system which, when enabled, allows the computer to share files and printers so that they can be accessed by other computers in the network. By default File and Printer Sharing is also turned on when the network type is specified as private.

Network Discovery and File and Printer Sharing are automatically disabled when the network type is set to public.

Network Discovery and File and Printer Sharing are two different settings. It is recommended that they must be enabled or disabled in contrast with each other according to the requirements. In most production environments, administrators do not allow their computers to be discovered by other computers in a network, but they allow trusted users to access the resources and send print commands to the shared printers on a Windows 8 computer. This can be done by disabling the Network Discovery and enabling File and Printer Sharing.

How to Manage Network Discovery and File and Printer Sharing?

In order to manage Network Discovery and File and Printer Sharing in Microsoft Windows 8, steps given below must be followed:

1. Log on to Microsoft Windows 8 computer with the administrator account.
2. From the **Start** screen, click **Desktop** tile.
3. On the desktop screen, right-click the **Network** icon from the system tray at the bottom right corner of the window.
4. From the context menu, click **Open Network and Sharing Center**.
5. On the **Network and Sharing Center** window, click **Change advanced sharing settings** option from the left pane.
6. On the **Advanced sharing settings** window, expand **Private** profile settings.
7. From the displayed options, click to select **Turn on network discovery** radio button under **Network discovery** section to enable network discovery.

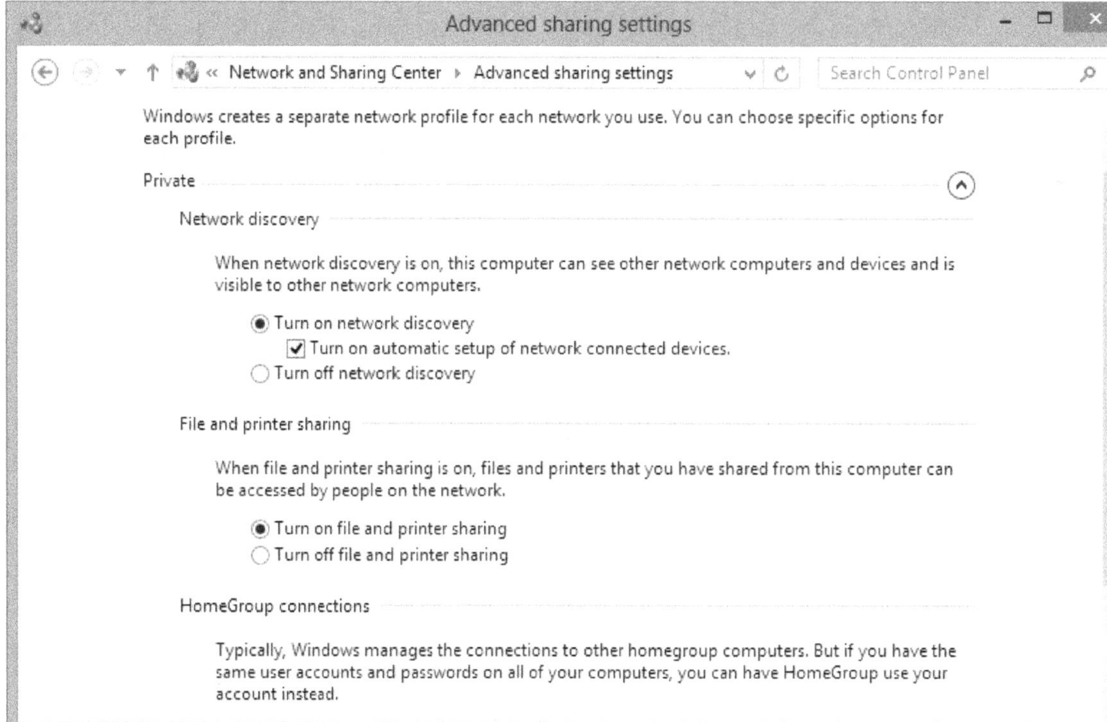

8. Under the **File and printer sharing** section, click to select **Turn on file and printer sharing** radio button to enable file and printer sharing.
9. Although it is not recommended to turn on network discovery and file and printer sharing on **Guest or Public** network profiles, if administrators want they do so by repeating the steps 7 and 8 by expanding **Guests or Public** profile settings.
10. Click **Save changes** button when done.

Enable Internet Connection Sharing (ICS)

Introduction to Internet Connection Sharing (ICS)

Internet Connection Sharing (ICS) is a feature in Microsoft Windows 8 that allows one Internet connection to be shared within multiple computers that are connected to the network. In order to enable ICS on a Windows 8 computer, the computer must have at least two network interface cards (NICs) installed in it. The first NIC of the computer must be connected to the Internet connection line, and the second NIC of the computer must be connected to a central device, which is further connected to other computers on the network. Sometimes second NIC can also be connected to another computer directly, if the Internet connection is to be shared only within two computers.

Once the above mentioned scenario is properly set up, administrators can then enable ICS on the NIC that is connected to the Internet. As ICS is enabled on first NIC, Windows 8 automatically assigns a static IP address to the second NIC (that is connected to the central device or to the other computer). The IP address range that Windows 8 uses to assign static IP address to the second NIC is 192.168.137.1 with the subnet mask 255.255.255.0. Moreover, once ICS is enabled on the NIC that is connected to the Internet, the second NIC automatically turns into a mini DHCP server and starts assigning dynamic IP addresses to all client computers that are connected to it. The dynamic IP addresses that the second NIC assigns to the client computers belong to class C range and start with 192.168.137.2 and the subnet mask 255.255.255.0.

How to Enable Internet Connection Sharing (ICS)?

In order to enable Internet Connection Sharing (ICS) on a Windows 8 computer, make sure that the computer has at least two NICs installed in it and one NIC is connected to the Internet. Once verified, steps given below must be followed to enable ICS on the computer:

1. Log on to Microsoft Windows 8 computer with the administrator account.
2. From the **Start** screen, click **Desktop** tile.
3. On the desktop screen, right-click the **Network** icon from the system tray at the bottom right corner of the window.
4. From the context menu, click **Open Network and Sharing Center**.
5. On the **Network and Sharing Center** window, click **Change adapter settings** from the left pane.
6. On the opened **Network Connections** window, right-click the NIC that is connected to the Internet.
7. From the displayed context menu, click **Properties**.
8. On the opened NIC's properties box, go to the **Sharing** tab.
9. On the **Sharing** tab, check **Allow other network users to connect through this computer's Internet connection** checkbox.

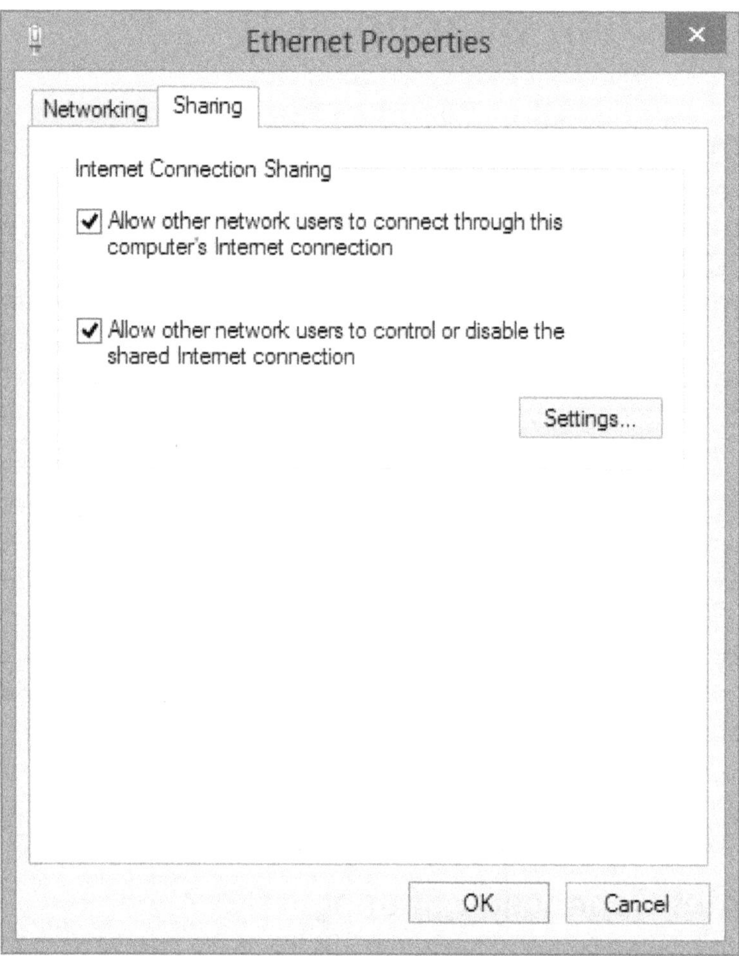

10. Click **OK** to enable ICS on the computer.

To disable Internet Connection Sharing (ICS), steps 1 to 10 can be followed, while unchecking the **Allow other network users to connect through this computer's Internet connection** checkbox when on step 9.

Change (ICS) IP Address Range

Introduction to Internet Connection Sharing (ICS) IP Address Range

In Microsoft Windows 8, when Internet Connection Sharing (ICS) is enabled on an NIC, the second LAN card automatically turns into a mini DHCP server and assigns itself a static IP address that belongs to 192.168.137.0 network address with the default 255.255.255.0 subnet mask. The static IP address that the second NIC automatically assigns to itself is 192.168.137.1. Since the NIC is converted to a mini DHCP server, it also starts assigning dynamic IP addresses to all the client computers that are connected to the local computer, on which ICS has been enabled. The dynamic IP addresses that the second NIC assigns as a mini DHCP server belong to the same range, i.e. 192.168.137.0 network address and 255.255.255.0 subnet mask.

In small scale industries or some medium scale organizations, this default configuration and the IP address range works perfectly fine and no further modifications are required to be done by the administrators. However in the organizations where the IP addressing scheme of 192.168.137.0 network address already exists, this default configuration might create conflicts when automatic IP addresses are assigned to the ICS client computers. In such situations, administrators may want to modify the default IP address range that mini DHCP server of ICS assigns to the client computers.

How to Change the Default IP Address Range in ICS?

In order to modify the default IP address range while using ICS in Microsoft Windows 8, steps given below must be followed:

1. Log on to Microsoft Windows 8 computer with administrator account.
2. From the **Start** screen, click **Desktop** tile.
3. On the desktop window, press **Windows** + **R** keys simultaneously to initiate **Run** command box.
4. In the opened **Run** command box, type **REGEDIT** command and press **Enter** key.
5. On the displayed **User Account Control** confirmation box, click **Yes** to grant the consent to open **Registry Editor** with elevated privileges.
6. On the opened **Registry Editor** window, from the left pane, locate and click to select **HKEY_LOCAL_MACHINE\SYSTEM\CurrentControlSet\services\SharedAccess\Parameters**.
7. Once **Parameters** key is selected from the left pane, from the right pane, double-click **ScopeAddress** string.
8. On the opened **Edit String** box, specify the first IP address of the new IP address range in the **Value data** field. (E.g. 192.168.0.1)

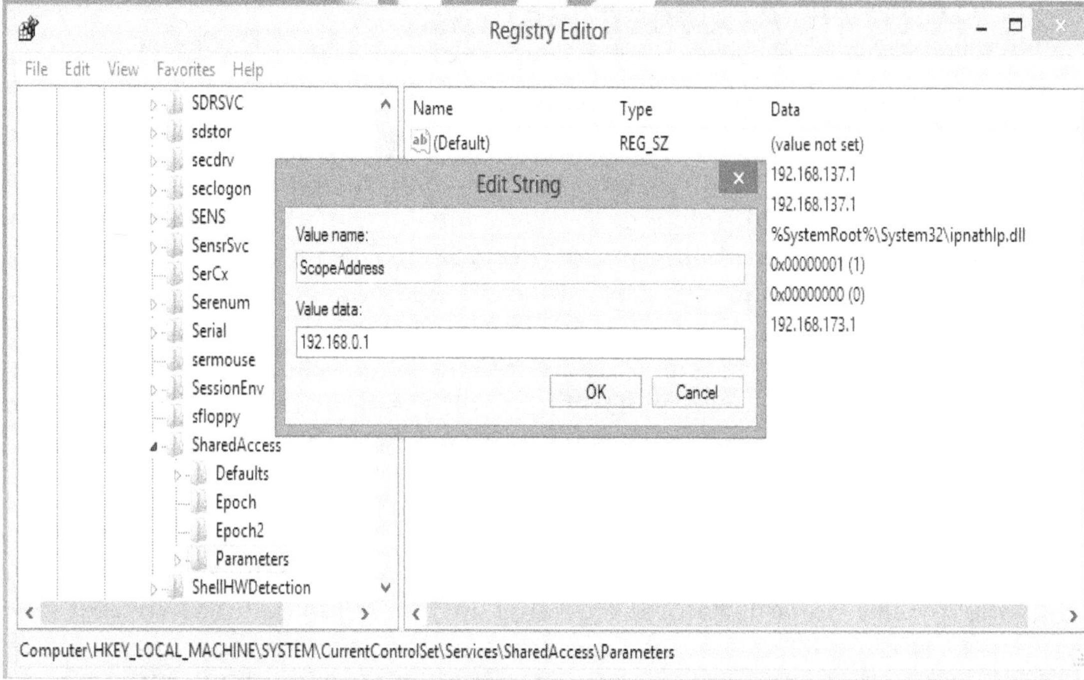

9. Click **OK** and close **Registry Editor**.
10. Restart the computer to make the new settings applicable.

Note: *Even though the IP address range for the DHCP service (mini DHCP server) can be modified, the 255.255.255.0 subnet mask still remains the same and cannot be changed whatsoever.*

Manage Password Protected Sharing

Introduction to Password Protected Sharing

When Microsoft Windows 8 is installed, by default password protected sharing is enabled which prompts remote users to provide the password of an authenticated user account before Windows allows them to access the resources of the computer through the network.

Password protected sharing is enabled for security reasons. When administrators disable password protected sharing, remote users who try to access resources on a local computer through the network are not required to provide the password. The reason behind this is that when password protected sharing is disabled, the local Guest account (which is disabled by default) gets enabled and the users who try to access the resources remotely are automatically granted the permission to log on to the computer using the credentials of the Guest account. When this happens, the remote users are granted with all the privileges that a Guest account has. In other words Password Protected Sharing and the state of Guest account are inversely proportional to each other. This means that when Guest account is enabled, Password Protected Sharing is automatically disabled and vice versa.

Note: *In order to maintain security of a Windows 8 computer, it is recommended that Password Protected Sharing must not be disabled, and Guest account must not be enabled.*

How to Disable or Enable Password Protected Sharing?

In order to disable or enable Password Protected Sharing in Microsoft Windows 8, steps given below must be followed:

1. Log on to Microsoft Windows 8 computer with the administrator account.
2. From the **Start** screen, click **Desktop** tile.
3. On the desktop screen, right-click the **Network** icon from the system tray at the bottom right corner of the window.
4. From the context menu, click **Open Network and Sharing Center**.
5. On the **Network and Sharing Center** window, click **Change advanced sharing settings** option from the left pane.
6. On the **Advanced sharing settings** window, expand **All Networks** settings.
7. From the displayed options, click to select **Turn off password protected sharing** radio button under the **Password protected sharing** section.

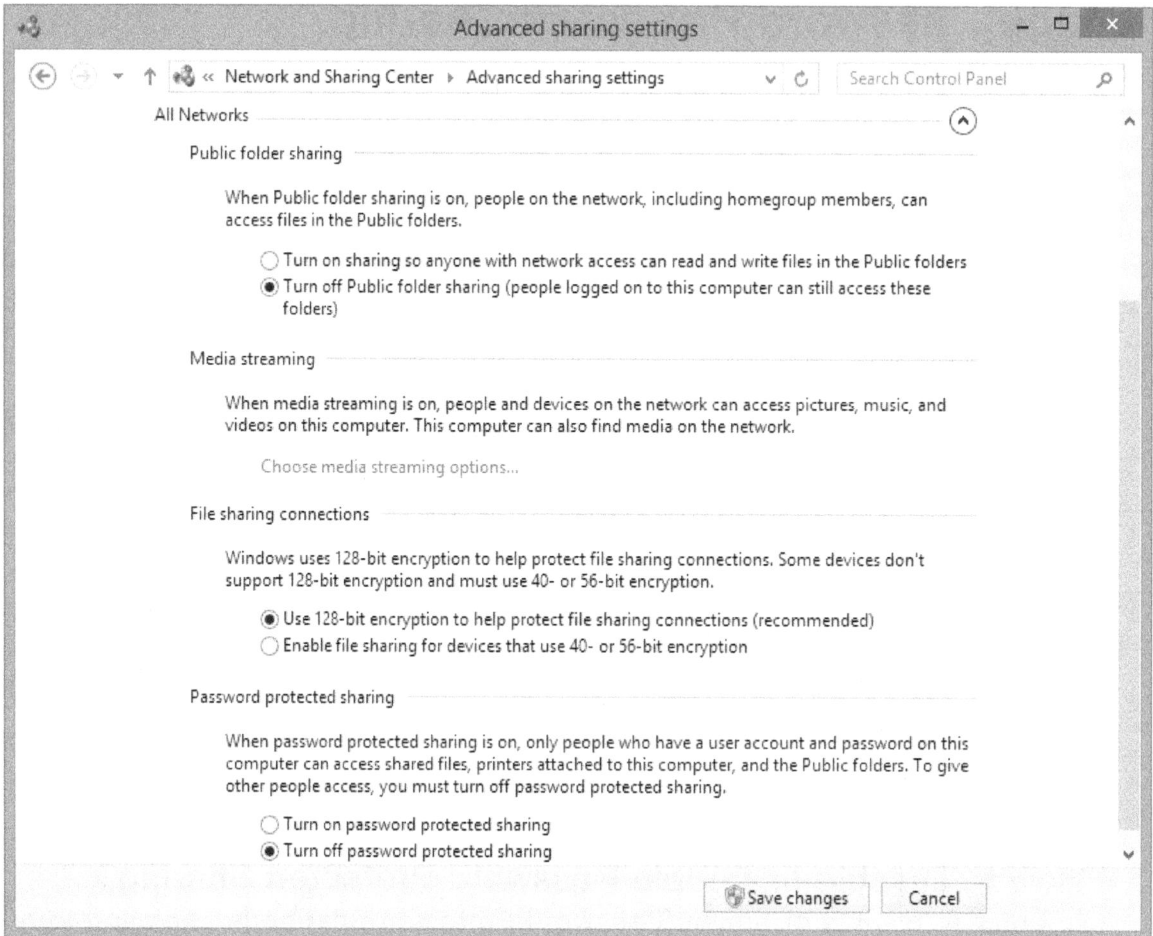

8. Click **Save changes** button to disable password protected sharing feature.

To re-enable password protected sharing, steps 1 to 8 can be followed, while selecting **Turn on password protected sharing** radio button when on step 7.

Enable Network Access for Administrative Shares

Introduction to Administrative Shares

Administrative share is a concept through which users can access secured locations (system drives, Windows folder, etc.) of a remote computer even if the locations are not shared. This happens because even if the drives are not manually shared by the users, they are still accessible to the remote users, provided they have administrative privileges on the computer. When users try to access a secured location on the remote computer through the network, the remote computer prompts for administrative credentials. When appropriate credentials are provided, the remote computer allows the user to access the secured locations.

In order to access the secured locations remotely, users must type the Universal Naming Convention (UNC) path of the remote computer along with the drive letter where the secured location exists followed by a $ sign. The $ sign represents a hidden share on the remote computer. By default all drives of the remote computers are administratively shared and the share is hidden. Therefore in order to access the drives, the entire UNC path to the drive of the remote computer must be typed followed by a $ sign. Users can type the UNC paths of the remote computers in the address bar of any window, or in the Run command box.

In legacy versions of operating systems, such as Microsoft Windows XP, it was quite easier to access secured locations using administrative shares and by providing appropriate credentials when prompted. Things are a bit complicated in Microsoft Windows 8. When a user using Windows 8 computer tries to access an administratively shared location on another remote Windows 8 computer, only the administrator credentials are required to be provided in order to gain access. However if a user tries to access Windows 8 computer remotely from any other version of Windows, for example Microsoft Windows 7, access to Windows 8 computer is denied even if administrative credentials are provided when prompted. The reason behind this is that Microsoft Windows 8 does not allow its resources to be accessed by other users using any other version of operating system, even if they provide administrative credentials while using administrative shares.

In order to allow users of other versions of Windows to remotely access Windows 8 using administrative shares, registry settings in Microsoft Windows 8 computer must be modified.

How to Enable Network Access for Administrative Shares?

In order to enable network access for administrative shares in Microsoft Windows 8, steps given below must be followed:

1. Log on to Microsoft Windows 8 computer with administrator account.
2. From the **Start** screen, click **Desktop** tile.
3. On the desktop screen, press **Windows** + **R** keys simultaneously to initiate **Run** command box.
4. In the **Run** command box, type **REGEDIT** command and press **Enter** key.
5. On the **User Account Control** confirmation box, click **Yes** button to provide the consent to open **Registry Editor**.

6. On the **Registry Editor** window, from the left pane, locate
7. **HKEY_LOCAL_MACHINE\SOFTWARE\Microsoft\Windows\CurrentVersion\Policies\System**.
8. Once located, click to select **System** container from the left pane.
9. In the right pane, right-click anywhere and from the context menu, go to **New**.
10. From the displayed submenu, click **DWORD (32-bit) Value**.
11. Rename the newly created DWORD (32-bit) Value as **LocalAccountTokenFilterPolicy**.
12. Once renamed, double-click **LocalAccountTokenFilterPolicy**.
13. On the opened **Edit DWORD (32-bit) Value** box, in the **Value data** field, change the value from **0** to **1**.

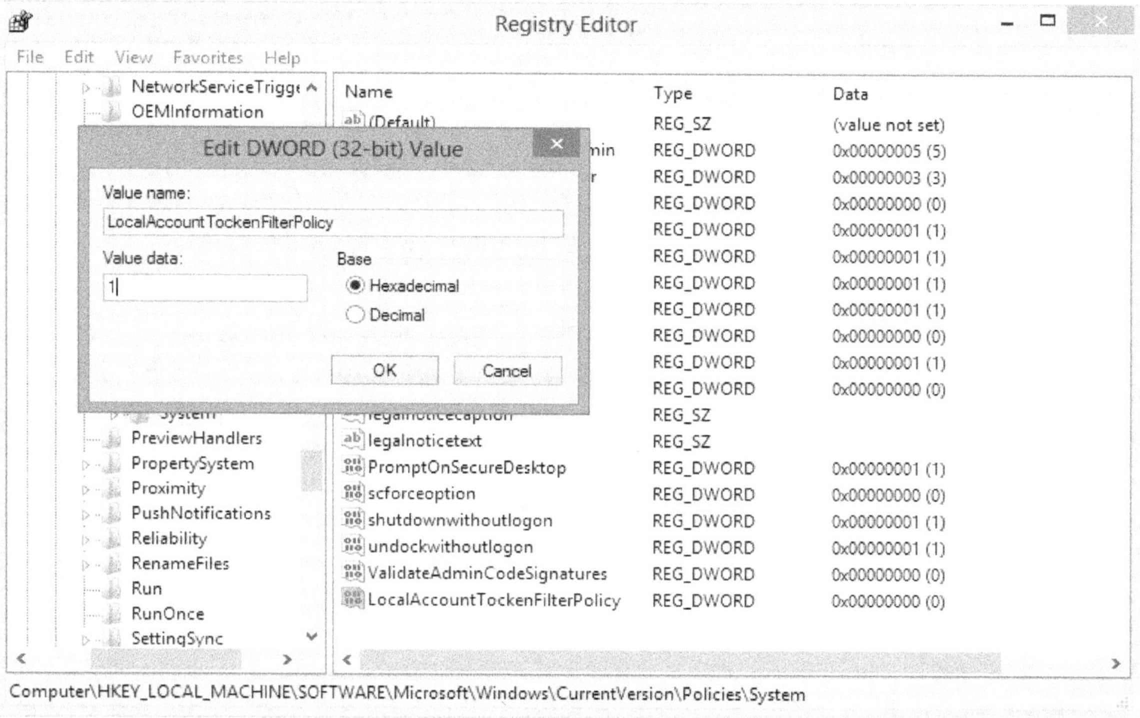

14. Once done, click **OK** to save the changes.
15. Close **Registry Editor** window and restart the computer to allow the changes to take effect.

To disable network access for administrative shares, steps 1 to 7 can be followed, while double-clicking the **LocalAccountTokenFilterPolicy** DWORD and replacing **1** with **0** in the **Value data** field. In order to allow the changes to take effect, the computer must be restarted after clicking **OK** in the **Edit DWORD (32-bit) Value** box and closing **Registry Editor** window.

Manage Encryption for File Sharing

Introduction to Encryption for File Sharing

When file and printer sharing is enabled on Windows 8 and remote users try to access shared files from the computer, the communication and transaction that takes place remains encrypted by default. The default 128-bit encryption level is quite fine when remote computers have Windows 8 or Windows 7 installed on them. However if legacy versions of operating systems or the devices that do not support 128-bit encryption are configured to access files or folders from a Windows 8 computer, the default encryption level might prevent users from accessing the shared objects. In order to allow a flawless communication between Windows 8 computer and the legacy versions of operating systems and/or devices, default encryption level must be reduced so that even the older operating systems/devices can decrypt the encrypted information after receiving the data.

How to Manage Encryption for File Sharing?

In order to manage encryption for file sharing in Microsoft Windows 8, steps given below must be followed:

1. Log on to Microsoft Windows 8 computer with the administrator account.
2. From the **Start** screen, click **Desktop** tile.
3. On the desktop screen, right-click the **Network** icon from the system tray at the bottom right corner of the window.
4. From the context menu, click **Open Network and Sharing Center**.
5. On the **Network and Sharing Center** window, click **Change advanced sharing settings** option from the left pane.
6. On the **Advanced sharing settings** window, expand **All Networks** settings.
7. From the displayed options, click to select **Enable file sharing for devices that use 40- or 56-bit encryption** radio button under the **File sharing connections** section.

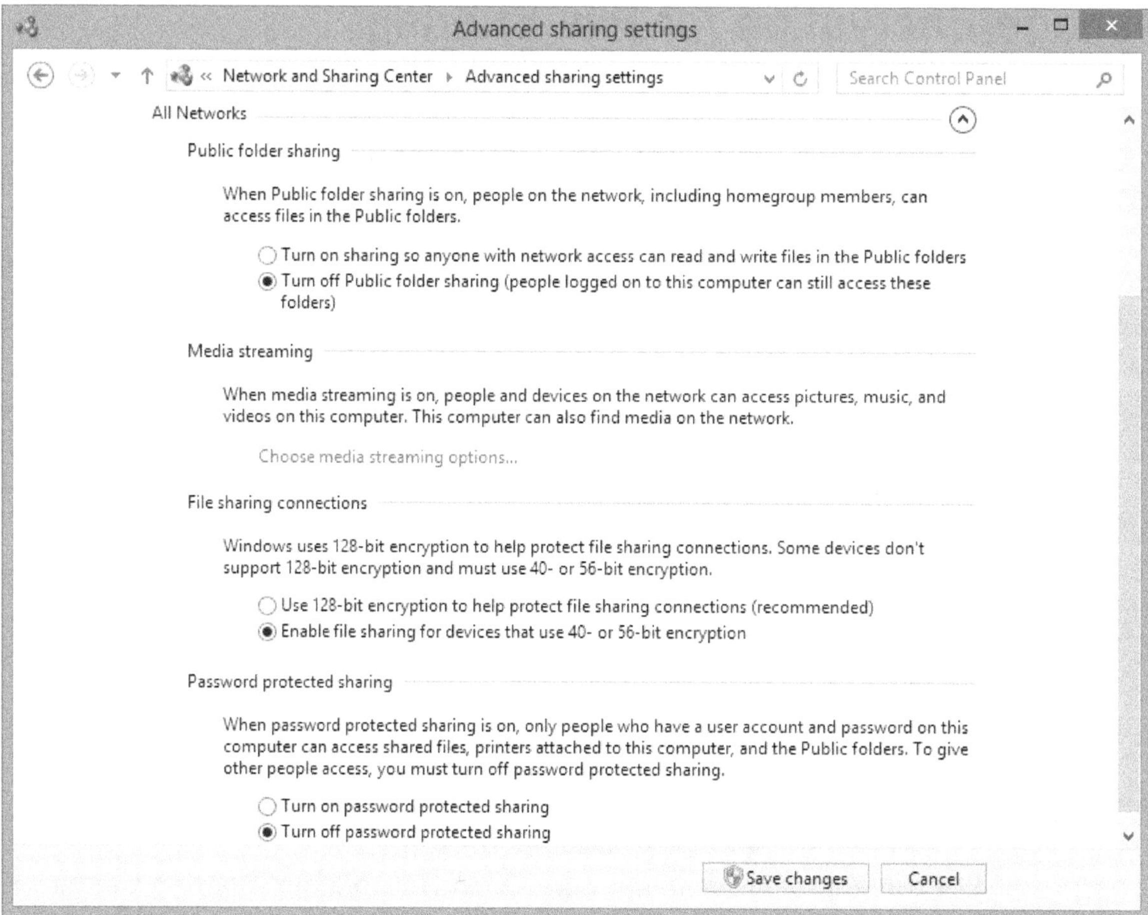

8. Once done, click **Save changes** button to save the modified settings.

To set Windows 8 back to its default file sharing encryption configuration, steps 1 to 8 can be followed, while selecting **Use 128-bit encryption to help protect file sharing connections (recommended)** radio button when on step 7.

Share a Folder

Introduction to Folder Sharing

When a Windows 8 computer is connected to a network, it is expected that the resources that reside on the local computer are allowed to be accessed by the users using other computers on the network.

In order to allow remote users to access objects (files or folders) from a Windows 8 computer, folders must be shared and appropriate NTFS and share permissions must be set on them. When a folder is shared, Server Message Block (SMB) protocol is used in the background. If file sharing fails, it is quite likely that it is because of SMB protocol.

How to Share a Folder?

In order to share a folder in Microsoft Windows 8, steps given below must be followed:

1. Log on to Microsoft Windows 8 computer with administrator account.
2. From the **Start** screen, click **Desktop** tile.
3. On the desktop screen, click **File Explorer** icon from the taskbar.
4. On the opened **Libraries** window, navigate and locate the folder that is to be shared.
5. Right-click the located folder and from the context menu click **Properties**.
6. On the opened folder's properties box, go to **Sharing** tab.
7. On the **Sharing** tab, click **Advanced Sharing** button.
8. On the **Advanced Sharing** window, check **Share this folder** checkbox.

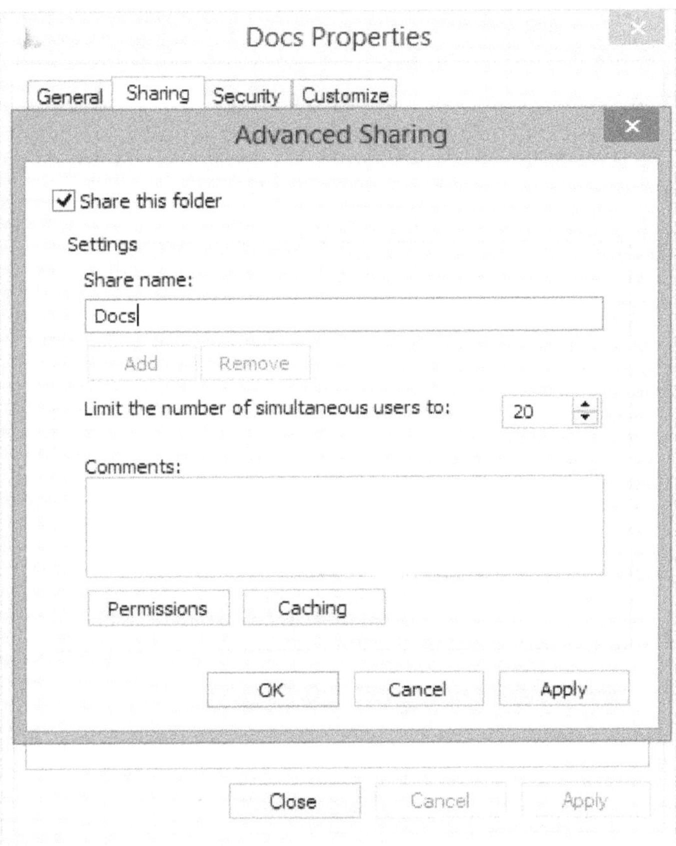

9. Optionally, **Add** button can be clicked under **Share name** field to specify a different share name for the folder.
10. Optionally, **Permissions** button can also be clicked to set share permissions on the selected folder.
11. Once done with the configurations, click **OK** button to enable sharing on the selected folder with the specified settings.
12. Back on the folders properties box, click **Close** button.

To un-share a folder, steps 1 to 8 can be followed, while unchecking **Share this folder** checkbox when on step 8. **OK** button must be clicked to un-share the shared folder and **Yes** button must also be clicked on any warning box that appears.

Set Share Permissions

Introduction to Share Permissions

Share permissions are the privileges granted to the remote users or groups in order to make local files and folders accessible to them. When a folder is shared, by default 'Read' permissions are set for 'Everyone' system group. This makes the folder accessible to everyone who accesses the system from a remote computer via network. If administrators want, they can set other share permissions on the object in order to grant higher level of privileges to the remote users. The other share permissions that administrators can set on an object are:

- **Full Control** - When this level of permission is set on a folder for any user or group, that user or group gets unrestricted privileges on the folder. The user or the members of the group can read, modify, delete and modify NTFS permissions for the contents of the folder.
- **Change** - When this level of permission is set on a folder for any user or group, that user or group gets all the permissions of 'Full Control' except for managing NTFS permissions for the contents of the folder.
- **Read** - As mentioned above, 'Read' permission is set for 'Everyone' system group and allows any remote user to view the contents of the folder, and read the files that the folder contains.

Unlike NTFS permissions that are five (for files) and six (for folders) in numbers, share permissions are only three in numbers and can be set only on the folders. In other words, administrators can only share the folders that reside in a computer and not the files (using Advanced Sharing). However Microsoft Windows 8 also allows administrators to share individual files using Sharing Wizard, provided that the files reside any container that belongs to the logged on user's profile folder itself. For example, Documents folder, Videos folder, etc. Sharing Wizard is mostly used to share documents and other personal data in HomeGroup network environments.

In most corporate environments, administrators prefer setting share permissions using 'Advanced Sharing' that allows them to set permissions granularly. Share permissions work along with NTFS permissions, and the effective permissions that apply on the users or groups are the most restrictive ones. For example, if NTFS permissions for group A are set as Read, Write and Modify on a folder IMPORTANT, and the share permissions for the same group on the folder are set as Read, if any user that belongs to group A tries to access IMPORTANT folder from the network would get Read permission on the folder.

Since NTFS permissions can be configured more granularly as compared to the share permissions, it is recommended that administrators should set share permissions to Full Control for Everyone group and then configure NTFS permissions as per the needs for individual users or groups. This practice gives more options to the administrators while setting the security permissions on the folder.

How to Set Share Permissions?

In order to set share permissions on a folder in Microsoft Windows 8, steps given below must be followed:

1. Log on to Microsoft Windows 8 computer with administrator account.
2. From the **Start** screen, click **Desktop** tile.
3. From the desktop screen, click **File Explorer** icon from the taskbar.
4. From the opened **Libraries** window, navigate and locate the shared folder for which share permissions are to be set.
5. Right-click the target folder after locating and from the context menu, click **Properties**.
6. On the folder's properties box, go to **Sharing** tab.
7. Click **Advanced Sharing** button from the **Advanced Sharing** section.
8. On the opened **Advanced Sharing** box, ensure that **Share this folder** checkbox is checked.
9. Click **Permissions** button.
10. On the opened box, add or remove users or groups as required, and set appropriate share permissions as planned.

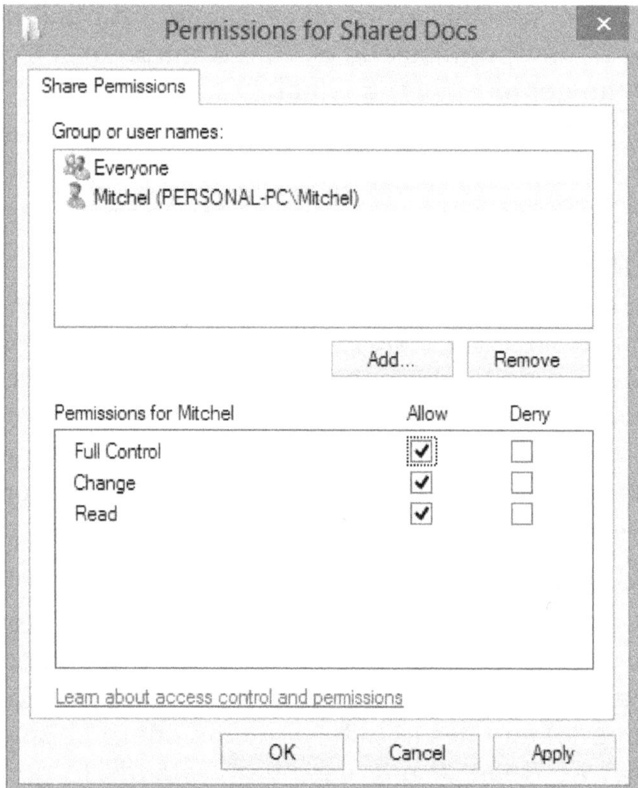

11. Click **OK** when done, and back on **Advanced Sharing** box, click **OK** again.
12. Back on the folder's properties box, click **OK.**

Share Streaming Media

Introduction to Streaming Media Sharing

When Microsoft Windows 8 is installed on home computers, especially when there are multiple computers in a home and are connected to each other, users may want to enable sharing on their personal information so that users on other computers can access the data. Home users' personal information may include images, audio files, home videos, etc. Since images are just as other normal files and are small in sizes, they can be remotely accessed without consuming a lot of bandwidth. Decent amount of bandwidth is mostly consumed when audio files and videos are remotely accessed.

In order to avoid network congestions in both homes and production environments, Microsoft Windows 8 allows users to enable streaming media sharing. When streaming media sharing is enabled, the shared media files can be accessed flawlessly from the remote computers.

How to Enable Streaming Media Sharing?

In order to enable streaming media sharing in Microsoft Windows 8, steps given below must be followed:

1. Log on to Microsoft Windows 8 computer with any account.
2. From the **Start** screen, click **Desktop** tile.
3. On the desktop screen, right-click the **Network** icon from the system tray at the bottom right corner of the window.
4. From the context menu, click **Open Network and Sharing Center**.
5. On the **Network and Sharing Center** window, click **Change advanced sharing settings** option from the left pane.
6. On the **Advanced sharing settings** window, expand **All Networks** settings.
7. Under **Media streaming** section, click **Choose media streaming options**.
8. On the **Media streaming options** window, click **Turn on media streaming** button.
9. On the opened window, make sure that **Allowed** checkbox opposite to **Media programs for this PC and remote connections** option is checked.

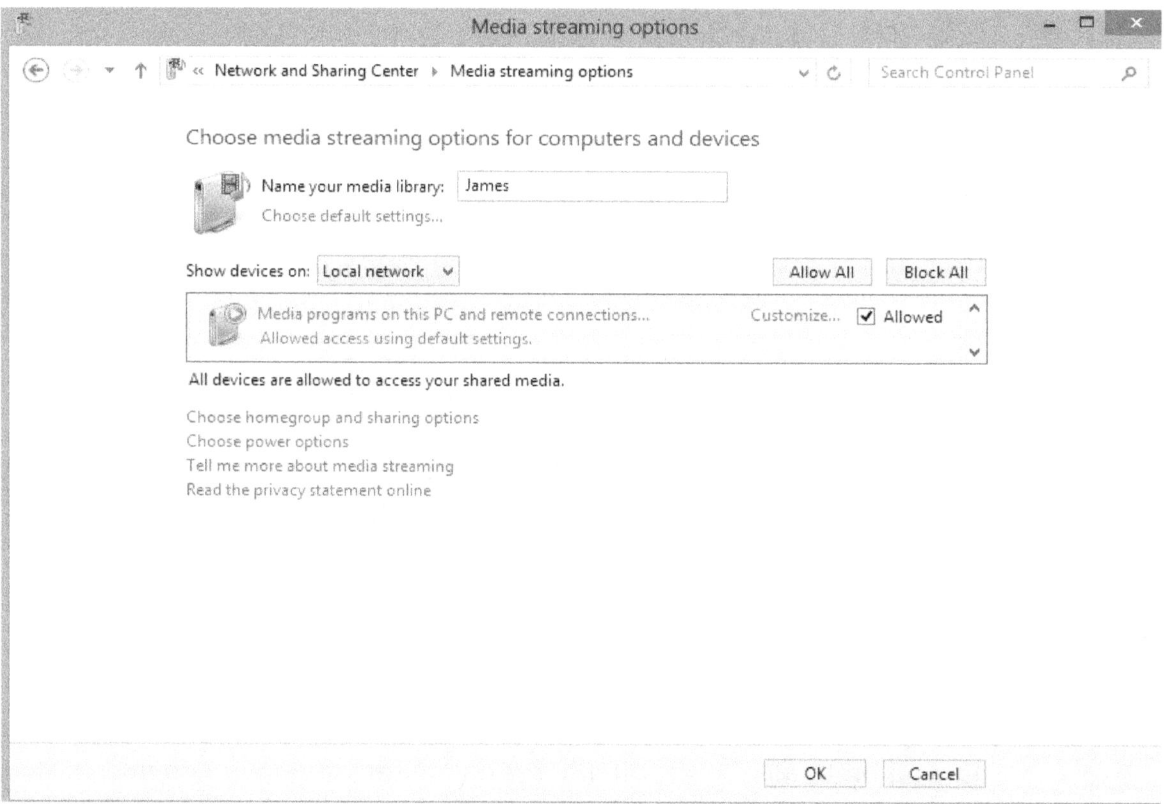

10. Click **OK** when done.

To disable streaming media sharing, on the **Media streaming options** window, click **Block All** button and click **OK**.

Create a HomeGroup

Introduction to HomeGroup

HomeGroup is a network location type that is mostly used in home environments. Since Windows 8 is designed for home users as well, when there are multiple computers in a home, users can create HomeGroup in order to share their personal data with other family members who use different computers.

In order to create a new HomeGroup, IP version 6 (IPv6) must be enabled in the installed NIC (by default it is enabled and users do not have to make any modifications at all). Moreover the current network type must be set to Private while creating a HomeGroup (the network location type is automatically set to Private as soon as a Windows 8 computer is connected to the Internet).

Once a HomeGroup is created, users can share their documents, videos, pictures, etc. with other home users by enabling sharing. As soon as HomeGroup is created, Windows 8 asks users to specify the type of data they want to share with other people who belong to the same HomeGroup.

In one subnet (home network) only one HomeGroup can be created. When there is no HomeGroup available in a subnet, all the computers that belong to the same network are eligible to create a new HomeGroup. However, as soon as any one of the available computers in a network creates a HomeGroup, all other computers of the network lose their ability of creating a HomeGroup, and can only join the existing one.

When a HomeGroup is created, the process automatically generates a password and displays it on the display screen. The displayed password is required by other computers in order to join the created HomeGroup. The HomeGroup password is case-sensitive.

How to Create a HomeGroup?

In order to create a new HomeGroup in Microsoft Windows 8 computer, steps given below must be followed:

1. Log on to Microsoft Windows 8 computer with any account.
2. Make sure that the computer is connected to active Internet connection.
3. From the **Start** screen, click **Desktop** tile.
4. On the desktop window, hover mouse to the bottom right corner of the screen.
5. From the displayed options, click **Settings**.
6. From the **Settings** pane, click **Control Panel**.
7. From the **Control Panel** window, click **Network and Internet** category.
8. From the **Network and Internet** window, click **HomeGroup**.
9. On the **HomeGroup** window, click **Create a homegroup** button.
10. On **Create a Homegroup** window, click **Next**.
11. On **Share with other homegroup members** window, from the containers' drop-down list, choose the appropriate option to enable or disable sharing.

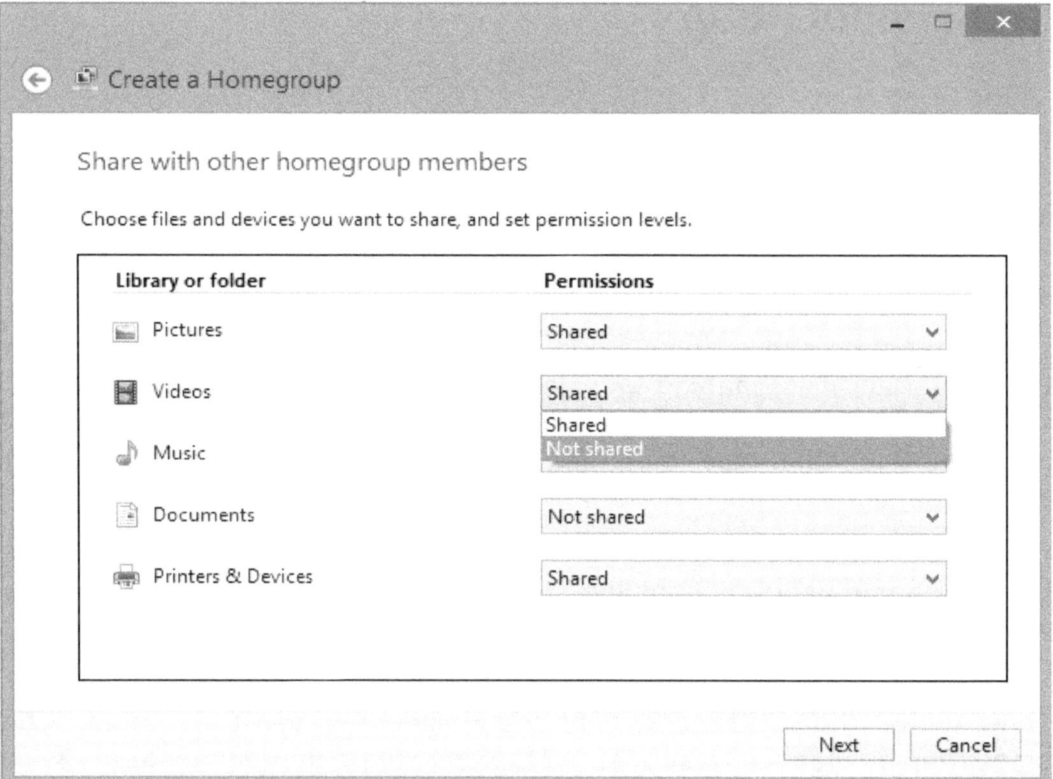

12. Click **Next** to proceed.
13. From the next window, write down the displayed HomeGroup password.

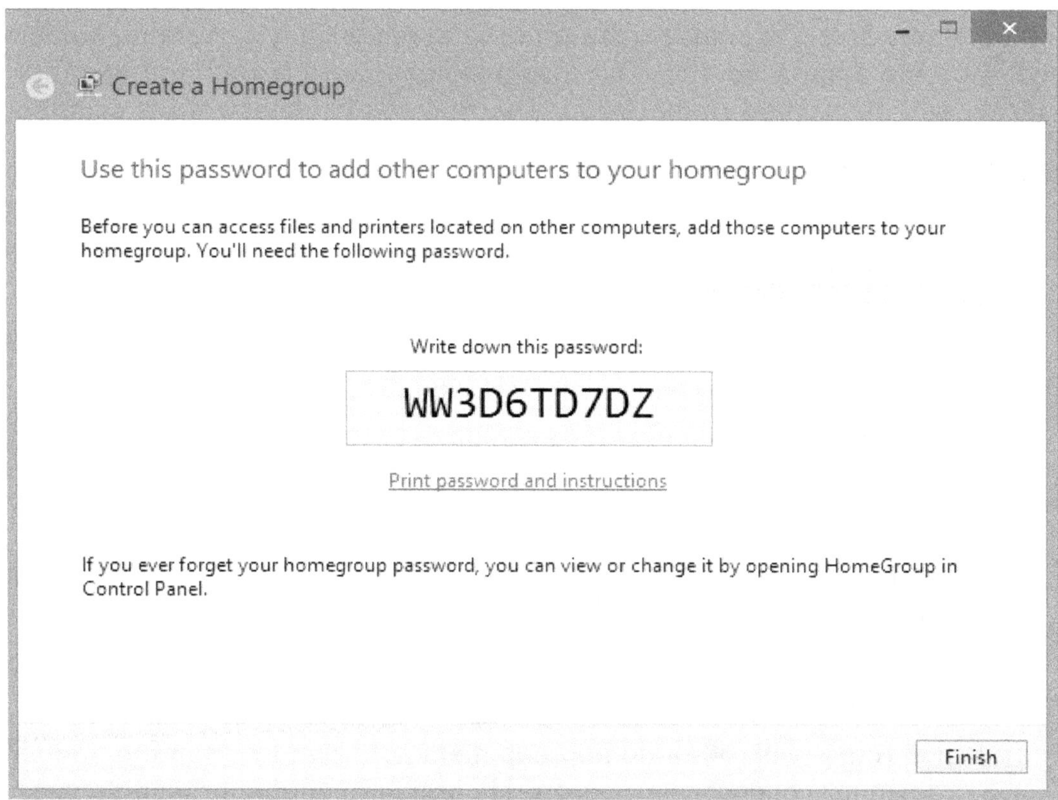

14. Click **Finish** to create a HomeGroup.

Join a HomeGroup

Introduction to Joining a HomeGroup

Windows 8 computer can join any HomeGroup available in the network as long as it belongs to the same subnet. Even in cases when a HomeGroup has been created on Windows 7 computer, process of joining Windows 8 computer to that HomeGroup is same.

While joining Windows 8 computer to an existing HomeGroup, the computer's network type must be set to Private (Windows 8 automatically sets the network type to Private as soon as it is connected to the Internet).

To join a computer to an existing HomeGroup, user must provide the appropriate password that was displayed on the main computer while creating the HomeGroup. (Refer to the previous lesson for details).

How to Join a Computer to an Existing HomeGroup?

In order to join Microsoft Windows 8 computer to an existing HomeGroup, steps given below must be followed:

1. Log on to Microsoft Windows 8 computer with any account.
2. Make sure that the computer is connected to active Internet connection.
3. From the **Start** screen, click **Desktop** tile.
4. From the desktop screen, hover mouse to the bottom right corner of the window.
5. From the displayed options, click **Settings**.
6. From the **Settings** pane, click **Control Panel**.
7. On the **Control Panel** window, click **Network and Internet**.
8. On the **Network and Internet** window, click **HomeGroup**.
9. On the opened **HomeGroup** window, click **Join now** button.

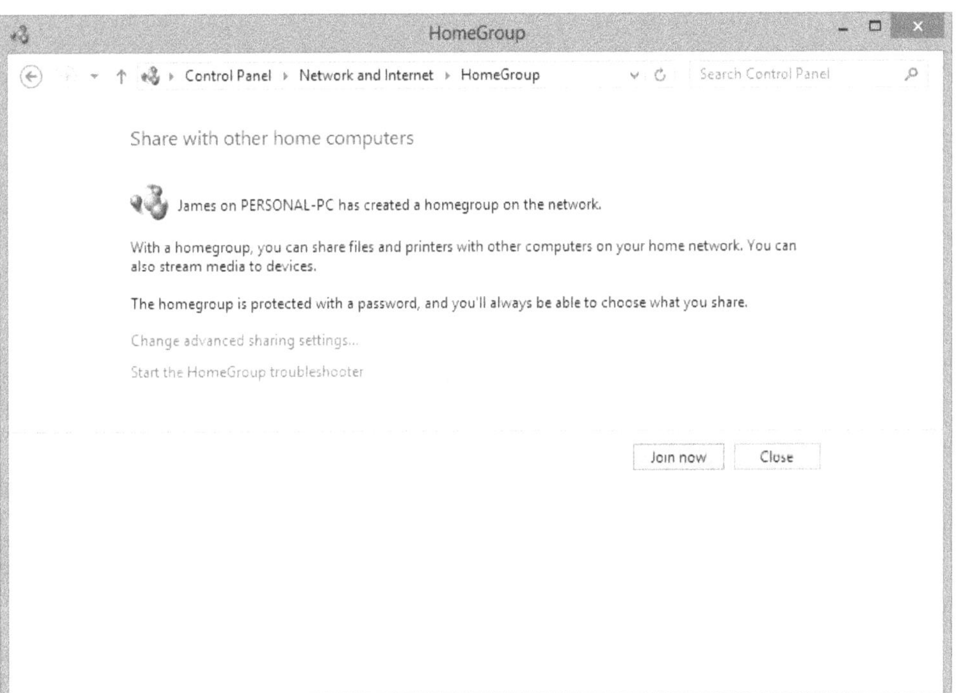

10. On the **Join a Homegroup** window, click **Next**.
11. On the next window, from the drop-down list, set the permission for the data that is to be shared with other HomeGroup members.

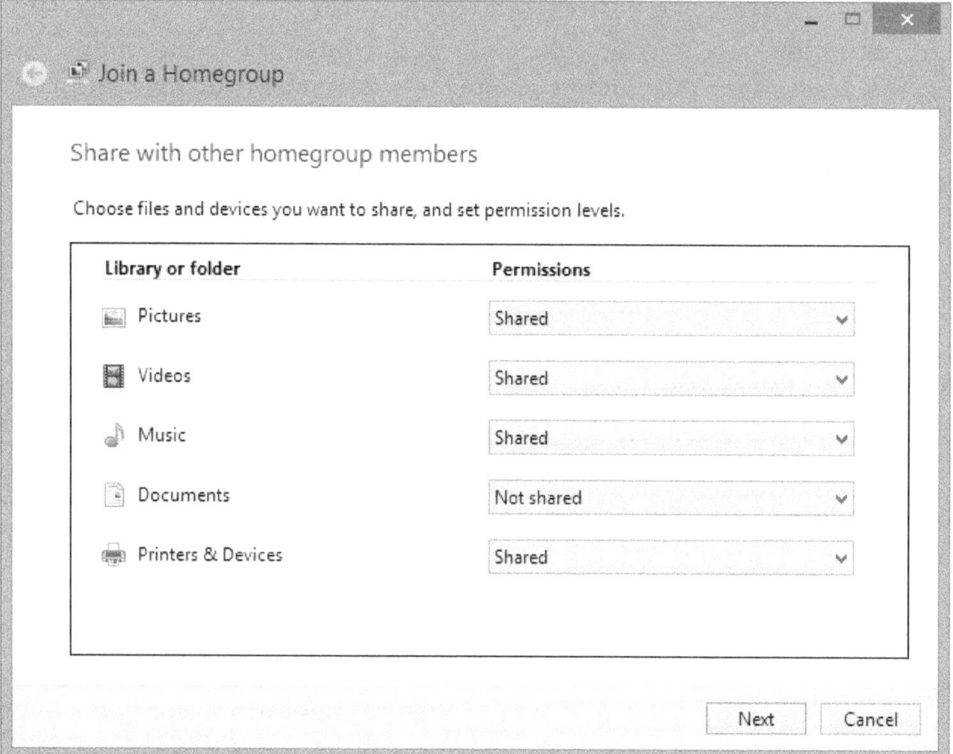

12. Click **Next** to proceed.
13. On the next window, in the **Type the password** field, provide the HomeGroup password that was displayed on the computer where the HomeGroup was created.

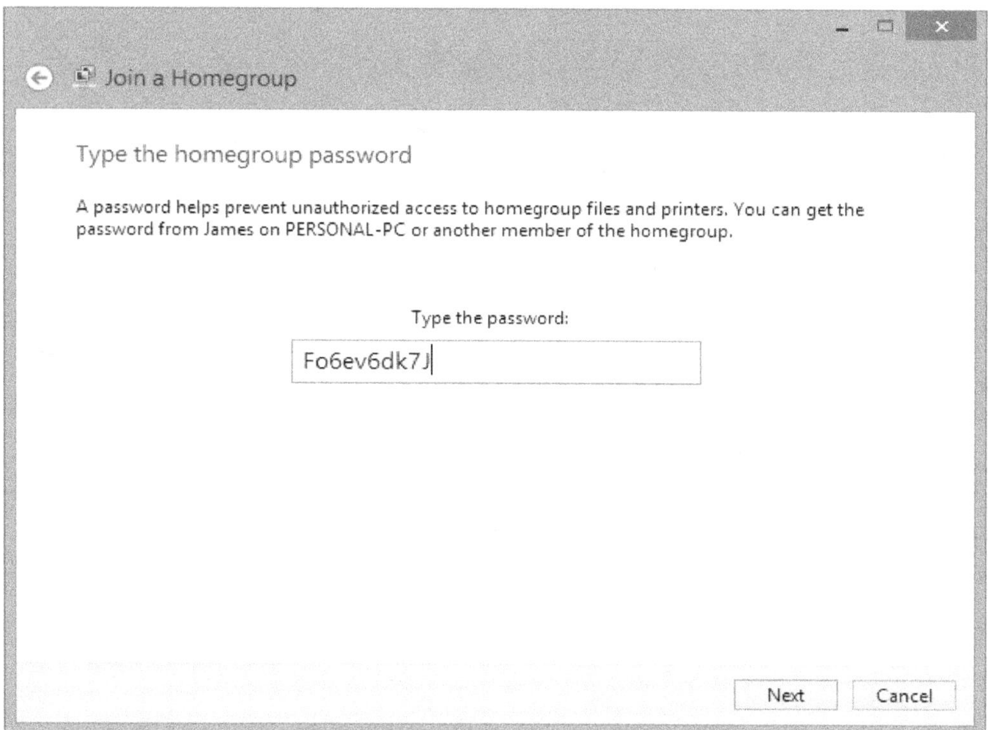

14. Click **Next** to join the computer to the HomeGroup.
15. On the next window, click Finish.

Add Computer to an Existing Domain

Introduction to a Domain

In production environments where there are more than 25 computers connected to each other, it becomes essential for the administrators to establish a domain-based network setup. A domain in an organization can be thought of as a logical empire objects (computers and other network devices like network printers, etc.) of which are managed and controlled by a central and most powerful computer, technically known as a domain controller.

A domain controller is a network operating system that is installed on a computer with decent hardware configuration, and in which Active Directory Domain Services (AD DS) have been installed and configured to manage the entire network from a central location.

In order to manage multiple Windows 8 computers from a central server, i.e. domain controller, the computers must be added to the domain. When Windows 8 computers are added to the domain, they become client computers to the domain controller. Apart from being managed centrally from a domain controller, once Windows 8 computers are added to the domain, domain user accounts' credentials can be used on the client computers to log on to the domain.

In order to add a Windows 8 computer to an existing domain, a user must have administrative privileges on the local computer and the credentials of at least domain user account of the domain on which Windows 8 computer is to be added. Moreover, proper IP address and the address of the DNS server of the domain must also be specified on the client computer before it can be added to the domain.

How to Add a Windows 8 Computer to an Existing Domain?

In order to add a Windows 8 computer to an existing domain, verify that the computer has been assigned with the IP address and is able to communicate with the domain controller exists. Also make sure that the correct DNS server address has been specified in the NIC's properties box. Once the above mentioned specifications are verified, steps given below must be followed:

1. Log on to Microsoft Windows 8 computer with local administrator account.
2. From the **Start** screen, click **Desktop** tile.
3. On the desktop screen, click **File Explorer** icon from the taskbar.
4. On the opened **Libraries** window, right-click **Computer** icon from the left pane.
5. From the displayed context menu, click **Properties**.
6. On the opened **System** window, under the **Computer name, domain, and work settings** section click **Change settings**.
7. On the opened **System Properties** box, make sure that **Computer Name** tab is selected.
8. Click **Change** button.
9. On the **Computer Name/Domain Changes** box, under the **Member of** section, click to select **Domain** radio button.

10. In the enabled field, type the FQDN or the NetBIOS name of the domain to which the computer is to be added.

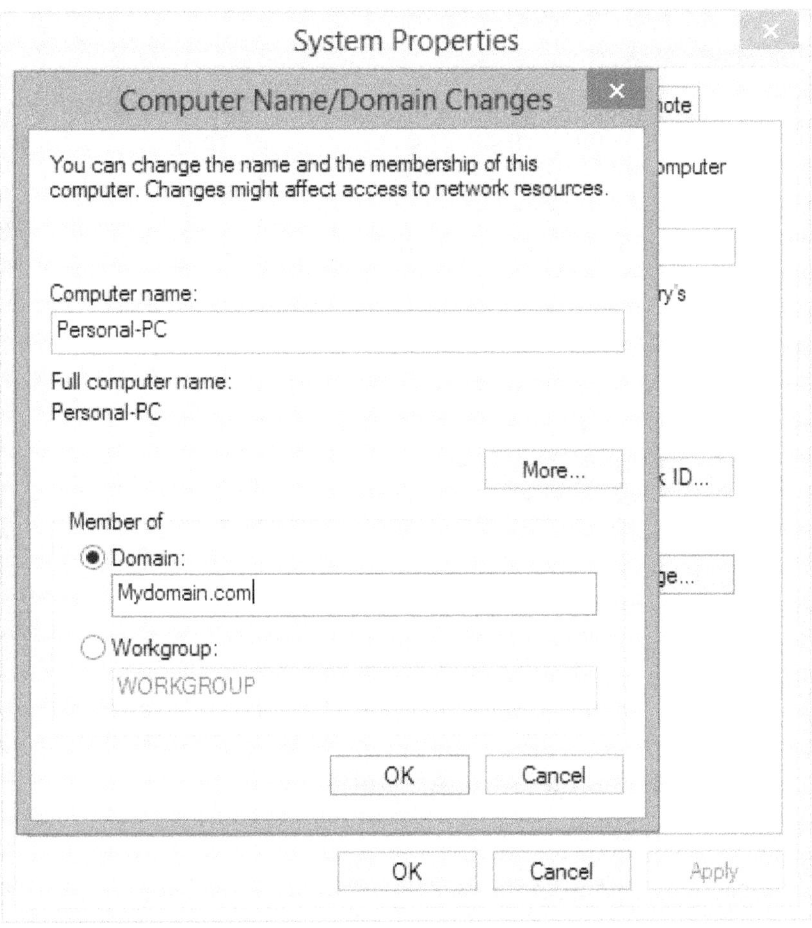

11. When prompted, provide the credentials of the domain administrator or domain user account in the displayed box.
12. Click **OK** button.
13. Restart the computer after receiving welcome message in order to allow the computer to make appropriate changes.

To remove a computer from a domain, steps 1 to 9 can be followed, while selecting the **Workgroup** radio button and specifying the name of the workgroup in the enabled field. **OK** button must be clicked after typing the name of the workgroup, and the computer must be restarted to allow the changes to take effect.

Enable Telnet Client

Introduction to Telnet Client

A Telnet client is a computer that is capable of establishing a Telnet connection to a Telnet server. By default Microsoft Windows 8 is not configured to be used as a Telnet server or a Telnet client. In order to initiate and establish a Telnet connection from a Windows 8 computer to a Telnet server, the Telnet client feature must be enabled. Once Telnet client feature is enabled, Telnet connection can be established using the command line interface.

Why Telnet Is Important?

As mentioned above, Telnet connection is established using command line interface. When administrative credentials are used to establish a Telnet connection, remote computers can be managed by sending the commands through the command line interface using the established connection. Since the commands are just the text characters, they do not consume as much of network bandwidth as graphical user interface (GUI) consumes when the remote computers are managed through remote desktop connections. In other words, with the help of Telnet connections, organizations can remarkably reduce the consumption of network bandwidth while administering remote computers on the local area network or through the internet.

By default Telnet uses port number TCP 23 which must be enabled on both the computers between which the Telnet connections is to be established.

How to Enable Telnet Client?

In order to enable Telnet client in Microsoft Windows 8, steps given below must be followed:

1. Log on to Microsoft Windows 8 computer with administrator account.
2. From the **Start** screen, click **Desktop** tile.
3. On the desktop screen, hover mouse to the bottom right corner of the window.
4. From the displayed options, click **Settings**.
5. From the **Settings** pane, click **Control Panel**.
6. From the **Control Panel** window, click **Programs** category.
7. From the **Programs** window, click **Turn Windows features on or off** option under the **Programs and Features** category.
8. From the opened **Windows Features** box, check **Telnet Client** checkbox from the displayed list.

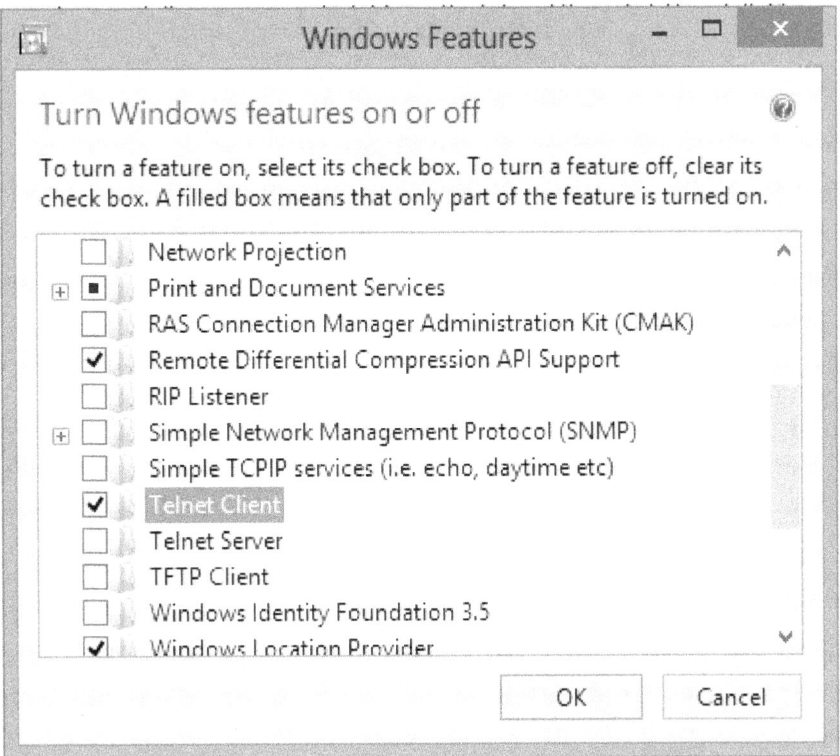

9. Click **OK** install the telnet client.

To disable telnet client feature from the computer, steps 1 to 9 can be followed, while unchecking the **Telnet Client** checkbox when on step 8. All opened windows and boxes must be closed after the successful completion of the task.

Establish a New Ad Hoc Wireless Connection

Introduction to Ad Hoc Wireless Connections

While establishing a wireless network connection, any one of the two available wireless network topologies is used. The two wireless network topologies are:

- **Infrastructure** - This topology is used to establish a wireless network connection when a Wireless Access Point (WAP) is available in the network. When Infrastructure topology is configured, all the computers that are connected wirelessly can communicate with each other through the Wireless Access Point, hence using it as a central device. Benefit of using a Wireless Access Point in wireless network topologies is that it provides 300+ Mbps bandwidth when configured with IEEE 802.11n standards. In order to avail the above mentioned bandwidth, both the Wireless Access Point and the wireless NICs on the client computers must be able to support IEEE 802.11n standards.
- **Ad Hoc** - This topology is used to establish wireless network connection when no Wireless Access Point (WAP) is available in the network. In ad hoc wireless network topology, all client computers connect to each other directly, hence forming a sort of wireless mesh topology. In most laptop PCs that are used in homes, users do not prefer buying Wireless Access Points. They instead establish ad hoc wireless connections that prove to be quite cost effective in home networks. The only drawback that ad hoc wireless connections have is that in ad hoc connections, wireless data transmission is not as secure as it is in Infrastructure topology, and the Wireless connection speed is comparatively slow than that of Infrastructure topology.

Establishing an ad hoc wireless network connection is a bit complicated as compared to establishing an Infrastructure topology. Administrative credentials must be used in order to establish an ad hoc wireless network connection on a Windows 8 computer.

How to Establish an Ad Hoc Wireless Network Connection?

In order to establish an ad hoc wireless network connection in Microsoft Windows 8, steps given below must be followed:

1. Log on to Microsoft Windows 8 computer with administrator account.
2. From the **Start** screen, hover mouse to the bottom right corner of the window.
3. From the displayed options, click **Search**.
4. From the **Apps** screen, right-click **Command Prompt** under **Windows System** category.
5. On the opened command window, type **NETSH WLAN SHOW DRIVER** command and press **Enter** key.
6. From the displayed results, verify that the value of **Hosted network supported** is **Yes**. (If it is **No**, administrators must update the wireless NIC driver).
7. Type **NETSH WLAN SET HOSTEDNETWORK MODE=ALLOW SSID=<SSID-NAME> KEY=<PRESHAREDKEY>** command and press **Enter** key.

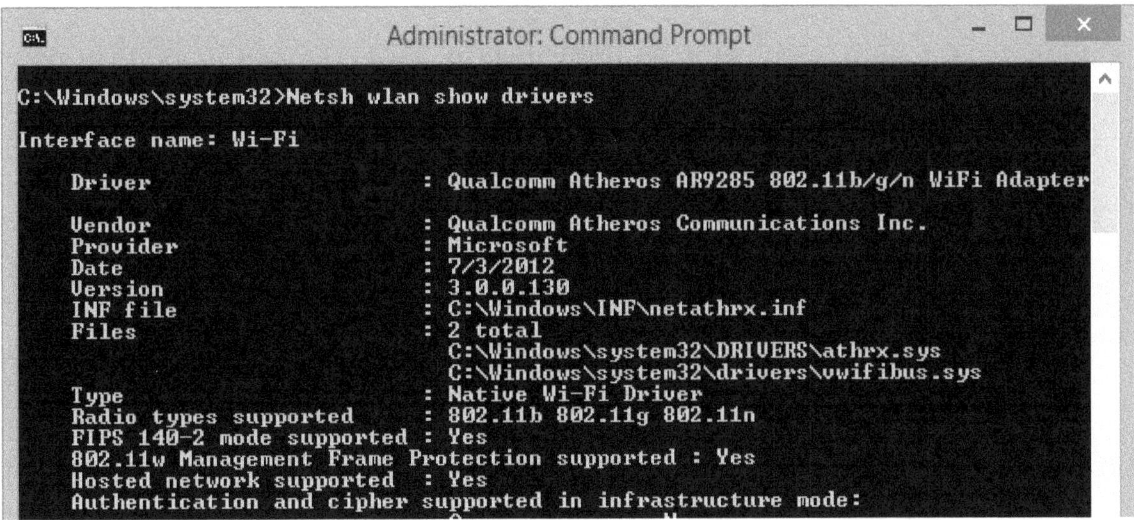

8. Type **NETSH WLAN START HOSTEDNETWORK** command and press **Enter** key.
9. Once done, provide a unique IP address to the newly created virtual Wi-Fi NIC.
10. The SSID of the created Ad hoc wireless connection would be displayed on the other wireless network devices and would be ready to get connected

To remove an ad hoc wireless network connection, steps * to * can be followed.

CHAPTER 12:

WORKING WITH REMOTE DESKTOP

Enable Remote Desktop

Introduction to Remote Desktop

Remote Desktop is a feature in Microsoft Windows 8 that allows locally logged on users on one computer to remotely access another computer that may reside anywhere else in the network. When a remote desktop connection is established, the entire console (desktop screen) of the remote computer is displayed on the monitor screen of the local computer. This enables users on the local computer manage the remote PC without leaving their own seats.

When users try to establish a remote desktop connection to a remote computer, they are displayed with a logon box in which they must provide the administrative credentials of the remote computer, to which the remote desktop connection is to be established. For example if user 'A' is a local administrator on a computer 'C1' and user 'B' is the local administrator on the computer 'C2', when 'A' logs on locally on 'C1' and tries to establish a remote desktop connection to 'C2', on the displayed logon box, 'A' must provide the credentials of 'B' to establish a successful remote desktop connection to computer 'C2'.

Remote Desktop uses Remote Desktop Protocol (RDP) and TCP 3389 port number to establish a successful remote desktop connection. The interface from where a remote desktop connection can be established can be initiated by typing MSTSC command in the Run command box.

Because administrative credentials are required to establish a successful remote desktop connection, users get unrestricted privileges on the remote computers when the connection is established. Moreover as the connection is established, any locally logged on user on Windows 8 automatically gets logged off from the computer.

Before establishing remote desktop connection, Remote Desktop feature must be enabled. In order to enable the Remote Desktop feature it in Microsoft Windows 8, administrative credentials are required. Remote Desktop feature can be enabled for the network setup that has older versions of Windows (e.g. Microsoft Windows XP) running on some or all computers, or for the network setup that has only the computers running Microsoft Windows Vista and above operating systems in them.

How to Enable Remote Desktop?

In order to enable Remote Desktop in Microsoft Windows 8, steps given below must be followed:

1. Log on to Microsoft Windows 8 computer with administrator account.
2. From the **Start** screen, click **Desktop** tile.
3. On the desktop screen, click **File Explorer** icon from the taskbar.
4. On the opened **Libraries** window, right-click **Computer** from the left pane.
5. From the displayed context menu, click **Properties**.
6. On the opened **System** window, click **Remote settings** option from the left pane.
7. On the **System Properties** box, make sure that **Remote** tab is selected.
8. On the **Remote** tab, under **Remote Desktop** section, click to select **Allow remote connections to this computer** radio button.

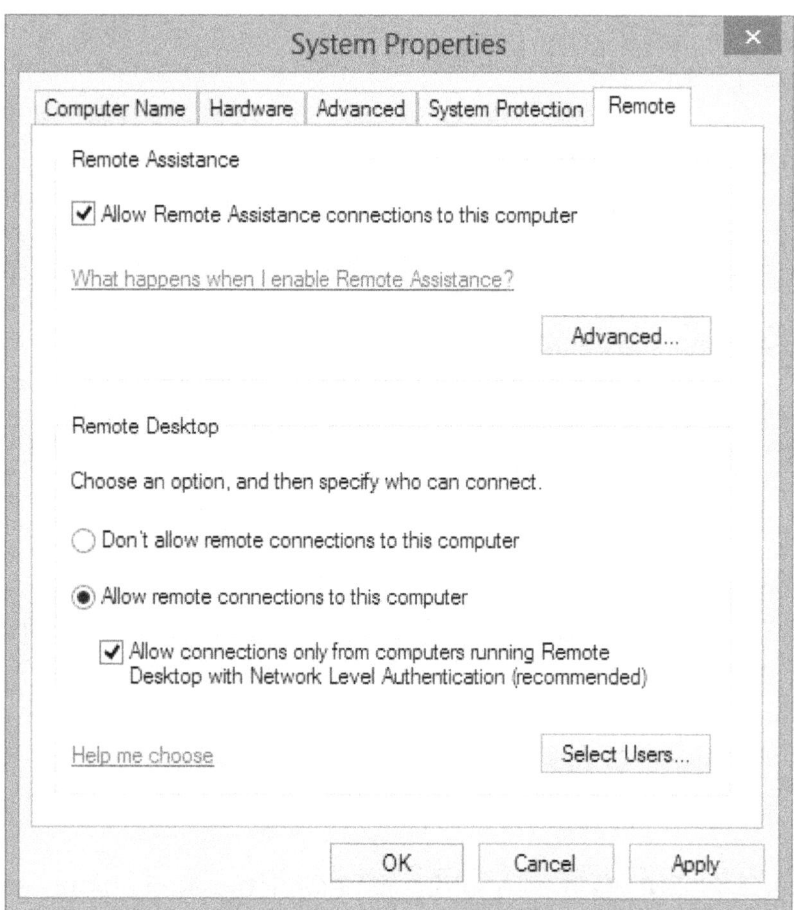

***Note**: In case the network setup consists of Windows Vista, Windows 7 or Windows 8 computers only, administrators can also check **Allow connections only from computers running Remote Desktop with Network Level Authentication (recommended)** checkbox to enhance the security. Also, in case the computer is configured to hibernate or go to sleep mode when it is not in use, Windows displays a warning box while enabling Remote Desktop feature. Administrators are recommended to take appropriate action according to the type of network setup and the utilization of Remote Desktop feature to avoid connection failure or abrupt and unwanted remote desktop session termination.*

9. Click **OK** to enable Remote Desktop feature.

To disable Remote Desktop feature, steps 1 to 9 can be followed, while selecting **Don't allow remote connections to this computer** radio button when on step 8.

Initialize and Use Remote Desktop Client

Introduction to Remote Desktop Client

As mentioned in previous lesson, in order to establish a remote desktop connection, Remote Desktop feature must be enabled on the remote computer. Moreover, appropriate firewall rule must be added to the Windows Firewall exception list (mostly done automatically in Microsoft Windows 8).

Once Remote Desktop feature is enabled, a built-in Remote Desktop Client program must be initiated to establish a remote desktop connection to the remote computer. Remote Desktop Client program should be initiated on the computer from where a remote desktop connection is to be established.

No elevated privileges are required on the local computer to initialize Remote Desktop Client and to establish a remote desktop connection to the remote computer. However, as mentioned in previous lesson, while establishing a remote desktop connection, users must provide administrative credentials of the remote computer to which remote desktop connection is to be established.

How to Initialize and Use Remote Desktop Client?

In order to initialize and use Remote Desktop Client program to establish remote desktop connection to a remote computer, steps given below must be followed:

1. Log on to Windows 8 computer from which a remote desktop connection is to be established to the remote computer.
2. From the **Start** screen, click **Desktop** tile.
3. On the desktop screen, press **Windows** + **R** keys simultaneously to initiate **Run** command box.
4. On the opened **Run** command box, type **MSTSC** command and press **Enter** key to initiate **Remote Desktop Connection** client program.
5. Once initiated, on the opened **Remote Desktop Connection** box, in the **Computer name** field type the name or the IP address of the remote computer to which remote desktop connection is to be made.
6. Click **Connect** button.
7. On the opened **Windows Security** box, provide the administrative credentials of the remote computer.

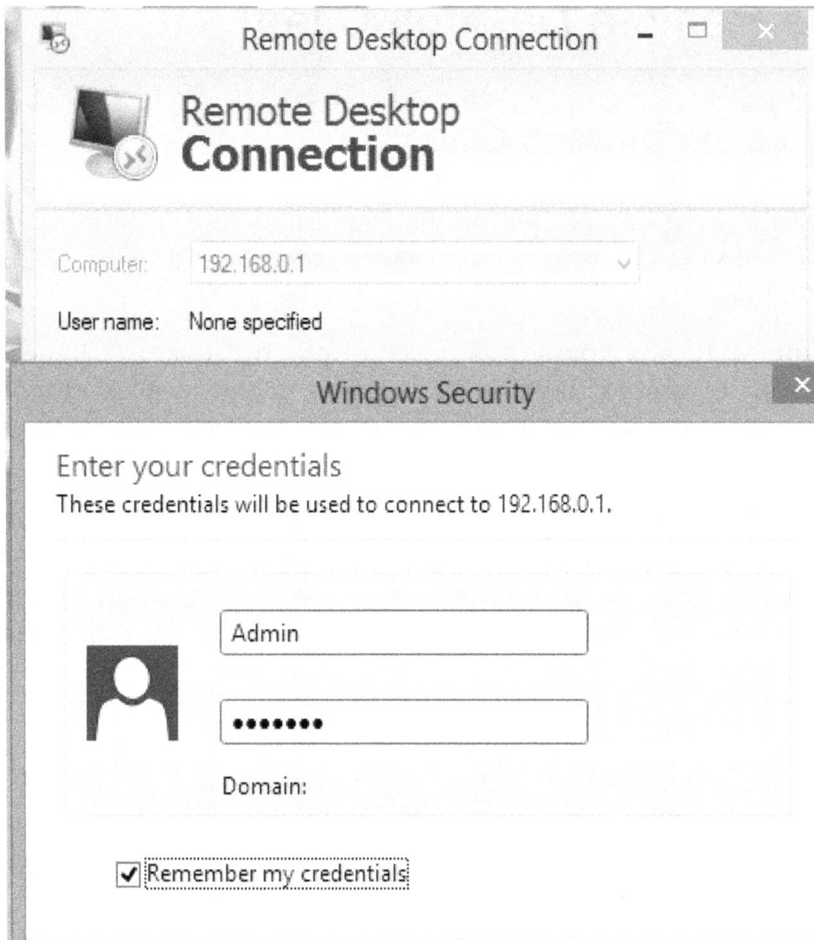

8. Optionally, **Remember my credentials** checkbox can be checked to allow Windows to store the provided credentials in order to eliminate the requirement of typing username and password every time a remote desktop connection is established.
9. Click **OK** to proceed.
10. On the displayed certificate error box, check **Don't ask me again for connections to this computer** checkbox and click **Yes** to establish a remote desktop connection to the remote computer.

Save a Remote Desktop Connection (.RDP) File

Introduction to Remote Desktop Connection (.RDP) File

A remote desktop connection (.RDP) file is a saved file that administrators mostly save in order to eliminate the requirement of providing computer name/IP address and the administrative credentials of the remote computer every time they establish a remote desktop connection.

A saved remote desktop connection file has .RDP extension, and once it is double-clicked, a remote desktop connection to the remote computer is automatically established. For example if administrators know that they would establish remote desktop connection to 'ABC' computer on a regular basis, they can save an .RDP file for the 'ABC' computer. Every time the saved .RDP file is double-clicked, a remote desktop connection to the 'ABC' computer is automatically established.

Note: Although Remote Desktop Client allows administrators to save the credentials of the remote computers, in production environments administrators are strongly recommended not to do so in order to maintain the security of the network and of the remote computer.

How to Save a Remote Desktop Connection (.RDP) File?

In order to save a remote desktop connection (.RDP) file in Microsoft Windows 8, steps given below must be followed:

1. Log on to Windows 8 computer on which an RDP file for remote desktop connection is to be saved.
2. From the **Start** screen, click **Desktop** tile.
3. On the desktop screen, press **Windows** + **R** keys simultaneously to initiate **Run** command box.
4. On the opened **Run** command box, type **MSTSC** command and press **Enter** key to initiate **Remote Desktop Connection** client program.
5. Once initiated, on the opened **Remote Desktop Connection** box, in the **Computer name** field type the name or the IP address of the remote computer to which remote desktop connection is to be made frequently.
6. Click **Show Options** button from the bottom of the box to view advanced features.

7. Under the **Connection settings** section on the **General** tab, click **Save As** button.
8. On the opened **Save As** box, navigate to locate the target location where the RDP file will be saved.

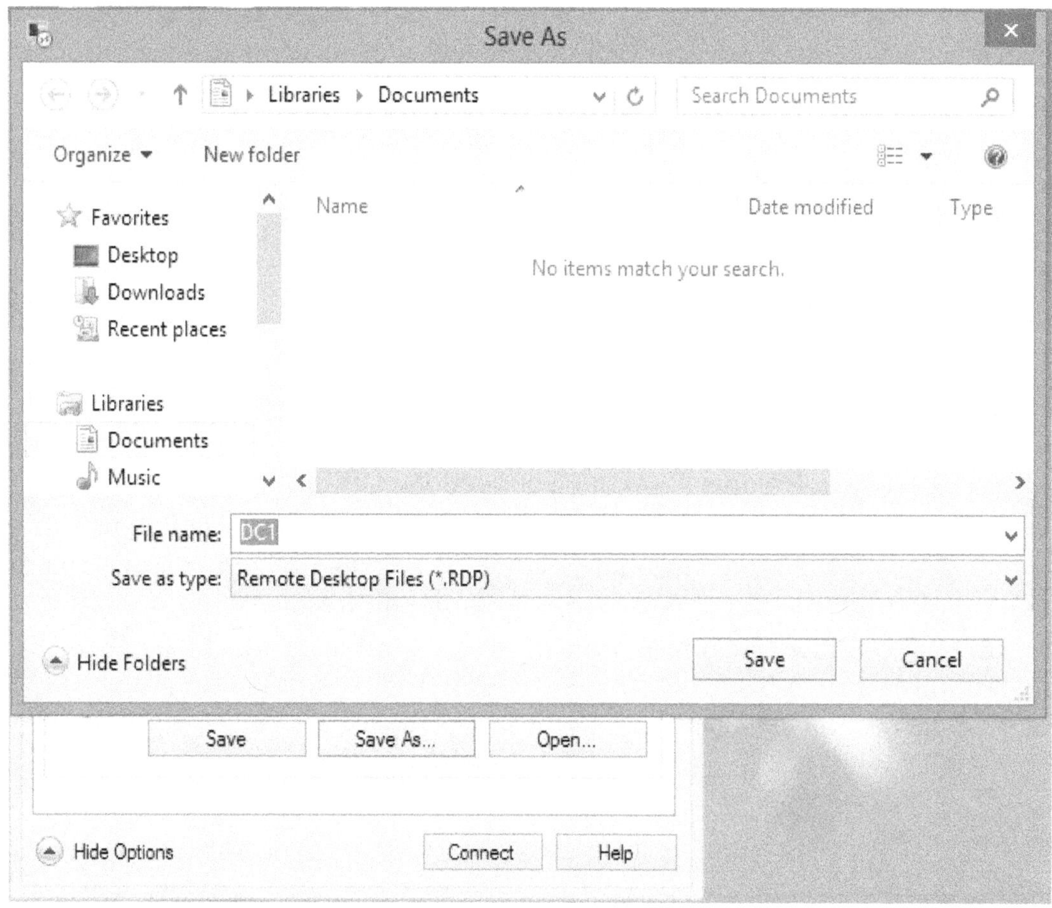

9. In the **File name** field, specify a name for the RDP file and click **Save** button.

Customize a Saved Remote Desktop Connection File

Introduction to Customizing Saved Remote Desktop Connection (.RDP) File

As mentioned in previous lesson, Microsoft Windows 8 allows its users to save a remote desktop connection (.RDP) file that can be used to establish a remote desktop connection to a remote computer automatically and quickly.

There might be times when users might want to modify the saved information in the RDP file. Modifications that users might want to make in the saved RDP file might include alterations in the IP address, changes in the saved credentials, etc. Remote Desktop Client allows users to make modifications in a saved RDP file, hence eliminating the requirement of creating a new RDP file with the modified settings right from the scratch.

How to Customize a Saved Remote Desktop Connection (.RDP) File?

In order to customize a saved remote desktop connection (.RDP) file in Microsoft Windows 8, steps given below must be followed:

1. Log on to Microsoft Windows 8 computer with administrator account.
2. From the **Start** screen, click **Desktop** tile.
3. On the desktop screen, click **File Explorer** icon from the taskbar.
4. On the opened **Libraries** window, navigate and locate the saved RDP file.
5. Once the RDP file is located, right-click the file and from the displayed context menu, click **Edit**.

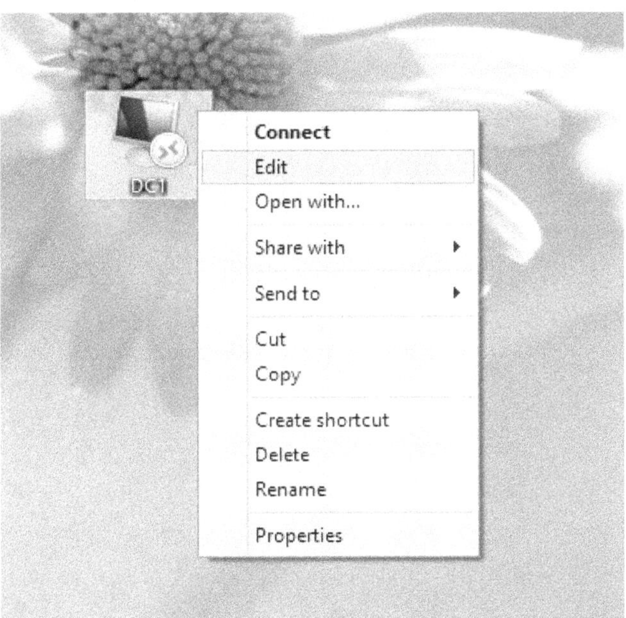

6. On the opened **Remote Desktop Connection** box, make appropriate modifications as desired.
7. Once done, under the **Connection settings** section on the **General** tab, click **Save** button to save the existing RDP file with the modified changes.

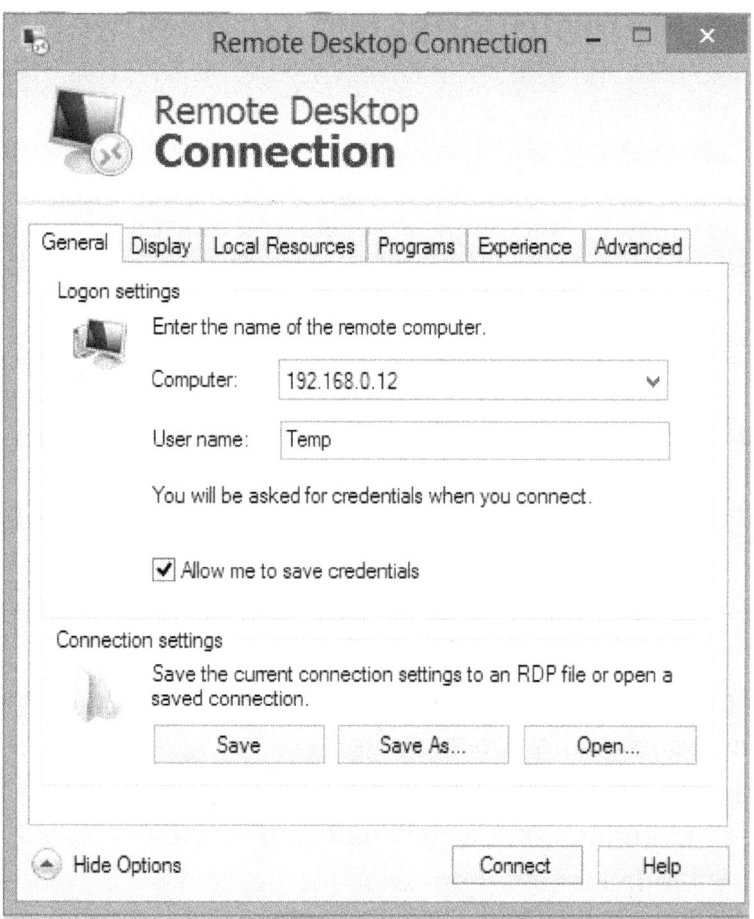
Remote Desktop Connection
Remote Desktop
Connection
General
Display
Local Resources
Programs
Experience
Advanced
Logon settings
Enter the name of the remote computer.
Computer:
192.168.0.12
User name:
Temp
You will be asked for credentials when you connect.
Allow me to save credentials
Connection settings
Save the current connection settings to an RDP file or open a saved connection.
Save
Save As...
Open...
Hide Options
Connect
Help

Improve Remote Desktop Connection Graphics

Introduction to Remote Desktop Connection Graphics

In Microsoft Windows 8, by default the Remote Desktop Client program is configured to detect the connection quality automatically and establish the remote desktop connection according to the detected quality. This default configuration is best in most cases as users can experience optimum performance when the quality is detected automatically. However, sometimes due to automatic quality detection, administrators may experience decreased graphics. An example of decreased graphics may be that when a remote desktop connection is established, desktop wallpaper of the remote computer is not displayed.

In such situations, while establishing remote desktop connection to a remote computer, administrators can modify the Remote Desktop Client settings and can manually specify connection quality in order to experience improved graphics when a remote desktop connection is successfully established.

Note: *When high connection speed is specified in the remote desktop client program and a remote desktop connection is established using the modified connection speed, almost all GUI oriented features of the remote computer are displayed on the console window that is displayed on the local computer screen. If the LAN connection does not have enough speed as manually specified in the remote desktop client program, remote desktop connection performance might decrease and users may experience reduced remote desktop performance.*

How to Improve Remote Desktop Connection Graphics?

In order to improve remote desktop connection graphics in Microsoft Windows 8, steps given below must be followed:

1. Log on to Microsoft Windows 8 computer with administrator account.
2. From the **Start** screen, click **Desktop** tile.
3. On the desktop screen, press **Windows** + **R** keys simultaneously to initiate **Run** command box.
4. In the opened **Run** command box, type **MSTSC** command and press **Enter** key.
5. On the opened **Remote Desktop Connection** client program, click **Show Options** button from the bottom of the box.
6. From the displayed advanced options, go to **Experience** tab.
7. On the **Experience** tab, under the **Performance** section, select **LAN (10 Mbps or higher)** option from the **Choose your connection speed to optimize performance** drop-down list.

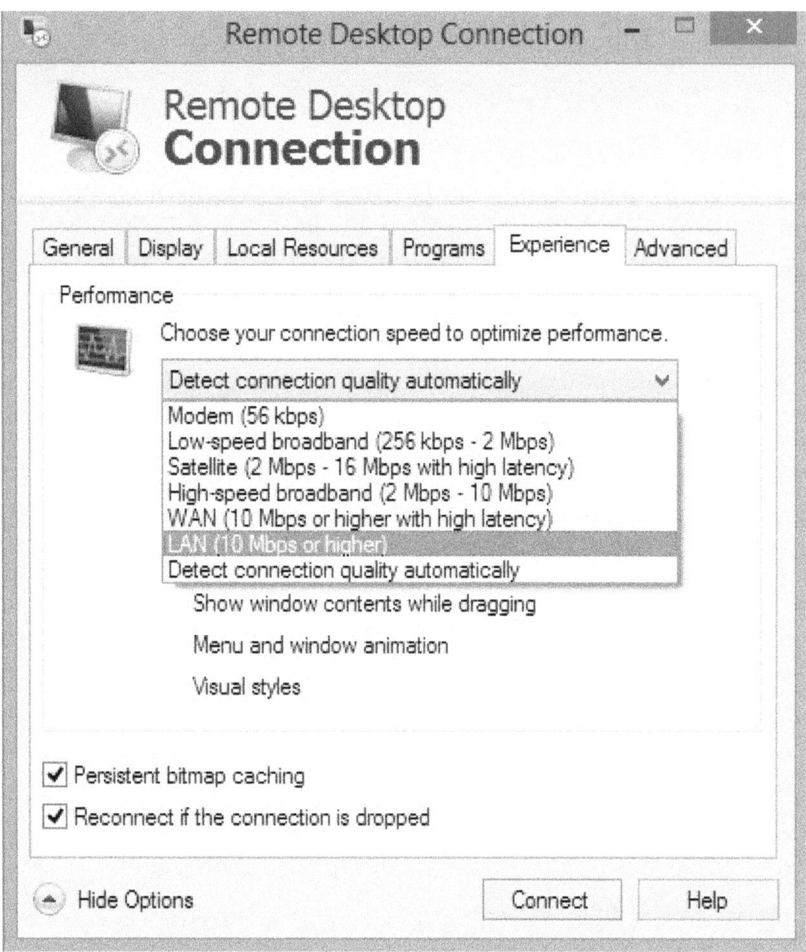

8. Click **Connect** button to establish remote desktop connection with the modified settings.

***Note**: Make sure to provide the name or IP address of the remote computer, to which remote desktop connection is to be established, before clicking **Connect** button.*

Manage Clipboard Mapping

Introduction to Clipboard Mapping

When a remote desktop connection is established, users work on the console of the remote computer exactly the way they would work if they were logged on to that computer locally. After a successful remote desktop connection is made and users copy any object on the remote computer, logically the object must be copied to clipboard of the remote computer only. However users can enable clipboard mapping so that every time an object on a remote computer is copied, it is saved in the clipboard of the local computer, i.e. from where the remote desktop connection has been established.

Enabling clipboard mapping while establishing a remote desktop connection allows users to copy and paste objects from the remote computer to local computer and vice versa. In other words, an object that is copied on the remote computer using remote desktop connection can be pasted on the local hard disk drive of the local computer, from where the remote desktop connection was initiated, and vice versa.

How to Enable Clipboard Mapping?

In order to enable clipboard mapping in Microsoft Windows 8, steps given below must be followed:

1. Log on to Microsoft Windows 8 computer with administrator account.
2. From the **Start** screen, click **Desktop** tile.
3. On the desktop screen, press **Windows** + **R** keys simultaneously to initiate **Run** command box.
4. In the opened **Run** command box, type **MSTSC** command and press **Enter** key.
5. On the opened **Remote Desktop Connection** client program, click **Show Options** button from the bottom of the box.
6. From the displayed advanced options, go to **Local Resources** tab.
7. On the **Local Resources** tab, under **Local drives and resources** section, check the **Clipboard** checkbox. (If it is already checked, leave all the settings as default).

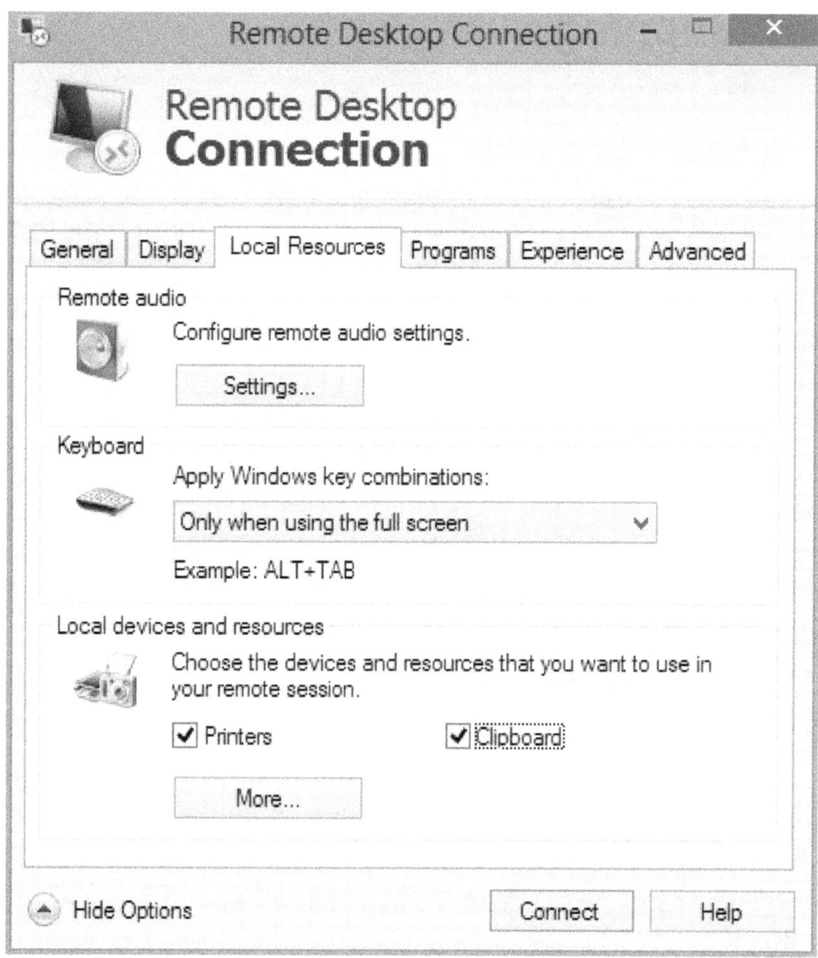

8. Once done, click **Connect** button to establish a remote desktop connection with the mapped clipboard.

***Note**: Make sure to provide the name or IP address of the remote computer, to which remote desktop connection is to be established, before clicking **Connect** button.*

Manage Local/Removable Drive Mapping

Introduction to Local/Removable Drive Mapping

Just like clipboard mapping that was discussed in previous lesson, local drive or a locally connected removable drive mapping can also be enabled before a remote desktop connection is established to a remote computer. Benefit of enabling drive mapping while establishing a remote desktop connection is that all the local drives that are mapped are displayed as mapped network drives on the remote computer.

Since the drives of a local computer are displayed as mapped network drives on the remote computer when a remote desktop connection is established, users can easily copy the objects on the remote computer and paste them in the drives of the local computer that are displayed on the remote computer as mapped network drives.

How to Manage Local/Removable Drive Mapping?

In order to manage local/removable drive mapping while establishing a remote desktop connection, steps given below must be followed:

1. Log on to Microsoft Windows 8 computer with administrator account.
2. From the **Start** screen, click **Desktop** tile.
3. On the desktop screen, press **Windows** + **R** keys simultaneously to initiate **Run** command box.
4. In the opened **Run** command box, type **MSTSC** command and press **Enter** key.
5. On the opened **Remote Desktop Connection** client program, click **Show Options** button from the bottom of the box.
6. From the displayed advanced options, go to **Local Resources** tab.
7. On the **Local Resources** tab, under **Local drives and resources** section, click **More** button.
8. On the opened box, expand **Drives** tree.
9. From the displayed drives list, check the checkboxes representing the drives that are to be mapped to the remote computer.
10. To map removable drives as well, check **Drives that I plug in later** checkbox from the **Drives** tree. Also, expand **Other supported Plug and Play (PnP) devices** tree and check **Devices that I plug in later** checkbox to map other removable drives to the remote computer as well.

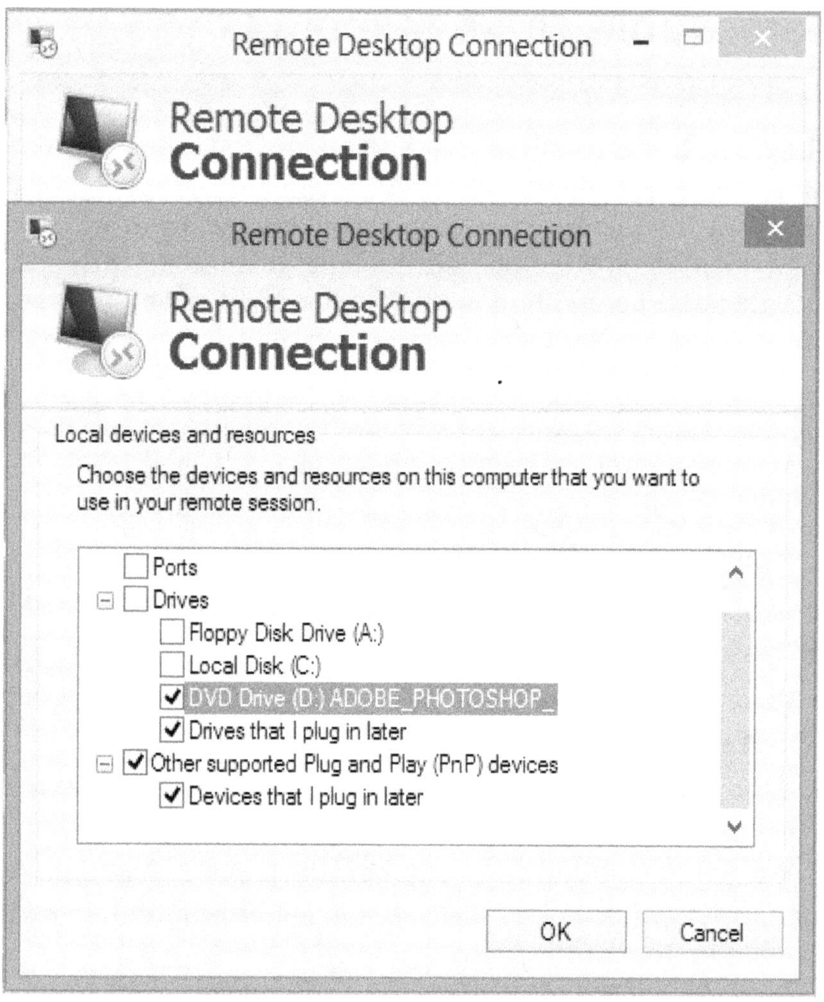

11. Click **OK** when done.
12. Back on **Remote Desktop Connection** box, click **Connect** button to establish remote desktop connection with mapped drives.

***Note**: Make sure to provide the name or IP address of the remote computer to which remote desktop connection is to be established, before clicking **Connect** button.*

Manage Audio

Introduction to Managing Audio

Before a remote desktop connection is established, users can configure audio settings of the remote computer in the Remote Desktop Client program. Using Remote Desktop Client, users can configure what happens to the sound output when an audio file is played on the remote computer during the remote desktop session. Users can also configure microphone settings to manage audio input during remote desktop connection. User can choose any one of the available options mentioned below:

Audio Playback Settings

- **Play on this computer** - When this option is selected, every time an audio file is played on the remote computer, its output can be heard on the local computer from where the remote desktop connection has been initiated.
- **Do not play** - When this option is selected, even if an audio file is played on the remote computer, no audio output is heard on either the local computer or on the remote computer.
- **Play on remote computer** - When this option is selected, an audio file that is played on the remote computer can be heard on that computer only.

Audio Recording Settings

- **Record from this computer** - When this option is selected, any voice input on the local computer is recorded on the remote computer.
- **Do not record** - When this option is selected, no voice input on local computer is recorded on the remote computer.

In most production environments 'Do not play' and 'Do not record' options are selected, whereas in home computers users can select any of the available options as required.

How to Manage Audio?

In order to manage audio before establishing remote desktop connection, steps given below must be followed:

1. Log on to Microsoft Windows 8 computer with administrator account.
2. From the **Start** screen, click **Desktop** tile.
3. On the desktop screen, press **Windows** + **R** keys simultaneously to initiate **Run** command box.
4. In the opened **Run** command box, type **MSTSC** command and press **Enter** key.
5. On the opened **Remote Desktop Connection** client program, click **Show Options** button from the bottom of the box.
6. From the displayed advanced options, go to **Local Resources** tab.
7. On the **Local Resources** tab, under **Remote auto section**, click **Settings** button.
8. On the opened box, click to select appropriate radio buttons as desired from **Remote audio playback** and **Remote audio recording** sections.

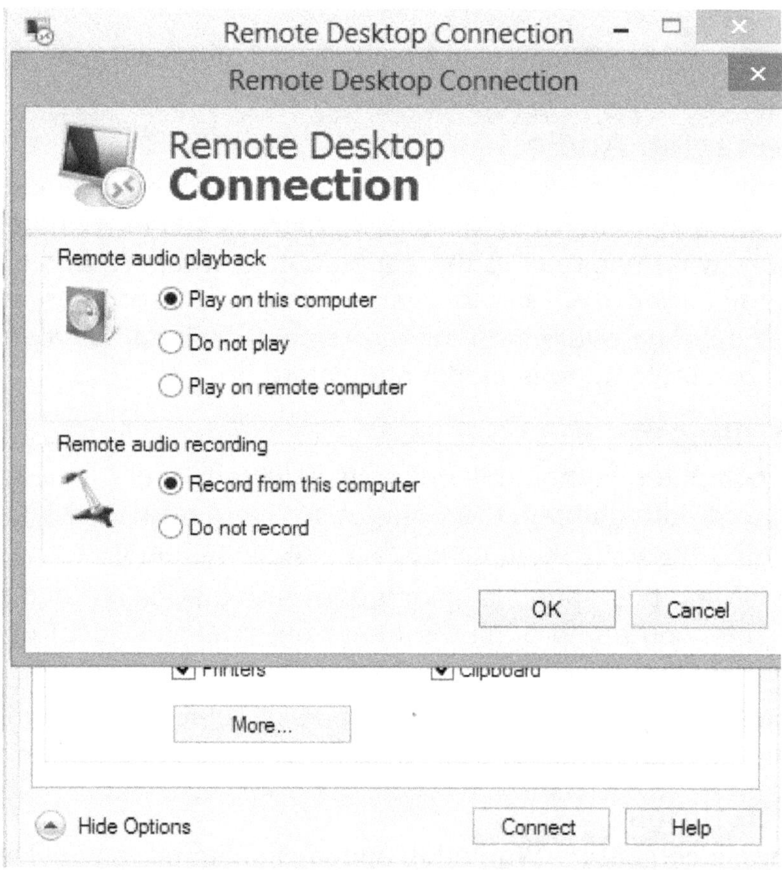

9. Click **OK** when done.
10. Back on **Remote Desktop Connection** box, click **Connect** button to establish remote desktop connection with configured audio settings.

***Note**: Make sure to provide the name or IP address of the remote computer, to which remote desktop connection is to be established, before clicking **Connect** button.*

Use Remote Assistance

Introduction to Remote Assistance

Remote Assistance is a feature in Microsoft Windows 8 that allows locally logged on users to invite any other experienced person to the computers if they are stuck with something, or are facing some troubles while using any application or a feature.

Just like Remote Desktop feature, Remote Assistance also uses Remote Desktop Protocol (RDP) and TCP 3389 port number. Difference between a remote desktop connection and remote assistance connection is that in remote assistance, a locally logged on user invites a remote user to establish a connection. Moreover, when a remote assistance connection is established, the console of a local computer is displayed on the remote computer, and the locally logged on user and the remote user both can see the same desktop screen simultaneously.

Another difference that a remote assistance connection has is that the user who is invited to establish a remote assistance connection is granted with the privileges of the locally logged on user who has invited the other user. For example if user 'A' who is a standard user on the local computer 'C1' has invited user 'B' to establish a remote assistance connection, user 'B' would receive standard user privileges on the 'C1' computer. Also user 'B' will be able to access only the resources to which user 'A' has been granted the permissions.

As far as security aspect is concerned, the user who has invited the other user for remote assistance can terminate the connection at any moment by pressing the 'Esc' key.

Ways to Establish a Remote Assistance Connection

Users can be invited to establish a remote assistance connection through:

- By using any Remote Assistance oriented instant messaging program (such as Windows Live Messenger)
- By creating and sending the invitation file through e-mail
- By creating and sending the invitation file through local area network
- By using Easy Connect

How to Invite for Remote Assistance?

In order to invite a user for remote assistance in Microsoft Windows 8, steps given below must be followed:

1. Log on to Microsoft Windows 8 computer with any account.
2. From the **Start** screen, click **Desktop** tile.
3. On the desktop screen, hover mouse to the bottom right corner of the window.
4. From the displayed options, click **Search**.
5. From the **Apps** screen, in the **Search** pane in the right, type **Remote Assistance** in the **Apps** field.

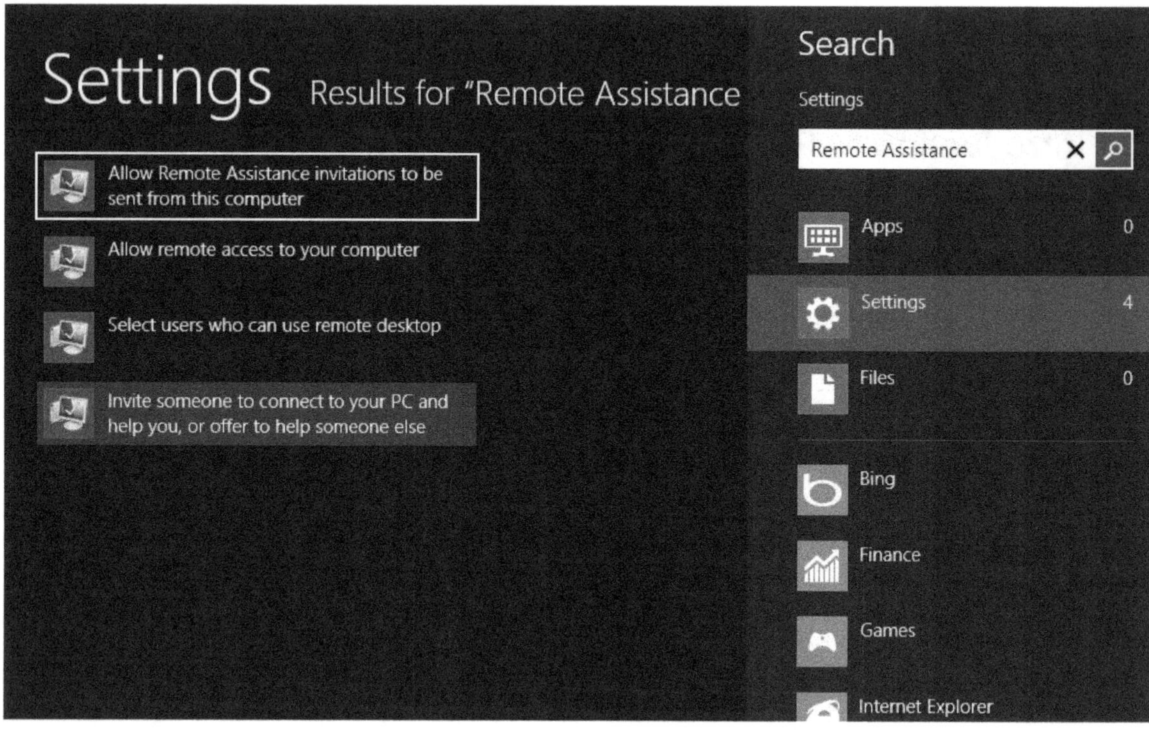

6. From the available search scope options, click to select **Settings**.
7. From the displayed **Settings** options in the left, click **Invite someone to connect to your PC and help you, or offer to help someone else** option.
8. On **Windows Remote Assistance** window, click **Invite someone you trust to help you** option.
9. On the next window, click **Save this invitation as a file** option.
10. On the **Save As** box, navigate for the destination location where the remote assistance invitation file is to be saved.
11. In the **File name** field, specify a name for the invitation file and click **Save**.
12. On the opened box, note down the displayed password.

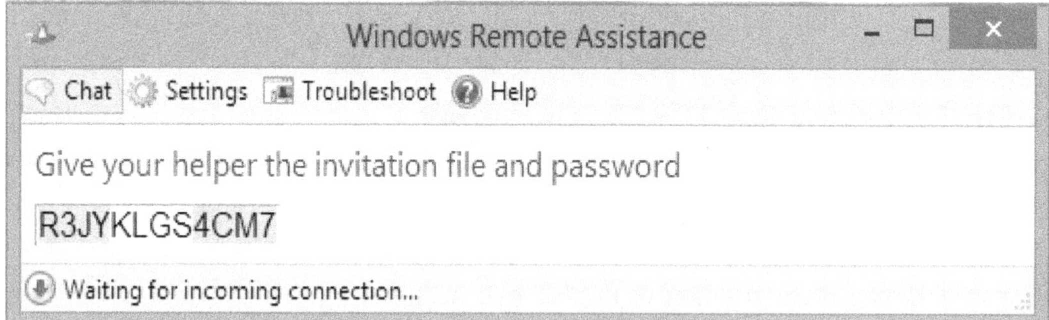

13. Finally send the previously created invitation file and the password to person who is to be invited to help.
14. The invited person must double-click the invitation file and provide the password when prompted, to establish a remote assistance connection.

CHAPTER 13:

BACKUP & RESTORE

Back Up Files and Folders

Introduction to Backing Up Files and Folders

Microsoft Windows 8 allows users to back up their files using new feature named File History. Backed up files and folders are stored in a system reserved space from where they can be restored when required. By default, 5% of system space is reserved for data backup. In fact, when files or folders are backed up in the system reserved space, the timestamp is used to calculate the version of the objects (files or folders). When users modify the files or folders and change their contents, since the timestamp is updated accordingly, version of the object that was previously saved in the system reserved space is considered as its previous version. In order to restore the object, users can go to the 'Previous Version' tab in the object's properties box and can restore the previously backup the version from the available previous versions list.

In Windows 8, by default File History feature is turned off and the interface displays that no usable drives are present on the computer even if the hard disk drive is present. When an external drive is connected to the computer, or a shared folder on a network location is added to the list, it is displayed as a usable drive and then administrators must manually turn on File History feature. When File History feature is turned on for the first time, it starts saving the files in the added location or drive. File History feature allows users to schedule the backup process that automatically saves the files in the system reserved space as per the specified time intervals.

How to Backup Files/Folders?

In order to backup files or folders in Microsoft Windows 8, steps given below must be followed:

1. Log on to Microsoft Windows 8 computer with administrator account.
2. From the **Start** screen, click **Desktop** tile.
3. On the desktop screen, hover mouse to the bottom right corner of the window.
4. From the displayed options, click **Settings**.
5. From the **Settings** pane in the right, click **Control Panel**.
6. On the **Control Panel** window, click **System and Security**.
7. From the **System and Security** window, click **File History**.
8. On the **File History** window, click **Select drive** option from the left pane.
9. On the **Select Drive** window, click **Add network location** button to store the backup copy of the data on any network location. Alternatively, an external storage media such, as a USB drive can also be connected to use it as the storage location of the backed up files.
10. On the **Select Folder** window, navigate and locate the shared folder residing on any remote computer.
11. Once located, click **Select Folder** button.

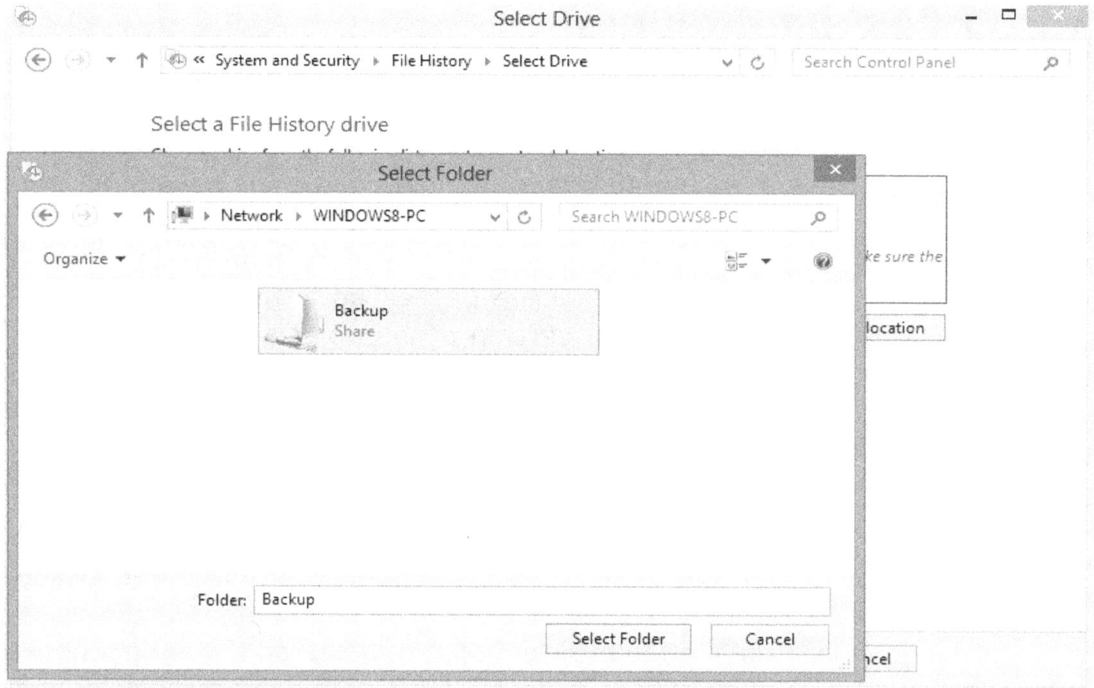

12. Back on **Select Drive** window, click **OK**.
13. Back on **File History** window, click **Turn on** button to enable **File History** feature and initiate the data backup process.

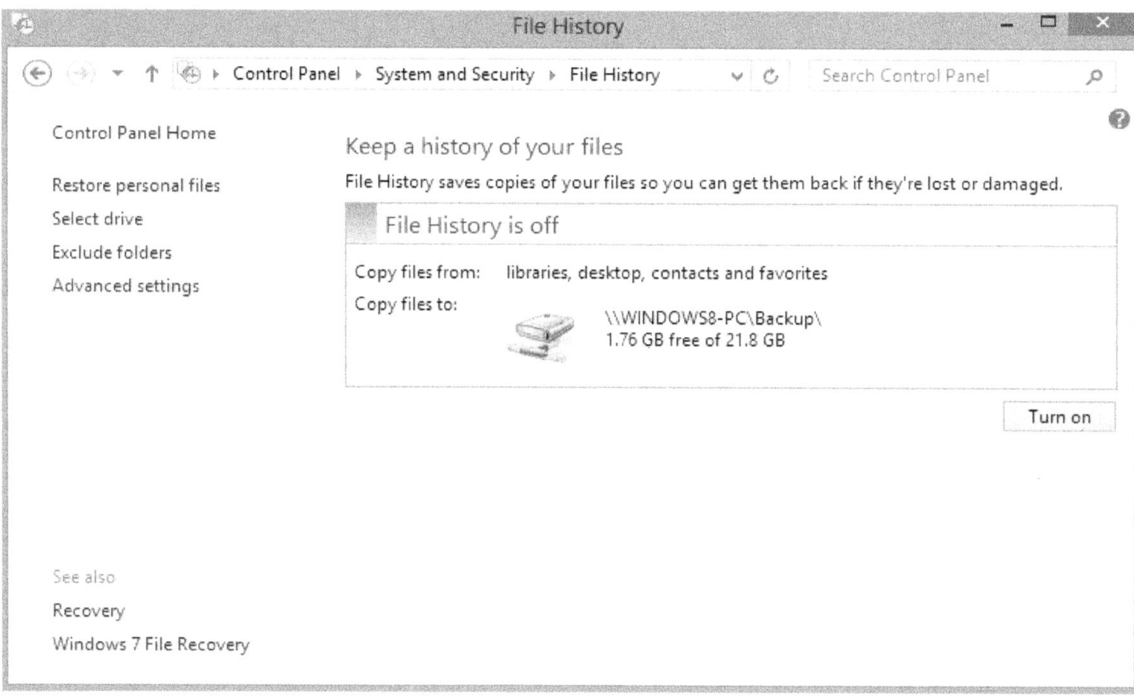

Create Restore Points

Introduction to Restore Points

Restore points are the snapshots of the states of the operating system to which Windows can be rolled back in case it fails to function as expected. Although restore points are automatically created at specific time intervals, administrators can modify the automatic restore point creation schedule, in Microsoft Windows 8. Moreover, administrators can also create restore points manually.

In Windows 8, by default creation of restore points is enabled for the system drive and the feature must be enabled manually for all other volumes that the hard disk drive may have. When Windows 8 computer is restored to a restore point, only the settings of the computer are rolled back and any users' personal data remains intact.

All restore points are saved in system reserved space which is by default set to 3% of the total size of volume. This means that every time a restore point is created, it is saved in the system and the amount of space it consumes is deducted from the system reserved space. For example the total system reserved space is 500 MB and a system restore point is 200 MB in size and is saved in the system reserved space, the system reserved space will then have 300 MB of free space. When the entire 500 MB of system reserved space is consumed, and a new restore point is created, the very first restore point is automatically removed from the computer to make room for the newly created restore point.

How to Create a Restore Point Manually?

In order to create a restore point manually in Microsoft Windows 8 computer, steps given below must be followed:

1. Log on to Microsoft Windows 8 computer with administrator account.
2. From the **Start** screen, click **Desktop** tile.
3. On the desktop screen, click **File Explorer** icon from the taskbar.
4. On the **Libraries** window, right-click **Computer** from the left pane.
5. From the displayed context menu, click **Properties**.
6. On the opened **System** window, click **System protection** option from the left pane.
7. On the **System Properties** box, make sure that **System Protection** tab is selected.
8. On the **System Protection** tab, from the displayed list of available drives under **Protection Settings** section, click to select the drive for which a restore point is to be created.
9. Once selected, from the bottom of the **System Protection** tab, click **Create** button.
10. On the opened **Create a restore point** box, type a name for the new restore point in the available field.

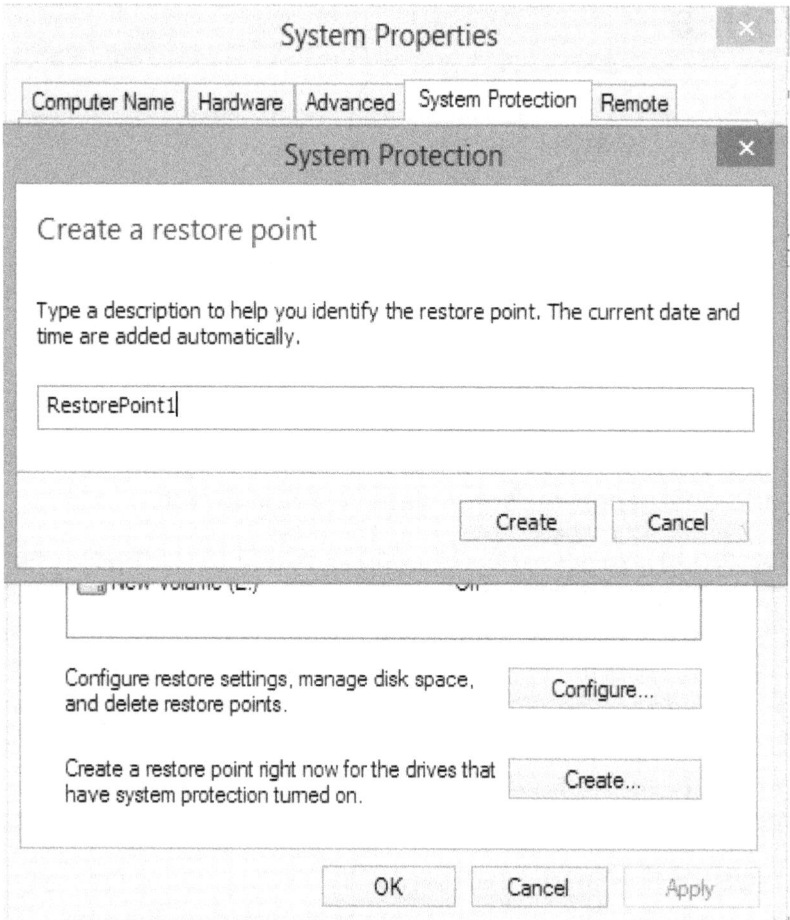

11. Click **Create** button to create a new restore point with the specified name.
12. Close all the opened windows and boxes when done.

Restore Computer to a Restore Point

Introduction to Restoring a Computer to a Restore Point

Once a restore point is created in Microsoft Windows 8 computer, the computer can be restored to it in order to get the system settings back to the state at which the restore point was created. Since multiple restore points can be created on a Windows 8 computer, while restoring the computer, administrators must select the desired restore point from the displayed restore points list. It is recommended that the computer should be restored using the most recent restore point to get the latest settings back in use. Situations when administrators may want to restore a computer to a previously created restore point may include, corrupt device drivers, crashed Windows registry, in appropriate computer settings, etc.

When a system is restored to restore point, only the system settings, device drivers, Windows registry and other computer configurations are rolled back to the previous state. Users' personal data remains unaffected and intact during the system restoration process whatsoever.

How to Restore a Computer to a Restore Point?

In order to restore a Microsoft Windows 8 computer to a previously created restore point, steps given below must be followed:

1. Log on to Microsoft Windows 8 computer with administrator account.
2. From the **Start** screen, click **Desktop** tile.
3. On the desktop screen, click **File Explorer** icon from the taskbar.
4. On the **Libraries** window, right-click **Computer** from the left pane.
5. From the displayed context menu, click **Properties**.
6. On the opened **System** window, click **System protection** option from the left pane.
7. On the **System Properties** box, make sure that **System Protection** tab is selected.
8. On the **System Protection** tab, under the **System Restore** section, click **System Restore** button.
9. On the opened window, click **Next** button.
10. On the next window, from the displayed restore points, click to select the one to which the system is to be restored.

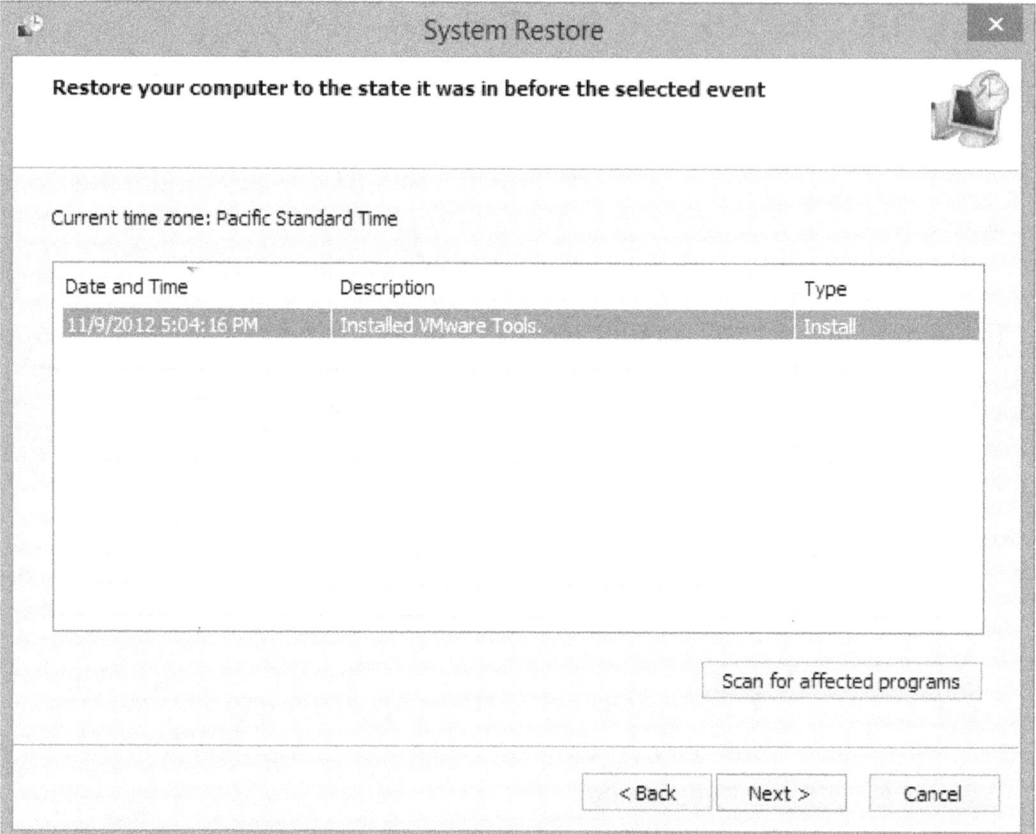

11. Once selected, click **Next** button to continue.
12. On **Confirm your restore point** window, review the settings and the restore point using which the computer will be restored.
13. Click **Finish**, and on the displayed confirmation box, click **Yes** to restore the computer to restore point.

Delete Restore Points

Introduction to Deleting Restore Points

As mentioned in previous lesson, when a restore point is created, it consumes some space in the system reserved area. When multiple restore points are created, the entire system reserved space gets completely consumed. When another restore point is created after the full consumption of the system reserved space, the very first restore point is automatically deleted to make room for the new system restore point.

Apart from automatic deletion of the system restore points, sometimes administrators might want to manually delete them for security reasons or to free some space in a system reserved area.

How to Delete Restore Points?

In order to delete restore points in Microsoft Windows 8, steps given below must be followed:

1. Log on to Microsoft Windows 8 computer with administrator account.
2. From the **Start** screen, click **Desktop** tile.
3. On the desktop screen, click **File Explorer** icon from the taskbar.
4. On the **Libraries** window, right-click **Computer** from the left pane.
5. From the displayed context menu, click **Properties**.
6. On the opened **System** window, click **System protection** option from the left pane.
7. On the **System Properties** box, make sure that **System Protection** tab is selected.
8. On the **System Protection** tab, from the displayed list of available drives under **Protection Settings** section, click to select the drive whose restore points are to be deleted.
9. Once selected, click **Configure** button.
10. From the displayed box, click **Delete** opposite to **Delete all restore points for this drive** label.
11. On the displayed warning box, click **Continue** to delete all restore points for the selected drive.

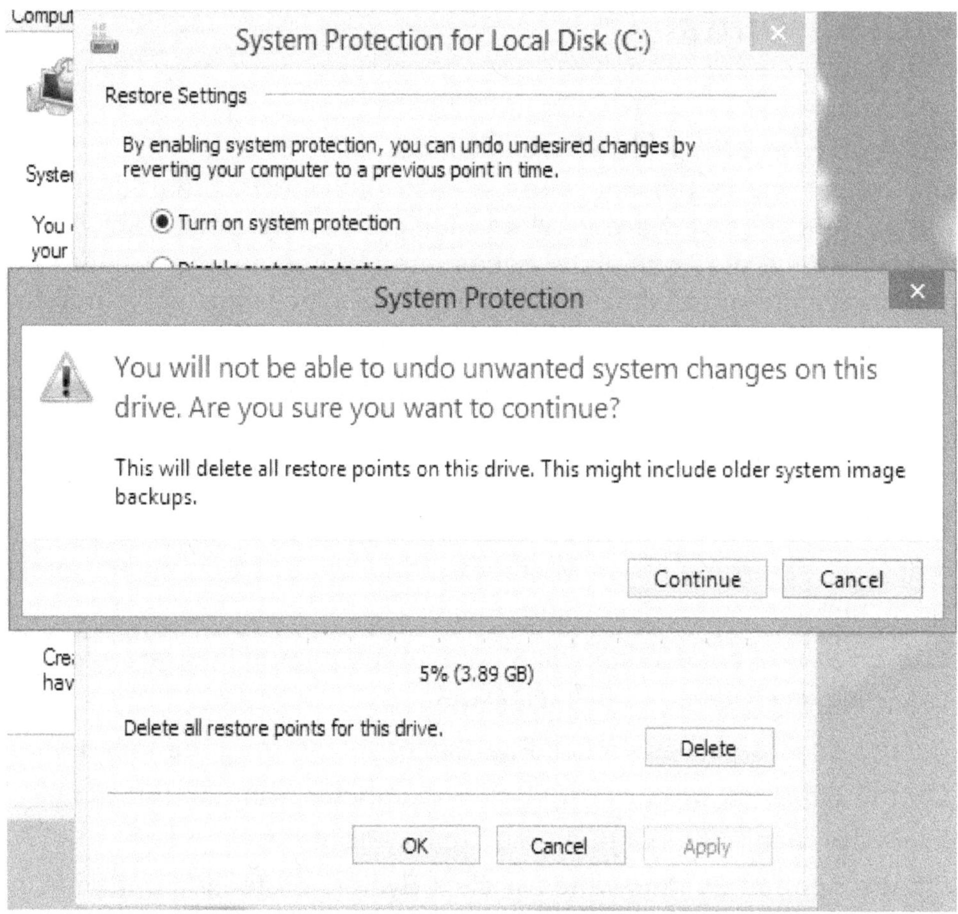

12. Back on the previous box, click **OK** and back on the **System Properties** box, click **OK** again.

Disable System Restore Point Creation

Introduction to Disabling System Restore Point Creation

As mentioned in previous lesson, when a restore point is created, it consumes some space in the system reserved area. Also, if administrators want they can enable and schedule automatic restore point creation to reduce administrative overheads.

In production environments automatic system restore point creation is quite helpful as the computers in organizations likely contain sensitive information. On the other hand, since home computers are not expected to have important data in them, automatic and scheduled restore point creation can be disabled to gain some extra space in the hard disk drives and reduce the consumption of resources that Windows otherwise consumes when automatic restore point creation is enabled.

Disabling restore point creation is an administrative task and elevated privileges are required to complete the process successfully.

How to Disable Restore Point Creation?

In order to disable restore point creation in Microsoft Windows 8, steps given below must be followed:

1. Log on to Microsoft Windows 8 computer with administrator account.
2. From the **Start** screen, click **Desktop** tile.
3. On the desktop screen, click **File Explorer** icon from the taskbar.
4. On the **Libraries** window, right-click **Computer** from the left pane.
5. From the displayed context menu, click **Properties**.
6. On the opened **System** window, click **System protection** option from the left pane.
7. On the **System Properties** box, make sure that **System Protection** tab is selected.
8. On the **System Protection** tab, from the displayed list of available drives under **Protection Settings** section, click to select the drive on which restore point creation is to be disabled.
9. Once selected, click **Configure** button.
10. From the displayed box, under **Restore Settings** section, click to select **Disable system protection** radio button.

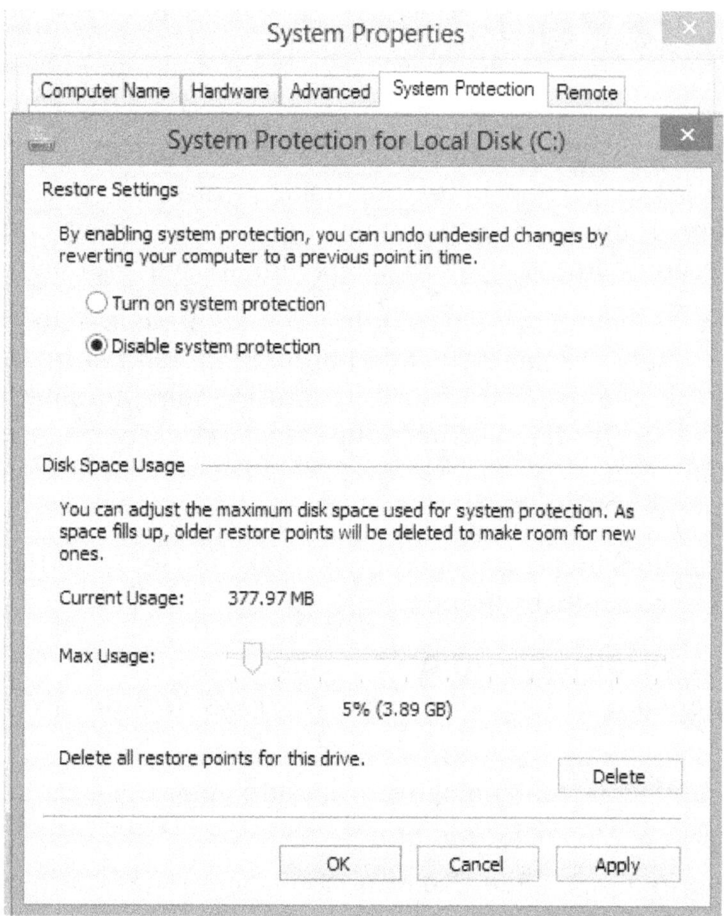

11. Once done, click **OK** and on the displayed warning box, click **Yes** to confirm the changes.
12. Back on **System Properties** box, click **OK** again.

To re-enable restore point creation, steps 1 to 12 can be followed, while selecting **Turn on system protection** radio button when on step 10.

Create a System Image

Introduction to System Image

A system image is a snapshot of entire operating system that can be created either using any third-party application or by the help of a built-in feature in Microsoft Windows 8. When a system image is created, the entire image is saved in a file. The system image file can be saved at a different network location, and external hard disk drive, or in any other volume of the local hard disk drive.

Since a system image contains all files and folders and the entire operating system files, it is quite large in size (depending on the applications and data stored in the operating system) as compared to the snapshots captured while creating restore points.

In order to restore a Windows 8 computer from the system image, the computer must be externally started using the Windows 8 bootable media. Once the system is started using bootable media, the system image file can then be located and opened in order to restore the system back to the state when the system image was created.

In most home and production environments, administrators install a fresh copy of Windows 8 operating system, install all the required applications and programs, and then capture the system image of the entire system drive. Since the computer is not expected to have corrupt files or virus programs right after the fresh copy of an operating system is installed on it, the system image that administrators create also remains error and virus free.

When Windows 8 fails to start or gets infected by viruses, administrators can restore the operating system from the system image that they have previously created. When this is done, the error free image of the operating system is restored, hence making the computer as fresh as it was when the fresh copy of the operating system was installed on it.

How to Create a System Image?

In order to create a system image of Microsoft Windows 8 computer, steps given below must be followed:

1. Log on to Microsoft Windows 8 computer with administrator account.
2. From the **Start** screen, click **Desktop** tile.
3. On the desktop screen, hover mouse to the bottom right corner of the window.
4. From the displayed options, click **Settings**.
5. From the **Settings** pane in the right, click **Control Panel**.
6. On the **Control Panel** window, click **System and Security**.
7. From the **System and Security** window, click **File History**.
8. On the **File History** window, click **Windows 7 File Recovery** option from the bottom of the left pane.
9. On **Windows 7 File Recovery** window, click **Create a system image** option from the left pane.
10. On **Create a system image** window, click to select the radio button representing the destination location where the system image is to be saved. (Existing volume in the local hard disk drive for this demonstration.)

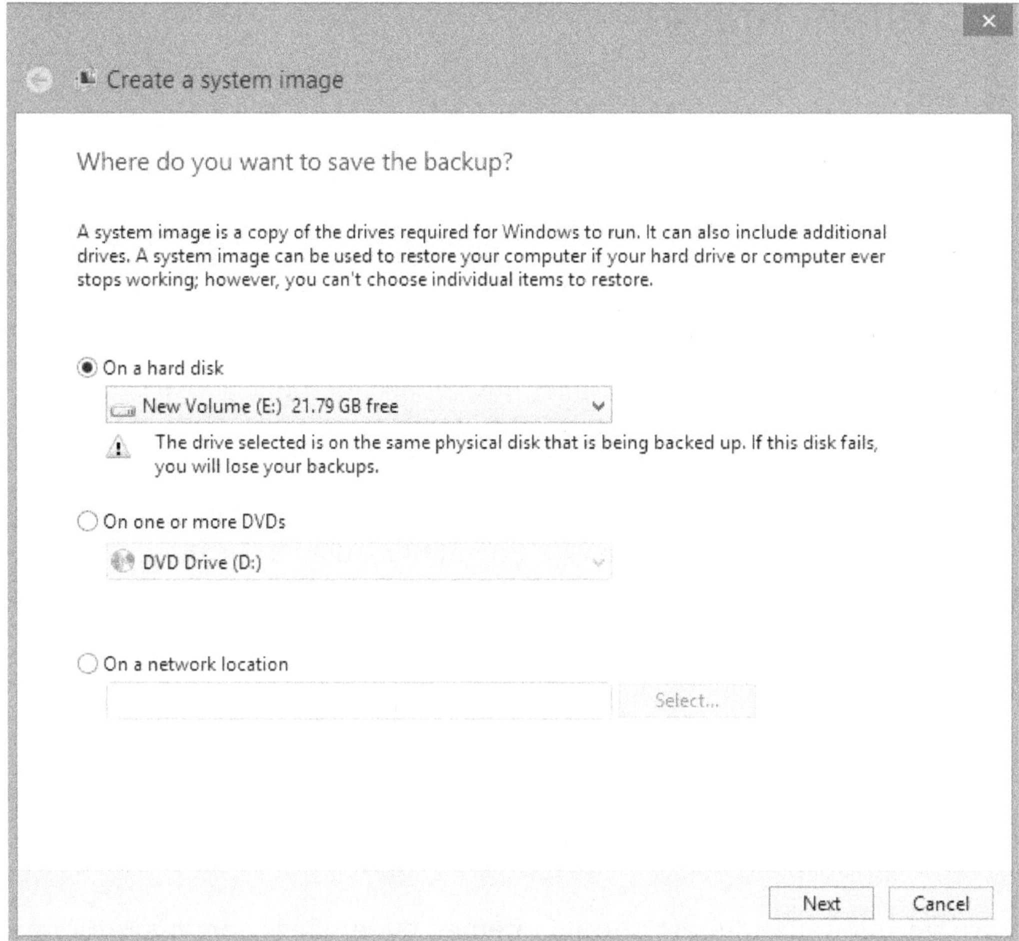

11. Click **Next** when done.
12. On **Confirm your backup settings** page, click **Start backup** button to initiate the backup process.
13. Once the system backup image is created, on the displayed **Create a system repair disc** box, click **No** to skip system repair disc creation process. Alternatively, **Yes** button can also be clicked in case administrators want to create a system repair disc.
14. Back on **Create a system image** box click **Close** button.

Restore a System Image

Introduction to Restoring a System Image

As mentioned in previous lesson, when a system image is created, it can be used to roll back the system to the state when the image was created. This ensures that the operating system gets free from errors and allows users to work flawlessly and smoothly.

In order to restore a system image, the computer must be restarted using the Windows 8 bootable media. Once restarted using bootable media, the image can then be located and the system can be restored from that image file.

How to Restore a Computer from a System Image?

In order to restore a Windows 8 computer from a system image, steps given below must be followed:

1. Start the computer with bootable Windows 8 installation DVD.
2. On the displayed box, click **Next**.
3. On the next box, click **Repair your computer** option from the bottom left corner.

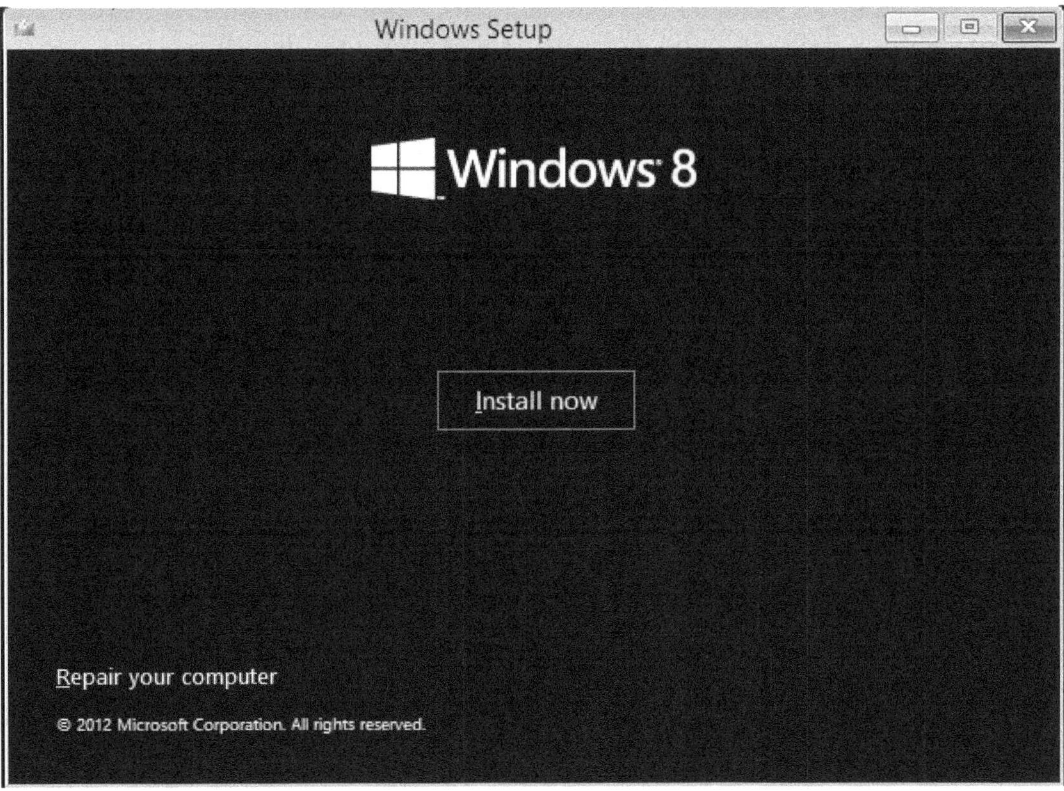

4. On the **Choose an option** window, click **Troubleshoot** option.

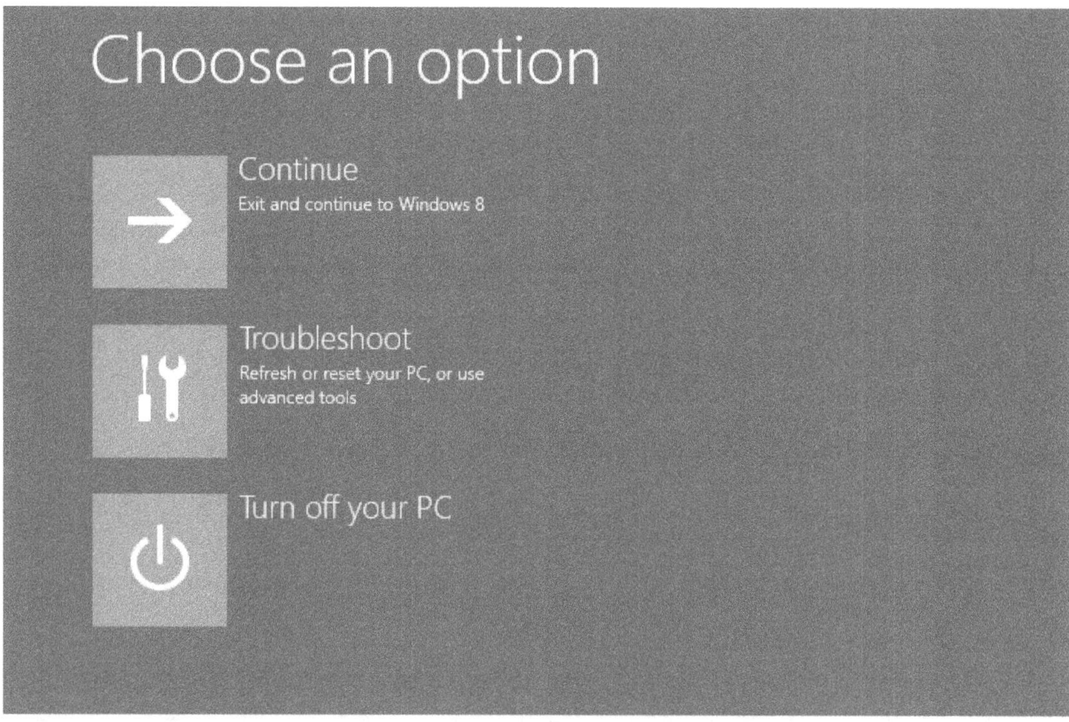

5. On the **Troubleshoot** window, click **Advanced options**.

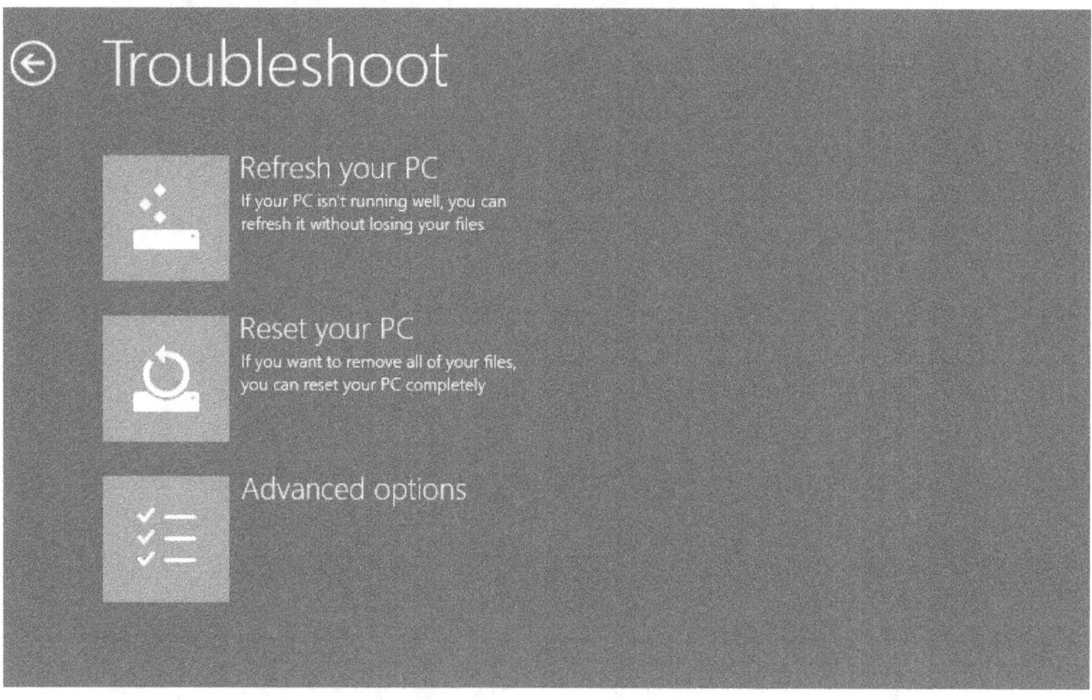

6. On the **Advanced options** window, click **System Image Recovery** option.

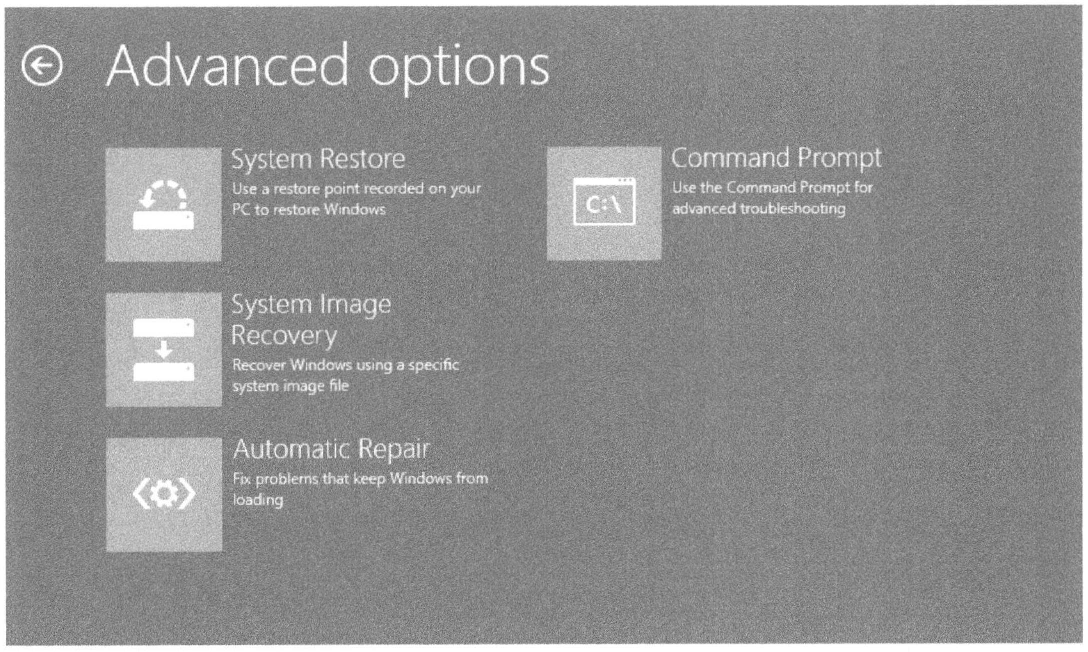

7. On the **System Image Recovery** window, click **Windows 8** from the **Choose a target operating system** list.

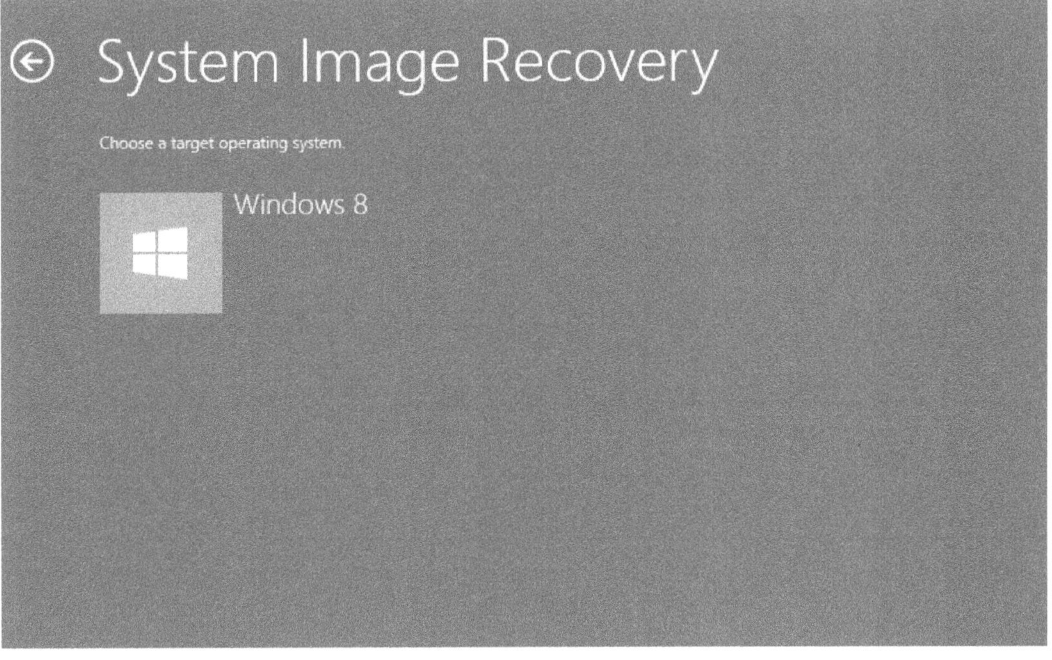

8. Once Windows scans and detects the most recent system backup image, click **Next** on the **Re-image your computer** box.

   Note: *In most cases, Windows automatically detects a previously created system backup image for recovery, and displays its details in the* ***Re-image your computer*** *box. In case administrators want to restore the computer from a different system backup image, they can select,* ***Select a system image*** *radio button and follow on-screen instructions thereafter.*

9. On the **Choose additional restore options** box, leave everything as default and click **Next**.

10. On the next box, view the displayed details and click **Finish**.
11. On the displayed confirmation box, click **Yes** to restore the computer from the selected system backup image.

Create a System Repair Disc

Introduction to System Repair Disc

A system repair disc is a CD or DVD that administrators can create using Windows 8 built-in tool. System repair disc contains the operating system's important files that are required to boot the computer initially. System repair disc is used when the computer crashes or fails to boot. During the system failure, administrators must insert the system repair disc and boot the computer with it. BIOS of the computer must be configured to boot from the CD/DVD drive before using the system repair disc.

When a computer is booted with system repair disc, it allows administrators to restore the computer to an earlier restore point, restore Windows 8 using system image, etc. Administrators can choose any of the available options according to the situation they are in.

Creating a system repair disc requires administrative credentials and only administrators of Windows 8 computer can do so.

How to Create a System Repair Disc?

In order to create a system repair disc, steps given below must be followed:

1. Log on to Microsoft Windows 8 computer with administrator account.
2. From the **Start** screen, click **Desktop** tile.
3. On the desktop screen, hover mouse to the bottom right corner of the window.
4. From the displayed options, click **Settings**.
5. On the **Settings** pane, click **Control Panel**.
6. From the **Control Panel** window, click **System and Security** category.
7. From the **System and Security** window, click **File History**.
8. On the **File History** window, click **Windows 7 File Recovery** option from the left pane.
9. On the **Windows 7 File Recovery** window, click **Create a system repair disc** from the left pane.
10. On the **Create a system repair disc** box, choose the appropriate disc burner from the **Drive** drop-down list.
11. Ensure that a blank disc (CD or DVD) is inserted in the appropriate drive.
12. Click **Create disc** button to create system repair disc.

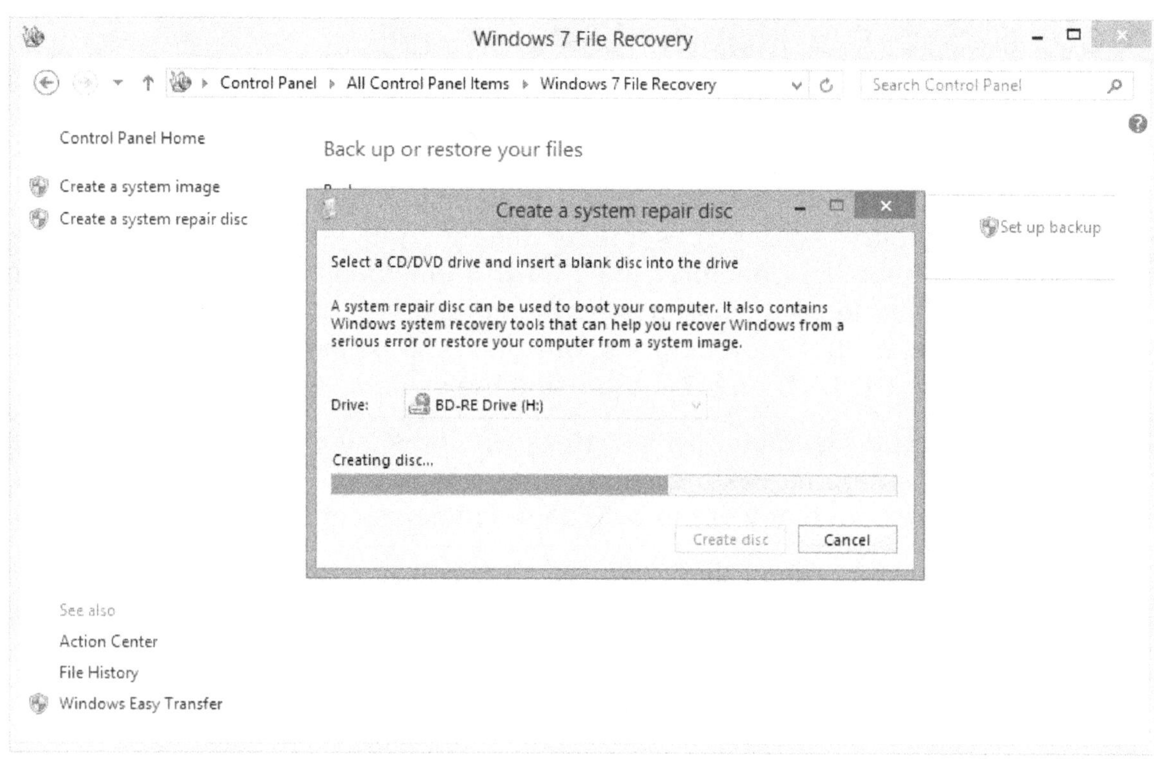
Windows 7 File Recovery
Control Panel > All Control Panel Items > Windows 7 File Recovery
Search Control Panel
Control Panel Home
Create a system image
Create a system repair disc
Back up or restore your files
Set up backup
Create a system repair disc
Select a CD/DVD drive and insert a blank disc into the drive
A system repair disc can be used to boot your computer. It also contains Windows system recovery tools that can help you recover Windows from a serious error or restore your computer from a system image.
Drive:
BD-RE Drive (H:)
Creating disc...
Create disc
Cancel
See also
Action Center
File History
Windows Easy Transfer

Create a System Recovery Drive

Introduction to System Recovery Drive

A system recovery Drive is a new feature in Microsoft Windows 8 that allows administrators to recover Windows 8 computer if it fails to boot or crashes. Unlike system repair disc, that allows administrators to repair a computer using various repair tools, system recovery drive can be used to recover the entire operating system. A system recovery drive is a USB flash drive. Administrators can choose either to refresh or reset the computer.

System recovery drive's creation process allows administrators to copy information from the recovery partition that the computer system may have. Doing so allows the administrators to refresh or reset the computer during complete system failure.

In order to recover a system using system recovery drive, the computer must be configured to boot from a USB media. This configuration can be done by accessing the BIOS of the computer.

Like creating a system repair disc, creating a system recovery drive also requires elevated privileges and only administrators of Windows 8 computer can do so.

How to Create a System Recovery Drive?

In order to create a system recovery drive, steps given below must be followed:

1. Log on to Microsoft Windows 8 computer with administrator account.
2. From the **Start** screen, click **Desktop** tile.
3. From the desktop screen, over mouse to the bottom right corner of the window.
4. From the displayed options, click **Settings**.
5. From the **Settings** pane, click **Control Panel**.
6. On the **Control Panel** window, click **System and Security** category.
7. From the **System and Security** window, click **File History**.
8. On the **File History** window, click **Recovery** option from the left pane.
9. From the **Recovery** window, click **Create recovery drive**.
10. On the displayed **User Account Control** confirmation box, click **Yes** button to grant the consent to open the wizard using elevated privileges.
11. On the **Recovery Drive** window, click **Next**. Alternatively, **Copy the recovery partition from the PC to the recovery drive** checkbox can also be checked to copy the contents of recovery partition to the recovery drive before clicking **Next** button.
12. On the **Select the USB drive** window, click to select the drive that is to be used as system recovery drive.

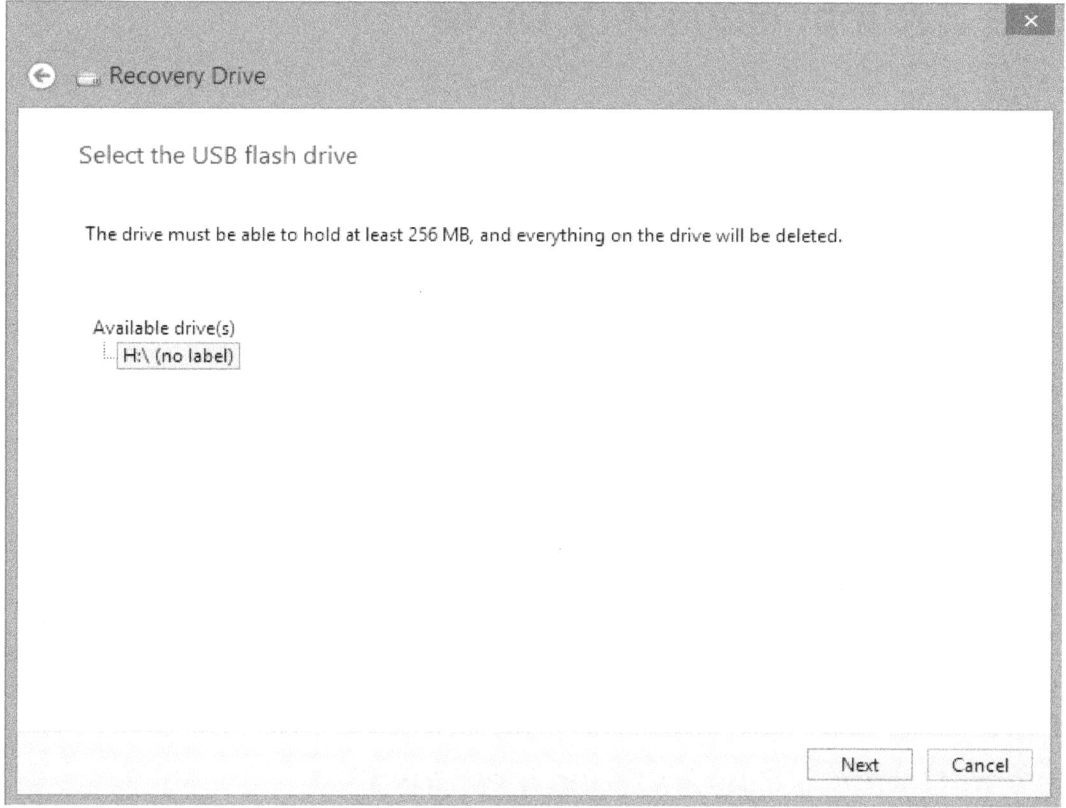

13. Click **Next**.
14. On **Create the recovery drive** window, click **Create** button to create a system recovery drive.
15. On **Creating the recovery drive** window, wait till the recovery drive gets prepared.

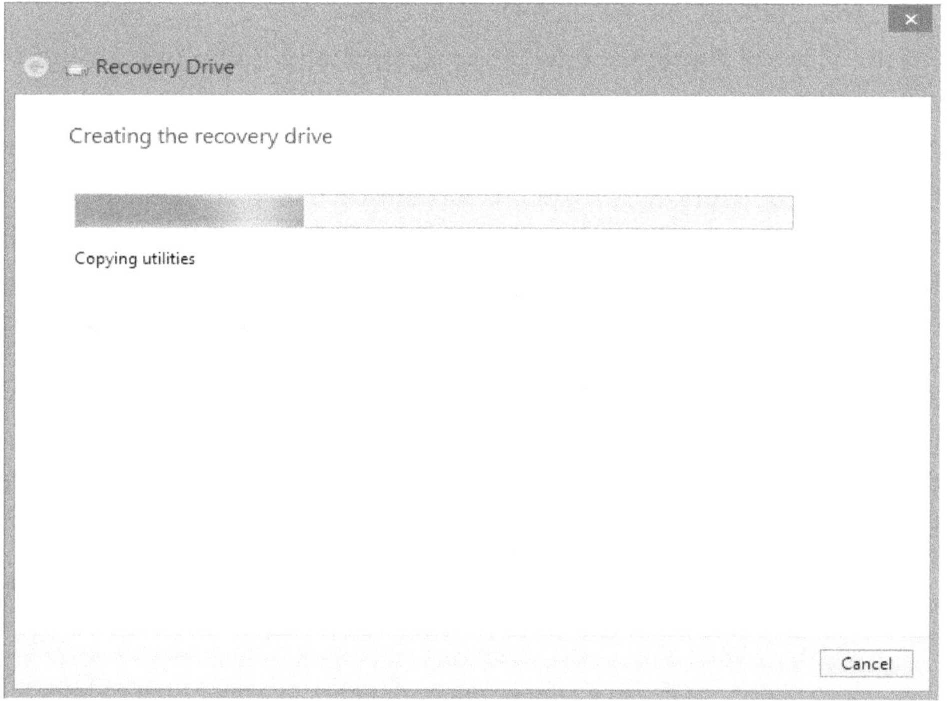

16. Once done, click Finish button.

Re-schedule Backup

Introduction to Re-scheduling Backup

When administrators turn on File History feature in Microsoft Windows 8, the operating system automatically schedules itself to back up the files every hour. Even though this automated backup scheduling this frequently is resource intensive, it is quite helpful in most production environments. However in homes, it might not be necessary to back up data so often as home computers are not expected to contain sensitive and important information. In such cases, administrators can re-schedule automatic backups in home computers in order to reduce additional resource consumption.

Re-scheduling backups in Microsoft Windows 8 is an administrative task and elevated privileges are required to complete the process successfully.

How to Re-scheduled Backup?

In order to re-scheduled backup in Microsoft Windows 8, steps given below must be followed:

1. Log on to Microsoft Windows 8 computer with administrator account.
2. From the **Start** screen, click **Desktop** tile.
3. On the desktop screen, hover mouse to the bottom right corner of the window.
4. From the displayed options, click **Settings**.
5. From the **Settings** pane in the right, click **Control Panel**.
6. On the **Control Panel** window, click **System and Security**.
7. From the **System and Security** window, click **File History**.
8. On the **File History** window, click **Advanced settings** option from the left pane.
9. On the **Advanced Settings** window, under the **Versions** section, select the desired backup frequency from **Save files every** drop-down list.

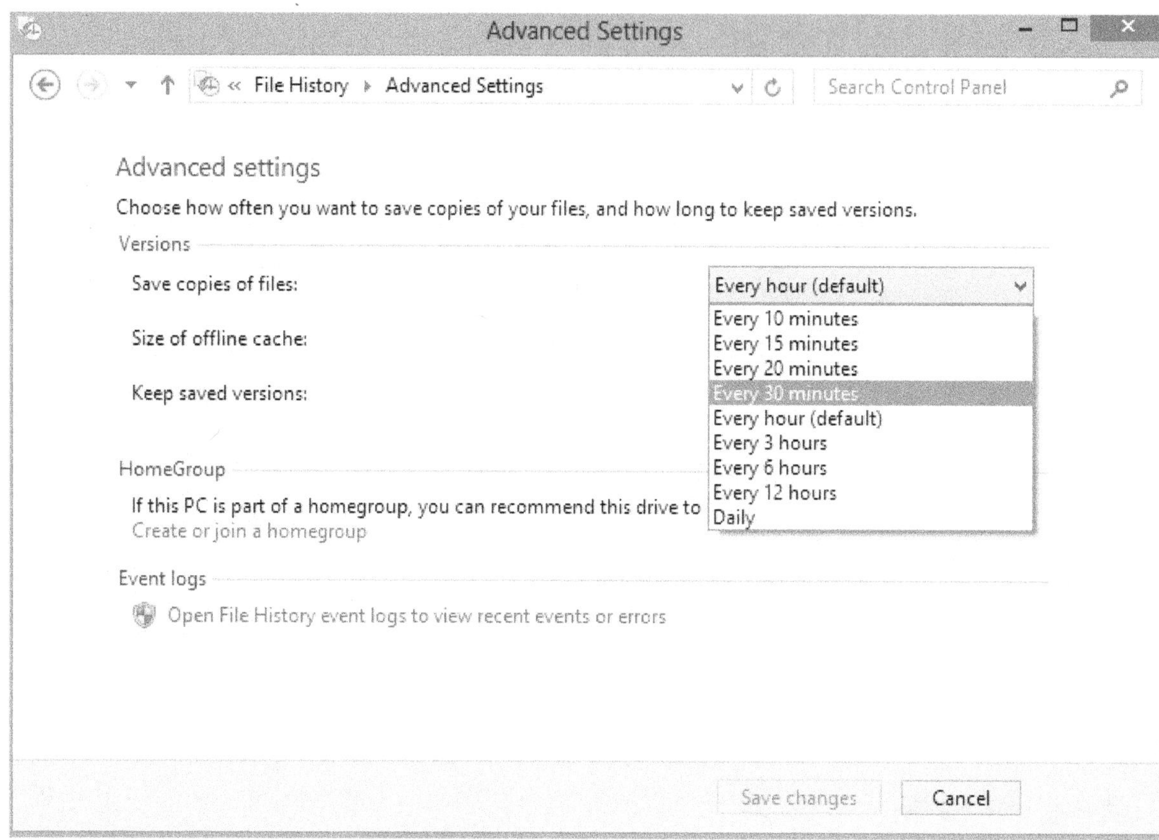

10. Click **Save changes** when done.

Backup Windows Registry

Introduction to Backing Up Windows Registry

In all Microsoft operating systems, Windows registry plays an important role in smooth functioning of the OS. Windows registry is considered the backbone of an operating system without which the OS would not be able to perform as efficiently as it really does. If some specific entries of Windows registry are tampered with or if they get corrupted due to any reason, the entire operating system crashes and fails to boot.

As administrators install/uninstall applications on a Windows 8 computer on a regular basis, the installation and un-installation process affects Windows registry. If because of any reason the registry file gets corrupted, the administrators may end up crashing their computers, hence losing their important and sensitive data for good.

Although Microsoft Windows 8 automatically creates a virtual store that contains a user specific copy of Windows registry for every user account that the computer has, Microsoft still recommends that the Windows registry must be backed up on a regular basis in order to avoid system crashes and/or boot failures. Backup of Windows registry is stored in a single file that has .REG extension. After Windows registry is backed up, it can be restored in case it gets corrupted because of any reason.

How to Backup Windows Registry?

In order to backup Windows registry in Microsoft Windows 8, steps given below must be followed:

1. Log on to Microsoft Windows 8 computer with administrator account.
2. From the **Start** screen, click **Desktop** tile.
3. On the desktop screen, press **Windows** + **R** keys simultaneously to initiate **Run** command box.
4. In the opened **Run** command box, type **REGEDIT** command and press **Enter** key.
5. On the **User Account Control** confirmation box, click **Yes** to provide consent to open **Registry Editor**.
6. In the **Registry Editor** window, from the left pane, click to select **Computer** from the top of the tree.
7. Click **File** from the menu bar and from the displayed list, click **Export**.

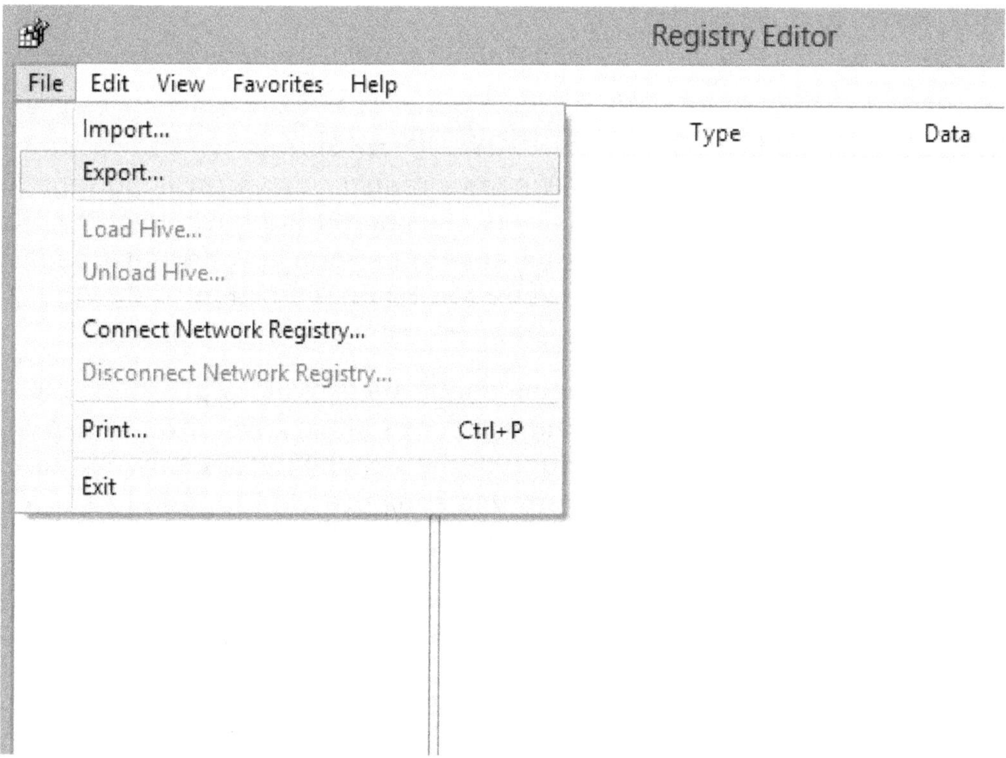

8. On the **Export Registry File** box, navigate to locate the destination where the backed up registry file is to be saved.
9. In the **File name** field, type a file name for the exported registry file.
10. Click **Save** button to export Windows registry.

Restoring Windows Registry

Introduction to Restoring Windows Registry

As mentioned in previous lesson, when Windows registry is backed up, it can be restored if computer crashes and/or fails to boot. When Windows registry is backed up, the backup is stored in a single file that has .REG extension. While restoring, the backed up Windows registry file is imported back to its original location, i.e. the system drive of the operating system.

Restoring Windows registry might sometimes display an error message telling that not all registry entries were imported. This makes sense because when computer a boots, Windows uses the registry and some of its entries are used by the OS. This prevents registry importing process from updating those entries.

How to Restore Windows Registry?

In order to restore Windows registry in Microsoft Windows 8, steps given below must be followed:

1. Log on to Microsoft Windows 8 computer with administrator account.
2. From the **Start** screen, click **Desktop** tile.
3. On the desktop screen, press **Windows** + **R** keys simultaneously to initiate **Run** command box.
4. In the opened **Run** command box, type **REGEDIT** command and press **Enter** key.
5. On the **User Account Control** confirmation box, click **Yes** to provide consent to open **Registry Editor**.
6. In the **Registry Editor** window, from the left pane, click to select **Computer** from the top of the tree.
7. Click **File** from the menu bar and from the displayed list, click **Import**.

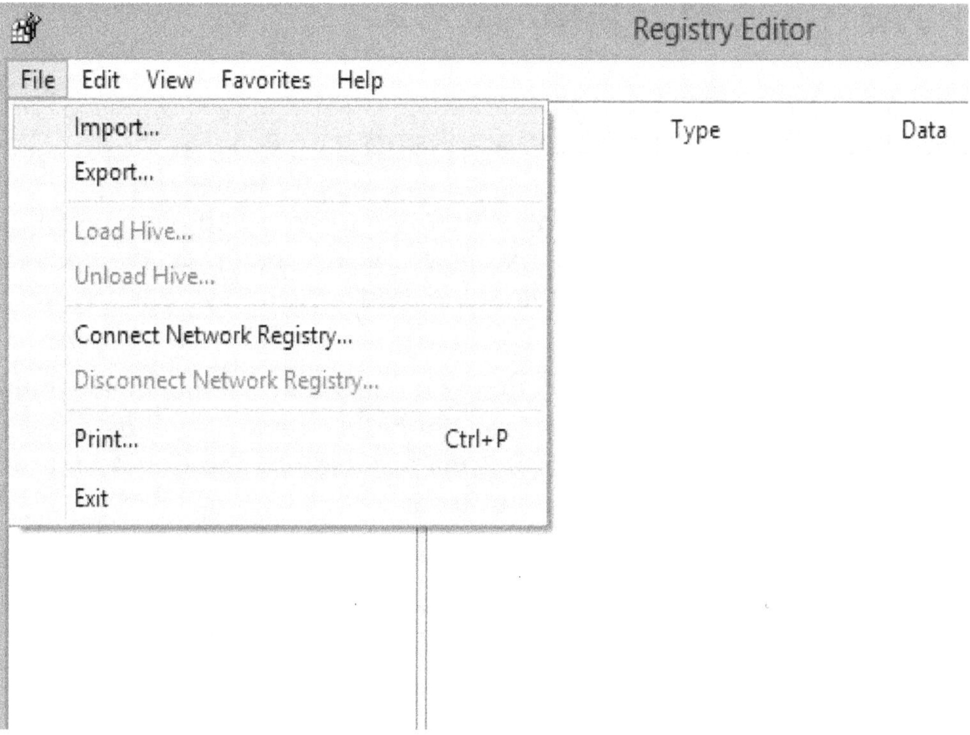

8. On the **Import Registry File** box, navigate to locate the destination where the backed up registry file is saved.
9. Once the backed up file is located, click to select the file and click **Open** button to import the registry.
10. Click **OK** on the displayed error message box and restart the computer.

Alternatively, the exported registry file can be right-clicked right from its location, and **Merge** option can be clicked from the context menu. On the **User Account Control** confirmation box, **Yes** button must be clicked and on the **Registry Editor** confirmation box **Yes** button must be clicked as well to merge the backed up registry file with the existing one. **OK** button must be clicked on the displayed error message box and the computer must be restarted.

Customize Reserved Disk Space

Introduction to Reserved Disk Space

In Microsoft Windows 8, the reserved disk space is used to hold restore points. By default the reserved disk space is set to 3% of the total size of the volume (partition). Once the entire reserved space is consumed, the very first restore point is automatically deleted in order to free up some space for the new restore point, in case it is created ether automatically or manually.

In production environments, since computers are likely to have sensitive information, administrators might want to create restore points on a regular basis in order to eliminate the chances of system unavailability due to abrupt or sudden system crashes.

Keeping this in mind, sometimes the default reserved disk space might not be sufficient enough to hold all restore points. Therefore, administrators might want to customize the default reserved disk space size so that additional restore points can be created.

How to Customize Default Reserved Disk Space?

In order to customize default reserved disk space in Microsoft Windows 8, steps given below must be followed:

1. Log on to Microsoft Windows 8 computer with administrator account.
2. From the **Start** screen, click **Desktop** tile.
3. On the desktop screen, click **File Explorer** icon from the taskbar.
4. On the **Libraries** window, right-click **Computer** from the left pane.
5. From the displayed context menu, click **Properties**.
6. On the opened **System** window, click **System protection** option from the left pane.
7. On the **System Properties** box, make sure that **System Protection** tab is selected.
8. On the **System Protection** tab, from the displayed list of available drives under **Protection Settings** section, click to select the drive for which default reserved disk space is to be customized.
9. Once selected, click **Configure** button.
10. From the displayed box, under **Disk Space Usage** section move the slider right or left to increase or decrease the system reserved space respectively for the selected volume.

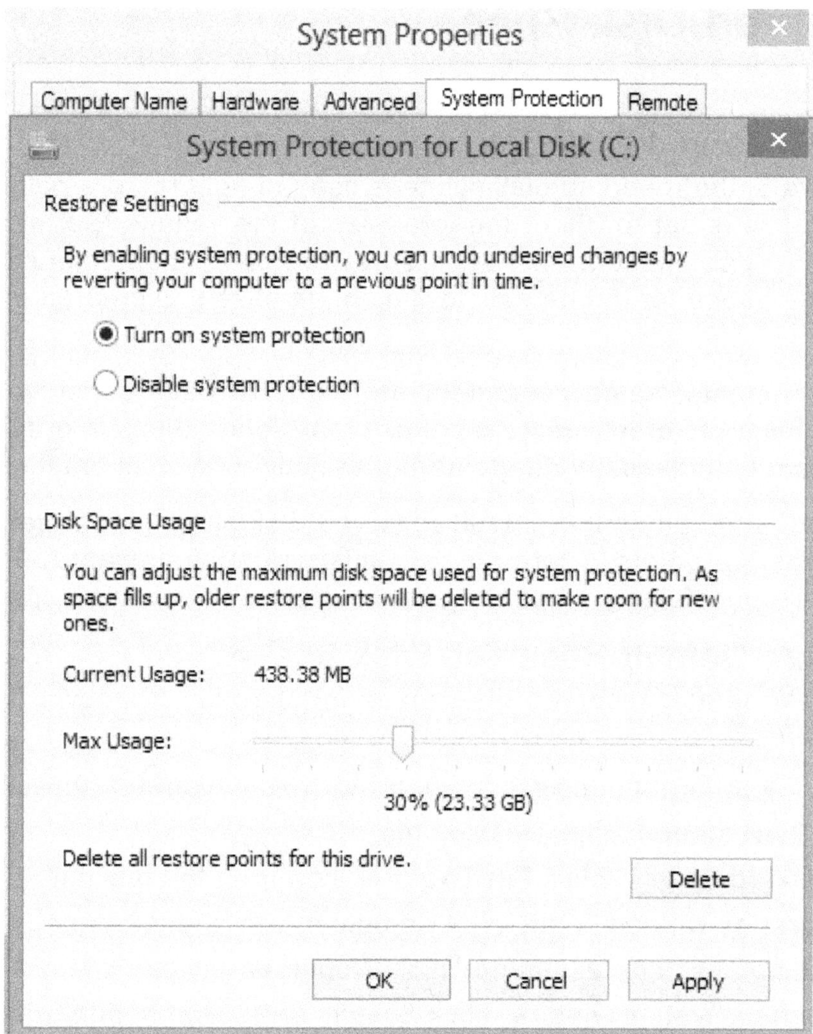

11. Click **OK** when done and back on **System Properties** box, click **OK** again.
12. Restart the computer when done.

CHAPTER 14:

MONITORING, MAINTAINING & TROUBLESHOOTING

Check If the Operating System Is 32-Bit or 64-Bit

Introduction to 32-Bit and 64-Bit Operating System

Number of bits in an operating system means 2^n number of bits of data that the OS is capable of reading at a single given time. When a 32-bit operating system is installed on a computer that has 64-bit processor, the operating system is capable of reading/writing (sending and receiving) 2^{32} bits of data at a time. Even though the processor can process 2^{64} bits of data at a time, because of the 2^{32} bits limitation of the operating system, the processing efficiency is reduced. On the other hand if a 64-bit operating system is installed on a computer that has 64-bit processor, the operating system is capable of sending 2^{64} bits of data to the processor for processing, hence exploiting the efficiency of the processor to its full.

When a laptop PC is purchased, in most cases it has 64-bit operating system installed in it. Because of 64-bit operating system, users can install other 64-bit Microsoft-based or other third-party applications in order to experience fast and efficient processing. In any case, if users are still confused about the bit numbers of the operating system that their laptop PCs or desktop computers have, Windows 8 allows them to identify if the OS is of 32-bit or 64-bit.

32-bit and 64-bit are sometimes also referred to as x86 and x64 respectively. In some cases these terms are used interchangeably.

How to Check If the Computer Has 32-Bit or 64-Bit Operating System?

In order to check if a computer has 32-bit or 64-bit Microsoft Windows 8 operating system installed in it, steps given below must be followed:

1. Log on to Microsoft Windows 8 computer with any account.
2. From the **Start** screen, click **Desktop** tile.
3. On the desktop screen, click **File Explorer** icon from the taskbar.
4. On the opened **Libraries** window, right-click **Computer** from the left pane.
5. From the displayed context menu, click **Properties**.
6. On the **System** window, under the **System** section, the operating system's bits can be seen in front of **System type** label.

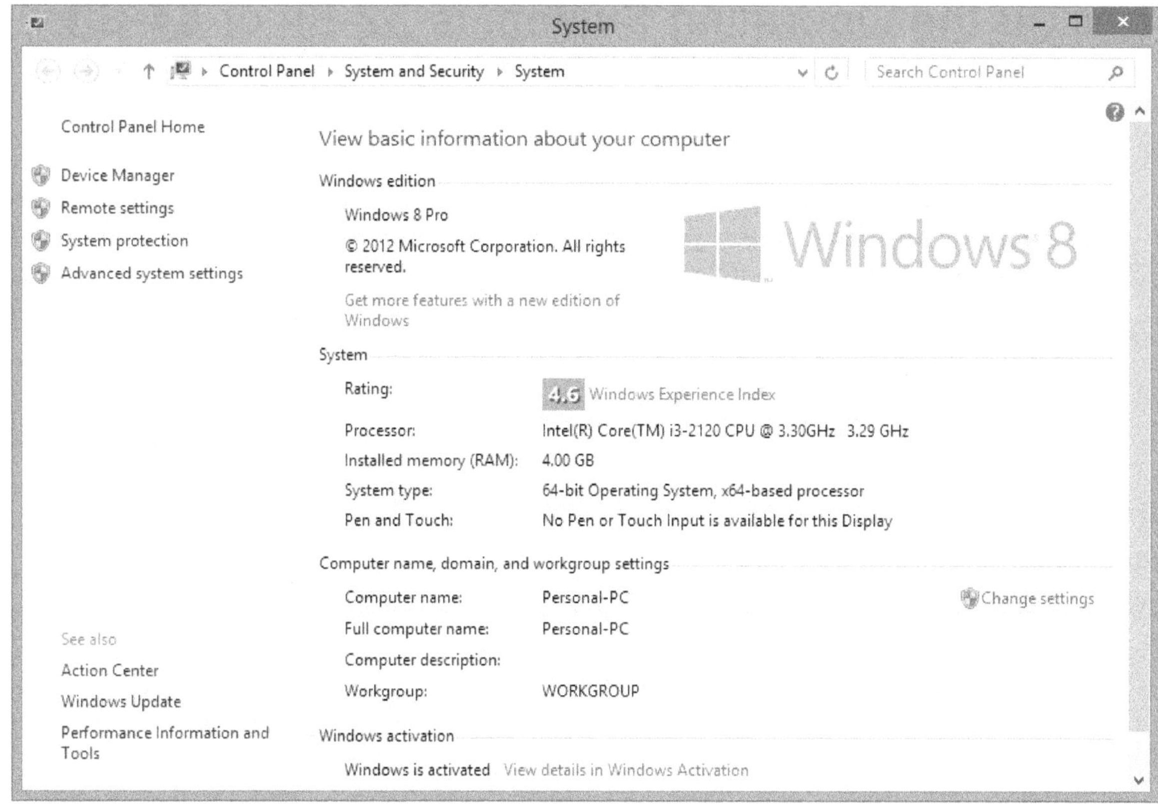

7. Close the window when done.

Get System Rating

Introduction to System Rating

System rating in Microsoft Windows 8 computer is the assessment of hardware resources that a computer has. System rating in Microsoft Windows 8 can be seen by going to the System Properties window. System Properties window can be accessed by right clicking the Computer option from the navigation pane in the left on the Libraries window. Libraries window can be initiated by clicking on File Explorer icon that is available in the taskbar of the Microsoft Windows 8 desktop screen. When system rating of a computer is assessed in Microsoft Windows 8, it includes:

- **Processor** - System rating of processor is assessed on the basis of calculations that a processor can perform per second.
- **Memory (RAM)** - System rating of the memory is assessed on the basis of operations the physical RAM can perform per second.
- **Gaming graphics** - System rating of the graphics is assessed on the basis of 3D output that the graphics card can produce while using high graphic oriented applications or games.
- **Graphics** - System rating of graphics is assessed on the basis of the efficiency the graphics card can provide while displaying Aero feature of the operating system.
- **Primary hard disk** - System rating of primary hard disk drive is assessed on the basis of rate at which the data is transferred to and from the drive.

When Windows 8 is installed on a computer, by default no system rating is assessed and therefore the system rating is displayed 'unrated'. In order to get the exact and accurate system rating, the assessment test must be initiated manually after the successful installation of the operating system. During the assessment test, the computer must be plugged in to the direct power supply. Once Windows 8 has successfully assessed system rating, it can be seen in the System Properties window. Although system rating is assessed for every above mentioned component individually, overall system rating is displayed on the basis of the component with the least rating. For example if Processor rating is 4.9 and all other components that the operating system has assessed have the 5.0 or above ratings, the overall rating of the computer will be 4.9.

Advantage of running system rating assessment test is that users can easily notice the weak hardware component that their systems have and can replace the device as per their conveniences.

How to Get System Rating (Run Assessment Test)?

In order to get system rating on to Microsoft Windows 8 computer, steps given below must be followed:

1. Log on to Microsoft Windows 8 computer with administrator account.
2. From the **Start** screen, click **Desktop** tile.
3. On the desktop screen, click **File Explorer** icon from the taskbar.
4. On the opened **Libraries** window, right-click **Computer** from the left pane.

5. From the displayed context menu, click **Properties**.
6. On the **System** window, under the **System** section, click **System rating is not available** option (if using for the first time after installation) or click **Windows Experience Index** option (to re-run the assessment) opposite to **Rating** label.
7. From the **Performance Information and Tools** window, click **Rate this computer** button (if using for the first time) or click **Re-run the assessment** to get the latest and updated system rating for the computer.

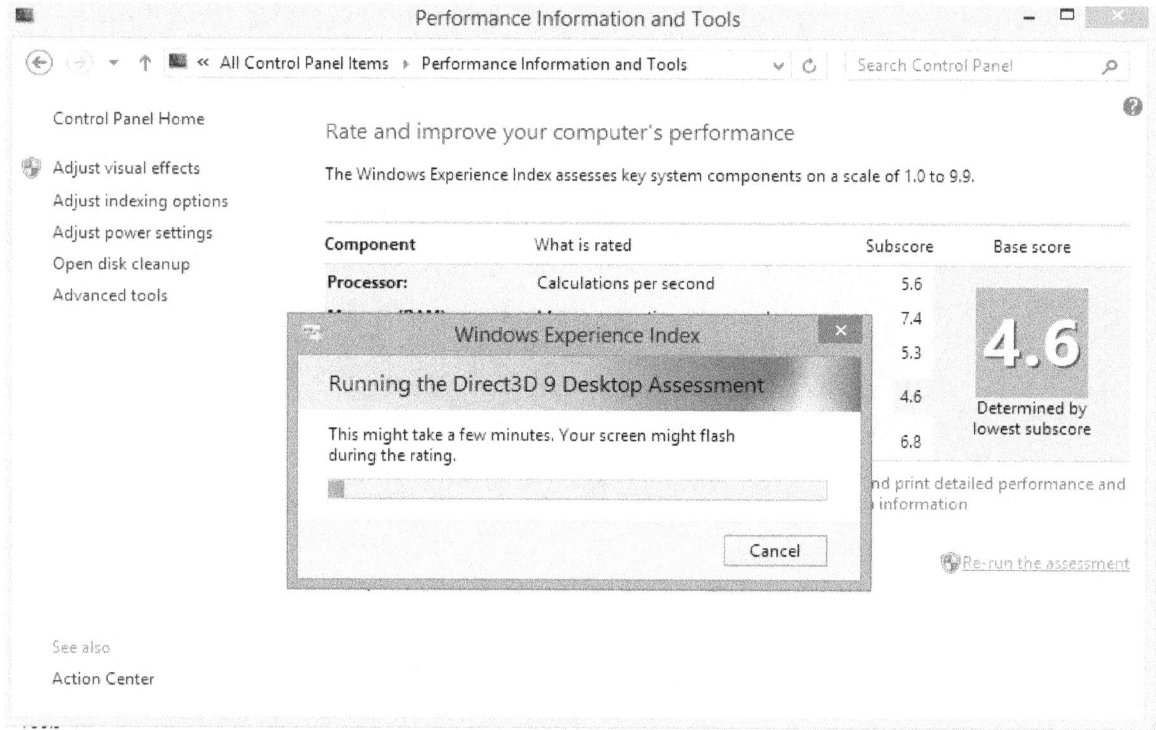

8. Close the opened window when done.

Generate System Health Reports

Introduction to System Health Reports

System health reports are the results of the assessments that the administrators of Windows 8 computer may have executed in order to assess the efficiency of the components that the computer has. When system health assessment is initiated, the feature diagnoses the workload on the memory, and other hardware components. After diagnosing the workload, a system health report is generated, which can then be used by the administrators to assess the utilization of the resources that the computer has.

In case users experience reduced performance while using Microsoft Windows 8 computer, system health reports can also help administrators to find out the installed component that is being over used by the users. Once the programmatic component is located, administrators can take appropriate steps to resolve the problem.

How to Generate System Health Reports?

In order to generate system health reports in Microsoft Windows 8, steps given below must be followed:

1. Log on to Microsoft Windows 8 computer with administrator account.
2. From the **Start** screen, click **Desktop** tile.
3. On the desktop screen, click **File Explorer** icon from the taskbar.
4. On the opened **Libraries** window, right-click **Computer** from the left pane.
5. From the displayed context menu, click **Properties**.
6. On the **System** window, under the **System** section, click **Windows Experience Index** option opposite to **Rating** label.
7. On the **Performance Information and Tools** window, from the left pane, click **Advanced tools**.
8. On the **Advanced Tools** window, click **Generate system health** report from the displayed tools list.

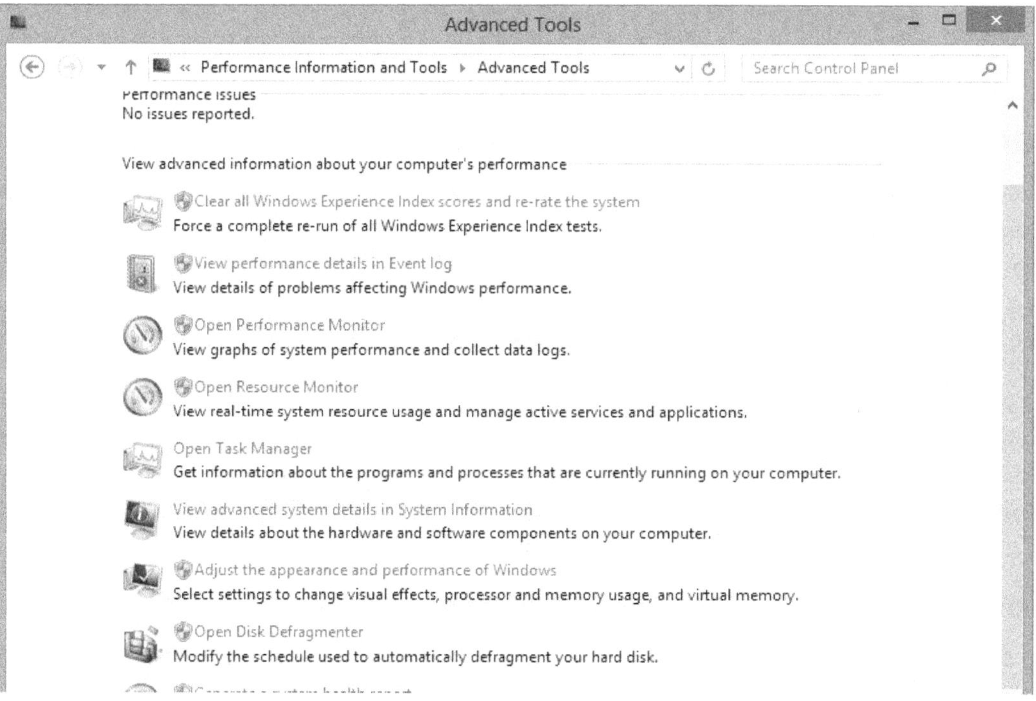

9. On the **Resource and Performance Monitor** window, wait till the system health report is generated. (Progress can be viewed under **Report Status** section.)

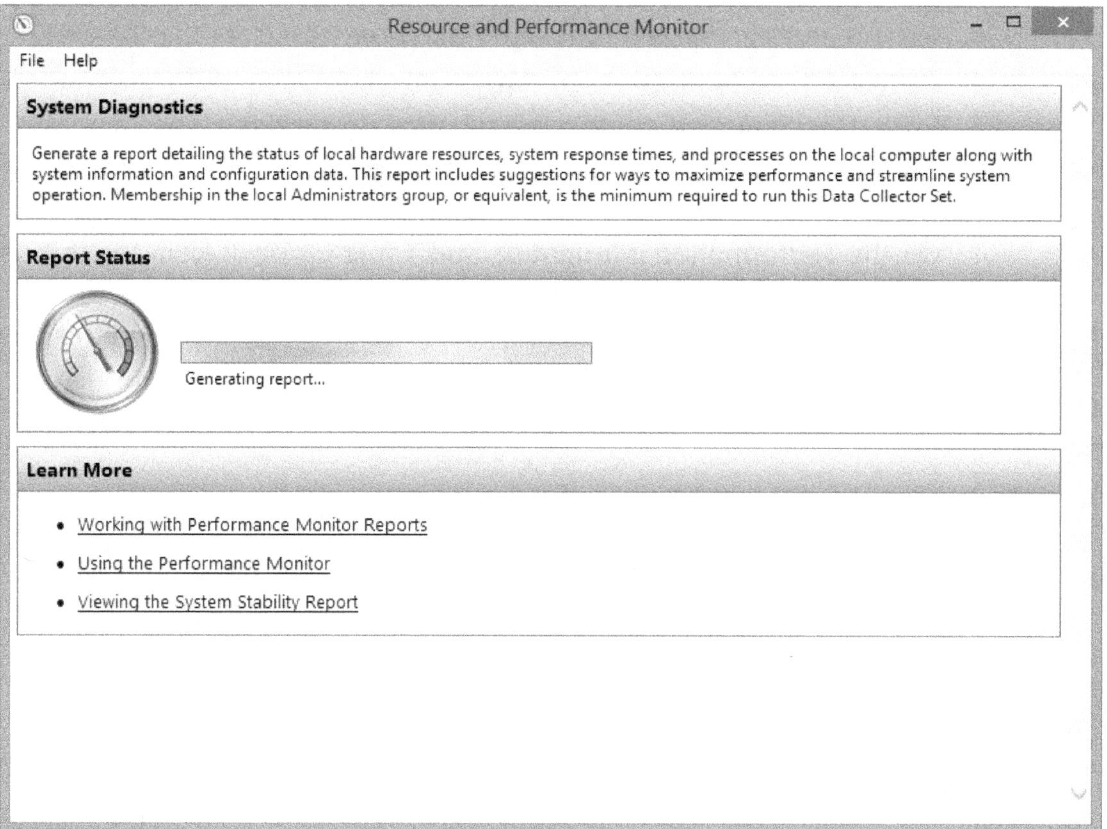

10. Once the report is generated, categorized results can be viewed on the **Resource and Performance Monitor** window.
11. Close all the opened windows when done.

Get Graphical Representation of HDD Usage

Introduction to Graphical Representation of Hard Disk Drive Usage

Being a secondary but permanent memory of a computer, hard disk drive plays an important role in improving the performance of an operating system. Efficiency of a hard disk drive can be decreased when the system drive (the partition on which the operating system is installed) is overpopulated with unwanted applications and files, leaving no or very less free space for the system files to expand when in use.

Normally hard disk drive usage cannot be seen until a specific tool named Performance Monitor is initialized and is configured to display the hard disk drive usage graphically. With the help of graphical representation of hard disk drive usage, administrators can assess and verify the reduced performance of the hard disk drive. Once the cause of the decreased performance is diagnosed, administrators can take appropriate steps to resolve the issue.

How to View Graphical Representation of Hard Disk Drive Usage?

In order to view graphical representation of hard disk drive usage in Microsoft Windows 8, steps given below must be followed:

1. Log on to Microsoft Windows 8 computer with administrator account.
2. From the **Start** screen, click **Desktop** tile.
3. On the desktop screen, click **File Explorer** icon from the taskbar.
4. On the opened **Libraries** window, right-click **Computer** from the left pane.
5. From the displayed context menu, click **Manage**.
6. On the opened **Computer Management** snap-in, from the **System Tools** category in the left pane, expand **Performance**.
7. From the displayed options in the expanded list, expand **Monitoring Tools** and click to select **Performance Monitor**.
8. From the right pane, click plus sign (+) from the toolbar displayed at the top.

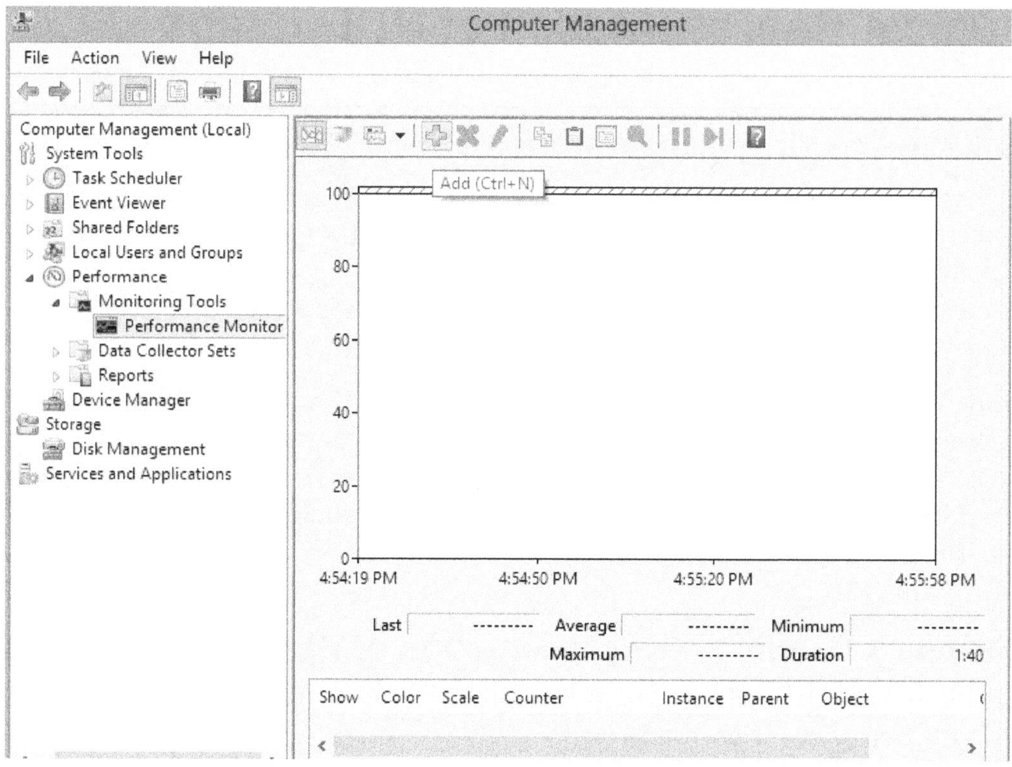

9. On the opened **Add Counters** window, under the **Available counters** section, ensure that **Local computer** option is selected in the **Select counter from computer** drop-down list.
10. From the displayed list, expand **PhysicalDisk**.
11. From the displayed options, click to select **Disk Transfer/sec**.

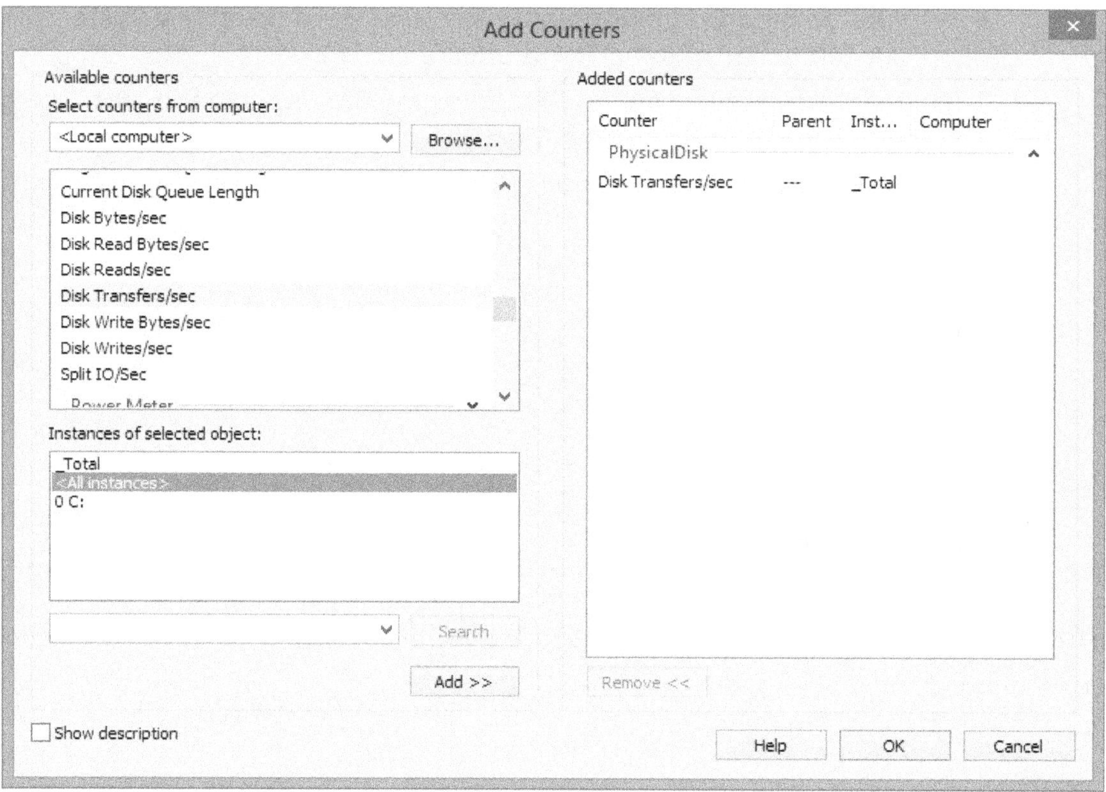

12. From the **Instances of selected object** section, make sure that **_Total** is selected.
13. Click **Add** button from the bottom to add the selected counter to the **Added counters** list in the right.
14. Once done, click **OK**.
15. Back on the **Computer Management** snap-in, disk transfer rate can be monitored by viewing the displayed graph in the right pane.

Graphical Representation of Processor's Idle Time

Introduction to Processor's Idle Time

When Microsoft Windows 8 is installed on a computer and the computer is in use, the best performance of the computer is considered when its CPU usage does not exceed 5% to 10%. A processor's idle time is inversely proportional to its percentage of usage. This means that the more percent of CPU is used the lesser idle time it has. When processors idle time is decreased, it means that there are some unwanted applications, scripts and/ or viruses that are affecting the performance of the computer.

Although there are several third-party tools available that can assess the processor's idle time, a built-in feature in Microsoft Windows 8 named Performance Monitor can also be used to graphically view the idle time of a running processor.

How to Get Graphical Representation of Processor's Idle Time?

In order to get graphical representation of processor's idle time in Microsoft Windows 8, steps given below must be followed:

1. Log on to Microsoft Windows 8 computer with administrator account.
2. From the **Start** screen, click **Desktop** tile.
3. On the desktop screen, click **File Explorer** icon from the taskbar.
4. On the opened **Libraries** window, right-click **Computer** from the left pane.
5. From the displayed context menu, click **Manage**.
6. On the opened **Computer Management** snap-in, from the **System Tools** category in the left pane, expand **Performance**.
7. From the displayed options in the expanded list, expand **Monitoring Tools** and click to select **Performance Monitor**.
8. From the right pane, click plus sign (+) from the toolbar displayed at the top.
9. On the opened **Add Counters** window, under the **Available counters** section, ensure that **Local computer** option is selected in the **Select counter from computer** drop-down list.
10. From the displayed list, expand **Processor**.
11. From the displayed options, click to select **% Idle Time**.

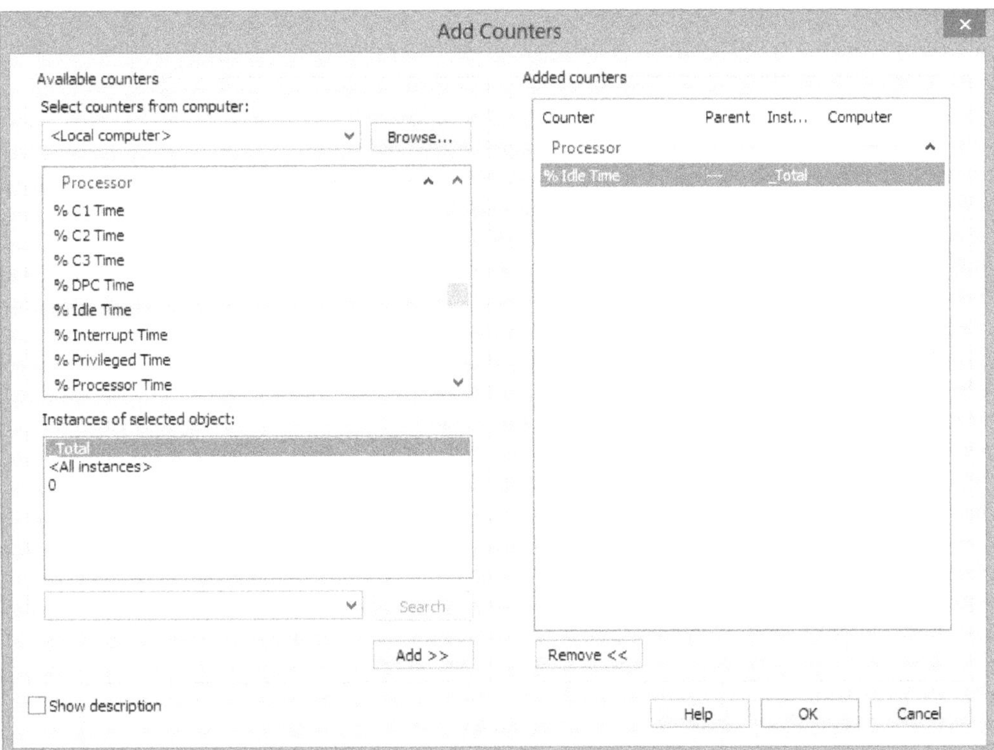

12. From the **Instances of selected object** section, make sure that **_Total** is selected.
13. Click **Add** button from the bottom to add the selected counter to the **Added counters** list in the right.
14. Once done, click **OK**.

15. Back on the **Computer Management** snap-in, processor's idle time can be monitored by viewing the displayed graph in the right pane.

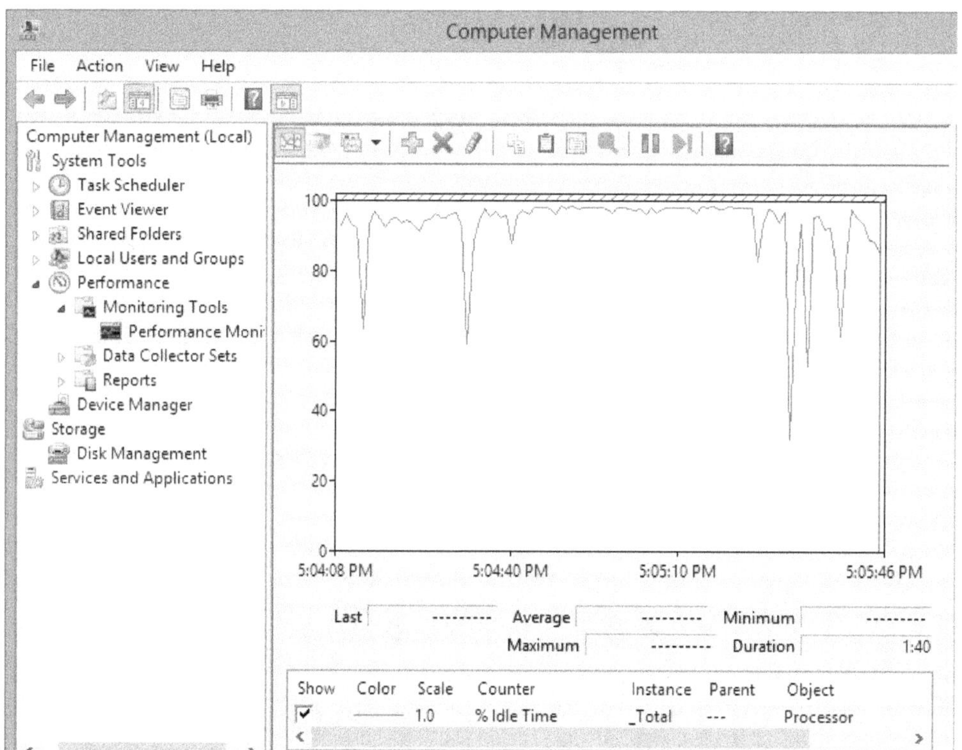

DirectX Diagnostics

Introduction to DirectX Diagnostic Tool

DirectX Diagnostics Tool can be used to view the information of the components that a computer system has. When DirectX Diagnostic Tool is initiated on a Microsoft Windows 8 computer for the first time, a Windows Hardware Quality Lab (WHQL) confirmation box is displayed on which users are recommended to click 'Yes' button in order to let the tool verify if all the drivers are digitally signed. If users click 'No', the DirectX Diagnostic Tool still gets initialized but without the verification of digitally signed drivers. Once appropriate button is clicked on the confirmation box, DirectX Diagnostic Tool box is displayed on the computer screen. The DirectX Diagnostic Tool box has multiple tabs and each tab displays the information about a specific component that is installed in the computer. For example the 'System' tab (first tab) displays the information of the system along with the version of DirectX the operating system has. 'Display' tab displays the information of the graphics card that is installed on the computer along with its corresponding driver version. In the same way, when the 'Sound' tab is clicked, the information about the speakers (in laptop computers), the sound card, and the version of the installed driver can be seen. Finally, when 'Input' tab is selected, users can view the information about the keyboard and mouse used as input devices.

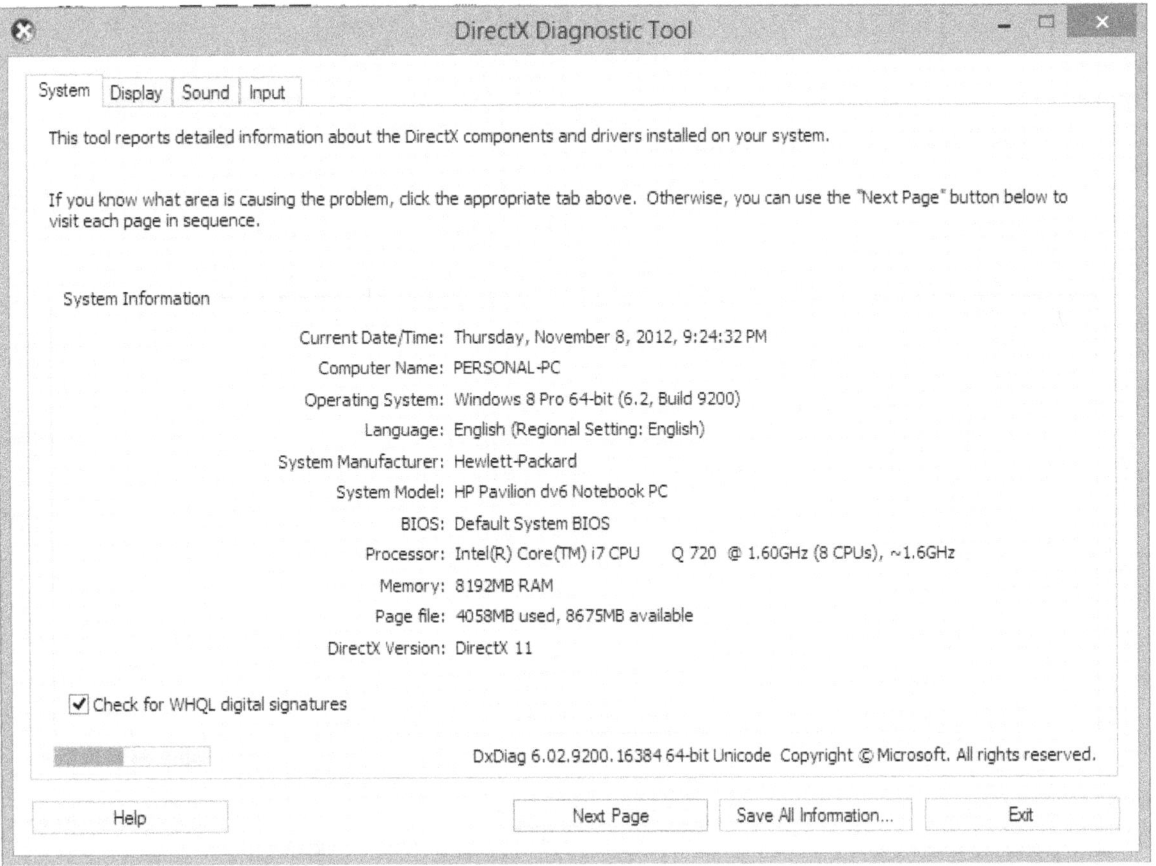

How to Run DirectX Diagnostics?

In order to initiate DirectX Diagnostics Tool box in Microsoft Windows 8 computer, steps given below must be followed:

1. Log on to Microsoft Windows 8 computer with administrator account.
2. From the **Start** screen, click **Desktop** tile.
3. On the desktop screen, press **Windows** + **R** keys simultaneously to initiate **Run** command box.
4. In the opened **Run** command box, type **DXDIAG** command and press **Enter** key.
5. On the displayed **DirectX Diagnostic Tool** box, click **Yes** button to allow Windows check the digital signatures of the installed drivers.
6. On the opened **DirectX Diagnostic Tool** window, required information can be viewed by selecting the appropriate tabs.
7. Close **DirectX Diagnostic Tool** window when done.

Create Custom Views in Event Viewer

Introduction to the Custom Views in Event Viewer

Event Viewer is a built-in feature in Microsoft Windows 8 that contains the logs that are generated when any event is triggered on the computer. When any problem is to be diagnosed that users and administrators face while using the computer, administrators mostly refer the logs that the Event Viewer contains. In other words, Event Viewer plays an important role in production environments when before dealing with the problems, diagnosing them becomes important.

When Event Viewer is initialized, it contains several logs that are generated because of thousands of events that are triggered while using Microsoft Windows 8. Because of the endless number of logs that the Event Viewer has, it becomes quite challenging for the administrators to locate a particular log that is related to the problem they are trying to resolve.

To overcome the above mentioned problems, Event Viewer allows administrators to filter the logs that it has by creating custom views. By creating custom views in the Event Viewer, administrators can specify the type of log that they are looking for. This filters the available logs in the Event Viewer and displays the only ones that are related to the issues, solutions of which the administrators require.

How to Create a Custom Views in Event Viewer?

In order to create custom views in Event Viewer in Microsoft Windows 8, steps given below must be followed:

1. Log on to Microsoft Windows 8 computer with administrator account.
2. From the **Start** screen, click **Desktop** tile.
3. On the desktop screen, click **File Explorer** icon from the taskbar.
4. On the opened **Libraries** window, right-click **Computer** from the left pane.
5. From the displayed context menu, click **Manage**.
6. On the opened **Computer Management** snap-in, from the **System Tools** category in the left pane, expand **Event Viewer**.
7. From the displayed options, right-click **Custom Views** container.
8. From the context menu, click **Create Custom View**.

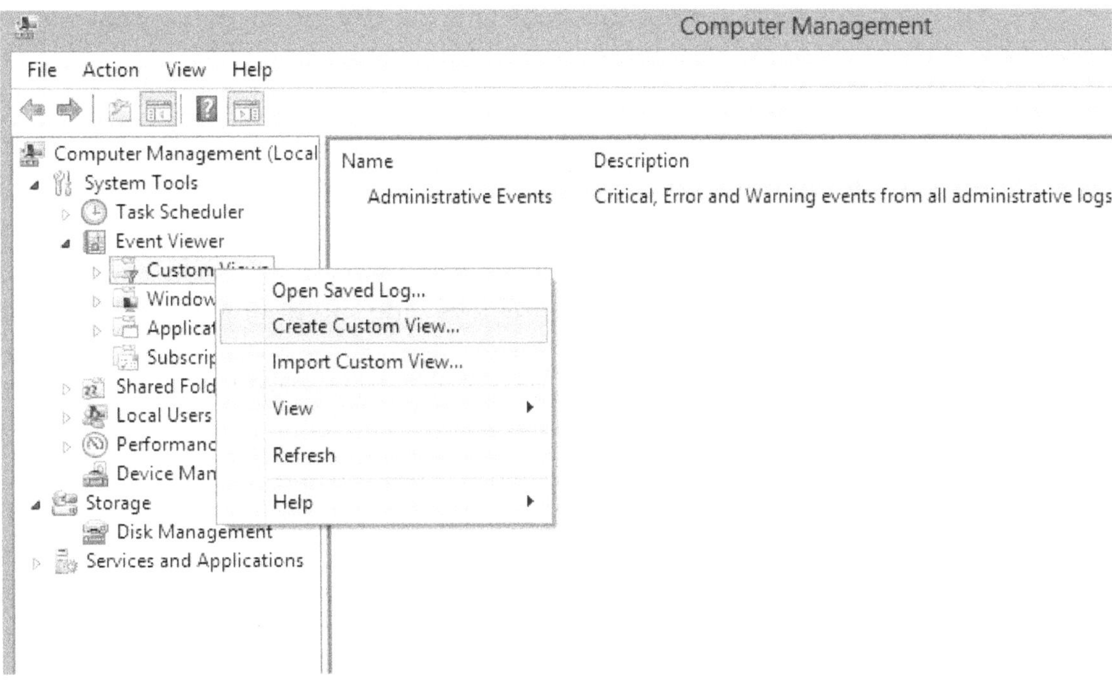

9. On the opened **Create Custom View** box, make sure that **Filter** tab is selected.
10. Choose the appropriate time from the **Logged** drop-down list.
11. Check the checkboxes as desired, representing the type of events that should be displayed in the custom view.

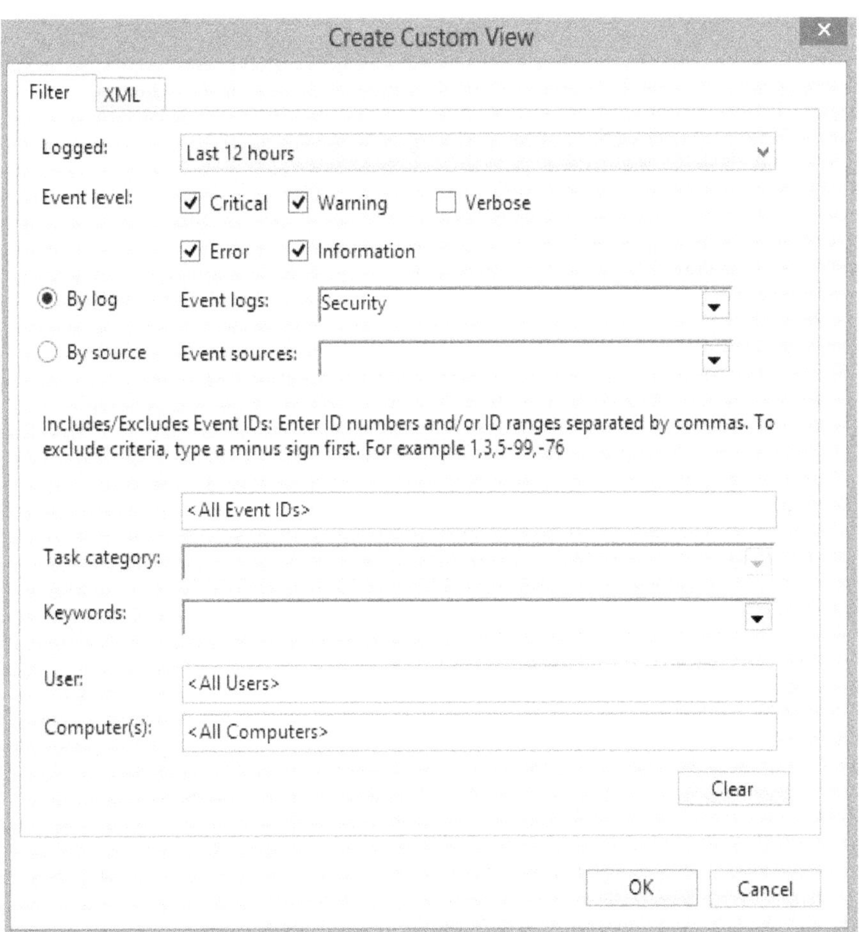

12. Click to select appropriate radio button (**By log** or **By source**) and choose the desired option from the corresponding drop-down list.
13. Click **OK** when done.
14. On the opened **Save Filter to Custom View** box, specify a name for the custom view in the **Name** field.
15. Type a brief description about the created custom the in the **Description** field. (Optional)
16. Click **OK** to create the custom views with the defined specifications.

Note: *In order to view the contents of the custom view,* ***Custom Views*** *container must be expanded in the* ***Event Viewer*** *tool and the desired custom view must be clicked.*

Use Resource Monitor

Introduction to Resource Monitor

Microsoft Windows 8 has a built-in feature named 'Resource Monitor' with help of which administrators of the computers can monitor the usage of the resources that a computer has. Some of the major sources in a computer system are CPU, hard disk drive, memory, etc. In homes, users generally use lightweight applications, and mostly they run one application at a time. Even if they play heavy and resource intensive games, they play them only for a couple of hours, and during that period they initialize no other application on the computer.

The case is different in production environments. In organizations, a computer system may have multiple resource intensive applications and administrators may use all of them simultaneously. When this happens, it is likely that the performance of the computer may decrease. In order to assess the utilization of the resources and the impact of utilization on the performance, administrators can use 'Resource Monitor'.

With the help of 'Resource Monitor', utilization of the resources can be seen graphically and in the real-time. This helps administrators to diagnose and locate the programmatic application or a file. Once the programmatic object is located, administrators can then take appropriate steps to resolve the issues.

How to Initiate and Use Resource Monitor?

In order to initiate and use 'Resource Monitor' in Microsoft Windows 8, steps given below must be followed:

1. Log on to Microsoft Windows 8 computer with administrator account.
2. From the **Start** screen, click **Desktop** tile.
3. On the desktop screen, click **File Explorer** icon from the taskbar.
4. On the opened **Libraries** window, right-click **Computer** from the left pane.
5. From the displayed context menu, click **Properties**.
6. On the **System** window, under the **System** section, click **Windows Experience Index** option opposite to **Rating** label.
7. On the **Performance Information and Tools** window, from the left pane, click **Advanced tools**.
8. On the **Advanced Tools** window, click **Open Resource Monitor** from the displayed tools list.
9. On the opened **Resource Monitor** window, the desired tab can be clicked to view the usage of that particular resource. (Graphical representations of the usage of the resources can be viewed in the right section of the window.)

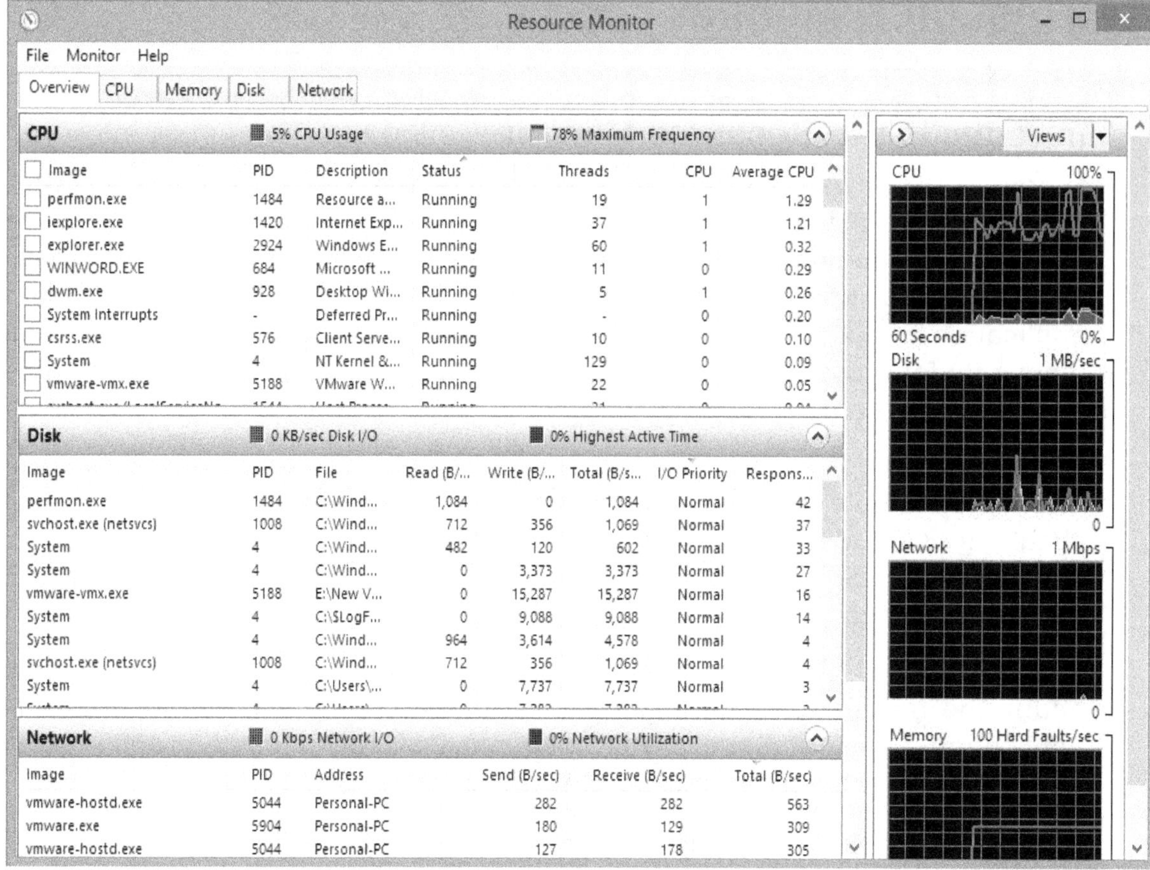

10. Close **Resource Monitor** window when done.

Get Desktop Screen Back If Not Visible

Introduction to the Desktop Screen

While using Microsoft Windows 8, there might be times when the desktop screen of the operating system is not displayed when the computer starts. Sometimes the desktop screen also vanishes if any opened application stops responding. When this happens, most users and administrators restart their computers to get the desktop screen back. When the computer is restarted in such situation, it is likely that the computers are powered off abruptly, hence increasing the chances of corrupting the system files of the operating system. If this same process is repeated multiple times, the chances are that the hard disk drive may generate bad sectors in it.

Why Desktop Screen Vanishes?

When a Windows 8 computer starts, because of the Metro UI, it is quite unlikely that the desktop screen would not be displayed when the Desktop tile is clicked on the Start screen. More chances are that the desktop screen would vanish if any running application fails to respond. In either case, the reason behind the desktop screen not being displayed is that process named 'Explorer.exe' is not initialized at all during the system boot or it stops functioning due to application failure. In order to get the desktop screen back, 'Explorer.exe' process must be initialized manually.

How to Get Desktop Screen Back?

In order to get desktop screen back in Microsoft Windows 8, steps given below must be followed:

1. Log on to Microsoft Windows 8 computer with the user account on which the desktop screen is not visible.
2. Once logged on, even if the **Start** screen is not visible, press **Ctrl** + **Alt** + **Del** keys simultaneously.
3. From the displayed options, click **Task Manager**.
4. From the bottom of the opened **Task Manager** box, click **More details** button.
5. Click **File** from the menu bar at the top.
6. Click **Run new task** from the displayed options.
7. On the opened **Create new task** box, in the **Open** field, type **EXPLORER** command and press **Enter** key to get the desktop or **Start** screen back.

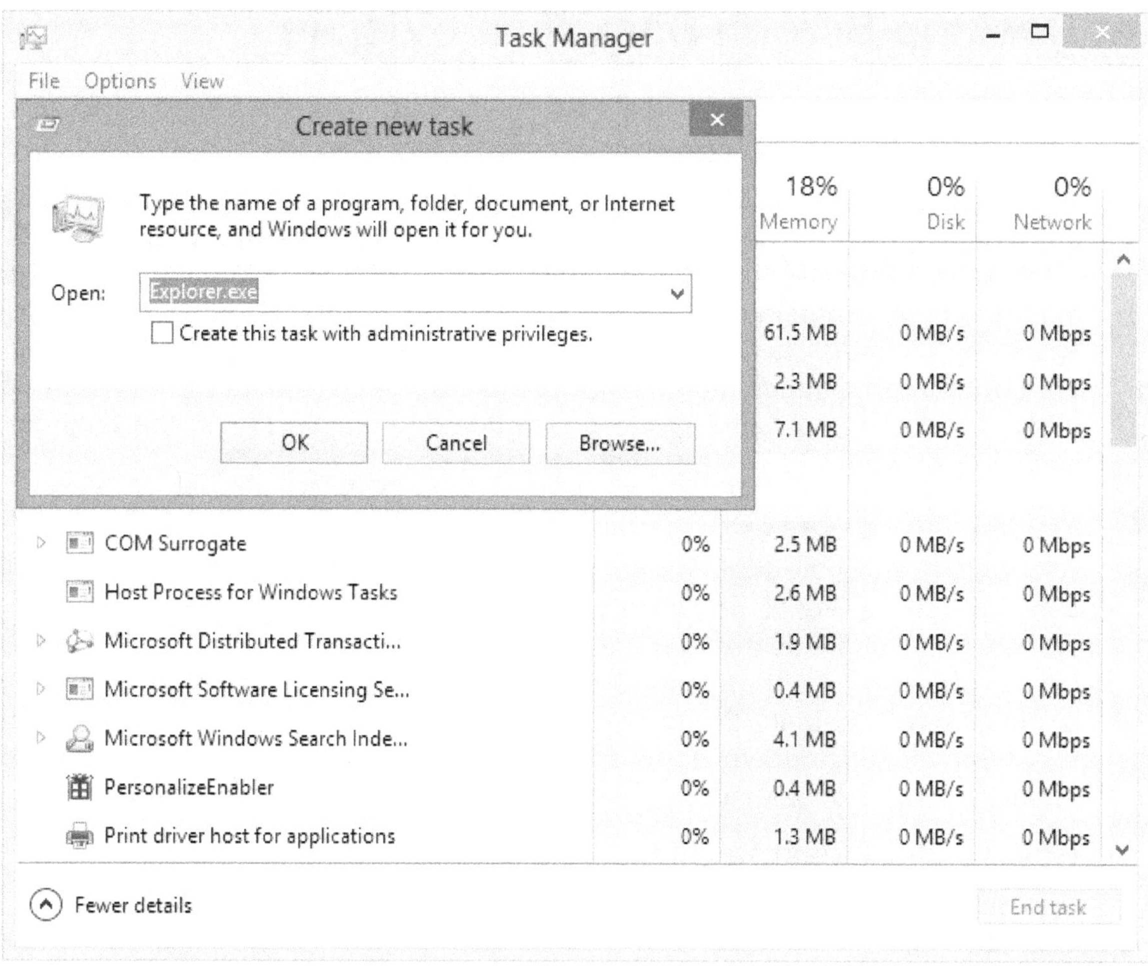

8. Close the **Task Manager** when done.

End Running Processes

Introduction to Ending Running Processes

When Microsoft Windows 8 operating system starts, there are several built-in processes that automatically initiate and run in the background. Moreover, when users manually initiate any application, its corresponding process also gets initiated and starts utilizing the resources of the computer (processor and memory). If a computer has sufficient amount of memory and decent processor, all initiated applications run quite smoothly, whereas if the memory and/or the processor are not sufficient enough to handle multiple applications, some of the applications might stop responding, hence putting the system to the unstable state. In such situations the processes of the non-responding applications must be ended forcefully.

Note: *Some running processes cannot be terminated even if administrator account is used to log on to the computer. The reason behind this is that those processes are used by the system, which does not allow even the administrators to end them whatsoever.*

How to End a Running Process?

In order to add a running process in Microsoft Windows 8, steps given below must be followed:

1. Log on to Microsoft Windows 8 computer with administrator account.
2. From the **Start** screen, click **Desktop** tile.
3. On the desktop screen, right-click the taskbar.
4. From the displayed context menu, click **Task Manager**.
5. From the bottom of the opened **Task Manager** box, click **More details** button.
6. Once done, make sure that **Processes** tab is selected.
7. From the displayed running processes list, right-click the one that is to be ended.
8. From the context menu, click **End task** to end the selected running process.

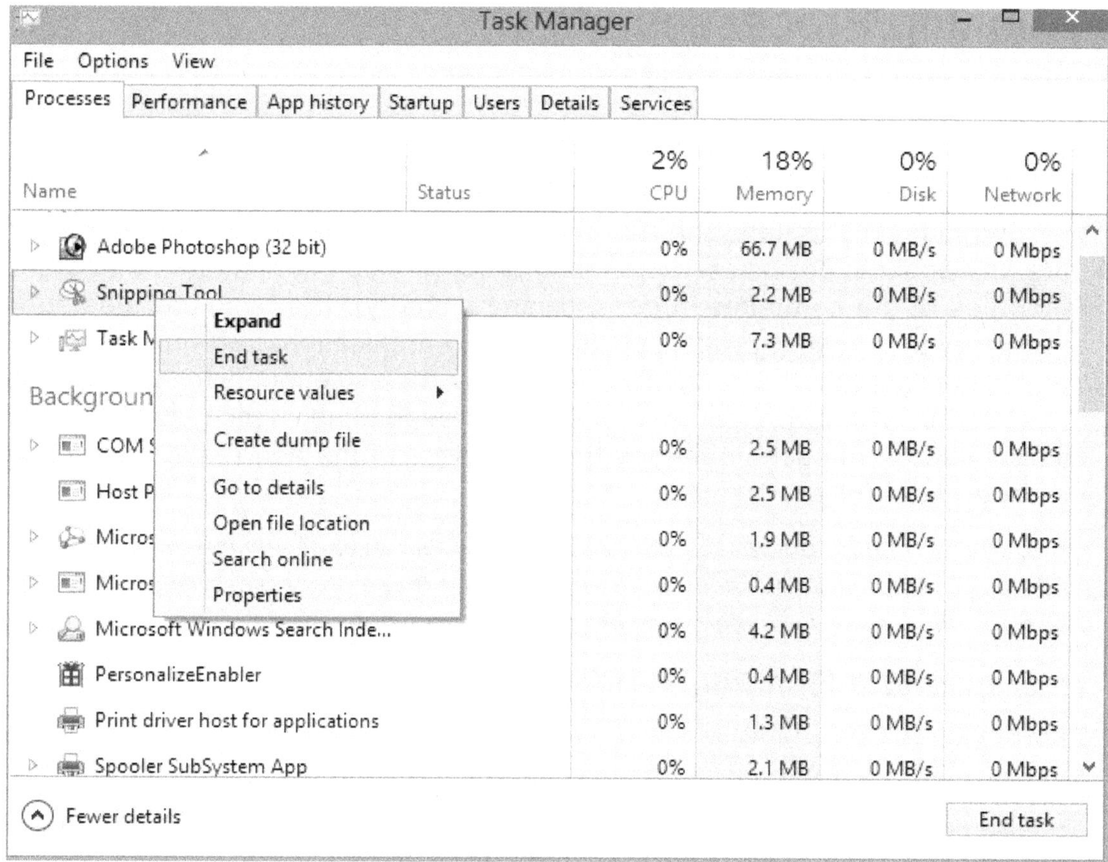

9. Close **the Task Manager** when done.

Optimize and Re-Schedule Optimization Process

Introduction to Optimization (Defragmentation)

In Microsoft Windows 8, the term 'Defragment' has been replaced with 'Optimize'.

Optimization is the process in which all the fragmented files that are stored in the hard disk drive are relocated to the most contiguous clusters to increase the performance of the hard disk drive that further increases the overall performance of the computer.

When a file is saved in a hard disk drive, the operating system fragments the file and stores each fragment of the file in a separate cluster. When the hard disk drive is new and no data is present in the clusters, all the fragments of the file are saved in the contiguous clusters (clusters in a series). When multiple files are saved, they occupy the available clusters in the hard disk drive. In such situation, when the first file is modified and the data is added to the file, its size increases. While saving the file, its fragments may not be saved in the contiguous clusters. When this process is repeated multiple times (daily several files are saved, modified and deleted), it becomes hard for the hard disk drive to read the scattered fragments of the file from the different locations.

Even if the contiguous clusters that reside between the fragments of a file become empty (by deleting the file whose fragments were stored in the contiguous clusters of the first file), the fragments of the first file still do not get relocated to the contiguous clusters automatically. This makes challenging for the hard disk drive to read the fragments of the file from different locations, which decreases the reading and writing speed of the hard disk drive, hence remarkably reducing its performance.

In order to maintain the efficiency and performance of the hard disk drive, Microsoft strongly recommends that the hard disk drive must be optimized on a regular basis. In order to reduce administrative overhead, in Microsoft Windows 8, the hard disk drive is scheduled to get optimized (defragmented) automatically on a weekly basis. This default configuration can be overridden as per users'/administrators' conveniences. In homes, it is recommended that users must optimize the hard disk drives manually regularly in case they have disabled the default scheduled auto optimization.

How to Optimize (Defragment) and Re-Schedule Auto Optimization (Defragmentation)?

In order to optimize and re-schedule auto optimization in Microsoft Windows 8, steps given below must be followed:

1. Log on to Microsoft Windows 8 computer with administrator account.
2. From the **Start** screen, click **Desktop** tile.
3. On the desktop screen, click **File Explorer** icon from the taskbar.
4. On the opened **Libraries** window, right-click **Computer** from the left pane.
5. From the displayed context menu, click **Properties**.
6. On the **System** window, under the **System** section, click **Windows Experience Index** option opposite to **Rating** label.

   *On the **Performance Information and Tools** window, from the left pane, click **Advanced tools**.*

7. On the **Advanced Tools** window, click **Open Disk Defragmenter** from the displayed tools list.
8. On the opened **Optimize Drives** box, from the displayed drives list, click to select the one that is to be optimized.
9. Click **Optimize** button to start disk defragmentation process.

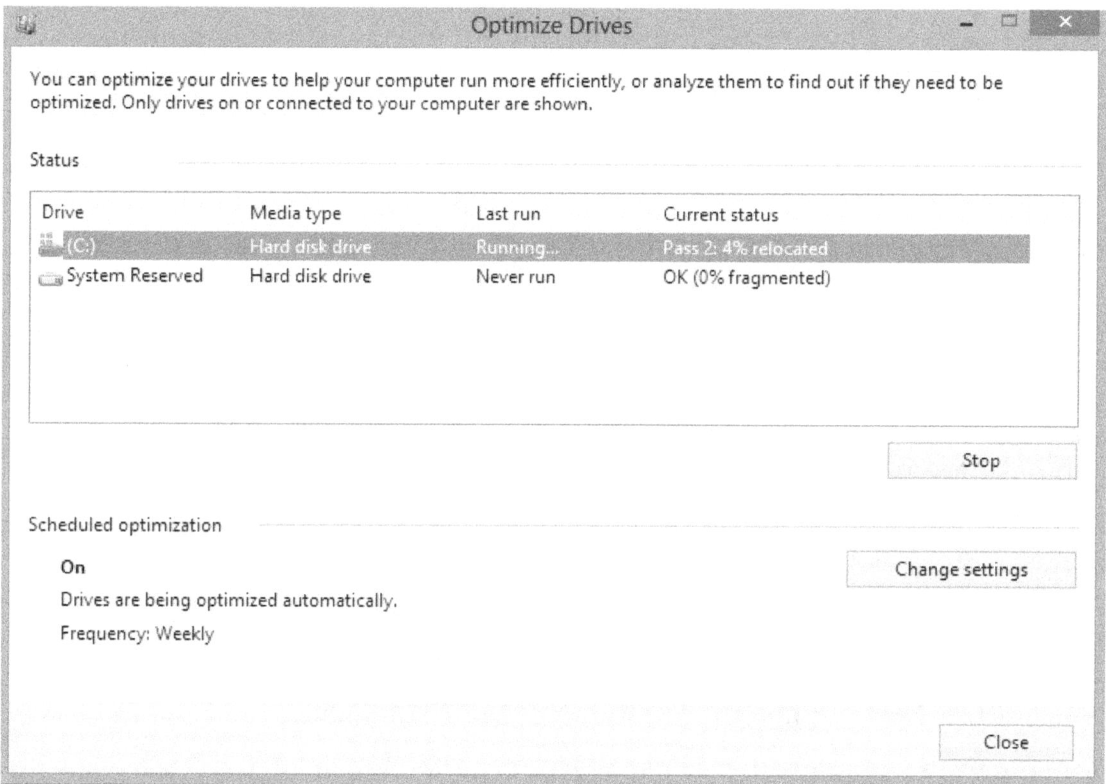

10. In order to modify the auto-defragment schedule time, click **Change settings** button from the **Scheduled optimization** section.
11. On the opened box, choose the appropriate schedule time from the **Frequency** drop-down list.

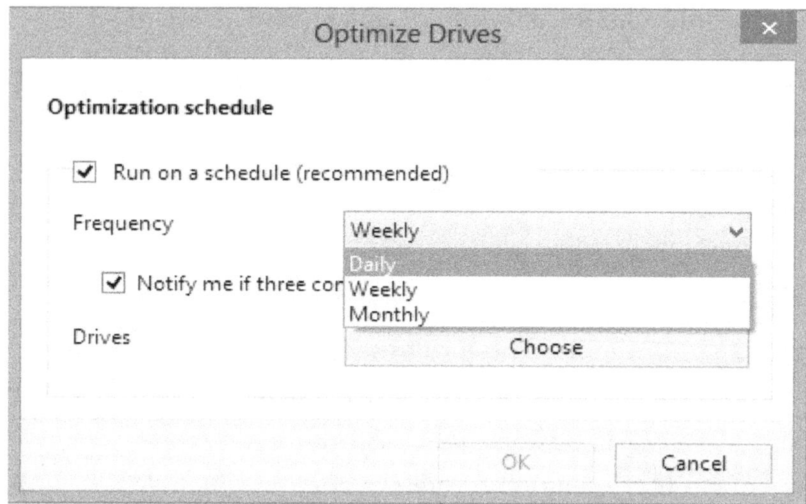

12. Click **OK** when done and back on the **Optimize Drives** box, click **Close**.
13. Close **Advanced Tools** window when done.

Disable Auto Optimization

Introduction to Auto Optimization

When Microsoft Windows 8 is installed, by default it is configured to automatically initiate the hard disk drive optimization process on a weekly basis. This auto optimization scheduling is quite helpful in production environments as it remarkably reduces administrative overhead which administrators otherwise would have to face if they were to optimize the hard disk drive of the computer manually on a regular basis. On the other hand, in homes this automated optimization scheduling might not be appreciated as it is resource intensive and the computer must be turned on at the scheduled time of automatic optimization. Therefore many users might want to disable the auto optimization feature while using Microsoft Windows 8 at homes.

How to Disable Auto Optimization?

In order to disable auto optimization in Microsoft Windows 8, steps given below must be followed:

1. Log on to Microsoft Windows 8 computer with administrator account.
2. From the **Start** screen, click **Desktop** tile.
3. On the desktop screen, click **File Explorer** icon from the taskbar.
4. On the opened **Libraries** window, right-click **Computer** from the left pane.
5. From the displayed context menu, click **Properties**.
6. On the **System** window, under the **System** section, click **Windows Experience Index** option opposite to **Rating** label.
7. On the **Performance Information and Tools** window, from the left pane, click **Advanced tools**.
8. On the **Advanced Tools** window, click **Open Disk Defragmenter** from the displayed tools list.
9. On the opened **Optimize Drives** box, click **Change settings** button from the **Scheduled optimization** section.
10. On the opened box, uncheck **Run on a schedule (recommended)** checkbox.

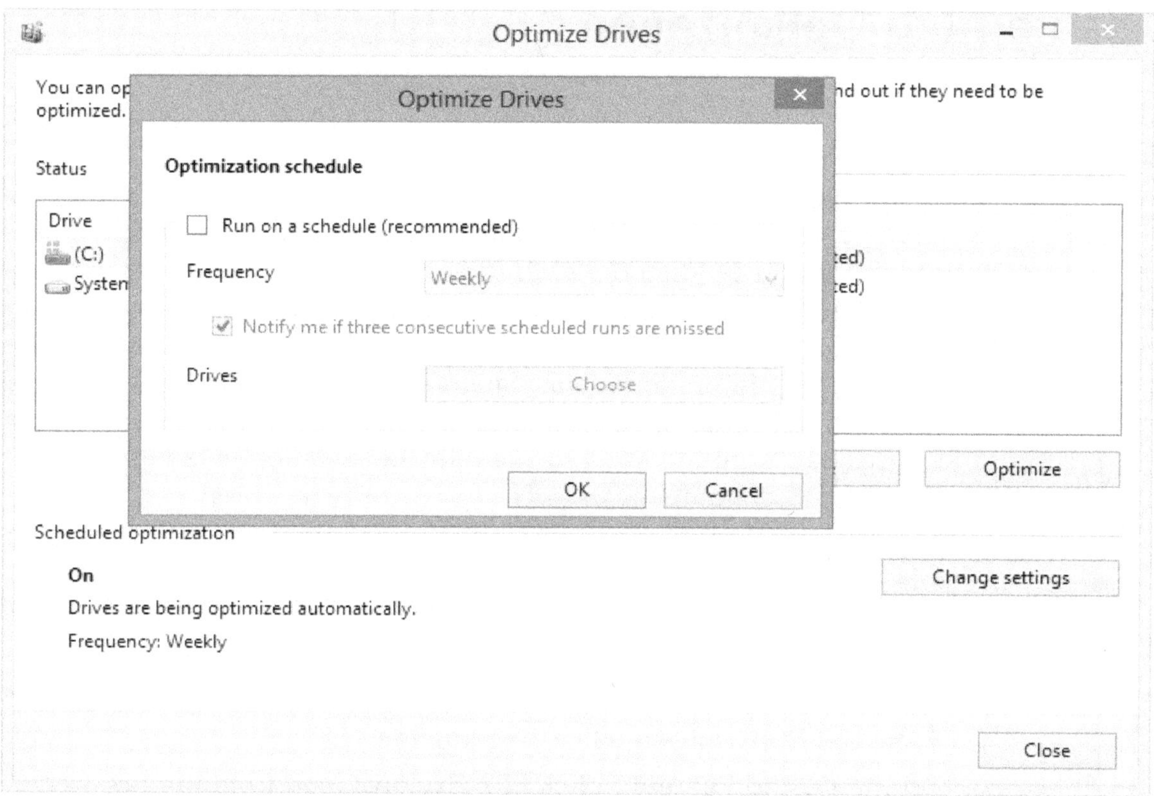

11. Click **OK** when done to disable automatic defragmentation (optimization) process.
12. Back on the **Optimize Drives** box, click **Close**.
13. Close **Advanced Tools** window when done.

To re-enable auto optimization, steps 1 to 13 can be followed, while checking the **Run on a schedule (recommended)** checkbox when on step 10.

Use Problem Steps Recorder (PSR)

Introduction to Problem Steps Recorder (PSR)

Problem Steps Recorder (PSR) is a built-in tool in Microsoft Windows 8 that allows users to record the steps if they find any trouble while performing some task. Problem Steps Recorder captures a sequence of screenshots every time a mouse is clicked. All captured screenshots are saved in an .MHT file that can be opened in the Internet Explorer, which is the built-in web browser in Microsoft Windows 8. Moreover, while using Problem Steps Recorder users can also add comments to the recorded steps to support the screenshots and make the help desk people understand the problem more clearly.

Once users have recorded the steps and they stop recording, they are displayed with a box to specify the name of the file. Once they specify a file name, a zip file is created that contains the .MHT file.

How to Initiate and Use Problem Steps Recorder (PSR)?

In order to initiate and use Problem Steps Recorder (PSR) in Microsoft Windows 8, steps given below must be followed:

1. Log on to Microsoft Windows 8 computer with administrator account.
2. From the **Start** screen, click **Desktop** tile.
3. On the desktop screen, press **Windows** + **R** keys simultaneously to initiate **Run** command box.
4. In the opened **Run** command box, type **PSR** command and press **Enter** key.
5. On the opened **Steps Recorder** application, click **Start Record** button to begin recording the steps.

   Note: *While recording,* ***Add Comment*** *button can be clicked to add a comment and the mouse can be used to select the area or a control for which the comment is to be added. Also, the recording can be paused for a short while by pressing* ***Pause Record*** *button.*
6. Once the recording is done, click **Stop Record** button to stop recording.

7. From the displayed options in the toolbar, click **Save** button.
8. On the **Save As** box, navigate and locate the destination where the recorded file is to be saved.
9. In the **File name** field, type a unique name for the .ZIP file in which the recorded file will be saved.
10. Click **Save** when done.
11. Close the **Steps Recorder** application.

Fix Device Drivers

Introduction to Fixing Device Drivers

After the successful installation of Microsoft Windows 8, administrators must install the drivers of the devices that the computer has. In most cases the motherboards that users purchase are shipped along with their corresponding driver installation discs that contain all the drivers for the devices that are integrated on the motherboards. On the other hand, when a laptop PC is purchased, the drivers for the installed hardware devices must be downloaded from the vendor's website. In either case, in absence of appropriate device drivers, no hardware devices can be used, hence making the computer system almost unusable.

When device drivers are installed on a computer, and the computer is used for a couple of months, it is likely that because of the frequent manipulations and modifications in Windows registry, the driver files may get corrupted and as a result, the devices may fail to work. When this happens, administrators of the computers must fix the device drivers so that the devices can start functioning again.

Sometimes administrators of the computers might update the device drivers when they find the new version of the driver available online. When administrators do so, and if the new version of the driver is not compatible with the device, the device may stop functioning. Even in this case, the driver of the device is required to be fixed by the administrators.

Every time a device driver is updated with the newer version, Microsoft Windows 8 automatically creates a backup of the current device driver before initializing the update process. In case the updated driver is not compatible with the hardware device, administrators can rollback the device driver to its previous version. In case rollback option is not available, administrators are then required to uninstall the new driver, and reinstall the older device driver right from the scratch.

How to Fix Device Driver?

As mentioned above, device drivers can be fixed either by reinstalling the drivers or by rolling them back to their previous versions. Steps given below must be followed to reinstall and rollback the device drivers on the Microsoft Windows 8 computer:

Reinstalling Device Driver:

1. Reinstalling a device driver requires that the driver must first be uninstalled from the computer. Lesson '**Uninstall a Device Driver**' from the chapter '**Manage Hardware Devices**' in this book can be referred to do so.
2. Once the driver is uninstalled, it can be reinstalled from its installation disc or any other storage media in which the installer file has been saved.

Note: *Administrator account must be used to log on to the computer to uninstall and reinstall a device driver.*

Rolling Back Device Driver:

1. Log on to Microsoft Windows 8 computer with administrator account.
2. From the **Start** screen, click **Desktop** tile.

3. On the desktop screen, click **File Explorer** icon from the taskbar.
4. On the opened **Libraries** window, right-click **Computer** from the left pane.
5. From the displayed context menu, click **Manage**.
6. On the **Computer Management** snap-in, under **System Tools** category from the left pane, click to select **Device Manager**.
7. In the right pane, expand the category of the devices to which the target device belongs.
8. Right-click the target device from the expanded list and from the displayed context menu, click **Properties**.
9. On the device's properties box, go to **Driver** tab.
10. On the **Driver** tab, click **Roll Back Driver** button to roll back the driver to its previous state.

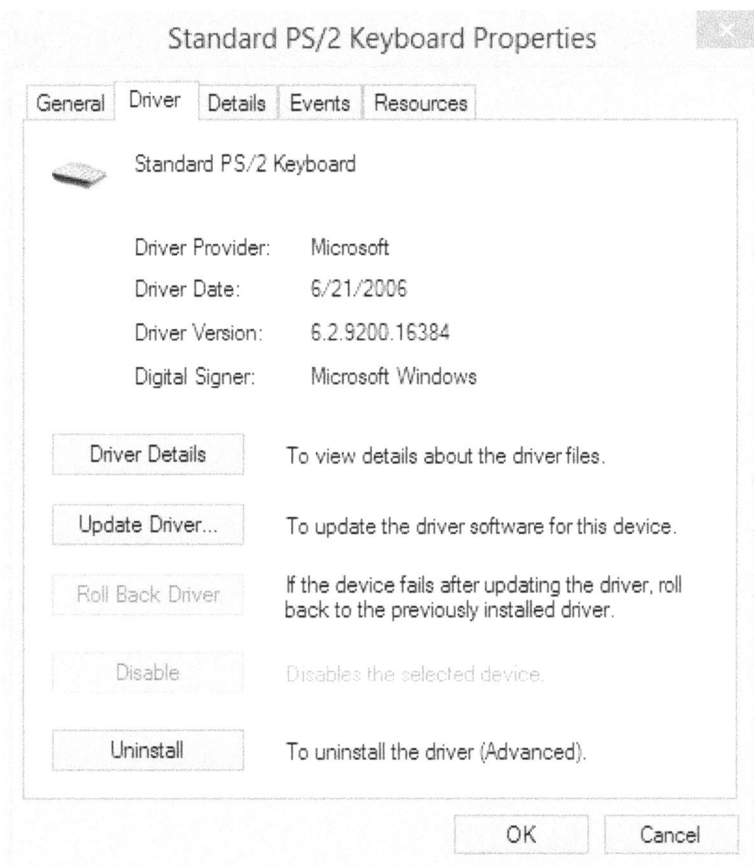

11. Accept any confirmation box that appears to continue the process.
12. Once done, restart the computer.

***Note: Roll Back Driver** button would remain disabled if the device driver has not been updated up earlier. (As displayed in this demonstration).*

Monitor LAN Card Usage

Introduction to Monitoring LAN Card Usage

When a computer is connected to the network, it is expected that it will be allowed to communicate with other computers that belong to the same network. In homes, since there are limited numbers of computers, it is unlikely that network congestion would ever take place. On the other hand, when a Windows 8 computer is used in production environment, the chances are that the NIC installed in the computer might face heavy network traffic while communicating with other computers on the network. In some cases, it is also possible that the NICs might face bottlenecks.

When network congestions occur, users may experience reduced network performance which may be reflected in the form of slow Internet speed or decreased local area network connection speed. In either case, it becomes a challenging task for the administrators to assess the main cause of the slow performance, i.e. either the performance is decreased because of the bottlenecks or due to faulty cables or some problem with the Internet connection itself.

In order to diagnose the bottlenecks, administrators can monitor the LAN card usage with the help of Task Manager in Microsoft Windows 8.

How to Monitor LAN Card Usage?

In order to monitor LAN card usage in Microsoft Windows-based, steps given below must be followed:

1. Log on to Microsoft Windows 8 computer with administrator account.
2. From the **Start** screen, click **Desktop** tile.
3. On the desktop screen, right-click the taskbar.
4. From the displayed context menu, click **Task Manager**.
5. From the bottom of the opened **Task Manager** box, click **More details** button.
6. Once done, go to the **Performance** tab.
7. On the **Performance** tab, click **Ethernet** from the left column.
8. LAN card usage can be monitored through the displayed real-time graph in the right.

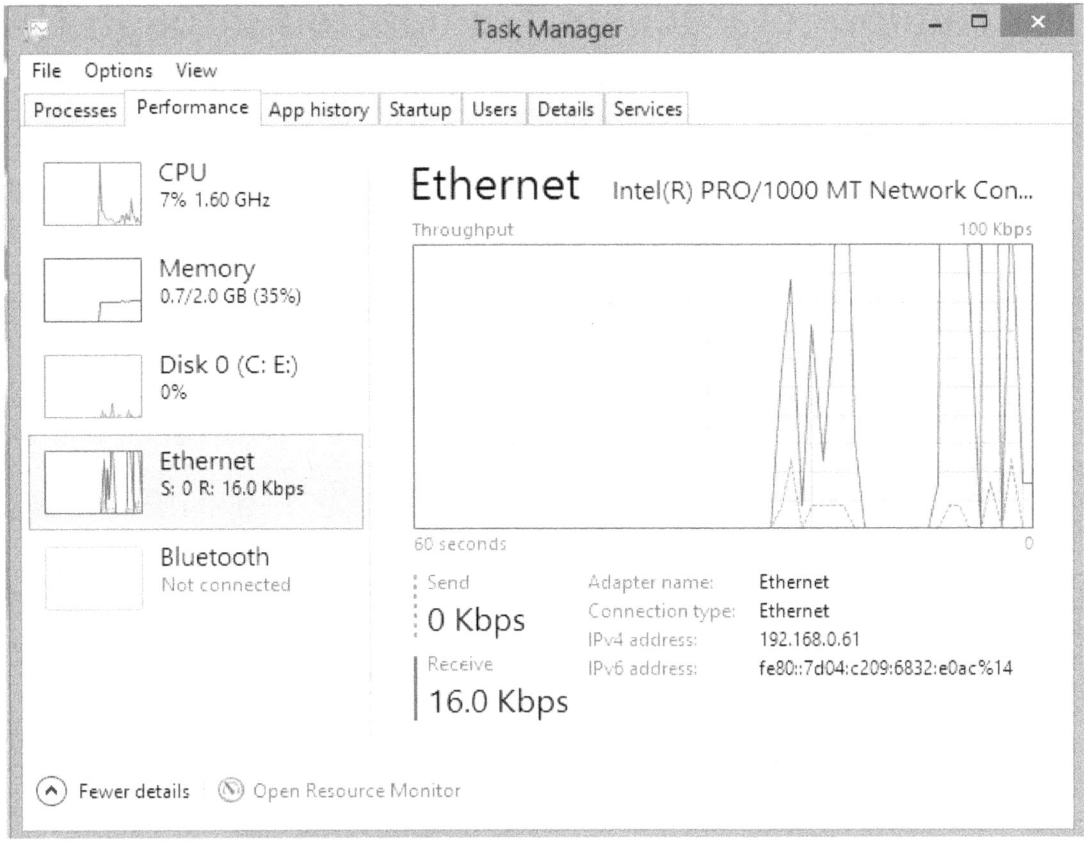

9. Close the **Task Manager** when done.

Monitor Number of Packets Transferred through NIC

Introduction to Packet Transfer Monitoring

In the previous lesson, Windows Task Manager was used to monitor the NIC usage. The process mentioned in the previous lesson was fairly good for the administrators and/or home users if the network interface cards are just to be diagnosed for the network congestions and bottlenecks. However the method does not provide detailed information about the number of packets that are transferred to and from the computer when it communicates with other computers on the network.

Microsoft Windows 8 helps administrators overcome this limitation and allows them to assess the network traffic usage by monitoring the amount of packets that are transferred to and from the NIC that is installed on the computer. In order to accomplish this task, 'Performance Monitor' is used.

How to Monitor Number of Packets Transferred through NIC?

In order to monitor number of packets that are transferred through an NIC in Microsoft Windows 8 computer, steps given below must be followed:

1. Log on to Microsoft Windows 8 computer with administrator account.
2. From the **Start** screen, click **Desktop** tile.
3. On the desktop screen, click **File Explorer** icon from the taskbar.
4. On the opened **Libraries** window, right-click **Computer** from the left pane.
5. From the displayed context menu, click **Manage**.
6. On the opened **Computer Management** snap-in, from the **System Tools** category in the left pane, expand **Performance**.
7. From the displayed options in the expanded list, expand **Monitoring Tools** and click to select **Performance Monitor**.
8. From the right pane, click plus sign (**+**) from the toolbar displayed at the top.
9. On the opened **Add Counters** window, under the **Available counters** section, ensure that **Local computer** option is selected in the **Select counter from computer** drop-down list.
10. From the displayed list, expand **Network Interface**.
11. From the displayed options, click to select **Packets/sec**.
12. From the **Instances of selected object** section, click to select the NIC that is to be monitored. Alternatively, **<All Instances>** option can also be selected to monitor all the NICs installed on the computer.

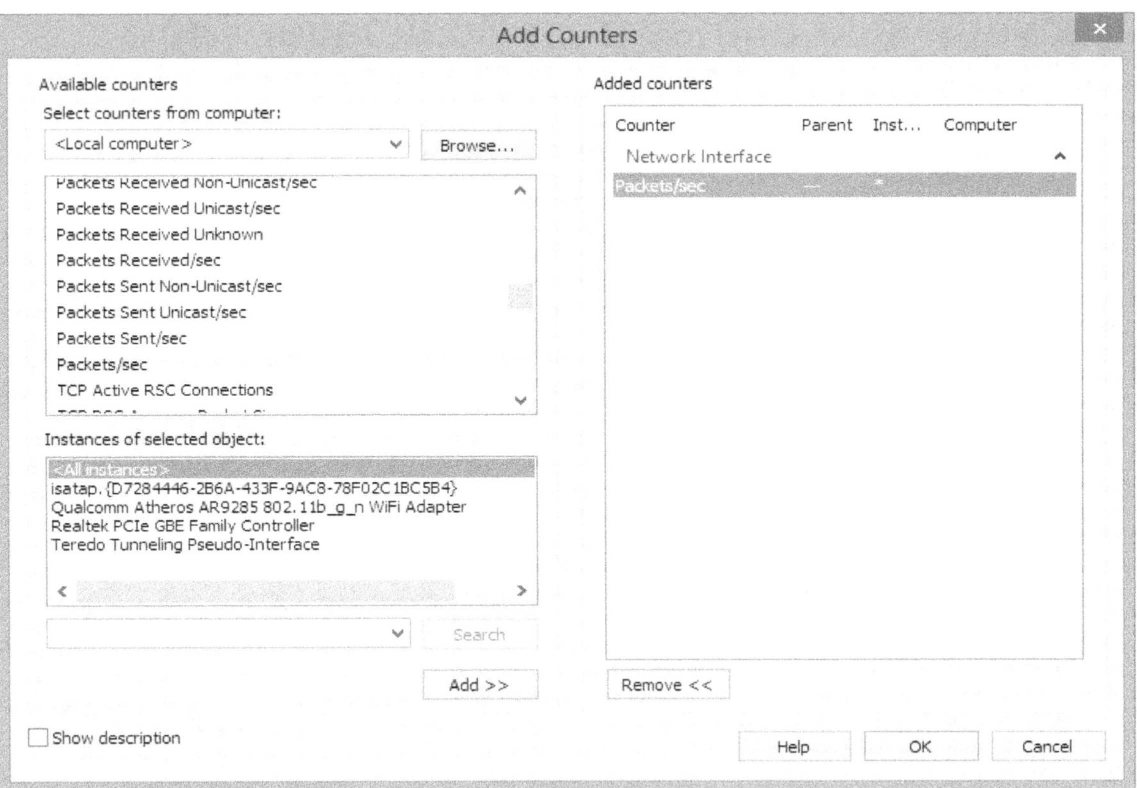

13. Click **Add** button from the bottom to add the selected counter to the **Added counters** list in the right.
14. Once done, click **OK**.
15. Back on the **Computer Management** snap-in, NIC can be monitored by viewing the displayed graph in the right pane.

Remove Invalid Entries from Bootloader File

Introduction to Invalid Entries in Bootloader File

When working with Microsoft Windows 8, it is quite likely that after using the operating system for a couple of months its performance reduces, and sometimes the OS starts behaving obnoxiously. In order to rectify the issues, administrators try several things and in most cases they end up reinstalling the operating system without removing the older one. When this happens, due to any misconfiguration, sometimes two entries of the same operating system are added to the bootloader file and every time the user starts the computer, both the entries are displayed on the computer screen. Since the second entry points to the newly installed Windows, the first entry becomes invalid and it becomes important for the administrators to remove that invalid entry from the bootloader file.

How to Remove Invalid Entries from Bootoader File?

In order to remove invalid entries from a bootloader file in Microsoft Windows 8, steps given below must be followed:

1. Log on to Microsoft Windows 8 computer with administrator account.
2. From the **Start** screen, click **Desktop** tile.
3. On the desktop screen, press **Windows** + **R** keys simultaneously to initiate **Run** command box.
4. In the opened **Run** command box, type **MSCONFIG** command and press **Enter** key.
5. On the opened **System Configuration** box, go to the **Boot** tab.
6. On the **Boot** tab, click to select the invalid entry from the displayed list.
7. Click **Delete** button and accept any confirmation message that appears.

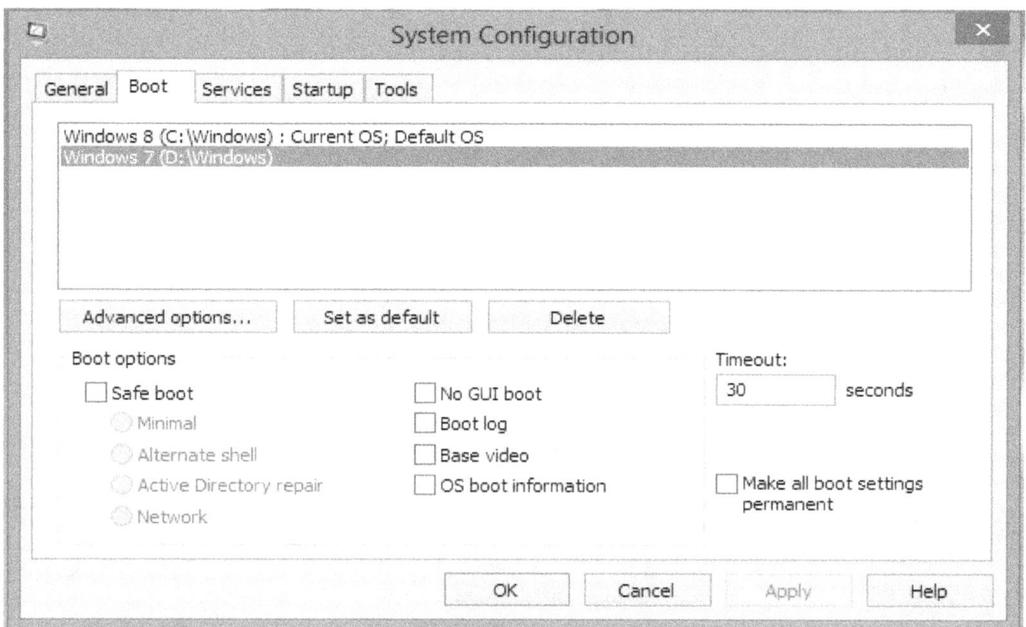

8. Back on the **System Configuration** box, click **OK**.
9. Restart the computer when done.

Fix Master Boot Record (MBR)

Introduction to Master Boot Record (MBR)

Master Boot Record (MBR) is the area in the hard disk drive that contains the addresses of the boot files. When a computer is powered on, in order to boot Microsoft Windows 8, its booting files must be loaded into the memory. Booting files are stored in the clusters in the hard disk drive and when the boot process of Windows initiates, the operating system reads the MBR to get the addresses of the clusters where booting files of the operating system are stored. Once the booting files are located, they are then loaded into the memory, hence allowing the operating system to boot successfully.

Sometimes computer fails to boot, the most likely reason can be errors in MBR that prevents the computer to locate the booting files to load into the memory. Therefore, in order to bring the computer back to the running state, administrators must fix the Master Boot Record.

How to Fix Master Boot Record (MBR)?

In order to fix Master Boot Record (MBR) in Microsoft Windows 8, steps given below must be followed:

1. Start the computer with bootable Windows 8 installation DVD.
2. On the displayed box, click **Next**.
3. On the next box, click **Repair your computer** option from the bottom left corner.
4. From the **Choose an option** window, click **Troubleshoot**.
5. From the **Troubleshoot** window, click **Advanced options**.
6. From the **Advanced options** window, click **Command Prompt**.
7. On the command line window, type **BOOTSECT /NT60 C:** command and press **Enter** key.

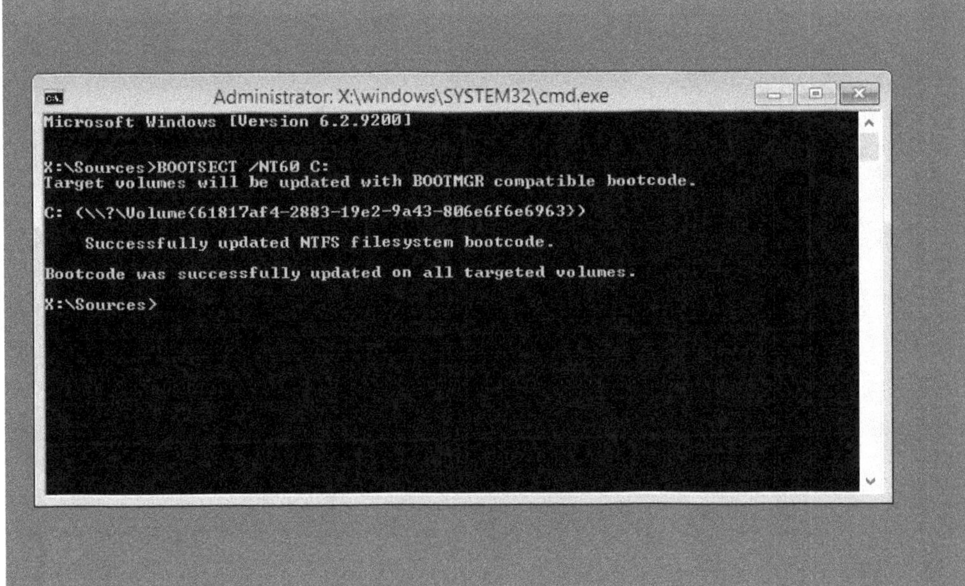

8. Once the command is successfully executed, close the command window and restart the computer normally.

Fix Bootloader File

Introduction to Bootloader File

Bootloader is the most important file without which the operating system cannot boot. As mentioned in previous lesson, when the computer starts, it looks into the MBR of the boot device (mostly a hard disk) and locates the booting files that reside hard disk drive. Once the booting files are located, it is the bootloader file that initiates and performs further booting process.

When Windows fails to boot, the problem might be either in the MBR or in the bootloader file. In order to fix MBR, previous lesson can be referred, however in case fixing the MBR doesn't work and the operating system still doesn’t boot, the other likely reason can be a corrupt bootloader file. When bootloader file gets corrupted, administrators must manually fix the errors in the file.

How to Fix Bootloader File?

In order to fix Microsoft Windows 8 bootloader file, steps given below must be followed:

1. Start the computer with bootable Windows 8 installation DVD.
2. On the displayed box, click **Next**.
3. On the next box, click **Repair your computer** option from the bottom left corner.
4. From the **Choose an option** window, click **Troubleshoot**.
5. From the **Troubleshoot** window, click **Advanced options**.
6. From the **Advanced options** window, click **Command Prompt**.
7. On the command line window, type **BOOTREC /FIXBOOT** command and press **Enter** key.

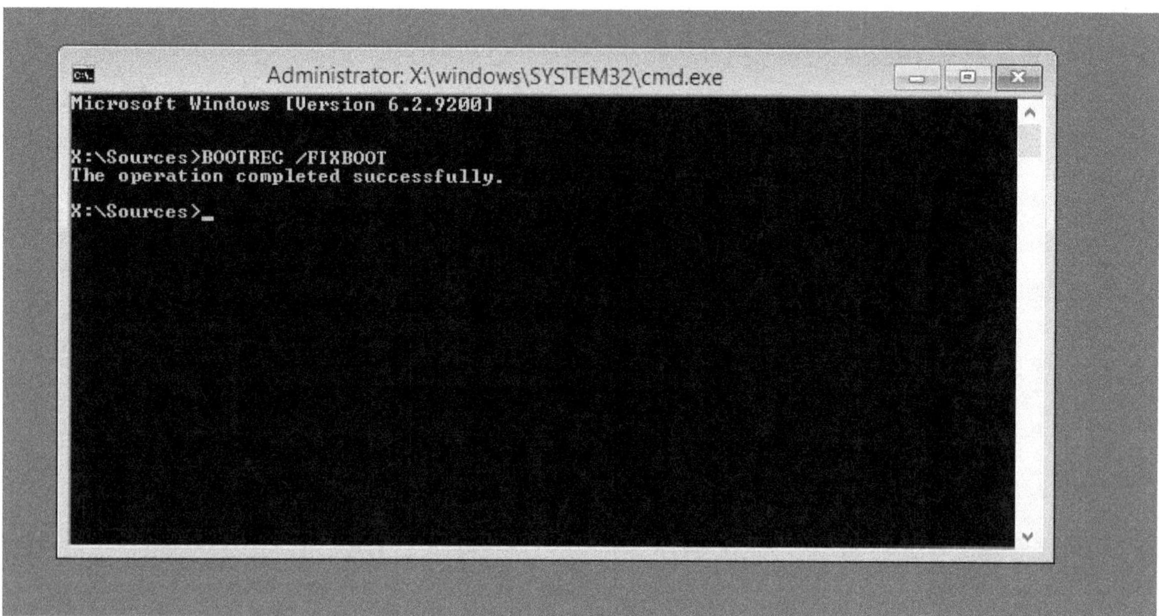

8. Once the command is successfully executed, close the command window and restart the computer normally.

Start Windows in Safe Mode

Introduction to Windows Safe Mode

Safe mode in Microsoft Windows operating systems is the boot process that allows the OS to initiate and run only the necessary services and processes that are required to start the computer and function normally. Optional processes and services are not initiated when Windows starts in safe mode.

Administrators of Microsoft Windows 8 computer might want to start Windows in safe mode when the operating system requires troubleshooting. For example if administrators have installed an application that automatically gets initiated every time the computer boots, it cannot be uninstalled when Windows is booted normally because Windows uses the files of the application, thus have exclusive access to them. In such cases administrators can boot the computer in safe mode so that the application does not get initiated along with the operating system, hence allowing them to remove the application without hassle.

How to Start Windows in Safe Mode?

In order to start Microsoft Windows 8 computer in safe mode, steps given below must be followed:

1. Log on to Microsoft Windows 8 computer with administrator account.
2. From the **Start** screen, click **Desktop** tile.
3. On the desktop screen, hover mouse to the bottom right corner of the window.
4. From the displayed options, click **Settings**.
5. From the bottom of the **Settings** pane, click **Change PC settings** option.
6. On the **PC settings** window, click to select **General** category from the left pane.
7. From the right pane, under **Advanced startup** section, click **Restart now**.

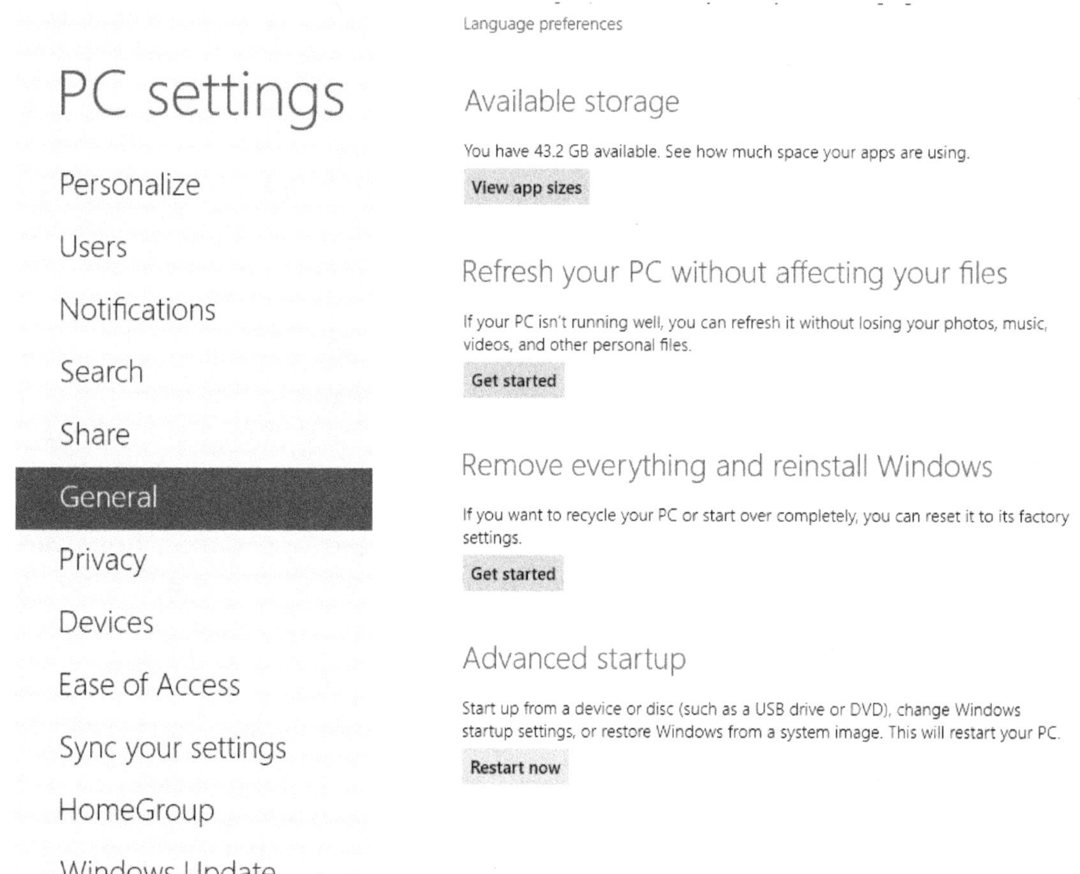

8. On **Choose an option** window, click **Troubleshoot**.
9. On the **Troubleshoot** window, click **Advanced options**.
10. On the **Advanced options** window, click **Startup Settings**.

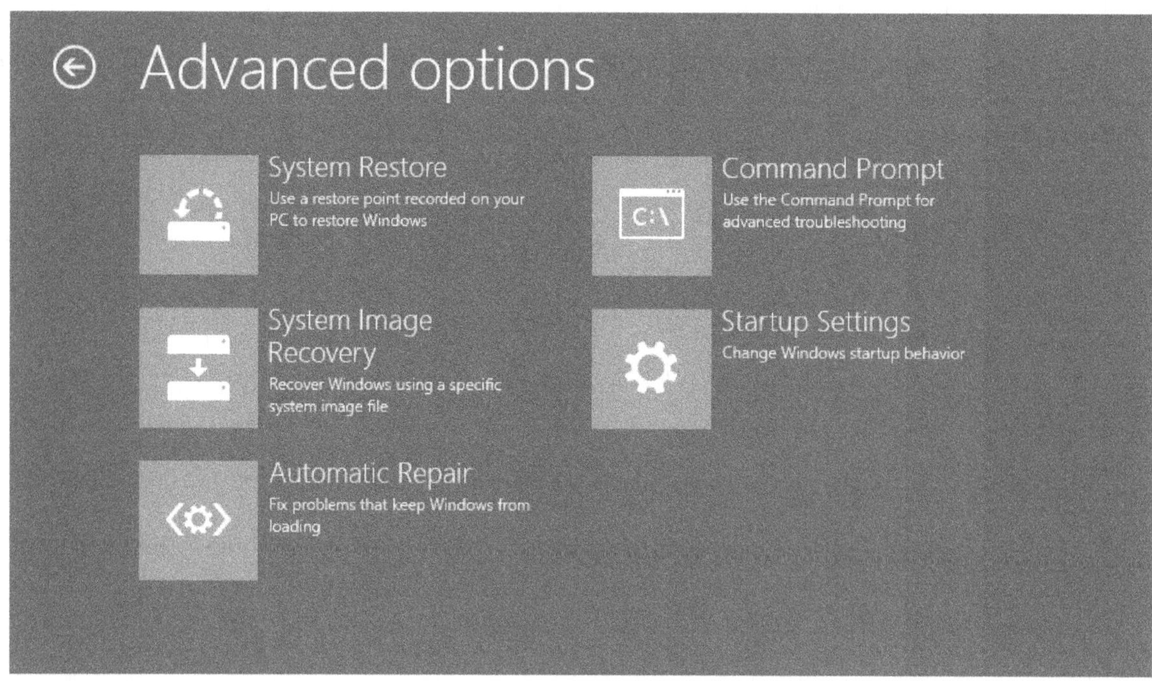

11. On the **Startup Settings** window, click **Restart**.

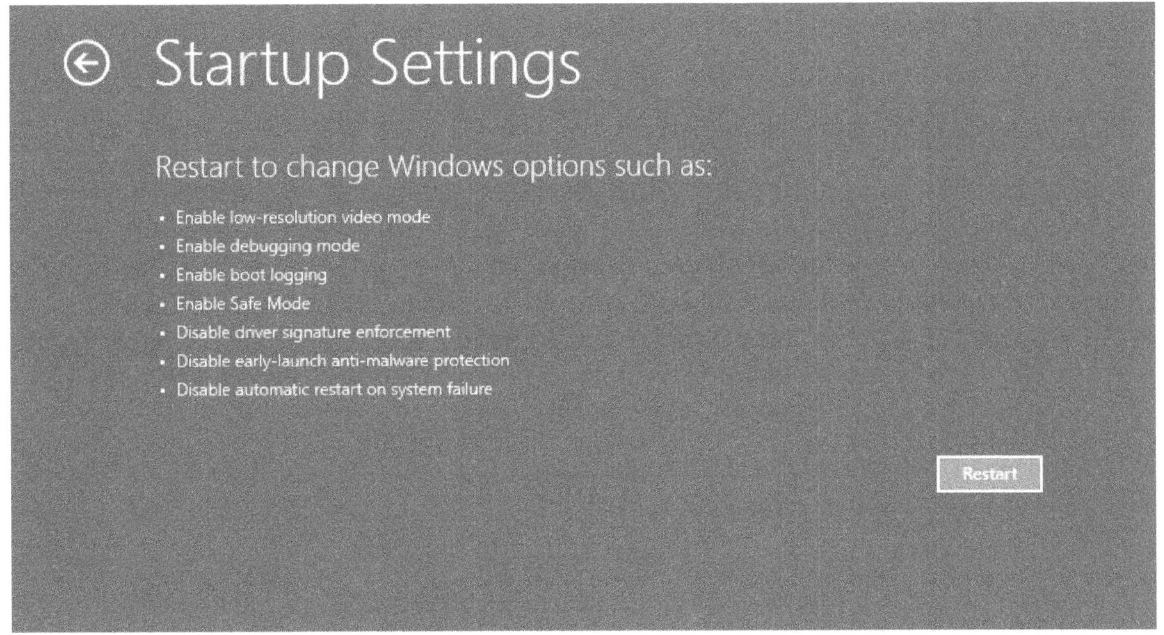

12. On the opened **Startup Settings** window, press the corresponding number (number 4) from the displayed list using number keys on the keyboard to start the computer in safe mode.

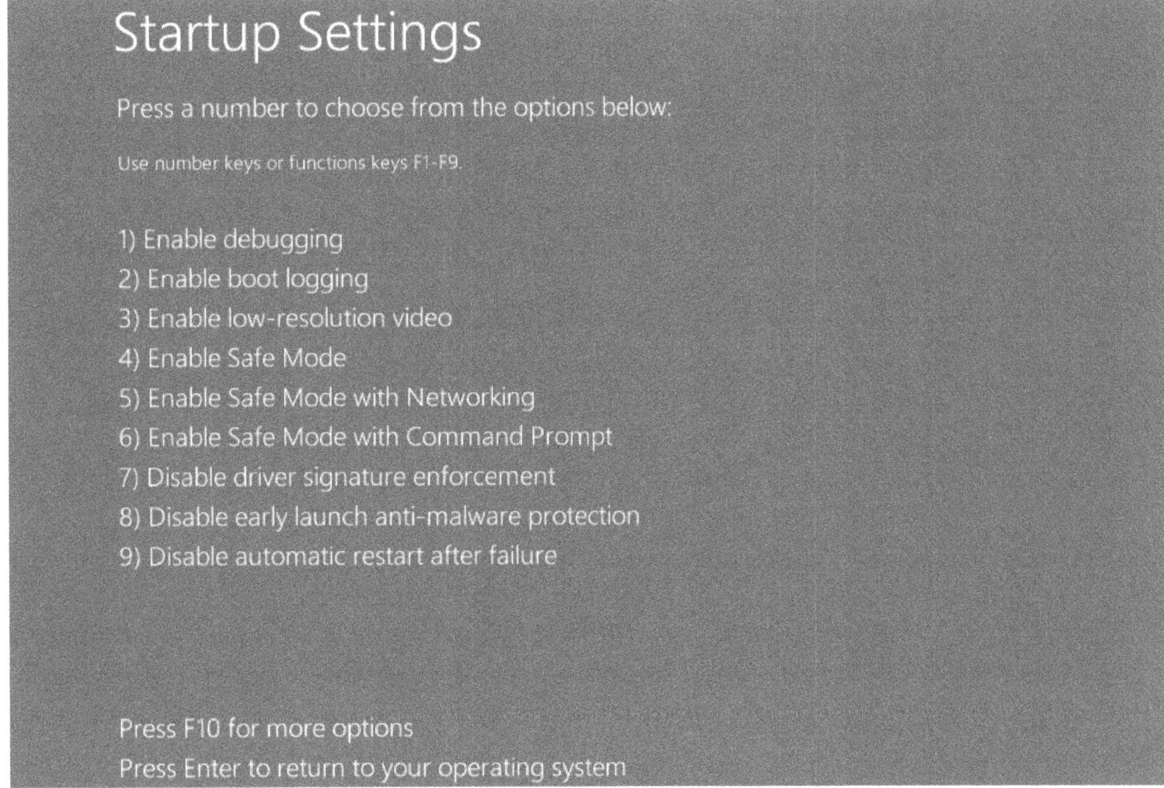

Delete Unwanted Services

Introduction to Services

Services in Microsoft Windows 8 help the operating system to run various tasks and enable several features that are otherwise not accessible if their corresponding services fail to boot or are disabled. An example for such a service is 'Print Spooler' that allows the documents to be spooled (buffered in the memory for easy printing) when the print command is sent to the printer. By default the state of 'Print Spooler' service is 'Started' and its 'Startup type' is set to 'Automatic', which means that the service would be initiated automatically every time the computer starts.

Startup of every service that the Windows operating system has can be configured to any one of the following available types:

- **Automatic (Delayed Start)** - When the startup type of a service is set to this option, the service does not get initialized along with the boot process of operating system. Instead, it gets initiated after the operating system has completed its boot process and the Windows is started. This reduces the boot time that Windows take, hence booting the operating system faster.
- **Automatic** - When the startup type of a service is set to this option, the service automatically gets initialized along with the boot process. Startup types of most services are set to 'Automatic' so that any feature that the service enables can be available for use as soon as the Windows starts.
- **Manual** - When the startup type of a service is set to this option, the service must be manually initialized every time its corresponding feature is required to be used in the computer. Sometimes if the startup type of the service is set to 'Manual', it gets started automatically if its corresponding feature is required by any installed application.
- **Disabled** - When the startup type of a service is set to this option, the service does not get initialized whatsoever. In case the corresponding feature of a disabled service is required by any application or the administrator, its startup type must be set to 'Manual' or 'Automatic'. After the startup type of a disabled service is set to 'Manual' or 'Automatic', the service must be started manually for the first time after its startup type has been changed.

Since all above options allow users to configure the services and their startup types as per their own preferences, it is quite unlikely that users would ever want to delete any service from Windows. Moreover, deleting a service is not at all recommended until it has been added because of any unwanted malicious script or corrupt application.

How to Delete a Service?

Before deleting a service from the Microsoft Windows 8 computer, make sure that the service is stopped and is not in use. Once confirmed, steps given below must be followed to delete the unwanted service:

1. Log on to Microsoft Windows 8 computer with administrator account.
2. From the **Start** screen, click **Desktop** tile.
3. On the desktop screen, hover mouse to the bottom right corner of the window.

4. From the displayed options, click **Search**.
5. On the opened **Apps** screen, locate and right-click **Command Prompt**.
6. From the advanced options displayed at the bottom of the window, click **Run as administrator**.
7. On the **User Account Control** confirmation box, click **Yes** button to open the command window with elevated privileges.
8. In the command line window, type the **SC DELETE** command followed by the name of unwanted service and press Enter key. (E.g. **SC DELETE BTHSERV**)

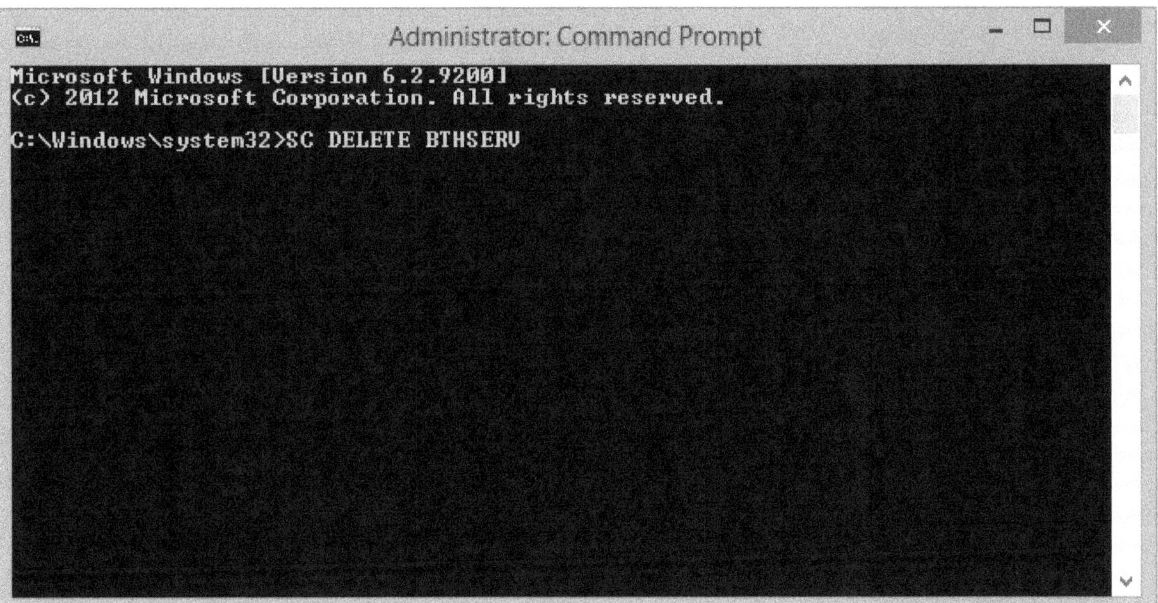

Rectify MSI Installer Error

Introduction to MSI Installer Error

After Microsoft Windows 8 computer has been used for a couple of months, it is likely that some registry entries might get corrupted or some of them might automatically get added or deleted because of some applications or malicious scripts. The most common error that users face in such cases is that Windows does not allow them to install any other application due to 'MSI Installer Error' and displays errors like 'Installation of MSI failed', etc. 'MSI Installer Error' occurs due to an entry in Windows registry which, when deleted, resolves the issue and allows the applications to be installed on the computers without hassle.

Since the rectifying process requires registry modifications, elevated privileges are required and therefore administrative credentials must be used to perform the task successfully.

How to Rectify MSI Installer Error?

In order to rectify 'MSI Installer Error' in Microsoft Windows 8, steps given below must be followed:

1. Log on to Microsoft Windows 8 computer with administrator account.
2. From the **Start** screen, click **Desktop** tile.
3. On the desktop screen, hover mouse to the bottom right corner of the window.
4. From the displayed options, click **Search**.
5. On the opened **Apps** screen, locate and right-click **Command Prompt**.
6. From the advanced options displayed at the bottom of the window, click **Run as administrator**.
7. On the **User Account Control** confirmation box, click **Yes** button to open the command window with elevated privileges.
8. In the command line window, type the **REG DELETE HKLM\SOFTWARE\MICROSOFT\SQMCLIENT\WINDOWS\DISABLEDSESSIONS /VA /F** command and press **Enter** key.

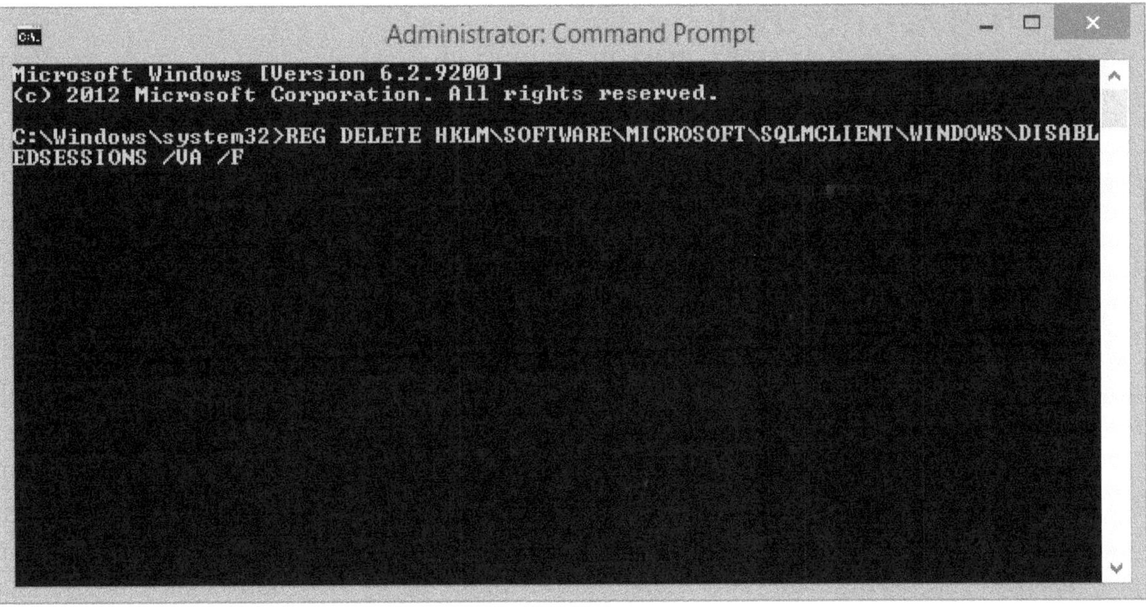

9. Once the command is successfully executed, close the command window and restart the computer.

Refresh a Computer

Introduction to Refreshing a Computer

Microsoft Windows 8 has a new feature that allows administrators of the computer to refresh the operating system if it starts behaving obnoxiously. In order to refresh a Microsoft Windows 8 computer, the computer must be booted externally from the Windows 8 bootable media. After the computer is started externally, 'Repair your computer' option must be clicked in order to get to the appropriate option.

When the computer is refreshed, all computer settings are set to the default configurations, hence making the computer as fresh and error-free as it was right after the installation of the operating system. While refreshing Windows 8, the process does not remove any users' personal data, and neither the Apps from Microsoft store are deleted. However the Apps that administrators have installed manually from a CD/DVD or from the Internet are automatically removed from the computer while refreshing.

How to Refresh a Computer?

In order to refresh a Microsoft Windows 8 computer, steps given below must be followed:

1. Start the computer with bootable Windows 8 installation DVD.
2. On the displayed box, click **Next**.
3. On the next box, click **Repair your computer** option from the bottom left corner.
4. From the **Choose an option** window, click **Troubleshoot**.
5. From the **Troubleshoot** window, click **Refresh your PC**.
6. On **Refresh your PC** window, click **Next**.
7. On the next window, click **Windows 8** from the **Choose a target operating system** list.
8. From the next window, click **Refresh** button to start the process.

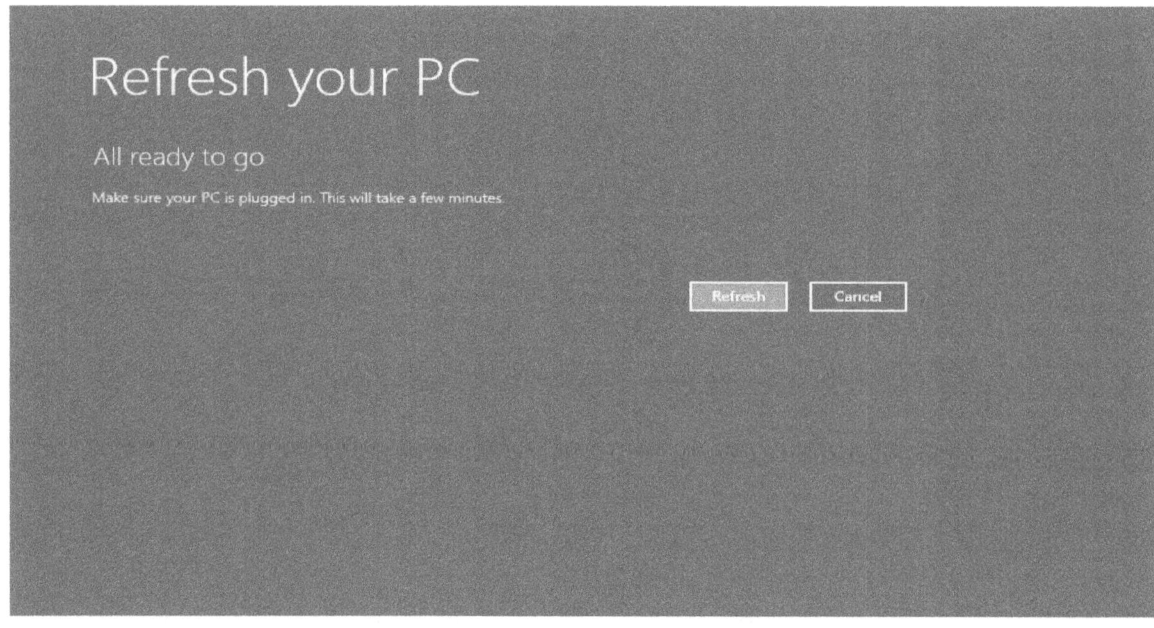

9. Wait till the Windows 8 computer is refreshed before start using it normally.

Reset a Computer

Introduction to Resetting a Computer

Microsoft Windows 8 has a new feature using which administrators can reset the computer in case it starts behaving obnoxiously. In order to reset a Microsoft Windows 8 computer, the computer must be booted externally from the Windows 8 bootable media. After the computer is started externally, 'Repair your computer' option must be clicked in order to get to the appropriate option.

When a Windows 8 computer is reset, all users' personal data and the installed Apps are deleted and the computer settings are set to their default configurations, hence making the computer as fresh and error-free as it was right after the installation of the operating system.

How to Reset a Computer?

In order to reset a Microsoft Windows 8 computer, steps given below must be followed:

1. Start the computer with bootable Windows 8 installation DVD.
2. On the displayed box, click **Next**.
3. On the next box, click **Repair your computer** option from the bottom left corner.
4. From the **Choose an option** window, click **Troubleshoot**.
5. From the **Troubleshoot** window, click **Reset your PC**.
6. On **Reset your PC** window, click **Next**.
7. On the next window, click **Windows 8** from the **Choose a target operating system** list.
8. From the next window, click **Only the drive where Windows is installed** option to reset only the system drive of the computer.
9. On the next window, click **Fully clean the drive** option to fully reset the computer and make it completely error free. Alternatively, **Just remove my files** option can also be clicked to quickly erase users' personal files from the computer.
10. On the next window, click **Reset** button to start the reset process.

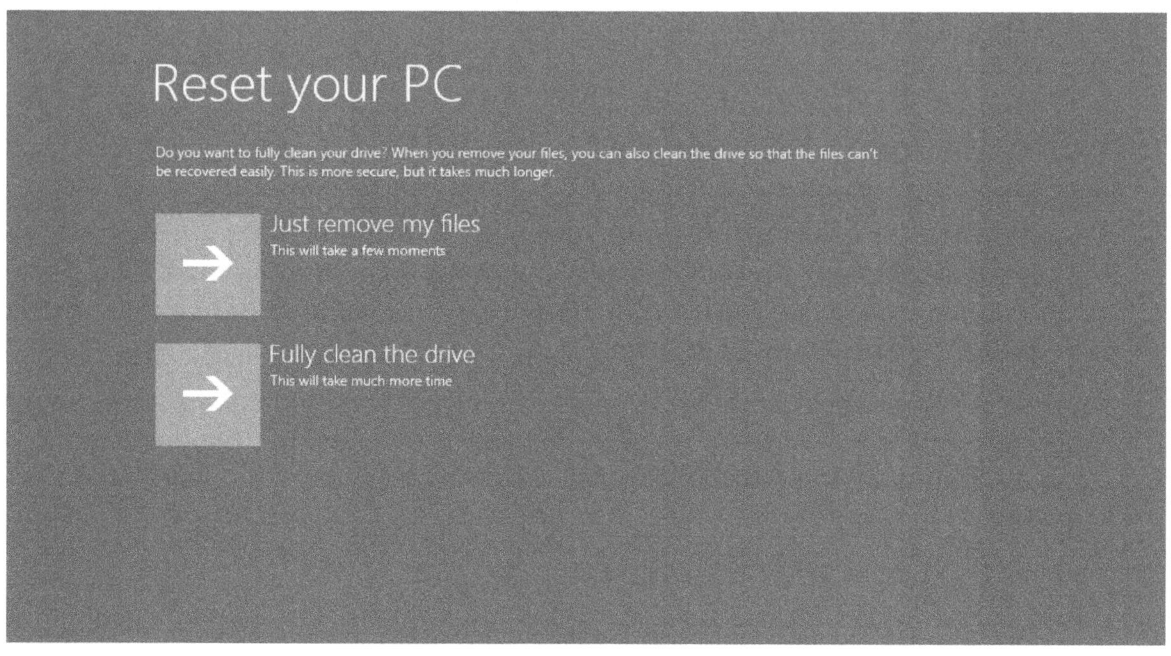

11. Wait till the Windows 8 computer is reset before start using it normally.

Cannot Open a Webpage (Wrong DNS Cache Entry)

Introduction to DNS Cache

DNS cache is a temporary memory in the DNS that holds the resolved queries (URLs of the websites that it has searched for and has found successfully) for a predefined period of time. Duration for which a resolved query can be considered valid in the DNS cache of DNS client is specified while configuring the DNS server.

Sometimes hackers also configure their own DNS servers that maintain records of the fake sites that resemble the genuine ones. For example 'A' has configured a DNS server and has created a DNS record named www.site1.com but has specified a different (false) IP address for the website. Moreover while configuring the DNS server, 'A' has also specified that the records are to be considered valid for 100000 seconds. When this record is fetched by the DNS clients while looking for www.site1.com, they get redirected to the IP address specified in the DNS record. Since the DNS client has successfully resolved the query (fake one), it adds the resolved query to its DNS cache for 100000 seconds. Every time a user types www.site1.com in the address bar of the web browser, the computer redirects the user to the false IP address, hence preventing the computer from opening the genuine website.

To solve above mentioned problem (when a webpage is not getting displayed or the wrong website is getting opened), administrators can erase the DNS cache in order to re-fetch the correct IP address for the desired website.

How to Erase DNS Cache?

In order to erase DNS cache from Microsoft Windows 8 computer, steps given below must be followed:

1. Log on to Microsoft Windows 8 computer with administrator account.
2. From the **Start** screen, click **Desktop** tile.
3. On the desktop screen, hover mouse to the bottom right corner of the window.
4. From the displayed options, click **Search**.
5. On the opened **Apps** screen, locate and right-click **Command Prompt**.
6. From the advanced options displayed at the bottom of the window, click **Run as administrator**.
7. On the **User Account Control** confirmation box, click **Yes** button to open the command window with elevated privileges.
8. In the command line window, type the **IPCONFIG /FLUSHDNS** command and press **Enter** key to erase DNS cache.

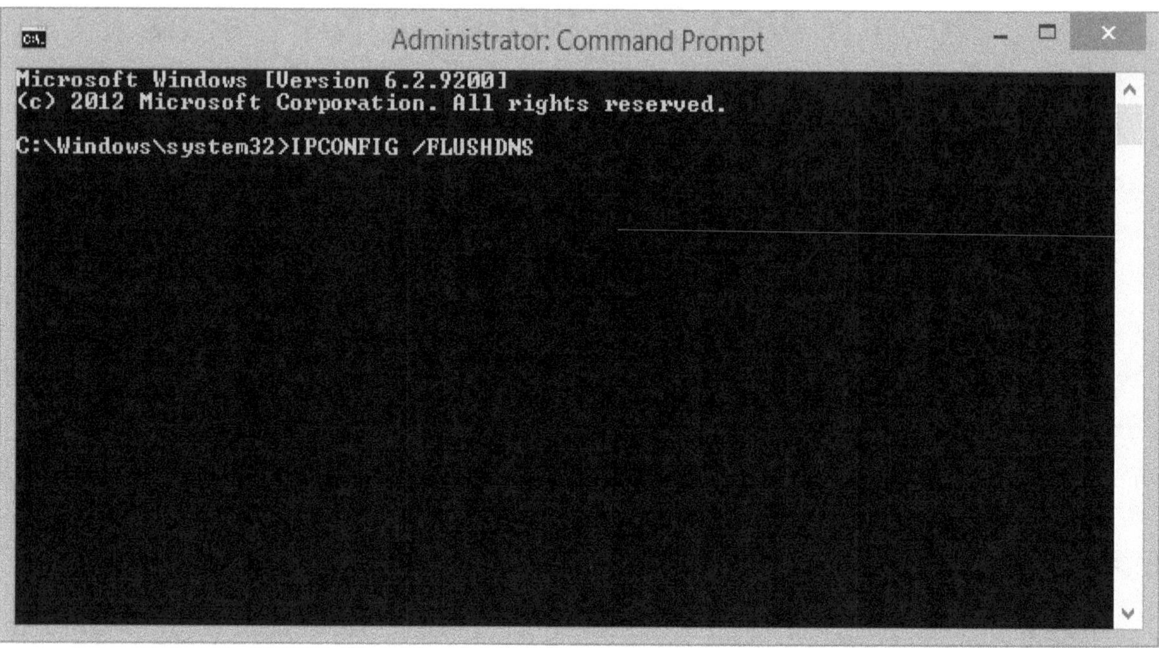

9. Close and reopen the web browser to start surfing the Internet.

Prevent Application Initialization at Computer Start up

Introduction to Preventing Application Initialization at Computer Start up

When administrators use Microsoft Windows 8, it is expected that they would also install several applications to ease out their works. Such applications may be developed by Microsoft itself or by different vendors. When such applications are installed, many applications automatically configure themselves to be initialized automatically every time the computer starts.

Such characteristic of some applications is important to keep the computer run smoothly and flawlessly. However, since the applications also consume system resources, such as RAM and processing, administrators may want to disable some of them from getting automatically initialized at computer start up.

Moreover, if because of any reason the computer gets infected with any virus program that automatically gets initialized at system start up, administrators can prevent it from doing so in order to experience flawless performance of the computer without re-installing the Windows. Although this method is not very reliable every time, it can still give some relief to the users and the computer for a short while.

In pre-Windows 8 operating systems, applications could be prevented from getting initialized at start up from the 'Startup' tab of 'System Configuration' box, which could be initiated by typing 'MSCONFIG' command in the 'Run' command box or 'Search' box. In Windows 8, this task can be done from the 'Task Manager' box itself. Nonetheless, administrative privileges are still required to perform the task.

How to Prevent Applications from Getting Initialized at Computer Start up?

In order to prevent applications from getting initialized at system start up, steps given below must be followed:

1. Log on to Microsoft Windows 8 computer with administrator account.
2. From the **Start** screen, click **Desktop** tile.
3. On the desktop screen, right-click the taskbar.
4. From the displayed context menu, click **Task Manager**.
5. From the bottom **Task Manager** box, click **More details** button.
6. From the extended **Task Manager** interface, go to **Startup** tab.
7. From the displayed list of applications, click to select the one that is to be prevented from getting initialized at computer start up.

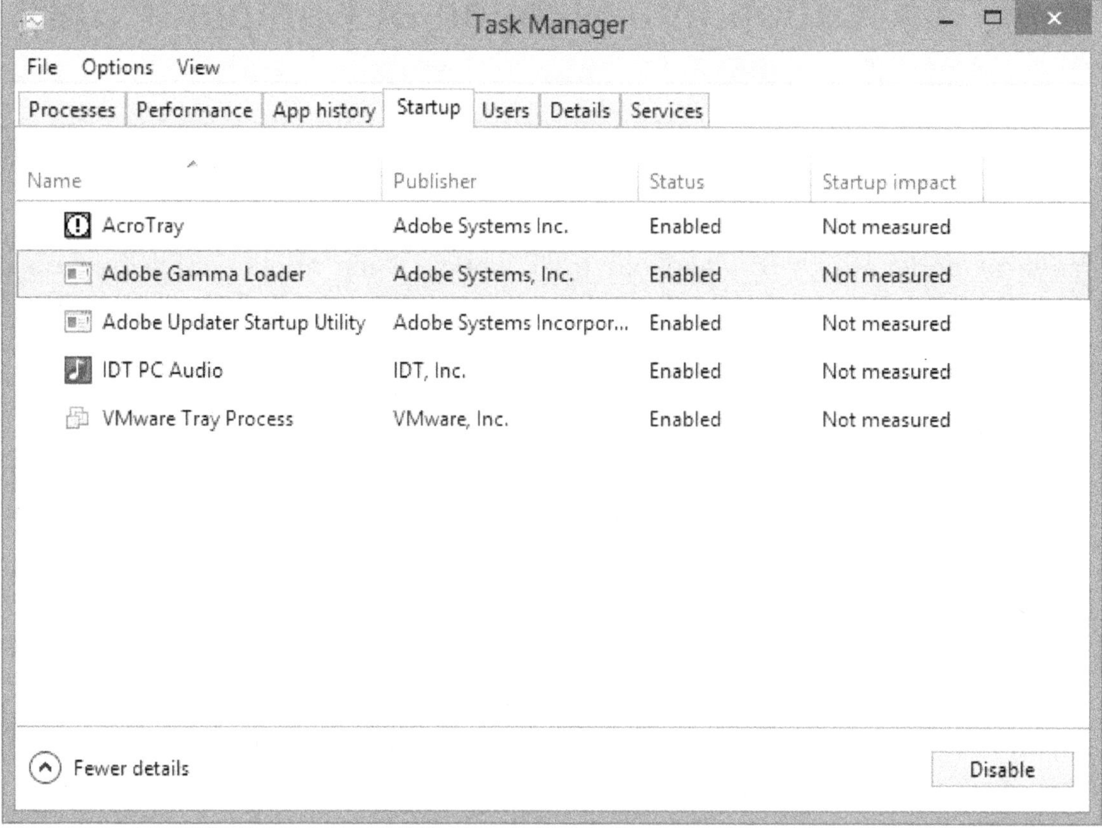

8. From the bottom of the **Startup** tab, click **Disable** button.
9. Click **OK** when done and if required, restart the computer to experience the modified settings.

To re-enable the disabled application, follow steps from 1 to 9 while clicking **Enable** button when on step 8.

www.ingramcontent.com/pod-product-compliance
Lightning Source LLC
LaVergne TN
LVHW060132070326
832902LV00018B/2756

* 9 7 8 1 4 8 1 0 6 7 0 3 4 *